Instructions On Psychological Skills

Joseph M. Strayhorn, Jr., M.D.

Psychological Skills Press

Wexford, Pennsylvania

Published by
Psychological Skills Press
263 Seasons Drive
Wexford, PA 15090
www.psyskills.com

Second printing October, 2002
Author's email address: joestrayhorn@juno.com.
Thanks to Rob Kyff for editing this book.

Publisher's Cataloging-in-Publication
(Provided by Quality Books, Inc.)

Strayhorn, Joseph M.
  Instructions on psychological skills / Joseph M.
Strayhorn, Jr. – 1st ed.
  p.cm.
  Includes index.
   ISBN 1-931773-00-9

   1. Self-help techniques. 2. 3. Problem solving –
Problems, exercises, etc. 4. Adjustment (Psychology)
I. Title.

BF632.S77 2002   158.1
                          QBI33-307

Contents

Introduction

What is mental health? It's being able to do well the things we need to do to handle life. These include productivity, joyousness, kindness, honesty, fortitude, good decision-making, and so forth. I call these psychological skills.

People can find themselves deficient in some of these skills for any of several different reasons (heredity, various aspects of the environment, free will?). But whatever the reason, it's almost always possible to get better at these skills by systematically working at them. Working at these skills can make people more likely to be happy, productive, and free of symptoms. Psychological skills can be taught, learned, practiced, modeled, and instructed, just as any other skills can.

This volume gives ideas on how to do the skills well, as well as some sales pitches on why it's important to learn to do them well. Many of the ideas expressed here are gained from my own experience as a psychotherapist, trying to help people live in a more psychologically healthy way. Many of the ideas are gleaned from various different writers in the fields of psychology, psychotherapy, self-improvement, performance enhancement, and philosophy.

One way to use this book is to read it from start to finish. The advantage of this strategy is that all the skills are important, and the time invested in learning about all of them is well worth the effort. The other way to use this book is to pick out the psychological skills of highest priority now, and to study the sections dealing with those skills. The advantage of this strategy is that you can focus on the skills you're most motivated to learn at any certain time. In this way you give yourself a "skills axis diagnosis": you figure out which skills are highest on your priority list. Then you work in a concerted way on these skills.

This book can stand alone. It can also be used with other materials. *Exercises for Psychological Skills* goes into detail on practice exercises for the psychological skills listed here. *Programmed Readings on Psychological Skills* provides fictional models for the psychological skills.

The next pages reproduce the psychological skills axis, the list of sixty-two skills that forms the structure of this book and my other writings on building psychological skills. This list is also the basis of the table of contents of this book. I present the form of the skills axis that asks you to rate yourself on how skilled you are for each of these. As you read and learn more about what constitutes skill in each of these areas, your rating may change.

The psychological skills inventory

This questionnaire will allow you to rate the "psychological skill" strengths and weaknesses of yourself or someone else. Each item will ask you to rate the degree of skill in a certain area. Please rate each item according to the following scale:

0 = No skill
2 = Very little skill
4 = Some, but not much skill
6 = Pretty much skill, moderate amount of skill
8 = High amount of skill
10 = Very high amount of skill

Please rate all items.

Group 1: Productivity
_____1. Purposefulness. Having a sense of purpose that drives activity
_____2. Persistence. Sustaining attention, concentrating, focusing, staying on task
_____3. Competence-development. Working toward competence in job, academics, recreation, life skills
_____4. Organization. Organizing goals, priorities, time, money, and physical objects; planfulness

Group 2. Joyousness
_____5. Enjoying aloneness. Having a good time by oneself, tolerating not getting someone's attention

_____6. Pleasure from approval. Enjoying approval, compliments, and positive attention from others
_____7. Pleasure from accomplishments. Self-reinforcement for successes.
_____8. Pleasure from your own kindness. Feeling pleasure from doing kind, loving acts for others
_____9. Pleasure from discovery. Enjoying exploration and satisfaction of curiosity
_____10. Pleasure from others' kindness. Feeling gratitude for what others have done
_____11. Pleasure from blessings. Celebrating and feeling the blessings of luck or fate
_____12. Pleasure from affection. Enjoying physical affection without various fears interfering
_____13. Favorable attractions. Having feelings of attraction aroused in ways consonant with happiness.
_____14. Gleefulness. Playing, becoming childlike, experiencing glee, being spontaneous
_____15. Humor. Enjoying funny things, finding and producing comedy in life

Group 3: Kindness
_____16. Kindness. Nurturing someone, being kind and helpful
_____17. Empathy. Recognizing other people's feelings, seeing things from the other's point of view
_____18. Conscience. Feeling appropriate guilt, avoiding harming others

Group 4: Honesty

_____19. Honesty. Being honest and dependable, especially when it's difficult to be so

_____20. Awareness of your own abilities. Being honest and brave in assessing your strengths and weaknesses

Group 5: Fortitude

_____21. Frustration-tolerance. Handling frustration, tolerating adverse circumstances, fortitude

_____22. Handling separation. Tolerating separation from close others, or loss of a relationship

_____23. Handling rejection. Tolerating it when people don't like or accept you, or don't want to be with you

_____24. Handling criticism. Dealing with disapproval, criticism and lack of respect from others

_____25. Handling mistakes and failures. Regretting mistakes without being overly self-punitive

_____26. Magnanimity, non-jealousy. Handling it when someone else gets what you want

_____27. Painful emotion-tolerance. Avoiding "feeling bad about feeling bad."

_____28. Fantasy-tolerance. Tolerating mental images of unwanted behavior, confident that you will not enact them

Group 6: Good decisions

6a: Individual decision-making

_____29. Positive aim. Aiming toward making things better. Seeking reward and not punishment

_____30. Thinking before acting. Thinking, rather than responding impulsively or by reflex, when it's useful to do so

_____31. Fluency. Using words to conceptualize the world: verbal skills

_____32. Awareness of your emotions. Recognizing, and being able to verbalize your own feelings

_____33. Awareness of control. Accurately assessing the degree of control you have over specific events

_____34. Decision-making. Defining a problem, gathering information, generating options, predicting and evaluating consequences, making a choice

6b: Joint decision-making, including conflict resolution

_____35. Toleration. Non-bossiness. Tolerating a wide range of other people's behavior

_____36. Rational approach to joint decisions. Deciding rationally on stance and strategies for joint decisions

_____37. Option-generating. Generating creative options for solutions to problems

_____38. Option-evaluating. Justice skills: Recognizing just solutions to interpersonal problems

_____39. Assertion. Dominance, sticking up for yourself, taking charge, enjoying winning

_____40. Submission: Conciliation, giving in, conceding, admitting one was wrong, being led

_____41. Differential reinforcement. Reinforcing positive behavior and avoiding reinforcing the negative

Group 7: Nonviolence

_____42. Forgiveness and anger control. Forgiving, handling an insult or injury by another

_____43. Nonviolence. Being committed to the principle of nonviolence and working to foster it

Group 8: Respectful talk, not being rude

_____44. Respectful talk, not being rude. Being sensitive to words, vocal tones, and facial expressions that are accusing, punishing, or demeaning, and avoiding them unless there is a very good reason

Group 9: Friendship-Building

_____45. Discernment and Trusting. Accurately appraising others. Not distorting with prejudice, overgeneralization, wish-fulfilling fantasies. Deciding what someone can be trusted for, and trusting when appropriate

_____46. Self-disclosure. Disclosing and revealing oneself to another when it's safe

_____47. Gratitude. Expressing gratitude, admiration, and other positive feelings toward others

_____48. Social initiations. Starting social interaction; getting social contact going

_____49. Socializing. Engaging well in social conversation or play.

_____50. Listening. Empathizing, encouraging another to talk about his own experience

Group 10: Self discipline

_____51. Self discipline. Delay of gratification, self-control. Denying yourself present pleasure for future gain

Group 11: Loyalty

_____52. Loyalty. Tolerating and enjoying sustained closeness, attachment, and commitment to another

Group 12: Conservation

_____53. Conservation and Thrift. Preserving resources for ourselves and future generations. Forgoing consumption on luxuries, but using resources more wisely. Financial delay of gratification skills

Group 13: Self-care

_____54. Carefulness. Feeling appropriate fear and avoiding unwise risks

_____55. Habits of self-care. Healthy habits regarding drinking, smoking, drug use, exercise, and diet

_____56. Relaxation. Calming yourself, letting the mind drift pleasantly and the body be at ease

_____57. Self-nurture. Delivering assuring or care-taking thoughts to yourself, feeling comforted thereby

Group 14: Compliance

_____58. Compliance. Obeying, submitting to legitimate and reasonable authority

Group 15: Positive fantasy rehearsal
_____59. Imagination and positive fantasy rehearsal. Using fantasy as a tool in rehearsing or evaluating a plan, or adjusting to an event or situation

Group 16: Courage
_____60. Courage. Estimating danger, overcoming fear of non-dangerous situations, handling danger rationally
_____61. Depending. Accepting help, being dependent without shame, asking for help appropriately
_____62. Independent thinking. Making decisions independently, carrying out actions independently

Some versatile ways of increasing psychological skills

Before launching into the individual skills, let's list some of the ways people can help themselves or other people to get better at these skills.

I have in various places referred to the "Methods of Influence Axis": a list of ways in which people influence each other or themselves. Here's that list:

Methods of Influence

1. Objective formation, or goal-setting

2. Hierarchy (or figuring out a series of small steps to the goal)

3. Attribution (or attributing to yourself or believing you have the capacity to attain the goal)

4. Modeling (seeing and hearing examples of the skill in question)

5. Practice (rehearsing positive examples of the skill)

6. Reinforcement and punishment (getting rewards for good examples, and non-reinforcement or possibly punishment for bad examples, of the skill)

7. Instruction (reading or hearing about how to do the skill well)

8. Stimulus situation control (putting yourself in situations that tend to bring out good examples of the skill)

9. Monitoring (measuring and keeping track of progress in the skill)

These general influence methods can be remembered by the mnemonic OH AM PRISM.

Let's go into a little more detail about influence methods.

Goal-setting involves convincing yourself, really selling yourself, on the value of getting better at one or more of these skills. If you review times when you have made mistakes in your life, and these mistakes have produced negative outcomes, and if you can see that the unhappiness would have been avoided had you been more proficient at a certain skill, then it's helpful to preserve these painful insights: they give you motivation to improve at the skill.

Goal-setting involves much more than just saying, "Yes, I'd like to get better at this." It involves being able to see and hear in your mind how and why your life would be better if you had more of the skill in question.

One activity that helps goal-setting is the "internal sales pitch." You write down the reasons you want to get better at a certain skill. You list the benefits in as much detail as you can. You review these benefits periodically, and add to them. You memorize them, and go over them in your mind frequently. You also frequently affirm to yourself that you want to get better at the skill. All the other techniques I'll list here or discuss in the rest of the book take work, and to do that work you have to motivate yourself.

This brings up another part of goal-setting. Goal-setting does not simply mean saying, "I'd like to get better at this," but rather saying, "I'd like to get better at this so much that I'm willing to devote x amount of time to this goal on a regular basis." If x is zero, you really haven't adopted a goal.

You may need to get more information in order to motivate yourself for your goal. You may need to hear how other people have improved their lives by attaining the goal. You may need to make a foray, and do some experimentation, and get a taste of how your life is better when you do positive examples of the skill than when you don't.

Hierarchy means figuring out a series of small steps you can take toward the goal, rather than having to attain it in one giant leap. In all of education, you can accomplish much more if there are way stations. In piano, you start with "Mary Had a Little Lamb" and gradually work your way up to "Clair de Lune." If you tried the high-level piece as your first venture, you would get too discouraged. Similarly, in learning concentration skills, for example, you don't expect yourself to be able to concentrate fully on the most boring text for five hours straight. Rather, you might start out with five minutes of concentration on a fairly interesting text.

Attribution means refusing to see yourself as someone who is permanently bad at a skill, someone incapable of improving. Instead, you attribute to yourself the capacity to improve. Rather than saying to yourself, "I'm bad at concentrating, and I will always be that way," you say to yourself, "I haven't YET developed my concentration skills as much as I want to."

Modeling means exposing yourself to examples of the skills in question. The book "Programmed Readings for Psychological Skills" gives concrete examples of these skills. There are many other places where you may find these models; gather them and hold onto them. Real-life models of other people are very useful; fictional or biographical models will also do nicely. Whatever method you can use to get the positive pattern into your memory bank in concrete, vivid detail will serve the purpose.

Modeling is an ongoing activity, not just something you do once. A method of both modeling and practicing is making up and writing down your own stories that model psychological skills. You can take these from

1) good examples you do in life,

2) good examples you *wish* you would have done in life rather than what you did,

3) good examples you have seen other people do,

4) good examples other people should have done instead of what they did,

5) good examples from fiction,

6) good examples fictitious characters should have done instead of what they did, and

7) inventions of your own imagination.

If you can collect models of the way you want to think, feel, and behave, and frequently run them through your memory bank, you greatly increase your chances of improving the skill in question.

In the models you acquire, pay attention not just to visible behaviors, but also to invisible ones: the thoughts and the emotions. Oftentimes what you say to yourself and what you imagine play a big role in determining how you feel and act.

Practice of the positive patterns is crucial for growth in psychological skills. When we have bad habits, we have to try to give even greater habit strength to alternative positive patterns. The only way I know to reliably do this is repetitive practice.

There are several ways to practice psychological skills. One is by simply going out in real life and doing good examples of them. Another way is by role-playing your desired behavior – either alone or with someone else – using drama to practice.

And a third way I call fantasy rehearsals. In fantasy rehearsals done in the most productive way, you actually speak or write out a description of the situation, of the thoughts you want to have in response to the situation, the emotions you want to feel, and the behaviors you want to do. The sources of positive patterns for fantasy rehearsals can be the same as I listed above as sources for positive modeling stories.

You speak a fantasy rehearsal as if it were happening right now: "I am in this place, and someone is saying this to me, and now I think to myself this, and this, and this. And I'm feeling this way, and I'm saying this, and doing this. Hooray, I'm glad I handled it this way!"

Make sure you fantasy rehearse the desirable pattern, that is, what you want to do, rather than rehearsing what not to do. Doing lots of rehearsals is to psychological skills what doing lots of repetitions of lifting weights is to bodybuilding. If you can master the technique of fantasy rehearsal, you have an extremely valuable skill at your disposal.

Reinforcement means trying to get yourself rewarded for doing the positive patterns of thought, feeling, and behavior. One mechanism is internal, self-reinforcement. This means remembering to celebrate in your mind when you have done something good.

Another reinforcement mechanism is to find someone to tell your successes about and to do this regularly. It helps to keep a diary of your positive patterns, because then you can celebrate them by yourself or with someone else over and over.

Some people even use tangible reinforcement for themselves. If I do this much of the desired behavior, I allow myself this much candy, this much purchase of a new thing, this much time doing a luxury activity. If you have the self-discipline to withhold reinforcers from yourself and give them only when you have done a certain amount of positive activity, such a tangible reinforcement program can be truly beneficial.

Instruction means paying attention to ideas about how to master the skills and why mastering them is important. Reading this book is one way of getting such instruction. Often instruction is as much a matter of reminding yourself of something you already know as it is of learning something new. For this reason, in the really important skills, I recommend reading the instructions repeatedly.

Stimulus situation control means you try to find situations and environments that bring out positive patterns. If someone wants to practice concentration on written material, that person will probably find the stimulus environment of a library more conducive to the skill than the environment of the living room of a fraternity house with lots of other people present, watching television and talking.

Monitoring means measuring your skill, repeatedly, over time. You make an imagined or real graph and see whether your skill is going up, going down, or staying the same. One way to measure your skill is simply to rate it. On a scale of ten, how much skill do you have at this, where 0 is none, and 10 is a very high amount. In giving yourself this rating, you take into account the specific examples that have happened lately: the examples of situations you have handled skillfully, and those you have handled unskillfully. How much does the first predominate over the second?

If, in addition to giving yourself a rating, you can more objectively measure some part of the skill in some way, by all means avail yourself of that. You can obtain a certain measure of relaxation by seeing how relaxed you can get your forehead muscles according to an EMG biofeedback machine. You can measure concentration by seeing how sustained, accurate, and fast you can be in a skill such as touch-typing. You can also measure concentration by seeing how long, how accurately and how quickly you can read paragraphs of standard material and summarize them.

You can measure courage skills by seeing how long and how comfortably you can expose yourself to something you were unrealistically afraid of before. When you notice progress in the skill, then you can celebrate and feel good, and use reinforcement to help yourself along.

The twelve types of thoughts

In various parts of this book I refer to twelve different categories of thoughts. This way of classifying thoughts is useful for work in very many different skill areas. The major idea is that you can choose the types of thoughts you want to use, on the basis of which ones are most helpful in accomplishing what you're trying to do. You don't have to continue thinking thoughts that have become habitual and reflexive. If you have some habits of thinking certain types of thoughts too much or too little for your own good, you can change those habits.

Here are the twelve types of thoughts, with an example of each.

1. Awfulizing. This situation is terrible. I don't think I can stand this.

2. Getting down on yourself. I did something really bad. I am bad. I did something stupid. Why did I have to be so stupid?

3. Blaming someone else. That person did something really bad. Why did you do that stupid thing? He is an idiot.

4. Not awfulizing. Even though this is not preferable, I can take it. Even though this is undesirable, it's not the end of the world.

5. Not getting down on yourself. I made a mistake, but I don't want to punish myself too much for it. I can forgive myself. I don't want to put my energy into making myself feel bad.

6. Not blaming someone else. That person did something I didn't like, but I don't want to punish him more than is wise. I don't want to keep putting my energy into thinking how bad he is.

7. Goal-setting. Here are my priorities in this situation: . . . Here's what I want to try to make happen now: . . .

8. Listing options and choosing: How can I reach my goal? I can do this . . . or that . . . or this other idea . . . the advantages and disadvantages are . . . Here's the one I think is best.

9. Learning from the experience: Next time this happens, I'll know to handle it this way: . . . I learned from this something I can use next time . . .

10. Celebrating luck: I'm glad this thing happened to happen, because . . .

11. Celebrating someone else's choice: I'm glad this person decided to do this thing, because . . .

12. Celebrating your own choice: I'm glad I did this thing, because . . .

In any given situation, it's possible (though it's sometimes a stretch) to think any one of these twelve types of thoughts. One useful exercise is to generate each of the twelve types of thoughts about a wide variety of different situations. This helps in realizing that there are many possible ways to think and that you can be flexible in choosing.

Awfulizing, getting down on yourself, and blaming other people are sometimes useful thought patterns. But many people greatly overuse one or more of them. Replacing them with some of the others is often a very helpful thing for people to learn to do.

Goal-setting and listing options and choosing are components of the rational problem-solving and decision-making process. If people can get very oriented to making the best decision possible out of all the available options, their lives are often greatly improved.

Learning from experience is a reason for optimism. As we go through life, our experiences teach us how to handle our next experiences more skill-fully.

Celebratory thoughts are very much at the center of what constitutes happiness. Celebrating your own choice is a way of reinforcing yourself for the wise and good actions you do. Such self-reinforcement makes it more likely that you will repeat those wise and good actions.

Group 1: Productivity

I list productivity first among all groups of psychological skills for an important reason: it's possible to increase any other psychological skill, if only you're willing to work at it. A person can improve almost any problem, if only that person is willing to take constructive action and do something about it. We live in a world where information is available as never before. There is very good advice to be had on the handling of psychological problems, career problems, medical problems, financial problems, and all sorts of other problems – if people can only get themselves to read it. The major catch is that reading is work

Let's think of two major ways in which people respond to a problem, an unmet need, or a feeling of dissatisfaction with the way things are. I don't have enough money; I don't have good enough friends; the world is too violent; people are too selfish; I am not expert enough at what I do; my life is too disorganized; I feel as though I'm wasting time; my family life is too full of conflicts; I want to make a greater contribution to humanity – these are some of the problem-recognition thoughts that are basic to all our lives.

Some people have developed what I call the dissatisfaction-to-effort connection: they harness the feeling of dissatisfaction to generate energy toward productive activity. It's as if

there's a connection in the brain between the recognition of an unmet need and effort aimed at meeting it.

When the person with this sort of connection doesn't have enough money, she feels impelled to start reading and talking with people about how to get highly valued skills, make more money, save more, invest wisely. And after lots of information gathering, she starts plugging away at concrete efforts.

When the person with this sort of connection finds himself lonely, he starts gathering information about how to find and make and keep friends, listing options for constructive action, choosing carefully, and then energetically enacting those options.

When the person with this sort of connection finds herself dissatisfied with her performance in school, she reads and talks with people about how to improve her schoolwork, considers various plans, chooses carefully, and works diligently at the plan she has chosen. The people who seem automatically to connect unmet needs with productive effort are very lucky.

The other major way of responding to unmet needs is the one that most of us have to overcome. In this pattern, the dissatisfaction we feel produces bad feelings without generating effort to improve things. Sometimes, the bad feelings even create an urge toward escapism, which aims us away from constructive efforts. We can call this the dissatisfaction-to-escapism connection.

For example, a man feels dissatisfied with having too little money and too little success; he escapes these bad feelings by watching movies and drinking alcohol. A woman feels bad about not having friends; her bad feelings lead her to withdraw from people even more. A boy receives negative feedback on his schoolwork, and this makes schoolwork so unpleasant for him that he avoids it all the more.

So much depends upon whether we can feel that connection between problems and efforts toward solutions – between having goals and working toward those goals – between things that need to be changed and what we can do to change them.

One of those things is whether or not we feel depressed. Depression is usually experienced as a state of having given up. The fundamental depressing idea is "Things are bad, and I can do NOTHING about it." The fundamental anti-depressing idea is not "Things are perfect as they are; I don't need to do anything." Rather, the fundamental anti-depressing idea is, "Things can be improved, and there are various OPTIONS I can choose from; which one I choose matters; I will try to enact the best options I can."

Here are other paraphrases of the fundamental anti-depressing idea: "What I choose to do and think makes a big difference." "The name of the game is to pick the best way of handling any situation I'm given." "No matter what happens, I'll exert whatever effort it takes to make the best of it." "Whatever situation I'm in, constructive effort of the right kind can make at least a little difference in how things go." "I feel like exerting effort to make things better."

I list four skills in the productivity group. The first is maintaining a sense of purposefulness, a feeling of being called toward goals. The second is being able to exert effort toward those goals, in a persistent, concentrated way. The third is gradually developing your own competence at whatever it takes to accomplish your goals. And the fourth is staying organized, so that your effort can focus itself rather than being scattered in all directions. Self-discipline is another very important productivity skill, but it's important enough to be put in its own group. Let's study the first four one by one.

Skill 1: Purposefulness

It has been said that "He who has a *why* to live can bear almost any *how*." The skill of purposefulness is having that sense of *why*. What am I doing all this for? What are my goals? Why do I want to achieve them?

This surely must be one of the most important of psychological skills. If you don't know where you want your actions to take you, how can you make meaningful choices and decisions? If you don't know what you're aiming for, how can you get there? Without a sense of purpose and direction, you tend to drift, or just react to whatever comes along, or pursue goals that leave you disillusioned and unhappy. The skill of purposefulness is about consciously choosing how you want to direct your effort.

People seem constructed to want certain things

We can choose what goals we want to strive for, what purposes in life we want to adopt. There is a great deal of freedom in our choosing. But our brains appear to be set up with certain built-in motives. Some of these are very obvious: the need to breathe, eat, drink, sleep, and keep warm. Almost as obvious are needs to protect ourselves from physical injury and danger, to keep ourselves from getting hurt. The most basic pleasure and pain mechanisms of our bodies are set up so it feels good to meet our basic physical needs, and it feels bad not to meet them.

In today's world most of our basic needs require money. So the wish for money is tied to basic physical needs, although money can also facilitate the achievement of most of the others as well.

Less obvious, but probably just as much built into the brains of most people, is the wish to bond with other people – to make friends, to belong to a stable family or group of some sort, to have a "social network." People can survive as hermits, but it's not very easy. The wish to get people's approval is probably linked to this very basic need for social belonging.

The instinct to find a mate and pass our genes on to the next generation certainly operates for all non-extinct species of animals, including human beings. Sexual wishes are built into almost all human beings. Other motives also ultimately derive from the instinct to preserve the species. It's likely that the desires to be in love with a mate, to have children, and to nurture and protect children, are for many or most people built-in motives over and above sexual desires.

Another common motive, both in humans in animals, is getting the power to influence others. There is probably something built into our brains that makes it pleasant to affect other people, rather than to have them act "as if we didn't exist." It could be that much of the motivation for sports contests and all sorts of other competitions derive from the basic wish to be powerful.

The wish for competence, to figure out how to do something effectively, is another motive that appears fairly universal. This meshes with the desire for acceptance and approval by a social network. The areas in which we want competence are largely determined by what our social group deems useful. The desire for understanding, for figuring out what is going on, is closely linked to competence.

The word "achievement" is often used to describe the accomplishments that tend to bring approval and power and demonstrate competence.

Aesthetic motives are people's wishes for beauty in the world around them: to hear beautiful music, to experience the beauty of nature, to live in a pleasing building. The wish to create beauty is for many people a motive separate from simply experiencing it.

Last on this list, but most admired, are altruistic motives: the wish to help others, to make other people happy, to make the world a better place, and to achieve our full potential to contribute to humanity.

A psychologist named Abraham Maslow put forth the idea that people's needs and wishes seem to fall into a certain order, so that we can concentrate best on the "higher" needs when the "lower" needs are taken care of. For example: It would be hard, and usually not a good idea, to focus on creating a beautiful symphony if you were very thirsty and without water. Likewise, if you were standing in the street and a fast car started coming at you, you would need to focus on protecting yourself; the question of how to eliminate world hunger can wait at least until you get to the sidewalk.

Let's list some of the motives I've mentioned so far:
1. Breathing, eating, drinking, sleeping, keeping warm, etc.
2. Health, safety, avoiding injury and danger, self-protection
3. Money
4. Social belonging, having friends, being part of a group, affiliation
5. Getting the approval and esteem of others
6. Attracting a mate, being in love, romantic or sexual wishes.
7. The wish to have and/or to nurture children.
8. Power, influence, prestige.
9. Achievement
10. Competence, understanding.
11. Experiencing and creating beauty
12. Making others happy, making the world a better place.

Knowing, or at least theorizing, that these motives seem to be part of most human beings does not solve the problem of how to pick goals that are worthy of us. For each of these basic motives, there are ways to tap into them that get us into trouble, especially when one of the first eleven motives is allowed to grow to large proportions and is disconnected from the twelfth one, that of making others happy. Let's look at some of the trouble-making directions these motives can lead to.

Addictions

The capacity for physical pleasure is built into our brains to make sure we meet our basic physical needs. It feels good to eat, because we need food. But people, in their ingenuity, have discovered ways to stimulate the pleasure centers in the brain more directly, through a variety of drugs. The pursuit of physical pleasure through drug-taking can become so reinforcing that it crowds out other activities and creates addictions. The person whose main purpose is trying to find where the next dose of a pleasurable drug is coming from has a purpose that is unworthy; it detracts from the ability to help others.

There are activities other than drug-taking that give momentary pleasure despite being harmful in the long run. Many people get addicted to the excitement of gambling. Overeating can resemble a drug addiction.

In avoiding or getting over problems of addiction to pleasurable experiences, self-discipline is called for. Self-discipline is the ability to pass up pleasure for the sake of doing what is right or doing what is best in the long run. Later in this book there is a separate chapter on the skill of self-discipline.

Anxiety

The wish to protect oneself from danger is a motive that essential to survival. The feeling of fear exists to give us a signal that danger needs to be avoided. Sometimes when fear gets too prominent, other goals are interfered with. Those of us who are afraid to go out in public, who are afraid of contamination of anything we touch with germs, who greatly fear going over a bridge or being in the dark, need to re-channel or turn down fear. Doing this takes courage skills, which are discussed later in this book.

Money as an end rather than a means

Money is certainly worth striving for, as a means toward buying food, clothing, shelter, health care, and other necessities, and even some luxuries. However, when the motive to make money is not connected to the motive to make people happier, people can find themselves making money by taking it away from others, by means that are legal or illegal. If the whole goal of life is making money, then it's just as good to make money by marketing horror films to young children as it is by helping poor children learn to read.

A radical "free market" theory of economics would argue that the person who makes the most money does the most social good. People must want what they get from that person, or else they would not spend the money. And if the person makes more money than someone else, he or she must be supplying people with more of what they want.

In order to accept this reasoning you have to believe that all people spend their money in a rational way, a way that maximizes long-term happiness. But there's plenty of evidence that this isn't true, as when a parent spends all the family's money on illegal drugs instead of the children's basic needs. Similarly, each year Europeans spend about $50 billion on cigarettes; the world would be much better off if no cigarettes were made. More money does not necessarily mean more good.

Consumerism

While some people are obsessed with getting money, others (sometimes the same people) are obsessed with spending it. The motive of consumerism is summarized by a bumper sticker: "The person who dies with the most toys, wins." If you drive a car that is twice as expensive as your comparison person, you win in the car department. If your house costs twice as much as theirs, you win there. If you wear shoes that cost $200, whereas someone else wears "fake" ones that look almost the same but cost $40, you win there too. If there's a certain toy that is the rage this year, and you can get it for your child, you win.

You win if you can afford an even faster computer, a bigger swimming pool, a more exclusive club, a more exclusive school. Or in a different variation, you win if you can get a bet-

ter deal on this thing or that. You win if you save hundreds of dollars (by spending a few other thousands). In another variation, you win if you get the new version. This type of consumerism is summarized by, "Be the first one on your block to own one."

Consumerism is the orientation to life that is preached to us constantly in advertising. Our senses are repeatedly bombarded with messages that we need to buy something else. For many people the amount that is bought is limited only by the amount of money they have.

A sign of a culture that worships consumerism is the emergence of a new service: a person you can hire to help you figure out how to remove the clutter from your home after you have bought so much stuff that you don't have enough space to live in any more.

Seeking acceptance by whatever group you can get it from

We naturally want to be included in groups. Without a deeper sense of purpose, people can get caught up in the goal of simply pleasing whatever group they happen to find themselves among, usually by conforming to whatever behavior that group does. If they are among the fans of a certain celebrity, they will fawn over that celebrity; if they are among gang members, they try to please the gang; if they are among the drug subculture, they'll try to please the other drug users, and so forth.

Many people fall into this conformity trap, simply imitating the people around them. If the neighbors pour lots of chemicals onto their lawns, then they do too. If their coworkers steal things from the store, then they do too. If other kids at school all avoid being seen with their parents, then they must also. If they find themselves among a group of productive and honest and kind people, they can be lucky enough to try to imitate them in order to gain acceptance. But what they really need is not to have luck dictate the group they're in, but to choose a group to fit in with according to what they want to accomplish.

Tribalism

This is another harnessing of the need to affiliate with others in groups. Tribalism is the rule of life that says, "I'll protect my tribe from the enemy intruders," or "I'll help my tribe conquer the enemy." For centuries people have organized themselves into groups that defend themselves against other groups, so it's not surprising this is the primary motive of life for some people. One of the troubles with making this orientation toward life your primary motive is that, when enemies don't happen to exist at the moment, they must be created if life is to be meaningful. People can come up with paranoid ideas — the Jews are undermining our culture, there are communists hiding everywhere in our culture, all the blacks are trying to take us over, all the whites are constantly plotting against us. Many lives have been lost in wars created by the tribal mentality. And, sadly, when one group has the tribal mentality, other groups are often forced to adopt it for their own defense.

Getting famous

Seeking fame without asking whether the actions that accomplish it are good or bad for others is another distortion of the motive to have a social network, belong to a group, be known by others, and get approval. The rule that summarizes this purpose in life is "Become a household name." The more people who know who you are, the more points you get. According to this orientation, the currency for meaning in life is publicity. The mass communication media become the arbiters of who is good and important.

It's true that fame can often help people who are doing or providing something good to reach more people with it. But if the desire for fame is disconnected from the desire to help, there are multitudes of bad ways to get famous, as is demonstrated by picking up any newspaper. Being part of a scandal or doing a horrible, violent act will probably get your name known by more people than spending a whole lifetime working for peace, justice, or understanding.

Attractiveness

Many people have as the major purpose in life, looking good. This especially applies to young women, even in this liberated era. This is not surprising, given that many people, especially young men, evaluate young women almost totally according to how they look. There is a biologic basis to the worship of attractiveness; attractiveness of the body has a correlation with health and reproductive potential. Probably for this reason, evolution has built the brains of those in the reproductive years to be on the lookout for mates with certain physical characteristics. But the culture and the media reinforce the notion that attractiveness is the most important thing about a person, perhaps even more than our brain structure does.

Numerous studies have found that people act more favorably toward attractive people than toward unattractive ones, in all sorts of ways having nothing to do with choosing a mate. People are more interested in pleasing attractive people. Based on this, it's not irrational for any human being to try to look his or her best.

The worship of attractiveness can become an obsession. One element of attractiveness is having a body weight in the zone that the culture considers most beautiful. Many people become so obsessed with controlling their weight that this goal consumes energy best spent on more worthy goals. Eating disorders such as anorexia and bulimia can sometimes be greatly helped if the person can seriously ask herself the questions, "Am I here on earth for any reason other than to control my weight?

Am I here for a reason other than making myself look a certain way? Is eking out a few more attractiveness points all there is to life? Isn't there anything more important than that, to which I can devote myself?" People obsessed with their looks might do well to study the models of people who, despite not looking particularly good, have done good things and have been happy.

Maximally widespread sexual activity

I use this phrase to refer to the purpose for living (much more commonly pursued by males than females) that can be summarized as, "The larger the number of attractive sexual partners I can have, the better." Some people have argued that evolution has built into males a motive to spread their genes as widely as possible. Others point out that role models, such as James Bond, who are admired even by young boys, model something very far from a monogamous life style. Whatever the influence of culture or instinct, people need to use the thinking parts of their brains to consider what is best for themselves and for other human beings.

Power, disconnected from ethics

Social groups have pecking orders. Some people devote their lives to obtaining a position that keeps anyone from pecking them and allows them to peck whomever they want. From the empire builder who wants to acquire more and more businesses to the barroom brawler who wants to make sure he can beat any of the drinking crowd in a fight, this driving purpose can result in positive or negative action, depending on how that dominance is won.

The motive to have power and influence over another person can result in very evil behavior. People who make other people miserable just for the fun of it, who bully others, probably do it out of a misguided harnessing of the power motive. Bullying for the sake of power assertion seems to be much more common among males than among females.

On the other hand, like all the other motives, there are ways to link the desire for power with the desire to help. For example, if a judge attempts to become more powerful by getting a reputation as the most fair and just resolver of conflicts she can be, she is attaining power in a pro-social way.

Proficiency in violence

This world is fortunately civilized enough that, in most places, individuals get power by means other than proficiency in violence: by their knowledge, their skills, their money, and so forth. But, for much of human history and in many settings, the acquisition of power has been brutal, and the one who has had the most power to do harm has prevailed.

Many people, especially young boys, have a distorted view of how useful proficiency in violence is. "The person who is best at fighting, shooting, martial arts, etc., is the hero who prevails." This is the message sent to millions of little boys each day in "action and adventure" movies and video game adaptations of such movies.

One of the simplest plots of video games, repeated over and over, is the fight between the hero and the villain. If it moves, you should shoot it, kick it, or otherwise dispose of it. Our culture worships the actors who portray violent heroes. This orientation to life is one of the worst possible ones for people to adopt.

Achievement in not very useful fields

The achievement motive lies behind many great things people have accomplished. However, it's good to select carefully what you want to achieve success at. For example, it seems that a large number of little boys have their hearts set on someday participating in professional sports. This is not surprising, given the fame, fortune and approval given to the greatest sports heroes. Those boys need to consider, however, not only the very small chance they will ever be successful in professional sports, but also whether society is best served by effort devoted to defeating someone else in a game, as opposed to effort aimed at preventing war, hunger, poverty, violence, ignorance, disease, and the destruction of the environment.

Wasteful objects of beauty

The motive to create and appreciate and own beauty has been the source of much of the artistic and musical treasures of the world. The desire to preserve the beauty of nature is a motive that we partly depend upon for the preservation of the world.

On the other hand, spending huge amounts of money and effort on building an ornate temple, creating lush palaces, acquiring fantastically expensive art works, idolizing rock music stars, creating and buying lovely clothes – all this seems wasteful in a world where many people are hungry, sick, illiterate, poor, or violent.

Nothing in particular

Before leaving this incomplete list of types of goals and purposes that can cause trouble, we should mention a very common one: not having any particular goal or purpose. This results in boredom with existence, and the feeling that there isn't much point in anything. The word *ennui* describes this state. Someone may be enrolled in school, for lack of anything better to do, but not really be motivated to work. Someone may have a job, but not be able to find any point in it. Someone may have relationships that provide temporary satisfaction, but the relationships seem meaningless, the satisfaction fades, and the person is left with a sort of emptiness. Even the people who are struggling with meeting the basic survival needs of existence are probably happier than the people who can't see any point in anything.

Connecting all other motives to the helping motive

So far, I have mainly recounted ways in which the basic human motives can get us into trouble. But these same motives can drive us to the highest and most worthy and best behavior, to meeting our full potential. Here, I believe, is the most important idea of this chapter: All the basic human motives can be harnessed wisely, provided they are connected to the one I listed last on the list – helping others, being kind, making the world a better place.

Wonderful things can happen when the motives I listed work in partnership with the wish to make things better for other people. For example, it can be a wonderful thing to make lots of money, if that money is made by doing things that truly make people happier, and the money is also used in ways that reduce suffering and cruelty or otherwise increase happiness. Setting up social networks and making oneself valued by others in the social network can be an extremely positive activity, if the network exists for purposes that make sentient beings better off.

Working toward great achievement is a wonderful direction for life, if the achievement fosters happiness. Even meeting the basic needs of taking care of our own health and safety is a more meaningful calling if we can remind ourselves that the point of such self-care is at least partly to preserve our ability to bring happiness to others.

The central idea of making people happy

What should we do, what is good to do? This is the subject of ethics.

A summary statement of ethics that is good enough for most purposes is the Golden Rule. One version of it was stated by Confucius somewhere around the year 500 B.C.: "Is there any one maxim which ought to be acted upon throughout one's life? Surely the maxim of loving kindness is such: Do not unto others what you would not have them do unto you." Other versions reside in the sacred writings of all the world's major religions.

In order for the Golden Rule to make sense, we have to tack on an assumed qualification: "Do unto others as you would have them do unto you, *if you were in their circumstances*." For example, if I'm a surgeon I find it ethical to operate on people whom I wouldn't want to operate on me! If I'm a parent I find it ethical to put a very young child in diapers and a high chair, despite not wanting to be so dressed and seated myself. To give a less trivial example: perhaps one person places a very high value on his reputation, and thus would like to be locked up if he shows any signs of mania or similar illnesses that affect his judgment. But his preference does not automatically give him the right to use this rule with people who are in different circumstances and who do not share his preferences.

Two of the major schools of ethical philosophy are represented by the "utilitarians," and the "Kantians." Let's examine each of these briefly.

Here are some words from John Stuart Mill, one of the utilitarian philosophers. The following is from *Utilitarianism, Liberty, and Representative Government*, first published in 1863. I'll quote Mill's words, and then offer my more simple-minded translation.

"The creed which accepts as the foundation of morals, Utility, or the Greatest Happiness Principle, holds that actions are right in proportion as they tend to promote happiness, wrong as they tend to produce the reverse of happiness. By happiness is intended pleasure, and the absence of pain; by unhappiness, pain, and the privation of pleasure . . . All desirable things (which are as numerous in the utilitarian as in any other scheme) are desirable either for the pleasure inherent in themselves, or as means to the promotion of pleasure and the prevention of pain."

Or in other words: Mill believes that if you want to know whether an action is right or wrong, you have to ask, "What are its effects?" Given the choice between two actions, according to Mill, you should choose the one that causes the most happiness to result.

In the same work, Mill writes this: "As between his own happiness and that of others, utilitarianism requires him to be as strictly impartial as a disinterested and benevolent spectator. In the Golden Rule, we read the complete spirit of the ethics of utility. To do as you would be done by, and to love your neighbor as yourself, constitute the ideal perfection of utilitarian morality."

In other words, Mill's philosophy requires that you take into account other people's happiness just as much as your own, just as is suggested by the Golden Rule.

Mill goes on to write a long sentence, part of which I'll quote: "Education and opinion, which have so vast a power of human character, should so use that power as to establish in the mind of every individual an indissoluble association between his own happiness and the good of the whole; especially between his own happiness and the practice of such modes of conduct as regard for the universal happiness prescribes; so that not only he may be unable to conceive the possibility of happiness to himself, consistently with conduct opposed to the general good, but also that a direct impulse to promote the general good may be in every individual one of the habitual motives of action, and the sentiments connected therewith may fill a large and prominent place in every human being's sentient existence."

To put this more simply: Mill wishes for a world in which people are trained to feel good about making others feel good. He imagines a world in which people are in the habit of thinking, "Will this action have a good effect for those concerned?"

Another very influential ethical philosopher, (who used language even more difficult than that of Mill!), was

Immanuel Kant. Part of Kant's ethical philosophy was the notion you should not use people, as though they were just ways for you to accomplish things, without taking into account their own welfare as an end in itself.

Another famous ethical guide given by Kant is called the "categorical imperative," as follows: "Act only on that maxim through which you can at the same time will that it should become a universal law." In other words, don't act on principles that you want everybody else to avoid. For example, if I find myself thinking, "I'll lie to anyone whenever it meets my purposes," but yet I think, "People shouldn't lie to me!" then that's a clue that I'm not living up to Kant's rule.

If you think about Kant's rule enough, it seems to get back to the general idea of trying to make others happy, trying to act toward them using principles that you wish they would use in acting toward you – the basic spirit of the Golden Rule again.

When we speak about doing good for "others," are we speaking just about other people, or should we include nonhuman animals? I would certainly vote for including nonhuman animals – preventing cruelty to them, being kind to them. Should all animals receive equal value? I would vote "no" on this: for example, I value the lives and feelings of dogs and gorillas more highly than those of fleas and mosquitoes. Nonetheless, a reasonable ethical system should at least consider the welfare of all sentient beings, even if we don't want to give them all equal standing.

Concern for others as the smartest way to look after yourself

Some have argued that if you're interested only in maximizing your own happiness, the best "game" to adopt for your own amusement is, "Let's see how happy I can make others." (This is assuming that you don't also forget about the other motives, such as keeping warm, remembering to eat, getting enough money, and so forth.)

Why should making other people happy be such a good way of becoming a happy person? Because it's a goal that can be attained in many different ways; because people tend to want to make you happy back when you make them happy; because there may be something built into the brain that makes happiness result from people's helping each other. But whatever the reason, people have observed that the people who are most content, who have the least need to drug themselves, who have the best lives, tend to be those oriented to making the world (or their small corner of it) a better place.

The happiest people are a rather unselfish bunch. But they are not masochists. They usually don't renounce their own needs totally. They know that it's hard to go on making others happy when they themselves are miserable.

Happiness is the process of reaching goals; it's not having everything you want already

People seem to be happiest when they want something very much, and their actions are achieving that goal, bit by bit. People do not seem happiest when they have already gotten everything they could possibly want, and there is nothing they have to do to get anything. In fact, the situation where there is no connection between the effort they exert and the payoffs they receive is downright depressing. The phrase that students of human behavior use to describe the situation where getting what you want is very closely tied to the effort you exert is *contingent reinforcement*. When your reinforcers, i.e. rewards or payoffs, depend on the effort you exert, they are contingent. When you get, or fail to get, the reinforcers no matter what you do, the reinforcers are noncontingent. A state of psychological well-being seems often to accompany contingent reinforcement.

It's good to have goals harnessed to several motives

One of the most important ideas of this chapter is that the wish to make other people better off is at the heart of worthy goals. If some means of making people better off can also tap into other sources of motivation, then that's all the better. It's like having an airplane with several different engines. If one fails, the others will be capable of supplying the energy.

Let's imagine a young adult applying to medical school who asks himself, "Why do I want to be a doctor?" He figures that the medical profession allows him to help other people and make the world a little better place. But a variety of other motives probably also get harnessed. He wants to keep eating, to provide for his own safety, to get money; to get a position of power and influence, to get understanding of processes that are very interesting to him, and competence at important skills. In addition, he hopes that the achievements he makes in his profession will bring him a certain amount of fame, and that he will have no trouble maintaining a positive social network. He hopes that his profession will make him more attractive to a mate, and that he will be able to get into a marriage where his wishes for love and sexuality and his wishes to have and nurture children are met. Finally, he hopes he will get enough money from his job to be able to live in surroundings where the beauty of nature is nearby. Thus, all of the major motives we have listed in this chapter are involved in his wish.

We could go through the same analysis with most other jobs and many other hobbies. Why does a person exercise regularly? She wants to preserve her own health; she wants to make herself more attractive; she enjoys the social network she has formed with other people who exercise; she enjoys the experience of natural beauty she gets while running cross-country or hiking;

she saves some money by doing physical tasks herself rather than hiring other people to do them. She nurtures her children by going for walks with them and playing soccer with them. She knows that she is making the world a little better place by sharing these positive experiences with them and other people.

If you can find goals that can tap into several of the various sources of motivation listed in this chapter, you're likely to find those activities especially meaningful.

Some ways of helping

If someone has the overarching goal of making the world better, and making sentient beings happier, it's necessary to pick some specific ways of doing this. What are some worthy goals? I offer these, not as a complete list, but just as some examples.

1. Contributing to a positive emotional climate within your own family or social network, by saying kind and cheerful words to others, by doing work that assists others, by being a good listener for others, by modeling joyousness for others.

2. Teaching other people the skills they need in order to be happy.

3. Writing or otherwise communicating useful information to others.

4. Making discoveries about the world, seeking out the truth through scientific observation.

5. Meeting people's basic needs for food, clothing, shelter, health care, safety, and nontoxic environments.

6. Helping people to solve conflicts and make joint decisions peacefully and justly.

7. Working toward ending violence of all sorts.

8. Preserving the environment, not poisoning or destroying it.

9. Making artistic creations that people can enjoy and benefit from.

10. Meeting people's needs for goods and services that, while they are not essential, enrich life and make it more fulfilling.

11. Allowing communication, transportation, transactions and manipulation of information to take place, and with convenience.

12. Preserving life and health through safety measures, and preventive and curative interventions.

This list can surely be enlarged. These are the types of goals that are readily are connected to making the world a better place.

Here's a purposefulness exercise. Generate a list of various specific human activities, and try to rank order them. Which contributes the most to the welfare of the world? Which next most?

Here's a similar exercise. Suppose you were a government official, with a billion dollars to spend. What possible uses could you put this money to, and how would you rank order them in terms of helping humanity the most?

Do you feel you have an overarching purpose in life? Do you have a very central general goal? If you do, it will be useful to write down that goal on paper, carry the paper with you, and pull it out often to read it. Ask yourself, to what extent are your actions in accordance with your overarching purpose? This is a good way of keeping on track.

Skill 2: Sustaining Attention to Tasks

The skill of sustaining attention to tasks goes by several names, among them "persistence skills" and "concentration skills." With all of these labels, we'll talk about the skill of focusing attention on one thing long enough to get the results you want. Examples include paying attention to homework long enough to get it completed, concentrating on a problem long enough to get it solved, concentrating on what someone is saying long enough to understand what she is telling you, concentrating on reading well enough to understand thoroughly.

Learning versus pharmacological approaches to attention

Concentration comes much easier for some people than for others. Some people who find concentration very hard and who have certain other symptoms get a diagnosis of attention deficit disorder. A good bit of evidence shows us that difficulties in concentration – like almost all other aspects of our personalities – have a hereditary component. People whose moms and dads had a hard time concentrating tend to have a hard time concentrating themselves. The fact that attention difficulties can be hereditary implies that there is something biological, located in our brains, that makes concentration easier for some people and more difficult for others.

Some people take these facts and infer from them that attention problems can only be helped by medication. This inference is a serious error. Learning is a way of changing the biology of our brains, just as medication is. Every time we learn anything, our brains are physically changed by that learning. Sometimes that learning is even visible to the brain imaging methods available today. In one experiment, teaching people with obsessive compulsive disorder to face the situations that tended to bring out compulsions, without giving in to the temptation to do compulsions, produced changes in brain activity that were visible with a method of brain imaging. Training in attention skills is likely to change brain physiology as well.

Unfortunately, training in concentration skills for someone who is very low in natural concentration talent (e.g., someone with a fairly high degree of attention deficit) is a very time consuming process. People should probably think not of several hours to learn it, but several hundred hours.

The current scientific literature on attention problems is rather negative about the possibility of helping attention problems by skill training. But there has hardly ever been a published study in the treatment outcome literature where the subjects received several hundred hours of focused training in a skill.

When I have examined the literature on skill training for attention deficit disorders, the longest trainings are in the neighborhood of forty hours, and often even these hours are not spent in concentration exercises per se. Consequently, most of the published studies haven't tested the hypothesis that several hundred hours of practice and work could produce big improvements.

Is it realistic to expect anyone to work for hundreds of hours on anything? Current psychotherapeutic treatment emphasizes extremely "brief treatment." But people do work for hundreds of hours on many skills. We see lots of people who are capable of playing musical instruments such as the piano or violin; it's estimated that these take close to a thousand hours of practice to learn to play fairly well. We see lots of people on sports teams who practice hundreds or even thousands of hours to achieve excellence. We routinely see people who have learned calculus; to get to this stage requires several hundred hours of training in mathematics skills. What if we approached any of these skills with the attitude that if you couldn't learn them in twenty to forty hours, you should give up on a learning-based approach to them? We'd be giving up on all of them. Similarly, we should not give up on learning based approaches to attention skills.

This belief, by the way, does not imply that medicine is not useful. Indeed it should be used when the benefits exceed the risks. But a discussion of the risks and benefits of medicine is not a topic for this book.

A sales pitch for concentration skills

Is it really worthwhile to spend hundreds of hours working on concentration skill? The answer is yes, for two reasons. First, concentration skill is so crucial to success in so many areas. Second, it's possible to work on concentration while at the same time working on other goals, namely schoolwork, reading, or using any other skill requiring concentration.

Why is concentration skill so important? One reason is that in today's culture, most people spend a good portion of the first parts of their lives in school. Much of people's feeling about success in life comes from how well they do in tasks of reading, remembering things that were read, solving math problems, writing coherently, and so forth. If you're going to spend much of your life in activities that put a high premium on concentration skills, you'd better get good at concentration.

But even after school, a vast majority of the most pleasant and high-paying jobs involve dealing in information. A doctor who listens to symptoms and diagnoses an illness is an information-handler. A lawyer who listens to the circumstances of a case, is familiar with the law that is relevant to it, and presents this information in court, is an information-handler. A writer, computer programmer, composer, or artist delivers an information product.

A business executive inputs information relevant to the business, and outputs information in the form of decisions, and earns his salary for dealing in information. An accountant takes in information and rearranges it in a form that is relevant, for example, to taxpaying decisions. A scientist reads the available information on a question, and searches out more information.

A minister or priest or rabbi deals in the information present in religious writings, and figures out how to apply such information to current questions of living. An engineer takes information about materials and techniques and applies them to decisions of design and production of things people need. All of these information-handlers must concentrate in order to input and output their information well.

Concentration is crucial not only in work and school, but also in human relations. One of the basic skills of forming good relationships is being able to listen to another person. If you can't keep your mind on what the other person is saying, if you aren't patient enough to hear them out, it's much more difficult to create a good relationship.

And finally, there are hundreds of tasks of daily living where concentration skills make the difference between frustration and pleasure. It takes concentration, for example, to deal with and organize the papers that come in the mail, to remember where we put things, to remember what to take where, to organize what to do by what times.

For all these reasons, I believe that work on concentration skills should be a part of the universal curriculum for all people, not just those with diagnosed attention problems. However, it's usually the case that *neither* those with attention deficit disorder nor the general population group receives any systematic training in concentration.

The connection between boredom and low concentration skills

A very frequent complaint by people with low skills of sustaining attention is that something or other is boring. Almost everyone has the skill of sustaining attention to interesting, fascinating tasks that are not too hard, not too easy, but just at the right level of challenge. What really challenges this skill is "boring" tasks such as reading very difficult material, working at things that are quite complex, working at things that don't yield results quickly. If you are good at this skill, you are hard to bore, because you have the patience to find something interesting in nearly every task.

Sometimes people feel bored when they feel a task is too easy. But after you already know how to do something, if you want to get really great at it, you have to practice over and over so the performance will come more automatically, and you can focus your attention on doing it with true excellence. So it's necessary to learn to tolerate the boredom of doing something that's already easy again and again.

Sometimes people feel bored when a task is too hard. For example, suppose there is a very hard problem, and you have to keep thinking about it in lots of different ways, but still the answer doesn't come. If you don't have the patience to stick with the task and tolerate the frustration of not being able to get it, you won't be able to get really hard things done. But when you learn this skill of persisting at hard tasks, you can accomplish far more than you ever thought possible.

Someone who can't stand boredom sometimes does what we call "sensation-seeking behavior." This means the person tries to create some sort of excitement that will relieve his boredom.

Sometimes people get this excitement by starting an argument with someone. For example, the person creates a ruckus by refusing to do something that someone else wants, or unreasonably insists that someone do something. For some people even unpleasant arguments are better than boredom. These people can greatly improve their relationships with people by learning to tolerate low-stimulation situations better.

If you're not skilled at sustaining attention and tolerating low stimulation, it's less pleasant for you to get information simply through a string of words. You're reading a string of words right now. You listen to a string of words whenever you go to a class and hear a teacher lecture. The person who can't tolerate low stimulation is more dependent upon visual images, especially visual images that change much more rapidly, such as in a television program or a movie or video game.

What improvement in concentration means

As we improve in concentration, we improve in at least three different ways. We can keep our minds on:
1. less exciting material,
2. with greater focus,
3. for a longer time.

Thus, when I move from being able to focus only on movies and video games, to being able to focus on reading very exciting books such as mystery novels, I'm improving my attention skills. When I go from exciting books to less exciting ones (such as *Instructions on Psychological Skills)*, I'm also improving attention skills. When I can do any of these activities without my mind's traveling to other thoughts so often, that's improvement. And when I move from being able to focus from five minutes to fifteen minutes to an hour to two hours, I'm improving by another measure. It's good to monitor each of these three variables as you work on concentration skills, and to celebrate any time you get better in one way while holding the other two constant.

Is our culture becoming less skilled in concentration?

Some writers have raised the possibility that, as a culture, we are losing the skill of sustaining attention, as we become more accustomed to rapidly changing stimulation. Perhaps we are getting used to seeing television and hearing music and getting all sorts of other stimuli from electronic inputs, such as video games, so frequently that we are losing the ability to read and listen to words.

As Neil Postman has noted, the debates between Abraham Lincoln and Stephen Douglas in 1858 were phrased in language very much as someone would write, and yet the audiences of the day seemed to tolerate listening to these debates for three or four hours, taking a break and then continuing to listen for another three or four hours. Postman argues that it's almost inconceivable that an audience of today could sustain attention that long. Comparing the lengthy and attention-demanding works of Shakespeare or Verdi with today's television shows makes us wonder about what is happening to our collective attention spans.

Concentration exercises

1. *The self-observation exercise.*

The first exercise doesn't ask you to sustain a focus at all, but just to observe what you are focusing on. You practice the skill of self-observation.

To do this exercise you first simply sit and close your eyes. (Or ride on an exercise bike, and leave your eyes open.) Let your mind do whatever it wants to. In other words, let your mind drift. If you want to think about some one thing, do so. If you want to flit from one thing to the next, that's fine.

The only thing that makes this an exercise is for you to reserve a little bit of your mind to observe what the rest of it is doing. Ask yourself the questions, "What am I thinking about now?" "What images are going through my mind now?" "What feelings am I having now?" Start out by doing this for short periods of time, for example, a minute. After the minute is up, recall what you thought about, and then report this to someone. Gradually, you can do this for more and more minutes.

What is the point of this? If you are going to gain in the ability to focus, you first have to have awareness of what you are focusing on. Have you ever let your attention drift away from what you wanted to be focusing on, without discovering this until perhaps five or ten minutes or more later?

The point of the self-observation exercise is that, if you get off task, you'll know it more immediately. If you notice yourself getting off task as soon as you do it, you can bring yourself back very quickly.

You want to be fully immersed in what you are doing, except for saving a very small portion of your mind to observe yourself. If you save too much, you'll be so self-conscious that you don't perform as well. But if you don't save any, you have no way to monitor yourself and know how well you are doing. You learn how to save just the right amount of neuronal energy for self-observation by seeing what maximizes your performance over repeated efforts. We'll talk more about that later.

2. *Self-observation out loud.*

Here's a variant of the self-observation exercise. In this one, you do the same thing; only this time you say aloud what you are thinking about. You describe in words any images that flash on the screen of your consciousness. You say out loud any thoughts you are thinking. You name any feelings you are having.

This is a difficult one. Talking your thoughts certainly affects what thoughts you have. But that's OK. The main thing is to practice conscious awareness of what is going through your mind. The more you do this, the more you are set up to realize when you are concentrating on one thing, and when you are drifting from one thing to another.

3. *Shifting focus on purpose.*

In this concentration exercise, you pick something to focus your attention on, such as your own breathing. During the exercise you will turn your attention to your breathing, then to anything else you want, then back to your breathing, then back to anything else you want. You keep shifting the focus, on purpose, about every thirty seconds or so.

The point of this exercise is to get practice at consciously directing the focus of your attention. As you do this exercise, feel what it's like to direct your attention toward something, and to feel your mind respond.

For example: I focus on my breathing for a few seconds. Then I turn my attention to looking at my telephone answering machine, and my mind turns to some of the messages I've received. Then I turn the attention back to my breathing, and feel the dryness in my nostrils as the air goes in, and the moisture in my nostrils as the air goes out. Now I look at a clock, and watch the second hand moving around the clock face. I do this, thinking about the passage of time on various scales, and then I direct my attention back to my breathing.

The point of this exercise is to practice getting your attention to go where you want it to. So much of the time, our attention "is drawn" by external stimuli rather than directed from within. We walk into a room, and the television attracts our attention. Someone speaks to us, and that draws our attention from the television to the person's voice. Then the doorbell rings, and that pulls our attention to it.

But by practicing the conscious directing of your attention, you strengthen the "executive" part of the brain that tells the rest of it what to focus on. You want this executive to be in charge, and you do not want to have your attention held hostage to whatever external stimuli happen to be going on at the moment.

There are several variations on this exercise. You can, if you wish, select two things to pay attention to, and alternate between the two of them; for example, you read a book for a minute and then relax your muscles for a minute. Or you do math problems for a minute and then spend a minute looking at the blackness that happens when you close your eyes. You can pick long periods between the shift of focus, or short periods such as three or four seconds.

4. *The concentrate, rate, and concentrate exercise.*

In this exercise, you do anything that requires concentration: reading, typing, math problems, writing, dancing, solving chess problems, playing the piano. But you stop every few minutes and rate how well you concentrated on the task. If you concentrated well, you try to remember what you did with your brain that let you concentrate so well. If you did not concentrate well, you notice that, and resolve that, on the next trial, you'll emulate a time when you did concentrate well. Then you go back and concentrate again.

If you wish, you can use the following scale to answer the question "how much" concentration:

0 = None
2 = Only a little
4 = Some, but not much
6 = Pretty much
8 = High amount

10 = Very high amount

What's the idea behind this exercise? In explaining this, let's think about the skill of shooting foul shots in basketball. Most good basketball players spend a good bit of time practicing these important shots.

But let's imagine that a player went to practice foul shots blindfolded and earplugged so that he couldn't tell whether the shot went in or not, whether it was to the right or left or too high or low. The practice session wouldn't be nearly so productive, would it? Because the *feedback loop* would not be closed, the information on each shot would not get back to the learner.

I believe this is the way most people practice concentrating when they do homework or read a book – without closing the feedback loop. That is, they try to concentrate, but they never raise the questions to themselves, "How well did I concentrate then?" "Was that one of my best concentration efforts lately, or was it average, or not so good?" Rather than thinking about these questions, they are thinking about the subject matter at hand, or else they're off on something else. But seldom do they get a concentration rating.

When you do periodically give yourself a concentration rating, you close the feedback loop. You are like the basketball player now practicing with the blindfold off.

I've written some computer programs that ask you to practice typing letters or typing the answers to math fact problems. You can set the period of practice for whatever time you want – say two minutes. During that time you practice, and the computer keeps track of how well you are doing. At the end of each trial, the program prompts you to rate your concentration during that trial. When you are done, the program computes a correlation coefficient to see how your subjective concentration rating correlates with your objective performance. These programs are meant to help you notice when you are performing well or poorly, and to take that into account when judging your own concentration.

But you don't need a computer program to do the concentrate, rate, and concentrate exercise. In one variation, you can study with another person. You can read something and answer questions on it, or write something, or work problems. The other person notices how much you are accomplishing. Every few minutes you stop and rate your concentration, and you compare it with the other person's rating of how much you accomplished. In another variation, you work alone. You simply stop every few minutes to rate yourself, remember the moments of highest concentration, and resolve to emulate those during the next trial.

5. *The reflections exercise.*

We will discuss reflections in a chapter on the skill of empathic listening. But here we use reflections in the service of gaining concentration.

Let's first describe the version you do with another person. Your partner's role is to either read or speak to you. The simplest way to do this is for your partner to read to you from a book. Your partner stops every so often, maybe every sentence, maybe every paragraph. You respond with a "reflection" of what your partner read. How do you do a reflection? You can use one of the following prompts and fill in the blank.

Prompts for Yourself to Do Reflections

So you're saying _____?
What I hear you saying is

_____.

In other words, _____?
So if I understand you right,

_____?
It sounds like _____.
Are you saying that _____?
You're saying that _____?

What you're doing is saying back what you heard the other person read or say.

Your partner's response can be simply "Yes," if you heard correctly, or "No," if you didn't. If the answer is "No," then your partner should read it again, and let you try again.

Alternatively, the partner can rate the accuracy of your reflection on a 0 to 10 scale. You can again use the rating scale for "How much," asking the question "How much accuracy was there in the reflection?"

0 = None
2 = Only a little
4 = Some, but not much
6 = Pretty much
8 = High amount
10 = Very high amount

If you can keep doing this activity over time, shooting for
1. more accurate reflections,
2. of more difficult, complex, and unexciting material,
3. for a longer and longer time,
then you are almost sure to improve your concentration skills. This exercise is very hard work, but it's worth it. It's really a variant of the concentrate, rate, and concentrate activity. And that activity in all its variants is to concentration-building as pushups and weightlifting are to muscle-building.

6. *The reflections exercise with reading rather than listening.*

In this exercise, rather than listening to someone read or speak, you read a paragraph yourself. After finishing the paragraph, you paraphrase out loud what you recall from it. If you're lucky, your personal concentration trainer, a very fast typist, can transcribe this for you.

If you've done a great deal of the concentrate, rate, and concentrate activity with typing, you're a fast typist yourself and can summarize the main idea of the paragraph in writing. Later you can look back at how your summaries compare with the original para-

graph, and see if over time you are getting more and more accurate.

7. *Constructing your own test, and taking it.*

This exercise is another variant of the concentrate, rate, and concentrate exercise. Suppose you are studying a book. Like the other variants of the concentrate, rate, and concentrate activity, you don't try to passively absorb information. You do something that tests or measures how well you are concentrating. You do a task that's impossible to do without concentrating on the information.

A task I recommend is pretending to be a teacher and actually writing a test on the material that you are studying. With each sentence you read, you think, "Can I make a question out of this?" Having to make that decision tends to keep your mind on the task. If you get to the end of a paragraph and the answer to the question "What question can I make about this" is "I have no idea because I wasn't tuned in," then you've received valuable feedback. You've closed the feedback loop. On the other hand, if you can think of a really good test question about the material, that's important feedback too.

Then, when you finish writing the test, you get more feedback on your concentration effectiveness by taking your own test and writing out the answers. Then you grade it and practice answering any missed questions until you can get them correct. At any point, if you don't remember or understand the material well enough to complete a step in the process, you go back and study it again, and see if you can do so the second time around.

You are constantly giving yourself feedback about your concentration as you complete this whole process. My guess is that people who take the time, energy, and concentration to use this technique will see big increases in their mastery of the material. If you're a student, I would guess that using this technique would improve your grades.

7. *The return to the central question exercise.*

This is another way of completing the feedback loop, seeing how well you are concentrating. Here the measure of your concentration is how well you can keep churning out answers to a question with many answers. I learned this exercise from a yoga book; this is a technique yogis use to develop their skills of mind-control.

The yoga book described starting with a question that can trigger lots of thoughts. If you want, you draw a circle with a question inside it, and lots of arrows going outward from the circle. Now, for each of the arrows, you think of an idea. After you think of that idea, you return to the central question and see whether you can think of another. You keep going until none immediately come to mind.

Even when you think you have run out of ideas, you keep pulling for new ones. You resist the urge to give up and go on to something else. You also resist the urge to go off on a tangent from one idea to the next without returning to the concept in the center of the circle. The skill of persisting on one focus until maximal benefit has been obtained before shifting to another focus is a central skill this exercise practices. (It also exercises the skills of divergent thinking and option-generating.)

Although the spatial image given in the yoga book is one of a circle with lines going outward from it, an equally good way to do the exercise is to put the central concept at the top of the page and list the offshoots of it on successive lines down the rest of the page. In other words, make a list.

In the yoga book, there is an example for concentration on the concept of "cow." The question was defined as, "What is anything you can say about a cow?" The thinker might start with a list something like this:

Usually gentle
People use it to get milk
Usually lives on farms
Eats grass and clover
Makes mooing sound
Hides can be brown, black, or reddish
Hides sometimes used to make leather

If you do this exercise, you will perceive the difference between the way you think while doing it, and the more tangential course that our thoughts often take. This course may be represented as follows:

Cows --> Give milk --> A milk shake would taste good --> I saw Mary Jones last time I got a milk shake --> Mary Jones's brother plays the guitar --> I saw someone break his guitar on stage --> They're smashing up that vacant house on the corner -->

Letting the thoughts drift from one to another without any "return to the center" has many useful purposes, and is not to be discouraged; the point is that the style of thought with "return to the center" is also useful and should be in the repertoire. Let's give another example of it.

Suppose the question is, "How can violence be reduced?" You can do the same concentration exercise, sitting and thinking about the question, writing down one possible answer after another, but always returning to the main question after every possible answer. The list someone would make might look like this:

How can violence be reduced?
> Teach problem-solving skills
> Reduce availability of guns
> Reduce violent models in the media
> Form a world court or world government
> Educate people better, for useful work
> Teach parenting
> Improve dispute-resolution systems in community
> Reduce the demand for illegal drugs
> Remove children from violently abusive parents more quickly
> Teach people about heroes of peace and heroes of kindness
> Provide fictional models of peace and kindness
> Help teachers promote kindness in classrooms
> Remove violent criminals from rest of society
> Put more law enforcement officers into action
> Promote a universal second language for reducing misunderstandings among nations

Returning to the central question and continuing to search one's mind for items to add to the list is the essence of the exercise.

Suppose you make this exercise a little more complex. After listing ideas, you arrange them some rational order. You can generate a list of ideas that are subtopics of the ideas previously generated, and more subtopics of these, as far as you want to go. This then becomes the structure known to writing teachers as an outline. The exercise can get transformed into writing a book! Teaching people to organize their own thinking through writing is indeed a useful antidote to skill deficiency in concentration.

8. *Returning to the central question with options or consequences.*

Two particular types of central questions that are very worthwhile to think about have the following formats. First: "Here is a situation. To respond to it, what options can you think of? Second: "Here's an option someone is considering. What possible consequences could come from doing that option?" In some of the materials I have written that are companions to this book, there are many problems, each with several options listed; in another section there are many actions listed, each with several possible consequences. If you wish to, you can test your own option or consequence lists against the ones I generated for these hypothetical situations or actions.

Generating options and predicting consequences are very important parts of the decision-making and problem-solving process. By using these sorts of questions for the return to the central question exercise, you're able to practice concentration while at the same time practicing problem-solving.

Listing options and listing possible consequences are not the only parts of the decision-making process that are useful to practice with the return to the central question exercise. When you read the section on decision-making, you'll see several other processes that are central to making good decisions. These include listing your goals for a certain situation, listing the factors that are important to maximize or minimize, listing the advantages and disadvantages of a certain idea, and oth-

ers. Any listing can be used for the return to the central question exercise, but these decision-making maneuvers are particularly useful to practice in this way.

9. *The good will exercise.*

Here's another useful concentration exercise: the exercise of good will. This is similar to the technique of relaxation using a mantra that we will look at more thoroughly in the chapter on relaxation skills. In relaxation using a mantra, you do something repetitively with your mind, such as to say a word or gaze at an object. If you notice that your mind has drifted away from the mantra, you gently direct your attention back to the mantra. In the good will exercise, the mantra is mentally directing good wishes toward yourself and other people, one by one.

You close your eyes and relax. Then you think about someone, possibly yourself. You direct good wishes toward yourself:

May I become the best I can become.
May I give and receive compassion and kindness.
May I live happily and productively.

Now think of someone else, and picture that person clearly. Go through these three wishes for that person. Then will that these wishes come true for that person.

May she become the best she can become.

May she give and receive compassion and kindness.

May she live happily and productively.

Let your mind range from one person to the next, and spend some time willing these positive outcomes for each of these people. If you find your mind straying from the activity (for example, you find yourself making a grocery list in your mind instead), reinforce yourself for noticing what your mind is doing rather than punishing yourself for getting off track, and swing back to the exercise of good will.

What's the point of this exercise? You're doing an exercise in concentration whenever you try to keep your mind on something and monitor whether you are succeeding or not. The good will exercise is useful also because of what you're accomplishing at the same time. To practice willing good for yourself and others improves your skills of kindness, empathy, forgiveness, conflict resolution, purposefulness, and various other skills, as well as concentration.

When I do this I try to remind myself of images of wise holy people whose good wishes for people are mental and spiritual and cooperative rather than superficial and material and competitive. Thus, good will for the happiness of my friend may be that, in her tennis game tomorrow, she will experience joy and peak performance and conduct herself in a way that betters the world, rather than wishes along the lines of "I hope she beats the pants off those snooty opponents of hers."

10. *Fantasy rehearsals.*

I've discussed the technique of fantasy rehearsal at several points in this book. When doing fantasy rehearsals, you picture and describe to yourself a certain situation, and you run through your mind an image of yourself doing the thoughts, emotions, and behaviors that you would most like to do in that situation. You are practicing in your imagination the best possible response to a certain situation, once you have decided what that response is.

The main purpose of fantasy rehearsal is to practice positive patterns of thought, emotion, and behavior in your imagination, and make yourself more likely to carry out those positive patterns in real life by such practice. But to do this exercise requires concentration, and thus it can be used as a concentration exercise. If you concentrate fully on fantasy rehearsals every day, your concentration skills are likely to increase.

The principle of fantasy rehearsal is used very frequently in sports psychology. Some of the earliest research in fantasy rehearsal involved sports performance. In several studies, athletes were divided into two groups, and one group was asked to practice their performance in their imagination, while another group was asked to do something irrelevant to their performance. After some time of this, the group that practiced in imagination did better in a real-life performance test than did the comparison group.

In doing fantasy rehearsals, it's good to go through the following steps, as remembered by the mnemonic STEBC. STEBC stands for situation, thoughts, emotions, behaviors, and celebration. You imagine yourself in a certain concrete situation. If there is someone saying something to you, you imagine a particular person, not just a generic person. You make the image as vivid as possible. You describe the situation and the events up to the choice point where you will respond.

Next you talk to yourself about the situation. You tell yourself rational, reasonable thoughts. Some of these thoughts are in sentences you say to yourself. Some are in visual or auditory images.

You can practice new patterns of emotion just as you can practice new patterns of thought and behavior. If you want to feel differently in situations from the way you currently feel, and if you are sure that the new emotional reaction is better and more preferable, then you can visualize yourself feeling that new way in the situation, and practice that new emotional response.

Do you want to feel brave in a situation in which you formerly felt scared? You simply imagine yourself feeling brave. It might help to recall another situation in which you felt brave, and transfer that pattern of feeling into the situation. Or you might imagine someone else feeling the way you want

to feel, as a stepping-stone into imagining yourself feeling that way.

Then you imagine yourself behaving the way you want to behave in the situation: saying things to other people, moving in the way you want to. There are two points of view from which to visualize yourself doing these things. In one position, you see things as if from your own eyes. In another position, you see your imaginary self as if from the eyes of an outside observer, or as if you were watching a video of yourself.

The C in the mnemonic STEBC stands for celebration. In your imagination you hear yourself congratulating yourself for doing the desirable pattern, just as you would like to congratulate yourself in real life. Then you are done with the fantasy rehearsal, and you can celebrate having done it. So two celebrations are in order.

There are two ways of doing fantasy rehearsal: silently and out loud. In silent fantasy rehearsals, you simply sit and relax and do the rehearsal in your imagination. If a trainer wants to get feedback on what the trainee imagined, the trainer can ask the trainee to recall and report on what was imagined after the silent fantasy rehearsal is over.

In the fantasy rehearsal out loud, you put into words everything that you are visualizing and saying to yourself, while the fantasy rehearsal is taking place. You speak as if you are experiencing the situation in the present, not the past or the future. This technique is a wonderful one because it lets the trainer hear exactly what is going on in the trainee's mind. If the trainee is trying to rehearse positive patterns but is actually rehearsing fairly negative patterns, the trainer can hear it. If the trainee's mind is drifting off onto extraneous ideas, it's obvious to the trainer. And when you do fantasy rehearsals out loud, you yourself can hear when they start and end. For this reason usually when I refer to fantasy rehearsals, I mean fantasy rehearsals out loud.

What does a fantasy rehearsal sound like? Let's give some examples.

Here's a fantasy rehearsal of a situation calling for frustration tolerance. "I'm at the computer, and I'm writing an assignment. I've been working at this for half an hour. Oh no, the power for the whole house has gone off, including the computer! And I hadn't saved what I'd written since I started! I think I've lost everything I wrote! Now the power has come back on now, and I can look. Yes, I've lost it all. Well, this is an opportunity for me to practice frustration tolerance, all right. I learned something from this. Next time I'll save what I've written really often. And when I can afford it, I'm going to buy an uninterruptible power supply. But how can I handle this now? Let me relax. It's just a half hour's work down the drain; it's not the end of the world. It's not as if someone is about to drag me off and kill me. What are my options? I could go and do something else for a while, and give myself a break. Or,

while what I wrote is fresh in my mind, I could write it back again, as fast as I can, this time saving it every few minutes. I think I'll do that. Even though I'm disappointed that this happened to me, I'm not devastated. I'm feeling OK. Now I'm writing as fast as I can, before I forget. I'm saving, and writing some more. Hooray for me. I'm handling this really well. And hooray for me for doing this fantasy rehearsal!"

Did you notice in this fantasy rehearsal how the person talked about the situation (at the computer, etc.), the thoughts (this is an opportunity, etc.), the emotions (disappointed, not devastated, feeling OK), the behaviors (writing, saving), and the celebrations? This fantasy rehearser went through the STEBC.

Now let's model a fantasy rehearsal of another frustration, this time at the hands of someone else. This is from the point of view of a schoolchild.

"I'm at school, and I'm going to sit down at lunch. A kid in my class looks up at me as I walk by with my tray, and says, 'Hi, fat pig,' with a real impudent-looking smile. Here's an opportunity to practice frustration tolerance, because I didn't feel like being teased or taunted right now. Well, it isn't as if I'm in the middle of a civil war and people are burning down my family's village. I can handle this. This I can take. I want to relax my muscles and think fast about how to react to him. The urge to pour my drink right on his head is occurring to me, but if I did that

I'd just get into trouble and maybe start a fight. I could ignore him, and if I can't think of anything else better to do, that's what I'll do. I think I'll just give him a smart aleck remark back, without being too hostile about it. I want to just have some fun horsing around with him. So I'm saying to him, 'Bye bye, skinny pig!' and I walk on past him and sit down with my friends. I'm hearing some other people laughing at what I said, and I feel good about how I handled it. I wasn't mean to him, and I didn't make too big a deal out of this. Hooray for me for handling this frustration well, and hooray for me for doing this fantasy rehearsal!"

Again, in this fantasy rehearsal we had the situation (at school . . .), the thoughts (I can handle this . . .), the emotions (fun horsing around, without being too hostile), the behaviors (I'm saying to him . . .), and the celebration (Hooray for me . . .). Again, the fantasy rehearser included all the STEBC.

Now let's listen to a third fantasy rehearsal out loud. "I'm playing checkers with my friend, and I really want to beat him, because he's been acting cocky. He's making a move where I have to take a jump. And now he can jump two of my men. I'm behind. Now I'm in another bad situation. I've lost enough men now that there's no way I can win the game. OK, this is a chance to practice frustration tolerance, because I really wanted to win. But let's keep this in perspective. Losing one checkers game is not something that's too much

for me to handle. I can take this just fine. Let me relax, and get this game over with, and maybe try again. What are my options about how to act? I want to be gracious about it, and so I'm congratulating him on some good moves. It won't do me any good to blame him for my losing. What can I learn from this? Let me remember those good moves that he made, and see if I can find a chance to do them myself sometime soon – maybe even in the next game. I want to relax my muscles and just take it easy. I'm finishing up this game, and I'm saying, 'Good game. Want to play again?' and I feel pretty lighthearted about this. It's just a game, anyway. I'm glad I handled it this well, and I'm glad I did this fantasy rehearsal!"

Again, let's think of the STEBC. Situation: losing at checkers. Thoughts: lots of them, including "I can take this" (not awfulizing), listing options, learning from the experience. Emotions: lighthearted. Behaviors: congratulating on good moves, saying good game, wanting to play again. Celebration: I'm glad I handled this well.

Another type of frustration is being treated unfairly. Let's listen to a fantasy rehearsal of this. "I'm in class at school, and the teacher has his back turned and is writing on the board. The guy next to me makes a loud and long yawning noise. The teacher, without even turning around, calls out my name and says, "Go to the principal's office. Now." I'm looking at the guy next to me, but he isn't about to confess. I say to the teacher, 'Could I tell you something first?' The teacher says, 'Out of here, right now.' OK, I realize this is totally unfair, and I'm totally innocent. But worse things have happened to people in the world. It's not as if I'm going to have to go to jail. There will be some other people who heard it and can back me up if it comes down to that. So I want to relax. What are my options now? I could continue to protest, but I think that would just get me in worse trouble. I want my behavior to be totally above reproach. So I think I'll just get up and go to the principal's office. I'm walking down the hall now, and I'm reminding myself that this isn't so bad. What are my options? When I get to the principal's office, I can sit down and plan how I'm going to explain, and make my case really well. I want to be very polite to the secretaries in there and to the principal. I don't want to sound like I'm perfect, but just to say that this time, I happened to be innocent, and the teacher made a mistake, but I can forgive him for that. I'm feeling confident that I can keep cool throughout this whole thing. Now I'm explaining things to the principal, and I'm being very respectful. I'm mentioning that other people can probably back me up, and telling her their names. I can see the principal doesn't know whether to buy my story or not, but if she doesn't, I can handle that, too. I want to come out of this with a reputation for being able to keep cool no matter what

happens. I feel calm. I'm glad I handled this in this way."

Again, we have the situation (in class . . .), the thoughts (What are my options?), the emotions (I feel calm), the behaviors (I'm explaining it to the principal), and the celebration (I'm glad I handled this . . .).

If we abstract from lots of useful fantasy rehearsals, we can make some skeleton outlines of how to do them for certain sorts of situations. If we get too upset or angry in a certain type of situation, we should practice frustration tolerance; if we get too scared, we should practice courage. If we do the pleasurable but unwise thing instead of the less pleasurable but wiser thing, we should practice delay of gratification. If we fail to feel good about what is celebration-worthy, we should practice celebrating. Here are four outlines for how to fantasy rehearse these sorts of situations.

Steps in practicing handling frustrations

1. Situation:
    Describe the situation. What are the sights, sounds?
2. Thoughts:
    Here's an opportunity.
    How bad is what happened? When I compare this to the worst that has happened to people, how does this stack up? Not awfulizing.
    Not getting down on myself. Not blaming someone else.
    Listing options and choosing.

Learning from the experience.

Let me remember a time when I handled a situation like this well. I want to see and hear it in my mind.

I want to relax.

It will be an accomplishment if I can tough this out and handle it well.

I want to speak to myself and to others in a calm voice.

3. Emotions:

If I feel angry, that doesn't mean I can't act reasonable.

I imagine myself feeling the way I want to feel: confident, excited, determined, resigned, calculating, proud of the way I'm handling this, or . . .

4. Behavior:

I'm doing the option that I chose. I'm doing something that makes sense.

5. Celebration:

Hooray, I did a good job!

∎■■■■■■■■■■■■■■■■■■■■■■■■■■■■∎

Steps in practicing courage

1. Situation:

Describe the situation. What are the sights, sounds?

2. Thoughts:

Here's an opportunity.

What bad could happen? How bad is it? How likely is it? How much danger am I in? If I'm in danger, I want to protect myself. If I'm not, I want to tough out this situation.

Let me remember a time when I handled a situation like this well. I want to see and hear it in my mind.

I want to relax.

Not awfulizing.

Listing options and choosing.

It will be an accomplishment if I can tough it out.

3. Emotions:

If I feel scared, that doesn't mean I'm in danger.

I'm feeling brave, confident, happy, relaxed, excited, or having fun.

4. Behavior:

I'm doing the option that I chose. I'm doing something that makes sense.

5. Celebration:

Hooray, I did a good job!

■■■■■■■■■■■■■■■■■■■■■■■■■■■■■■■

Steps in practicing delay of gratification

1. Situation:

Describe the situation. What are the sights, sounds?

2. Thoughts:

Here's an opportunity.

What are the reasons for doing the less enjoyable vs. the more enjoyable option? (Visualize benefits of delaying gratification, visualize consequences of not delaying gratification)

How bad is what I have to endure by delaying gratification now?

Let me remember a time when I handled a situation like this well. I want to see and hear it in my mind.

It will be an accomplishment if I can tough this out and handle it well. It will toughen me for the future.

What gratification can I give myself, to celebrate finishing this?

It won't kill me to do the less enjoyable option.

If I really play my cards right, maybe I can figure out a way to enjoy this.

I want to reinforce myself for every step along the way.

3. Emotions:

I feel determined.

I imagine myself feeling the way I want to feel: confident, excited, resigned, calculating, proud of the way I'm handling this, or . . .

4. Behavior: I'm doing the option that I chose. I'm doing something that makes sense.

5. Celebration: Hooray, I did a good job!

Steps in responding to desirable situations

1. Situation:

What is the situation? It's desirable, relative to what?

2. Thoughts:

I don't want to let this opportunity pass.

Did I help bring this about? If so, hooray for me.

Did I help bring this about? If so, I want to rehearse what I did.

Did someone else help bring this about? If so, I'm glad for what they did.

Did it happen just by chance? If so, hooray for my good luck.

3. Emotions:

If I helped bring this about, I feel proud.

If someone else helped bring this about, I feel grateful.

If it was just lucky that this happened, I feel blessed.

4. Behavior:

Maybe I can let my tone of voice and my actions reflect those good feelings.

5. Celebration:

I'm glad I remembered to respond to this situation in this way.

How do you maximally turn fantasy rehearsals into concentration exercises? You can do a variant of the concentrate, rate, and concentrate activity by seeing how clearly and vividly you can imagine the situation and your response to it. You might want to use the following scale:

0 = No image at all
2 = Very vague and dim image
4 = Some vividness, but not much
6 = Moderately clear and vivid
8 = High degree of clarity and vividness
10 = Very high degree of clarity and vividness

It's not necessary to see the image with very high vividness in order to get a lot out of the fantasy rehearsal. What is necessary is that you simply stay on task with the fantasy rehearsals, for a long enough time to get lots of practice. So another way to rate your performance is to rate the answer to the question, "How well did I keep my focus on what I was doing," after each fantasy rehearsal, and to keep track of how long you can keep up your focus on fantasy rehearsals in general. If the numbers go up and up over time, you're seeing yourself get better at concentration.

There's another good way to do fantasy rehearsals – in writing. You list the situations, the choice points to which you would most like to improve your response. Then for each you write out the description of the situation, and then the thoughts, emotions, behaviors, and celebrations with which you'd like to respond. You can revise this fantasy rehearsal, add many others to it, and read them out loud or silently many times.

You can even fantasy rehearse yourself concentrating. You imagine yourself tackling difficult material, imagine getting the urge to drift away, thinking, "Hey, I want to get back on task," feeling confident, starting to use a technique such as writing questions (described above) to pull your mind back on the subject, and celebrating getting back on track.

To summarize: concentration skill can be built up through exercise and practice, just as muscles can be built up the same way. The exercises of this chapter are highly recommended. But just as when exercising to build muscles, you have to keep at them for a long time before seeing visible results. Persistence is required, even in building persistence skills!

Overcoming work block

Sometimes the problem is not so much persisting at work, as starting the work in the first place. Sometimes procrastination is the greatest enemy of accomplishing anything. Here are some ideas about how to get yourself started working.

1. Avoid all-or-none thinking. One of the biggest barriers to getting started working is the idea that it has to come out perfect on the first try. If I believe it's terrible if I produce work that is flawed in any way, that's a major obstacle to doing anything at all. On the other hand, if I think along the lines of "This is only a first draft; I can always revise it later," or "I'll do a practice run, and the real thing will only come later," then I give myself permission to work toward the "good enough" level by successive approximations. Successive approximations, or getting better and better the more you work at something – is the way most good things get produced.

2. Discriminate between "pain as a signal to protect yourself," "pain that should be desensitized," and "pain that should be tolerated." Sometimes it's really painful to start working on something. But you can desensitize the feeling of work aversion by continuing to expose yourself to the work. By contrast, the pain from having freezing hands outside in winter is pain as a signal to protect yourself.

3. Try not to use avoidance and repression to get rid of the pain from work aversion. Avoidance means stay-

ing away from the work situation. Repression means making yourself forget about the work, shoving it out of your mind. One way of facing the task head on is to include it on a written to-do list and look at that list often.

4. Using prolonged exposure to desensitize the pain associated with work. In the chapter on courage skills, I speak about using prolonged exposure to the scary situation to get over phobias. Quick and brief exposures won't work nearly as well. How long is prolonged enough exposure? You want to keep in the unpleasant situation until the "subjective units of distress" rating drops to a fairly comfortable level.

5. Avoid "emotional reasoning." Emotional reasoning is drawing a conclusion about the way something is in reality from the way you happen to feel about it. "I don't feel like doing this work, therefore I can't," is an example of emotional reasoning. You can change that to, "I don't feel like doing this work. But what I feel right now is not so important. What's important is accomplishing my goals."

6. Use internal reinforcement to increase the pleasure of working: self-statements like, "Hooray, I've gotten started"; "Good. I'm getting something down; that's progress"; "Hey, this revision improved it. Yes! I finished it!"

7. Avoid internal punishment statements while working. Avoid saying to yourself, "What a piece of junk this is. How can you even think of showing this to anybody?"

8. Translate internal "critical parent versus rebellious child" dialogues into more rational adult dialogues. For example, some people have dialogues going on inside their own heads that sound something like this:

Critical Parent: "You lazy bum; you should be working . . ."
Rebellious Child: "Shut up and leave me alone!"

Adult self-talk goes more like this: "If I want to produce this result, this is the work that will bring it about . . . Of the various possibilities for allocating time to this task, which one will work out the best for me?"

9. Use self-run contingency programs. For example: I allow myself fifteen minutes of TV watching for each hour of work I do. I allow myself to surf the Internet only when the to-do list for today is written and each item checked off. I allow myself to play chess this week only when I've done ten hours of writing during the previous week. I'm feeling the urge to avoid working by getting something to eat; I'll reward myself with eating when I've done thirty minutes of work. I allow myself to read whatever I want for an hour when I've done two hours of goal-directed work.

10. Consider contingency programs in cooperation with someone else. For example: I'll give you $200. I'll get $5 back for every day I do a minimum of two hours of work, between now and December 1.

11. Place a high value on self-discipline. Self-discipline is defined as the ability to get yourself to do what is best to do even when you don't feel like doing it. Wish frequently for increased levels of self-discipline, and celebrate greatly any evidence for improvements in this skill.

12. Visualize positive fantasies of accomplishing the goals in question. Cultivate daydreams of celebration and self-congratulation after the accomplishment.

13. Practice the "internal sales pitch" for doing the work and accomplishing the goals. Review the pros and cons of working toward the goal. Affirm that it's worth working for – or else decide that it isn't worth it, and drop it! Not all tasks are worth doing, but some are; your goal is to make careful decisions about which you want to spend your energy on.

14. Avoid real-life critical parent-rebellious child dialogues. That is, try to stay out of the situation where someone nags you to work, and you tell him or her to leave you alone. If someone irritates you by nagging you to work, it's too easy to spite him or her by being lazy.

15. Practice relaxation techniques. (See the chapter on this skill.) Use these methods to reduce negative emotion that gets in the way of working.

16. Allocate adequate play and fun time, so that you don't activate a rebellious part of yourself that needs a break. Ideally, you can let that play and fun reinforce the work. As an example of this idea: this is a beautiful day, and I want to take a long walk with my dog. I allow myself to do this as a reinforcer when I've spent two hours working on my thesis.

17. When you have decided not to work, avoid getting down on yourself for not working, but enjoy that time, so as to replenish your store of self-discipline. Telling yourself you should be working and not doing it probably depletes your store of self-discipline.

18. When there are experiences of successful accomplishment, recall those and mentally rehearse them in order to help yourself repeat them. Visualize positive experiences of goal accomplishment frequently to help deepen the groove of this pattern.

19. Keep a log of time spent working on goals, and study this log frequently. Study what makes the imaginary or real graph go up or down. Celebrate increases in this over time.

20. Celebrate each event for which you made a resolution and formed an intention and actually followed through with it.

21. Get into your mind models of courageous use of self-discipline, and meditate upon these; then visualize yourself acting similarly.

Skill 3: Competence Development

A very important competence is getting yourself more competent! Knowing how to get better at skills is one of the keys to living life well. I like to divide these skills into four groups. The first is psychological skills, the ones we have been talking about here. The second is work skills – doing things that are directly useful and/or that help to make a living: doctoring, scientific research, bricklaying, cleaning up a house, and so forth. Third are academic skills – reading, writing, mathematics, the foundation skills used in information-processing tasks. Fourth are recreational skills – playing basketball, playing chess, paddling a canoe, playing a piano, holding parties.

What results in happiness? One of the major contributors to it is a good match between the challenges we face and the skills we possess to face them. When our skills are too low relative to the challenges life gives us, we tend to be scared or frustrated. Few experiences are more unpleasant than being expected to do things that we don't know how to do. On the other hand, when our skills are high relative to the challenges we encounter, we tend to get bored. The ideal zone, where skills are equal to the challenge, we can call the "challenge zone."

It's much easier to be very skilled and to find more difficult challenges for yourself than to be very unskilled and to find easier challenges. So if you want to be able to get into your challenge zone and to be happy, learn to do things very competently.

Let's first talk about competence in work. Many people are not nearly as happy as they could be, because they don't know how to do their work well enough. When you are not good enough at your work, it's unpleasant. Unpleasant memories of work can lead people to avoid thinking about work when they get time off, rather than honing their skills. This is the vicious cycle of failure that we talked about in the chapter on handling mistakes and failures. The way out of this vicious cycle is to "tough it out" and take the time and energy that it requires to become really expert at your work.

Some people get stuck in their own incompetence because of a misguided idea: the notion that you do your learning during the school years, and then you stop learning and apply what you learned in school to your work. According to this idea, there is a stage in life for learning and a very different stage for working.

But this idea is misguided for several reasons. First, no school can anticipate all that you need to know to do a certain type of work. You must constantly fill in the gaps. Second, the knowledge that we have about how to do most jobs well is constantly accumulating; if you cease to learn, you deliver an ever more obsolete product or service.

It requires self-discipline to keep on learning once you are in the work place. You get strong economic incentives to do more work, rather than spend time learning how to do it better. For example, a doctor gets paid for seeing patients, but does not get paid for studying textbooks and journal articles. But the doctor who stops studying gradually becomes less and less competent, and his work becomes less and less gratifying.

Now let's move to the academic arena. People in our culture spend a good part of their lives being evaluated on how well they can read, write, spell, do math, remember things, figure out things, and generate ideas. Since all these skills are trainable ones, it's wise to train yourself until you're very good at these academic skills. For some people this will be a quick task; for most people it will take a great deal of repetitive work.

For the person who is somewhat behind in any of these skills, the most rational course of action is to cultivate the skill of repetition-tolerance and to plug away at refining these skills. For example, the person who writes only very slowly and with great discomfort can learn to write faster and more comfortably with a great deal of concentrated practice in writing. Yet there are many students who are very hampered by their poor writing skills, who never do any concentrated practice in writing. Some students bemoan the fact that they are bad at math and hate math, without spending any time catching up on unlearned skills. They are spending their lives working at a level that is too hard for them – spending their lives in the frustration zone. That's no way to live. They need to drop back to easier tasks that lie within their challenge zone, but to work steadily enough that their challenge zone gradually moves up to what life is presently requiring of them.

Some students rationalize the lack of effort to achieve success by pointing out the meaninglessness and irrelevance of many of the tasks that school requires. When I think back on my own education, and I recall having to memorize the state capitals or the dates for battles in wars, or the army leaders who fought these battles, I agree that education typically fosters much meaningless memorization. When I recall reading novels and plays and getting asked on quizzes which characters said certain quotations, I regret the time and brainpower that was focused on these activities, and I wish that I could have been reading material like that in this book! These wishes reflect my own tastes, however; it's difficult to get people to agree on what is meaningless and meaningful. Each activity I felt was a total waste was regarded by at least some other people as extremely valuable.

And yet most people in the school-aged years (with the exception of some homeschoolers and some people in alternative schools) find that the game of learning whatever their course requires them to learn is the "only game in town." The choice is as follows: is it more fun to play the game to win, play the game to get by, or play the game and lose? Not playing the game is not a permissible option.

For most people, playing the game and winning is the most enjoyable way to experience education. This means trying hard to do whatever tasks are required, to succeed at whatever is defined as success. And while some tasks are meaningless, the basic activities of reading, organizing thoughts through writing, doing math, and learning about the world and human beings, can be the most meaningful, pleasant, and wonderful activities that can be done. (Please see the skill of pleasure from discovery.) And for the truly useless memorization and the other meaningless tasks that education requires, it may be helpful to remind oneself that they are no more meaningless than goals such as propelling a ball over a line or between two posts or over a net.

Now let's turn our attention to competence in recreational activities. Recreational activities were invented because they had the capacity to be fun, and almost all of them are more fun if you're more proficient in them than if you're less proficient in them. This is true across areas as diverse as playing checkers, doing ballroom dancing, making quilts, playing sports, singing, playing musical instruments, gardening, and making machines work. In almost every area of recreational endeavor, there is a group of people who are interested in that activity. One gains status in that group by proficiency in the skill in question. Since getting proficient at one or more of these activities is a pleasure that life offers to us, it's often worthwhile to avail ourselves of this pleasure.

Dominance hierarchies and competence in sports and other skills

In a world where diseases need to be cured, poverty, violence and warfare need to be solved, and environmental destruction halted, surely the attention, effort and money devoted to spectator sports must seem baffling. Why do sports generate so much intense interest? Part of the answer to this, as well as a lot else that goes on in adolescent and young adult culture, lies in an understanding of "dominance hierarchies."

Dominance hierarchies have been studied by ethologists, the students of animal behavior. Imagine a flock of birds in which the more dominant ones can peck the less dominant ones without getting pecked back. Imagine that you can actually rank order the individual birds in the group according to who wins when a dispute comes up between them. This image accounts for the fact that the more common term for dominance hierarchy is "pecking order."

Young males of many species, including humans, literally fight with one another to win a favorable position on the dominance hierarchy. This position determines how much they get of scarce resources, including the ability to mate with the females of their choice. The advantage to the species of such competitions is that the "fittest" members of the species preferentially pass their genes to the next generation.

But groups where males must literally kill each other for positions on a dominance hierarchy must pay a very big price for such competition. If they can evolve a less costly way of establishing dominance hierarchies, they will have an advantage over other groups. Accordingly, a very interesting phenomenon in the animal kingdom is competition on a more symbolic and less lethal basis. Certain species of goats literally butt heads, but without killing each other, to establish a position on the dominance hierarchy by how much force they can muster in knocking the other back. And in other contests in the animal kingdom, contestants do things that somehow pick the fittest animals for reproduction, without having to kill off the rest. These contests are proxies for violent encounters.

In some ways, sports contests among adolescent males serve as similar sorts of proxies. I remember being teased and picked on by a classmate in early high school. When we both wound up on the wrestling team and I met him on the wrestling mats, he was impressed enough with my wrestling that the teasing ceased. In this instance, I advanced on a dominance hierarchy, not by fighting with him, but by having a sports experience very similar to fighting, in which the probability of serious injury or death was minimal.

Throughout most of human evolution, the disrespect or abuse you had to take or did not have to take from another human being depended upon the skills fairly accurately measured by a wrestling match or a football contest – strength, agility, speed, competitive spirit. Brute physical force would prevail in most unresolved disputes. And to this day, this remains true in certain subcultures. Sports contests then became very useful as a proxy method of determining the dominance hierarchies, with all the advantages of fighting to death or to unconsciousness, with none of the disadvantages.

The last few centuries of human civilization have somewhat altered the rules about dominance, and have developed other means than brute physical force for attaining power. The invention of courts and political power, the invention of money and economic power, the growing dominance of information and expertise as a source of power, and on a grosser level the invention of guns, have all reduced the importance of physical strength and agility.

In fact, a very rude awakening awaits many athletes in today's culture. They enjoy a high place on the dominance hierarchy in high school and perhaps college, where their athletic exploits are celebrated. But immediately upon graduation, unless they're good enough to join a very small group of highly paid professional athletes, they find their sports skills relatively useless. The ability to make money, to command a prestigious job, to be an expert in something, to have skills in dealing with people, to command economic, political, social, or information-based power, has suddenly replaced sports as the determiner of their position on the dominance hierarchy. They find themselves subservient to the same nerds they had bullied while in school. The athletic skills that had been at the center of their identity undergo a rapid devaluation.

Of course, not all high school and college kids are unaware of what awaits them upon emergence into the work world. And for this reason, as well as others, the dominance hierarchies are not determined by sports alone. People in schools and colleges attain favorable positions on dominance hierarchies by being smart, having good social skills, being politically astute, and having other abilities, as well as through sports.

What are the practical implications of this? My advice to adolescents who are uncomfortable with their positions on the dominance hierarchy of their social group (a vast number of people) is to ask themselves several questions. First, what skills determine the position in their group? What weight is given to sports, academic skill, social skill, displays of wealth, ability to organize groups, etc.? Second, what are their own potentials in these areas? Is there some skill that can be developed by effort?

Third, if they were to expend this effort, would it be worth it? Is there a less costly way of defending themselves against a low position on the dominance hierarchy, for example by dropping out of the hierarchy altogether and associating with someone other than same-age peers (a very difficult task for many adolescents in our culture), or by dropping out of the hierarchy and getting support from one or two peers who form their own subgroup? These dominance hierarchies are intensified by the nature of school culture; some adolescents have escaped them by participating in homeschooling.

The final piece of advice before leaving the notion of dominance hierarchies is that amidst all this struggle and competition for position, somewhere there are activities and skills that really are useful to people. The beacon of trying to produce the greatest possible good should supersede the wish for dominance, although to the person who is being cruelly dominated, escaping victimization comes first.

How do you get to be a high achiever?

If you want to be a high achiever in work skills, academic skills, recreational activities, and psychological skills, how should you go about doing it?

Here are some guidelines on becoming an "achiever" in whatever area you wish. I've put them in the form of a rating scale.

Checklist for Achievement

Rate the extent to which you follow each of the following guidelines.

0 = None
2 = A little
4 = Some
6 = Pretty much
8 = A high amount
10 = A very high amount

_____1. Clearly define what the goal is. Visualize very clearly what it would look like to achieve it. Hear what it would sound like.

_____2. Sell yourself on the benefits of obtaining that goal. Write these down, and review them frequently, using the "internal sales pitch."

_____3. Read books, listen to speeches, get consultations, and otherwise educate yourself about how to achieve in this area.

_____4. Make a very detailed plan for achieving the goal. Write this down as well. What are the steps?

_____5. Allocate the time for achieving the goal. Toughen yourself to the fact that to devote more time to any goal, you will have less time to spend on something else.

_____6. Anticipate the obstacles that could prevent your success, and make a plan for surmounting them.

_____7. Set up a system for monitoring how you're doing, over time, preferably involving another person who will be pleased with your success.

_____8. Use fantasy rehearsal to practice doing what you need to do to achieve the goal.

_____9. Spend a great deal of time in real-life practice of the skills you need for success.

_____10. Work steadily, keeping the vision of the goal and its benefits in mind. Put in the number of hours of work required to accomplish the task, according to the most realistic estimate you can make, and don't give up until you have spent at least that number of hours.

_____11. For each piece of work that you do, celebrate and try to feel good; use your self-reinforcement skills.

_____12. Review your plan often, and revise it if necessary.

_____13. Place the responsibility for success or failure in yourself rather being too quick to blame someone else or something else. Look for the ways in which you're in control of your fate. See the solutions to failures as actions that you can take.

_____14. When doing practices, homework assignments, workouts, etc., define your goal in terms of your own proficiency rather than in terms of simply completing the task. For example, if you finish the required ten math problems but still feel shaky on solving that type of problem, do more until you feel proficient.

_____15. Train yourself to concentrate on tasks for longer and longer periods of time, going immediately back to where you were if you're interrupted and avoiding interruptions as much as possible.

_____16. Make demands on yourself that are not too harsh, not too lax, but in a happy medium.

_____17. Have in mind role models who have achieved in your field, and learn all you can about how these people were successful. In other words, don't feel you need to reinvent the wheel. If you can learn success skills by imitation learning rather than by prolonged trial and error, go for it!

_____18. Cultivate the self-discipline skills to work for success that may not come for a long time, rather than doing things that are more pleasurable at the moment.

_____19. Interpret each failure as information, as feedback, showing you that you need to do something differently the next time. Avoid getting demoralized by setbacks.

_____20. Practice controlling the degree of arousal or excitement you have, so that you can relax when you need to and get psyched up when you need to for highest performance. (The chapter on the skill of relaxation has more on this.)

_____21. Measure your performance frequently, so you can congratulate yourself and feel good about each upward movement toward more proficient performance. Avoid the pattern of not measuring your performance for fear of revealing to yourself less than perfect skill.

_____22. Cultivate social networks of people who admire achievement in your chosen area, people who will reinforce your achievement. Conversely, avoid hanging out with those who are envious or jealous of achievement and thus tend to punish it.

_____23. Cultivate the ability to enjoy expending effort in your field, taking pleasure in seeing how well you can do.

_____24. Avoid long-term failure and mistakes that actually harm people. But don't let the burning desire to succeed induce a fear of failure that keeps you from having the gumption to try things. This is especially true when a mistake would be embarrassing but would not hurt anyone, and when you could learn something valuable, even from failing.

_____25. Avoid the pattern of not trying your best to succeed for fear of exposing something other than a "great potential."

_____26. Cultivate repetition-tolerance. No matter who you are, there are almost certainly areas of achievement that come slower for you than for someone else. If the skill is important but doesn't come easily for you, often this means only that you'll have to do many more repetitions to master it than some other people might need. If you're good enough at repetition tolerance, this needn't stand in your way.

_____27. Learn to organize time, papers, and objects, and practice the self-discipline to apply that learning. Many people could achieve much more if they would apply what is widely known about organization skills. (Please see the chapter on these skills in this book.)

_____28. If you really have a low aptitude for a certain skill useful in achieving an important goal, even despite a reasonable degree of repetitive practice, consider forming a partnership with someone else who does have high skill in this area. Such cooperation can mean you don't have to become proficient in every skill yourself.

If you really want to accomplish a goal, see how high you can boost these ratings. If you can keep them high enough long enough, you dramatically increase your chances of achieving the goal.

Academic achievement

Here's a list of suggestions for academic achievement. This one overlaps a lot with the more general checklist for achievement in any area. If you can rate the extent to which you follow each of these suggestions as very high, the chances for success are great.

Checklist on academic achievement

Please rate the extent to which you do each of the following.

0 = None
2 = A little
4 = Some
6 = Pretty much
8 = A high amount
10 = A very high amount

_____1. Do you write down your assignments very clearly?

_____2. Do you get a clear image in mind of what assignments are to be done, not just on a day-to-day basis, but also for the next couple of weeks or months, and even an image of what you should accomplish by the end of the course?

_____3. Do you have a regular time in your schedule for academic work?

_____4. Do you allocate enough time to attain superior achievement?

_____5. When you do your work, are you in a place that is free from distractions, so that you can concentrate?

_____6. Do you check all your academic work after it's completed, working for error-free products?

_____7. Do you work on long-term projects far enough ahead of time that you don't have a crisis just before the project is due?

_____8. If you're not performing well enough in a subject, do you adjust upward the amount of time you spend working on that subject?

_____9. In writing assignments, do you use the GIOW framework? (Concentrating, in turn, on Generating ideas, deciding which to Include, deciding how to Order them, and deciding how to Word them?)

_____10. In studying mathematics, do you read, slowly and carefully, each word in a text that explains the concepts?

_____11. In studying mathematics, do you keep doing problems of a certain sort until you have "overlearned" the skill of doing that sort of problem?

_____12. In studying for subjects where you will have to remember facts, do you find ways of practicing doing things with those facts rather than just passively reading them? (Examples: making up questions about them and answering them; figuring out what their implications are; debating about them, with a friend or with oneself; figuring out what the scheme of organization of them is, as in, for example, making an outline of them.)

_____13. If you have subjects that depend upon lecture notes, are you good at note-taking? Are your notes complete enough, intelligible enough, organized enough?

_____14. Do you give every assignment and test enough effort to attain high success?

_____15. Do you make up practice tests and take them, to prepare for the tests you will take?

_____16. Do you remind yourself frequently of the benefits of achieving your desired goals?

_____17. Are you able to maintain a high desire to achieve your goals?

_____18. When you don't do as well as you want on something, do you let your disappointment mobilize your energy to do better in the future, rather than getting demoralized and discouraged?

_____19. Are you able to take pleasure in working toward your goals, and to reinforce yourself for your progress?

_____20. Are you able to take real pleasure in sharing your achievements and successes with at least one other person?

_____21. Are you very organized about remembering to turn in every assignment on time?

Steps in writing: G I O W

One of the most important academic competences is writing well. A common mistake people make when writing is trying to do everything at once rather than breaking the task up into more manageable bits. If you try to do everything perfectly all at once, you'll fail unless you have so much writing experience that this skill comes by second nature. Many people fall into the trap of criticizing themselves so much while writing that the job is very unpleasant. Writer's block, a state where you can't work up the gumption to get anything written, is usually a disorder that results from too much self-criticism. But if you concentrate on one step at a time, and reward yourself for completing that step, without worrying about the subsequent ones until later, the process will be much more enjoyable.

Here are the four steps as I see them. First, you generate a several ideas about what you want to say. Then you decide which of them to Include and which to discard from this particular piece of writing. Third, you figure out what Order to put them in, and, fourth, you concentrate on Wording. This process of Generation, Inclusion, Ordering, and Wording = GIOW. Let's look at a few more ideas on each.

Generation of ideas

In this stage you simply get down on paper (or in the word processing file) all the ideas that come to your mind. Do NOT worry about whether they will all fit into your essay. Do NOT worry about what order they come in. Do NOT worry about how they are worded. Do NOT think about grammar or punctuation. You're simply trying to brainstorm and get ideas down so you won't forget them.

Inclusion of ideas

In this stage you decide that some of the ideas you have put down deserve to be in this essay, and others don't. If you're composing with a computer, separate them into two sets. If you're writing, you can mark out or cut out the parts you want to delete or keep. Don't worry about what order the ideas go in or how they are worded.

Ordering of ideas

In this stage you figure out a logical sequence for the ideas. What logically comes first, second, third, and so forth? The structure of an outline is often useful at this stage. Don't worry about how the ideas are worded.

Wording of ideas

In this stage, with everything in order, you now think about the wording of your ideas. You concentrate on making them very clear to the reader. You check spelling, punctuation and grammar during this stage.

....

The order of these stages minimizes the chance of wasting time. For example, it's a waste of time to worry about how a sentence will be worded, if you eventually decide it won't be included.

The higher-order competence of competence development

Suppose a person teaches himself typing, piano, using a piece of computer software, and probability and statistics. These are all particular skills, that we can call first-order competences. But in learning first-order competences successfully, the person is practicing habits that will carry over to other competences as well. These are such things as sitting down and reading about how to do something, practicing something until it's mastered, using self-reinforcement for progress, using self-discipline to make himself work, learning from failures, and others listed above.

To the extent that these habits can then be generalized to the next first-order competence the person wants to learn, he has learned a second-order competence – how to get good at doing whatever he chooses to do. It's a happy thought that with each competence you learn, you will find it easier to learn the next one! The next time you're trying to get good at doing something, it may also be useful to recall the methods you used to get good at something else. Perhaps you can aid the generalization process by consciously recalling the positive moves you made.

Skill 4: Organization

Here's a formula to predict how fully you accomplish any of your goals – in work, academics, personal relations, skill development, or anything else.

Accomplishment = Talent x Effort x Luck x Organization.

The organization part is the subject of this chapter. (The work part is covered in the sections on self-discipline and persistence. Innate talent and luck are by definition things we can't change.)

You can be close to a genius, AND you can work very hard, but if you're disorganized, your efforts will not bear the fruit they should. You'll be wasting your time working on the wrong things, never figuring out what the right things are or never getting around to them once you've figured them out. Or it'll be so unpleasant looking for the things or papers you need that it will be hard to get yourself to work. Or you'll not have the money you need to accomplish your goals because your finances are too disorganized.

Organization is the skill that makes work and whatever talent you have pay off in really accomplishing what you want.

Lack of organization skills by people in charge of the safety of others has cost countless people's lives. Some disasters, such as the explosion of the space shuttle *Challenger*, have been linked not so much to evil or bad luck as to disorganization. Lack of organization skills by people in positions of financial responsibility has cost the jobs and the life savings of countless people. There are huge numbers of students who fail to achieve to their maximum performance, not because of stupidity but because of disorganization. Organization skills can and do make the difference between success or failure, poverty or wealth, for countless people.

The key to organization is making plans and following those plans. The plans involve managing: 1) objects, 2) paper, 3) time and tasks, 4) money, and 5) your own thoughts.

Organization skills are necessary because we do not have infinite memory. If it were possible to remember the position in which every piece of paper had been placed, there would be no need for file cabinets; if we could remember every appointment, there would be no need for appointment calendars. But because the complexity of life exceeds what we can hold in memory, we need customs and habits that are brain-extenders, ways of enlarging our effective memory or minimizing the drain upon it. Or put another way, having good organization skills can make us act in smarter ways without having to get a brain transplant. Put another way, poor organization skills can result in stupid acts by smart people.

There is, however, a price to be paid for organizing. Things don't automatically get organized just because you know how to organize them. It takes a certain amount of time, every day, to put things in order, to plan tasks, and to do the other jobs of organizing. Unless the time to accomplish these tasks is allocated and spent, it will not do any good to know the principles of organization. Furthermore, the jobs of organizing are not nearly as much fun as some other things one could be doing. Thus, it takes self-discipline to spend time planning and organizing rather than just going ahead and doing.

Here are some of the basic principles of organizing:

1. Benefit from having routines. For example, try to make a routine time and place for doing a certain activity, and try to have a routine places for certain things to be kept. And most essentially, there should be routine times allocated to organization itself.

2. Group related things together, whether they are ideas, or papers, or objects.

3. Put things in writing, so that you don't have to rely on your memory.

4. On complicated or important tasks, make plans for what is going to happen, and then carry out those plans, rather than trying to plan and carry out the plans at the same time.

Making time for the tasks of organizing

Organizing oneself consists of several activities that take time to do. These are:

1. Taking your physical objects, deciding where they should go, and putting them there.

2. Taking pieces of paper, deciding where they should go, and putting them there.

3. Organizing time and tasks: writing your goals, writing the tasks you want to do, ordering their priority, estimating how long they will take, and scheduling when you're going to do them. Also, looking items written in the to-do and appointment book frequently enough to remind yourself to do them; and celebrating the accomplishment of tasks.

4. Keeping records of monetary income and expenses, and making calculations about these.

5. For important decisions, organizing your thoughts by writing them down and revising your writing.

None of these tasks do themselves, no matter how much you know about organization. Sometimes disorganization is taken as a sign of attention deficit disorder. How much time per day are you willing to spend on these tasks? If the answer is zero, then there's no need to resort to attention deficits as the explanation for disorganization. In order to be organized, one must be willing to spend at least some time, regularly, in organizing.

Organizing physical objects

If your work area is too cluttered up, you might be tempted to run away from it rather than work in it. And if you can't find the materials and tools you need to do your work quickly, your work becomes much less pleasant.

The basic principles of organizing objects are simple:

1. Make a "home" for each object, where that object will go when it's not being used.

2. Group related objects together, and make their homes as close as possible to the place where they will be used.

3. Establish customs of putting objects back into their homes as soon as they are not being used any more, rather than doing so only when the space becomes so cluttered that there's no more room.

4. Don't acquire so many objects that it becomes a needlessly complex task to keep them organized. In other words, de-clutter yourself.

No one has time to waste on looking for objects like keys, wallet, appointment books, pens, glasses, coats, and so forth. With objects like these, it's a good idea to have only two or three places you permit them to be. For example, my keys when not being used are either in a certain pocket or in a certain box, and nowhere else. My reading glasses when not being used are either

in a shirt pocket or the same box; my computer glasses are in the backpack. My warm coat when not being used is hanging in the front hall closet. If I can resist the temptation to put these down anywhere else, I will not have to look for them.

In deciding upon a "home" for an object, I often think to myself, "If I forgot what the home for this object was and wanted to pick the most logical place to start looking for it, where would I look?" This often is the answer to where its home should be.

Organizing paper

In this world of paperwork, it's difficult to overestimate the importance of having a file cabinet with organized files. I think the best way to organize files is to have a title for each file folder, and to put them all in alphabetical order. At regular intervals, you process incoming paper by taking each piece and either doing something with it, filing it, or throwing it away.

Let's suppose the piece of paper is something you want to do something with at a later time. In that case, you file it and at the same time make an entry in your to-do book and appointment calendar that will remind you what to do with this piece of paper, and where it's filed. For example, you might write, "Order book for math course. See to-do file for order form."

Two useful file categories are the "to-do" file and the "holding" file. The to-do file is for the papers corresponding to tasks you can do as soon as you can get to them; the holding file is for tasks that can only be done at some specified time in the future.

Suppose that someone writes you a letter, and you want to reply to it whenever you can. That would go into the to-do file. You would put on your master to-do list (which we'll talk about in the section on tasks), "Reply to Mr. X's letter (to-do file)."

Suppose you get in the mail a plane ticket you will use in three weeks. Then you would put it in the holding file, and make an entry on your master to-do list something like "11/21: flight to Cleveland, (ticket-holding file)" and on the day for 11/21 in the appointment book, you would write down something like "3:27 p.m., US Air fl. 43 to Cleveland, arrive 4:30 pm. Ticket holding file." Now this piece of paper has been processed and you don't have to remember anything additional because of it – all you have to remember is to look at your notebook, which you already do anyway.

What about things that should happen by a certain time, for which other people are responsible, things that should be taken care of without action from you? For example, what if you send back a piece of merchandise, and you're supposed to get a refund within a couple of weeks? Or what if someone promises you over the phone that a certain very important job will get done by such and such a time?

In such cases, it's good to do just the same sort of thing that we spoke of with the airline tickets. When you send in your piece of merchandise for the refund, keep a copy of the mailing slip or notes on when it was sent and where, and put these in the holding file. Then make an entry on your master to-do list something like this: "Verify receipt of refund from X-store, see notes holding file." If the refund comes, then you can look at the holding file and make sure the refund is in the right amount, and check this item off your to-do list. If the refund does not come, then you're reminded of this by seeing the unchecked item on your master to-do list.

Or in the case where someone has promised to do something very important by a certain date, during the conversation you take notes on what will be done by what time. Then you file those notes in your holding file, and make an entry on your master to-do list, for example, "By 11/30, printer to return galleys of book. Holding file." And on the to-do list for 11/30, write in something like "Call printer if galleys not back by today – holding file." Now you have something to remind you in case the person you're dealing with isn't organized himself.

As with putting physical objects into their homes, one of the requirements for organizing is spending time putting papers in the proper file folders and file drawers. Is this fun? Not particularly. But it has a major payoff. Doing work that is not particularly pleasant for the sake of future gain is the skill of self-discipline. This skill is connected very closely to the skill of organization.

Managing time and tasks: goal-setting

One of the great benefits of organizing oneself comes from setting goals for the future and systematically working toward them. This enables you to be "proactive" rather than "reactive," that is, simply reacting to the events that come up. When one is proactive, one develops a vision of a desired future and tries to bring that vision into effect. There are several aspects of being proactive that are worth thinking about.

Let's suppose you're a student, and your goal is to get better grades in your course work. The first step is setting the goal: realizing you want the outcome to take place, realizing things would be much better if you got better grades. In order to know what you're going after, however, it's not sufficient to have just a vague image of what you want; it has to be very concrete. Rather than just thinking, "I want to do better," proper goal-setting involves getting an image of specific, concrete examples of what you will be seeing and hearing if the goal is achieved. Do you want to make straight A's? Do you want to make the honor roll?

A second part of goal-setting is heightening your desire for the goal by dwelling on the benefits that would occur if it were achieved. Simply ac-

knowledging, "Yes, I suppose I'd like that to happen," is not sufficient for setting a goal; it's important to sell yourself, to convince yourself how important it is that the goal be achieved, because to achieve it you will have to do lots of work.

In selling yourself on the goal of getting better grades, you imagine that it will be more fun taking tests, it will be more fun reading your report card, it will be fun to be acknowledged by certain classmates, it will be fun seeing your family members pleased, it will feel good to know you have credentials that will help you get to the next step of your education, etc. If you can't convince yourself that the goal is worth the work, maybe some other goal is more important to you.

Another important part of goal-setting is generating some optimism – summoning the basic faith that, given enough work, you can achieve the goal at least to some degree. If you believe there's really nothing you can do that will affect anything, it's hard to do the work necessary to achieve a goal. If you believe your incomplete success of the past occurred because of fixed traits in you that will never change, it's a good idea to work on changing this attribution. Some people have been able to radically change their lives for the better, and those people are made of the same type of protoplasm that everyone else is made of.

But you can't accomplish everything. Every time you work on a goal, you're choosing *not* to work on certain other goals. For this reason, it's crucial to invoke a well-grounded value system, to decide what goals are really most important. Is it more important to get good grades, or to gain popularity? Is it more important to get the absolutely top grades, or to contribute to the community by volunteer work? Is it more important to succeed in schoolwork or in athletics?

Sometimes such choices are very difficult. Is it more important to foster progress toward world peace, or to increase good feeling in the family by, for example, spending time in light-hearted recreation? Is it more important to preserve harmony with a spouse, or to enjoy one's favorite hobby? Sometimes people can choose "both of the above" when making goal decisions; sooner or later, however, something has to be eliminated because of limited time and energy.

One approach to choosing worthy goals is to value those goals that make oneself and other people most happy in the long run – those that make the world a better place. This is the ethical rule of creating the greatest good for the greatest number, the utilitarian philosophy.

Another approach is to choose goals using a principle that you would want all people to use. This is using Kant's categorical imperative. Religious principles almost always contain elements of these two ideas.

Here's a menu to prompt you when you're pondering what goals are important to you.

Goals Menu

For Workers:
Would you like to get more proficient at any aspect of your work?
Would you like to allocate your work time differently, to produce a better effect?
Are there work achievements you would like to accomplish?
Would you like to change any of your work habits, e.g. punctuality, establishing routines, permitting fewer or more interruptions, etc.?

For Students:
Are there any subjects you would like to get stronger in?
Would you like to get your academic work better organized?
Would you like to get better grades or get other recognition for academic achievement?
Would you like to be able to study better?
Is there something you would like to learn about or learn to do?
Would you like to log in more, or less, time studying?

For Students, Re: School Behavior
Are you making life pleasant for your teacher(s)? Would you like to do this more?

Are you making life pleasant for your classmates? Would you like to do this more?

Do you have a good reputation at school for behaving reasonably? Would you like to do this more?

Athletics and/or Health and Fitness

Any accomplishments you want to make in sports?

Any sport you want to get more skilled at?

Any particular sports skills you want to get?

Do you want to get more exercise? If so, how?

Do you want to improve your eating habits? If so, how?

Are there other health habits or attitudes you want to strengthen, such as non-use of alcohol or tobacco or others?

Hobbies and Other Skills

Do you want to take up any new activities, such as playing a musical instrument, learning to use a computer well, reading and learning about a new subject, hiking, cycling, etc.?

Are there particular skill goals you have in any activity?

Or do you have a goal of simply spending time enjoying some activity?

Relations with Family Members

Are you pleased with the way you get along with each person in your family?

Whom in your family would you like to get along better with?

What would be happening less often, and what would be happening more often, if you got along better with that person?

Is there someone in your family you would like to spend more time doing fun things with?

Social Life and Relations with Friends

Would you like to make more friends?

Would you like to have a best friend you're closer to?

Would you like your time with a friend to be more fun?

Would you like people you don't know really well to like you better?

Personal Development:

What would you like to do to improve yourself?

How would you like to make yourself a better person?

What psychological skills would you most like to get better at? (Looking carefully at the menu of psychological skills will be helpful in making this decision.)

Religious involvement

Would you like your religious life to be improved in any way?

Service to Humanity, Making the World a Better Place

Would you like to be of more service to humanity?

Would you like to be of service in some particular way?

Would you like to learn more about how to be of service to humanity?

Are you interested in a cause such as nonviolence, reducing poverty, improving the environment?

∎∎∎∎∎∎∎∎∎∎∎∎∎∎∎∎∎∎∎∎∎∎∎∎∎∎∎∎∎∎

After setting the goal, getting a concrete picture of what its achievement would look like, selling oneself on the importance of achieving it, and generating optimism that it can be achieved, what's the next step? A next important step is devising some way of *measuring* or *monitoring* the progress toward the goal.

For someone playing the game of academic achievement, or for a track runner or competitive swimmer, such measurement is relatively easy: the grades on the report card, or the time that it takes to cover a certain distance. For goals such as increasing your enjoyment of acts of kindness or building your frustration tolerance, the measurement has to involve more judgment. But giving some sort of score to how well you do in these tasks, or keeping a record of how many and what sort of positive examples you're doing, will help in the crucial task of monitoring progress.

The next step is making a plan as to how the goal will be achieved. What are you going to do to bring about the desired result? How much time, at exactly what times of day, do you want

to devote to working on your school-work? For goals having to do with other people, it's good to think about the nine methods of influence remind yourself how to bring out change in people's habits. (These are the methods recalled by the mnemonic *oh am prism*, and discussed in the introductory chapter of this book.)

When planning, it's useful to anticipate some of the obstacles that might obstruct progress toward the goal, and figure out how to get around these obstacles. For example, an obstacle to getting good grades might be that if I do poorly on one test, I might demoralize myself to the point that I give up and stop working. I can get around that obstacle by telling myself ahead of time that I don't want momentary setbacks to deter me from my long-range goal.

Another obstacle might be that people in my class may tease or even harass me if I get good grades, and I might bow to this pressure and do less well, in order to be liked by them. I want to get around this obstacle by cultivating relationships with people who will celebrate and admire my successes rather than punish them. I also rehearse saying to myself, "If they want to discourage me from achieving, I don't care what they think."

Likewise, I anticipate the obstacle that fatigue keeps me from studying as much as I want to, and plan to use some twenty-minute relaxation and exercise sessions at crucial times to renew my energy.

In planning how to overcome obstacles, and solve problems, consider the skill of individual decision-making, which is discussed in this book.

The next step in achieving goals is to execute the plan, to do the work that was planned, while frequently monitoring progress toward the goal. If progress takes place, make sure to celebrate it thoroughly, to renew your energy for further work. If progress does not take place after a reasonable amount of time, return to the problem-solving or decision-making process, and decide how to modify the plan.

(It's often difficult to decide what a reasonable amount of time is – whether to stay the course or change tactics. Information on how long it takes for the solution to work is crucial in making this decision.) Persist in this process until the goal is attained.

It's useful to *write down* your goals. What things would you like to accomplish in your lifetime, and in the foreseeable future? If you take the time to answer this question in writing, your time will be well spent.

In setting goals, it's sometimes useful for someone to think of the following categories: career, financial security, strength of support system, relations with family, child-rearing, relations with friends, health and fitness, personal development, and contributions to humanity.

One element people often neglect when goal-setting is that of cultivation of their own relationships, their own social network. Who are the people most important to maintain continuing closeness with? Most of us spend time with people based on proximity or chance rather than a conscious effort to be with the people most important to us. In writing goals, a useful consideration is maintaining close relations with certain specific people, listed by name.

If you write your goals and post them in front of you, and look at them as you plan your daily activities, you will have a means of keeping yourself centered on what is really important to you.

Organizing time and tasks: the logistics

Once you have devoted time to figuring out what goals you have, the task is to translate those goals into daily activities that make progress toward the goals.

Part of being organized is to have and use a to-do and appointment book. For the student, this takes the form of an assignment book. I use a four-inch by six-inch spiral notebook, one for each month, with two pages allocated to each day. When you open the book to any day, you see the appointments written on the right hand page, and the daily to-do list on the left page.

In the front of the notebook is the "master to-do list." This is where you write down everything, of any sort, that needs to be done. In other words, whenever you think of anything you need or want to do, write it down on the master to-do list.

Then each day you make a daily to-do list. On the appointment page, you have written down any activity that is scheduled. Each evening you can review what you're scheduled to do the following day. Then, for the time that is not scheduled, you can look at the master to-do list, and also your list of long-range goals, and put on the daily to-do list page the additional things you want to get done. Throughout the day, you then refer to these two pages.

After you make the to-do list, order the priority of the tasks. That is, write 1 by the most important item; write 2 by the next most important, and so forth. You do this because you never know exactly how long things are going to take, so you never know whether you're going to get through all the items on your to-do list. But if you get the most important ones done, then at least you're putting your effort into the areas that will pay off the most.

Another reason for doing the items in the order of the priority list is that by doing so you train yourself not to put off unpleasant or difficult activities. When a task's number comes up, you do it, like it or not.

Here's a game useful to play with yourself. After making your daily to-do list and ordering the priorities, you look at your scheduled activities, and figure out how much time you have to devote to your to-do list items, and predict how many you will get done.

Then, put a mark by the last item you predict you will finish. Then at the end of the day, see how your prediction compared with your actual accomplishment.

There's a major benefit in seeing how your prediction compares with the actual accomplishment: you gradually get better and better at predicting how long something will actually take to do. Being able to predict this accurately then allows you to make plans both for the long run and the short run. It enables you to make commitments to other people that you can more easily keep.

When you finish an item on the to-do list, check it off, and congratulate yourself for finishing it, and try to feel good about what you have done! If you can train yourself to feel good when you finish an item, you will get much more done.

When you're making a to-do list, it's better to break down large tasks into small parts, so that you'll be able to check off an accomplishment and feel good about it more often. For example, rather than having one item for "Do income taxes," you could have separate items for "Sort out papers in tax file," "Find canceled checks for deductible items," and so forth. Breaking a job down into small parts is often a very important step in overcoming resistance to getting it done.

What if, as the day goes on, you decide that some task not on your to-do list is what's most worth doing? The to-do list of course can be revised at any point during the day. Some people write newly-arisen tasks on their to-do list and check them off, sometimes even after they've done them, just to aid in self-reinforcement.

When you do a task so automatically and routinely that you don't need even to think about whether and when to do it, your reward is not having to write it down. For example, most people never write, "Brush my teeth" on their to-do lists, because it becomes an automatic ritual.

Establishing routines

Which of the following sounds more pleasant for you?

To do laundry when you notice that no clean clothes are left, or to schedule laundry at certain regular times each week?

To pay bills and process paperwork when you wake up in the middle of the night wondering if the phone will be cut off, or to have a certain scheduled time once a week for bills and paperwork?

To write your daily to-do list whenever you can remember it, or to have a certain routine time in the daily schedule for writing it?

To call the doctor and try frantically to get a new prescription the day your blood pressure medicine runs out, or to schedule a routine way of renewing it regularly?

To wash the dishes when there are no clean ones left, or to wash them routinely after every meal or once a day?

To change the oil in your car when you start hearing strange noises or seeing warning lights come on, or to do it at regular intervals?

In the first instance, the stimulus to do the task is some sort of unpleasant circumstance; in the second instance, the stimulus is a regular habit or something on an appointment calendar. My observation is that having regular routines rather than reacting to the negative consequences of letting tasks go is a much more pleasant way to live.

In many families where there are insufficient routines, these tasks become the source of much irritation and feelings of frantic emergency. It will be useful for family members to sit down together with pencil and paper and decide together what routines they wish to adopt, to write them down, and review them frequently. If the routines save time, energy and effort, keep them; if they cause discord and contention, make a different plan.

What's the routine for laundry? for dishwashing? for homework-doing? for cooking and mealtimes? for bedtimes? for buying of supplies? If some task causes a hassle repeatedly, raise the question of what the system is for accomplishing it, and try to arrive at a system that will eliminate the hassle.

Using task analysis and fantasy rehearsal

How long does it take you to get organized into a new routine? For example, if you're a student, how long does it take you to get a routine established that will let you get the right books and papers where they should be at the right times? If you're a worker, how long does it take you to get to the right place with the right stuff in hand or in briefcase?

If the answer is "Never" or "Too long," task analysis combined with fantasy rehearsal might help.

Task analysis means writing down the steps in carrying out a procedure, such as completing a day of school, performing a surgical operation, or cleaning a house. You take a procedure or complicated process, and break it down into its individual parts. Let's illustrate task analysis with a silly example. Here are the logistics of getting a drink of water from the kitchen sink.

1. Walk to the kitchen cabinet.
2. Open it.
3. Get a glass.
4. Walk to the kitchen sink.
5. Turn on the cold water.
6. Let it run until it's cold.
7. Stick the glass underneath the stream of water.
8. When the glass is full, take it out.
9. Turn off the water.
10. Lift the glass to the lips, and drink the water.
11. Go back to step five if still thirsty.
12. If not still thirsty, put the glass in the sink and walk away.

(I could have had the drinker wash the glass out, dry it, and put it away, but I'll let the drinker be lazy, so we can keep it simpler.)

I left out a step, between steps 3 and 4. Can you figure out what it is? It's not easy to write a task analysis and remember all the steps the first time. Writing the task analysis forces you to think really hard about what the steps are. If I were editing and revising this task analysis, I would include closing the cabinet door, so as to avoid hitting myself on the head with it. Thinking about these steps and writing them down helps you to get a very clear image of exactly what goes on in the process.

If you've ever written a computer program, you'll recognize that writing a task analysis is like writing a computer program.

Let's do an imaginary task analysis for someone in high school who has a locker in the hall, switches classes every period, and finds it convenient to stop by the locker before each class. This student likes to carry a book bag to all classes.

Let's start the task analysis as the school day begins.

1. Pick up book bag I left on my desk last night and check one more time to make sure all my books and papers and

my assignment book are in it. Take it with me to school.

2. Before the first class, stop by my locker. Check what books, pencils, pens or papers I need for the first class, and put them into the book bag.

3. At the first class, turn in my homework paper when asked to do so. When I get a homework assignment, take my assignment book out of the book bag, open the assignment book to that day's date, write the name of the subject, and write the assignment carefully. (If there is no homework, write "none.") Check to make sure I wrote the assignment correctly. Return assignment book to the book bag.

4. Do steps 2 and 3 before all the other classes.

5. Before going home, stop at my locker and open my assignment book. Look at each assignment and make sure the books or papers I need to do each assignment are in my book bag. Take the book bag home.

6. At homework time, sit at my desk and read the first assignment from my assignment book. Get out of the book bag what I need to do it. Do it. Check it off in the assignment book. Then put the completed paper back in my book bag, in the file folder for that subject.

7. Do the same thing with the other assignments until all are finished.

8. Return the book bag to the top of my desk.

If there's a procedure you do repeatedly and you keep forgetting steps, it's a good idea to write a task analysis. The next job is to go over the task analysis repeatedly and memorize it. Next, you very vividly imagine yourself carrying out the procedure or do fantasy rehearsals of it.

Here's how a fantasy rehearsal might start for the task as analyzed above.

"It's morning, and I'm about to leave for school. I'm seeing my book bag on my desk, and I'm checking to make sure all my books and homework papers are in it. I'm picking it up and taking it with me. Now I'm at school, and it's before my first class. I'm stopping at my locker. I'm pulling my assignment book out of my locker and looking at it. I see what I need for my first class, and I'm making sure I've got that book in my book bag. I'm glad I checked carefully. Now I'm at my first class, and the assignment is written on the board. I pull my assignment book out of my book bag, and I write the name of the subject and copy the assignment. I'm checking it very carefully; yes, I've got it right, good for me . . ."

As you do a fantasy rehearsal, remember to congratulate yourself for carrying out the steps well.

If you find the way the task analysis is set up just doesn't work very well in real life, then you can go back and revise the task analysis again, and improve the process. Then you practice the new plan in imagination.

When there is no problem with logistics or organization in the procedure, your reward is that you can file away or throw away your task analysis and stop doing fantasy rehearsal.

Reducing error in tasks

Before a pilot takes off in a plane, she refers to a list of things to check and checks each thing that could possibly cause trouble during the flight. The same thing can be done, mentally or on paper, with any other task: you make a list of all the things that have to be done right in order for the job to be successful, and you don't call the job finished until each one is checked off. Your checklist should cover all the errors you can think of.

An example might be the task of child-proofing an area of the house where there are infants or toddlers. The checklist might have items such as the following: 1) Are there no matches and lighters available to the child? 2) Are no firearms available? 3) Are there no knives, ice picks, or other sharp objects available? 4) Are there no poisonous substances or medicines available? 5) Are there no heavy objects that can be pulled over or pulled down onto the child? 6) Are electrical outlets plugged? 7) Are there no opportunities for the child to get to a place high enough to be seriously injured if he fell? 8) Are there no objects small enough to be swallowed or choked on? 9) Are there no plastic bags that the child could suffocate from inhaling? 10) Is the temperature of the hot water from the faucet turned down enough that expo-

sure to it would not burn the child badly? (This is not a complete list.)

There's a big difference between error-reduction using a checklist as mentioned above, and compulsive checking rituals or nervous worrying. The error-reduction method I'm advocating allows you to focus on one type of possible error at a time and feel secure that all have been checked once you've completed the list. Compulsive checking involves trying to think about too many aspects of the job at one time. When compulsively checking, someone can't remember what has been checked and what hasn't and tries to make up for this disorganization by repetition.

Organizing communications with other people about tasks

In organizing your communication, a major goal is to place as few demands as possible on the other person's memory.

If the procedure you want someone to do is too much to hold in memory, write it down for them. Writing it down also prevents a good bit of telephone tag and a good bit of misunderstanding of verbal messages.

Keep unnecessary information to a minimum. If we call the most important points the "signal" and the most unimportant points the "noise," then you want your utterances to have the highest possible ratio of signal to noise.

Suppose someone asks, "Why didn't you buy a new cartridge for the printer when you were at the office supply store?" If you say, "The store was out of them," that utterance has a high signal-to-noise ratio.

The following utterance, on the other hand, has a low signal-to-noise ratio: "Well, I went down to the place about 2 p.m., no, I think it must have been about 3 p.m.; that's right, it couldn't have been 2:00 because I was still in a meeting until just a little before 3:00 – anyway, when I got there – it's the place where we always get supplies down on Meyran Avenue – I looked all over the place, and at first it was hard for me to believe that they would have been out, because I've been going there for at least a year, and I don't think there's been one other time that I couldn't find any, but I asked the clerk, who wasn't in a very good mood today . . ." In this example, the essential message is buried in a sea of irrelevant detail.

Deciding to take on a new commitment to a task

Here is an important principle that accounts for a substantial portion of human unhappiness: *People continue to take on new commitments to tasks until they are performing incompetently in at least one, if not all, of them.* If people are performing successfully, other people will ask them to take on new things to do and often offer rewards for doing them. People tend to say "yes" to such commitments.

A psychotherapist who establishes a reputation for very thorough and competent work tends to have more and more patients referred to him, to the point where he can't keep up with who is who.

An executive who establishes a reputation as a competent and thorough director of an organization is invited to be on more and more boards of directors, until she doesn't have time to understand an organization she is directing.

A full-time mother who establishes a reputation for organizing activities for parents and children to do together takes on so many projects that there is little time left to relax informally with her child.

A couple enjoy their first child so much that they have four more, and find that, with their other commitments, they can't give any of their children the time and attention they deserve.

Of course, it's possible to avoid new commitments, but it takes real effort to do so.

Each person has only a finite amount of time and energy. As the commitments proliferate, something has to be sacrificed. Sometimes the task that gets sacrificed is spending quality time with family. Sometimes it's enjoying time to oneself. Sometimes it's the task of getting adequate sleep. Sometimes it's the least urgent commitment someone has made to someone else, or sometimes the least urgent five commitments.

Just as organizing objects is easier if you can avoid owning so many of them, organizing tasks is easier if you think carefully before taking on another one. Are you on top of things now? Is your stress level in a very comfortable zone? How much time will the new commitment take? With that time no longer available, will you still be on top of things and at a comfortable level of stress?

This is the way to think before taking on a new commitment. The way *not* to think is simply to say, "Would this be interesting or worthwhile or profitable?" You must not only think of the returns, but of the investment of time and energy needed to reap the returns.

Organizing money

Just as the disorganization of time and tasks leads to very unpleasant outcomes, such as the failures of businesses and marriages, so does the disorganization of money.

Most of the works I've read on managing money ask people to spend a lot of time making a very detailed budget and figuring out how much money does go and should go to each category of expenditure. But it seems that very few people in the real world can consistently muster the energy to do this. Perhaps the labor that such a task requires isn't justified by the payoff. Is there a simpler and easier way to get a handle on managing finances?

Many people have no real money management system at all and would do well to adopt the following "minimalist" approach to financial organization, rather than taking on a very detailed and laborious system.

This minimalist system doesn't require that you add up expenses and income. It doesn't require that you categorize expenses into groups. It isn't even necessary to record your expenditures and income in order to use it, although that is necessary for other purposes.

In the most minimal of minimal systems, you simply calculate your financial net worth at regular intervals, say once every few months. You add up the amount you have in any accounts and subtract anything you owe.

The change in net worth from one month to the next represents the same number you would get if you were to keep a detailed record of all your expenses and all your income and compute the total of income minus expenses.

Under this system, any fluctuation in stock or bond prices is considered to be either income or expense. You don't count the value of consumption items, such as china or cars, or anything else except a house when calculating net worth.

If the trend of the net worth figure over the long term is upward in the amount you want it to be, you don't need to waste a lot of time on further recording and calculation.

If you have investments that fluctuate in value, you might want to get a handle on how much of the change in net worth is due to fluctuation of investment value and how much is due to the excess of income over expenditure. By doing this, you don't, for example, lull yourself into living far beyond your means during periods when the investments fluctuate upward.

To track this in a simple way, you put your income into a checking account and make your expenditures from it. You have your investments in a brokerage account. You record every transfer you make between the checking account and the brokerage account. If the net transfer from checking to brokerage is positive, you can meet expenses without relying on your investment income. If it's negative, then you have to make some further calculations to see under what circumstances your expenses will be adequately supported.

Of course, expenditures vary from month to month, and there may be some months where the change in net worth is negative, balanced by other months where the number is very positive. But by tracking net worth over time, you get an overall picture of your financial status. If you're in the black by a sufficient amount to prepare for retirement, future emergencies, future college expenditures, and so forth, then you're finished with this minimalist money organization procedure.

If you're not sufficiently in the black, then you need to add income or cut expenditures. If you need to cut, then there usually needs to be discussion among family members on which

expenditures may be cut and which may not. In the minimalist procedure, you simply go out and cut whatever you can cut and see what happens. If this doesn't work, then you go to the detailed budget figures, keeping track of food, clothing, phone, electricity, etc. But your reward for sufficient thrift is not having to do this.

Organizing thoughts

Organizing your own thoughts is perhaps the most difficult, yet important, organizing task of all. When some people think or talk about their own lives, they are so scattered that their thoughts can never seem to get anywhere. They can flit from one thing to another seemingly endlessly. They seem to spend more time on irrelevant details than on important facts. They can talk at high speed for a long time, and then stop for breath and think, "Now what was it I started out to tell you about?" Such jumping from one tangent to another is called "tangential thinking." This way of thinking is very frustrating, for the person trying to listen to it or read it, but even more so for the person who is thinking it!

What are the characteristics of organized thoughts? You deal with various questions or topics one at a time. You pose a question and then try to marshal all the evidence and ideas necessary to answer that question, before going on to the next question or topic. If there are subtopics under a certain topic, you try to deal with those one at a time, too. You try to do things in some logical sequence. You try to finish one thinking task, in some sense or another, before taking up the next.

How do you learn to organize your thoughts better? One way is to practice writing them down. Why do elementary school teachers help students learn to make outlines of their essays? It's because the principles of writing a coherent essay are exactly the same as those of thinking in an organized way.

One special case in which organized thinking is useful is when people are making decisions or trying to solve problems in their lives. Here's an outline for thinking about these decisions:

Outline for organizing thoughts about decisions

1. What is the problem? How can I best describe the situation? What are the RELEVANT details about this situation, the ones that have some chance of affecting what I decide? Whom does this problem affect?

2. What are my goals? That is, what do I want to happen as a result of my efforts to solve this problem?

3. What options can I think of? That is, what are the various alternative solutions I can imagine?

4. What are the advantages and disadvantages of the best of those options?

5. Which option or options appear to be the first choice at this time?

6. If I don't have enough information to make a good choice now, how can I get more information?

7. If I have made a choice, what are the specific details of my plan? What am I going to do, with and to whom, where, and when?

8. How am I going to follow up to see whether my plan worked or not?

Organizing thinking means not trying to do everything at once. I believe that therapists can be very helpful to people sometimes, just by handing them a piece of paper with these questions on them, and helping the person think about one question at a time, with one problem at a time. In doing so, they promote the process of organized thought.

For more on the skills of organized decision-making, please see the chapter on decision-making.

Organization skills checklist

Are you willing to allocate time, regularly, to putting objects in their homes, filing papers, writing to yourself about goals and tasks, and organizing money? _____

Do you declutter your life by acquiring and keeping no more objects and papers than you really need?

_____

Do you have a "home" for each object, especially the important ones? _____

Do you have adequate file space to keep organized files of all papers you want to keep? _____

When you receive a piece of paper that calls for some action later on, do you file the paper and make a note in your master to-do list of what you have to do, with a note in parentheses of where the piece of paper is filed?

_____

Do you make written lists of your long-term goals? _____

Do you periodically ask what is really important in life and revise your goal list accordingly? _____

Do you have one, and only one, "appointment and to-do" book that is almost always near you? _____

Does the appointment notebook have in it adequate space to write daily appointments and daily to-dos and to see both of them without having to turn pages? _____

Do you keep a master to-do list, of all tasks to be done? _____

Do you make a to-do list each day? _____

Do you put numbers by your tasks to be done, to order their priorities? _____

Do you check each task off the list as you do it? _____

Do you remember to feel good when you check a task off the to-do list? _____

Do you make error-reducing checklists for important tasks, consisting of all the things that need to be right for the job to be complete and check them before finishing the task?

_____

Do you create regular routines, and do recurring tasks according to a schedule rather than waiting for some negative consequence to prompt you to do it? _____

In adjusting to complicated routines, do you write out a task analysis and do fantasy rehearsals? _____

Do you communicate complicated procedures to other people in writing rather than straining their memories? _____

Do you have a high "signal-to-noise ratio" when you communicate with other people? _____

Before taking on a new commitment, do you carefully consider

whether you will have the time and energy to do it well, and say no to it if the
resources aren't there? _____

Do you calculate, each month,
the change in your net worth and adjust
your use of money according to what
those numbers tell you? _____

When you're thinking about
problems, do you try to think about one
question at a time or one problem at a
time? _____

Group 2: Joyousness

The skills in the joyousness group have one thing in common: the ability to feel good about some type of situation, or the ability to generate pleasure when some sort of thing happens. Can you enjoy both being by yourself and having positive interactions with others? When you get things accomplished, and when you do good things for others, does it make you feel good? Can you enjoy learning and discovering things? Does it make you feel good when other people are nice to you? Can you enjoy affection and gleefulness and humor?

There are two basic mechanisms for motivation of behavior: production of good feelings, or avoidance of bad feelings. Basic pleasure mechanisms are a major portion of what keeps people going. It's hard to motivate yourself if you don't anticipate that your action is going to bring at least a little bit of good feeling. To get enjoyment, you not only need to have good things happen to you – you also need receptivity to those good things, the ability to feel good about them.

It's nice if you can rig things so you're operating more on a "happiness economy" than a "pain economy." That is, it's good if you're often thinking, "Hey, something good happened; I feel good! Let's see if I can make it happen again!" rather than thinking, "Oh no, this bad thing happened, I feel bad. Let's see if I can avoid it or escape it."

Many of the pleasures and pains we experience are self-delivered. We create our own pleasure by saying things to ourselves. I give myself pleasure, for instance, when I say, "Hooray, I helped someone out. I did a kind act that was in keeping with my highest values!" But the same act would give me pain if I were to say, "I did a kind act. I was a real sucker. That person took advantage of me without giving me anything in return."

Fortunately, many of the pleasures in this group are able to be cultivated. You can learn to say things to yourself, to interpret what goes on, in a way that helps you feel good about the things that are very useful to feel good about.

Skill 5: Enjoying Aloneness

The skill of enjoying aloneness is obviously useful when there's no one else around. But it's also very useful when people are near but are not paying attention to you. So we might call this skill 'handling inattention' as well as enjoying aloneness.

Why is this such a useful skill to have? Let's talk about some of the problems people get into when they are not good at the skill of handling aloneness and inattention. A preschool-aged child who is not good at handling aloneness and inattention feels driven to get constant attention from his parent or caretaker. When the parent is on the telephone, the child feels the need to interrupt. When the parent is trying to get some work done, the child struggles to get 100 percent of the parent's attention. After a while, the parent begins to get irritated and worn down by this. Sometimes the parent's irritation brings out real misbehavior from the child.

When a child reaches school age, low skill in handling aloneness or inattention can cause him to have trouble getting independent work done, even when the child has all the academic skills necessary. Because the child has a craving for constant interaction, three or four minutes into doing math problems the child finds another child to poke or grab a pencil from or talk to. The child tends to get lots of disapproval from teachers. This can create a vicious cycle where the disapproval makes the child perform worse, and the worse performance brings on more disapproval. The teacher and students may perceive this child as bad, when really his motive is not to create any trouble. It's simply to interact and not be alone.

As people grow into the older school years, and then adolescence and adulthood, low skill in handling aloneness can be a big barrier to getting work done. There is a great deal of work that any person will need to sit down and do by himself. The adolescent needs to do homework, the adult needs to pay bills, do taxes, pay attention to insurance, and so forth. The professional needs to study how to do his job better.

Low skill in handling aloneness also makes someone feel worse when separation, rejection or criticism occur, particularly if someone has put all their eggs in the basket of one relationship. If I am very good at handling aloneness, I still may not like the separation. But at least I'm able to give myself some happiness by doing things by myself while I am repairing my social support system.

How do you cultivate the skill of handling aloneness? First, remember that cultivating this skill doesn't mean becoming a "loner." You want to have a social support system, but at the same time you want to enjoy solitude. If you remind yourself that the solitude won't be forever, it's much easier to tolerate.

A second aid is to cultivate the art of internal dialogue: the art of thinking in words. For example, the person who has to do lots of solitary work talks to himself about it. "Let's see. I have a whole pile of papers that I have to process. Which is the most important of them? I definitely want to get through this one before the time that I have is up. Where is one that I can get out of the way quickly? Why don't I start with that one just to get myself a little momentum? Then for the second task, I'll tackle the big one . . . Hey, I'm making some progress. I'm doing productivity! This is hard, but I'm moving along on it."

Such self-talk can make it easier to be alone. Thinking in words provides an experience somewhat like talking with another person. Thus cultivating self-talk helps in this skill, just as we've already mentioned it does in the skill of self-nurture or tolerating separation.

If you extend the idea of thinking in words, you arrive at writing. People who like to write can spend hours by themselves. They have a dialogue with themselves that probably provides some of the good feelings of dialogue with other people. Thus practicing writing is probably a good way to practice the skill of tolerating aloneness.

Another skill that aids in tolerating aloneness is imagination. Some people who have been prisoners of war in solitary jail cells have coped well with their solitude by creating very extended and elaborate imaginary activities. One such prisoner reportedly played a very good golf game soon after he returned home from years of imprisonment. When asked how he could possibly have kept his game up to such a high level, he reported that he had spent much time playing golf in his imagination while in his jail cell.

Self-talk, writing, and imagination all are specific examples of what we can call cultivating an "inner life," a set of things one can do in one's mind when one is alone. In another example, a prominent mathematician who has a long wait at a doctor's office, "does mathematics" to pass the time, pursuing ideas where he last left off with them.

To what extent do you have an "inner life" that you can enjoy? Try this experiment if you want to get more information on this question. Just sit, without reading, listening to music, playing a video game, talking to anyone, or even looking around, and let your mind do something enjoyable or productive. How long can you do this, and how enjoyable or productive can you make this time? In other variations of this experiment, permit yourself to walk, but without the Walk-man music earphones. Or permit yourself to use pencil and paper (or computer and word processor) to keep track of your ideas. Or get yourself out into nature, and let yourself look around at it all you want while you think.

If you find these sorts of exercises excruciatingly boring—if you experience the overwhelming urge to turn on the music video station or the video game or to get off to an action and adventure film—if you get a mounting feeling of impatience after only a few minutes—then you don't have much of an inner life.

The skill of handling aloneness requires practice just as any other skill does. There are archetypal stories of people spending time by themselves to emerge more enlightened or with more of an inner life than before. Henry David Thoreau's description of his days in solitude at Walden Pond is a classic example of this. There are biblical stories of going off by oneself before coming back to share enlightenment with others: Jesus' forty days in the wilderness, Jonah's days in the whale's belly, and so forth.

It's not necessary to do something dramatic, such as to travel to the remote mountains of Tibet, to "find yourself," cultivate an inner life, and strengthen the skill of aloneness. In various forms of meditation people practice a retreat from interaction and external stimulation, wherever they happen to be. In some forms 15 or 20 minutes once or twice a day of cultivation of the inner life is the regimen for meditation. Such regimens are also useful in relaxation; the skill of relaxation and that of handling aloneness are very much linked.

No amount of skill in handling aloneness will make it superfluous to have a social support system. In other words, people still need other people. Paradoxically, getting and keeping a support system is probably easier if the need for other people is less desperate. If you have a serenity born of being comfortable with your own inner life, you can enter only those relationships you choose rather than having to take any you can get. A strong inner life can make what you have to say to others less superficial. Being comfortable with yourself makes you more able to handle separations and rejection and criticism.

How else can you cultivate the skill of handling aloneness? Any sort of practice of activities you can do alone gives practice in the skill.

Let's quickly catalog some of these activities: reading, writing, doing mathematics, going for walks, appreciating nature, thinking about ideas, imagining stories, thinking about life decisions, exercising, practicing skills, playing music, doing solitary work, sports such as cross country skiing, swimming, weight lifting, hitting a tennis ball against a wall, looking at art work, creating art works, solving puzzles, fiddling with computers, recalling past experiences, imagining future experiences, thinking about whatever is highest and best in the universe.

Someone who wants skill in handling aloneness would do well to pick some or all of these activities and simply practice doing them. The person's mission is to find the mental maneuvers that will make these activities most fulfilling and enjoyable to himself.

We live in a world where cultivating an inner life is quite difficult for many people. This may be because the distracting stimuli from television, movies, video games, recorded music, and others are so pervasive and so available that you have to consciously try to get away from them if you want to be with yourself.

I would guess that the skill of handling aloneness, the cultivation of an inner life, is an antidote to various sorts of problem behavior, among them the addictions. Alcohol, drugs, cigarettes, overeating, and compulsive sex are methods of self-stimulation, methods of escaping the unpleasantness of just being with oneself. I would hypothesize that the person who can enjoy being with himself is less vulnerable to these. Other thrill-seeking or stimulus-seeking behavior such as fast and dangerous driving, getting into fights, impulsive stealing, and others might be dramatically reduced in a population that cultivates enjoying their own inner lives.

Skill 6: Pleasure from Approval

This skill is one of the intermediate steps on the path toward development of self-reinforcement skill, the ability to congratulate yourself for kind and productive acts. Before you learn to congratulate yourself, you usually must learn to take pleasure in other people's congratulations. Only after you've learned that crucial skill can you internalize both the congratulating and the pleasure from your own congratulation, so that you're reinforcing yourself. If you want to help someone feel good about self-congratulation, an important step is to help him feel good about someone else's congratulation.

I call the skill of taking pleasure from approval an intermediate step toward self-reinforcement rather than the first step. That's because the first step in developing the skill of pleasure from approval is learning appropriate trusting and depending. If you let someone else fulfill some of your needs, you develop more of a wish for that person's approval.

So the steps are these. First, the person (hopefully, the child) learns to depend on someone. Second, the person learns to feel good about the approval of the person he is dependent on. And third, the person cultivates an internal voice that can give approval and can create the same sort of good feelings he derives from the approval of the person he depends on.

The skill of feeling good about other people's approval is only useful when the other people have rational and good standards for giving approval. If other people give approval for success in violent exploits or deception, for the use of illicit drugs, or for sexual promiscuity, then the skill of feeling good about other people's approval doesn't get you far. But if you have the skill of taking pleasure from approval, at least you have the chance of being in a relationship with someone whose approval is based on good and useful standards.

For many people, the skill of pleasure from approval is easy. For these people it goes without saying that when someone praises you or approves of you, you feel good. But for others, barriers stand in the way of this skill.

Let's think about some of those barriers. One of them occurs in people with a big fear of failure: the fear of raising standards. Here's an example. Someone does some math problems. Someone else says, "Let's check these . . . Hey, you got them all right! Congratulations! You're really good at this sort of thing." And the person, instead of feeling good, feels bad. Why? The person is thinking, "Uh oh. Now I'll be expected to get them right from now on. If I don't do that, I'll be a failure. That will be terrible."

In other words, the person fears that success and approval elevate the standard to which he'll be held. Undoing some of this fear of failure may be the key to promoting enjoyment of approval in people with this sort of pattern.

Another source of displeasure from compliments is a fear of being influenced by someone else. Such fear may stem from strong anti-authoritarian attitudes or skill deficiencies in submission and compliance. The attitude, "I don't want anyone else influencing me in the slightest," can make you resent the very idea of another person evaluating your performance in any way.

Thus person A says, "You really did a good job." Person B thinks, "Who are you to tell me whether I did a good job or a bad job?" Thus, sometimes cultivating skills of submission or compliance is key to getting skills of pleasure from approval.

Sometimes people with very anti-authoritarian attitudes respond better to what the semanticists call "report language" rather than judgment language. "When you sang those songs, I felt so good," is the language of report. "You're an excellent singer; your vocal control is exceptional" is the language of judgment. Report language has also been called the use of "I statements" or "I messages," such as, "When this happened, I experienced this because of that." We spoke earlier about delivering critical messages in this format; sometimes it's also best to express approval in this form as well. But any person who can't enjoy compliments unless they're in this form is too picky.

In a similar vein, some people don't enjoy compliments because, when they hear one, their first thought is, "What is this person trying to con out of me now?" People can get cynical about compliments, particularly when they've spent lots of time with con artists who compliment them only to make them feel more inclined to grant a request the con artist makes.

Here the task is the skill of trusting. This means not making generalizations from experiences with con artists and not assuming that everyone in the world is a con artist. Trusting means learning that sometimes people have unselfish and honest motives for delivering approval.

Some people, especially children, are more reinforced by excitement than approval. Perhaps because they have a novelty-seeking gene, or perhaps because they haven't spent enough time cultivating the skills of handling low stimulation, they are more reinforced by someone's yelling "Hey, what do you think you're doing!" than by someone's calmly saying, "You did a good job. I'm proud of you."

If someone is more reinforced by excitement than by approval per se, it makes sense for people to try to give approval in an excited tone of voice and to give disapproval in an unexcited tone of voice. Perhaps, over time, the coupling of excitement and approving words will help the child learn to be reinforced by approval, even when it's not delivered with great excitement.

What really deserves approval? It's making the world, even if only a very small part of it, a better place. The more a society can collectively give approval for those actions that truly do increase long-term happiness, the better the society will be.

We're living in a society where boxers and football players, whose main skill is delivering violent blows to another human being, get much more approval than the mother or the preschool teacher who fosters psychological skills in children. The actor who plays in action and adventure movies modeling rampant acts of mayhem and destruction gets hugely more approval than the person who works in a mediation center. When the President of the United States bombs or invades a country, the effect, for the short term at least, seems to be a meteoric rise in approval ratings.

Thus the quest for approval is not a perfect beacon to guide behavior. "Hoard the esteem of your fellows" is a good guide for living only to the extent that your fellows know what's worthy of approval; sometimes it appears that this is seldom the case. Nonetheless, being able to take pleasure from the approval of some people you deem wise and good is a crucial psychological skill.

Skill 7: Pleasure from Accomplishments

The next skill on the list is using self-reinforcement for your accomplishments. This skill can be divided into two parts. The first is congratulating yourself, sometimes by literally saying, either out loud or with self talk, "Hooray for me! I did something good. I'm glad I did that." The second part is feeling good about the congratulations you deliver to yourself.

What is an accomplishment, anyway? I think it's useful to discriminate between acts that actually make the world a better place, actually help people, and acts that demonstrate your potential to help people. If you graduate first in your class, that's an accomplishment. But who is directly better off because you did it – other than your relatives who get to brag about you? Unless you've gone to an unusual school, the work you've put into tests and projects has only demonstrated your potential to help people and has not directly helped anyone.

Suppose someone goes to school all his life and dies with eight Ph.D.s. This person has demonstrated his potential to do good in eight different ways, but unless he's actually done good for someone in one of those ways, no one is any better off for it. In fact, he has absorbed the resources of the world in the form of teachers' investments in him, without producing a payoff on those investments. Or suppose someone

scores extremely highly on an IQ test, or runs a race faster than anyone else. Who has been helped? These accomplishments demonstrate mental and physical potential to do things that will actually help people, but they don't directly make people better off. The real value of an accomplishment is measured by the extent to which people are happier because of something you've done.

I believe education should be radically restructured so that children and adolescents, instead of spending the first parts of their lives simply demonstrating abilities that will equip them to do good in later years, should be given much more of an opportunity to actually do good and useful things for other people. It's very desirable, however, for children – and other people – to be able to feel good about either type of accomplishment.

It's widely known that the reinforcement of approval and congratulations can drastically increase a positive behavior. There have been lots of studies of the following sort. You measure how often someone does something. Then you start giving the person approval each time he does that thing. If the approval really is reinforcing, the person starts doing the thing much more frequently. Then, when you withdraw the approval, the person does it less frequently, and, when you reinstitute the approval, the frequency goes back up.

This sort of experiment demonstrates that the behavior is influenced by approval. But it's worrisome that the behavior gets less frequent so fast when the external approval is withdrawn.

Suppose the subject in the study is a six-year-old child, being reinforced by a twenty-six-year-old adult for doing or saying nice things. If we want that child to keep on doing and saying nice things, do we have to keep up the external approval, so that when the child is sixty years old, the eighty-year-old adult is still following him around giving approval for positive behaviors?

Somewhere in the process of becoming an adult or a mature person, you should learn to deliver a good bit of positive reinforcement to yourself. If you do this, you'll be able to maintain positive behaviors on a "leaner schedule of external reinforcement" than those available in behavioral studies.

The first part of the skill of self-reinforcement is remembering to say to yourself, "I did a good job," when you do so. Sometimes people have been taught that they should not boast or brag; this resistance to bragging prohibits them even from congratulating themselves silently. Sometimes people can't deliver these self-congratulatory statements because they have the idea, "I shouldn't congratulate myself until the task is fully finished." Most tasks, in some large sense, are never fully finished. They can always be improved

upon, or they can be seen as one step in a larger process that should be continued.

Recognizing the little milestones that are best to congratulate is an art. If you wait for the entire task to be finished, you don't get enough reinforcement. If you reinforce yourself indiscriminately for everything you do, you lose your sense of direction. It's a real art to figure out what really moves you closer to your goal, what is a step in the right direction.

Just as the proof of the pudding is in the eating, the decision on how much self-reinforcement is best is made on the basis of what makes you perform best. Sometimes going down blind alleys is a very important part of an accomplishment. In writing a book, for example, writing paragraphs that will never show up in the final version can be crucial steps toward the final product.

The second part of this skill, namely, being able to feel good about the approval you give yourself, is a more subtle art. It depends upon the ability to trust your judgment, to trust your own decisions about what is worthwhile and good. If you think, "I can't make any competent decisions about anything," then why should you feel good about your own decision that you deserve to feel good? Thus, gaining some confidence in your ability to make competent decisions can be a very important step in the skill of self-reinforcement. Over and over we see how interdependent these various skills are.

The shaping game

I invented the shaping game to simulate the process of giving approval for successive steps toward a goal. It's meant to give practice in several skills: expressing positive feelings to others, feeling gratitude for good things others do, using differential reinforcement, and feeling good about others' approval. Ultimately, it's also meant to help with the skill of self-reinforcement. So let's arbitrarily decide to talk about it here.

Here are the rules of the game.

1. There are two people. The "shaper" thinks of some behavior for the "shapee" to do, and writes it down, without showing the shapee.

2. The object of the game for the shaper is to give clues so the shapee can do that behavior.

3. The object of the game for the shapee is to do that behavior. (Both players have the same goal. Thus this is a cooperative game rather than a competitive one.)

4. The shapee usually begins the game by doing things like walking around, touching things, and saying things, i.e., trying out behaviors to see what gets reinforced.

5. The shaper can give clues only by approving things the shapee has already done. For example, the shaper can say things such as, "I like it that you turned that direction," or "That's good that you moved your hand upward."

6. Criticism, suggestions, or commands are against the rules. Only positive reinforcement for behaviors already completed is permitted.

When you're the shaper, you have to withhold criticism and rely on positive reinforcement. You have to decide what constitutes a movement closer to the goal behavior. If you let a significant movement go by without reinforcing it, you don't win the game as quickly. On the other hand, if you reinforce everything indiscriminately, you don't help the shapee figure out what to do.

You also have to reinforce quickly after the shapee does the behavior, so that the information comes at the most useful moment. You have to cultivate pleasure in the shaper's being successful, rather than being so much into the competitive mentality that you enjoy seeing your fellow player frustrated or stumped.

You have to make your approval specific: for example, saying "I'm glad you looked at that book" works better than "That was good." It's good if you can express different degrees of reinforcement in your voice, getting very excited about big movements or those particularly close to the goal.

When you're the shapee, you have to pay attention to the approval rather than simply exploring the environment. You have to remember what you got the approval for, and keep acting in ways consistent with that. You have to stay goal-oriented, trying to get more and more approval, rather than just aimlessly wandering. If you try something and it doesn't get the approval, you have to be ready to drop it and try something else.

You have to have enough energy to try things fast enough that you have a chance of going in the right direction – nothing fails at this game so much as immobility. If you're going to be most successful, you have to get yourself to want the approval, to feel good about it, to go after it.

If you take these subskills of playing this game and think about them in the context of the messages we give ourselves and how we respond to them, all of these apply to the skill of self-reinforcement. They also apply to the skill of using differential reinforcement with another person. Playing the game is a good way to get a mental pattern laid down that will be useful in these real-life skills.

Unlike in the shaping game, in real life it's sometimes a good idea to use some critical statements both to oneself and to others. Some studies have looked at what sorts of statements happy and productive people say to themselves, particularly the proportion of positive evaluative statements to negative ones. The proportion of positive statements is not one hundred percent, but there are usually many more positive statements than negative ones. I think eighty percent positive is a good portion to shoot for. When people are very depressed, they often have close to one hundred percent negative self-statements.

The positive behavior diary

Sometimes we're too busy doing something to reinforce ourselves for doing it. Sometimes the best thing to do is to recall the positive thing later on, and say to ourselves, "Hey, that was something good I did! Hooray!"

If you're consciously working on the skill of self-reinforcement, it's good to do an exercise of keeping a positive behavior diary. You write down the good things you did, and you celebrate them. Or, if you don't want to write them, you can dictate them into a tape recorder. Or you can contact a significant other and just tell that person. The most important thing is having a structure that lets you recall those acts and put them into words. If you can make a permanent record of them, that's great too.

Then you can do an exercise wherein you recreate those positive acts in your own fantasy, doing a fantasy rehearsal of them. You practice celebrating, congratulating yourself for the positive behavior; you have time in your rehearsal even if you didn't have time in real life.

If you keep a permanent record of these positive behaviors, you can go back and celebrate them days, weeks, or years after having done them.

There are several benefits of this exercise. It promotes storage in memory as well as fantasy rehearsal of the most positive parts of your behavior for the day. This tends to strengthen those behaviors in your repertoire. It also gives lots of practice in self-reinforcement.

Skill 8: Pleasure from Your Own Kindness

Which psychological skill, if drastically increased in all people, would go the furthest to make the world a better place? The ability to take great pleasure from acts that make other people happier would have to rank high on the list. It's because this is such an important skill that I make a separate slot for it, despite the fact that we've already talked about the skill of kindness itself. In addition, we've already talked about the skill of taking pleasure from accomplishments, and I argued in that section that the best accomplishments are those that help others. But despite the redundancy, it's important to focus the mind specifically on feeling good about making others feel good.

A world, a community, a classroom, a family, or a pair of friends or lovers who greatly enjoy being kind to one another is probably a happy unit of people. The skill of taking pleasure from making other people happy blends the two major goals that this manual has emphasized: bringing happiness to others and being happy oneself. If you have cultivated strongly enough the skill of making yourself happy by making other people happy, you can accomplish both of these goals simultaneously.

Many pleasures are cultivated. People cultivate the ability to take great pleasure in certain types of music, in watching plays, in gourmet food. The person who has cultivated the ability to take great pleasure particularly in the finest of a certain set of things is a connoisseur. People can cultivate pleasure in stimuli that at first are aversive, such as tobacco smoke or wine.

If you can cultivate the things you take pleasure in, it makes sense gradually to become a connoisseur of making others happy. Unlike smoking and drinking, it's not harmful; unlike watching plays or listening to music, it tends to make people want to reward you and do nice things to you in return. If you take pleasure in making others happy to the point that you would do it with no reward, then the gratitude or compensation you receive are gifts.

How do you cultivate the ability to take pleasure in something? You spend time thinking about the distinctions between one variation of it and others. You look for, observe and concentrate on the pleasurable feelings you get from it, so as to heighten those. You talk with other connoisseurs about the object of your pleasure, and you let the pleasure of socializing spill over into the object of your interest. You talk about the good qualities of various examples of the object. You get into the habit of thinking positive thoughts about the object. If people can do this for wine, why can't they do it for acts of kindness?

Motives for kind acts

Here's a classification of why people do kind things for each other.

1. Fear of punishment. The first possibility is the fear of being punished if you don't act in a prosocial way. A parent says to the child, "You share that toy with your brother or else I'll take it away." Or the employee thinks, "I had better smile and speak very pleasantly to my boss, or else I'll get fired."

2. Wish for a tangible reward. A parent says, "If you share with your little brother, I'll give you an ice cream cone later on." Or, a real estate sales person gives a fruit basket, a card and a nice visit to someone whose parent has died. The real estate salesperson hopes that he will be asked to sell the parent's house and get a commission for doing so. For another example, a child in school tries to help everybody so he can get the citizenship award at the end of the year.

3. Wish for a positive interpersonal climate. This is the desire to be kind, because of the knowledge that reciprocity is a rule in human relationships. People tend to be kind to those who have first been kind to them. For example, someone is nice to family members because he knows this sets a tone that helps the others be kind as well. He is kind because he wants to live in a family with a good emotional climate.

4. Belief that creating happiness is good and taking pleasure from doing so. This is the desire to make others happy even when there are no obvious rewards for yourself. This is using the skill of this section – the skill of taking direct pleasure from creating happiness.

It's my informal observation that groups where the third and fourth motives prevail are the happiest ones; the ones where the second motive prevails are the next most happy; and the ones where the first motive prevails are the least happy.

Total reliance on the first motive, the fear of punishment, can lead to vicious cycles in which the first person is punishing the second person for being unkind. But the second person rightly perceives that punishment as unkind, and punishes the first. Now the first has more reason to punish the second. The escalation of this process is responsible for murder, warfare, and a great number of the other ills that human beings inflict upon one other.

The second motive, the wish for tangible rewards, is the driving force for exchange, trade and capitalistic economies. When it's taken to its logical extreme, people do good things for others in exact proportion to others' capacities to reward them, usually with money. Taken to its logical conclusion, this motive leads to systems where power, not love, is the driving force in human interactions. I have occasionally seen very successful business people who have tried to run their personal and family lives on this principle. Sometimes the desired behaviors are produced, but the feelings of love, loyalty and attachment seem to be lacking.

The third motive, the wish for a positive emotional climate in the group, is somewhat more principled. It's still a self-seeking motive, but it recognizes that one can only attain one's own ends through helping other people attain theirs. One problem that arises when this motive is not supplemented by the fourth one is that you have little motive to be kind to people outside the groups you're in.

For example, a white, upper middle class person using this motive may be kind only to those in his family, country club, and church, but viciously discriminatory against the poor, racial minorities, and others he perceives he will never depend upon for the quality of his own emotional climate.

The fourth motive, the wish to create happiness simply because of a belief that it's good to do so and a highly cultivated pleasure in doing so, is the "highest" motive. People who have this motive can take pleasure in helping others without being subject to resentment and bitterness if the others don't feel grateful enough.

One caution regarding this motive: avoid becoming an "enabler." An enabler is one who, through help and kindness that seem good in the short run, actually reinforces or prevents the punishment of someone else's irresponsible behavior, and thus sustains it. Thus it's necessary to think about the other person's long-term happiness, not just giving him what he wants in the short run.

A second caution: it's possible to be exploited by selfish individuals. Con artists abound in the world. Anyone who takes pleasure from kindness should also be aware of the need for self-protection and appropriate assertion.

Despite these problems, if most people could greatly raise the strength of the motive to do kind acts simply because of a cultivated pleasure in them, the world would be immeasurably helped.

Other tips on cultivating this skill

How do you develop the skill of pleasure from your own kind acts? Connoisseurs, or specialists in taking pleasure from a certain source, do several things: concentrate, look for the pleasure, talk with other people about it, get into the habit of thinking positive thoughts about the object of pursuit.

The habit of thinking positive thoughts takes us back to our familiar classification of thoughts. "Celebrating your own choice" after doing a kind act reinforces you for doing it. "Celebrating someone else's choice" increases your gratitude and raises your desire to do something kind.

But taking the deepest pleasure from kindness probably requires having a strong ethical belief system, based on religion or philosophy, that being kind is right, good, what one ought to do. In addition to having this belief, pleasure from kindness probably also requires frequently reminding oneself of this belief.

It's not without reason that many religions of the world encourage daily prayers that remind people how important it is to be kind. I believe that daily repetition, from an early age, of the Golden Rule and related ethical principles, such as the sixteen groups of skills that form the basis for this book, is an important element in a child's upbringing, and one that appears very much absent in most families in current American culture.

Another skill central to taking pleasure from kindness is empathy. It's hard to take pleasure from making someone else feel good when you're oblivious to how you're making others feel. Empathy involves putting oneself in some other person's place, taking that person's perspective, and imagining very completely how she must feel. The use of the Golden Rule or the greatest good for the greatest number rule relies on empathy: I can't decide what is good for another person unless I can see things from that person's point of view.

A very important way that people learn the skill of pleasure from their kind acts is by having received kindness, particularly from parents, but also from peers. Experiencing someone's obvious pleasure in doing something kind for you with no other reward accruing is a very powerful experience for most people. In a process called "identification with the aggressor," people who have been treated unkindly tend to imitate that aggression, particularly toward those less powerful than they. The same process tends to take place, fortunately, with kind behavior as well. We can call this "identification with the benefactor."

Another way people learn this skill is by observing models, rather than directly experiencing them. This can take place in symbolic models, such a stories, plays, television shows and movies. Of course, models can also present the opposite of this skill, namely, taking pleasure in someone else's misfortune, or taking pleasure in thwarting, defeating, and upsetting someone else. A society that is serious about improving itself will seek to produce multitudinous models of people feeling good about their acts of kindness to other people.

We should note that the tendency to enjoy producing distress in others, to laugh at others' misfortunes, to take pleasure in others' pain, is the diametric opposite of the skill of pleasure from acts of kindness. In my opinion the tendency to enjoy producing pain and distress in others is the worst quality that a human being can possess. When this behavior is extreme, we call it sadism. It deserves the title "evil." Unfortunately, the tendency to take pleasure in other people's misfortunes, particularly in the defeat of someone set up to be viewed as an opponent or enemy, is extremely widespread in our culture.

Another way in which people learn the skill of enjoying acts of kindness is by internalizing external approval for kind acts. Suppose a child often hears a parent saying something like this: "I think you made that person feel good when you did that. I was proud to see that. I like it when you make other people happy."

When the parent says this in an excited and enthusiastic voice, both the excited, enthusiastic emotion and the ideas of approval are stored in memory. Internalization means that the child's inner speech duplicates these ideas when the child performs a kind act with the parent not around. The internalized image of the parent in the child's head can say, "I'm proud of you. It makes me feel good when you do things like that."

Different brands of happiness

When we think about creating happiness in other people, we should think of several brands of happiness. Or perhaps it's more accurate to think of a rating scale where happiness is rated on a continuum. On one end of the spectrum is short-term, superficial pleasure from actions that have bad effects in the long term. On the other end of the spectrum is happiness that evokes a permanent increase in the quality of life for oneself and for other people. In cultivating the skill of pleasure from kindness, we want to feel more pleasure about producing higher-rated happiness.

To illustrate: A dealer in cocaine and heroin can be pretty certain he is giving people what they want and making people feel good, in the short run. But in the long run, he is contributing to the destruction of their lives. Thus the happiness he creates gets a low rating on our quality of happiness scale.

For another example: Someone creates a violent action movie, in which the filmmaker's art leads to pleasure in the bad guys' violent deaths. The film may produce short-term pleasure in the viewers, at the expense of long-term damage to their personalities, and the promotion of the practice of sadistic pleasure in other's misfortunes.

Likewise, a professional baseball player provides entertainment, but the long-term effects of his trade are debatable. For most viewers, watching baseball games probably falls into the category of harmless amusement without much effect on the personality one way or another.

At the other end of the spectrum is creating happiness by, for example, supplying essential food to hungry people, creating a vaccine that will prevent a horrible illness, reattaching a severed limb, doing a job of parenting that teaches a child to get competent at all the psychological skills, inventing a psychotherapeutic procedure that helps thousands of people get over depression, discovering an economic principle that helps millions of people escape poverty, articulating a philosophy that helps lots of people live better lives, and so forth. Creating the best and most worthwhile happiness brings numerous benefits. It causes a person to feel happy, to make other people happy, and to help other people to make other people happy. A good educator, for example, helps students to be more competent in ways that not only make the student happy, but also help the student to make others happy.

The contagion of this skill and of its opposite

I mentioned earlier that people learn this skill from having others enjoy being kind to them. The implication is that the skill of taking pleasure from your own kindness is a contagious phenomenon. It spreads from one person to another.

In just the same way, its antithesis, taking pleasure from other people's pain, is also contagious. When someone is sadistic to you, that person tends to make it pleasurable to hurt him or others you see as being like him.

I find that reminding myself of the contagiousness of these patterns helps in cultivating the skill of pleasure from kindness. It's useful, and accurate, to imagine that a contagion of pleasure from kindness is competing with a contagion of sadism. Showing people the ability to enjoy kind acts carried out toward them scores some points for the positive pattern in this competition and contributes to a better world.

Skill 9: Pleasure from Discovery, Love of Learning

Some developmental theorists belief there is an innate drive in people to discover things, to find out more about how the world works, and to become more competent in dealing with the world. These scientists think the drive toward competence is hard-wired into our brains, just as hunger, thirst, sexual urges, and the urge to breathe are. If you watch a preschool-aged child, you will see almost constant exploration, as well as near constant work on language acquisition.

If you watch adults amusing themselves, you will often see the amassing of a great deal of information and competence, although it isn't always useful for the betterment of the world. There are people who can recall minute facts of baseball statistics and others who have learned vast numbers of intimate details about movie stars' personal lives. There are countless others who have become supremely competent at video games. Although educators wish this drive toward learning and competence could be channeled in the service of science, mathematics and writing, the drive to discover and learn is very much alive and well.

Given the time and aptitudes available for us, it's entirely possible to have a society full of people who are very knowledgeable and competent in all sorts of useful arenas. If the skill of pleasure from discovery were fully and expertly fostered in our society, we could have a whole culture of people who were very competent at skills such as medicine, law, accounting, statistics, business management, plumbing, carpentry, machine repair, art, music, dance, and many other useful fields, not to mention the study of psychological skills. With enough fostering of pleasure from discovery, we could have a very highly educated culture. Perhaps with enough pleasure from discovery going on, people would not turn so often to some of the less healthy pleasures, such as gambling or drugs.

The person who becomes hooked on the pleasures of discovery is a lucky person, especially in this information age. For such an individual, a library, a bookstore, or the Internet can become a vast playground offering great amounts of pleasure and enjoyment. The ability to take pleasure in these pursuits also confers upon the person who takes such pleasure a certain immunity or a certain resistance to the pain of separation and rejection. The pleasure of discovery can be done in solitude. When solitary pleasures are available, the pain of losing part of the social network is less intense.

On the other hand, people who share pleasure in a certain type of discovery are often drawn into strong social bonds. In fact, one of the qualities that makes discovery pleasurable is the ability to report upon it, to talk about it with other human beings, and to make a social activity out of it.

Pleasure from discovery is different from pleasure from accomplishments. Another way of putting this is to say that achievement motivation is different from curiosity motivation.

The person who learns mathematics so that he can do well on a test or use math to do something great is acting from achievement motivation. The person who learns mathematics purely because of the beauty and inherent interest of it is acting from curiosity motivation. You can have both of these motives at the same time.

The person with a great deal of curiosity motivation is probably going to enjoy education more than the person who is driven only by achievement motivation. For the person with lots of curiosity motivation, learning is a pleasurable end in itself. For the person driven only by achievement motivation, it's a means to an end.

There are many sources of pleasure from discovery. One of those sources of pleasure comes from finding that a lot of unwieldy information that would clutter up the brain very quickly can be dramatically condensed. It's very pleasurable to boil down all that information into one little but powerful principle that does the job all by itself.

For example, let's suppose you're interested in how hard you have to push on things to get them to move at certain speeds. You take lots of meas-

urements: you use different forces to pull and push on things of different sizes, and you see how fast they go after certain periods of time. After accumulating extensive data and studying it, something falls into place. You discover that the speed an object accelerates is proportional to how hard you push on it, divided by how much it weighs. You get a very short equation like F=ma (Force equals mass times acceleration).

Then you find that every one of the measurements and bits of information you collected can be explained by this equation. When you go out and do another experiment, the data from that experiment are also consistent with the equation. Part of the pleasure from this discovery is knowing that you don't have to fill your head with hundreds of bits of information to be able to understand why things go at certain speeds.

Incidentally, the person who discovered the relationship between force, mass, and acceleration was Isaac Newton. The relationship we just mentioned is Newton's second law of motion. Newton himself seemed to take pleasure from discovery. He compared his life's work to a child exploring a seashore and finding pretty shells.

Another element that makes discovery pleasurable is the ability to predict and control the future. This pleasure is similar to the pleasure of pretending to do magic. Most magic tricks involve being able to predict or control something in a way that is a mystery to someone else. For example, the magician doing a card trick is able to predict what card will turn up, when it appears that this should be unknowable. When the magician throws several scarves into a hat and pulls them out all tied together, the magician seems to be able to control something in a way that seems impossible.

But many of the discoveries people have made let us do magic without trickery. Try to imagine what the world was like before certain discoveries, and then imagine these discoveries being introduced, and experience in your mind the wonder that people felt.

Being able to communicate instantly with someone thousands of miles away (through a telephone) is like magic. Being able to see inside a person's body with x-rays and other imaging techniques is like magic. Being able to concoct a drug that will cure an illness is like magic.

Or imagine that you saw a piano for the first time, and were able to plink around on it, and become curious about what it was for. Then imagine that someone came in and played a beautiful song on it. It's like magic without the trickery.

All these pieces of learning allow us to control something that, without such learning, would be uncontrollable. The person who learns the technique of any of these is being let in on the magician's secrets. Our basic desire to be able to control what is happening probably accounts for some of the pleasure of discovery.

How much should we worry about work destroying pleasure from discovery?

There are two opposing theories about the development of the love of learning or the love of any other activity. One theory is that you create long-term distastes for an activity by forcing people to partake in that pleasure when there is absolutely no appetite for it.

Many people grow up to like the taste of lima beans, but if a child is forced to eat more and more lima beans until he finally gags and vomits, he may avoid them from then on, if he is able to, and have a life-long aversion to them.

To give another example, there was one mildly successful method of helping people quit smoking, in which the researcher would get them to rapidly smoke cigarettes past the point where they wanted any more, to the point where they made themselves sick. For a while, at least, this tended to diminish the pleasure of smoking and helped people to quit. Unfortunately, the strength of nicotine addiction is usually too great for this sort of experience to overcome it.

The second major theory is that, by doing an activity a lot, you increase the long-term taste for it, even though, in the short run, it might not have been pleasant.

One version of this process is sometimes referred to as gaining "functional autonomy" of a motive after external motives have brought about lots of experience in the activity.

Most people report that their first puff of cigarette smoke is not a pleasant one. It's done only in response to the external motivation of social pressure. But when this external motive causes someone to inhale cigarette smoke frequently enough, a chemical addiction sets in, and the habit becomes highly reinforced by the chemical effects. The motive to inhale the smoke becomes "functionally autonomous" and intrinsically reinforcing, whereas it wasn't at the beginning.

The idea is that in order to become hooked on an activity, you first have to just do it, for whatever reason, enough times. When you do it enough, the motive to do that activity can take on a life of its own.

Here's another example, which like cigarette smoking is of pathological behavior rather than positive behavior. There are some men who report they were forced to wear girls' clothing during childhood. Someone did this to them as a form of humiliation. Yet, rather than developing a conditioned aversion that would lead them to avoid women's clothing forever, they somehow got hooked on wearing women's clothing in a pattern called transvestism.

So it's not true, apparently, that we automatically hate to do what we are forced to do in an early age. In fact, sometimes the words "repetition compulsion" are used to describe the fact

that we feel compelled to repeat those early experiences.

Here's another example. Suppose a girl is raised by a harsh and abusive father. A simple, conditioned aversion model would suggest that this girl would be extremely unlikely to pick a harsh and abusive husband. But it certainly appears that people who live with abusers in childhood wind up married to abusers more often, not less often. The repetition compulsion often seems to win out over conditioned aversion.

Can the same process occur with learning, discovery and competence development? I recently read a small biography of the great composer Beethoven. What were his initial experiences with music like as a child? Were they highly positive ones, designed to set up a lifetime of positive associations? On the contrary, Beethoven's father used an abusive manner to force his son to play the piano. The father liberally used humiliation and physical punishment, sometimes coming home drunk in the middle of the night and waking up his son to make him practice. A simple conditioned aversion model would make us think such experiences would set up a lifetime of conditioned aversion and avoidance of anything musical. Obviously, this effect did not predominate.

When I think of some of the enduring pleasurable activities of my own life – running, playing music, reading, writing, working with patients – for each of these, there were many times when external contingencies forced me to do much more of the activity than I had an appetite for. In the case of running, this reached the point of literally vomiting. In the case of medical training, the coercion to do very large amounts of work for extended hours when one would like nothing better than to quit working and sleep is a long-standing part of medical training.

All these experiences did not induce in me a long-standing conditioned aversion. On the contrary, it seems that learning to tolerate huge doses of these activities may have increased my enjoyment of normal doses of them.

What psychological process may explain this? Perhaps it's the process of habituation, discussed more fully in the section on fear reduction. In doing an activity, certain pieces of feedback are unpleasant, while others are pleasant. In the case of running, for example, the unpleasant feedback is the bodily sensation of fatigue. In the case of writing, the unpleasant sensations are mental fatigue or restlessness.

By doing large amounts of these activities, you get the chance to habituate, to desensitize yourself to these unpleasant sensations. It's the same mechanism whereby the person who's afraid of elevators has his fear habituate more readily when he exposes himself to the elevator for long periods of time than when he does so only for short periods.

Something more obvious happens when you spend extended periods of time working at a learning task:

competence development takes place. When I practice the piano for hours on end, I get better and better at it. So later on, I have more skills in that activity, and the more skills I have, the more capacity for enjoyment I have.

These ideas suggest we shouldn't worry that doing too much work will produce conditioned aversions. Perhaps large amounts of work may enhance the skill of pleasure from discovery, by producing habituation to fatigue and by building competence. If you want to take great pleasure in discovery and learning, it will be just fine to spend fairly large amounts of time working at discovery and learning, even if such work produces a feeling of great fatigue. At the same time, it's also a good policy to search for the intrinsic sources of pleasure from learning and discovery and to rely on them as much as possible.

The importance of staying in the challenge zone

If too much work poses no threat to the skill of pleasure from learning, here's something that does pose a threat: working at the wrong level of difficulty.

Imagine opening a mathematics textbook five levels above your understanding and then trying to do the problems at the end of a chapter. Both the chapter and the problems are unfathomable; they might as well be written in a foreign language. How long would you work at the problems until your love of attempting this task began to wane?

Or imagine beginning a course on how to become a more intelligent reader of great literature, only to find that the first six weeks will be spent filling out workbook sheets on the alphabet?

Frustration and boredom come from working at too difficult or too easy a level of challenge. But when you're working at the level that is not too hard, not too easy, but in the "challenge zone," it becomes much easier to cultivate the love of learning.

A wonderful gift to every child would be a continual exposure to academic learning challenges that were just the right level for that child. But in classrooms, particularly large ones, with children of widely differing abilities, it's very difficult for a teacher to engineer that feat.

Learning for a purpose other than the game of academics

What do I mean by the "game of academics"? It's doing academic tasks, such as tests and papers, to get a good grade, win a high class rank, prove yourself smarter than the average peer, and, if you do well enough, earn some awards and recognition. There's nothing inherently bad about this. If the thrill of winning and proving yourself smart can work to help people enjoy chess competitions, why not test-taking and paper-writing competitions?

But something very important is lost when the game of academics becomes the only motivation available for learning. What's missing is the idea that discovery and learning are tools that let you make the world a better place, not just prove how smart you are.

Also missing are two other ideas: that, even if you aren't a winner at the game of academics, your learning can often let you make the world a better place, and that being a winner doesn't guarantee your learning will make the world a better place.

For example, one child has great difficulty learning how to read and gets bad grades in reading. But he finally catches on and learns to read easy books. When he does so, he uses this knowledge to read to his younger sister. He does this with love and patience and greatly helps his younger sister.

By contrast, another child has great natural talent, so he picks up reading easily and gets great grades. But he has no desire to help his younger sister, and he spends his time honing his skills at video games.

Or, in another example, a high school girl learns sign language. Even though she is not at the top of her signing class, she continues to practice, and she is able to help many deaf people by interpreting for them and by helping deaf children develop language skills.

On the other hand, a person who's at the top of her sign language class spends her time learning Russian, Chinese, and French, and is able to brag about how many languages she knows; it turns out that she never uses any of them to actually help anyone. If she takes great pleasure from using these languages over the years, then at least she has been learning for something other than the game of academics. But, if after the last test has been passed, she does not return to these languages and gradually forgets them, it seems she has engaged in a meaningless exercise.

In my way of thinking, it's misguided to educate children for years and years, sometimes for a couple of decades, without ever asking them to use their learning in ways that actually make someone better off. The fact that knowledge gives you power to make people better off goes a long way toward increasing the love of learning.

The internal sales pitch on discovery and learning

When working on any of these sixty-two psychological skills, a useful technique is the "internal sales pitch." This is a mental listing of the benefits of getting good at the skill. When you review the benefits of the skill often, you increase your motivation.

What is so good about learning, discovering, and figuring things out anyway?

Often people are taught things without realizing why what they're learning is so good to know, or even realizing why discovery in general is such a great thing. Most children, for example, will never realize that people

have been burned at the stake as witches because they were blamed for causing misfortunes such as floods and epidemics. Such ignorant persecutions ended only when people discovered the true causes of floods and epidemics.

Discovery of how to build and make the incredible variety of tools we use in living means that we don't have to live in huts and shiver through cold winters. Discovery of ways of dealing with mental illness means that we have techniques for helping severely ill people other than locking and chaining them up. It also means that a vast number of less severe psychological problems can be dramatically alleviated, so as to make a great difference in people's lives.

Whenever we receive effective medical care, whenever we communicate with people far away, whenever we use transportation or any device, we are benefiting from discovery and learning. When people are able to cultivate philosophies that help them to live harmoniously with one another rather than in eternal warfare, they are using discovery and learning. In short, discovery and learning elevate human life above an animal existence.

In formulating the internal sales pitch, then, it's useful to think of any pleasurable or useful activity that you can do, and to think of the discoveries and learnings that make it possible.

But another way to formulate the internal sales pitch is more oriented toward oneself. If I have the power to cultivate pleasures in myself, I can gradually make it more and more pleasurable for me to add patterns of knowledge and competence to my brain. And why should I? Because the more things I know how to do well, the more able I am to deal with the world successfully. The more I know how to handle in a competent manner anything that comes up, the more fun life is. It's much more fun dealing with situations you know how to handle well than dealing with situations you can only handle poorly! So it's learning that makes all the difference.

I might also add to my internal sales pitch that knowledge or competence is the most important factor that determines my ability to make an income, to support myself, and to buy food, clothing, and shelter. In our culture, income tends to increase in proportion to education.

Using the nine methods of influence – on yourself

In trying to cultivate the skill of taking pleasure from something, it helps to have the nine methods of influence all lined up so you want to do that thing. We spoke earlier of these nine methods, which you can remember by the mnemonic OH AM PRISM: objective formation, hierarchy of steps, attribution, modeling, practice, reinforcement and punishment, instruction, stimulus control, and monitoring. Let's briefly review how you could use these methods to help yourself enjoy learning.

Objective formation. You can get it clearly in your mind that you would like not only to learn and discover a lot, but also to cultivate great pleasure in this process, to become a connoisseur of learning.

Hierarchy of steps. This means that, whenever you try to learn something, try to arrange the challenges you face in a hierarchy of difficulty. That way, each step will prepare you for the next ones, and, if you do the steps in order, none of them will be very difficult. Finding a good teacher is partly a matter of finding someone who knows what this hierarchy of steps looks like and can help you find the right spot for you, the spot that lies in the challenge zone.

Attribution. Here the word "attribution" refers to what traits and qualities you attribute to yourself, that is, how you think of yourself. Try to avoid attributing things to yourself such as "I hate math" or "I'm no good at writing" or "I can't get interested in psychological skills." It's better to think to yourself, "I haven't yet learned to enjoy this subject. But if I do, that will be great."

Modeling. Try to develop a group of peers who highly value leaning and discovery. When you see other people delighting in learning and sharing their learning with one another, it will be easier for you to take pleasure in learning. This is probably the main reason for spending the money to go to a "good" college: you purchase a group of peers who are selected to value learning. If you can't get enough real-life people around you who love learning, perhaps next best is to expose yourself to symbolic models.

Practice. The more you practice trying to learn and discover as well as trying to enjoy the process, the more likely you are to succeed at it.

Reinforcement and punishment. The more reinforcers you arrange to occur after learning and discovery, the more likely you are to enjoy it. There are several classes of reinforcers. We've already mentioned the intrinsic reinforcers, such as the beauty of mathematical relations, that are best appreciated by trying to tune into them. Similarly invisible are the self-reinforcing sentences you say to yourself, such as "Hooray! I discovered something important!" or "Hooray! I learned something good to know!" There are also social reinforcers, such as being able to talk with peers about something you've learned and to experience the pleasure of interacting about this. Another social reinforcer is experiencing the approval of your teacher or tutor. There are the reinforcers of being able to use the learning to do something useful, i.e. to help someone. There are reinforcers having to do with the game of academics, such as winning math contests.

Instruction. Getting instruction on the art of pleasure from discovery is exemplified by reading this chapter!

Stimulus control. This means arranging the things you see, the things in your reach, so as to foster the goal you're working toward. An environment conducive to love of learning might be one where there are lots of good books around that offer instruction on all sorts of subjects at all levels of complexity, with computer resources and learning-oriented software, mathematical tools, writing instruments, musical instruments, board games such as chess or Scrabble that exercise the mind, and so forth. Another element of the stimulus environment conducive to love of learning is the absence of distractions that grab one's attention away from learning and discovery: violent or high-stimulation television shows playing in the background, loud music playing in the background, loud arguments between people, or violent or high-stimulation video games tempting one away from pursuits requiring more concentrated effort.

Monitoring. That which gets measured gets improved, goes the saying. One possible way of monitoring progress in this skill is keeping a log of the major learnings and discoveries you make and of how much pleasure you were able to take from them. The more rapidly you can accumulate examples, the more progress you're making in this skill.

Skill 10: Pleasure from Others' Kindness, Feeling Gratitude

The twelve types of thoughts are relevant to this skill.

1. Awfulizing
2. Getting down on yourself
3. Blaming someone else
4. Not awfulizing
5. Not getting down on yourself
6. Not blaming someone else
7. Goal-setting
8. Listing options and choosing
9. Learning from the experience
10. Celebrating your own choice
11. Celebrating someone else's choice
12. Celebrating luck

The skill of feeling gratitude is fostered by doing lots of "celebrating someone else's choice." It's fostered by spending time thinking, "I'm glad this person did this nice thing for me"; "I'm lucky this person's labor contributed to my welfare in this way"; "Thank you for doing that." The emotion of gratitude is very closely linked to love. It's a very positive, warm feeling toward another person. Thus, people who are good at this skill tend to be more loving people than people who aren't good at it. They tend to have more positive feelings toward other people.

The opposite of this skill is over-entitlement and taking for granted

What is the opposite of the skill of feeling gratitude? It's the habit of taking for granted what other people have done. For example, two family members have an angry argument. Then, the emotion of anger causes a "cognitive filter" to go into effect. A cognitive filter means that certain types of thoughts pass into your consciousness and other types are filtered out.

Suppose that after the angry disagreement, the family member can see very clearly the times when the other person was lazy and didn't do his work. But somehow "filtered out" of mind are the memories of times when the other person *was* industrious, and *did* do his work. Then the person remembers the times when the other person was critical and hostile. But he forgets the times when the other person was supportive and friendly.

This selective filtration of memories can then produce a "cognitive distortion": an idea such as, "This person is simply a burden on me and never benefits me at all." This process can destroy love between people and destroy relationships.

The antidote to this destructive process is cultivating the skill of remembering the positive acts of the other person and feeling good about them, even when they are mixed in with some undesirable acts. This is often difficult. But cultivation of this skill can make the difference between being a person who loves and a person who is bitter.

One of the enemies of human happiness is our tendency to take good things for granted. Unless you try hard not to do this, you will start to accept any good thing that someone regularly furnishes for you as simply part of your environment and cease to celebrate it.

Suppose two people start living together, and one of them simply starts doing the laundry for both of them, without asking anything in return. At first, the person who gets his laundry done feels grateful. But then, after a while, he takes the task for granted.

Then one day the other person gets so busy that she can't do it. He says to her in an angry voice, "Where are my clean clothes?" What has happened?" He has adjusted his expectations to be in accord with what he has been given. He has gradually begun to feel entitled to the gift that he received, which leads him to feel angry if he doesn't get it, rather than grateful when he does get it.

When I discuss the skill of choosing fair and just options for solutions of two-person problems, I mention the entitlement syndrome. I mention that the antidote to it is rational thinking about what is a reasonable expectation of another person, what is too low an expectation, and what is too much entitlement feeling. All this is another way of saying that it's good to stop and remind yourself not to take for granted the things other people do for you.

The entitlement syndrome is a very serious malady. A person feels no gratitude for the things others do – the thought is, "I was entitled to this, at the very least. In fact, I deserve much better!" Thus rather than feeling grateful and happy, the person feels cheated and indignant most of the time. The thought "Hooray! Someone did something that helped me!" is crowded out by the alternative thought, "Hey! Why isn't that person doing more to help me?"

The person with the entitlement syndrome tends to be reinforced by other people who temporarily buy into the person's ideas of what he deserves and give it to him. But, after a while, people tend to get fed up. They tend to think, "You're a bottomless pit! I can never give enough to satisfy you for very long! I'm getting out of this relationship!"

Most of what we have was furnished by someone else

As I write this, I'm using a computer. Every part of this machine was invented by someone else, assembled by someone else, delivered to me by someone else. The software I'm using, someone else wrote for me. The eyeglasses that let me see the screen better were invented by someone else long ago. Another person figured out what strength of glasses I need, using instruments furnished by lots of other people. Some other people put the glasses together, and others delivered them to where I could pick them up.

Just a minute ago, when I banged my foot against the leg of a chair, it didn't hurt my toe, because of the shoes that someone very long ago invented, that someone more recently designed, that some people put together, and that people delivered to me. And the same thing goes for the chair I'm sitting in, the water fountain that came in handy a while ago, the building that's keeping the rain off me, and on and on.

But the objects are only a part of it. Several people taught me how to read and write and type. Very large numbers of people taught me the ideas that I'm writing, and other people gave *them* ideas. Almost everything I know, other people taught me. Someone (my wife) is taking good care of my children while I'm writing, so that I can do this. And I also have to thank the obstetrician who delivered me, for not damaging my little head on my way out into the world, so I can write today, as well as my parents for thousands of actions that kept me alive and prepared me to do this, and my friends and family members for being supportive enough that I can feel good enough to muster productivity.

I could go on like this for many pages if I let myself. To summarize: if I were to assemble in one place, all the people living or dead who have in some way assisted in what I'm doing right now, I feel sure they could not fit into a very large stadium. Thinking about things in this way tends to make me feel very grateful.

But someone might object as follows. "It's true that people have done things that have served me, but they didn't do it because they wanted to help me out. They were simply trying to make a buck, or make a discovery that would make them famous, or some other selfish reason. I don't feel grateful to the surgeon who saved my life – she just did it because she was trying to make money, and she enjoyed doing it. The public health specialist who discovered a vaccine that kept me from being killed in an epidemic was just trying to win the Nobel Prize. The mother who took care of me and fed and clothed me and consumed herself with my welfare for many years simply did this because her maternal instincts made her feel good about doing it."

If you accept the notion that there's no reason to feel grateful for anything if the person who gave it to you received a payoff for doing so, you very seldom feel grateful. Expecting that people should do things for you out of completely unselfish motives is a recipe for unhappiness and disappointment.

A good way to be happier is to rejoice at anything someone else has done that has helped you, whether the person's motive was selfish or not. (You can rejoice even more when someone acts unselfishly in your behalf.) If the person had a selfish motive that somehow ended up being harnessed in the helping of you, you can rejoice that the world happened to be rigged up so that this would happen. Perhaps this is more "celebrating what happened to happen" than "celebrating the other person's choice," but it still is cause for rejoicing.

Gratitude and positive reinforcement

The skill of feeling gratitude is the foundation for the skill of helping to influence someone positively by giving approval. Parents are often advised to give positive reinforcement when they see their children do something good. But if you simply mouth the words, "I liked it when you did that," without first taking pleasure and feeling pleasure and gratitude about what the child did, then the reinforcement usually isn't very reinforcing.

For this reason, if you're a parent it's useful to tune up the parts of your personality that actually feel pleasure and gratitude over the good things that the child does. When you feel that gratitude, the positive reinforcement will be much easier to deliver in a sincere way, and you'll be able to help your child do good things more frequently.

(If you're a child, the same thing goes in feeling gratitude toward and giving approval to your parent! Part of your job as a child is to help your parent behave well! And the same goes for your brothers or sisters or friends!)

The skill of feeling gratitude for what others have done is the same skill that people use when they master the art of finding the good parts of other people. People all have many sides to their personalities. Try to find the noblest and best, and the most enjoyable portions of other people. If you can focus on those best parts, you can at least enjoy people more. You may even wind up bringing out positive patterns in some people so much that other people benefit, as well. Finding, noticing, recognizing, and appreciating the best aspects of other people is a true gift. Like all other psychological skills, it can be cultivated by working at it, by practicing it, by monitoring how you do at it, and so forth.

In many families, people participate in a regular ritual of thanksgiving at meal times. I think it's also useful for families to include a regular ritual of thanksgiving to one another. I have advocated that parents do this for children in a ritual called "the nightly review." In this ritual, parents recount to the child stories of the positive examples of any psychological skills the child has done that day. As the child gets older, the nightly review can be converted into a more egalitarian ritual, where all members of the family recall and recount the positive actions of the others. They can also include positive actions they themselves have carried out.

Skill 11: Pleasure from Blessings

The skill of pleasure from blessings is the result of frequent practice of "celebrating luck." In addition to celebrating our own accomplishments and celebrating what other people do for us, we will maximize our happiness if we also remember to celebrate things that happen by luck.

In the section on feeling gratitude, I mentioned that people tend to reset their happiness thermostat so that they take things for granted and forget to feel good about them. The antidote to this is consciously to remind oneself to celebrate blessings. In addition, it helps to cultivate the frequent thought that "the way things are isn't the only way that they could be," especially when this thought brings on wonder, awe and gratefulness about the way things are.

Have you given thanks lately for the ratios of forces between the elementary particles of the universe? If you haven't, I seriously recommend it! Physicists have classified a large number of elementary particles that make up our universe. They've also discovered four basic forces that act on them: gravity, (what makes apples fall off trees), electromagnetic attraction and repulsion (what makes sodium and chloride stick to each other in a salt crystal, what makes a compass needle point north), and two nuclear forces (one of which can get protons to stick together inside the nucleus of an atom, even though their positive charges ought to repel each other).

Without even getting into complicated physics, it's easy to imagine sets of elementary particles and forces between them that would make it impossible for life or even simple chemical reactions to exist. For example, suppose there were only one type of particle, each of these particles repelled all others, and there were no such thing as a force of attraction. Then the universe would consist of particles acting very much like atoms of an inert gas like helium – spreading out as far as they can get from one another, not reacting with one another, not making any other chemicals, not supporting life, not doing much of anything very interesting.

Or how about universe number 2: there are several particles that all attract each other, and no force of repulsion. Then the particles gradually all come together in one very compact ball, and there they sit. Again, this is not a very interesting universe.

Or here's an even simpler scenario, universe number 3: there are no elementary particles. There is no matter or energy at all. There's a universe made of empty space that just sits there for eternity.

There's something about the universe that doesn't like such a boring set up. So it's possible for chemical reactions to take place. Not only that:

you can have a certain sort of chemical reaction that tries to keep itself going on purpose and even tries to reproduce itself! (It's life!)

As if that weren't enough, these little units of chemical reactions can actually see, hear, taste, smell, and touch the other things going on around them and can actually look at and think about themselves doing that! (That's consciousness!)

To top it all off, they can care about the other little units that are around them, and want to do kind things for those other little chemical units. (That's love!)

If I weren't one of those units, I wouldn't have bet a nickel on such a thing being possible!

Looking at things this way makes the fact that human beings really can live happily among one another even more amazing and beautiful. It also makes it seem an even greater tragedy when people can't take advantage of the incredibly rare opportunity we've been given, and when the chance to be alive is wasted in unhappiness and hostility.

The mental maneuver of imagining what other forms of the universe there could be, and contrasting these with the form we are lucky enough to be alive in, can be a prototype for taking pleasure from blessings. Whatever is good about life does not necessarily have to be that way. If you imagine how life would be without that blessing and contrast that with how things are, you can take more pleasure from your blessings.

You can do the same form of maneuver with elements of existence other than the universe itself. It's very possible to imagine human beings with no capacity for appreciation of music of any sort. Why do our brains have the property that sensing sound patterns of certain types causes us such pleasure?

What about the phenomenon of humor? It would be very easy to imagine a world or society where people acted like little computers and there was no such thing as laughter or humor. But we are given the gift of having this source of pleasure in our lives. Exactly the same thing can be said about friendship, love, sexuality, appreciation of nature, and religious and philosophical experiences.

We can even say the same thing about the phenomenon of locomotion. We could have evolved from trees! We could be stuck in one place, able to sense the fact that we are present, but not to move around.

Perhaps one of the benefits of reading and writing science fiction is that we gain the capacity to imagine that life could be greatly different than it is. When we take that altered perspective, we can more fully appreciate life as it is.

But it's not necessary to turn to science fiction if you seek alternate images of life. News reports of people undergoing tragedy and terrorizing one another abound every day. While it's never desirable to take pleasure in other people's misfortunes, learning about the types of misfortunes that can befall other people can help you to appreciate your own blessings.

Is it possible to have an accident that severs my spinal chord and paralyzes me from the neck down? I can be thankful this hasn't happened to me. Are there countries beset by war and poverty and famine? I want to celebrate that this is not my fate. Are there earthquakes and floods and hurricanes? I give thanks that I have escaped these.

Are there atrocities that human beings have committed toward one another? Among the grief, repulsion and sorrow I may feel, and the obligation to work toward a nonviolent world, I also want to reserve some room to give thanks that the hostility I have experienced in my life pales by comparison.

Taking time occasionally to make a mental catalog of the misfortunes one has been spared of, simply by fate, is a very worthwhile exercise.

Skill 12: Pleasure from Affection

The skill of pleasure from affection means being able to enjoy touching, stroking, patting, and hugging, and to enjoy sexuality when appropriate.

A very common reason why husbands and wives fail to enjoy affection with each other is that they are angry at each other. Some unresolved conflict causes one or both of them not to be in the mood for affection. If this goes on for very long, it can start a vicious cycle, in which one or both of them also becomes angry about the lack of affection, and the angry climate in turn makes affection even less likely.

In discussing psychological skills we constantly see how interdependent they are – how much they affect each other. The skill of pleasure from affection is highly dependent on the skill of interpersonal problem-solving and joint decision-making. Great amounts of practice and learning in such conflict-resolution skills, together with overcoming any resistance to applying those skills to sexual issues, will go a long way toward overcoming such vicious cycles.

Sometimes adults have great difficulty with the skill of taking pleasure from physical affection even when the relationship with a spouse is otherwise in good shape. Usually when this is the case, some type of fear stands in the way. Thus improving this skill is very much related to the fear-reduction

strategies I speak of in the chapter on courage skills. Psychotherapists help people get over fears of sexuality or affection by using the same principles used in overcoming fears of heights, fears of public speaking, and so forth.

For children, the skill of pleasure from affection has its counterpart in the ability to enjoy being touched, hugged, kissed, or held by someone who is trusted and loved. Deficiencies in this skill in children often don't come to much attention until later, unless they are combined with other skill deficiencies.

What are some fears that can block the pleasure from affection? Sometimes a fear about nonsexual touching is that it will progress into an undesired sexual situation. People who have been subjected to unwanted sexual touching or overtures can easily develop such fears. Another obstacle to pleasure from affection is the experience of coercion. Having to submit to someone else's affection, even of a nonsexual nature, without choice, may produce a conditioned aversion.

Such aversion may also result if physical touching has been paired with some other unpleasant experience. For example, if you're a child who has been picked up several times by someone who has then dropped you, you probably don't like being picked up! The skill of trusting is closely bound up with the skill of pleasure from affection. Many of the experiences that breed difficulty in pleasure from affection also breed difficulty in trusting.

Being directly taught that affection or sexuality is wrong, disgusting, sinful, etc. can also be responsible for aversions people have. Where would the idea come from that sex is bad or disgusting? Messages about sexuality in our society are very mixed, for reasons that are fairly obvious. On the positive side: pleasant sexual relations between husband and wife are conducive to happy marriages, and happy marriages are good for children and for society in all sorts of ways. Pleasant sexuality between a husband and wife tends to bring out feelings of love and caring.

Conversely, marital discord that is fostered by unhappy sexual relations can provoke all sorts of other problems. Another not-so-minor advantage of sexuality is that the survival of the human race depends upon it. It's for a good reason that centuries of evolution have made sexuality feel so pleasant, and have made the drive for it strong. It's a source of great pleasure that most people decide not to miss out on.

On the other hand, you have to be very picky about when to act on sexual urges. Sexuality with the wrong person can make you wind up in jail (e.g. for statutory rape), with a deadly disease (e.g. AIDS), with a nondeadly but incurable disease (e.g. herpes genitalis), with a divorce (resulting from an extramarital affair), with a destroyed reputation, or with an unwanted pregnancy. So it's necessary to inhibit sexual urges except in carefully chosen conditions.

Therefore with sexuality, as with all other biological urges, people must undergo a good deal of learning not to always do what comes naturally. It should come as no surprise then that sometimes the learning of inhibition spreads too far, and once one gets into a relationship where it's desirable and good to have a sexual relationship, e.g. marriage, the inhibition persists.

Once someone experiences inhibition of sexual desire or performance, then another factor can start coming into play: fear of failure or performance anxiety. A vicious cycle can begin, as follows. Someone worries about whether his performance will be good enough and starts worrying and concentrating on observing himself. This sort of thought pattern is not conducive to enjoyment of affection, so the performance anxiety inhibits performance, which increases fear of failure, in a vicious cycle.

Therapists have lifted people out of this vicious cycle by helping them redefine what success and failure really mean in the area of sexual affection. If both members of a couple cultivate the belief that any pleasant exchange of physical affection is a "success," rather than thinking, "It's a success only if it happens in this particular way," performance anxiety drops.

No matter how much each member of a couple can enjoy affection, a certain choice point for joint decision-making is sure to come up sooner or later. The solution to this problem can be central to the harmony of the couple. The problem is: one member of a couple desires sexual activity at a given moment, and the partner does not. What are the options? What is reasonable for people to expect of one another? Which option will make things best in the long run? Obviously if people can solve this problem in a way that doesn't leave them angry at each other, their chances of happiness are greatly increased.

Sometimes the fear of unattractiveness significantly impairs rational solution of this problem. Specifically: partner A for some reason lacks sexual desire or sexual performance when partner B desires it. Partner B takes this as an affront to his or her masculinity or femininity or attractiveness. This can produce a lot of negative emotion.

Now A starts to realize that a lot is at stake in sexual performance: not only having a good time, but also B's self-esteem! This can increase A's performance anxiety. If B feels insulted and expresses anger at A, and A says angry words back, the conditions are ripe for many vicious cycles that result in conditioned aversion to sexuality.

Since the world of post-pubescent people is largely made up of people who wish not only to experience sexual pleasure but also to see themselves as attractive, such vicious cycles are extremely prevalent. This creates a seemingly improbable situation: two people who are biologically capable of pleasant sexuality, who initially chose to be in a sexual relationship with each other, now avoid sex altogether or almost altogether because the attempt to solve the interpersonal decisions involved brings too much anger or shame.

One theme of this book is that rationality is key to psychological health. Rationality is defined as choosing what to do based on your best information and best calculations of what will make things turn out best. It's the application of logical thought to life management.

Often the area of sexuality is one where rationality seems particularly difficult. This is especially true with respect to the sexuality of adolescents. Some of the fiercest conflicts between parents and teenagers revolve around the issue of sexuality, when parents attempt to deny that their offspring have become beings with sexual wishes.

Sexual urges arise with great strength for many adolescents. For the average male, and for at least some females, sexual desire is never greater than it is during adolescence. A rational society would spend a good bit of energy coming up with good solutions to the question: what are adolescents to do with those urges? How can there be reasonable and nonharmful ways for young people to ready themselves for married relationships with long-term sexual satisfaction? This book will not attempt to answer this question, but the question should be grappled with rationally, and with dialogue between adolescents and their parents and other adults. It's not appropriate for young people to get all their lessons in what sexuality is supposed to be from popular music and movies.

The option of attempting to inhibit all sexual thought and activity through the exercise of self-discipline poses dangers of the "forbidden fruit syndrome," as discussed in the next chapter. Performing some psychological maneuver meant to turn off sexual urges (such as attaching great fear and disgust to the arena of sexuality) poses the danger that the maneuver may not be readily reversible when later it becomes appropriate to enjoy sexuality. In addition, this maneuver is often a recipe for a great deal of internal conflict that can be painful and harmful.

Imagining appropriate and loving sexual experiences and masturbating to these images, in privacy, is an option that should be rather uncontroversial as one possible answer to the question of what to do with sexual urges when sexual activity with a partner is not desired or appropriate. Adolescents should get the message that masturbation is normal and not harmful, physically or psychologically – and if the sexual fantasies that accompany it involve loving, caring, and committed relationships, the "fantasy rehearsal" can have positive effects.

The most rational solutions to problems of sexuality obviously take into account the welfare of both of the participants. For this reason it's good to be aware of some differences in the sexual psychology of males and females. On the average, females tend to have their feelings of affection more conditioned upon the quality of the relationship. By contrast, the biological makeup of males predisposes them to focus less on relationships and more on the relatively more simple elements of physical attractiveness and physical pleasure.

Females often find themselves having sexual experiences that lie outside the positive relationship that would make them most happy. Sometimes adolescent females in particular can delude themselves into thinking they're permanently loved and cared for by a sexual partner. They can delude themselves into imagining that their partner has all the positive qualities they would like in a permanent relationship. Then they may find their emotions shattered when their vision of the relationship turns out to have been an illusion.

At other times, females are pressured or persuaded to engage in sexual encounters that are obviously not within a caring relationship. Often a large challenge for an adolescent female is to resist social pressure toward exploitative casual encounters. A challenge for males is to cultivate the attention to quality of relationships that seems to come more naturally to females.

The skill of pleasure from affection, like so many other psychological skills, is best nurtured when people are

genuinely interested in each other's
welfare, and when they think rationally
about that welfare, and enact what they
rationally decide – in other words, when
the skills of kindness, good decisions,
and self-discipline abound.

Skill 13: Favorable Attractions

What do you find attractive in another person? The answer to this question can be crucial to the quality of life, and even, in some cases, to the continuation of life itself.

The skill of favorable attractions means the answers to the questions "Whom do you want to be in a relationship with" and "Whom do you feel attracted to?" are helpful to you. Do you want friendships with people who treat you kindly and considerately and who are trustworthy and dependable? Do you want relationships with people who are interested in doing the same sorts of things you are and talking about the same sorts of things you're interested in so that you have a realistic prediction that you and this other person can have lots of fun times together? Do you want someone who is good at the psychological skills described in this book, a person able to handle well the situations the relationship encounters?

Or, are there more convoluted motivations for getting into relationships that are much less likely to lead to long-term happiness? What are some of these other motivations?

Sometimes people seek someone who will dominate and control them. Sometimes perhaps this is a way of seeking a parent they never had, or sometimes it may represent a compulsion to repeat an experience with a very domineering parent they did have.

Likewise, some people are looking for someone to dominate and control. One problem with this form of attraction is that it runs up against a fairly universal human wish for freedom that tends to emerge sooner or later. Sometimes when people get into relationships based on highly unequal power, the less powerful person gradually develops the skill of independent thinking. The person then ceases to wish to be controlled so much. Unless the other person can simultaneously change, the relationship is in trouble. This problem formed the plot of Henrik Ibsen's play, *A Doll's House*.

Another problem with such relationships is that the more dominating person begins to find it's a lot of burdensome work to be in charge of another adult's life as well as his or her own. The dominating person sometimes starts to resent the other's dependence. Sometimes this happens to people who start out looking for someone to take care of and nurture. For example, a woman with a strong need to "mother" people gets into relationships with men who are "losers" out of a desire to mother these men. She would do better to get into a relationship with a "winner" and spend her time mothering children instead of mothering an adult.

Another basis for attraction that often fails to work out in the long run is the wish to gain admiration from an imaginary or real audience. For example, a beautiful girl who is very interested in intellectual matters and prevention of violence and drug abuse is asked out by a boy who is aggressive, anti-intellectual, into the bar scene, and captain of the football team. These two stick together for a while because she enjoys the prestige from her friends in dating the captain of the football team and he enjoys prestige from his friends for dating someone so good-looking.

If the two of them don't realize soon enough that their attraction is not based on something more substantive than the approval of peers who will be scattering to the winds, they are likely to find themselves in a very unhappy marriage.

The motivation for approval from an imaginary or real audience is allied to the motive of overvaluing physical attractiveness. The valuing of physical attractiveness when choosing a mate is probably to some extent hard-wired into the human brain. Some argue that sensitivity to physical attractiveness is something that evolved in the human species because it tends to draw us toward mates who are healthy and who have reproductive potential, and thus natural selection favored those who were attracted to mates who look "attractive."

But the motive for attractiveness in a mate can go far beyond this. Some people choose mates who are stunningly attractive but totally spoiled or otherwise unsuited to be in a relationship.

People choose such a mate, not because they need someone so attractive for themselves, but because they want their mates to be a visual advertisement for their own desirability. They are motivated by what others will think about the attractiveness of their mate. But the admiration of strangers can't begin to compensate for unpleasant hours spent in a relationship where people don't really enjoy each another.

Another unhealthy motivation influencing attractions is the syndrome in which "you only want the ones that you can't get." Suppose someone is not confident of his or her own desirability. The person believes, "No one who is very attractive to other people would choose me." The corollary, then, is that anyone who would choose me is not worth having. If she is so hard up that she would pick me, she must be a loser.

This belief system leads to no satisfaction with a relationship, but an endless need to go from one relationship to the next. The grass is greener on the other side of the fence, and you have to keep crossing from one field to another forever.

For the person with this syndrome, it's futile to keep on looking. The only thing that will help is cultivating the opposite idea: "I am worthy of being in a relationship. The people who choose me are the ones I'm likely to be the happiest with, because they enjoy things about me."

The opposite side of the same coin is the syndrome of "I'll take whatever I can get." Again, this exists in a person who views herself as undesirable. Then if someone comes along who seems to find her attractive, she is swept away, in love with the notion of being found attractive, not necessarily with the other person. She temporarily blinds herself to the reality that he is not a good person for her.

A similar unfavorable motivation for relationships is overly great fear of separation or abandonment. Someone who is desperately afraid of being left might choose someone who is a "loser" or someone who also appears desperately afraid of abandonment, thinking, "This person is so afraid of being alone or so incompetent at making it alone that the person will never leave me."

But it's always unstable when a relationship is held together by the skill deficiencies of the two people. What happens when one of them gains in skills of independent thinking and handling separation? This might provoke a great deal of anxiety in the other person. This person might find ways of sabotaging his mate's movements toward personal growth, strength, and confidence. "I'll kill myself if you leave me" is but one of the unpleasant binds one can be placed in when one is moving toward psychological strength in a relationship held together by fear of abandonment.

Now let's talk about two other motives for unfavorable attractions, particularly unfavorable sexual attractions. These two motives cause a great many problems for human beings. One is the drive toward novelty, and the other the attraction of the "forbidden fruit."

I read recently of a very attractive young actor, involved with an extremely attractive girlfriend, who was arrested for employing a prostitute. Over the years I've read several times about powerful political figures who, despite being married to beautiful wives, have destroyed their careers by having sexual relations with other women. If the lure of novelty and the lure of forbidden fruit are at least partial motivators for these acts, the powerful and famous are certainly not alone in dealing with the problems caused by these unfavorable attractions.

The lure of novelty refers to the condition in which someone in a more or less stable sexual relationship finds the attractiveness of any sexual partner other than his mate enhanced, simply because that person has the virtue of being someone new. Some researchers have demonstrated that this effect seems to take place in certain animals that, for example, can engage in sexual activity to the point of fatigue and inactivity with one sexual partner, but then actively resume it when put with a novel sexual partner. Some theorists have postulated that males who have been hardwired to the lure of novelty transmit their genetic material in greater abundance, and thus the lure of novelty is selected for.

On the other hand, certain animal species that have endured selection pressures for the same number of centuries as all others mate for life with one partner. And certain theorists argue that the protection and nurturing of children by both parents places children at enough of a survival advantage that monogamy is most advantageous.

At any rate, at this point in history no one has found a way of using gene therapy to decrease the attraction of novelty and increase the attraction of stability in sexual relations, so the major tool at the disposal of human beings is the power of the cerebral cortex, the thinking part of the brain, to influence the rest of the brain. It's probably true that if someone deeply desires not to be so attracted to novelty and to be happier with stability, one can influence one's own attractions.

The lure of the "forbidden fruit" is something that can be particularly difficult to deal with. This motive dictates that a person is particularly attractive as a sexual partner especially because there are good reasons *not* to be in a sexual relationship with that person. Instead of "You only want the ones that you can't get," this motive dictates, "You only want the ones you *shouldn't* get." This motive is inimical to marriage in two ways: it decreases the attractiveness of the spouse who is not forbidden, and it increases the attractiveness of everyone else.

How could such an ill-serving motive get started? Let's try to understand some possibilities.

One possibility has to do with association learning in adolescence and a not very successful answer to the difficult question I posed earlier: what are adolescents supposed to do with their sexual urges?

Suppose an adolescent tries to resist all sexual urges and to define all of sexuality as forbidden. Suppose the urges now reach the level at which he fails to resist them, and he engages in sexual activity of some sort, whether masturbation alone, sexual touching with someone else, or sexual intercourse. Then he repents of this weakness and again tries to avoid all sexual activity. Once again, the biologic drive gets the better of him, and he yields to it. This cycle repeats itself many times.

What is happening each time this takes place? The person has periodic experiences of great pleasure, each of which immediately follows a decision to engage in forbidden activity. The laws of learning would predict that not only sex, but also engaging in a forbidden activity, are being reinforced.

Doing the forbidden will gradually take on secondary reinforcing characteristics. The phenomenon of secondary reinforcement is the same sort of thing that happens if you click a clicker just before you give an animal a piece of food. Soon the click itself acts as a reward. If the conditioned association between doing something forbidden and sexual pleasure becomes strong enough, forbidden sex may continue to be associated with greater pleasure than permitted sex is, once some sexual activity is permitted.

Here's another reason for the attraction of forbidden sex: the reduction or elimination of performance anxiety. One of the inhibitors of sexual enjoyment can be fear of failure: "What if my sexual performance isn't good enough?" Sex therapists sometimes find, for this reason, that prohibiting sexual intercourse paradoxically leads to it. If it's a thoroughly bad enough idea to have sex with a certain person, then one has a good reason not to want to perform sexually and less reason to fear not performing. The mind is saying, "I really shouldn't do this," rather than "Uh oh. What if I don't do this well?"

Here's another reason for the attraction of the forbidden fruit: the relation between deprivation and strength of reinforcement. To use an analogy, people who diet to the point of extreme hunger and who then break down and eat chocolate mint cookies have had an experience of extreme pleasure associated with the cookies. Their brains remember this, particularly if it happens repeatedly. The cookies become much more reinforcing than if the person were not dieting.

Similarly, if the forbidden sexual relationship is avoided as much as possible but only engaged in when the desire for it's at its height, it becomes more reinforcing than sexuality that may be enjoyed ad lib.

These reasons for the lure of "forbidden fruit," incidentally, may also operate with chemical addictions and other addictions, as well as the addiction to forbidden sexuality.

Being conditioned to respond sexually only in response to situations where it's not a good idea to be sexual, i.e., the forbidden fruit syndrome, is an example of a very unfavorable attraction. It's probably the most common unfavorable attraction.

But there are attraction patterns that are even more unfavorable. The worst thing for sexual arousal to be associated with is hostility or harm or violence, either to another or to oneself: sadism or masochism.

Sadism and masochism are sometimes the products of early sexual conditioning, when someone is sexually exploited during childhood. The pairing of sexual and violent stimuli in movies may also raise the incidence of sadistic or masochistic sexual learning.

Suppose that an adolescent male's first exposure to a very sexually arousing experience comes from a depiction of sexuality in a movie scene that is also very violent. The sexuality is an unconditioned stimulus for sexual arousal; the violent images are not, at that time, particularly associated with sexual arousal.

But suppose the adolescent gets this image firmly fixed in his mind and then for a long time afterward calls up this image for sexual fantasies. Then each time those fantasies are paired with sexual arousal, the conditioned association between the violent images and sexual arousal is strengthened. If the association becomes strong enough that he deliberately seeks out other similar stimuli, then a very dangerous association has been learned.

My conclusion from this sort of reasoning and from the forbidden fruit syndrome is that a good bit of attention should be paid to what sorts of images and situations become attached to sexual feelings, from the earliest dawnings of sexuality. From the first, sexual arousal should be paired with desirable features that one hopes will stay associated with sexual arousal throughout life. Or in other words, when one starts practicing sexual association learning, he or she should practice it in the right way.

Now, what is the right way? We've talked so far mainly about what constitutes unfavorable sexual association learning. What do you wish to be the stimuli that lead you to feel sexual arousal?

One might say, it's better to have sexual arousal conditioned to feelings of warmth, love and respect for the other person and good wishes for the other person's welfare than it is to have sexual arousal conditioned to hostility. But most of the people in the world for whom you will feel warmth and love and respect, will not be appropriate sexual partners, even if you restrict those people to adults. You can feel a great deal of respectful and kind feelings toward other people's spouses or your own blood relatives, for example, even though you aren't sexually aroused by these people.

So what is the crucial element that separates favorable attractions from unfavorable ones? It's the opposite of the forbidden fruit syndrome. It's good to associate with sexual arousal the thought "It would be a very good idea, good for myself, good for the other person, good for society, to enter into sexual activity with this person in this way right now."

In other words, in this state of favorable attractions, sexual arousal is subject to a go-ahead message, a message from the higher centers of the brain. Sexual arousal is ideally decreased by forbidden fruit status and increased by "permissible fruit" status.

If everyone could be blessed with such sexual associations, the world would be vastly improved. Our understanding of how to bring about such a state is in its infancy. But the first step is focusing on its desirability and thinking about it openly and rationally.

Skill 14: Gleefulness

Gleefulness is the skill of enjoying being playful, silly, and childlike. It's the art of having fun.

In our culture, children themselves are often given the message that being playful, gleeful, and silly is something that they should put behind them once they reach a certain age. They probably receive this message more frequently from other children than from adults. In any given peer group there are certain rules as to what is too childish to do at a certain age and what is permissible.

For example, many eight or nine-year-old boys consider it too childish to do dramatic play with toy farm animals, toy people, and so forth, even though this is a highly creative and imaginative activity that can fully tap into the highest intelligence. By contrast, this same age group often considers it not too childish to play a video game involving very simple hand/eye coordination tasks enacting people fighting. The notion that violence is grown-up and improvisational drama with toy people is for babies is very sad to see.

In my observation of children's culture, it also appears that children often strongly discourage one another from singing and dancing. Sometimes children become sophisticated enough to feel the power of making someone else self-conscious about singing or dancing. Yet they aren't sophisticated enough to realize that the criticism or derision they use to get this power kills a lot of fun. This too is a shame whenever it happens, because singing and dancing are elements of the skill of gleefulness that ideally should be available in abundance to all people.

As a culture we're ambivalent about the skill of gleefulness. To call an idea "silly" or to call someone "silly" is often very insulting. On the other hand, if you ask people to recall the most pleasurable and enjoyable moments of their lives, those moments often involved acting slaphappy or silly.

Inhibitions about gleefulness are often reduced by alcohol, and for many people this provides a major motivation to use alcohol. In many social situations, alcohol is a cue that gleefulness and playfulness are permissible. Sometimes, when a person is drinking alcohol, gleefulness and playfulness become more socially acceptable because it's seen as an excuse for the person's silliness. In addition, the physiological effect of alcohol can sedate some of the fears that would prevent gleefulness.

Unfortunately, many people who know how to be gleeful under the influence of alcohol don't know how to be gleeful without it. These people are thus dependent on alcohol in a way that is probably more difficult to break than an actual physiological dependence.

With both gleefulness and humor, it's important to be on guard against taking gleeful pleasure in other people's misfortunes or in frustrating or upsetting another person.

There is a fine line to be walked. On the one hand, it's great to be able to be gleeful and to use humor to transform your own misfortunes. When you slip on a banana peel in front of other people, it's great to be able to laugh rather than feel devastated. But when someone else slips and falls and does not laugh, and you do, you're being cruel. Developing too great a habit of enjoying others' misfortunes can result in sadism.

Many adults lose the ability to play with children. Playing is a complex art. It's complicated to explain in digital fashion to someone who isn't able to draw on memories of their own childhood or their own experiences with other children. When there are toy people to play with, many adults will start drilling the child on what color they are or how many there are. But it's much more fun and, in important ways, more educational to pick up a character and speak from the persona of that character to another character.

The skill of gleefulness and playfulness is related to what Eric Berne called the "natural child." The natural child is the collection of memories about how to be gleeful and playful. For people who feel they have lost the ability to be gleeful and would like to recover it, I would recommend watching someone interact gleefully with a pre-school age child and watching what the pre-school age child does in response. Then I would recommend imitating the best behaviors of both of them!

It can be therapeutic for an adult to get together with pre-school aged children and try to generate as much mutual fun as possible. What makes the child laugh? What makes the child smile? What makes the child want to have you do whatever you just did over and over again?

Is it hiding and seeking, chasing, doing acrobatics, putting on plays, pretending to be different animals, pretending play plots? Is it drawing or singing or dancing around?

The experiences that delight the young child are the experiences that later in life evolve into "serious" arts. Sculpture, painting, drama, music, and dance are great fun for young children to do.

Young children also have fun by exploring things, finding out how to take things apart and (less frequently) how to put them back together. They enjoy finding out what things do. They like to figure out the causal relationship between doing something and making something else happen. This is the playful child's predecessor of the engineer or the scientist. Retaining this playful component probably allows the adult scientist to have more fun and be more creative in doing science.

The person who wants to improve the skill of playfulness would also do well to spend some time playing competitive games or games with rules with grade-school age children. Some of them are masters of the skills that it takes to truly enjoy such games.

One of those is the ability to suspend disbelief and to ignore the arbitrary nature of the game. You have to do some pretending, for example, to get into the frame of mind to think it really makes a difference who has checkers left on the board at the end of a game. It's good, but only because you've agreed to pretend it's good. If you agreed it was best to be the first one to lose all your checkers, then it would be good to lose all your checkers first.

Some would say this act of purposefully injecting meaning into activity is a microcosm for what people do with life itself. If you define the goal of the game as making the world a better place and being happy doing it, you can play that game; if you define the goal as dying with the most consumer goods, you can play that too.

Other skills that enable competitive games to be approached with a great deal of playfulness and lightheartedness include the ability to take great pleasure from winning, but not a great deal of displeasure from losing.

A more complicated approach is to take displeasure from losing on a certain level, but on another level to take even greater pleasure in the drama of the "agony of defeat." To explain this mentality a little more: in our pretend world, it really makes a big difference who gets the most balls into the goal. If we lose, it's almost a symbolic dying. But in reality, it makes little difference where the balls end up. And part of the fun is in occasionally being able to experience the drama of dying, without any of the negative side effects (such as not getting to live any longer, your relatives' having to execute a will, and so forth).

Sports contests are drama, requiring imagination just as operas do. If you don't even pretend to care who wins or loses, there's no fun, just as if in the opera you don't pretend to care whether the pretend heroine dies or lives happily with her lover.

What are other elements of the skill of playfulness and gleefulness? Let's list some. One is showing off – doing something entertaining or interesting for other people and letting them watch. The two-year-old who dances around to entertain the adults in the living room, and the adult who dances on stage share this element. Part of the excitement is the risk: will they like it or not?

Another element is creativity: doing something unexpected, surprising, coming up with something off the beaten path to say or do. Another is imagination – pretending whatever is necessary to make the activity most fun. A fourth is emotionality – you don't do gleefulness from a stance of cold analytical thought.

And a final element is the social nature of gleefulness. It's possible to be gleeful by yourself, but it's much easier to enjoy the way people bounce gleefulness back and forth to one another, reinforcing one another for their lightheartedness.

How do you increase your gleefulness and playfulness skills? Sometimes the answer to this question follows the same paradigm as the familiar one we discuss in the chapter on courage skills: exposure that is prolonged enough to allow fear reduction.

What is the exposure to, and what fear is reduced? Exposure in this case is simply acting gleeful, playful, slaphappy, silly, or lighthearted. The fear to be reduced is the fear of being derided or ridiculed by others for such behavior.

If one is going to follow this paradigm, it's important to do two things: 1) pick people to be around who will not in fact deride or ridicule good gleefulness, but who will reinforce it; 2) pick ways of being gleeful that are not offensive or destructive.

As with all psychological skills, if you can find people to be around who can be good models of this skill, take opportunities to be around them and watch them. If you didn't have a lot of practice in good gleefulness as a child, it's never too late to start. Some people have vastly improved their lives by fostering the growth of their own "natural child" ego states, by consciously growing their abilities to be playful.

A lot of light can be shed upon the skill of gleefulness by the answer to the question, "In your family (or in your social network), what do people do for fun with one another?" Can you come up with answers to this question other than vacations and entertainment that others are paid to provide for you?

Or can you have lots of fun by making your own comedy with one another, singing with one another, dancing around in one another's presence, making up your own dramas with one another, recounting your own stories to one another? Can you be gleeful even while doing mundane tasks together such as cleaning up the kitchen? Can you simply go on a walk together and come up with all sorts of ways to make that fun?

Many activities are pleasurable in the short run but produce bad long-term effects: smoking, drinking, drug use, the wrong type of sexual activity, bingeing on junk food, entertainment violence, etc. A parent or teacher who seeks to teach young people to avoid these indulgences runs the risk of being seen as a joyless person who is missing out on all the fun in life. If that person wants to be a good teacher, he or she must show young people that it's possible to get great pleasure from life in non-harmful ways. He or she must demonstrate joy in living and in taking pleasure from the amazing things life has to offer.

I conclude this chapter with a "Menu of Mutually Gratifying Activities" that people have found useful to look at when seeking to increase their fun with one another. It's good to cultivate the ability to feel pleasure from these activities and others like them. I don't include watching television and other paid entertainment partly because these have their own advertising budgets already and partly because I want people to regain some of their capacity to entertain themselves successfully.

Menu for "mutually gratifying activities"

Social conversation, reading silently in one another's presence; reading aloud to one another, making up stories together; audiotaping stories; listening to audio-taped stories; putting on plays with one another; improvising plays with one another, discussing current events, telling jokes, listening to or trying to solve one another's problems, singing songs together, playing music together, dancing, acting, talking while taking walks together

Recording music, plays, comedy, or dances you have created

Exploring objects: With young children: Big things such as playground equipment, big rocks, hills, and trees etc., little things such as stopwatches, tape recorders, clocks, scales, boxes, pots and pans, toys. For older people, working on building or fixing gadgets together, engineering projects, carpentry projects.

Doing work together: cleaning and organizing, cooking, yard work, shopping, fixing things, paperwork, gardening – and socializing while doing so.

Academic activities: Doing homework together, reading nonfiction books to one another, doing tutoring activities or games, teaching one another, composing writings together; solving brain-teasers together

Playing Games: Games for infants and toddlers (repetitive sequences with suspense and celebration, e.g., peek-a-boo), board games, including psychological growth board games, card games, cooperative games, e.g., the shaping game, two-person solitaires, puzzles, thinking games such as quarto, password, twenty questions, Scrabble, Boggle, Mastermind, chess, checkers, charades.

Computer activities: Edutainment games, using other programs, programming, communicating by computer

Athletic Activities: throwing balls or Frisbees back and forth, trying to make the target (basketball, darts, archery, horseshoes), traveling sports: skating, skiing, cycling, swimming, track, traditional sports contests

Outdoor Life: hiking, camping, canoeing, observing the natural world: stars, animals, plants

Pets: Taking care of them, playing with them, training them

Arts and Crafts: drawing, painting, making stuff that's useful, fun, or pretty

Religious or philosophical activities

Hosting and attending social events: planning and putting on parties, getting together with friends for meals, hosting and attending social gatherings

Psychological Skill Exercises: doing the shaping game, the reflections exercise, joint-decision role-plays, the decisions game, the sentence completion exercise, the twelve-thought exercise, the cele-brations exercise, etc., together (see the volume entitled *Exercises for Psychological Skills*)

Skill 15: Humor

Humor is the skill of enjoying funny things and being funny yourself. Humor is fun. It's one of the things that make life worth living. Ralph Waldo Emerson, in defining success, started off with the phrase "to laugh often and much." Many of life's most pleasurable moments are those spent laughing.

On the other hand, derisive or sadistic humor is one of the worst aspects of human activity. Many people's worst moments are those when they are laughed at, made fun of, and derided. Many people live in fear of being laughed at by others. So humor, like most other things, can be misused.

Purposely saying things that make people laugh is usually quite reinforcing. But if you say something that insults someone for the entertainment of others and yourself, you're misusing humor. The person who is most skilled at the use of humor and the enjoyment of humor should apply the test that says, "Is this humor contributing to the greater good of humanity?"

There are many complex forms of humor and complex theories of humor. On the simplest level, though, laughter is a way of expressing pleasure just as crying is a way of expressing pain. I have seen this very uncomplicated level of laughter many times in young children. When one of my daughters was an infant, I would at times when she was hungry hold her in a horizontal position and carry her steadily toward her mother's breast. As she realized she was going to get what she wanted, she would laugh loudly.

I have listened to other children laugh loudly as they danced around in anticipation of getting a birthday cake or were picked up and played with in a way that was fun for them. There is no need to invoke any complex theories as to what this brand of laughter means. It's simply the expression of pleasure and fun.

Fairly early in childhood there begins to be a more complex form of humor. This involves colluding with someone – sharing a secret of some sort, sharing some ruse. For example, a father acts as if he is a monster or acts as if he is a puppy dog, and the child laughs at this play-acting.

Now the father is doing something that could be perceived as an attempt to fool the child. But the child is in on the ruse, and realizes the puppy dog act is just an act (meant to fool nobody in particular). If the child should perceive this as a genuine attempt to fool him, the emotion might be anger.

But at the moment the child realizes he is being recruited, not as the object of the deception, but as the co-conspirator, he feels pleasure in that realization. The realization takes this form: "We are both on the same side; we are both in this together; we both know the trick; we both know the secret code; we have both caught onto this deal."

This moment of realization – that the joker and the audience share an insight – is common to almost all forms of humor. Let's think about the pun or play on words. What did the ocean say to the beach? Nothing – it just waved. A word can be interpreted one way; a split second later there's the realization it can also be interpreted a second way. There's also the realization that the joker intended the audience to catch on to this. In the simplest case there is laughter and pleasure at this shared trick.

In a slightly more complicated situation, the audience groans at the pun as if to communicate, "That trick is too simple, or too stupid to engage me in an alliance with you. But if we won't form the full alliance of laughter, at least we can form a compromise alliance of mock pain, whereby you're now in on my trick that I'm not really feeling pain. I'm putting on an act that your act was painful."

Another form of the collusion-type joke is a mistake that isn't really a mistake. The joker acts as if he's doing certain things out of clumsiness, stupidity, bad luck, or insanity, when actually he's doing these things on purpose. The shared ruse is that the joker and the audience both know it's done on purpose.

Most slapstick humor is based on this sort of collusion. The clown slips on the banana peel repeatedly, and the audience takes pleasure in the knowledge that the clown is really putting on an act and not just simply having a very hard time staying on his feet. One actor puts a pie in another one's face; that one does a slow burn and then puts a pie in the other one's face. The shared ruse is the knowledge that these two people are not really angry at each other but are putting on an act they intend the audience to be in on.

Being in on the ruse is pleasurable for the audience and that pleasure gets expressed as laughter. Part of the artistry of the slapstick humorist is the combination of acting as if the situation were real while at the same time, giving unmistakable nonverbal signals that it's not real – as, for example, by directing a good part of the slow burn directly toward the audience, rather than toward the other actor. Appreciating the complexity of these mixed messages and feeling in on the trick is part of what contributes to the audience's pleasure.

The ruse that we are acting like enemies when we are really friends is the collusion behind a good deal of the humor in friendly teasing and insults that friends trade with one another. The pleasure comes from the knowledge that the other person is really on your side despite insulting you. This is the ruse that is behind the "roast," where the best friends of a person get together and insult him, and everyone laughs.

Another version of the mistake that isn't really a mistake occurs when the joker simply acts stupid or crazy and the collusion between the joker and the audience is that they both know the joker is doing it on purpose. For example, the child or the adult puts the pants on the head rather than on the legs in a way that would look rather pathetic if someone who was really crazy or stupid did it. But when someone pretending to be crazy or stupid does it, it's appreciated as funny.

Another version of the mistake that isn't really a mistake comes when someone overacts a role in a way that, on the first and most obvious level, would seem to be a mistake in acting, were it not for the fact that the actor and the audience both know the overacting is on purpose.

Collusion or conspiracy is also present in malicious forms of humor. For example, one person mocks the tone, manner, or volume of another person's speaking voice in a very uncomplimentary and exaggerated way. The audience, by its laughter, lets the joker know they're in on the conspiracy and they know he's not really speaking like that from his own persona, but that he is mimicking the other person. However, the collusion is a way of taking sides against the mocked person.

In sarcasm, the meaning of the words spoken would seem to indicate praise, but the tone of voice reveals that the opposite of praise is meant, such as in saying, "Oh, brilliant! That's just brilliant!" Again, the audience (sometimes present in reality or sometimes just imaginary) is colluding with the joker in a ruse where hostility takes the guise of friendliness. That's why sarcasm is often more painful than a direct insult: there's not only hostility, but collusion against you as well.

Finally, there's the perversion of slapstick humor – laughing at a mistake that isn't really a mistake. This is laughing at the true misfortunes of other people, for example, laughing when the person really does slip and fall and hurt himself or laughing at the tone of voice or utterances of an individual with brain damage.

When this happens, the person who is laughing is confusing show business with reality. Perhaps he has developed a conditioned association between misfortunes or mistakes and laughter, even when there is no element of mutual collusion or pretending. The person who does this is in need of improvement in the skill of empathy. Coming to an accurate realization that another person is feeling pain should at least help in preventing malicious laughter at other people's misfortunes.

How does one cultivate the skill of appropriate humor? The most valuable helper in such a skill is someone who laughs easily, who appreciates one's efforts at humor, who has a low threshold for appreciating something funny. Such a partner will reinforce your attempts at humor by laughing, and this, more than anything else, will help improve your comic skills.

What if there's no such person readily available? Then my recommendation is to try to become one yourself. Simply by directing the attention and looking for the funny aspects of what others say, and by reinforcing them for their comic efforts, you may be sur-prised at how entertaining they can be.

Group 3: Kindness

There are three skills in this group. The skill of kindness is simply doing kind acts. The skill of empathy provides one reason to be kind: you feel a portion of what the other person feels, so that it makes you feel good to help and feel bad to harm. The skill of conscience provides another source of good feelings about kindness and bad feelings about cruelty.

Conscience comes from feelings generated by your own standards of what is right and wrong about your own actions. Thus, if I see someone hurt, but it's not in any way my responsibility, I might feel empathic pain but not guilt. If I help someone I greatly dislike, I might feel pleasure emanating from my conscience but not from my sense of empathy with that person. The lucky person has both motives for kindness.

There are still other motives for kindness. One of these is the gratification of one's wish for power, for the ability to affect and influence others. The ability to have an impact by helping is a very positive harnessing of the power motive. The conglomeration of a variety of motives that lead one to enjoy acts of kindness has already been given its status as a separate skill, in the joyousness group. (The more important skills are, the more redundantly they are discussed here!)

Skills in other groups are very relevant to kindness. If one can't do friendship-building well, it's hard to form the relationships within which most acts of kindness take place. If one has very poor skills of forgiveness and anger control, the temptation to retaliate can override the urge toward kindness. If decision-making skills are very poor, people can harm people inadvertently and gradually become habituated to this unpleasant image. Like most of the skills discussed here, this one is highly interdependent with others.

Skill 16: Kindness

What do we mean by kindness? When you act kindly, you make someone else happier. Complimenting people, helping people get things done, smiling at people, helping to relieve people's pain – all these are kind things to do because they make people happier.

Sometimes what makes someone happiest in the long run is not what makes them feel best in the short run. For example, someone is taking care of a child. The child wants to eat nothing but candy and Popsicles and soda pop for lunch. In the short run, it might make the child happiest if you give him exactly what he wants. But true kindness is doing what's good for people in the long run. In this case, it's giving the child nutritious food rather than sugary treats.

How do we know what's good for other people in the long run? One of the main ways is to imagine ourselves in the other person's life, to try to see things from their point of view. Suppose I were this person, and I were really wise about what would make me happy in the long run. What would I want?

Thinking this way is called using the "Golden Rule." Other ways of saying the Golden Rule include "Treat other people as you would like them to treat you," and "Do unto others as you would have them do unto you." This rule shows up in the sacred writings of most of the world's great religions. It's an idea that was discovered by many different groups of people at many times and places long ago.

Whenever you're applying the Golden Rule, it's important to remember that other people are not exactly the same as you are. So a more complicated, but perhaps more accurate statement of the Golden Rule would be, "Look at things from the other person's point of view, and try to do what's best for that person in the long run."

Here's an example of looking at things from the other person's point of view. A boy likes folk music. His father dislikes folk music but loves classical music. The boy is picking a present for his father's birthday. He sees a wonderful folk music recording. Suppose he were to think, "Do unto others as you would have them do unto you; if I were having a birthday, I would really like this folk music recording, so that's what I should do for my father."

But of course he should think, "What would I like IF I were my father?" When he adds that second part, he realizes the classical recording would be better. So this act of kindness requires another skill; putting yourself in the other person's place, imagining what their wishes are, imagining what is going on in their minds. The art of putting yourself in the other person's shoes is called the skill of empathy. We will discuss this later.

Doing what's best for a person in the long run sometimes means saying no to what people want. Suppose, for example, I have a friend who gets drunk on alcohol and gets into big trouble when he does so. Suppose I'm old enough to buy alcohol, but this friend is not. The friend wants me to buy alcoholic drinks for him.

How would I want to be treated, if I were that person? If I were looking out for my short-term pleasure only, I'd want the other person to get me the alcohol. But if I were looking out for my long-term best interests, I would realize I'd be better off if the other person refused. So if we follow the rule of looking at things from the other person's point of view and trying to do what's best for the person in the long run, we would refuse to buy the alcohol for him.

The point where you figure you know the other person's long term best interest better than the person himself does brings up some sticky dilemmas about what really is best to do. Suppose I feel someone is about to become an alcoholic. And suppose I not only refuse to get alcohol for him, but I also physically force him not to drink or threaten to punish him with physical violence if he does. I tell myself this is in his long-term best interest and may even save his life.

Here the principle of doing what you think is in the other person's long-term best interest conflicts with another rule, namely that you should usually avoid hurting and threatening people. When is it right to make people do things they don't want to do because it's for their own good?

If you do make people do things they don't want to do, you'd better be sure it really makes the other person happier in the long run. You'd better make sure you aren't just indulging your own wish to be powerful and boss someone else around.

Many people have done cruel things out of a thought that they were doing it for someone else's own good. Many children, for example, have been injured by adults who told themselves the punishment they delivered was for the child's "own good."

Later, we'll talk more about ethical principles and deciding what really is the kind thing to do. But in many, many instances, it's not hard to decide what is kindest to do; the hard part is to do it.

Why is the skill of kindness so important? This is like asking, "Why is happiness so important?" Kindness is trying to make other people happy. If people could be kind to one another very much of the time, people would be much happier.

There's a story that is told about someone who had the fortune to take a tour of heaven and hell. When he went to hell to watch what was going on, he saw many people sitting at a big table. They had long spoons strapped onto their hands. They had a wonderful banquet with all sorts of wonderful looking food in front of them.

The trouble was that the spoons were so long the people couldn't get the food into their mouths. If you got some food onto the end of your spoon, you couldn't get it into your mouth – the spoon was longer than your arm.

(To make this story work you have to imagine that they couldn't get the food with their hands or their mouths, or hold the spoons farther down the handle; holding the spoons at the end was the only way to get the food.)

So everybody was miserable, because they wanted the wonderful food but couldn't get it.

Then this person took the tour of heaven. To his amazement, he found exactly the same arrangement. The people had the long spoons strapped onto their hands in exactly the same way. In heaven, though, the people were enjoying the food and having a great time. What was the difference? In the scene in heaven, the people were feeding one another.

This story illustrates that some people create a hell on Earth for themselves by only thinking about themselves. Other people create something like a heaven on Earth by being nice to one another. Often the difference between misery and happiness is as simple as whether people are being kind to one another or not.

Let's think about some of the ways in which people can be kind to one another. It's useful to do this so that you can systematically search for ways to be kind to other people.

Helping someone with a task. Someone is carrying something that's too big to carry by himself, and someone else helps him to carry it. Or someone has a big job to do, like cleaning up the house for a party, and someone else helps them do it.

As these two examples illustrate, the more you like to work, the more kindness you're able to show, because often kindness is doing some work that helps another person. Thus, the skills of self-discipline or delaying gratification and sustaining attention to tasks help in kindness.

Also, the more competent you are at some particular task, the more you're able to be kind. A plastic surgeon who had learned to correct disfigurements traveled to a poor country to perform operations for free. If he had not taken the time and effort to develop his surgical skill, he would not have been able to be kind in this way.

Explaining or teaching something. A person helps someone else figure out how to fill out a tax form. Or a person explains to someone how to do some math homework.

Sharing your knowledge and expertise is an important way to be kind to people. It can be a very kind act to help another person when that person needs to know what to do. Sometimes an even kinder thing is to give them your expertise so the next time they'll be able to do it on their own. You do this by teaching the other person to do something useful.

Being cheerful and upbeat. A way to be kind is having a tone of voice that communicates to another person, "I'm glad that you're around." Saying to someone, "Good morning. How are you? I'm glad to see you." in a cheerful tone of voice is a kind act. It lets that person know they're appreciated. Just saying "Hello" or looking at the person and smiling can be a kind act.

Physical affection. Another category of kind acts is physical affection, especially with people in your family. Going over and patting someone on the back, giving someone a hug or kiss, giving a back rub, just letting her know that you like her, that you want her to feel good – these are important acts of kindness.

Spending time with the person. One of the things that make people happy is to have someone fun to be with. We would all be lonely if we never had anybody to be with, and therefore, choosing to spend time with someone, either in play or conversation or while working together can be a kind act, something that makes someone happy.

Remembering special occasions. For example, remembering someone's birthday and sending that person a letter or card telling him, "Happy Birthday!" can make someone happy. It tells him, "I care enough about you. I'm interested enough in you to remember and to think

about you, rather than just forget about you."

Lending and giving. Being generous with your possessions and sharing your things or your money with other people is another way to be kind.

Withholding anger. Another way to be kind is to withhold an angry response even when most people would get angry. Let's imagine that the driver of a car says to his passenger, "Don't worry. I know how to get to this place." Suppose it's very important that they get there on time. The person who is driving makes a wrong turn and gets them lost, and they get there late.

It would be natural for many passengers to say, "You told me you knew how to get here! Why don't you plan these things better? Why do you take these turns unless you know where you're going?" and so forth.

Suppose, on the other hand, the passenger were to say, "Well, worrying about it won't get us there any quicker. I know you wouldn't have made the mistake on purpose, and I know you don't like getting here late any more than I do. So let's just concentrate on where to go now." Responding in that way is the kind act of withholding criticism.

Complimenting. It's kind to recognize when someone has done something smart or good and to point that out to her. For someone to recognize the smart or good things you do is one of the kindest things someone else can do for you. In the best of all possible worlds, people would probably be complimenting one another very frequently.

Listening. It's kind to listen empathically when someone talks. Here you express kindness by how accurately and attentively you listen and how much you really try to understand what the other person is experiencing. We'll talk more about this when we talk about the skill of listening.

This skill is really basic to the skill of kindness. If you're not able to understand something about the other person, you won't know what they need in order to be happy. If you aren't a good listener, you tend to assume that they're like you and that what makes you happy will make them happy.

Politeness. It's kind to say the words our society uses that all mean "I care about your feelings." Saying "please," "thank you," "excuse me," "you're welcome," etc., and doing so in a polite and respectful tone are acts of kindness. These contribute to a positive emotional climate in families and a good feeling among people.

Working for a good cause. You're being kind to others when, for example you work for an organization that's trying to clean up the environment or put an end to violence or poverty.

Let's list these categories of kind acts here:

Categories of Kind Acts

1. Helping with a task
2. Explaining or teaching something
3. Being cheerful and upbeat
4. Physical affection
5. Spending time with the person
6. Remembering special occasions
7. Lending and giving
8. Withholding anger
9. Complimenting
10. Listening
11. Politeness
12. Working for a good cause

Kindness begins at home

When people think about acts of kindness, they usually think about acts of kindness to strangers: helping the blind person cross the street, saving someone who is drowning, and so forth.

Kind acts to strangers definitely make the world a better place. Every time someone who doesn't know you and has no obligation to you at all does something kind to you, that person increases your faith that the world is a good place. That person teaches you that the world is populated by at least some people who are caring and nice. Every time you do a kind act for a stranger, you make the world a better place.

But, perhaps even more important and difficult are kind acts to your own family members. With a stranger, you do one thing quickly and it's appreciated, and your obligation is over. For the family member, maybe you help them out by doing some work around the house for her, knowing that same bit of work around the house is going to be there to be done again tomorrow and every day thereafter.

Maybe you get the urge to be kind by using an upbeat tone and a joyous tone of voice upon seeing someone. But then you remember the disagreement you had with your family member a while ago, and that makes it harder to do kind acts through cheerfulness. So it can be more challenging and difficult to be kind to family members than to strangers.

Even though more difficult sometimes, being kind to family members and close friends is very important. These are the people who make up your social support network. These are the people who depend upon you. You can make a big difference in their lives by gradually doing more and more acts of kindness for them.

Kindness is the opposite of cruelty

In realizing how important kindness is, it's helpful to be mindful of the problems caused by its opposites. The opposites of kindness are cruelty, hostility, hurtfulness, the wish to make others feel bad rather than good, and physical and emotional violence.

Any time you pick up the newspaper, you'll read stories about people hurting one another, killing one another, doing all sorts of cruel things to one another. Violence, cruelty, and hostility are the prime conditions that make life on this Earth unpleasant for so many people.

Kindness is the opposite of violence and verbal abusiveness. Promoting kindness serves to decrease violence, cruelty, and hostility.

Earlier, we spoke of a skill that is very closely linked to kindness: the skill of taking pleasure from your own acts of kindness, of feeling good when you're able to make someone else feel good.

But now, let's talk about the opposite of this skill, which presents a big barrier to the skill of kindness. Too often people learn to enjoy other people's pain and suffering.

Many, many people get lots of pleasure from watching people hurt one another. If this were not true, then there would not be such a huge market for violent entertainment – movies of people hurting and killing one another, video games involving hurting and killing, and violent sports such as boxing.

If you're really interested in the skill of kindness, really interested in seeing this skill grow in the world, really interested in seeing the skill of kindness crowd out people's taking pleasure from others' suffering, then you should think about the issue of violent entertainment. Is it right and desirable for people to be entertained by images of other people getting hurt?

A great deal of research has shown that people are influenced by their entertainment, even when they know that what they're watching is not real. This is because each time you send images through your mind, you are in a sense rehearsing them. Many people watch a lot of violent entertainment without ever doing anything violent. Nonetheless, studies have shown that the watching of violent entertainment leads to increases in real-life violence.

Motives for kind acts and stages of moral development

What are some of the reasons people are kind to one another? People can act kind for good or bad reasons. If I'm kind to someone because I want to get on her good side to sell her something, that's a different act than if I'm kind because I really am interested in her welfare and want to make her happy.

Looking at people's reasons for doing kind or unkind acts leads to ideas about stages of moral development. In the lowest stage, you don't necessarily act kind – you simply do whatever is most pleasurable to you. You don't even think about what the other person's needs are. We can call this stage hedonism or selfishness.

A little more advanced on the scale is the stage where people follow some authoritarian rule about being kind and decent to one another because an authority is going to reward or punish them accordingly.

Another motive for kind acts is called bargaining or reciprocity. I'm nice or kind to you because I want to get something back from you in return.

There are two ways to do this, however. One is bargaining for short

run pay-offs; I'll do this only if you do this back for me. The other is longer-term reciprocity. I'll do this for you without expecting any reward right now, but I'll expect that sooner or later you'll want to be nice to me in return. The longer the person's time range is, the more the person tends to act in a way that seems unselfish.

According to most moral development theorists, the highest stage on the scale of moral development is acting on principle. That is, you have in your mind a set of principles on how people should act toward each other, and you try to follow those principles. The Golden Rule – "Do unto others as you would have them do unto you" – is one example of such a principle.

We can also use the idea of stages to think about why people in families are kind to one another.

In families at the bottom end of this scale, family members are not nice to one another. They speak in a hostile manner, are physically violent, or otherwise do things that make one another unhappy without much effort to change these patterns.

In families at the next stage of this scale, family members act kind only to avoid punishment. For example, a child avoids hitting his sister because he knows he'll be put in time out if he does.

In the next stage, family members show kindness to get a fairly concrete or tangible reward. For example, a child knows that if he obeys and doesn't hit, he'll have a chance to go to a hockey game. Or a child acts very nice to a playmate because he wants the playmate to invite him to a fun party he knows the playmate will be having.

The next higher motive is a long-range wish to enjoy the benefits of a positive emotional climate. That is, a family member wishes to make the other people in the family happy so he will get caught up in the atmosphere of good will and sharing that is created; the person as well as other people will benefit from living in an atmosphere of positive emotion.

The highest motive in this categorization is simply seeking to feel good by making another person in the family feel good and happy. People thus try to make one another happy for that reason, without expecting any other external rewards.

As a rule, the higher family members can move their family along this scale, the happier this family will be and the less selfish in-fighting there will be among family members.

Deciding what is kind and good: ethical principles

The branch of philosophy devoted to questions of what is kind and what is good is called ethics. The ethical philosophers have asked the questions, "What should people do? And how can we decide what is good or bad?" Two ethical philosophers, Jeremy Bentham and John Stewart Mill, advocated the rule that people should try to make the total amount of happiness in the world as great as they could possibly make it. Since "utility" is another word for happiness, these philosophers have been called "utilitarians."

Sometimes it's hard to figure out what's going to increase people's happiness the most. Suppose you're playing with a preschool child. You have a ball, and you're trying to see how many times you can dribble it. The child says, "Give me that!" and starts whining and screaming, "I want it! I want it!" in a very unpleasant way.

What's the kindest thing to do in this situation? Someone who is purely selfish might think, "No. I want it, therefore I'm not going to give it to the child." and it's as simple as that. Someone who's a little more interested in trying to maximize happiness might think, "It'll make him happy to get it, and it won't make me terribly unhappy to lose it. I know I can handle losing it, apparently better than he can, so I'll give it to him."

But, someone who thinks in a still more sophisticated way might think, "Well, if I give it to him, I'm making him happy in the short run by giving him what he wants, but I'm also rewarding him for acting whiny and unhappy. So I might be decreasing his happiness in the long run, even though I may be increasing it in the short run. I think the kindest thing to do is to tell him to wait and give it to him in a few minutes, when has stopped whining and acting unpleasant."

Immanuel Kant also tried to figure out a rule to guide people into thinking what was kind and what was good. Kant's rule was called the "Categorical Imperative" and went something like this: "Act in such a way that the principle you're acting on is something you would want everyone to use."

For example, someone gets the idea of stealing a pencil from someone else in school. He says to himself, "The principle I am acting on is 'Take anything that belongs to anybody else whenever you want to.' Would I like people to act on that principle toward me, or everybody in the world to act that way? No, I wouldn't. Therefore I shouldn't act on that principle."

Some people believe Kant's Categorical Imperative is just another restatement of the Golden Rule.

Some people are easier to be kind to than others. Some people require a more principled person than others. Let's suppose there's someone everybody else really likes, and you can see why they like that person. This is a really nice person who's lots of fun to be with, has lots of friends, likes to laugh, and is generally a pleasant person. He's really easy to be nice to. Part of the reason it's easy to be nice to this person is that the person is so ready to be nice in return. So, people tend to want to be friends with this person just because everybody else is a friend with this person.

But, what about someone people tend to reject and look down on, some-times for bad reasons? Perhaps this person looks different or dresses different, or is too fat or skinny – something that makes them different from everybody else, but nonetheless, makes everybody else dislike them. Sometimes, people are scared to be nice to this person for fear people will think they're friends with someone who's rejected and then people will then reject them.

But the person who is really good at the skill of kindness and believes in kindness as a principle, rather than just out of what he can get back from kindness, will especially go out of their way to be kind to people other people dislike.

An even more severe test of the skill of kindness is the person who is actually mean and nasty toward you. The natural thing for most people to do when someone is mean to them is to want to be mean right back to punish them for it. Sometimes, though, when someone is mean to you and you're kind back to them, it has a very startling effect on the other person. It shows them that someone actually believes in the principle of kindness. That person can be ashamed of his meanness and be shocked into being nice. This is more likely to happen if other people see and admire the kindness that's being demonstrated.

Something like this happened in India when Mohandas Gandhi led a nonviolent revolution to free India of British rule. Gandhi and his followers refused to be violent even when the

British were violent. Eventually, it paid off.

On the other hand, usually the kindest thing to do for someone who's acting unkind is to stop them from doing so.

Suppose I'm an adult and a little boy comes in and starts hitting me, hard, for no reason. What's the kindest thing for me to do? Is it to turn my other cheek and let the boy pummel me? Is it to say, "If you'll quit I'll give you a lollipop?"

Or is it to say, "I'm not going to let you be violent," and to physically take both of the boy's hands and cross them over in front of him and hold him in the corner until he gets over the urge to be violent?

Whatever reduces his long-run tendency to be violent is probably the kindest thing to do for him. So the sterner response sometimes is actually kinder in the long run.

That's one thing that makes the skill of kindness difficult. Even if you're totally committed to acting in the other person's long-term interest, what is that interest? What will serve the other person best?

Here's another issue that makes the skill of kindness hard. Where do my own interests come in? What do I do when I have a choice between two actions; one makes the other person happier, but the other makes me happier? For example, suppose that by giving away lots of my money, I can make some stranger happier and make myself less happy? How do I balance my own happiness against other people's happiness?

If I make myself too unhappy, I reduce my ability to make other people happy. So I would defeat my own purpose by carrying unselfishness to an extreme. But on the other hand, when I buy luxury items while other people are unfed, unclothed and homeless, I can hardly think of myself as acting on the highest ethical principles.

A step in the skill of kindness: discriminating kindness from selfishness

In teaching children the skill of kindness, I find it useful to examine many stories in which people do something that's either selfish or unselfish. The child's job is to tell, first, whether the person acted selfishly or unselfishly, and, second, what the person might have done if he or she had acted the other way. There are lots of such stories in the book Programmed Readings for Psychological Skills.

One could construct an almost unlimited number of these stories. Here's an easy one. A boy who came to the United States from China has a name that's unusual for U.S. children. When another boy at this kid's school hears his name, he laughs and tells other kids what his name is and they make fun of it, in front of the boy from China.

Are they acting selfishly or unselfishly? Obviously, they are acting selfishly, because they are putting their own desire for amusement above consideration of the other child's feelings. If they acted unselfishly, they would suppress any urge to amuse themselves at the other child's expense and treat his name with respect.

After a learner has done a great number of exercises in discriminating selfish from unselfish acts, a next step is for the learner to construct a large number of stories like this for himself. This is a useful exercise for adults as well as children. Doing this exercise helps in heightening awareness of the opportunities for selfish and unselfish behavior that are presented to us constantly.

A longer list of ethical principles

The central task for the person who would understand these principles is to think about specific situations that are examples of times when they apply.

Productivity
1. Work; do useful things.
2. Prevent bad things from happening before they happen and promote good things' happening before they happen too.

Joyousness
3. Since good cheer is contagious, be cheerful if at all appropriate.

Kindness
4. The Golden Rule: Do unto others as you would have them do unto you.
5. The love your neighbor rule: Love your neighbor as yourself.

6. Kant's rule: Act using the principles you wish everyone would use.
7. You should treat people as important for themselves and not just use them for what they can get you.
8. The "greatest good" rule: Make as much happiness as you can. Or: Make the greatest good for the greatest number. Or: Improve the world as much as you can.
9. Don't destroy other people's property.
10. Don't treat people unkindly or unfairly just because they're different from you.

Honesty
11. Don't lie or deceive other people. Don't steal people's property or cheat them out of it.
12. Keep your promises.
13. When people make agreements with one another to exchange goods or services, they should keep these agreements.
14. When you have an agreement with someone, you should at least let the person know if you change your mind.

Fortitude
15. Avoid letting yourself feel so bad about little things that you're less able to do good.

Good decisions
16. Make the best decision you can, given all the information you can get. (But no one should be expected to make

decisions that turn out best all the time, because luck and chance often play a role.)

17. Don't spoil people by sacrificing too much of your own welfare for their unreasonable wishes.

18. Although you should beware of forcing other people to do things just so you can enjoy having power, sometimes it's right to make people do things they don't want to do.

19. Reinforce people's good actions and don't reinforce their bad actions.

20. Ethical decisions are important in proportion to how much happiness is at stake.

21. When you look at the effects of your actions, think about the precedents and examples you set for yourself and others, as well as the direct effects of the actions.

22. When two ethical principles conflict with each other, you should act to produce the best long-term result.

Nonviolence

23. Don't try to kill other people.

24. Don't try to physically hurt other people.

25. Don't threaten to kill or hurt other people.

Respectful Talk

26. Don't use words that cause emotional pain to others, without good reason.

27. Sometimes it's helpful to punish people for doing bad things. But beware of being cruel just to get revenge or enjoy having power.

Friendship-Building

28. Build positive relationships with people.

29. Help other people to build and maintain positive connections among one another.

Self-Discipline

30. To produce more happiness in the long run, you often have to do what you don't feel like doing in the short run.

31. To be in a relationship with someone, be willing to sacrifice some of what you feel like doing.

Loyalty

32. Reinforce people's kindness by being kind back to them.

33. You owe more loyalty to family members and friends than to strangers; but it's good to help any human being.

34. You owe more loyalty to people who have been kind to you than people who haven't, but it's good to help any human being.

35. You owe more loyalty to people who are doing ethical things than to people who aren't.

Conservation

36. People should use scarce resources (like money, time, labor) on necessities or things that are more important rather than luxuries or things that are less important.

Self-Care
37. Take care of your own health and welfare, so that you can help others.

Compliance
38. People have a responsibility to obey the law unless the law is bad.

Positive Fantasy Rehearsal
39. People should not take pleasure from watching other people do bad things to one another.
40. People should not rehearse bad acts in imagination just for excitement or entertainment.

Courage
41. You should not do something wrong and bad just because an authority tells you to do it.
42. You will often need to oppose another person if you want to do the right thing.

You'll notice that the categories used to organize these ethical principles are the same ones used to organize the psychological skills. This reflects the belief that the two seemingly separate questions, "How should we live in order to be psychologically healthy," and "How should we live in order to be ethical?" really have the same answer. Behavior that has good effects for oneself and others is both psychologically healthy and ethical.

Time spent in thinking about these principles is almost guaranteed to be time well spent. Time spent in think-ing about situations that come up in real life, and referring to the list of principles to decide which ones most apply, will also be time well spent.

Skill 17: Empathy

There are two parts to the skill of empathy. The first is becoming aware of what other people are feeling and experiencing and why. This means paying attention to the proper signals to make inferences about other people's emotions and what is causing those emotions. The second part is recreating in yourself to some degree the feeling the other person is having, that is, "feeling along with" the other person.

A very important portion of the skill is becoming aware of what effect your own behavior is having on the feelings of other people. If I pick up a little child and swing him around in the air, is he having a great time or is he terrified? The answer to this question is important in my relationship with him. If I can notice he's getting scared at the very first instant when fear enters him, then I can take corrective action immediately and put him down. Then the relationship is still in good shape. But if he begins to get terrified and I continue swinging him around, mistakenly thinking his screams signify delight rather than horror, our relationship is very much harmed!

Here's another example. Suppose I'm talking with a friend, and after going on and on for several minutes, I start to notice the signals that my friend is getting bored and impatient. If I then stop talking and yield the floor, the interaction is still in good shape. But if I ignore or miss the other person's signals and keep on talking, I can harm our relationship. This is particularly true if I do this repeatedly.

Sensitivity to positive feelings in other people is also important. Suppose I'm having a conversation about a subject I'm deeply interested in. The other person is giving off signals of great interest and pleasure in hearing about this subject. If I missed those signals, I might be thinking to myself, "I shouldn't burden this person by talking too much about this subject. I'll change the subject." If I pick up on the signals, I can become aware of finding a kindred spirit with respect to this particular topic; the relationship is greatly helped by that information.

Feelings of other people are signals to us, just as our own feelings are. Very often a negative feeling in someone else signals "Stop doing that," and a positive feeling signals "Keep on, keep going."

Just as with our own emotions, sometimes other people's emotions give us false signals about what we should do. It's usually a good idea to refuse to yield to the high-pressure tactics of sales people despite signs of negative emotion such refusal produces. It may be a great idea to take a violent toy away from a child, despite the fact that the child enjoys playing with the violent toy. People can be happy about bad things and unhappy about good things. Nonetheless, we can usually make better decisions if we can at least become aware of what the other person is feeling.

In exercising the skill of empathy, it's often not enough to recognize that someone is feeling something; you want to understand the source of the feeling: i.e., what is the situation the person is responding to, and what does the person think about that situation?

One important special case of this type of inference is deciding, am I the cause of this person's feelings, or do they arise elsewhere? For example, a father gets a grim expression on his face, when he's thinking about how he's being ordered to do something at work that he doesn't think is a good idea. A child, looking at his face, correctly infers that he's feeling angry and worried. But the child might incorrectly guess the father feels that way because the child said something wrong, when the father's feelings didn't have anything to do with the child.

This example also shows that the skill of empathy is not equal to the skill of mind reading! Sensitive and empathic individuals usually pay careful attention to nonverbal signs of emotion in other people: facial expressions, movements of the body, postures, and the volume, pitch, and tempo of the voice. But to achieve the greatest understanding between people, it's important to communicate using language. People need words to check out what people

are feeling and why, to ask one another about their feelings.

For example, one person says, "When I mentioned taking the airline flight, you got a worried look on your face. I imagined you might be worried about the safety of the airline flight." This type of utterance may be called a "reflection of feeling."

The other person could reply, "Yes. You're right. The whole notion of airline safety has come to bother me greatly, recently." On the other hand, the person could reply, "No. That wasn't it at all. I just realized as we spoke what day it is and realized that my tax return is due tomorrow. I'm not ready to send it in." Or the person could reply, "No. I'm not worried about plane safety; I'm worried about how much money we have, and I'm thinking we can't afford to fly off on a vacation."

The more one can check out what someone else is feeling and get accurate feedback, the more highly developed his empathy skills become. The person who checks out the other person's feelings can gradually build up a bank of data that leads to more accurate inferences from the other person's nonverbal communications. But this accumulating information never eliminates the need to check things out verbally with the other person, and having lots of positive experience with this maneuver is very useful for empathy skills. If the second person responds with irritation or anger whenever the first checks out a hypothesis about his feelings, the first person gets punished for trying to be empathic.

So far I've been talking about recognizing what other people are feeling and why. The second half of the skill of empathy is recreating that feeling in yourself, to some extent. This is the ability to "feel along with" someone else.

This includes feeling good about someone else's accomplishment and celebration; suffering to some degree along with someone who has been humiliated; feeling a portion of the pain and suffering someone feels from being brutally treated.

This part of empathy is one of the basic motivations people have to help one another and not to hurt one another. That is: I make someone else feel good because I can empathically feel some of that good feeling myself. I avoid making them feel bad, because I know I would empathically feel bad myself.

Feeling bad about someone else's suffering is subject to habituation and desensitization. People protect themselves from too much pain. When they see lots of suffering and injury, especially in a context where there's also some reason to feel good about it, the capacity for empathy can be decreased. This probably happens to many people as they get more than 20,000 media entertainment exposures to murders by the time they reach adulthood. In a culture where exposure to killing and injuring is a daily occurrence, the

ability to shield oneself from the empathic response to a victim's suffering becomes an adaptive skill. Thus, we may be developing a culture that is gradually becoming more and more insensitive to the suffering of others.

It's often useful to temper or limit the amount of suffering you experience in empathic responses, particularly if your job is helping distressed people. If most mental health or medical professionals truly allowed themselves to feel a large portion of the pain that each patient and patient's family member felt, they would be very unhappy indeed. Not only would they feel unhappy – they would probably compromise their ability to help the very people they're empathizing with.

To function at a high level requires that you aren't suffering from huge amounts of pain at the moment. Thus the skill of feeling along with another's painful feelings demands balance. You want the degree of "feeling along with" that produces lots of compassion, while still allowing the helping person to derive happiness and joy from any helping he can provide.

For example, most trauma surgeons do well not to be overcome with revulsion and grief upon seeing badly hurt people. Most of them probably become fairly desensitized to such negative feelings. This desensitization helps the surgeon respond with rationality in the operating room, in a way most helpful to the hurt person. Yet, if the surgeon totally loses the ability to feel along with the family members or the patient in the office, he has lost an ability that allows him to console and support.

There's something fundamentally different about the desensitization a helping professional experiences and the desensitization that occurs from entertainment violence. Desensitization to suffering so that we can be entertained by it robs us of a certain degree of our humanity.

The cooperative spirit and the competitive spirit

There's something we might call reverse empathy. Reverse empathy means you feel good about the other person's bad fortunes; you feel bad about his good fortunes.

Reverse empathy isn't something that's limited to psychopathic sadists. A version of it is present in any normal competition. When I'm in the middle of a championship tennis game, I feel bad when my opponent makes a lucky shot that wins, and I feel good when he can't reach the ball I've hit. His triumphs are my disappointments and vice versa. Our interests are by definition opposed to each other.

But if we are sensible and humane, we realize this opposition of interests is limited to tennis shots. I don't feel good if he injures himself after the game. I don't feel bad if his sick child gets well. I'm able to have a cooperative attitude toward him as a human being, despite a competitive attitude on the tennis court.

But often it appears that the competitive attitude spills over into areas where humaneness would require cooperation. It would be interesting to know how many sets of sibling pairs grow up feeling predominantly competitive. How many children get a good feeling, rather than a jealous feeling, when a sibling gets recognized for a success? This surely varies from time to time and from situation to situation.

It's probably possible, however, to characterize relationships as falling somewhere on the spectrum of having good will toward the other, versus having good will reversed by a competitive attitude.

How many adults feel predominantly in cooperation with their co-workers? How much of the time do they secretly exult when a co-worker fails? How many members of legislatures celebrate when fellow legislators who belong to a different political party do something good for the voters, and get recognized for it? How many workers at X hospital really feel good when someone at Y hospital, the competitor across the river, finds a new breakthrough that will help patients?

The prisoner's dilemma game: a model for cooperation versus competition

Suppose you and another person go into an experimenter's office. The experimenter says, "This is an experiment to determine when people choose to trust each other, and when they don't. You have the chance to win some money. Here's the deal. There will be five rounds in this game. On each round, you each write the word "trust" or the words "not trust" on a card, without letting the other see what you're writing. When you have both written, you show me and the other person what you have written. Here's how you then get paid:

If both write "trust," then each gets $2.

If one writes "trust" and the other writes "not trust," the one who wrote "trust" gets $0 and the one who wrote "not trust" gets $3.

If both write "not trust," then each gets $1."

It's now time to write on your card. What would you write?

If the other person has written "not trust," you get a dollar more by writing "not trust" ($1 instead of $0). If the other person has written "trust," you also get a dollar more by writing "not trust" ($3 instead of $2). So if you want to maximize your receipts, you should write "not trust" – right?

But there's another consideration. If you and your partner can both write "trust" each time, you'll each get $2 from the experimenter each round. But if you both write "not trust" each time, you'll each get a total of $1 from the experimenter each time.

In other words, if two of you can cooperate and stay out of the selfish or competitive mentality, you will each take home twice as much money as if you don't cooperate.

Is this game analogous to anything in life? When you look for the analogies, you find them almost everywhere. Here are some.

1. Two countries would like to spend their money on programs to raise the living standards of their citizens. If they could trust each other not to take arms against each other, they could do that. But because they can't trust each other, and out of fear that the other will be heavily armed and one's own country will not be, both maintain very expensive armies and armaments.

2. Two brothers are fighting over a toy. Both would benefit by taking turns and sharing the toy. But each of them predicts that if he lets the other have the first turn, the other will not yield possession when it comes time to give up the turn. So rather than sharing the toy, they continue to fight over it.

3. Two spouses are angry at each other. Each would like to make up and get on good terms again, if he could trust the other to do the same. But each fears that if he apologized and offered conciliation, the other would simply use that as evidence the problem was his fault. So rather than risk that, they remain at a cold standoff.

4. Two people are falsely accused of a crime. They are separated. Each is told that if he will testify against the other, he will get a reduced sentence. They would like to stand firm on

the story that neither of them is guilty. But each, out of fear that the other will testify against him, testifies against the other to get a reduced sentence. (It's from this situation that the game gets its name.)

I once did the prisoner's dilemma game with pairs of sixth grade children. When simply told what the rules were, most of them chose "not trust" most of the time. However, when I gave them different instructions, they chose "trust" almost all the time.

Here are the different instructions: "The two of you are on a team. There is another pair on a different team. See how much total money your team can get. The team with the most money at the end wins." In other words, if the two players could see themselves as being on the same team, competing against someone else, they could cooperate.

Another instruction that helps people to cooperate is this: "Feel free to negotiate deals and make agreements with each other. Take seriously your obligation to keep any agreements you make." With this instruction, people feel free to say to the other person, "Hey, let's double our money. I'll write "trust" if you promise you will too. How about it?"

I mention the prisoner's dilemma game in this empathy chapter because I believe it teaches people not to let an overgeneralized competitive mentality destroy their empathy. Play-ing the prisoner's dilemma game is a good exercise in learning to cooperate.

Other empathy exercises

The "guess-the-feelings" game, described in the previous chapter on awareness of your own feelings, is an excellent exercise in recognizing other people's feelings.

Taking turns with someone else talking and doing empathic reflections, as described in the chapter on the skill of listening, also gives great practice in empathy. One person tells about what-ever is on his mind. The second person responds with a reflection, such as "If I understand you right, _____." If the second person can use a reflection of feeling, such as "Sounds like you're feeling _____," the practice of empa-thy is even greater.

Here's another empathy exer-cise. It's a variation on guessing feel-ings. You pick about five feeling words as the multiple choices. Then the "por-trayer" of the feeling in question tries to use the tone of voice and the facial ex-pressions that portray that feeling, using a neutral syllable such as "la la la" so the content of the speech won't give away the answer. The guesser guesses the feeling. Both win if the guesser can guess correctly.

In real life, one of the barriers to empathy is simply failing to ask oneself the question of where the other person is coming from, what the other person is experiencing. Someone who has set a goal of increasing this skill would do

well to simply monitor the number of
times that he can ask himself, "What is
going on with this other person? What
is she experiencing?"

Skill 18: Conscience

Conscience skills are to guilt as carefulness skills are to fear and assertiveness skills are to anger. In each case the unpleasant emotion can sometimes spur you to act wisely, but too much of it can keep you from acting wisely.

Guilt, like fear and anger, is an emotion that developed for a good reason. It delivers a sting when you have done something to harm someone else, and tends to keep you from harming someone in the same way again. And if you're lucky, the anticipation of feeling guilty, when you contemplate a harmful act in your imagination, keeps you from harming someone in the first place.

People can do conscience skills badly in two ways. One is by feeling too much guilt over actions that either were not very harmful or could not have been foreseen as harmful. The second is by feeling too little guilt over actions that should have been foreseen as harmful.

Various psychological theories have invented words for these two types of errors. In psychoanalytic language, one would say someone with too much guilt had a harsh and punitive superego, and someone with too little guilt had an undeveloped superego or holes in the superego.

In the language of Transactional Analysis developed by Eric Berne, having too much guilt might be called having too strong a "critical parent" portion of the personality. Having too little guilt might translate into having too much of the "rebellious child." Karen Horney spoke of the "tyranny of the shoulds" looming over the person who has too much guilt. The person without a conscience has been referred to in the psychiatric jargon as a psychopath or sociopath.

The person who torments himself endlessly by feeling guilty about very small acts of harmfulness has a big problem. However, the opposite sort of problem is an even worse one to have. People who have no conscience or very little conscience tend to end up as criminals.

Most people probably have an inborn ability to feel guilty over harmful acts. Perhaps some people are born with a deficiency of this ability, while others are born with it and gradually desensitize themselves to guilt and thus get rid of it.

How does a person desensitize his ability to feel guilt? This happens in the same way any other sort of negative emotion is desensitized. You experience the guilt-inducing situation repeatedly without any negative consequence. Gradually the guilt habituates or goes away. You gradually do more and more harmful things without bad consequences to you, and you become progressively able to do harmful things.

Just as with desensitization of fears, desensitization of guilt can begin with acts carried out in imagination. Learning to entertain yourself with video games where you act out in fantasy many killings of other human beings is a workshop for the beginning steps of desensitization of the conscience. Watching models of people who are able to do destructive and violent acts without any remorse or guilt, as in the typical action and adventure movie, is another avenue for the beginnings of desensitization of conscience.

Some people without consciences can be very charming and friendly, and use these social skills to get people on their side. Sooner or later, however, the truth comes out that the person is purely selfish, and the person who has been tricked into trusting the person often comes to hate him.

The person without a conscience usually gradually learns that he is unable to rely on the love of other people, because his selfishness makes him unlovable. Therefore many people without conscience have a relentless pursuit of power. The reasoning seems to go, if I can't get others to treat me respectfully because of their love for me, I will get them to do so because of my power, because of their fear of what I am powerful enough to do.

Some psychopaths are smart enough to make their actions have good effects, not because they care about the people they are affecting, but because they see having good effects as another route to power. For this reason sometimes, ironically, these people do much

good. But more often, the person without conscience winds up in a jail cell. If you want to have decent relationships with people, you must pay the price of having a conscience and the occasional pain it causes.

Guilt should depend on intention as well as outcome

If you can build your own conscience, how do you want it constructed? What do you want to feel guilty over? When is an act deserving of guilt? Consider the following vignettes.

Suppose a father permits his adolescent daughter to go on a skiing trip with some very responsible friends. While skiing, the daughter is severely injured in an accident when the ski lift cable breaks.

Another father responds to pressure from his adolescent son and supplies alcohol to his son and his son's peers. The boys get very drunk and then drive their cars while drunk. The son crashes his car and is injured severely.

An adolescent boy has a peer who is a rival for his girlfriend. The boys are hunters, and the boy plans to rig up the rival's shotgun so it will go off and injure him. The father learns about this and helps the teenager do this deed, and indeed the other boy is severely injured.

Here's the question: which of those fathers should feel most guilty and remorseful? And which next most?

Here's the second question: suppose that the first daughter had been severely injured, but suppose that by luck, the boys in vignette #2 all drove home safely, and suppose the evil deed planned in vignette #3 didn't work and no one was hurt. Now who should feel most guilty?

Probably most people, myself included, would answer these questions by saying that regardless of the outcome, the third father is most guilty, the second is next most guilty, and the first is least guilty.

What's the principle that's involved here? It might be phrased this way: you're guilty depending upon your intention and motivation and not just the outcome of your action. The third father intended to do direct physical harm. The second father intended to be an accomplice to a crime of driving under the influence of alcohol, but did not directly will anyone's getting hurt. The first father only intended for his daughter to have a good time and get some good exercise.

The ways things turn out are partly because of our choices and partly because of luck or random chance. It's good to have our consciences deal with the choice portion, and not with the luck portion. We try not to feel guilty about things that are beyond our control, as sad as we might feel about those things.

The father in the first vignette would rationally feel very sad that his daughter had been hurt in the ski lift accident. It would be very natural for him to wish that by luck he had, for some reason, forbidden the trip. But it would not make sense for him to punish himself and get down on himself too much, because he made a decision with a positive expected outcome, given the information he had.

How does someone develop a more powerful conscience, if that person has become desensitized to having guilt about harming people, or somehow has never had much of an ability to feel guilt?

The person with guiltlessness has a problem similar to that of the person with fearlessness. He needs to work very hard to let the reasoning part of the brain do what the feeling part of the brain can't do well.

People with adequate guilt feelings would simply have a very strong emotional signal that says, "No! I couldn't harm someone else in that way!" But the person with too little guilt must go through more complicated steps. He must think, "This is a harmful act I'm contemplating. This is contrary to my values of trying to improve the world as much as possible. (Or even, this is contrary to my goal of self-protection.) Therefore I must not do it, even though I would not feel particularly guilty about doing it."

The reasoning part of the human brain is so powerful, that it's possible for people to make up for fearlessness or guiltlessness by calculating well. The difficulty for most people with fearlessness or guiltlessness is finding the motivation to do so.

All of the steps suggested in the previous section for developing carefulness skills are also useful in developing conscience skills. Both involve a process of sensitizing oneself to the possibility of harm and cultivating one's tendency to avoid harm. Carefulness is avoiding harm to oneself, and conscience is avoiding harm to others.

Another suggestion for the person who wants to cultivate a healthy conscience is to avoid letting oneself be entertained by harmful acts. The best way to overcome a negative emotion is through repeated and prolonged exposure to the situation that brings out that negative emotion, and to do so in a way that makes the experience enjoyable.

These ingredients are the very ones present when one watches violent movies or plays violent video games. Scrupulously avoiding such exposures, perhaps combined with actively campaigning against them, can resensitize one who has become desensitized.

I began to avoid exposures to entertainment violence after becoming aware of the compelling evidence for their harmfulness to society as a whole. Over time, I gradually noticed a reappearance of some of the revulsion to seeing violent acts to which I had previously been somewhat desensitized. Is such a revulsion desirable? I believe so. In the words of the ancient philosopher, Lao Tsu:

Weapons are the tools of fear;
decent people will avoid them
except in the direst necessity
and, if compelled, will use them
only with the utmost restraint.
Peace is their highest value.
If the peace has been shattered,
how can they be content?
Their enemies are not demons,
but human beings like themselves.
They do not wish them personal harm.
Nor do they rejoice in victory.
How could they rejoice in victory
and delight in the slaughter of others?
They enter a battle gravely,
with sorrow and with great compassion,
as if they were attending a funeral.

Group 4: Honesty

There are two skills in this group. Skill 19, honesty and dependability, has to do with not deceiving other people and with fulfilling promises to them. This skill enables other people to count on you in all their dealings with you.

Skill 20, awareness of one's own abilities, has to do with honesty with yourself. It's very difficult to be honest with yourself about the basic question, how good am I at this or that? What are the positive and negative examples of my skills in this area? Sometimes people who are very courageous in other areas do not have the courage to look this question straight in the eye.

Skill 19: Honesty and Dependability

Honesty and dependability are two somewhat different skills. Honesty is telling the truth and not deceiving people; dishonesty is lying, cheating, or stealing. Dependability is keeping your promises; lack of dependability is telling people you will do things and then not doing them.

Some people think that if children can learn not to lie, they are protected from getting into habits of any other sort of antisocial behavior, such as aggression, stealing, drug abuse, and so forth.

Why is lying so central to all other antisocial behavior? Because people don't like antisocial behavior and they tend to make you pay the consequences for it. You have to lie to escape the consequences for bad actions. If you never lie, you anticipate taking the consequences for any bad action you carry out, and usually it isn't worth it.

A wise observer once said that all human neurosis was based on the refusal to accept the truth of the proverb: "You can't have your cake and eat it too." Actions with benefits often have costs as well. You must often decide between dilemmas. You can enjoy eating the cake, but the price is that you won't have it any more. A person can enjoy getting a good grade on a test, but the price is that he will have to work hard. Someone can enjoy having a new computer, but the price is that he will have to pay money. A man can go out and gamble away money, but one price is that his family will be angry with him. You can win a game, but the price is that you have to practice enough to get better than your opponent.

When people lie and cheat, they try to have their cake and eat it too. The person wants a good grade on a test without paying the price of studying hard, so he cheats. Someone wants a computer without paying the money, so he steals it. Someone wants to gamble but wants his family not to be angry with him, so he lies about where he was. Someone wants to win the game without having worked hard enough to become better than the opponent, so he cheats at the game. In all cases, the person wants to have the cake and eat it too.

But there is a larger price that gets paid by lying, cheating, or stealing. Getting something without paying the price is a very seductive experience. It can very rapidly be habit forming. The price of dishonesty is that you develop the habit of more dishonesty. And if someone is dishonest often enough, it becomes almost certain he will get caught at it.

A relationship in which one of the parties has been discovered in a major lie is probably permanently changed. Once the precedent of truthfulness in a relationship has been broken, trust can sometimes never be fully regained. If trust is regained, it usually requires quite a long time.

Why is it so difficult to regain trust after a major lie? Part of the problem is that it's never possible to verify most of what other people tell us. If you discover that someone is lying on something you can verify, you lose confidence in the vast number of things that you can't verify.

The practice of lying has a long-term effect on the person doing the lying: the emotional aversion to lying gets desensitized.

The word "desensitization" means getting over a negative emotion that's connected with a certain type of situation by exposing yourself to it for a long time. When someone with a fear of public speaking gives many speeches, she usually desensitizes her fear. Similarly, the more you lie, the more you get over the feeling of shame, guilt, or fear you previously associated with lying.

Lie detector equipment measures bodily indicators of emotion. Lie detectors only work when people have an emotional aversion to lying – when lying makes them feel nervous, scared, worried or some such emotion. But, because the emotional response to lying can become desensitized, no lie detector works very well. The emotional aversion to lying is a large part of what is called conscience. The more you lie and get away with it, the more you lose your conscience.

The aversion to lying serves a very important purpose. Suppose you're in a situation where there's a short-term gain in doing something dishonest, but a possibility of very bad consequences in the long term. This is the classic situation where delay of gratification is called for. For the person who has negative emotion associated with lying, it's much easier to delay gratification, because it doesn't feel good to do the dishonest thing. But if you've desensitized that aversion, it becomes much more difficult to delay gratification. All of this is simply to say that one breaks down one's personal precedent of honesty at great peril.

When people weigh the risks and benefits of a dishonest act, if they do so at all, they usually don't take into account the effects of the act upon their own habit of honesty. Taking these effects into account can tip the balance to make a clear decision that the honest choice is the better one.

We have spoken earlier of Kant's categorical imperative: "Act on principles you wish everyone would use." It's hard to imagine someone would prefer that other people lie to them rather than tell them the truth. Most of the decisions we make rely on information obtained from other people. Therefore, to doubt the truthfulness of all information from other people makes decision-making – and life – very difficult. The person who wishes to lie but wishes other people to be truthful is wishing for a free ride on the custom of truthfulness. That person wants to benefit from others' truthfulness but not follow it himself. This is a fundamentally selfish position. One can't follow Kant's categorical imperative and be a liar.

How do people promote the skill of honesty in others? This skill involves not only feeling good about telling the truth, but also feeling bad about lying. To some extent, conscience is conditioned fear. Thus, honesty skills are fostered by growing up in an environment where almost all dishonesty is found out, resulting in very unpleasant consequences. Cultures that react to dishonesty with a great deal of shame and social rejection are much more likely to foster honesty than cultures that believe all people are OK, whether they lie or tell the truth.

On the other hand, a very punitive and unforgiving attitude toward lying dictates that lies can't be admitted. And punitive and unforgiving attitudes are perhaps as undesirable as lying itself is.

Parents sometimes foster lying quite readily when they ask who is responsible for a bad outcome and punish anyone who confesses. Here honesty is punished, and lying goes unpunished, and this fosters lying.

Reward and punishment contingencies are not the only factors in developing honesty versus lying. Also important is cultivating a strong belief system in which honesty is given a very high value and dishonesty a strong

negative value. People are more likely to adopt this value if it is strongly held by the members of one's support system, family, and community.

Is it ever ethical to lie or deceive? Unfortunately, for those who would like simple answers to ethical questions, lying is sometimes the most ethical choice available. If Nazi police were looking for people to put in concentration camps, which is better: to hide those people in your house and lie to the soldiers who are looking for them, or to tell the soldiers the truth when they ask if you know where they are?

Here the outcome in human happiness and human suffering is so strong in favor of lying that the breaking of the precedent against lying looms relatively small in the risk/benefit equation. The rule of doing as much good (and preventing as much harm) as possible in circumstances like this takes precedence over the rule against lying.

How does one practice the skill of honesty? Honesty skills are a special case of self-discipline skills, and they can be practiced with fantasy rehearsals just like other self-discipline skills. Here's a series of steps for the person who wants to work at his own honesty skills.

First: Make a list of situations that have led you to be dishonest in the past. Spend lots of time recalling those situations and writing them down. Make up other situations that are similar and any you can imagine that could happen in the future. Try to assemble a very large situation list. Here are examples of such situations:

1. I find an expensive jewel on the ground; I think I know who lost it. I could keep it or return it to the rightful owner.

2. I have accidentally broken something very expensive. No one has seen me do it. I am asked how it got broken. I could lie or tell the truth.

3. A cashier accidentally gives me the wrong change that is many dollars in my favor. Do I take it and walk away, or tell truthfully what happened?

Second: Having listed those situations, decide not only what you would like to do if these situations should come up again, but also decide how you would like to think and what you would like to feel. The thoughts you choose might include an "internal sales pitch" for honesty. The thoughts should remind you that choosing to be dishonest in this instance will set a precedent for your future dishonesty. And the thoughts probably should include some readiness to do some appropriate awfulizing and getting down on yourself if you're dishonest. The desired feelings should involve readiness to feel guilty if you're dishonest and readiness to feel very proud if you're honest.

Third: You repeatedly rehearse in fantasy those situations and the desired response to them. You can do this aloud, in writing, or just in imagination. Within the fantasy, you celebrate doing the right thing. After the fantasy is over, you are deserve to celebrate in real life for logging in another fantasy rehearsal.

The skill of dependability

Agreements and promises between people make the world go around. People constantly make agreements with one another. A husband promises his wife, "I will be home by 6:30 to take care of the kids so you can teach your night class." A child promises her father, "I will go outside just to get the mail, but I will come right back in." A businessperson promises another, "If you drive these oranges to our store, we'll pay you for them when you get here." A construction person tells someone, "I can finish building the addition onto your building by October 10."

What happens when people don't keep promises? The wife who is counting on her husband to come home and take care of the kids waits frantically, trying to decide whether to cancel her night class and break her own promise to be there, or to take her two small children along. The parent who expects the child in from getting the mail becomes scared when the child doesn't return, and makes frantic phone calls until he discovers that she decided to drop in on a friend. Or suppose the person who has driven a giant truckload of oranges 500 miles hears the store person say, "Oh, I'm sorry. We can't buy them; we changed our mind."

He becomes frantic, knowing that a market for these millions of oranges has to be found quickly before they all spoil. The person in the building schedules an important meeting for October 16, counting on the contractor's promise to be done by October 12, only to find that the space is still half built and still unusable. The person holding the meeting becomes frantic, knowing that other people were counting on being able to meet there.

People count on promises' being fulfilled because they very much need or want whatever is promised. When the promise is made, they make their plans accordingly. When the promise is not kept, they usually become very angry, because they have been very greatly disadvantaged.

Some people are not dependable because they are liars. Suppose a certain bidder on a job says, for example, "I can get this job done for you by October 10." But this bidder knows he cannot get it done by then; he is making a calculated lie. He knows that once you give the job to him, you're not going to back out if the job is completed late. Or someone says, "If you'll lend me this money I'll pay it back within two weeks," knowing that he has no intention of ever paying you back or seeing you again.

But some people are not dependable, not because of dishonesty, but because of disorganization. For example, a bidder for a job says, "I can get it done by October 10," and he really be-lieves that he can, but he underestimates the length of time it takes to do everything, even when it's not in his own self-interest.

Sometimes people are not dependable because of low assertion skills. Someone says, "Can you do this for me?" And the person, afraid to say no, says, "All right, I'll do it," temporarily using the defense of denial to convince himself that he really can do it. But he has accepted so many other jobs that he doesn't have time to do this one, and he has to renege on his promise once he can't deny the fact that the time just isn't there.

Dependability and honesty are the most valued traits in employees. Bosses love to have employees who keep their promises – those for whom they can feel very confident that they can believe the statement, "I will do this, or else let you know immediately if unforeseen things keep me from doing it." With employees like this, the boss can delegate certain responsibility to the employee and turn his energies to other things, knowing that the job will either get done or that there will be a report about its not getting done.

When such dependability is not there, then the boss has to remember when the task should be finished, go inspect the job at that time, check on whether it was done right, and take action when it isn't done. This often involves more work than simply doing it oneself. Even more often, it involves more work than firing the undependable employee and finding someone else more dependable. Thus, if being employed and producing an income is important, people would do well to cultivate dependability.

The importance of dependability is even greater for spouses than it is for the employer-employee relationship. Spouses count on each other not only to do the work that they promise each other to do, but also to be responsible in saving or spending money, to be responsible in caring for children, to avoid giving each other venereal diseases, to avoid humiliating each other in front of other people, and countless other things. When choosing someone to marry, a very important criterion should be, "To what extent does this person keep his promises?"

Part of the skill of dependability is feeling a strong sense of obligation once a clear promise has been made. This necessitates feeling some displeasure, some shame, embarrassment or guilt, when you don't keep a promise. People differ greatly in the contingencies they set up for themselves when they make a promise. For some people, saying, "I'll meet you at a certain time and place" means, "If I should forget about this, I would feel absolutely mortified." For other people, the same statement means, "If I should forget about this, then I suppose I'll have to reschedule for a different time." The person who feels strong mortification at breaking a promise gives himself an incentive to deliver on the next one.

As always, it's important to keep a healthy balance in how much pain and suffering one wants to inflict upon oneself. It certainly isn't healthy to feel suicidal over showing up ten minutes late for a lunch appointment. On the other hand, it's quite maladaptive to be able to forget totally about an appointment with someone and to feel no negative feelings whatsoever. A readiness to awfulize and get down on yourself at least a little bit when you break a promise is the mark of a healthy person.

Skill 20: Awareness of Your Own Abilities

The skill of awareness of your own abilities means accurately assessing your strengths and weaknesses.

I've mentioned that happiness is easiest to find in situations where the degree of challenge is well matched with your skill in handling the situation. Too much challenge relative to skill results in panic or frustration. Too much skill relative to challenge results in boredom or a feeling of wasting your talents.

With accurate knowledge of your skills and abilities, you can try to insert yourself into situations where you find that magical match between challenge and skill. By finding such a match, you'll not only enjoy yourself more; you'll also maximize your chances of increasing your skill.

Some people are confused by the notion of self-esteem. Some people believe that having high self-esteem is incompatible with thinking, "I'm not very skilled in this area." Some people seem to believe that having high self-esteem means you have to say, "I'm great in this," even when you're not.

But self-esteem, as a desirable trait, is probably best thought of as the desire to make oneself happy, to create a good life for oneself. If I want myself to enjoy life, that in no way rules out my belief that I'd make a lousy football announcer and an even worse football player. It doesn't rule out my belief that I'm not the best at anything. Although I may want to be extremely competent, even if I turn out to be an average, ordinary sort of person, I still deserve to be happy and occupy my place in the world.

The more you can accept your own imperfection, the more you'll be able to face the truth about what you're good at and bad at. The truth shall set you free. It's better to know that you're relatively unskilled in a certain area for several reasons. One is that you might feel more like working to improve yourself. Another is that you don't take on tasks that are doomed to failure by deceiving yourself into believing you're more competent than you are. And the third is that, by accurately knowing your areas of weakness, you can achieve humility.

Humility is classified in this skill area. Humility isn't a false devaluation of one's abilities, but rather the accurate perception that no one is great at everything. There's someone else who's better than you in almost every enterprise worth being competent in. Even if you're the best in the world for the time being, you will not remain at that pinnacle for long. The ravages of aging and mortality inevitably displace the reigning champion in any skill.

This psychological skill also involves the ability to know which environments you function well in and which environments you function poorly in. If you can find a niche where your strengths are harnessed and appreciated, and your weaknesses are not a big problem, you may be able to live your whole life happily without ever having to raise your performance in your areas of weakness to an average level.

Some people, for example, find themselves so fascinated and thrilled by chemistry, electronics and machines that they're able to work productively and joyously for nearly all their waking hours in these areas. But if they have to function in a social situation with a group of unfamiliar people, their oddities and eccentricities get them in trouble, or their inability to socialize well causes them pain.

Should they spend many hours working on social skills? Or should they find happiness by avoiding the situations that are most difficult for them and by exploiting their strengths? Exactly what balance there should be between finding a niche and improving one's weakness is something for each person to decide. But accurate knowledge of strengths and weaknesses helps in either case.

Being skilled or unskilled in a certain area involves many dimensions – even more than the sixty-two that form the focus of this book. Within the arena of social conversation, for example, perhaps a certain person has extremely good social interactions when he's with one or two other people and

thoughtful conversation is going on. The same person might not function nearly as well and be very uncomfortable in large, party situations. Knowing this about himself allows him to either avoid parties or to become more skilled at handling them. He can play to his strengths or work at reducing his weaknesses.

Some people function best in environments where there's low social stimulation and few interruptions by other people. These people would be quite happy being authors, spending lots of time writing in a room by themselves, or being researchers putting in lots of time alone in a laboratory. These individuals might be driven nearly crazy if they had a job as a worker in a hospital emergency room, where interruptions and multiple tasks that need to be prioritized are the rule rather than the exception. These people might also find great unhappiness as a teacher in a classroom with many young children.

Some people like risk, and others hate it. People who like the thrill of the danger of high stakes decisions would do better in the hospital emergency room or in entrepreneurial aspects of business where lots of jobs and money are at stake. Other people would find themselves unable to sleep at night if they were involved in such high-stakes operations.

Some people prefer their repertoires to be preprogrammed; others want to constantly reprogram themselves. If you're a reprogramming type, you might enjoy working with an improvisational drama troupe; if you're a preprogrammed type, you might be happiest putting in a thousand performances as the same character in a long-running play. The preprogrammed type might enjoy doing the same surgical procedure over and over again each day; or the reprogramming type might be happier doing research on new surgical procedures.

Some people are much better and some people are much worse than others in skills such as memory of spatial patterns, memory of vocabulary words, memory of musical pitches and rhythms, the ability to understand complex syntax, and so forth. The more you understand and accept your strengths and weaknesses, the more you can harness your strengths.

It's interesting to speculate on this: how much of the world's failure and incompetence comes from mismatches between people's talents and the situations they're in, as opposed to people's low talents across the board? How much comes from people's having inadequate training? All three types of problems, I would guess, contribute greatly.

But the mismatch problem is a sad one. Many people have not been well suited for success in school, but have managed to thrive and blossom once they got into a situation outside school, fixing cars, making inventions, or running businesses. But many others probably get so demoralized by school

that they feel they're not good at anything, and give up trying to find their niche.

Being aware of your own abilities is also the opposite of a pattern some people have, in which their self-concept swings wildly between grandiosity and a feeling of worthlessness. For example, a person experiences successes and feels he can do anything and his greatness is unlimited. But then, when he experiences a few failures, he feels that he can't do anything right.

Both of these perceptions come from overgeneralization. The person is unable to see the entire data set of his performances. Instead, he focuses on a subset of the data and exaggerates its significance.

Sometimes this pattern comes from the core belief that "To be anything but the best is horrible and humiliating." The successes lead one to believe that one can be the best; the failures cause this belief to come crashing down. The replacement belief that's more reasonable goes something like, "The better I am at this skill, the more I'll like it. If I'm good enough to help people and increase the happiness of the world, there's certainly no reason to feel bad."

Two other problems can cause these great swings in self-concept. Some people have a desperate need to be liked by others because of great fear of aloneness and abandonment, coupled with a great fear of having to trust and depend on another person. Thus, there's great conflict about being in relationships. There's a desperate need to see oneself as likable. When someone else gives signs of liking these people, they can feel on top of the world and worth a million; then, when the other people reject them or criticize them, their notions of their own worth come crashing down.

The belief that causes trouble here is something like, "I'm a worthless piece of garbage unless someone else (or perhaps, unless all the right people) really like me." A more helpful belief runs more like this: "It sure is more pleasant to have friends than not to. If I'm not good at making and keeping friends, I want to work on those skills. But until I have more people who like me, I can still survive and contribute to the world and even enjoy life."

Group 5: Fortitude

The joyousness group had to do with taking pleasure in the desirable situations we find ourselves in (or get ourselves into). The fortitude group is the other side of the coin: how do we handle it when the going gets tough? How do we handle undesirable outcomes?

There's a lot to learn about the general skill of handling unwanted events as well as about handling specific types of undesirable situations: separations, rejections, criticism, your own mistakes and failures, someone else's getting what you want, having bad feelings, and having unwanted mental images.

The central idea for coping with all these situations is to get tough, to handle them by something more constructive than wailing or whining or having a tantrum. The idea is to handle them with the brain engaged and with one question foremost in that brain: how can you make things turn out best? In other words, what's your best strategy? How can you take this unpleasant situation and make the most of it?

Skill 21: Fortitude, Frustration Tolerance

Fortitude, or frustration tolerance, is the ability to behave rationally and to feel reasonably OK despite adversity. It's dealing with unwanted situations, stressor situations, everything from not getting your way in a minor way to handling major tragedy.

In speaking about frustration tolerance we're not speaking about tolerating the emotion sometimes called frustration. We're speaking about things that happen that we wish had not happened. Those events are called frustrations, and our ability to handle them well is frustration tolerance.

Let's think of two ways of handling frustration badly. One way is by feeling too bad about the frustration, and the other is not feeling bad enough.

A person with poor frustration tolerance of the first sort might have a tantrum when things don't go right. She might yell at other people, get physically violent, or might get very sad and cry and wail and ask for nurture from other people. If she puts on these displays of feeling bad too often, other people will get tired of them and will turn against her.

The story of "The Boy Who Cried Wolf" reflects this pattern. In this Aesop's fable, a boy who was watching the sheep called out that a wolf was upon him and got people to come running to help. When this happened a couple of times with no wolf there, the people learned to ignore the boy's distress calls. Then, when finally there was actually a wolf, they still ignored the distress, and the sheep (and in some versions the boy) were eaten by the wolf.

This story illustrates the fundamental fact that negative emotions have social functions. Displays of anger give the other person the message that he should stop frustrating you. Displays of sadness and distress tell other people they should take care of you. Crying, for example, a built-in communication a child uses before he even learns to talk, says, "I'm experiencing frustration; please nurture me."

Display of negative emotions, are sometimes well described as acting out the need for nurture or acting out anger. A tantrum asks the other person to solve your problem, to give you what you want, either from fear of your anger if you're a powerful person, or from pity of you if you're the less powerful person.

Thus, negative emotions send signals to other people. They serve a second purpose: to send signals to oneself. Bad feelings tell us, "A problem is present! This problem needs to be solved!" The negative emotion not only signals that the problem is present, but provides a motivation to solve it, to make the negative emotion go away.

Suppose I see a little lump growing on my body, and I begin to feel scared that I might have cancer. My fear mobilizes me to go to the doctor and get the lump diagnosed. If the lump really turns out to be cancer, and it's caught early enough, my negative emotion has probably saved my life.

This brings us to the second way of handling frustration badly: by not feeling bad enough about it. Millions of people have noticed cancerous lumps but have said to themselves, "Oh, it's nothing. I won't worry about it." Some have paid with their lives for their lack of concern.

To give another example, a small group of people lack the capacity to feel physical pain. Far from being lucky, these people tend to burn, cut or otherwise hurt themselves badly, because they lack the pain signals that would tell them to change whatever is hurting them.

To give a very different example, a woman is married to a husband who is very verbally abusive. He often shouts obscenities at her over little things. She tries to be stoic, and actually succeeds in not making herself feel very bad about his behavior. But later she realizes that, by tolerating his behavior and not seeking to either change it or escape it, she has lost many years when she could have been much happier.

Here's another example. A couple has a son who is very aggressive, bullies other children, and cannot make friends. They tell themselves, "Boys will be boys," and manage not to feel very bad about it. Later they realize that, if they had become more distressed and had sought help, they could have affected his life for the better.

People who don't feel bad enough about unwanted situations or who don't mobilize themselves enough to deal with them often find it useful to "get in touch with their feelings," or to stop using defenses that keep them from feeling bad about bad. The people who feel too bad about unwanted situations need techniques that will let them turn down the negative emotion.

In many cases, a certain degree of negative emotion brings out the best performance in handling the problem situation. A group of researchers expressed this finding in what has been called the Yerkes-Dodson curve. This curve is a graph of how well a person performed a task as a function of how much anxiety the person felt. The curve forms the shape of an inverted U. That is, as anxiety increases, the person's performance at first gets better. But, as anxiety increases still further, performance gets worse. Low levels of anxiety helping in solving the problem, but at higher levels, it interfered with it.

The ideal level of skill in fortitude is reached when our negative emotion about a problem situation is just high enough to be helpful in solving the problem. When the negative emotion grows so large that it interferes with solving the problem, the ideal is to turn the negative emotion down; when the negative emotion is too low to mobilize energy to solve the problem, the ideal is to turn it up.

Let's put the task of frustration tolerance in different words. The psychologically healthy person rarely "makes mountains out of molehills" by feeling too much distress over little things. However, neither does she "fiddle while Rome is burning," or ignore really bad problems that must be solved.

(The expression "fiddle while Rome is burning" comes from a certain emperor of ancient Rome named Nero who, according to legend, spent his time gleefully playing his violin and ignoring the empire's problems. Those problems were getting more and more severe, and the empire was in big trouble.)

Or here's another pair of useful contrasts: some people overreact to frustrations (by feeling too bad, by getting too excited); other people underreact (by ignoring the situation, by shoving it out of their minds).

Sometimes people underreact to frustration in order to keep themselves from overreacting! Let's recall the example of the parent whose child has serious problems with aggression, who tells himself, "It's OK. Boys will be boys." It turns out that, when this parent finally does acknowledge the child's serious problem, he feels very ashamed, guilty, distressed and depressed.

He then realizes he was denying the problem and underreacting in order to protect himself from the overreaction that occurred once he had acknowl-

edged the problem. For this reason, sometimes the same techniques that help people stop overreacting to frustration can also help them to stop underreacting.

So in part, the skill of frustration tolerance is feeling emotion that's not too much, not too little, but somewhere in the right range.

But that's not all it takes for good frustration tolerance. When frustrations happen, the most important thing is to figure out what to do about them.

Frustrations are problems to solve, and the big task is to pick, from all the available options, one of the best ones, and then do that option. If the frustration is a problem between two people, then good frustration tolerance means doing good joint decision-making. If the frustration is an individual problem, then fortitude means doing good individual decision-making.

In the section on decision-making we'll speak about the meaning of rationality: planning, predicting, and calculating in order to choose the option that will make things turn out best. Fortitude is hard to separate from those skills. We can think of fortitude as the skill that allows us to enter the frame of mind where we can use good decision-making and problem-solving skills.

Why is fortitude so important? Because frustrations happen so often. No one has everything go her way all the time. If someone is in the habit of feeling overly bad about frustrations, that person is making herself much more unhappy than she needs to be. If someone feels overly bad too often, she usually can't help making other people feel bad too. If someone can't figure out rational, reasonable responses to frustration, that person will be doing unreasonable things a good portion of her life. Fortitude can make the difference between a happy life and an unhappy one.

How do you get better at fortitude? A good first step is simply to notice how you're presently reacting to frustrating situations, heightening your own awareness of what is going on with you. In doing this, you might make use of the STEB matrix. STEB stands for Situation, Thoughts, Emotions, and Behaviors. Behaviors includes visible behaviors such as things you say and do, as well as less visible bodily reactions of tightening muscles, trembling, sweating, heart pounding, and so forth.

So when I am noticing and recording (either in memory or in writing) what goes on with me, I can record it according to these categories.

For example:

Situation: I'm playing baseball, and I strike out.

Thoughts: This is horrible; everybody is thinking I'm a total idiot. I can't do anything right. I hate myself for being such a klutz.

Emotions: Shame, anger, embarrassment, self-hatred.

Behaviors: I tighten up muscles. My body feels a pain going through it. I kick the ground, throw the bat, cry loudly, and scream at people and push them away when they try to comfort me.

Or for another example:

Situation: I'm taking a math test, and several problems seem impossible to do.

Thoughts: Oh my God. I'm going to flunk this. I don't have any idea how to do these. I can't do it. I'm terrible at math. Let me out of here! But I can't escape! This is terrible. I have the visual image of getting back a failing grade, everyone laughing at me and pointing at me, adults being angry at me.

Emotions: Anxiety, shame.

Behaviors: I tighten up. I do the flight or fight reaction: my heart pounds, my hands sweat. I can't keep my mind on the problems. I fidget and try to concentrate but can't do it.

In addition to recording what happened, you might also want to record how good a job of frustration tolerance you think you did. Here are two all-purpose rating scales. The first is for rating how much of something there is, for example, how much emotional distress.

0 = None
2 = Very little
4 = Some, but not much
6 = Pretty much
8 = High amount
10 = Very high amount

The second rating scale is for rating how good something is, for example, how good a job of frustration tolerance you did.

0 = Very bad
2 = Pretty bad
4 = So-So
6 = OK
8 = Pretty Good
10 = Very good

For example, I might rate that, in the strikeout situation, I felt bad 10 on a scale of 10 and I handled the frustration 0 on a scale of 10.

It takes great honesty and courage to be able to acknowledge to yourself that you're not very skilled at something, and the skill of fortitude is no exception. Recognizing how you really are responding to frustration is often a very difficult task. One thing to keep in mind is that the worse your performance is now, the more you'll have to be proud of later when you improve your frustration tolerance skills.

One of the challenges in filling out the STEB matrix is noticing the thoughts. These are sometimes called "automatic thoughts." These are both the words you say to yourself and the images you present to yourself in your mind. They tend to be slippery. That is, they may come into your mind and be responsible for your feeling bad or acting inappropriately, but when you try to remember them later, they've slipped out of memory. Often you need to make a conscious attempt to remember them if you're going to be able to hang onto them. But this effort may be greatly rewarded, because people often find that changing these thoughts is the key to changing emotions and behaviors.

In describing your emotions, it's good to be familiar with the set of "feeling words" in the language. Here are some of them.

Some "feeling words"

Positive: accepted, amazed, appreciative, amused, awed, attracted, calm, cheerful, curious, close, compassionate, confident, contented, elated, excited, free, friendly, glowing, sympathetic, grateful, happy, hopeful, jolly, light-hearted, liking, loving, moved, playful, pleasure, pleased, proud, relaxed, relieved, satisfied, self-assured, serene, silly, slaphappy, tenderness, thankful, tickled, wonder

Negative: afraid, angry, annoyed, ashamed, bitter, bored, bothered, burdened, drained, brokenhearted, confused, impatient, disappointed, disgusted, displeased, disturbed, embarrassed, envious, startled, fearful, frazzled, frightened, frustrated, guilty, harried, hate, hopeless, horrified, hurt, impatient, irritated, jealous, lonely, low, pain, rage, regret, resentment, scared, self-critical, shocked, terrified, threatened, tormented, troubled, uncomfortable, uneasy, unfriendly, unpleasant, upset, worried

Other: amazed, astonished, awed, bewildered, concerned, flabbergasted, indifferent, excited, pity, worn out, suspicious, stirred, wonder

It's useful to become familiar with feeling words, because being able to identify the precise one that describes what you're feeling can give you good clues about what you need to do. If you're feeling drained or frazzled, you usually need to take on fewer tasks. If you're feeling lonely, you usually need to get together with a friend, or make one. If you're feeling confused, you usually need to spend time figuring things out or to get someone to help you figure things out.

In recording the situation, sometimes the task is not as simple as in the two examples above. Consider this situation: you think someone thinks you're thinking something bad about him! Take your time and tell the story of the situation in as great detail as you need to, to express exactly what it is you're responding to.

If you get to the point where you can keep a log of exactly what the situation was, and what your thoughts, emotions, visible behaviors, and invisible behaviors or bodily reactions were, then you're doing something very important in gaining the skill of fortitude: you're thinking about frustrating situations at times other than in the "heat of the moment." This is the great key to developing fortitude.

If you wait until the frustration occurs to think about it, the emotion you're experiencing will usually be too great to think very rationally. However, if you can allocate some time to think about frustrating situations when they have passed and you're calm and cool, you can think rationally about them. With enough practice, you can transfer that rational thinking into the frustrating situation itself.

Why should you think about frustrating situations once they're finished? Sometimes people say, "It's water over the dam. I can't change it now that it's in the past. I don't want to think about it any more." But it's highly likely you'll experience a very similar frustration again in the future. The person who struck out at the baseball game will strike out again. Or, if he quits baseball, he'll make a similar mistake in another sport. Or, if he quits sports altogether, he'll make a similar mistake in a social situation. By thinking about frustrating situations in the past, you prepare yourself for handling frustrations in the future.

But just noticing what you're thinking, feeling, and doing in frustrating situations is only the first step. I sometimes refer to this as the step called insight or awareness. The next two steps are called redecision and practice.

Redecision means deciding how you would like to think, feel, and behave if a similar situation comes up again. For example:

Situation: I strike out in baseball.

Thoughts: Even Babe Ruth struck out lots of times. It's not the end of the world. I did get some hits other times I was at bat. Other people can handle this; they don't hate me. And if anyone is angry with me for striking out, he'll just have to get over it. I think maybe I was swinging too late; next time I'll swing earlier. I did my best even if I didn't connect. This is only a game. I want to concentrate on the rest of the game. If I can handle this frustration calmly, that will be a cause for celebration.

Emotions: Embarrassed only 4 on a scale of 10. Determined to do better next time. Curious about what went wrong. Proud of trying as hard as I could even though I didn't connect.

Behaviors: Put back bat, walk calmly back to bench, don't avoid people's eyes. If someone says "That's OK," say "thanks." If someone harasses me give him a quick glare or ignore him. I play as well as I can from here on out, without letting this get me down.

In deciding what thoughts you want to have about frustrations, it's useful to think about the categories I've listed several other times in this book.

Types of Thoughts:
Awfulizing
Getting down on yourself
Blaming someone else
Not awfulizing
Not getting down on yourself
Not blaming someone else
Goal-setting
Listing options and choosing
Learning from the experience
Celebrating luck
Celebrating someone else's choice
Celebrating your own choice

Most of the thoughts people have when they overreact to frustration fall into one or more of the first three categories: awfulizing, getting down on themselves, or blaming someone else. When people learn to react more rationally to frustrations, they do more of the next six: not awfulizing, not getting down on themselves, not blaming someone else, goal-setting, listing options and choosing, and learning from the experience. And when there's a positive aspect to the situation, they do well to acknowledge that positivity by celebrating their own choice, celebrating someone else's choice, or celebrating what happened to happen.

For example, when the person struck out the first time and thought, "This is horrible: everybody is thinking I'm a total idiot," that was an example of awfulizing. When he thought, "I can't do anything right. I hate myself for being such a klutz," that was an example of getting down on himself.

The second time, when he thought, "Even Babe Ruth struck out lots of times. It's not the end of the world," that's an example of not awfulizing. When he thought, "I think maybe I was swinging too late; next time I'll swing earlier," that's an example of learning from the experience. When he thought, "I did my best even if I didn't connect," that was an example of celebrating his own choice. When he thought, "I want to concentrate on the rest of the game," that was an example of listing an option and making a choice.

Not awfulizing, not getting down on oneself, and not blaming someone else are, in my definitions, not just the absence of awfulizing or getting down on oneself or blaming someone else. They are active thoughts that consciously decide not to think in the other ways.

So not awfulizing is something like, "I can handle this; I can take it; it's not the end of the world, even though I don't like it." Not getting down on yourself is something like, "I don't want to punish myself and make myself feel overly bad, even if I did make a mistake." Not blaming someone else is something like, "I don't want to keep running through my mind how bad the other person is, even if that person did do something I don't like."

Not blaming yourself or someone else doesn't mean you have to assign blame elsewhere. Given the universal human tendency to assign blame somewhere, this is often hard to remember. Thus, not getting down on yourself doesn't have to be "I didn't make a mistake; this wasn't my fault"; it can be, "I did make a mistake; it was my fault; but I want to put my energy into making things better rather than making myself feel bad." Similarly, not blaming someone else doesn't have to be, "It wasn't his fault"; it can be, "It was his fault, but I still want to put my energy into making things better rather than into blaming him."

Now that you have figured out how you would like to think, feel, and behave in the situation, the next stage is practice. Frustration intolerance is a habit. You have to practice handling the frustration in the new way enough times that you develop a new habit.

You can do this through fantasy rehearsal. I recommend doing fantasy rehearsals out loud. In this technique, you imagine yourself in the situation and describe it as though it's happening right now. Then you say aloud your thoughts and describe your emotions. You describe what behaviors you're doing as if you're doing them right now.

For example: "It's a real game, not a practice. I have two strikes on me. It looks like a good pitch. I'm swinging! Uh! I missed. I struck out. Well, I don't like this, but it isn't the end of the world. I'm putting the bat down and walking away calmly. I'm glad I didn't throw it, and I'm glad I'm keeping cool. What can I learn from this? I think I swung a little too late the last time. I'm visualizing swinging a little earlier next time. I'm feeling determined to keep doing my best. I hear someone saying, 'Don't worry about it,' and I look at that person and say, 'Thanks.' I feel good about using good frustration tolerance."

If you really want to get better at fortitude, it's well worth your time to do ten or twenty fantasy rehearsals out loud, every single day, for a long time. This is work, but it will pay off.

You can also visualize fantasy rehearsals without speaking out loud. You can do these at any spare moment of the day: while you're waiting for a bus, while you're waiting in line for a drink of water, while you're riding in a car. You visualize yourself in the frustrating situation, and you practice seeing and hearing yourself thinking the desired thoughts, feeling the way you want to feel, and doing the desired behaviors. You want to run the desired pattern through your neuronal circuitry as many times as you possibly can.

Here's another way of practicing that focuses on the thought patterns. Make as long a list as you can of frustrating situations. Then practice making up a thought in each of the following categories: not awfulizing, not getting down on yourself, not blaming someone else, listing options and choosing, learning from the experience. Imagine handling the frustration well, and then make up a thought that would be celebrating your own choice about handling it well. If you do this enough times, you will develop a reflex tendency to think in these ways when a frustration occurs.

If there are frustrations that can be acted out with other people, then you can practice, not only in fantasy, but also with role-playing. If you do this, you might practice saying your thoughts quietly.

If you would really like to get better at fortitude, you can get better at it if you do these exercises enough. It requires a lot of self-discipline to do these exercises, and this is why "many are called but few are chosen" to increase greatly their fortitude skills.

For many situations and many people, there is underreaction: the problem is not too much awfulizing, but not enough of recognition of how bad the situation is. There is too much tolerance of a bad thing rather than too little tolerance of a minor thing.

For example, highway deaths claim tens of thousands of lives per year, and many of these deaths would be preventable through lowering of speed limits and using checkpoints for drunk driving. But many people have the attitude that the people who are killed or severely injured have simply had bad luck.

More than one out of every ten males is alcoholic. Handguns kill thousands in the U.S. The interpersonal climate in many schools is very hostile and psychologically damaging toward children with handicaps in social skills. Millions of children suffer brain damage from malnutrition, while others feel deprived if they don't have the latest expensive toys. Population trends predict growing environmental problems. Children in many inner cities have high rates of illiteracy. These are the sorts of situations that most people seem to be too complacent about, in my opinion.

Thus, one goal to pursue in thinking about unwanted events is to rate their undesirability in a rational way, in a way that keeps perspective and sees them in relation to other unwanted events that are also occurring. The psychologically healthy person neither overrates nor underrates unwanted events. The psychologically healthy person makes some sort of priority list: here are the ones most pressing for me to deal with; here are the ones I can put on the back burner; and here are the ones too trivial for me to even worry about.

Many people, perhaps most people in the world, could greatly benefit from some concerted work on their fortitude skills. Yet very few actually do this work. One of the things that keep people from doing the work is a process of self-deception, of tricking oneself into believing the work is not necessary or there's no problem or everything is someone else's fault or the steps might work for other people but not for me. Often we trick ourselves in order to get out of feeling bad about something in the short run. Unfortunately, tricking oneself often keeps the problem from being solved and makes things worse in the long run. The person with good fortitude skills tends to see things as more the way they really are, rather than tricking himself to avoid feeling bad in the short run.

It's good to understand the ways of tricking oneself to avoid feeling bad. These are called defense mechanisms. Let's think about some of them.

Defense mechanisms

In adjusting to unwanted situations, we can trick ourselves in various ways. One defense mechanism is called repression. This means you simply shove out of your mind some portion of reality and forget that it's true. You do this without being aware you're doing it.

For example, someone rides in a car with a driver who, every once in a while, closes his eyes, drifts toward the side of the road, and opens his eyes with a start only when the tires hit the "rumble strips" on the side of the road. Because it's unpleasant for the person to admit to himself that the person driving the car is falling asleep at the wheel, the person shoves these incidents out of his mind and tells himself that everything is OK.

If the person actually forgets these incidents, he is using repression. Repression keeps the person from feeling fear for his life, and this makes the car ride more pleasant. However, if the driver has an accident and gets everyone killed, the distortion of reality brought about by repression has come at a very dear price.

So it is for many of the defense mechanisms: not admitting the truth makes things more pleasant, but the loss of information about reality can be quite harmful in the long run.

A defense mechanism that overlaps greatly with repression, one that usually requires use of repression, is called denial. When faced with a painful reality, someone simply won't admit to himself that it's true, even when there's overwhelming evidence that it's true.

For example, the parent of a teenager denies the possibility that her son could be using illegal drugs. This denial occurs in spite of extensive evidence: an unmistakable odor of marijuana often comes from his room; his best friends are known drug users; money flows from his budget without anything to show for it; there are bags of white powders that occasionally turn up when the room is cleaned.

Because it would be too painful for the parent to admit the reality that the child is using illegal drugs, reality is distorted. The parent goes on feeling good. However, if the adolescent suffers very bad consequences for the use of drugs, consequences the parent could have prevented by constructive action, then the parent's denial has occurred at great cost.

Another way of tricking yourself is called rationalization. Here, when you want to believe something, you make up some rational-sounding arguments to convince yourself of it, even if it isn't true.

For example, someone has very important psychological skill deficiencies to overcome. The person has the opportunity to work with someone who has a very high chance of helping him overcome these difficulties, and the person more than sufficient money and time to expend on the task.

But because making progress on these problems requires work the person doesn't feel like putting out, he says things to himself like, "I'm not doing so bad. It's not as if they have to lock me up in an institution. Plus, this is expensive. And it isn't fun. It would make me happier putting in the time doing something I enjoy more."

In this way he convinces himself he's doing a rational thing by quitting work on these difficulties. Although the rationalization makes him feel better about his decision, the price he pays is that he continues to have the psychological difficulties.

Humor is sometimes used as a psychological defense mechanism. Someone slips on a wet spill and falls in a cafeteria. All the person's food and beverages fall onto the floor. Everyone, including the person who fell, laughs, despite the fact that the person's hip is hurting and most of the people laughing wish this hadn't happened to him. The laughter takes something that's unpleasant and somehow transforms it into something that brings out emotions of gleefulness. In the short run, this defense makes everyone feel better, because the laughter is more pleasant than the real or empathic pain they would be feeling if they weren't using the defense of humor.

The ability to laugh and get pleasure out of mistakes, failures, and mishaps of various sorts is the basis of slapstick humor. What possibly could be pleasurable about someone's putting a pie in someone else's face? What could be pleasurable about a clown's knocking another clown down when he turns around carrying a big board? We learn to use humor to feel pleasure instead of pain. A family has a "vacation from hell," but gets a lot of pleasure later telling about it and laughing about the mishaps they had.

Yet humor as a defense is also not without risks and costs. Our society has manufactured countless slapstick cartoons in which people slam each other with sledgehammers, run over each other with steamrollers, and do all sorts atrocious acts of violence against one another for humorous effect.

But, when children are exposed to enough slapstick humor, the tendency to imitate violent acts takes hold in some of them. With enough entertainment through mishaps, the capacity to empathize with another person's pain, to feel that pain, and to seek to relieve it rather than take pleasure in it, begins to predominate the culture. A culture filled with people who are entertained by other people's suffering is, when taken to the extreme, a horrible and frightening culture. Taking pleasure from others' suffering is known as sadism, and it's the worst possible trait a human being can have.

Another healthy defense mechanism is known as suppression. We might think of suppression as repression with an alarm clock on it. In using suppression, rather than permanently shoving a bit of reality out of your mind, you shove it out of your mind temporarily.

For example, an adolescent has diabetes. She hates the idea of being abnormal and different from her peers. If she simply denied or repressed the fact that she had an illness, she might avoid getting her insulin shots at the right time, avoid doing blood tests at the right time, and avoid doing dietary restrictions and adjustments of insulin dose to diet, and all the other arduous tasks that are necessary to handle diabetes successfully. The use of repression and denial with an illness that requires frequent self-care can literally kill you.

On the other hand, if she uses suppression, she might literally set an alarm watch to go off at certain times and do the work at those times. The rest of the time she consciously shuts out of her mind thoughts of being different from other people. The price she may pay for this defense is a wrenching pain each time the alarm watch goes off and she has to reawaken himself to the reality of her status as diabetic. If she can avoid suppression, she may be able to desensitize herself to the negative emotion connected with that realization, and even take pride in the fact that she is living successfully with the condition.

Another defense mechanism is called avoidance. Here the person feels bad about – for example afraid of – facing a certain situation or task. Rather than confronting those bad feelings, the person finds himself avoiding the situation and does something else instead.

For example, someone has a great fear of failure connected with trying mathematics, based on past experiences of failure. The fear of humiliation would face her if she were to sit down and do her mathematics homework. So, instead she tells herself there's a very important basketball game being played among the neighbors and the mathematics homework can wait. Then a variety of other important tasks postpone the mathematics homework further until it doesn't get done at all.

The next day in class, she experiences more humiliation when she hasn't done her homework and doesn't know how to do the problems. When this continues for a while and she continues avoidance, she finally uses avoidance in a more drastic way by cutting math class altogether. Again, the defense mechanism in the short run protects against psychic pain, at a long-term cost. In escaping the pain, the person also loses the benefit of dealing with the reality of the situation.

People who gain a lot from insight-oriented psychotherapy often help themselves a great deal by understanding their own defense mechanisms. Coming to understand how you trick yourself and avoid dealing with a certain part of reality, and gradually getting brave enough to deal with that reality, is an experience that enriches the personality. But sometimes it's a mistake to try to get rid of defense mechanisms without having more healthy coping skills in place to deal with the situations you now have to face head on.

Let's talk about some of the healthy coping skills of dealing with unwanted situations.

Correctly estimating probabilities and utilities

What is meant by estimating probabilities and utilities? Our perception of danger or of loss is proportional to our estimate of utility – how good or bad a thing has happened, or will happen – and probability – how likely is it this thing has happened or will happen. For example, a very shy person estimates there's a 99 percent chance that most people at a party would dislike him; he also estimates this would rank 99 in badness on a scale of 1-100 if it were to happen. If these estimates are correct, then the person is in grave danger if he goes to the party.

However, when the person stops to think about the evidence, he recalls that he has no evidence that anyone he's met at a party has disliked him. He re-estimates the probability that someone would dislike him at about five percent and the probability that everyone would dislike him as close to zero. He also decides that, even if everyone at the party disliked him, he would still have all his previous friends and family members, and he would probably not see the people at the party ever again. Thus, having everyone at the party dislike him would be bad a maximum of five on a scale of ten.

When he re-estimates the probabilities and utilities on the basis of the evidence, he realizes he's not in anywhere near as grave danger as he thought he was, and he feels much better.

The beauty of estimating probabilities and utilities to be closer to reality is that it's the opposite of using a psychological defense. Rather than denying a part of reality or cutting oneself off to a portion of reality, one is actually getting more realistic in one's thinking. When reality is actually better than the fantasy we've created in our minds, acknowledging the truth makes us happier.

To give another example, let's return to the person with mathematics anxiety. The person contemplates working with a tutor. The person may feel that it's 100 percent certain he won't be able to understand any math, and that this is bad 100 on a scale of 100. If this is so, the person is in grave danger.

But when he re-estimates, he thinks as follows: "I may not be able to understand what the rest of the class is working on, but it's very likely that by working with the tutor, I'll come to understand some things I didn't understand before. If there are things I try to understand but can't understand, how bad is that? It just means I need to work on simpler stuff for a while. Even if I can never get it, that isn't the end of the world. Lots of people manage to be happy without understanding this much math."

The person also thinks, "It's good that I do have a tutor to work with me." This re-estimation of utility and probability allows the person to approach the tutoring with less fear.

Such re-estimation of probabilities and utilities is at the heart of cognitive therapy. It's another way of talking about moving from "awfulizing" to "not awfulizing" thoughts.

Broadening the limits of the rating scale

What happens when we deal with frustrations that are not trivial, and a realistic appraisal suggests these frustrations have very negative consequences? For example, a child is in an accident, and he gets an injury to his leg, which results in his leg's being amputated below the knee. To this child, this frustration probably rates 10 on a scale of 10 when he compares it to the frustrations he has experienced before and those experienced by his peers, his family members, and anybody else he knows. If someone were to tell him, "It's not so awful," he would, according to his own experience reply, "But it is awful!"

A maneuver people sometimes successfully use in such circumstances is one we may call broadening the limits of the rating scale. By the rating scale, I refer to the scale by which we rate the goodness or badness of the situations we encounter. By broadening the limits of the rating scale, I mean redefining what 10 on a scale of badness is.

For example, someone who previously had defined 10 on a scale of badness as having to get an immunization shot might broaden the limits of that scale to define 10 as having all family and friends killed due to something that was his fault. When the limits are broadened in this way, whatever you're facing doesn't seem so bad in comparison.

This maneuver, in my observation, works decidedly better when someone decides to impose it on himself than when other people push it on him. Suppose the person who had the partial leg amputation hears other people say, "Cheer up! Just think, you could have lost all of both legs! Or you could have been killed!" His reaction would likely be a good deal of anger, and a thought along the lines of "That's easy for you to say, when you're walking around with both legs feeling good!" However, if the person uses this same strategy on himself, rather than hearing it from others, it can be tremendously useful.

This strategy is like a psychological defense in that it tends to reduce psychic pain. But unlike the defenses I mentioned earlier, it doesn't distort reality but instead opens the person up to a new part of reality.

The child with the amputation might imagine the following: "Suppose I lived in a country that was suffering famine and dire poverty. Then suppose a war arose between the races. Every day there were brutal killings and tortures going on. Suppose my family and I were desperately trying to escape. It looked as if we would all be killed and I would be mortally wounded and left to die a slow and agonizing death. But no, we escape! My family lives and is healthy! We get to a world where war is not happening and dire poverty is not a problem! I get this wound where I lose part of my leg, but I get good medical care and a device that will let me walk!" When he imagines this, the predicament he has found himself in seems not so bad by comparison.

The general principle is that happiness is relative to some standard of comparison. For this reason, many people seem to get happier when their circumstances get better, but after a short time in the new circumstances, they adjust their expectations and go back to their old balance of happiness versus misery.

For example, a person who lives in the housing projects imagines she would be ecstatic if she could be living in the suburbs. Meanwhile, a person in the suburbs is angry because her house doesn't have a swimming pool. She thinks she would be thrilled to live in Beverly Hills. Meanwhile, a person in Beverly Hills with a beautiful house and several cars feels dissatisfied because her next-door neighbor is more beautiful than she is.

The people in this example are creating a rating scale where the bottom of the rating scale is their current status, and the top of the rating scale is the situation they would like the most.

The relative nature of happiness is communicated by the saying, "Do you see the glass as half full or half empty?" When given half a glass of something good to drink, you can feel pleased or disappointed. You feel pleased if you were expecting nothing and you have half a glass. You feel disappointed if you were expecting a full glass and only got half a glass. Your pleasure is relative to your expectations, your definitions of points 1 through 10 on your rating scale.

The fact that happiness is relative means we can set the scale points however we want to. We are limited only by our imaginations' ability to compare ourselves to other imaginary situations. Suppose we could all rate our happiness relative to that of the person who is totally paralyzed, can't talk, is in agonizing pain 100 percent of the time, and who lives with the knowledge that he caused the deaths of all the people he loved through an act for which he was totally responsible. If we could compare our happiness to his, I would imagine most of us would feel quite content with our own lot.

If this is true, why don't we all walk around feeling total contentment all the time? This brings us back to the point made several times before: negative emotions evolved for a reason.

They evolved to signal us that problems need to be solved, and to motivate us to solve those problems. The person who is dissatisfied with living in the housing projects and wants to live in the suburbs might have a very useful negative emotion if she can harness it to motivate her to plan and work to achieve the goal she desires.

But, when negative emotions don't help us achieve our goals, and just make us miserable, broadening the limits of the rating scale is one technique some people can use to reduce that negative emotion.

The same technique, by the way, can be used to increase dissatisfaction with current situations if that is useful. An interesting experiment is to spend some time imagining what it would be like to live in a human society where violence was totally nonexistent. What conditions would produce such a society? How would it feel to live in that society? What other problems would be solved? Spending time imagining this tends to make one less tolerant of the violence that goes on all around us today.

Seeing projects and sub-projects in perspective

Here's another healthy way of increasing frustration tolerance. People have the capacity to create in their minds memory slots for projects, sub-projects, sub-sub-projects, and so forth. While we're working on a sub-project, we often make ourselves happy or unhappy according to how the sub-project is going. But keeping things in perspective means being able to step back and look at the larger project and not just the sub-project.

Let's look at an example. Suppose I'm playing a basketball game. Temporarily, I feel good or bad depending on how the game is going. If the man I'm guarding moves into position for a good shot, I feel a little anxiety that motivates me to move quickly to cover him. If I hit an important shot that wins the game, I feel elated. If I were to blow that important shot and lose the game, I would feel very disappointed. I'm allowing my emotions to be ruled to some degree by this game, because I have made it a sub-project for a little while.

What difference does it make, in the grand scheme of things, whether I win or lose, do well or do poorly, in this game? Almost none. But I temporarily invest some feeling of importance in how this game goes. And that's good, because otherwise I'd feel little emotion one way or the other. I want to risk feeling bad in order to have chance of feeling good about it.

But then, if I do things right, at some point I step back and realize that this game is only a tiny project. This isn't my whole life project. When I realize this, I put things in perspective.

If I lose a game and feel bad about that, I might next realize that I've just played the best game I've ever played, and feel good about that. In do-

ing this, I'm moving from the project of winning the game to the project of improving my own skills in the game.

Or, suppose I lose the game, and I played just as badly as I always have played, but I did get some exercise, and I feel good about that. In doing this, I'm moving my attention to the project of being physically fit and healthy and thereby prolonging my healthy life.

Something wonderful about our brains is that we can view things from different perspectives, from the perspective of different parts of the whole life project. If we do things well, we return to the larger and more important projects, and we put things into perspective.

I once read of a sports fan who killed an athlete who made an error in an important athletic contest. This is an extreme version of failing to shift attention between the sub-project of the moment and the more important project of living life well. The person who did this horrible deed failed to answer the following question: what is the larger purpose of winning this game? Is it proving the honor of the tribe represented by the team? Is it having a good time? Is it modeling physical fitness and concentration skills? Any of these larger projects are obviously not served by punishing a player with any violence.

At other times, the skill of frustration tolerance is best served by shifting attention from larger projects to sub-projects. For example, a person devotes his life to trying to reduce violence. As he looks at the rates of violence, he feels justifiably disappointed about progress made toward his overall goal.

But this doesn't mean his whole life is unhappy. The person still feels proud about various sub-projects he has taken on. He feels good about having successfully taught conflict resolution to many children. He feels good about having contributed to a growing recognition of the harmfulness of entertainment violence. He feels good about providing a model for other people of dedicating one's life to a worthwhile cause. If he does frustration tolerance well, he will focus on the successful sub-projects enough to keep his morale and his zest for living high. He will also focus enough on the progress yet to be made to stay dissatisfied with the overall progress and to keep working.

Competence in listing options, making decisions

When something unwanted happens, the rational person starts to figure out what to do. The decision-making process involves generating options, predicting outcomes, and selecting the option predicted to work the best.

Here's the central idea of this section: The distress that an unwanted situation causes is far less when the person is competent to make and enact a good choice in that type of situation. Thus, learning how to handle various unwanted situations competently is one of the foremost coping methods in developing frustration tolerance.

For example, someone gets a flat tire where help is not available. The person who knows how to change the tire and has practiced this skill before will find the frustration much less distressing.

Or, some people find themselves lost while taking a trip. The person who is good at, and enjoys, map reading and navigating will find this situation much less unpleasant than the one who is incompetent at navigating.

When faced with the frustration of having to assemble records for income taxes, the person who has a very organized record-keeping system is much less distressed than the one whose record-keeping is in disarray.

A student experiences an unexpected quiz at school. The student who has prepared for it finds it much less distressing than the one who hasn't looked at the material.

A couple adopts a child, who throws major tantrums when he doesn't get his way. If they are expert in differential reinforcement, they'll be much less distressed.

A kid gets teased by people at school. If he knows various techniques for dealing with this, he is much less distressed than if he doesn't know what to do.

Some bad weather damages someone's house. She's much less distressed if she has lots of money saved up that will let her rent some other place temporarily and get the house fixed.

Most of the psychological skills you're studying in this book are competences required to handle certain frustrations well or to prevent them. For example, many of the frustrations of life are interpersonal conflicts. Many frustrations – for example losing things, forgetting things – can be prevented by being well organized. Many frustrations are separations from or losses of one's support system. Thus separation tolerance skills are useful.

One of the skills is competence in academic, job-related and recreational skills. The person who spends lots of time getting good at her primary occupation encounters fewer frustrations at work or school and is more competent to meet these frustrations when they come up.

People who are good at decision-making skills, for example, by being able to use libraries, computer data bases and expert consultants, is more able to handle the frustration of facing a difficult decision. The person who is good at the skill of building and maintaining a social support network will be better able to withstand frustration, because she can obtain information from other people on what to do.

Learning from bad experiences

The final skill on our list of healthy coping methods for frustration is learning from experience. People signal themselves to use this one when they say, "Let's chalk this one up as a learning experience." Every unwanted thing that happens presents an opportunity for some learning, either about how to handle that situation when it comes up or how to prevent that situation from happening the next time.

People who are worst at learning from experience repeat the same types of mistakes over and over again. People who are better at learning from experience usually learn from their own experiences and avoid repeating the same type of mistake too many times.

People who are best at learning from experience learn not only from their own experiences, but also from those of other people. They are able to take in information from friends and family members and from literature on the topic and to use the collected information of other people in decisions.

Often knowledge comes from a bad experience, knowledge that will help prevent the same thing from happening again, if not for oneself, then perhaps for someone else. This can salvage the situation in some way and allow good to come out of bleakest and worst experiences.

For example, parents who have had children killed by gun violence band together to work for nonviolence. Their learning about the paramount importance of nonviolence and the tremendous grief caused by violence is harnessed in the service of good. The learning gets translated into information for others to use.

Or for a more everyday example, bad experiences and feelings often motivate a person to learn a competence. A six-year-old girl is teased by an older girl because she doesn't know how to play baseball. The younger girl feels quite hurt by this. In response, she works, practices and learns and develops her baseball skills to the point where she is quite confident.

In another example, a child is laughed at in school when he misses a math problem. He harnesses the embarrassment and shame and uses these bad feelings to motivate him to spend many hours at home working on math, practicing, testing himself, studying, contemplating. He returns after doing this with confidence and a feeling of mastery. The person who's able to use work toward competence-development as a "defense" against bad feelings has a wonderful coping skill in his repertoire. To use this coping method requires a great deal of self-discipline and concentration skill and the ability to work hard and long.

One of the tasks of learning from the experience is avoiding over-generalization. Suppose the parent of the child who died by gun violence concludes, "Everyone of the same race as my child's killer is to be avoided." This is generalizing, extending a conclusion based on one case to other cases where it doesn't apply.

Or, as another example, a child who has been teased and belittled by classmates concludes, "It's best to stay away from other kids altogether; they're all cruel bullies." It's better to learn nothing from an experience than to learn something that isn't so.

To conclude this discussion of coping techniques for fortitude: there are two divergent pathways in handling unwanted situations. One path involves shutting oneself off to information, as through the use of defense mechanisms. In doing this, one blinds oneself to various aspects of the situation or how good or bad it is.

The other set of coping skills has to do with opening oneself up to further information. Becoming aware of better or worse situations for comparison, re-estimating probabilities and utilities, putting the situation in a different perspective, learning more about how to solve the problem now, learning more about it for the future – all these involve taking in new information, looking at things in new ways. Handling frustration by shutting oneself off to information constricts the personality. Handling frustration by opening up to new information expands the personality.

Skill 22: Handling Separation

The skill of handling separation is a close relative of skills in independent thinking, handling rejections, handling criticism, and enjoying aloneness. All of them involve finding some way of doing OK without another person's being with you or approving of you. This set of skills is balanced against skills of friendship-building or relationship-building.

We build relationships, we invest loyalty in them, we decide to trust, and in doing that we take a certain risk that the relationship is going to end in some sort of separation. Maybe the person we build a relationship with will move away. Maybe that person will die. Maybe that person will decide to end the relationship. Whenever there's a relationship, there's the possibility it will end before you want it to.

To some extent, having a loving relationship rules out being totally comfortable with separation. But the skill of handling separation doesn't work against the skill of building relationships. Sometimes the fear of separation or rejection gets in the way of building relationships. A person with low skill in handling separation might think, "I don't want to risk trying to become friends with this person, because she might reject me and not want to become friends, or we might become friends and then I might lose her. If either of those things happened I couldn't take it, so

I'll just play it safe and not try to become friends."

The person with better skill in handling separation might think, "I'll take the risk of trying to become friends. There's always the chance of rejection or separation, but I can handle that if it happens." Thus the person with better skills in handling separation is better equipped to form relationships.

Being able to handle temporary and permanent separations in relationships is a skill that's very important in preventing depression. By depression, I mean the state of mind where you don't feel good even when good things happen; you don't have much energy to make good things happen; you tend to have worse sleep and worse appetite; you don't feel like moving around much. Life feels pretty bleak.

Sometimes people get depressed for no apparent reason. But many other times, people get depressed when someone separates from them or rejects them, particularly when the person is very close and important. But people differ in their ability to handle separations without getting depressed. How people respond to separation depends largely on how skilled they are in handling separation.

Another reason to become skilled at handling separation is that some relationships are simply bad for you. For example, sometimes people find themselves in relationships with people who become violent when they get angry. Getting out of such a relationship can literally save your life. A person who is skilled at handling separation will be more able to leave a bad relationship.

Another reason to become good at handling separation is that you won't have to be a hostage to anyone who threatens to end your friendship because you don't do what she wants. For example, a girl has two good friends at school. The first friend starts to dislike the second one. The first friend tells the girl, "I'm not going to be your friend if you keep liking your other friend." If the girl who hears this has good skill in handling separation, she'll be more able to say, "I'm going to keep liking both of you. You can do what you want about being friends with me."

And another reason to develop skills in handling separations and losses is to be able to cope with the deaths of parents, grandparents, other relatives and friends. If you have pets, you'll have to handle their deaths. If you're going to have to do handle these deaths, you might as well learn how to do it in a way that preserves, as much as possible, your ability to serve others and experience happiness yourself.

These are some of the "whys" of developing good separation tolerance. Now, let's talk about some of the "hows" of developing this skill.

One strategy for separation tolerance is "not putting all your eggs in one basket." This means not having just one relationship that you depend on to meet all your needs for other people. If you have just one relationship, naturally you feel more devastated when that relationship ends. And you feel more scared when there's a threat the relationship will end.

Even when two people have a close and positive relationship, such as a couple happily married for a long time, it would be unwise for either of them not to maintain close relationships with other people. If this is unwise for spouses who trust each other very much, it's even more unwise for teenagers who have just recently formed a relationship with someone. Yet very frequently teenagers put all their eggs in the basket of one very intense relationship and thus feel devastated when that relationship ends.

One of the keys to separation tolerance is cultivating a support network. A strong support network will still be there even after a separation from a beloved person occurs.

Romantic songs often celebrate putting all the eggs in one basket rather than having a "diversified portfolio" of relationships. It sounds romantic to sing things like "You're my world, you're every breath I take," or "I can't live without you," or "If you leave I'll just die." It doesn't sound nearly as romantic to sing, "If you leave, I won't like it, but I can take it, with the help of my other friends." But what is romantic and what is smart are often two different things.

Sometimes people feel guilty about cultivating new relationships when they have lost someone they love, for example, by death. We have spoken before about the skill of loyalty and not simply going from one relationship to another in a fickle way. But if cultivating new relationships to make up for a lost one helps someone to be happy and to make others happy, it hardly seems wrong.

Now let's talk about applying the twelve thoughts to the skill of separation tolerance.

1. Awfulizing
2. Getting down on yourself
3. Blaming someone else
4. Not awfulizing
5. Not getting down on yourself
6. Not blaming someone else
7. Goal-setting
8. Listing options and choosing
9. Learning from the experience
10. Celebrating luck
11. Celebrating someone else's choice
12. Celebrating your own choice

Let's illustrate these thoughts with a situation involving separation. Suppose I have a friend who's going to move to a different state. This is an unwanted event, but there are several desirable aspects of this imagined situation. The friend is a very good letter writer and enjoys writing letters and I do too. The friend's family and my fam-ily both have money they're willing to spend on long-distance phone calls. The friend has family back in this region and therefore will probably be back here once or twice a year.

Now let's think about the types of thoughts in the table. Awfulizing means saying to yourself things like: "Oh, I can't handle this! This is the end of the world. I can't take this! This is horrible! This is awful! I can't stand this! This is one of the worst things that has ever happened to anybody in the whole world!"

Whenever anything bad happens to us, it's reasonable to estimate how bad it is, to think, "How much have I been set back by this?" When someone exaggerates how bad it is and overestimates how harmful it is, the person is awfulizing.

Not awfulizing, on the other hand, is not just the absence of awfulizing thoughts. Not awfulizing is thinking about how bad the situation is with a sense of perspective. Not awfulizing thoughts go something like, "I don't prefer this, but I can handle it." What would not awfulizing sound like in the situation of the friend's moving away? It would be something like: "I sure don't like my friend's moving, but I can handle it. Lots of worse things have happened to people." Awfulizing tends to make us feel awful; not awfulizing tends to make us feel not awful, even though we still might not feel good about the situation.

Getting down on yourself means saying things like: "I'm a worthless person. I'm such a bad person. I just don't have what it takes. I'm a loser!" What would getting down on yourself sound like for the person whose friend moved away? It would sound like this: "Everything I do goes wrong. I can't even pick a friend right! Why should I even try anything anymore? I'll just botch it up." Getting down on yourself makes you feel ashamed or embarrassed or guilty or depressed.

Not getting down on yourself is not just the absence of getting down on yourself. It's actively thinking something like: "OK. I don't like what has happened, but I'm not going to punish myself for it. That wouldn't do any good."

Not getting down on yourself doesn't mean you can't admit to yourself that you made a mistake. For example, suppose I'm trying dangerous ways of playing with a friend and the friend falls and gets hurt. Not getting down on yourself doesn't mean that you say, "I didn't do anything wrong. It wasn't my fault." Instead, not getting down on yourself means being able to say, "I did do something wrong. I did do something that was my fault. But instead of putting my energy into making myself feel bad, I want to put my energy into making things better." (We'll talk in a minute about the thoughts that help you figure out how to make things better.)

Blaming someone else means you think things like: "That other person is such a bad person. I can't stand him. He's so stupid. He can't do anything right. It's all his fault." Here's what blaming someone else sound like, with our example of the person moving away: "How could he do this to me? He shouldn't be doing this. I hope he gets hurt when he drives away." Blaming someone else tends to produce emotions of anger, hatred, disdain, and dislike.

Not blaming someone else is not just the absence of these blaming thoughts. It's actively saying things to yourself like: "Okay, this person did something I don't like, but is it a good use of my energy to get down on them and condemn them and think about how bad they are? I think it isn't. There are more constructive ways for me to spend my energy." Not blaming someone else, even when they make mistakes, tends to turn the mind toward responses that do not include punitive anger.

Goal-setting means you think about what you want to make happen. For example: "What are my priorities? I want to keep in touch with this person. I want to preserve our relationship. I want to keep feeling good. I want to feel OK about strengthening other relationships."

Listing options and choosing means you actively decide what you want to do to make things better. In our example: "Let's see, how can I make things better? I can try to persuade my parents and their parents to let us visit each other for a week during the summer. We can write each other often. We can call each other on the telephone often. We can send emails to each other. I could try to figure out why their family has to move and see if I can prevent it. I can make more friends. I can spend more time with some of the friends I already have. I can enjoy spending time by myself more. What do I think about the advantages and disadvantages of these? Which ones of these do I want to try at this point?"

This sort of mental activity is the skill of decision-making. Deciding what to do about an unwanted situation is a very constructive way of using your energy.

Learning from the experience is another constructive way of using energy. Let's imagine that the person in our example is a teenager who has put all her eggs in one basket with this one relationship. She has stayed away from other relationships and invested all her emotional energy into this one. When the friend moves away, if the person is learning from the experience, she might think things to herself such as: "I learned something from this. Next time I won't put all my eggs in one basket so much. I'll cultivate a support system of several different people. That way I won't feel so bad when one person has to move away."

Another part of learning from the experience is practicing in imagination the thing you have learned. Our teenager might imagine herself making and keeping more friends.

When we use the word "celebrating," we're not talking about having a party. We're talking about the celebratory thoughts that go on in your mind. When someone thinks, "Hooray, this is good," that's a celebration, even though no one can see it.

Celebrating luck means saying "Hooray" to yourself about things that happen, not as a result of anybody's choice, but by chance. For example: "I'm glad my friend happens to have some family in this area. That way they will be back fairly often." Or: "I'm glad the long-distance phone rates have gone down recently. It isn't going to cost nearly as much to keep in touch."

Celebrating someone else's choice means saying to yourself "Hooray," or something like it, about another person's choices or behaviors. For example: "I'm glad my friend's parents are reasonable and will give some consideration to a summer visit. I'm glad my friend has cultivated the skill of letter writing and staying in touch. I'm really glad my mother has been supportive and understanding about this."

Celebrating your own choice means recognizing the good things you've done and congratulating yourself for them. In our example, the person might say to herself, "Hooray for me. I handled this separation pretty well so far. I'm glad that I have earned the money it takes for me to make lots of long-distance phone calls. I'm glad I've cultivated the skill of writing letters. I'm glad I've gotten to be good at making new friends so I won't have trouble filling the void."

As a general rule, many people who overreact to separations overdo awfulizing, getting down on yourself, and blaming someone else. .

Handling losses, for example, the deaths of loved ones

It's good to love. It's good to form relationships where we care about the other person, where we want the best for her, where we will miss her when she's away, when we appropriately depend on that person to meet some of our needs. But how then do we deal with it if that person dies?

The first thing is to realize that it hurts. It feels bad. It's supposed to feel bad. How could you love someone and at the same time think, "I won't feel bad if this person dies?" Some people do stay out of relationships to avoid any chance of that sort of hurt. But staying out of relationships is a huge price to pay for avoiding the grief of a loved one's dying. Most psychologically healthy people are willing to pay the price of risking the pain of grief, in order to be in a loving relationship with someone. "Is it better to have loved and lost, than never to have loved at all?" goes the old saying. The answer, for most psychologically healthy people, is yes. We all have limited amounts of time to be alive. It's much better to fill that time with loving relationships than

to stay alone because we fear the grief that comes when those relationships end.

Many people assume that a person who cries and looks very sad after a loved one's death is not handling the situation well. Sometimes when deaths occur people will put off telling the bad news to loved ones, for fear of making them feel bad. These attitudes and behaviors overlook the fact that, when a loved one dies, the point is not to avoid feeling bad. Sometimes when people tell someone of the death of a loved one and that person cries and feels great pain, the person who told him feels guilty, as if he did something wrong by making him feel bad. Again, this overlooks the point that feeling bad at the death of a loved one is almost inevitable and not something to try to avoid.

Let's think for a minute about why such bad feelings at the loss of a loved one might be wired into the human brain. When you love someone, you want that person not to get killed, you want to keep that person safe, you want to keep the person alive and healthy. Let's imagine a tribe of people who don't fear the death of loved ones and who don't feel bad when loved ones die. One very important motive for their trying to keep the other person safe and protected would be gone. This tribe would probably not do as well at protecting one another from harm. Our fear of loved ones' deaths and our grief after they have died are feelings that motivate us toward trying to protect those we love.

Fear and grief evolved for a reason. Like almost all bad feelings, they exist partly in order to motivate us to do things that are good to do.

Bad feelings also serve another purpose. They send a signal to other people. Angry feelings, for example, send a signal to other people to stop doing something that makes us angry. Sad feelings often send a signal to others to nurture us, to try to be kind to us and make the hurt less.

So, to summarize what I've said so far, the person handling a loss should not feel that bad feelings are bad and shameful and must be avoided. They exist for very good reason.

On the other hand, it's usually not good to be so consumed with grief that you can't do anything else but feel bad for a long time. In other words, it's good not to be immobilized by bad feelings, at least not for long times at a stretch. You still have to tend to life. If you're making a living, you have to keep doing it. If you're taking care of other people, you usually have to keep doing that. If you're educating yourself, you usually can't put your education on hold for a long time. So it's good to be able to keep functioning, keep making good decisions, keep working. It's good to be able to be cheerful with people and to smile at them.

How do people do this, when the thought of the death of the loved one makes them feel so bad? What many healthy people seem to do is to put the thoughts about the loved one and her death out of their minds for a while, and let them return later. This is a "defense" against bad feelings: it's something the mind can do to make itself feel less bad. It's *suppression,* or temporarily turning your attention elsewhere. You concentrate on something else long enough to get it done.

So for example, if my loved one has died, but I need to help someone else with a different problem, I concentrate for a while on helping the other person. Or I concentrate for a while on paying bills or deciding how much a house should be sold for. It's not being disloyal to my loved one to concentrate on other things long enough to get them done.

But when I use suppression, there are times when I don't have to concentrate on anything. My mind can drift. Then perhaps my mind goes back to the loved one I have lost, and again I realize I can never be with this person again. My mind drifts back to pleasant times we had together, and I realize that those times will occur no more. Perhaps my mind drifts back to the image of the person's dying, and if it was a painful death, I feel pain too at imagining what my loved one may have felt. All these thoughts are painful ones.

When these painful thoughts drift back into the mind, over and over, for several months, something gradually happens. Sometimes people refer to it as *habituation* of the bad feelings. Sometimes people refer to it as successful grieving. What happens is that the loss stops being so painful. The mind somehow adjusts to the loss. No one knows exactly how this happens. Perhaps the mind gradually realizes that the bad feelings have served their function. The mind may say something to itself like, "I've felt bad enough for long enough that if these bad feelings are meant to motivate me to protect the rest of my loved ones, I certainly have that motive. So I can stop feeling so bad."

Maybe this habituation is the same thing that happens in the brain when people get over being afraid of something. If you want to get over being afraid of something that isn't really dangerous, the way to do it is to experience that something for a long time, without escaping from it. If someone is afraid of swimming, the way to get over that fear is to gradually get into a swimming pool and learn to swim. If someone is afraid of being on elevators, the way to get over that fear is to get onto the elevator and stay on it for long enough for the fear to go down. Similarly, if someone wants to get over being afraid to think about the death of a loved one, the way to get over that fear is to think about it.

One of the benefits of successful grieving is that you can have a full set of memories of the pleasant times you had with your loved one, and you can take pleasure in those memories. Perhaps those memories will always be "bittersweet" – perhaps there will al-ways be some sadness mixed in with the pleasure. But you can remember the loved one in great detail and relive the experiences with that person in your mind.

When I think about my own death, and I imagine *being* a loved one who has died, it feels a lot better to imagine that my loved ones will be able to think back with pleasure on the good experiences we had together, than to imagine that they can't think about those things. This is partly from unselfish motives – I want thoughts of me to make my loved ones feel good, after my death as well as before, for their sakes. And it's partly from selfish motives. If people can remember me, think about me and talk about me with pleasure after I'm gone, there's in a sense part of me that continues to be. It's a way of getting a little bit of immortality, being pleasantly remembered for at least a while. I may be dead, I can think to myself, but there will be a representation of me that will live on in the memories of the ones I've loved.

Sometimes people try to take suppression to the point where they *never* think about the loved one they lost. Then the defense mechanism, the thing they are doing in their mind to try not to feel so bad, is called *repression* or *denial*. Repression means that you actually forget about something painful. Denial means that you try not to let yourself believe that it happened; you immediately shove all thoughts of the loved one out of your mind whenever those thoughts come knocking at your consciousness. "I don't want to talk about it" and "I don't want to think about it" are the watchwords of the person who is trying to use these defenses.

Why not simply use repression and denial indefinitely, and shove painful thoughts out of your mind for the rest of your life? There are several prices that are paid by trying to do that, and those prices can be very large.

For one thing, the memories of the loved one tend to be destroyed. This is because we tend to forget those thoughts that we never rehearse in our minds. Thus the positive memories of the loved one tend to die with her, when we use these defenses too much.

Second, many people have a vaguely uneasy or anxious or gloomy feeling from knowing, deep inside themselves, that there are memories and thoughts they must try not to think about for the fear of feeling very bad. It's perhaps like having a "live" electric wire in your room and knowing you must not touch it for fear of getting shocked. You can't feel really safe in walking around your room.

Third, there may be times when the defenses break down, for example during sleep, and there are nightmares that remind us that something has not been dealt with.

And there's a fourth reason. The total amount of bad feeling may become much greater if someone often attempts and fails to shove it out of the mind,

than if the person went ahead and faced the painful memories.

Let's explain this fourth reason by giving an example that is similar. Suppose a child is afraid of going to sleep by herself in the dark. She cries and protests every night about going to bed; she refuses to go to sleep alone; she goes into her parents' room when she wakes up. She doesn't expose herself to the feared situation and goes on fearing it for months or years.

Then one day she decides to face the scary situation, and simply stay in her room in darkness by herself without escaping the situation. She has a hard time. She is more scared than usual, because she knows she isn't going to use an escape route. But she succeeds in doing it for a night. Then she finds that each time she does this, the fear gets rapidly less and less. Within two weeks she is going to sleep by herself in her room without fear. If she had been able to face the scary situation earlier, she could have saved herself months and years of fearfulness.

The phrase "getting over the hump" applies well to this situation. If you were to draw a graph of the girl's fear, once she decided to confront what she was afraid of, there would be a hump right at the beginning, when the fear rose. But as she hung in there and stayed with the scary situation, habituation took place. The fear went down. And it was downhill from there. She got over the hump.

Why didn't she do it earlier? Because the hump was in her way. She wanted to protect herself from the higher fear that was in the hump, and, in doing that, she couldn't get down to the region where there was no fear.

But the point is that confronting the fear long enough for habituation to take place results in a much smaller quantity of fear being experienced. The same thing happens whenever we do the work necessary to get over any other fear.

The same thing occurs when people let themselves do "grief work," that is, let themselves think about the loved one they lost. At first, this is much more painful than if they had used repression and denial and shoved all painful thoughts out of the brain. But once they get over the hump, they don't have to keep feeling that intense pain that comes every once in a while to remind them to shove something out of their mind again.

Thus, there are some good reasons to let yourself go ahead and think about the loved one you lost. In fact, sometimes a good way to grieve is to sit down and write down or tape record the memories you treasure the most. This may take a long time. But it allows you to assemble these memories in a permanent form and consciously protect them from the workings of repression and denial. It also thoroughly exposes you to those memories, and forces you to allow some habituation to take place. If you write down your memories of the loved one, you have created something that can last as long as you live and as long as there are people who care about that person. Writing down the positive memories of that person can let other people be helped by the person's positive models. It gives the loved one another form of immortality, however minor that form may be.

So far I've been talking about all the good reasons to go ahead and remember the loved one, and not to defend oneself from the pain involved in doing so. But deciding when someone is ready to confront painful memories and painful feelings is a complicated determination for *other people* to make. At times, the bad feelings become so intense and so immobilizing that people need to use their defenses for a while.

People who study the grieving process talk about normal stages of grieving. In various formulations, the first stage is denial. The next stages involve negative feelings: anger, sadness. Sometimes the person tries to bargain with fate. The final stage is usually called acceptance. This means that the person, while not liking the reality of what happened, can accept its truth without feeling horrible. But the point I'm making here is that for many healthy people, there's a stage of denying some portion of reality for a while. This stage lasts different lengths of time for different people.

I remember a doctor who, when interviewing patients, even in a one-shot conversation with no planned follow-up, would follow the rule of pursuing the topics that would bring out the biggest display of bad feelings from the patient. This strategy was terribly misguided and unintentionally cruel. He used this strategy because he thought that confronting and not defending against negative feelings was a great thing, for the reasons I listed earlier. But what he didn't realize was that pushing someone into feeling bad feelings for a short time and then leaving them to their own devices to get out of them might only make them more afraid of the memories they had brought up, not less afraid.

Let's use another analogy. Suppose someone is afraid of swimming. To get over this fear, the person must expose himself to what he fears. He might gradually get to know and trust a swimming teacher and start in the shallow end with very elementary maneuvers while standing firmly on the pool floor. He might gradually increase his skills while in the shallow water, and only after having become something of a skillful swimmer, he might advance to the deep water. With each new challenge he takes on, there's some fear, but he stays in the situation long enough to habituate to it. The habituation to each new situation makes him that much more capable of taking on the next step.

Suppose, now, that someone were to reason, "Exposure to the feared situation was the central ingredient that helped this person get over his fear. Let's do it with someone else." So this would-be helpful person takes another person who is afraid of swimming and throws him into the middle of a deep swimming pool, pushing him back to the middle if the person ever manages to struggle to the side. The person very realistically fears that he will drown and chokes on some water. Finally, a lifeguard, fearing for the person's life, rescues him.

This person has now experienced a conditioning trial to teach him, not to be less afraid, but to be more afraid of the water. He has been put into a situation where he was very much afraid and where exposure to the water was associated with horrible feelings. He was reinforced, not for getting used to the situation, but for escaping it. We would predict that he'd be even more afraid of swimming than he ever was before.

This analogy is meant to communicate the point that if you're going to force someone to face a painful situation against his will, you had better know what you're doing, if you want to avoid doing more harm than good. It's a complex decision sometimes. Many times people have overcome fears by being forced to face a scary situation. Many times, for example, children have simply been forced not to stay in their parents' room at night, and they have overcome their fear of staying in their own rooms without voluntarily signing on to such a program. You don't have to volunteer to get "over the hump"; you can be pushed over it. But if someone pushes you into something from which you'll simply escape before getting any habituation, or something that's really and truly dangerous, the attempt to get you to confront the source of the bad feelings can backfire.

To put this point another way, "getting over the hump" usually takes some strength – not physical strength, but psychological strength. If you think you don't have that strength, sometimes the thing to do is to wait until the strength comes. At other times the thing to do is to build up the strength by getting over some humps that are smaller.

In the case of the person with the fear of swimming, the person might start with just sitting at the pool for a while, without even intending to go in. Having success at even this task might make it easier to take on the next one.

For the person who is grieving, the first task might just be to listen while other people talk about the loved one who died. Or it might be just to let the image of the loved one come into the mind for a while – not the image of the death, but the image of a pleasant time during life. Any task you can do successfully increases your strength to take on the next ones.

So when I spoke earlier about "knowing what you're doing" when helping someone else to grieve, often "knowing what you're doing" means figuring out a gradual progression, a hierarchy of steps, that starts out with something easy and gradually works its way up to something harder. If you're

helping yourself grieve, the same idea is very useful. Set a goal of being able to think about both the life and death of the loved one without feeling awful. But if you need to, work your way up to this goal in gradual steps.

Now let's look at some other ideas that may help the grieving person.

First, it's often useful to be easy on yourself for a while and allocate some time to the process. It's work. Like all other tasks, you can't take it on and do it while at the same time doing everything else you were doing. There's only so much time in a day. If you're going to add a job to your schedule, you have to subtract something else. If you're working to your maximum before taking on the job of grief work, you should consider lightening your load for a while if possible. Can some tasks be tabled for a while? You shouldn't expect so much of yourself that you have to deal with failure as well as grief.

Here's a second way of being easy on yourself: allow other people to help you. Sometimes people do a poor job of grieving because they feel they have to take on the task all by themselves. They may not want to talk to other people about it for fear of making them feel bad. They may be afraid they'll cry or make the other person cry. They may appear to be so strong that others see no need to give them outside support.

For this reason, sometimes when a loved one dies, all the family members have their own private grief processes, never sharing their thoughts with anyone else, not able to be helped by one another or to help one another. But if someone allows someone else to help him, he then makes the other person more comfortable in getting help in return.

So sometimes getting help from someone else not only does not hurt the other person; it turns out to be the most helpful thing you can do for them. Grief is easier to take if people who love one another help one another with the task. In the words of a popular song from a few decades back: "Lean on me when you're not strong./I'll be your friend. I'll help you carry on./For, it won't be long, till I'm gonna need someone to lean on."

The image of people helping one another, lightening each other's loads, is very different from the image of using the loss as an excuse to become lazy and selfish for a long time. Sometimes when people suffer a loss, they do feel as though the world should permanently bend over backward toward them out of sympathy, as though they were the first and only person who ever suffered the loss of a loved one. Sometimes people feel a right to be ill tempered at others and a right for others never to be ill-tempered back. You want to avoid facing a loss with the outlook of a spoiled brat. But this is very different from letting others do some taking care of you and from taking care of yourself.

Sometimes grieving people feel bad about not having been nice enough to the person they lost, or about times when they were angry with him, or about having neglected the opportunity to be with him while he was alive. Here the skill of forgiving oneself, of not getting down on oneself too much, can be a lifesaver.

But it's also an opportunity for learning from the experience, and applying that learning to present relationships. How would you like to act to your current loved ones if you knew they would die soon? If the perspective gained by a loss can help you to appreciate the people still in your life, it can provide something very valuable.

When we spoke of the different thought patterns people have in response to unwanted events, "not awfulizing" was one of those that come in very handy. How do you "not awfulize" in response to something you truly think is awful? If the word *awful* has any meaning, it surely applies to events such as a parent's experiencing the death of a child or the permanent and severe brain damage of a child. Is the mental maneuver we have called "not awfulizing" thrown out as a possibility in such cases?

No, it's not. The mental maneuver is called "not awfulizing" for short: it's really something like "choosing to believe that my powers of withstanding hardship and continuing to function are greater than any power this unwanted event has to defeat me." The person might say, "For me this is awful, but I still can withstand it. For the sake of the

215

remaining people I love, and for the
sake of myself, and to best honor the
memory of my loved one, I must handle
it, and I choose to."

Skill 23: Handling Rejection

Rejections are a type of separation. With a rejection, the person chooses not to be close to you, or not to like you, or not to do something with you, or not to continue the relationship with you. This is often harder than in separations where the other person had no choice, as in the example where a good friend had to move away. For rejections, it's at least possible to come up with the idea that "Maybe I'm just unlikable. Maybe everyone will dislike me," even though usually this idea is very unreasonable.

Any time you invite someone to do something and the person says "No" you are in a sense having a rejection. Of course, people say no to invitations for lots of reasons other than not liking you. They can have other plans, they don't like the activity you're doing even though they like you, they can be shy. Nonetheless, not liking you and preferring not to be with you is a possible reason why someone can say no to an invitation.

What else are rejections? Whenever you make a suggestion to a person and they turn it down, that's a sort of rejection. When you say, "I've got a good idea. Why don't you do this?" and the other person says, "No, I don't like that idea," that can be considered a form of rejection, although most of the time it's a pretty mild one. When a salesperson tries to sell something and the other person says no, that's in a sense a rejection.

The hardest type of rejection to take occurs when someone decides not to have a relationship with another person anymore. Divorce often involves the rejection of one person by another. Or when two people in an unmarried relationship decide to break off the relationship, usually at least one of them feels rejected.

Often children have to deal with painful rejections. Someone goes to sit down next to someone at lunch, and the person says, in an unfriendly tone, "You can't sit here. I'm saving this for someone else." Suppose the same child goes out to the playground where two captains are choosing people to be on their sides; this person gets chosen last and then only reluctantly. The teacher asks everyone to find a partner, and no one wants to be a child's partner unless no one else is available. This child is dealing with a major dose of rejection.

Making invitations without the fear of rejection

Handling rejection is one of the important skills in building and maintaining a support network. Many people don't make invitations to others, because they expect they would feel terrible if the other person said "No." Thus, they lead lonely lives and spend lots of time by themselves when they could have been in very good relationships with other people.

What can people do to become less afraid of inviting people to socialize? One guideline that will reduce the probability of rejection is to devise ways of having lots of social conversation before making an invitation. In a world where fear of strangers is often rational, a person being invited needs a "data base" to rely on before accepting any invitation.

The second guideline is that the first invitation should involve little risk for the person being invited. For example, a young man will be much more likely to get an acceptance from a young woman if his first invitation is to have lunch together, than if it's to go with him on a week-long skiing trip. A school-aged child will be more likely to accept an invitation if it's to come over and play for an hour or two than if it's to go with the family on vacation. When you don't know someone well, you want to get a small sample of his behavior before committing yourself to spending a lot of time together.

Another element of issuing invitations is to be flexible about the particular time, date, and place. Imagine a teenage boy who invites a girl to go with him to a certain event; the girl says she can't. He says OK, and the conversation ends. He now says to himself, "She just isn't interested," and feels afraid to invite her to anything else. It could be that she would have been very interested, but just had other plans, and

he didn't use strategies that would let him find that out. He would have been more likely to succeed if, instead, he had first chatted with her, then inquired whether she was interested in getting together at all, and if so, then looked at several different possibilities for dates, times and activities, exploring until they found a mutually acceptable plan. In just the same way, the school-aged child who invites a child to come over today, right now, will be less successful than the one who invites the other child to come over the first time both their schedules allow.

No matter how good the person is at inviting, there is always a chance the other person will not have room in her social network at that time or will not be interested in forming a relationship with the other person. In this case, the types of thoughts the inviter has are very important. Those thoughts will determine whether the inviter feels punished or devastated or scared of inviting again, or whether the inviter will simply chalk it up to fate and move along to make another invitation to someone else.

Let's suppose someone fears feeling totally devastated if invitations aren't accepted. What can a person do to get out of this pattern? The first step is simply becoming aware of the automatic thoughts. This means noticing the answers to the questions: "What am I telling myself?" What is my self-talk?" "If I imagine the other person's turning me down, what do I imagine myself thinking?" Usually when there are large negative emotions, the self-talk consists of awfulizing and getting down on oneself or blaming the other person in response to the fantasy of the rejection.

Here's a very important point. If you become aware that you're awfulizing or using other negative thought patterns, try not to compound the problem by getting down on yourself for that! Becoming aware of what you're thinking is the first and most important step in choosing new thought patterns. Try to say to yourself, "Hooray, I came to an important insight! This will help me!" rather than saying, "Look, I'm awfulizing; that's so stupid of me."

People who are sensitive to having invitations turned down may find themselves thinking things like the following: "If she turns down my invitation, that means she hates me. She thinks I'm a total idiot. And her evaluation of me is totally accurate!" as contrasted to, "If she turns down my invitation, there could be lots of reasons for that. But it doesn't mean I'm a bad person."

People who are sensitive to rejections might find themselves thinking, "Because this person didn't want to accept my invitation, no one will ever want to accept any invitations from me, and I will be totally alone and friendless for my whole life." This is a type of thinking error called overgeneralization. When people overgeneralize, they draw conclusions that are stronger than the data justify.

Another type of automatic thought might go as follows: "If I invite this person and he turns me down, I'll look totally stupid, and he will think I'm a fool." A much more useful substitute thought pattern is as follows: "If he turns me down, at least I probably have made him feel good by letting him know I was interested in getting together. It's a kind act, even if the invitation is turned down."

When people examine their automatic thoughts, they might find themselves imagining that the person who turned them down will tell huge numbers of people that the invitation was extended and rejected and that they will become the laughing stock of the whole community, and all eyes will be upon them, humiliating them. This thought contrasts with the much more realistic notion that most people couldn't care less whom I invite for what and whether that person accepts me or rejects me. They're more worried about themselves instead.

The automatic thoughts we've looked at so far that make people fear rejection are versions of awfulizing and getting down on oneself that we defined earlier.

Let's summarize the steps in revising your thinking toward more helpful patterns. These steps apply to solving many problems, not just that of being sensitive to having invitations turned down.

Step one is simply becoming aware of your thoughts. If you're not aware of them, if you don't focus any attention on them, they're capable of making you feel bad without your being able to do much about them. Once you become aware of them then you're ready to do something about them.

The next step is holding those automatic thoughts up to the light of critical examination. It's thinking, "Wait a second. How likely is this really to be true? What evidence do I have one way or the other on this?" For example, how many times have I ever seen groups of people standing around teasing someone for inviting someone to something and getting turned down?

The next step is figuring out what are more realistic or helpful thoughts. What would I like to tell myself in this situation?

It would be nice if these steps were enough to solve the problem. But they usually aren't. The reason is the force of habit. Even if you decide that in a certain situation you'd like to think a certain way, you won't automatically start doing it unless you practice. You have to build up a competing habit pattern that will replace the old habit pattern.

The next step, therefore, is somehow practicing or rehearsing the new ways of thinking.

One of the best ways of rehearsing is by using your imagination, or your fantasy. For example: I imagine myself inviting someone for something and having them turn down my invitation. Then I practice reminding myself

that I have performed a kind act by expressing interest in this person. I remind myself that I have not lost anything. I remind myself that I haven't just found out that my whole personality is rotten through and through. I see the situation as vividly as I possibly can, and then I practice saying to myself the new and better thoughts that I had decided upon. The more I do this in fantasy, the more I build up my habit strength in the more positive direction.

Sooner or later the practice should also take place in real life. So the next step is experiencing real-life situations and practicing the same new thoughts and behaviors that were done in the fantasy rehearsal.

We're still not finished, though. The final step is to celebrate the practice of a positive pattern, to congratulate yourself for doing something you know is a better way of thinking, feeling and behaving.

These steps will be useful with any or all of the skills discussed in this book. Devoting a little time each day to carrying them out, with whatever skill you want to work on the most, will be one of the most important habits you can develop.

Here are three words that summarize this process: insight, redecision, and practice. Insight means becoming aware of what you're doing and thinking; redecision means examining whether you want to keep doing and thinking it and, if not, what you would rather do and think instead; and practice means rehearsing repeatedly the pattern you think is better.

Handling rejections from close others

Now let's discuss the skill of a different type of rejection tolerance: handling rejections by people who do know you well. For example, a boyfriend or girlfriend breaks up with you, or someone you thought was a best friend doesn't want to be your friend any more.

Every day, teenagers who have experienced this sort of stress wind up in emergency rooms because they've done something suicidal. It's important not to use the thought patterns that make this sort of stress so devastating.

When people are devastated by such rejections, they usually have delegated to the other person the power to make them feel good about themselves. The thought pattern is, "I'm a wonderful person because this wonderful person thinks that I am." This is part of what romantic love is, and it can feel very pleasant. It's extremely exciting. Many popular songs celebrate this feeling. It's a way of achieving a "high" that is unlike any other. One can work oneself into the idea, "My whole reason for living centers around this one person."

One problem with this way of thinking, of course, is that it leaves you too vulnerable to rejection. If someone else is your entire world, then when that person rejects you, it feels as if the world has ended.

The antidote to this sort of pattern is to cultivate a set of rather unromantic but much more healthy and realistic ideas about what the reason for living is and what the basis for your own worth is. That is, one – but only one – reason for living is to have a good relationship with this person. Other reasons include having good relationships with other people, doing pleasant things by yourself, accomplishing things that help the world, doing kind actions for many other people, cultivating your own abilities to handle the world better, and so forth. The notion that there are multiple sources of pleasure and meaning in the world, and that the loss of any one of them should not be a devastating blow, is encapsulated in folk sayings such as "Don't put all your eggs in one basket," and "There are more fish in the sea."

If you don't put all your hopes for happiness on the shoulders of one person, do you ruin the relationship? On the contrary, many people have ruined relationships by becoming too dependent. If the first person has centered all of his life around the second person, and the second person doesn't reciprocate, the first might get very jealous and want the second to spend time with only him or her. The first might struggle to keep the second on too tight a chain. The second might finally rebel against this by leaving the relationship altogether. Thus, the person who fears separation too intensely may actually cause a separation to occur.

Marriage is a different relationship from any other, because the degree of commitment is very great. Many of the eggs must be put in one basket. But even so, it appears that, in almost all happy marriages, people have relationships and activities other than their spouse to fill some of their needs for companionship and a feeling of worth.

It's possible to carry the idea of diversification too far. Some people who are very afraid of rejections can't commit to any one major relationship. A healthy balance between loyalty to one or a few people, and a more diversified support network usually best meets the needs of most people.

Hostile rejection by a group

Now let's think about another circumstance where it's necessary to use the skill of handling rejection. This is the situation where someone is rejected by a group of people and is treated with hostility and disrespect. Sometimes this results from the person's behavior. For example, someone has not learned relationship-building skills, and this turns people against him.

At other times, a person's rejection by a group has nothing to do with his behavior. For example, sometimes people reject other people because of their race, their religion, their skin color, their gender, the appearance of their bodies, or their age. At other times people reject others because they're different from the group in ways that ought to be perfectly unobjectionable. For example, they choose not to use alcohol, they choose to pray before eating, they're interested in a hobby that others hold in contempt, and so forth.

As an example of the last category, a school-aged boy I know became interested in ballet dancing. This should have been perfectly harmless to anybody else. But the boys in his school, who perhaps felt insecure about their own masculinity, chose to reject him in a most vicious way.

We will speak more about responses to this sort of situation in discussing the next skill, that of handling criticism and disapproval. But let's mention here some philosophy that may be useful in handling such rejection.

It's useful to try to determine the reason for the rejection. In many cases the rejecters will be only too happy to make their reasons clear. If someone finds himself rejected for behaviors or habits that really should be changed, then it makes sense to work on changing them. To recognize this and do it often takes a very great deal of courage and maturity.

If a child finds himself in a situation where he is regularly subjected to great hostility and verbal and physical abuse, such as bullying, it should be up to the supervising adults to end that abuse. For example, the sorts of rejection and cruelty that many children experience regularly at school should simply not be permitted. At schools, adults should monitor what goes on among children, and children who persist in abusing another child, despite warnings, should experience consequences that are effective in ending the abuse, even if this requires expulsion from the school or isolation from other students.

In the real world, it's often very difficult to mobilize adults to control hostility among children; the phrase "boys will be boys" seems to be all that certain adults in authority can muster. The child who is abused by peers often has a political battle to fight. That child is greatly helped if he has strong allies in his parents.

It's not "too much entitlement," but "reasonable expectations," for a family to demand that a child be able to attend school without the experience of hostile, rejecting actions, either in the form of physical violence or frequent disrespectful talk. It should not be the job of a rejected child to somehow convert the rejecting peers to friends or admirers. The rule of law should prevail in schools, and the law should protect children from physical or verbal abuse at the hands of peers.

Although it's possible to compel people to refrain from active abuse, it's usually not possible to compel them to be friendly and accepting. The person who wins a political battle to stop active abuse may next find himself facing a situation of being silently shunned by others. At such times, simply leaving a social circle or leaving a school for an-

other one or for homeschooling may be the best options.

The existence of homeschooling helps us to realize that winning acceptance from same-aged peers in school is not the "only game in town." It's possible for some children to withdraw from that game and do quite well. The form of social organization in which twenty or more same-aged children are supervised by one adult at a time is only one possible social structure – it's not necessarily the highest and best.

Apprenticeship arrangements, with much more contact among adults and children, have been the prevalent social structure for education in many other times and places. It's possible for a child who has experienced quite traumatic rejection from school peers to become very successful as a homeschooler in constructing a mutually warm and supportive social network.

For the person experiencing rejection, who at least for the time being cannot escape the social environment where it occurs, it's useful to ponder the question: "Is it possible and desirable to go through life with everyone liking you?" Usually the answer is no. Probably more realistic is the following idea: If you're active enough and determined enough in getting goals met, there will be people who are threatened by you or are jealous of you, and will reject you. But as long as there's a certain number of good members in your support network – and for many people that minimum number is one – you don't need to be liked by everyone in the world." If you believe this, you will probably be better at handling rejection than someone who believes it's essential to be liked by everyone.

Here's another thought pattern important in handling rejection. Suppose I believe, "These other people know whether I'm a good or bad person. Whether they like me is the most valid measure of my worth as a person." Then I'm likely to feel terrible if they don't like me.

It's much more realistic to believe the following: "What other people think of me does give me feedback about how I'm affecting them, and I don't want to ignore that. It's fun to be liked, and I want to have that fun if I can. But people can make big mistakes, and they can be small-minded, petty, and fickle. People have been known to literally worship horrible people. I want to evaluate myself in some better way than trying to win a popularity contest. I want to get feedback from the wisest and best part of myself, or compare myself to the standards of the wisest and best writings, or get feedback from a small number of wise and good people. In this way I want to be above needing to please 'the crowd.'"

What about friendship-building skills, or social skills, as an antidote to hostile rejection by a group? In my experience working on these skills is more useful in preventing hostile rejection than in curing it. Once a situation of hostile rejection has started, something more than learning of friendship skills is usually necessary. Rejection can take on a life of its own, and the initial forays of the rejected person into improved social skills are often punished. The rejected child in particular desperately needs to have those budding attempts at improved friendship-building reinforced.

Skill 24: Handling Criticism

The skill of handling criticism includes dealing with disapproval, disagreement, teasing, verbal abuse, and all other forms of negative feedback about your behavior or yourself. It overlaps with skills of handling rejection.

It's useful to think about what the person making the criticism is trying to do. The critic may be purely trying to give information to change behavior, without any intention of making the other person feel bad. For example, a doctor says to a patient, "I'd like you to stop drinking grapefruit juice. It has something in it that you shouldn't take when you're on this medicine." Or a parent says to a child, "You look great! You'll look even better if you stand up straighter."

At other times the critic is trying to give information that's helpful, but hopes the person will also feel just bad enough about what he has done that the bad feeling will help the person change. For example, a parent frowns at a child and says, "Not so loud! You're hurting my ears!" This kind of criticism is meant to give information but also be a mild punishment.

On the other end of the spectrum from pure constructive criticism is pure malevolent criticism. Here there's no wish for constructively changing the other person's behavior, but a pure wish for the other person to feel bad. For example: The class scapegoat gets onto the bus, and another child screams at him, "Oh, you stupid dork!"

The critic can have other motives than the motive to help or the motive to hurt. Sometimes the critic is just trying to vent his own anger, to make himself feel better (although often this doesn't work, and makes the critic feel worse instead). For example: Someone finds a couple of balls sitting on the steps of her home. She screams out at her daughter, "How many times do I have to tell you not to leave balls on these steps? I have been screaming myself blue in the face, and still you just can't seem to get it! Someone could fall and break their neck. Why can't you hear that?"

Even more complicated are the situations where the critic pretends that the criticism is meant to help, when it really is not. For example: A manager in a company has just been severely criticized by his own boss and is feeling humiliated and angry. Then he sees some minor mistake his secretary has made, and he calls her in and criticizes her most cruelly. But he does so under the pretense of simply giving helpful, constructive feedback. This is difficult for the secretary, because she is being called upon to act as if the criticism is constructive, when its real intention is for the boss to vent his own feelings.

An even more useful way of classifying criticism is according to whether there's any useful information in it. Sometimes people can give us useful information out of cruel motives. For example, someone who dislikes me reads an article I have written, and out of a pure wish to humiliate me, criticizes everything he can think of about the article. But embedded in this criticism are several ideas I can use to make the article better and help myself. The decision about whether the criticism contains useful information is important in my response to criticism. If there's useful information, I want to use it to help myself. If there's no useful information, I want not to be hurt by it, perhaps by dismissing it in my mind.

Now let's consider an important question to ask oneself in preparing to deal with criticism. True or false: you should be perfect. If you believe that it's awful to have any imperfections, that it's terrible to make a mistake, that it's awful to have an undesirable habit, then each criticism is an attack or an assault.

Contrast this with the following belief: "I'm not perfect. I never will be. But I want to work constantly to improve myself. I want to get feedback about how to improve. Sometimes that feedback is painful to hear. But I want to make the most of it and use it as well as I can to improve myself." With this attitude, criticism, even if it has only a little useful information in it, can be seen as an opportunity.

Here's another very important attitude about criticism. True or false:

When someone criticizes me, I need to convince that person I'm really OK. The person who feels this is true can be hooked into a very unpleasant game by anyone who's cruel enough to enjoy the game. The game goes like this: the persecutor criticizes. The victim tries to convince the persecutor he's OK. The persecutor won't let him do it. The persecutor keeps winning, and the victim keeps losing. Here's an example among school children.

> Persecutor: You're stupid.
> Victim: I am not!
> Persecutor: You're not only stupid; you're in love with the teacher. I heard you say it.
> Victim: What? I did NOT say that! You're making this up.
> Persecutor (to another persecutor): Didn't you hear him say that?
> Second persecutor: He says it all the time.
> Victim: What? I don't say it all the time. You're out of your head.
> Persecutor: You're the one who's out of your head. They had to lock you up, you were so out of your head, didn't they?
> Victim: No! Where did you get that idea? I've never been locked up anywhere.

The poor victim is laboring under the sad illusion that his denials will be convincing to the persecutors. In fact what the denials do is to reinforce the persecutors for playing the game, and to make the game fun for them.

Contrast this with the dialogue that occurs when the victim strongly believes, "If you criticize me, I don't have to convince you that I'm OK," and "Just because you're making evaluations of me doesn't mean I have to prove my worth to you."

Persecutor: You're stupid.
Victim: Oh. You think so, huh?
Persecutor: I know so.
Victim: OK.
Persecutor: You say OK; that means you agree. Ha ha; you think you're stupid.
Victim: And I guess you think you're really smart.
Persecutor: You're not only stupid; you're in love with the teacher. I heard you say it.
Victim: I'll bet you have some better things to do than to play these games.
Persecutor (to second persecutor): Didn't you hear him say he was in love with the teacher?
Victim (to second persecutor): Are you going to join in this game too?
Second persecutor: You two settle this – I'm staying out of it.

If the second would-be persecutor notices that the victim doesn't play the game in a way that reinforces persecutors and thus refuses to join in, the first persecutor is clearly not reinforced

for his criticism. He'll be likely to try someone else the next time.

But let's imagine that the second persecutor decides to join in. The crucial aspects of the victim's attitude are nondefensiveness (he doesn't feel he has the need to defend himself) and low excitement (he acts bored with the whole game). A third technique is to talk about what 's going on, rather than responding to the specific accusations. Let's continue this dialogue assuming the second persecutor joins in the persecution.

Second persecutor: Oh, yeah, I hear him say he's in love with the teacher all the time.
Victim (To first persecutor): So now you've got him in on the game to help you out. OK.
First persecutor: You're out of your head, too. They had to lock you up, you're so out of your head, didn't they?
Victim: You think hard to come up with lots of different ways to insult someone, don't you? You really work at putting other people down.

The victim really refuses to be a victim, by refusing to get into the game of defending himself. The persecutor wants to play the game of "I'll make up criticisms, and you try to prove to me that they're not true." But instead, the victim comments on the persecutor's behavior, in a way that probably gives that behavior the punishment it so thoroughly deserves, and at least does not reinforce it. Some of the victim's responses can be classified as "criticizing the critic." This is certainly appropriate when the only motive of the critic is pure cruelty.

But the attitude of nondefensiveness, the thought that "I don't have to prove that I'm OK to everyone who suggests I'm not," is also very useful when the critic is trying to help, or has a legitimate gripe. Let's listen as Sam, the criticized person, uses nondefensiveness to try to get the useful information from his sister's criticism.

Sister: I wish you wouldn't be so lazy.

Sam: Boy, I sure wish I could be less lazy too. What particular lazy thing I've done has bothered you?

Sister: You leave your things all over the living room and the family room. And then when I have someone over to visit, if I don't want the place to look terrible, I have to clean up.

Sam: I see. You'd like me to put my things away. That sure is a reasonable request. Which things in particular have bothered you the most?

Sister: The main thing is when you take off your shoes and socks. It really bugs me to have to pick up those dirty and smelly things.

Sam: They can get dirty and smelly, all right, can't they? I can see how that would bug you. OK, thanks for telling me that. I'll try to remember.

Sister: Thanks, Sam.

Sam's sister had some useful information here. Suppose Sam's response to her initial criticism had been, "Me lazy? I spent the whole afternoon cutting the grass, while you were painting your fingernails!" Sam would not have received the useful information from the criticism that told him how to get along better with his sister, but probably would have had a nonproductive argument.

Having an attitude of nondefensiveness and a willingness to search for the useful part of the criticism lead someone to respond in a few ways that we can name, other than criticizing the critic. Let's call them

Agreeing with part of criticism
Asking for more specific criticism
Reflections
I want statement
I feel statement
Silent eye contact

We're already familiar with reflections from the previous discussion of the skill of empathic listening. Sam does a reflection in the earlier conversation when he says, "You'd like me to put my things away." He's restating her message to make sure he got it right, or to let her know he got it right.

Agreeing with part of criticism means that not only do you not defend yourself against a criticism, but also that you actively affirm at least part of it. Sam does this in the conversation above when he says, "I sure wish I could be less lazy too," and when he says, "They can get dirty and smelly all right, can't they?" It's great to practice agreeing with part of criticism if for no other reason than to remind yourself that you don't have to defend yourself against every critical statement. Agreeing with part of criticism takes the wind out of the sails of someone who wants to play the game of making you defend yourself. And when someone who has some useful information to give you, it can reduce the need of the other person to oppose you, and help the person to give you the useful information they have in a nice way.

We say agreeing with *part* of criticism because you don't necessarily have to join in with all of it. When someone says, "You're a worthless, rotten liar," it's agreeing with part of criticism to say, "I'm certainly not perfect." It doesn't go quite as far as the critic does, though!

Asking for more specific criticism helps the critic to deliver the useful information. Sam does this when he says, "What particular lazy thing that I've done has bothered you?" and when he later says, "Any things in particular that have bothered you most?" These let his sister know he really is interested in hearing the specifics of how she wants his behavior to change. If there are such particulars, he can decide if he wants to work on them. If a critic has no particulars, but is simply generally insulting your character, then at least you make it

clear that the general insults are not grounded in specific complaints.

Here's an example of asking for more specific criticism used in this second way:

The first kid gets onto the bus.
Second kid: You're a dork!
First kid: What sort of dorky thing have I done that causes you a problem?
Second kid: Nothing causes me a problem; you're just stupid, that's all!
First kid: So, nothing I'm doing causes you a problem, but you're putting me down anyway just for the fun of it, huh? Okay.

Here's another example of agreeing with part of criticism. Imagine that the first person has lent the second a book. The second person has had it for several weeks. The first person says, "I'd like to get my book back from you, please. And, in fact, I need it within the next two or three days, because I need it for something next week." Suppose the second says, "What? You expect me to get it back to you so quickly? You're so selfish!"

At this point most people would be tempted to respond, "What! ME selfish! Who is it that has had my book for weeks? You entitled, spoiled brat!" This version of criticizing the critic is being very defensive, not being nondefensive. The first person is trying to prove himself OK by trying to prove to the second that it's his fault. But this is a waste of time and energy. What he really needs is his book back, not to establish who's the good person and who's the bad person. Here's how he responds by agreeing with part of criticism:

First person: "Selfish? Well, I guess it would be possible for me to be more generous to you. But in this case unfortunately I can't do that. I need the book back soon."

When the first person says, "I need the book back soon," that is an "I want" statement. The first person simply says what he wants the other to do. The first person sidesteps the contest to determine who's the good person and who's the bad person, and sticks to the much lower-stakes issue of the return of the book. If the first person had counterattacked by defensively criticizing the critic, full-fledged verbal battle might have resulted, perhaps escalating into a physical fight. Many people have been killed over much smaller issues.

This is why, when criticizing the critic, it's usually best to be low-key and only mildly critical rather than attacking the critic so viciously that the critic now feels the need to defend himself and get revenge. Agreeing with part of criticism runs almost no risk of beginning that vicious cycle.

The "I feel" statement takes the form of the following: "When you do this, I feel this because of this." When someone really wants to level with the second person, this is often a form for her statement to take. For example: The first kid sits next to someone on a bus.

The second kid says to him with a mean tone, "Hi, vomit-breath!" The first kid replies, "I feel bad to hear you say that. I was hoping you'd be a friendly person."

Here's another example: A boss chews out an employee for making a very small mistake. The boss says, "Can't you do anything right?" The employee says, "When you say that it sure does make me feel humiliated and discouraged."

"I feel" statements can also prevent another unpleasant and destructive game. We might call this one "Can you avoid showing you feel hurt?" A first person is trying to make the other person feel bad; the second person is trying to retain her pride by trying not to show she feels bad, when she really does. The more the first person criticizes, the more the second person realizes she's losing at the game of not appearing to be touched by the criticism. Now the second person feels bad, not only because of the criticism itself, but also because of losing this game.

With an "I feel" statement, the second person communicates, "I'm not going to play that game. I'll readily acknowledge that your criticism has made me feel bad. There's no rule that I shouldn't feel bad about criticism."

If the critic is really trying to make the other person feel bad but is trying to pretend he just wants to help, then the second person's acknowledging the bad feelings weakens the power of this deceptive stance.

If the critic is purely trying to make the other person feel bad and feels no conflict over doing that, then the ready acknowledgment that he has succeeded at least takes some of the pleasure out of the game. The thrill of the chase vanishes when the other person acknowledges from the beginning that your goal is already achieved.

School children who have been scapegoated and criticized by peers are very frequently advised to ignore the critic. Frequently I hear from such children that ignoring doesn't work. It seems to me that ignoring often turns into a losing game of "Can you avoid showing you're hurt?" Here's an example.

First person: "Hey, dork head."
Second person: Resolutely looks in the other direction, clenches his jaw but does not speak.
First person (to a third person): Look at that airhead over there. He's so stupid he forgot how to talk.
The two people begin to laugh at the second person. Now the second person glares at them and looks away again, but still doesn't speak.
The first person sees from the glare and the resolute turning away again that the second person is losing at the game. The first person redoubles the insults, in order to get a definitive victory. Finally after many insults:
Second person: Shut up! Just shut up!

Now the first person laughs gleefully. What's so funny about being told to shut up? The laugh is a victory laugh. It's a laugh of "Yay, I won the game. You were trying to ignore me and not show my power over you, but you just couldn't do it."

If the second person wants not to engage in an exchange of words, he can avoid playing the game by doing what I call silent eye contact. The second person looks at the critic, with a studious, curious, or sad expression – not a glare of "I want to get you back," but more an expression of "I'm sorry you're like this." The critic can't play the game of "I'll bet I can get your attention," because he already has it. If the critic goes on insulting, the second person simply listens and looks. If the critic says, "Why are you looking at me," the second person might say, "Because I thought you were speaking to me."

Sometimes the advisors of children being victimized by their peers overemphasize the question, "How should you respond at the moment of being criticized?" Often a better question is, "How can you gain allies?" If such a child has friends who will be on his side, then getting criticism or ridicule is not so painful. Sometimes simply imagining these friends helps at the moment of criticism.

Sometimes these allies will be even willing to come to one's defense immediately when the critic goes into action. If three or four peers immediately disapprove of the critic when he starts in, that can be very effective in halting the victimization. In getting those three or four or more allies, of course, relationship-building skills are very important.

The task of responding to criticism is different depending on whether an audience is listening. A head of a country, responding to criticism by a reporter at a press conference, is putting on a performance for an audience, not just dealing with the reporter. The child who's taunted on the bus in front of many others is in a different game than the child being taunted by a friend visiting him alone.

The two-person situation is simpler to handle. It permits a good bit more "I feel" statements and agreeing with parts of criticism than the game of responding before an audience. An audience will have loyalties and sympathies, and often gives clear support to the person they like better. Thus, if the goal is not to be humiliated by criticism, one should arrange to be surrounded by the most sympathetic audience possible. If the goal is to do some joint decision-making and come to an understanding with another person, often it's best not to have an audience. There are exceptions to this, of course. For example, sometimes the audience is a therapist trying hard to promote and reinforce people's solving of problems wisely.

When you have heard useful criticism and you have responded to it nondefensively, often the most difficult part occurs afterward. For example, Sam has heard from his sister how much it bothers her when he leaves his socks and shoes lying around. He has agreed that he should work on this.

But if he doesn't give it another thought after the conversation, his sister will understandably grow cynical. He now has a task that challenges his self-discipline skills: actually putting the socks and shoes away when he would prefer to postpone that task indefinitely. It's easier to handle criticism if you know you have the self-discipline to improve your habits in ways the criticism shows to be useful.

When handling criticism, as well as anything else unpleasant, it's often useful to think, "What's the worst possible thing that could happen in this situation?" Sometimes the worst that could happen is being totally abandoned by one's entire support system and being left totally alone. Even when this is very improbable, it's good to know that it's survivable. Thus, the skills of handling and enjoying aloneness make it easier to awfulize less when being criticized.

Skill 25: Handling Your Mistakes and Failures

If you're interested in getting better at handling mistakes and failures, be sure to read the section on frustration tolerance and fortitude. Making a mistake or failing at something is a special case of a frustration. But in this section I'll give some specific tips on handling mistakes and failures other than those in the section on frustration tolerance. (I'll also repeat some of those that are just too important not to emphasize again.)

Two vicious cycles of failure

The fear of failure is paradoxically probably one of the most frequent causes of failure. It's one of the most frequent causes of people not achieving up to their potential.

How does this work? Someone, for example, a child, tries something and doesn't succeed right away. Maybe some other child who wants to bolster his own ego by criticizing someone else says things like "What, you can't do that? Where have you been? Come on, everybody can do that. Just do it! What's the matter with you? Here, watch me. See how easy it is? You do it. No, not like that!"

Unfortunately, many children – and, sadly, even adults – are ready to volunteer to produce such shame, humiliation, and embarrassment for someone who's trying something for the first time. So the person feels bad as a result of the initial failure. The next time he

tries, he's more self-conscious. He watches himself and wonders, "Am I going to succeed or fail?" This takes his concentration off the task he's trying to do. The nervousness and self-consciousness make it more likely that he will fail again.

Now, with failure leading to bad feelings and the bad feelings leading to a greater chance of failure, we have the makings for a vicious cycle. He fails more, and that makes him feel worse, and the bad feelings make him fail even more.

When the bad feelings get bad enough, few people can hang in there and keep trying. So now the person begins to use a defense mechanism we talked about in the section on frustration tolerance: avoidance. The person avoids trying the task he has failed at. He does something else, anything else. For example, let's say his early failures have been in math. He comes to associate math with feelings of shame and humiliation. So when there's math work to do, he avoids it unless he's compelled to do it.

Avoidance gets another vicious cycle started. The more the person avoids the activity, the less chance he gets to practice it. Other classmates who are practicing math, for example, get better at it, but his competence doesn't grow. So compared with other people, he gets worse and worse at it. The more he falls behind, the more assured is his failure, and the more he uses avoidance, thinking, "What's the use of trying at all?"

So we have two vicious cycles. They often occur together:

1. failure -> shame -> failure
2. failure -> shame -> avoidance -> failure.

These two vicious cycles take an enormous toll on human beings. If we could eliminate these vicious cycles, the world would be filled with immensely more competent and happy people than it is at present.

When I talked about frustration tolerance, I mentioned two patterns that aren't good: overreaction and underreaction. The same applies to failure and mistakes. People can feel not bad enough about some mistakes and failures.

Imagine you're going to get some surgery. How would you like it if your surgeon and your anesthesiologist were both doing their first operation, with no supervision, and they each had thoughts like this: "Failure is nothing to be ashamed of. If I fail at this operation, if the patient dies, I won't get down on myself. I'll just keep trying until I succeed." If you heard this sort of talk, would you head straight out the hospital door and look for someone else to do the surgery? I would.

So even though making mistakes and failures when you first start something is natural, an important task is to figure out how to make those mis-takes in a way that won't harm you or anyone else. For the surgeon, the operation can be done on people or animals who have already died, in simulation on a computer, by observing and assisting an expert, in fantasy rehearsal, under the watchful eye of an expert supervisor, and only after those dry runs, by doing the operation independently.

Finding the challenge zone

One of the keys to overcoming crippling fear of failure (if it is present), avoiding developing it (if it is not present), and developing skill at the maximum rate is called "finding the challenge zone." This means you take on challenges that are not too hard, not too easy, but just right for your present level of skill. The challenge zone is the level of difficulty that is just right for you now. The more you work in the challenge zone, the more your skills improve, and the level of difficulty you can take on gradually rises.

So the challenge zone of today may be too easy tomorrow. You gradually raise the level as you become more and more competent. If you work too long at too easy a level, you don't stimulate improvement, and you feel bored. If you're working at too hard a level, you feel frustrated, scared, or ashamed. But at just the right level of difficulty, you'll find much success and challenge, and it's pleasant to do the task.

Let's look at an example. A man is learning to play tennis. After having two or three lessons, he challenges the local tennis champion to a game; he doesn't win a single point. He feels frustrated and upset. He feels that way because he was not working in the challenge zone, but in the frustration zone.

On the other hand, the local champion finds the match boring. He hits the ball right past the beginner time after time and stands and watches as the beginner's serves go into the net or into the next court. The level of difficulty for him is at the boredom level. Each of them would do better playing an opponent who's closer to his level of skill.

(Or, they could stop the match, and the champion could give the beginner a lesson. The champion now gets into the challenge zone, not for tennis skills, but for teaching skills. In doing so he gives the beginner challenges that are in the challenge zone for him.)

Let's look at another example. A child is experiencing much difficulty in math class, where he's being asked to multiply and divide fractions. He's coming to hate and fear math. A tutor is called in to work with him and help him with his homework, but this doesn't help.

Finally someone gives the child a test that starts with the easiest items in math and gradually gets harder and harder. With this test, people discover the child is being assigned work that's way over his challenge zone. The child is taken out of the math class altogether, and a tutor works with the child starting with the types of problems the child can do correctly right now. Now the child for the first time in a long time experiences success at what he is doing in math.

Gradually the level of difficulty is raised higher and higher, and the child moves along the hierarchy. But now, at each level, the child has been prepared to be successful by what has gone before. The child works his way up to learning about multiplying and dividing fractions, but now he has enjoyed the journey.

If you're working on learning something and you feel too much failure, if it's possible, reduce the level of difficulty until the challenge feels not too hard, not too easy, but just right. Then work your way up from there.

Here's another example: A woman is learning to play the piano. She hasn't had time to practice, but the teacher has assigned harder and harder lessons anyway. Now she's reached a point where she's expected to play fairly hard songs that are almost impossible for her.

She decides to stop taking on any new songs, but to drop back to the point where the lessons were easy and work her way forward from there. When she does this, she enjoys piano playing. She gets back to the level that previously had been frustrating for her, but now she enjoys working at this level, because now it's the challenge zone for her.

It's often hard for people to realize what the problem is when they're not at the right level of difficulty and to negotiate with teachers or others to locate themselves in the challenge zone. This is often hard, even for skills with a clear hierarchical progression, such as doing math and playing the piano. It's usually much harder for more abstract skills, such as the psychological skills discussed here. But for these skills too, progress takes place best in the challenge zone.

For example: A certain child finds it very difficult to participate successfully in social conversation. In his eighth grade class, the demands for social correctness are so strong that he gets continually rejected and ostracized by peers.

His parents decide to take him out of school and homeschool him. He starts spending more time socializing with kind adults, whose demands for a certain style of social conversation are not as harsh as his peers at school. He volunteers at a nursing home and socializes with the residents there, and he experiences great success at being able to produce happiness in the residents by listening enthusiastically to them when they speak to him. He occasionally invites to his house a couple of kids his age who are not rejecting and share one of his interests, and they work together on electronics projects. He now has chances to practice social interaction in settings where he can experience success. He can gradually work his way up the hierarchy of difficulty, without being plunged over his head.

People's usual tendency when they find themselves at the frustration or panic level, i.e. at too hard a level of difficulty, is to use avoidance and conclude that they don't like the whole activity. Try to avoid doing this, and cultivate a reflex of saying, "The activity itself may be a good one; I might need to drop back to an easier level and work my way up."

Let's give yet another example. A person is very much out of shape, and is urged, for the sake of his health, to take up exercising. He joins an aerobics class where the other people are in much better shape than he is, and he can't keep up with them for even two minutes. He feels as if he's going to faint, and he feels humiliated. He starts to conclude that exercise is not for him.

But, if he has cultivated the reflex I'm talking about, he says to himself, "Wait. It's not that exercise is not for me. It's just that I started too high on the hierarchy of difficulty. Let me drop back to a comfortable level and work my way up from there." So he starts out the next day by taking a walk. He goes slowly, but even so, after less than a tenth of a mile, the exercise starts to become unpleasant. So he stops for the day.

But the next day he does it again, and he notices he can go a little farther before the exercise becomes unpleasant. Importantly, he celebrates the fact that he's made progress. The next day he can go a little farther and a little faster, and he can have two walks rather than just one. He gradually works his way up to walking a couple of miles, and then to jogging, and he eventually returns to the aerobics class, participating with enjoyment.

How do you know you're in the challenge zone? Sometimes tutors and teachers use the rule that if the learner isn't successful on at least eighty percent of the things she tries, she may be at too difficult a level. But the chance of success that's right depends upon the task, the stakes and your tolerance for failure.

If you're a surgeon doing operations, the challenge zone should be very close to 100 percent success. If you're just beginning to learn to hit tennis balls, you're luckier if you can tolerate missing eighty percent of them than if you have to have hit eighty percent of them to keep your morale up. If you're someone like Thomas Edison looking for a metal to use in light bulbs, you're eventually successful because you can tolerate close to 100 percent failure for many trials before finally finding the substance that works.

The challenge zone means you can keep your morale up and keep trying. If you're able to tolerate a high rate of failure when nobody is harmed and when that's the fastest way to get to where you want to go, you're luckier than if you become demoralized quickly with only a few failures.

Comparing performance with your past level, not just that of others

In the last section I gave examples of people who found themselves at a level of challenge that was too difficult for them. Their successful strategy was to drop back to the challenge zone and work their way up from there. But to do this successfully requires another very important coping strategy. This strategy is to feel good about doing something better than you did it before, even if other people can do it better still.

Let's suppose I'm a child with a reading disability. I'm in a classroom where the reading demands on me are way over my head – I'm in the frustration zone. Whereas the other kids can read words like *operation* and *crustacean*, I can't figure out words like *click* and *spill*. People decide to help me by moving me back to the challenge zone. I get together with a tutor and start with words like *fat* and *hat* and *cat* and work my way up. I start progressing. Soon I can read simple books; gradually I work my way up to more and more complex books.

When I start this process, I soon begin to see progress *relative to my previous level of skill*. However, *relative to my peers in the classroom*, I'm still failing miserably. The crucial element for the success of my improvement strategy is to feel good about my progress relative to my own previous skill and *not* to get down on myself about being behind relative to my peers. If I can't do this, if

I'm constantly comparing myself to other people and saying, "Oh, what's the use? I can never be as good as they are," then it's unlikely I'll be able to mount the effort necessary to succeed.

Knowing when to quit and when not to

"If at first you don't succeed, try, try again," goes the advice of the proverb. Persistence is of very great value in achieving success in anything. But what if you've tried and tried again several times, and you still meet with nothing but frustration? And what if there's no hierarchy of difficulty to move down? There are times when it's reasonable to give up. Deciding when the time to give up has come can be a difficult task.

Suppose I set the goal of becoming a professional basketball player. I work and practice, and I do make progress relative to my previous level of skill. But I notice that no one in my family is much over five feet tall, and all of us, including myself, are even more uncoordinated and slow than we are short! Gradually I notice that even if I practice three hours for every half-hour that my peers practice, they remain far better in basketball than I am.

Gradually I revise my goals and expectations for myself. I eventually become a great success at managing a small business, and I often enjoy driveway basketball games with my own family members. If I had gone on striving toward basketball stardom with my last ounce of courage and never-ending determination, I would have ended up wasting countless hours. I would have rediscovered the truth that to be a champion at certain things requires a certain degree of genetic endowment.

It's with considerable reluctance that I acknowledge there's a time and place for giving up. That's because people with the fear of failure and with low skill in handling mistakes and failures tend to give up way too soon and too readily. How does one know when to give up and when to persist?

The best answer I can give is to suggest conscious attention to the question and to the strategy of gathering any available information that will help in answering it. For example, suppose I would like to be able to play Chopin's *Heroic Polonaise* and other pieces of music at its level of difficulty, and I don't know the first thing about playing the piano. But I want to try. So I work for forty hours on learning to play the piano. After doing this, I notice that playing the Chopin piece is just as impossible for me as it was originally. Should I keep on, or should I give up?

Suppose I take time out from piano practice to find out how long it takes the average person to learn to play the piano well enough to play a piece like this. Suppose I survey several piano teachers, and the average estimate is a little over 1,000 hours of practice, with intense concentration.

This is exceedingly useful information to me. Do I want to play badly enough, and do I enjoy it enough, to log in that much time? If so, on I go, and if not, I can stop. But I've learned that I shouldn't conclude I simply have no native ability and should abandon the piano, and I've also learned that I shouldn't conclude that piano lessons and practice are worthless. This is especially true if I've learned to do a pretty respectable job on *Twinkle, Twinkle, Little Star* and *Go Tell Aunt Rhodie*.

Unfortunately, for most of the psychological skills on this list, no estimates are available of how long it takes to go from one level of skill to another. Suppose I know I'm very unskilled at concentration, and I want to spend time doing the exercises listed in this manual to improve my skills. How many hours should I log in before giving up? My own guess is that most people spend fewer than ten hours before deciding to discontinue practice, when the amount necessary to make dramatic improvement is probably closer to 1,000 hours. When I'm deciding whether to give up or keep trying, I should certainly take into account the importance of the goal. Concentration skills are much more vital to my life's success than, say, football skills.

But many boys with concentration problems log in hundreds of times more practice on football skills than on concentration skills. If there's a skill vital for living, it would seem folly to give up on improving it after only a few hours, for fear of wasting time, while meanwhile one is regularly logging many hours watching situation comedies on TV and other similar pursuits. For really vital life skills, so many people give up so soon that the standard advice of "Keep trying forever, never give up" may be closest to the truth.

Trying, trying again in a different way

If a strategy isn't succeeding, when should you change the course, and when should you stay the course? This is a similar decision to that of when to abandon the endeavor altogether. It's a decision on when to abandon one strategy in favor of another, or to supplement one strategy with another.

Again, you ideally should make this decision based on information about how long it takes successful strategies take to work. If, for example, someone has been working in psychotherapy for depression for 200 hours and still feels as bad as when he started, he would certainly want to know that a different type of therapy has worked in thirty hours or that a pill has worked when taken once a day for three weeks.

Where do you get this sort of information? From expert consultants, from the scientific literature, from other books that draw upon the scientific literature, from other people, from the library, from the Internet, and so forth.

Types of thoughts in handling failure

Let's look again at the table of types of thoughts.

Awfulizing
Getting down on yourself
Blaming someone else
Not awfulizing
Not getting down on yourself
Not blaming someone else
Goal-setting
Listing options and choosing
Learning from the experience
Celebrating luck
Celebrating someone else's choice
Celebrating your own choice

Let's think of the example in which someone is behind in math, drops back to the challenge zone, and works diligently to catch up. Here are some thoughts that might prove useful to him: "It's not the end of the world that I am behind. It's embarrassing, and I don't like it, and I'm going to work hard to change this situation. But I can take it." (That was Not Awfulizing.)

"I don't want to punish myself and berate myself about this. That would only make it harder for me to work at getting better." (That was Not Getting Down on Himself.)

"Even though I feel the urge to blame my teachers and blame the whole subject of mathematics, I don't want to use my energy in that way." (Not blaming someone else.)

"I want to use my energy in working to get better at math." (Goal-setting.)

"One option is to work an hour a day on this; another is to work two hours a day. One option is to go by my math book I use at school; another option is to use this different one." (Listing options and choosing.)

"Hmhh, I missed that problem. Why was my answer not right? I see, I have to multiply this number by both of the numbers in parentheses; that makes it work out right. And that makes sense when I think about some examples. I'll remember this for next time." (Learning from the experience.)

"Hooray, I've learned how to do this type of problem! I couldn't do it before, and now I can! That's progress! That's what I get for working hard and long!" (That was celebrating his own choice.)

"Thanks to my tutor for helping me! I'm glad she was patient with me today." (Celebrating someone else's choice.)

"I'm lucky this tutor was available at this time." (Celebrating luck.)

How likely will this person be to succeed in catching up in math, compared with the person who thinks in this way: "It's just horrible that I can't do what other kids can do. I can't stand being reminded of that." (Awfulizing.) "I'm just stupid. I'll never be able to do this, because I just don't have what it takes." (Getting down on himself.) "These stupid people who write math books. They just like to torture people. I hate them all." (Blaming someone else.)

How do people learn to do too much awfulizing and getting down on themselves and blaming others? Often they learn it by simply internalizing the things other people say to them when they fail or when they make a mistake. When they hear these things from other people often enough, they often say the things to themselves, as if they've been programmed. It can be helpful to realize that you're imitating someone else's sentences. Discovering this sometimes makes it easier not to keep saying them to yourself.

An accounting system for awfulizing or not awfulizing

How bad is a certain mistake or failure? It's sometimes useful to quantify this, by going systematically through a list and deciding what was lost, and what remains, in each category.

Life and limb: How badly was I injured? Were other people killed or injured? How permanent are the injuries? How much am I or they still able to function?

Money: How much money was lost? How much do I have left?

Time: How many hours will it take to repair this? How much time do I have left?

Relationships: What portion of the people in my social network who used to like me, now dislike me as a result of what happened? How many friends do I have left?

Reputation: How many people who don't actually know me think bad things about me as a result of this?

Capacity to do good: To what extent am I still able to contribute to the world and do good for people?

Predictability and control: How much control did I have over this? How well could I have predicted this would happen? How intentional was what I did, versus being accidental?

People spend lots of time feeling very bad about mistakes and failures where the harm done is negligible. And people have been able to withstand mistakes and failures where the damage in these areas has been very severe. The things I talked about in the section on frustration tolerance, under the topic of broadening the limits of the rating scale, apply here as well. Getting perspective on how the harm done by a certain mistake or failure stacks up against the worst experiences human beings have endured can be very helpful in withstanding the mistake or failure.

The four R's in responding to mistakes and failures

When we or other people make mistakes and fail at things, what responses are most useful? The four R's give a simple outline for useful responding.

Responsibility
Restitution
Redecision
Rehearsal

Responsibility is for some people the most difficult part of handling mistakes and failures. It's the ability to say, "Yes. I did do something I wish I hadn't done. This action was, at least, partially under my own control. It was not simply the fault of someone else who made me do it or the fault of circumstances. I made a choice that was not the best choice." This taking responsibility for the action is an important predecessor of the remaining steps. It's a difficult challenge for anyone who thinks he's perfect or needs to feel that way.

Restitution is trying to somehow make it up to the person one has harmed. For example, if a child hits his brother and gets a time out for it, this penalty has no benefit for the brother who has been hit. But the brother does benefit if the child who hit him is told to give the brother one of his favorite possessions in restitution. If someone steals something from a store, it doesn't do the shopkeeper any good for that person to stay in jail for a while, but it does do the shopkeeper good if the person pays the shopkeeper back for what was stolen three or five times over.

If a man speaks very disrespectfully to his wife, it doesn't do the wife any good for the man to punish himself by making a suicide attempt. What does do the wife some good is for the man to make restitution by speaking much more respectfully and being kind and considerate to the wife from then on.

Sometimes restitution is best determined by asking the victim of the harmful act what they would consider to be adequate restitution.

Does restitution have any meaning when the only person harmed is you? How do you make restitution to yourself for not studying and flunking a test? You can try to make it up to yourself, and undo whatever harm you have done to yourself, perhaps, for example, by working extra hard on the course. For some mistakes and failures there's no possibility of restitution because no one was harmed. If this is so, you can celebrate that!

Redecision means asking yourself, "What do I wish I would have done, thought, or felt instead of what I did?" It's important when thinking of revisions to one's behavior to think in terms of thoughts and emotions and not just behavior. I mentioned previously the STEB matrix. STEB stands for Situation, Thought, Emotion, and Behavior. What was the situation I encountered? What was it that I thought? What was it that I felt? How did I behave, in a visible manner, and what bodily reactions did I have inside? Redecision means to fill in the matrix, to decide how I want to react to the same situation when it or something like it comes up again.

Figuring out what's the best thing to do in a situation often takes a good bit of time, thought, and research. But doing so is a very constructive action to take.

Rehearsal means having fantasy rehearsals, role-playing rehearsals, or real-life rehearsals of the DESIRABLE pattern. That is, rather than running through your mind over and over what you did that was a mistake, you run through your mind what you'd like to do the next time a similar situation arises.

Habit strength is of paramount importance in determining what we do. I can make a clear decision that the next time a certain situation comes up, I want to do a certain new thought, emotion, and behavior. But if I have done the old pattern five thousand times and I haven't done the new one even once, my habit strength usually creates too much inertia. It often makes me do the old pattern the 5,001st time rather than the new pattern for the first time.

Fantasy rehearsal or role-playing rehearsal is one of the ways out of this habit trap. It's one way of doing work to prevent future mistakes and failures. And work is probably the best of all psychological "defenses." The person who learns a reflex of going through the four R's in response to mistakes and failures, and works very hard in doing so, has learned a habit that will serve him well throughout life. This is a special case of the more general dissatisfaction-to-effort connection –the tendency to take constructive action when problems exist – which is the opposite of depression, and which I have advocated several times in this work.

Skill 26: Non-Jealousy

Magnanimity, or non-jealousy, or tolerating someone else's getting what you want, is another special case of frustration tolerance. It's tolerating two frustrations at once: not getting what you want and seeing someone else get it.

A special case of this skill is *sharing attention*. When a child has a brother or sister, this skill presents many challenges. The first-born child, for example, who has been used to getting an undivided portion of the parent's attention, now has to share that attention with a younger sibling. At many moments, the parent is not only ignoring her, but giving the desirable attention to someone else. The first-born child has had the time until the second child's birth to develop a feeling of entitlement to the parent's undivided attention.

How does a feeling of entitlement develop? Partly it develops simply by being given something regularly. Let's imagine that every month you send someone a check for $100. Like clockwork, the check arrives on the first day of the month, with no explanation. Imagine that you do this for three years. Then, all of the sudden, you stop the payments. What do you imagine the response of the person would be?

Unfortunately, many people would respond with anger: "Where is my check?" and not with "I never deserved this in the first place; thanks for giving it to me as long as you did." It's part of human nature that what people receive regularly, they begin to feel is owed to them.

Many times, then, a first-born child will feel that her rightful share of the parent's attention (that is, all of it) is being stolen by the second-born child. The second-born child is also not immune to wanting 100 percent of the parent's attention. If both children get reinforced by the parent's attention when they are particularly demanding, loud, and upset, that is if the "squeaky wheel gets the oil," a family can have two or more kids who are really bad at sharing a parent's attention.

As with all of these psychological skills, one of the first and most important steps in making progress in it is learning the meaning of the words for it. A second step is learning that it's a highly valued skill in the household. If you can think to yourself, "My family members really like it when I share attention well," you're much better off than if you don't even have those words in your vocabulary. Now every time the child has to share attention, she's not just losing something; she's gaining the opportunity to practice and demonstrate a highly valued skill.

Another phrase that covers part of the skill of non-jealousy is *tolerating unfairness*. When the pie is divided up, someone else gets a somewhat larger piece than you do. Someone else gets paid a little more than you do when you're doing a little more work than he is. Liars and cheats seem to prosper, whereas an honest person has bad luck and no end of troubles. One person in the family has to do more work than another. (Or even, each family member sees himself as doing more than all the others.) A person is happy to work for X dollars an hour, until he sees that someone else is getting X+1 dollars an hour. Again, the skill involved is frustration tolerance, with the added twist of comparison to someone else and seeing him getting something that you want.

The skills of sharing attention and tolerating unfairness are much easier if someone keeps in mind the concept of *enough*. If I feel that I've gotten enough pie, it doesn't bother me that someone else got more. If I can feel that I've had enough of my parent's attention, it doesn't bother me to see my sibling getting some of it. If I can feel that my salary is enough, I don't lose sleep over the information that someone is getting more (although I might use that information to help me in negotiations for a higher salary).

The idea that you can have enough, independent of what someone else has, is a viewpoint that aids in developing nonjealousy. The alternative to the viewpoint is as follows: "The person who gets the most, wins; and the person who gets the second most, loses."

Perhaps the second point of view is fostered in American culture by our tendency to put children into competitive sports as soon as or sometimes before they're able to keep up with the score. In such an environment, you learn quickly that scoring six goals is defined as a loss if the other team scores seven goals. You get a disapproving reaction from others if you try to suggest that six goals are enough, and your team really didn't need any more.

Or perhaps the absence of the notion of *enough* gets fostered in classrooms, where children are judged in comparison to their peers. If you're in a second grade classroom and reading at second grade level, that's not good *enough* if your peers are all reading at third and fourth grade level.

At almost any given time, a certain type of toy figure is the fad among children in the United States. How bad it can feel for some children to have only twenty of them, when peers or siblings have forty of them. Fortunately for the toy company, few children seem to have the notion that there is an *enough* associated with a certain number of these toys.

I saw a bumper sticker on an expensive car that made it a self-parody of the competitive attitude: "The person who has the most toys when he dies, wins." Many people pursue life as if this were literally true, competing with the neighbors or whatever other comparison group there is for more consumer goods – or if not for goods, then for power, prestige, or whatever else.

There are times when the competitive drive can be a very good and powerful motive for very useful accomplishment. It has not developed without a good reason. But if a person constantly finds himself upset, angry, and miserable because someone else has gotten a little more of something than he did, I would suggest that he spend time meditating on the meaning of the word *enough*.

Another part of non-jealousy is handling being the excluded one in a love triangle. For example, two males want to bond with one female; the female accepts one of them and rejects the other. For the rejected male to handle this requires more than the skill of handling rejection that we talked about earlier. Being excluded from a love triangle means not only that you don't get the love of the person you want; you also have to see, or at least can imagine, someone else's getting it. Some people have gone into rages of jealousy over this image, and there have been numerous murders spurred by such jealousy.

Having to deal with being the excluded third in a triangle is probably most intense when the desired relationship is that of romantic love and marriage. But in milder versions, the situation almost always occurs when three people spend time with one another. Sooner or later, two of the people will make an alliance that excludes the third person at least a little bit. Learning to keep your equanimity while being an excluded third is very important for psychological health.

Very simple ideas sometimes help when you find yourself the excluded third. Among them are: "there are other fish in the sea," which translates to "I do not have to make one person my entire social support system"; "tomorrow is another day," which translates to "the alliance that I find myself left out of today may change by tomorrow." The simple words to "Skip to My Lou" contain solace for the rejected third person: "Lost my partner, what'll I do? . . . I'll find a new one, a better one too!" And finally, being alone is not the end of the world. Sometimes "he travels fastest who travels alone."

As with all the other skills in this group, one usually wants to turn down the bad feelings that can come from a situation, but not to totally turn them off. To feel nothing but a cavalier apathy when one has lost a lover to someone else suggests that one's skill of loyalty has been sacrificed. The central idea for all these frustration tolerance skills is that you want to feel only as much bad feeling over a bad thing as is necessary for the bad feeling be an optimal signal and motivator, but not so much bad feeling that you immobilize yourself and interfere with your life's progress and your ability to do good.

Skill 27: Painful Emotion Tolerance

Talking about this skill can generate some sentences that require concentration. How about these: Painful emotion tolerance is the skill of feeling bad, without feeling bad about feeling bad. It's letting the first feeling bad be pain enough without generating more bad feeling.

Here's an example. Suppose two people are set to give a speech a group of people. They both feel anxiety: hearts pounding, hands sweating, a trembling feeling, and a worry that maybe they will look like fools. Let's suppose they each feel the same amount of anxiety.

Suppose the first person says to himself, "Oh no! I'm starting to get this terrible feeling! I can't stand this! What am I going to do! I can't make it go away! I've got to make it go away! But I can't!"

Suppose the second person says to himself, "This fear doesn't feel good. But I can handle it. I think I'll be able to give a good enough speech anyway. I've got everything written out, so even if the fear interferes with my ability to think, at least I can still read."

The first person is set up to go around the vicious cycle of painful emotion. This vicious cycle goes like this: First you feel bad. Then you feel scared or disappointed or worried or some other bad feeling about feeling bad. This makes you feel worse. Then you notice yourself feeling not only

bad, but worse, and this creates more bad feeling. This vicious cycle could be halted with better skill in painful emotion tolerance.

The second person demonstrates better skill in painful emotion tolerance. The second person doesn't like feeling fear but is prepared to gut it out. The second person also does something very important: he is defining success as being able to give a good enough speech, with or without the bad feeling, whereas the first is defining success as getting rid of the bad feeling. This is a very important difference in philosophy.

To make this philosophy a little more general, the second person has a philosophy of "The most important thing is to have the effect I desire on the world around me, and I'm willing to put up with a great deal of discomfort if necessary to do that." The first person's philosophy is more along the lines of "The most important thing is to feel good."

If your definition of success is to make the world a better place or some such external criterion, rather than to make yourself feel good, you're much less likely to hop onto the vicious cycle of painful emotion.

Let's look at some more examples of the vicious cycle of painful emotion. Some people misinterpret the feeling of the flight-or-fight response to be a feeling of impending death! Someone's heart starts to pound and he feels short of breath. He thinks to himself, "Maybe I'm having a heart attack. Maybe I'm going to die!" These are very scary thoughts. These thoughts lead to even greater anxiety, and the vicious cycle has started.

Or, someone else feels the flight-or-fight response and he thinks to himself, "I'm going crazy. I'm going to need to be locked up. I'm going to be held in a straight jacket. I'm going to be screaming. This is going to last for the rest of my life." These thoughts make him even more scared.

The feeling of fear is not the only painful emotion that can participate in this vicious cycle. People who get down on themselves and feel guilty and make themselves worthless can go around in a similar vicious circle. Suppose a person makes a mistake and gets down on himself and feels guilty and worthless. Then he notices how he is feeling discouraged and guilty and he gets down on himself for this, thinking "I'm feeling horrible again, over something little. This means there's something wrong with me. I'm defective. No one else does this, just me." Then he feels even more discouraged and worthless.

The first vicious cycle we described was "awfulizing about awfulizing"; the second one was "getting down on yourself for getting down on yourself." Both vicious circles are made greater by people's noticing the negative emotion in themselves and the physiological effects of that emotion, and responding with awfulizing or getting down on yourself in response to those effects.

Another frequent vicious cycle involves the fear of the effects of losing sleep. This cycle often starts when someone is worried about something going on. The worry keeps the person from falling asleep. Then the person thinks, "Oh no. I'm not falling asleep. I'm going to be sleepy or grumpy or have a headache (or something else) tomorrow. I can't take this." Now he has something else to worry about, and that worry also tends to keep him awake. He tries very hard to get to sleep, and fails, and this is more worrisome still.

People who do research on sleep find that the best advice for people in this state is to get up out of bed, quit trying to go to sleep and do something until you're sleepy. My recommendation is to do useful but boring work. (The task I use is to sort through piles of mail and get bills paid.) If there is a worrisome or pressing life problem, then I recommend working on it by organizing your thoughts in writing. You return to bed when you feel a little tired, and if you don't get to sleep in 20 minutes, get back up and do something useful again. If the plan is to get up and get some work done in the event of sleeplessness, then it's possible to look at sleeplessness with a different attitude. Rather than "I can't take this," one can say, "Here's a chance for me to accomplish something. I'll feel good about having gotten this work done. If I feel sleepy or out of sorts tomorrow, that's tough, I'll cope."

The vicious cycles I've mentioned so far are mediated by a response to negative emotion with more negative emotion. Other vicious cycles are mediated by avoidance. The fear-of-failure vicious cycle is one I've mentioned before. Someone experiences failure and feels very bad about failing. In response, he avoids the whole endeavor. Because he avoids it, he gets no practice at it. Avoiding practice leads the person to be still less competent than those who have practiced and thus to more failure. If the person can muster the skill of tolerating painful emotion enough to confront the skill he's not good at, and practice it, he can gradually improve at it and start building upon successes.

Another sort of vicious cycle involves using a substance to numb psychic pain. For example, a man has problems in his relationships at home and problems with his performance at work. He feels bad about both of these. To numb his pain, he drinks alcohol. When he does this, he doesn't feel so bad for the time being. However, he impairs his judgment and does things that worsen his relationships with family members and impairs his job performance even more. So now there are more bad feelings and still more reasons to drink to numb those. Again, if he could muster the painful emotion tolerance skills to work on the problems he

has at home and at work and gradually make things better, he could escape this vicious cycle.

There are vicious cycles that revolve around physical pain as well as psychic pain. Suppose someone starts to get a headache. In order to avoid the pain, the person tightens up and braces his muscles. But this tightening up only makes the pain worse. But this worse pain provokes even more tightening.

Here's another vicious cycle involving physical pain. Someone gets a pain that doesn't go away. The person responds by ceasing to do activities or work, and this gives him more time on his hands. When he spends lots of time doing nothing, he has less to distract him from the pain, and the pain seems still worse. He avoids more and more activities, to the point where he has little to think about but his pain.

The chapter on courage skills presents techniques for overcoming fears or compulsions. If you have an unrealistic fear, the best way to get over it is to expose yourself to the situation you fear long enough for the fear to go down. If you have a compulsion, the best way to get over it is to expose yourself to the situation that makes you want to do the compulsion, but endure the bad feeling of not doing the compulsion. You do this long enough for the bad feeling to go down, without escaping the situation.

What's the main problem that most people have with doing these things? It's mustering the skills of painful emotion tolerance and putting up with discomfort long enough for the discomfort to go down.

The skill of painful emotion tolerance is helped by certain philosophical beliefs we've mentioned earlier. If you believe, "The only important thing is how I feel," then feeling discomfort and pain seems like a momentous event. If you believe, "The most important thing is that I do things that make me better off and make the rest of the world a better place," then my bad feelings are less important – and I can make them less important by trying not to let them interfere with my doing worthy actions.

The skill of painful emotion tolerance requires some careful discriminations or good answers to the question: should this situation be toughed out, or should I try to escape it? Sometimes painful emotion is a signal that you should do something very quickly to protect yourself from danger. As is discussed in the courage skills chapter, you want to engage in rational self-protection when there really is danger, and you want to tough out the unrealistic fear when there isn't danger.

Suppose someone is outside on a very sunny day and notices her skin getting more and more red and painful. Suppose she says to herself, "I think I'll just have to exercise my painful emotion tolerance skills and tough out this pain I feel in my skin." She would be making a large error. The pain is a very accurate signal that something wrong is happening and she needs to take corrective action.

Skill 28: Fantasy Tolerance

Fantasy tolerance is the skill of tolerating unwanted images or ideas that intrude into your mind.

Why is it useful to cultivate this skill anyway? There are good reasons not to spend much time imagining yourself acting in ways you must not act in real life. Throughout this book I've emphasized the use of fantasy practice. When you imagine a pattern of thought, emotion, and behavior, you can strengthen your tendency to act that way in real life. It's good if your fantasy helps you practice patterns that will be useful to you rather than patterns you must avoid. For this reason, I recommend, for example, that people avoid indulging themselves in pleasant fantasies of being violent toward their enemies.

But sometimes people have images pop into their heads that are the direct opposite of what they want to happen. A high school student gets an image of vomiting all over classmates. A priest gets an image of himself committing blasphemy. A very moralistic person gets a fantasy of inappropriate sexual activity. A mother gets an image of doing something violent to her child.

Perhaps the two main areas of intrusive images are sexuality and violence. Sex is very different from violence. It is very desirable, perhaps the most desirable goal of humanity, to aim for a world without violence. But if the species is to continue, no rational person would want to aim toward a world without sex. Yet, in sexuality as well as violence, most people would have no difficulty in conjuring up images that, if enacted, would result in much trouble and harm.

If you have never had an intrusive fantasy image, I'd like you to do a quick experiment to help you empathize with those who have. Could you please try very hard *not* to think about a polar bear? Try not to let the visual image of the bear's white fur or the auditory image of a growling sound or the sound of the word "bear" come anywhere close to your consciousness. Take a few seconds to do this.

Most people fail when they try hard not to think of something. And the harder they try, the more likely they are to fail. Why? Because when you try hard at any task, you tend to monitor whether you're succeeding or not.

Suppose you were offered a big reward for doing twenty push-ups with your body perfectly straight. While performing, you'd be thinking, "Is my body straight? Here goes number thirteen, fourteen, am I still straight?" Likewise, when you're trying not to think of the polar bear, such monitoring thoughts go something like this: "Am I thinking about a bear? Is it a white one? . . . Oops, I thought about that bear again."

When a fantasy image elicits a great deal of shame, guilt or fear, it usually causes people to self-monitor all the more strongly. The image then can become all the more persistent. The more it comes, the more the person worries about it. A vicious cycle gets started, and the person now has what's called an "obsession": a thought that comes over and over in an unwanted way.

The crucial idea to remember is that the energy that perpetuates this unwanted thought is derived from the shame, guilt, and fear associated with the thought and the strong wish to be rid of the thought.

How can we end this cycle? The best way is to deplete the energy source. If the person can start thinking, "OK, it isn't the end of the world that this idea pops into my mind," victory over the obsession has begun. If the person can think, "I'm not going to try to get it out of my mind – I'm just going to let it run its course," the victory is more assured. If the person can think, "I'll just direct my energy, not to getting it out of my mind, but toward doing what's best to do while it runs its course in the background," then victory is even closer. If the person thinks, "What do you know? I can do what I need to do, even while this thought goes on in my head. Even if it doesn't go away very quickly, I can still lead a useful and pleasant life," then the problem is all but solved.

Here's a basic belief that helps you voice these ideas: it's good to have a wider range of permissible fantasies than permissible behaviors. In fantasy, for example, you can generate a wide range of options, before you zero in on one to really carry out. When you're solving a problem, it's good to be able to think of many more things you might do than options you actually will do.

Sometimes thinking of a silly or ridiculous option might free up your thinking to allow you to land on one that really is workable. Bad actions and real-life events are much more harmful than bad fantasy images. Wouldn't you prefer to have someone have a fantasy of killing you than to actually kill you? If you're like me and would rather have a million people fantasize killing you than have one person actually do it, that's pretty strong evidence for this proposition.

Sometimes fantasies of bad behavior can have a signal function, just as painful emotion can have a signal function. For example, a mother starts getting hostile and violent fantasies toward her child. The image comes to mind of throwing the child in the trashcan and getting on a plane to Brazil. When she asks herself why she would get such fantasies, she acknowledges to herself that she is starting to resent the degree to which the child is tying her down and totally restricting her freedom. She decides the fantasy is telling her she wants to escape from responsibility for just a little while. When she thinks rationally, she decides she should not be quite so perfectionistic about baby sitters as she has been. She has required so much of a baby sitter that literally no one on Earth has qualified. She completes a very thorough evaluation of potential baby sitters and selects a very competent one to stay with her child while she at least goes to see a good Brazilian movie!

Her fantasy was telling her something about herself. Because she had the fantasy tolerance skills to be able to step back and look at it and examine it and ask the question, "What useful information, if any, is this fantasy giving me?" she could make productive use of the information her fantasy generator was giving her.

Sometimes strategies other than those I've mentioned are useful in dealing with intrusive images. If you have lots of intrusive violent images, it's good to take an inventory of the amount of violence you view in the media. Violent images in the media can, for example, work their way into nightmare images.

Another source of intrusive images is real-life traumatic events. People who have had very horrible experiences sometimes have the memories of those experiences come back and produce strong negative emotion, either triggered by some reminder or just "out of the blue." The basic strategy of not trying to resist the image, but letting it run its course, is often useful with these posttraumatic images.

With both obsessions and posttraumatic images, sometimes the best strategy is not only letting the scary image run its course, but also trying deliberately to bring it to mind, under safe and supportive circumstances, so you can get used to it. Sometimes it's good to bring the image to mind while simultaneously doing something else. This demonstrates to yourself that you can make voluntary, purposeful actions even with the unwanted image going through your mind.

The word "habituate" means "to get used to it," or to have such prolonged exposure to something fearful that it doesn't to scare you so much. In the chapter on courage skills I discuss more thoroughly the basic fear-reduction technique of exposure to the scary thing. I underscore the fact that, for exposure to work, it has to last long enough for the fear to decrease somewhat. If you escape from the exposure just when you're most scared, the fear may be strengthened rather than weakened.

Group 6: Good Decisions

In any given situation, how do we choose which thoughts, emotions, and behaviors are the best? The "good decisions" group encompasses many important psychological skills oriented toward this crucial goal.

This group is divided into two parts, individual decision-making and joint decision-making. In individual decision-making, the question on the table is, "What am *I* going to do?" For joint decision-making, the question is, "What are *we* going to do?"

The skills of joint decision-making have also been put in the category of conflict resolution, problem-solving, or dispute management skills. If the skills are used most expertly, joint decisions can be made before they become conflicts, problems, or disputes.

Skill 29: Positive Aim

Positive aim means trying to make circumstances better rather than worse in the long run. It means really wanting to improve things, rather than wanting to make things turn out badly or fail. Some people seem to have motives to make things worse. What possible motives could these be?

In the chapter on relaxation, we discuss sensation-seeking or stimulus-seeking as one such motive, For some people with very high needs for stimulation, the excitement generated by getting people to yell at you is more reinforcing than their anger is punishing. For extreme stimulus-seekers, irritating people and getting people to hate you is sometimes just a side effect of constantly seeking stimulation rather than approval. The remedy for this problem is to improve the skill of handling low stimulation. The issue here is not getting relaxed, but finding it pleasant to be relaxed.

Children who grow up in a sensation-seeking culture where violent movies and violent video games are daily fare can become convinced that kindness, solving problems, peace and nonviolence are simply no fun – they are not entertaining. This can be a very important source of the problem of lack of positive aim. A child in today's culture usually needs strong counter-indoctrination if the child is to become convinced that helping people avoid violence, settle problems peacefully and get along harmoniously with one another is even a desirable goal. A steady diet of kind interactions and rational problem-solving makes for a much better life than it does stage drama or movie drama. Confusing what is entertaining to watch with what is reasonable to do is easy in a world that relies so heavily on entertainment value as the criterion for goodness.

A second motive for making things worse rather than better springs from low skills in tolerating aloneness and inattention, combined with low skills in social initiations. In this case, social interaction of a hostile nature is sometimes better than no social interaction at all. For example, a kindergarten child desperately wishes to play with peers, but he doesn't know how to get started with it. So he comes up and knocks over the structure they're building out of blocks, with a teasing grin on his face. If the other kids yell at him and chase him, he laughs with delight. But once they start to shun him and ignore him, he's very unhappy indeed. The remedy for this sort of problem is a course in the skills of tolerating inattention (enjoying aloneness) and in social initiations.

Another motive for making things worse is being hooked on pity. Sometimes someone wants approval or some sort of positive regard from other people, and cannot tolerate disapproval, rejection or criticism. But suppose the person is also deficient in the skills of work-related activities, social conversation, recreational activities, and other behaviors that win approval from other people. The person may find that getting pity from other people is the most reliable way of acquiring positive interaction. So the person gets himself into some sort of pitiable condition in order that nice helpers can minister to him. There are some marriages that are built on this type of relationship: one person needs to be pitied and rescued, and the other person has a constant need to be in the helper role. One problem with these relationships is that the rescuer tends to burn out. The other is that the pitied person needs to keep failing in order to preserve the nature of the relationship.

Sometimes people who *are* competent at getting approval and attention from others in appropriate ways get hooked on pity anyway. The good feeling of being cared for and nurtured takes on an addictive quality.

A similar sort of motive is using self-destructive actions to make a cry for help, sometimes when asking for help in more appropriate ways is not acceptable to the person. For example, an adolescent hates her school. She would like to admit that the situation is intolerable and ask her parents to send her somewhere else. But she would feel too ashamed of asking for help in such a straightforward way. She makes a sui-

cidal gesture as a way of acting out her need for nurture and mobilizing people to help her.

Using self-destructive actions to get people to feel guilty and avoid separating from you, when you have a big fear of separation, is another similar motive. For example, someone is about to be rejected by a boyfriend. But when she makes a suicide attempt, the boyfriend gets back together with her and tries to help her. The boyfriend would feel too guilty if she really killed herself, so for the time being he resolves to just stick with her. Of course, later when the fear of her suicide gets less, the same problems resurrect themselves. The remedy for her is to increase the skills of separation tolerance.

Here's another brand of the wish for self-harm or failure. Someone has been reinforced so much for getting hurt or experiencing difficulties that the motive to do badly achieves some sort of functional autonomy. The motive becomes capable of sustaining itself with no reinforcement or at least very little. For example, a young child is ignored a good part of the time by a parent, except when he falls down and hurts himself or gets hit by someone and starts crying. When he is hurt, sick, or being treated badly, the parent is quite attentive. The parent's use of differential attention in this situation tends to reinforce the child's tendency to display (and feel!) negative emotion rather than go for the situations and the outcomes that will produce positive emotion.

Another brand of low skill in positive aim comes when someone has been convinced, somehow, that she is a bad person who's not deserving of good things. She adopts a core belief that the only possible outcomes for her are negative ones. One of the nine major influence methods we've discussed is attribution. Some children grow up hearing negative attributions about themselves most of the time, e.g., "You're no good. Nothing good is ever going to become of you. You can't do anything right."

Sometimes the child gradually develops a belief system about himself and about his position in the world that goes something like this: "It's impossible that things will turn out well; my role in life is to continue to screw things up." The person can get so familiar with the role of "loser," so used to it, that to step out of it into the role of the successful and happy person would feel strange, scary, unfamiliar, undeserved, or not right in various other ways. Sometimes the person never brings this belief system to conscious awareness. But the remedy is to put the belief system into words, and to challenge and question it and look for the evidence for and against it.

Another reason for low skills in positive aim is tied to fear of failure. The person fears a success would elevate the standards by which she is judged, so that future attempts will be judged failures more often. The thought pattern goes like this: "If I make great grades in school, everyone will expect me to do well from now on. They'll be angry with me if I don't succeed. But without any big success, people maintain their expectation that I'll always hover on the brink of failure."

On many occasions, I've seen teachers and parents reacting to a child's success with tone of "Aha! Now I've got you!" The thought pattern is, "You did it! Now we know you can do it. Now we're not going to tolerate any of this nonsense from here on out!" The child who expects this sort of reaction to successes is given a strong disincentive to success.

Thus, one way of helping this brand of low positive aim for parents and teachers is to acquire a "shaping attitude." The shaping attitude means you celebrate successes, but don't make a big deal of failures. The person interacting with those who have a shaping attitude has everything to gain by success and nothing to lose by failure.

In addition to reshaping the external reinforcement contingencies for success and failure, another part of the remedy for this particular brand of problems with positive aim is for the person to improve his skills in handling mistakes and failures. If the person is in the habit of seeing a failure as something to learn from, as something that will make success in the next similar challenge more likely, then it's less likely that he'll fail in order to avoid having his standard raised.

Yet another brand of low skills in positive aim comes from being caught up in a sub-culture that approves of self-destructive or painful behavior. For example, certain work subcultures give approval only to those who work eighty-hour weeks. Some people in such a work culture may not want to subject themselves to such a grueling routine. But their fear of disapproval, fear of rejection, or insufficient problem-solving and decision-making in finding other options, combined with strong external reinforcement contingencies, make these people act masochistic.

As another example of self-destructive subcultures, I've seen some groups of adolescents where slamming your fist into a wall (sometimes breaking hand bones) was considered a macho thing to do. The person who did this would gain, at least in his own mind, a certain reputation: being intense, having very powerful emotions, and being able to exert strong force. When the opinion-makers of the group became enlightened enough to redefine hitting walls as a stupid act rather than a macho act, the frequency of wall-hitting went down.

Here's another classic explanation for masochistic behavior: physical pain acquires secondary reinforcing qualities by being repeatedly reinforced by the cessation of rejection and hostility. Throughout childhood, the person repeatedly does the same disapproved behavior. Then the person is subjected to extremely painful rejection, hostility and withdrawal of friendliness and support by his parents. Then the person is physically punished. Immediately after the physical punishment, the parents consider the person to have suffered enough for his sins. The withdrawal of friendliness and giving then ceases, and the hostility and rejection are over.

Thus, the infliction of pain comes to be associated with the cessation of the unfriendliness. If the person with this sort of conditioning in childhood then later on experiences from other people love, concern, and helping attitudes immediately after getting an injury of some sort, especially a self-inflicted one, the connection is reinforced further.

A final mechanism for masochistic behavior is going overboard on self-discipline. In the chapter on self-discipline we mentioned the pleasure principle – do what feels best in the short run – versus the reality principle – do what produces the most long-term good and happiness. Some people so strongly avoid being ruled by the pleasure principle that they adopt a "pain principle": whatever would feel best in the short run, do the opposite of it. "No pain, no gain" becomes the ruling principle of life.

The extreme use of self-discipline is often reinforced by attaining goals. For example, someone in an endurance sport, such as distance running or swimming, is reinforced for endless grueling practice by winning races. Sometimes athletes fail to discriminate how much self-denial is too much and ruin their careers, for example, by running on an injured leg to the point of permanent injury. Similarly, in business, working compulsively can be rewarded by making money. Failing to discriminate how much self-denial is too much can lead to the workaholic's finding himself without real relationships with family or friends.

Thus ends my catalogue of mechanisms whereby people can seem to be motivated to make things worse for themselves rather than better. If you recognize yourself in any of these patterns, the insight into the pattern can be helpful in avoiding it. I believe that these patterns are very common and that at least one of them exists to some degree in almost all of us.

As with all maladaptive patterns, one approach to overcoming this one is not to spend much time analyzing and figuring out what one is doing wrong, but simply to mount a large effort to do things right. You might repetitively affirm to yourself several things, as follows: "I wish strongly to have things turn out well." "I aim for choices that will make me and others happiest in the long run." Then each day, try to act in accordance with these affirmations, and monitor your success day after day. Trying very hard to do the positive pattern of making things come out well can sometimes steamroll right over the complex dynamics that would make you want to do badly.

Skill 30: Thinking before Acting

What's the difference between the skill of thinking before acting and that of decision-making? Decision-making is the skill of thinking *well* and *proficiently* about what to do. Thinking before acting is just thinking *at all* about what to do. Thinking before acting is necessary for good decision-making, but not sufficient for it. However, just starting to think *at all* is often the step that's left out by most of us when we mess things up badly.

Thinking before acting is the opposite of impulsiveness. Impulsiveness means doing the first thing that pops into mind without considering the consequences and without considering other options. People who do dangerous things without thinking beforehand need to improve in this skill. Danger can include physical danger or danger to reputation or relationships. The skill of thinking before acting has a good deal of overlap with the skill of carefulness.

One central element of thinking before acting is simply becoming aware that you have arrived at a choice point. In working with people with impulsiveness problems, many times I've asked the question, "What are some choice points you've encountered lately?" Often the answer is "There are none." If someone feels as though he's not encountering any choice points, that probably means he's choosing more or less by reflex or unconscious action. Actually, if you're awake, you're at a choice point. The only question is how important the choice point is.

Let's say I'm sitting and chatting with someone. His decision to walk into the same room with me represented one choice point. The decision to sit down rather than to remain standing was another choice point. The decision to listen to my question rather than hold his hands over his ears was another choice, and the decision to answer with the words "There are none" was another.

Every utterance made to anyone represents a choice point we're making. Every movement we make in any direction represents a choice to do that movement in that direction as contrasted to going in a different direction. The decision to get out of bed in the morning is a choice. The decision to brush your teeth in the morning is a choice. Every meal involves a choice of whether or what to eat. Every day involves a choice of how much work to do and when to keep working versus when to call it quits. Every social encounter involves a choice of how friendly to be, how dominating to be, how much interest in the other person to communicate, and a host of other variables. Every day involves a decision about how to use the time allotted to that day and what items to put on the agenda.

Every moment of the day involves a choice point as to what posture to assume in that moment. Do you have any money? Then you have to choose whether to save it or spend it, and how to do either of these. Each time we are exposed to any sounds or sights, we have a choice as to what we want to pay attention to, what we want to focus on, how strongly we want to concentrate. At any given instant, each act of driving a car involves how fast to go, which route to take, how closely to be watching the other drivers on the road, when to pull out into traffic, when to change lanes, etc. We are literally at a choice point every waking moment.

At any given moment we can use decision-making tactics to try to maximize the expected outcome of the choice. Or, we cannot bother to do this, and just do what comes naturally. There are lots of times where doing what comes naturally is good enough. The heart of the skill of thinking before acting is selecting the choice points where we want to think, and separating those out from those where it's fine to do what comes naturally.

Let's think about what determines what we do "naturally." One determinant is the force of inertia or habit. Doing what comes naturally often means doing whatever I've done before in similar circumstances. If I've handled a certain situation very successfully many times before, then I can afford to go on automatic pilot. If not, I'd better think.

Another determinant, discussed in the chapter on self-discipline, is the pleasure principle: whatever feels good at the moment. A third determinant of what comes naturally is what other people are doing. Whether we like it or not, most of us are like sheep in many ways; a certain mob psychology is basic to most people.

A fourth source of doing what comes naturally is the models that have become deposited in our memory banks. For example, the parent who was screamed at a great deal by a parent during his childhood often finds it very difficult not to reenact those screams in parenting his own children. When we decide what to do, we search through the images that have been laid down in our memory banks, and if there are a vast number of memories of a certain type – for example, hostile screams – we will have to exert more effort to search for different images.

Becoming aware of these different determinants of doing what comes naturally will help us to realize what we are up against when we want to really think before acting. When doing what you've done before, what feels good, what others are doing, and what you've seen and heard the most are NOT the best things to do, then it's crucial to stop and think before acting.

Here are some other clues that it's important to think before you act.

1. When you have the urge to do anything violent.

2. When you might take a drug – including alcohol or tobacco.

3. When you might go fast in a car, boat, or anything else.

4. When you might go into a high place from which you could fall.

5. When you might do something you don't want someone else to know about.

6. When you might tell a secret or promise to keep a secret.

7. When someone is very angry with you or you're very angry with someone.

8. When you're in the presence of a gun or other weapon.

9. When you might have a sexual encounter.

10. When you might make a promise to someone else, especially a major one.

11. When the news media are interested in what you're doing.

12. Whenever there's physical danger for any reason.

13. When you're about to make a policy that will affect a good bit of other people's behavior.

14. When you have the urge to criticize someone strongly.

You might want to think about what items should be added to this list. These items alone, I would guess, cover a large portion of the situations where people make their most damaging mistakes. In fact, I would suggest, as an exercise, doing fantasy rehearsals of remembering thinking before acting in several sorts of situations like those above.

What are some other exercises? One is to sit and list in detail the choice points you've encountered on a given day. Start with the decision to get out of bed, and go to the decision about whether to wash your face or go to the toilet next, and proceed. The purpose of this exercise is to train yourself to recognize choice points.

The next exercise involves deciding which choice points have been important ones in your life. Go through and think about times when there has been unhappiness and failure, or times when there has been happiness and success. Recall the choice points that led to these outcomes, and recall what you chose. Write out the choice point as a short problem statement. Keep going until you can say, "If I had made a good decision at each of these choice points, my life would have been much better than it is now."

For practice, you can add to the list of choice points for by creating imaginary choice points and writing them down. Fantasy choice points can be as useful as real ones.

Here are a couple of examples of what written versions of these choice points might look like:

You are in school. A classmate has just taken an expensive instrument from a science lab. He wants to pack away the instrument, but can't find his backpack. He says, "Let me borrow

your backpack for a while, will you?"
What options can you think of?

You are at work. Your boss
gives you a very harsh lecture for what
you regard as a very small mistake.
What options can you think of?

You have a best friend. Another
friend says to you, "I'm going to tell
you something, but promise you won't
tell your friend, OK?" How could you
reply?

There are many problem situations written in the booklet I wrote
called the *Options and Consequences
Book*. But this exercise calls upon you
to make up the problems, not to respond
to problems someone else has written.
This gives you exercise in identifying
and formulating choice points, which is
often a more difficult stage in the process than deciding upon them once
they're formulated.

Another exercise is to take hypothetical situations and practice listing
options and choosing among them,
picking the best way you can to respond
to each of them. Still another is to consider a certain option for a certain situation and to practice listing the possible
consequences of that action. These are
the exercises for which the *Options and
Consequences Book* was created. Making lots of decisions on hypothetical or
real problems consciously and systematically is an antidote to the pattern of
acting without thinking.

Skill 31: Verbal Fluency

Anthropologists have studied how the words in a language tell us about the thoughts and the world view of the people who speak that language. For example, a language spoken by natives of the Arctic regions contains many words for different types of snow. The fact that this culture developed so many different words for snow indicates that people in this culture are accustomed to doing a lot of thinking about distinctions between one type of snow and another.

You don't have to go to distant cultures to realize that, when people develop ways of thinking about things, they develop words for those ways of thinking. A doctor or anatomist will think about arteries, arterioles, capillaries, venules, and veins, whereas a layperson may simply think about blood vessels. Someone will not get far in dealing with computers unless he knows about ram and bytes and baud. Dancers invent terms like ball-change, fifth position, and rock step. Musicians think in terms of keys, tempo, staccato, and vibrato. Mathematicians speak of equations, variables, derivatives, cosines, and pi. Whenever there is any area of knowledge, there are words invented to describe the concepts that are the building blocks of those ideas.

In fact, it would be very difficult to develop specialized knowledge without inventing a vocabulary to express it.

Words are units that let us think about things. Knowing words lets us have thoughts we could not otherwise think.

This idea applies as much to psychological skills as it does to any other area of knowledge. For example, it's hard to think, "I'd like to get better at frustration tolerance" if you don't have a word in your vocabulary that means frustration tolerance. It's hard to think, "Do I want to stick up for my own way, or give in," if "sticking up for your own way" and "giving in" are not phrases that are in your vocabulary. It's easier to think, "I want not to get down on myself so much and spend more energy listing options and learning from the experience," when you have words in your vocabulary for these types of thoughts.

It's easier to think, "OK, this is a situation that is bad maybe 2 on a scale of 10, but certainly nowhere approaching 10," when you have in your vocabulary what 2 and 10 on a scale of 10 mean. It's easier for someone to take pleasure in his acts of kindness when he knows fully what acts of kindness mean, and can give concrete examples of them. Preschool children can learn to problem-solve more easily if they know the word *or*, as in "I could grab the toy away, OR I could ask for it."

The language of psychological skills is meant not to be a specialized language for mental health professionals but a language for all people to think about how they are handling situations.

Learning words can be a big step on the way toward becoming more psychologically skilled. This is especially true for children whose vocabularies are often less formed than adults. But it's true for adults as well. The strategy is, what sorts of thoughts are necessary to do a psychological skill well, and what words are necessary to think those thoughts? If a person is to celebrate his using a good pattern of thought, feeling, or behavior in a certain psychological skill, that person needs a name for the psychological skill and a name for the good pattern he used.

Part of the *Exercises for Psychological Skills* book is a glossary of words useful for psychological health skills. If people who don't know these words can gradually learn their meanings, they will be better equipped to think the thoughts necessary for psychological health skills.

Narratives

One of the subskills of verbal fluency is accurately observing and then being able to narrate the events that happened in one's life. I've placed a major emphasis in this series on being able to think about the situations one experiences, the thoughts, emotions, and behaviors that one does in situations, and being able to decide whether new sets of thoughts, emotions, or behaviors are more desirable, and then to rehearse those new sets of thoughts,

emotions, and behaviors. Or, to look at those situations, thoughts, emotions, and behaviors and decide, "I handled this well," and then to celebrate and further rehearse that positive handling of the situation. This is a generic program for psychological development.

However, the foundation for all this activity is registering, remembering, and narrating the stories that constitute these situations and the reactions to those situations. Some people with adequate enough vocabularies are nonetheless deficient in telling about things that happened to them, the true stories of their experience. To paraphrase George Santayana: If you can't remember and narrate the past, then you're doomed not to learn from it. Failing to learn from experience is exactly what seems to happen to people who are most deficient in the skills of remembering what happened to them and then telling about it.

Sometimes people can narrate portions of stories that happened to them, but they don't choose the correct starting point. For example, a child tells the story of an argument that happened between herself and her mother. She says that her mother screamed out and called her a nasty name, and, in response, she hit her mother. That's all that happened, according to the narrator. When you hear the story from a few other observers, however, you find that the story really began when the mother asked the child to start her homework. The child yelled a defiant "No!" at her mother. The mother then took the child by the hand to walk to the child's desk. The child pinched the mother on the hand with her fingernails. The mother screamed out in pain and anger. In response to this, the child hit her mother. The full version contains a chain of events that are causally related to one another, starting with a conflict over homework. The child's version left out the conflict over homework, the child's defiance, and the escalation of hostility.

What is the advantage of being able to tell the whole story to yourself? When you can do this, you're in a much better position to learn from the experience. The child who remembers the story only as "My mom was mean to me, and I hit her," might have as the only take-home message from the experience, "I wish I didn't have such a mean mommy." But the one who can narrate the whole story can think, "One lesson from this is that I need to figure out how to deal better with starting my homework. I also need to be able to handle it better when my mom makes me do something. I also need practice in keeping cool instead of getting so angry."

Poor narrators often fail to grasp causal relations. The child in the previous example may be at a total loss to say what the cause was of the mother's screaming at her. Many decisions involve making causal inferences. Much has been said in the literature of experimental and empirical research methods about how you draw causal inferences. Each human being is an amateur scientist who draws causal inferences and then tries to use those to control the things that are happening in life. Without recalling and narrating to yourself the data of experience, it's impossible to figure out what causes what.

Automatic thoughts

Throughout this book I've spoken of how useful it is to consciously choose thoughts. Do I want to awfulize or not awfulize, learn from the experience, list options? Is what I'm thinking now what I want to think, or do I want to choose a different way of thinking? Automatic thoughts are often expressed, not in clear language, but as fleeting images. Very negative thoughts tend to harm emotions and behaviors, and then quickly be forgotten. But putting automatic thoughts into clearly articulated words allows you to submit those thoughts to be tested for truth or falsehood. When people participate in cognitive therapy, they usually write down their automatic thoughts so they can consider them more thoroughly. Getting the thoughts clearly into words is the first step in altering them favorably.

Recognizing the logic or illogic of your thoughts

Another benefit of putting your experience into words is recognizing when your ideas are internally consistent, or whether you're trying to tell yourself something that's clearly contradicted by something else.

Here's an example: A counselor and a client have the following dialogue.

"Are there any problems you want to work on?"

"No, things are going pretty well."

"Is there anything you want to change about yourself?"

"No. I like myself pretty well. I'm pretty satisfied with the way I am."

"How happy are you now?"

"Pretty happy."

"Has anything changed in your life recently?"

"No, things have been going along about the same."

"How long ago was it that you wrote that suicide note and made that suicide attempt?"

"About a week I guess."

Obviously something doesn't add up here. If nothing has changed, how can life be going well now, yet bad enough to warrant a suicide attempt a week ago? When you can use words to conceptualize the world, you're at least in better position to recognize that you may be blinding yourself to part of reality.

Succinctness

Another subskill of using words well is narrating succinctly. This is the ability to tell a story with only the essential details. Some people with great skill deficiency in this area get started narrating but go in a tangential way from one detail to another without con-veying the point of it all. Others with less skill deficiency get to the point, but only after wasting a great deal of time recounting unnecessary details.

This skill, like many of those involved in this verbal fluency category, involves a multitasking activity of the brain. On the one hand, you're remembering the event and translating the images into a verbal narration. On the other hand, you're occasionally switching back to ideas about what the purpose of your narration is in the first place and constantly checking and comparing whether your narration is serving the purpose. Doing both of these tasks involves holding a fair amount of information in working memory.

There's another type of multitasking that goes on in expert communication with others. The narrator has images in mind of what happened during an event, but the person hearing or reading the narrative starts without the information the narrator has. The narrator must constantly store in memory what the audience has heard so far, and compare that with the memories the narrator himself has. If the narrator assumes knowledge that the audience doesn't have, the narrative may not make sense. On the other hand, if you don't remember what you have told and what you haven't, succinctness is difficult because you tend to say things over and over.

Criteria for coherence

Coherent use of language is language that makes sense. What makes language coherent? Let's list several criteria.

1. Information not relevant to the goals of the communication is left out, so as not to confuse the listener (even, or especially, if the listener is yourself)!

2. The information has a "one thing at a time" quality. That is, you present one point, give the information that supports or undermines it, then go to the next point, and give the information that relates to it. This is in contrast to skipping around from one idea to a supporting detail for another idea, then to different idea, so that you're trying to deal with everything at once.

3. The points are in some sort of logical sequence. If you're narrating a story, one possible logical order is chronological, although many narratives of course have made good use of flashbacks. If you're speaking about a problem, a possible logical order is the narration of the circumstances, a summary of the problem, a consideration of the goals, a generation of options, a discussion of advantages and disadvantages of the options, and a choice of an option. If you're making a logical argument, and some points depend on previous ones, you defend the previous points first. For example, suppose someone is arguing that guns should be less easily available. Which point should come first: that there is a need

for gun control, or that a certain plan is practical and workable? The point about the need for gun control comes first because, if the listener is not convinced of the need, it's a waste of time to think about particular plans.

4. The individual words and individual sentences in the communication are chosen so they make sense.

5. There are enough concrete examples that it's clear what you mean by the abstract words you use. When you say, "He tried to increase his productivity with edible reinforcers," you might also add, "For example, he would let himself eat one piece of mint candy for every hour he spent writing his book." Concrete words are words that call to mind particular images of pictures or sounds. Eating one piece of mint candy and working on writing a book for an hour are concrete images; edible reinforcement and productivity are more abstract terms.

Exercises for fluency skills

1. Vocabulary learning. The glossary of terms for psychological skills, present in *Exercises for Psychological Skills*, was created to include words that are relevant for making sense of the world, making decisions, and thinking about your own psychological growth. I recommend learning these words by playing games with them. For example: Two people make a list of about ten of these terms. They take turns making up sentences that leave out the word, and see if the other

one can guess what word goes into the blank. But the game is a cooperative one: the object of the game is to help the other person guess correctly, and not to stump the other person.

2. Practice narrating events from your life. Tell about the situation, the thoughts, the emotions, and behaviors that took place (the STEBs).

One special case of this is celebrations: times you made a good choice. Another special case is regrets: telling about a choice you regret. This exercises your skill of handling mistakes and failures.

Tell about the event that happened in elaborate enough detail that it's a real story. Tell it succinctly enough that there's not unnecessary distracting information.

3. Practice expository language about events in your life. In this exercise, you depart from narration and make up an essay about some aspect of your experience. Here are some ways that expository language starts out. "I think people should more often . . ." "It would be good if it happened that . . ." "Here are some reasons why this might have happened . . . " "Here are some reasons why this should be done . . ." "Here's a proposal I'd like people to think about . . ." "Here's how to do this, to make it turn out best . . . " "Here are some thoughts I want to keep in mind about this . . . " "Here's my analysis of what's really going on in this situation . . . " "Here are some of my learnings from this event."

Both narratives and expository language about events in your life can be done either orally or in writing. Most forms of psychotherapy give people practice in using language in this way about their lives, without making them use the self-discipline to write it out. If the above exercises were writing assignments done hundreds of times during a student's education, the student would greatly benefit from it. (However, this presupposes the teacher can respond with adequate confidentiality, nonpunitiveness, and just the right degree of demand for technical excellence in writing for the student's current skill. These are very big "ifs.") The habit of using language, especially written language, to study your own experience and learn maximally from it, could be an extremely useful habit to develop.

Skill 32: Awareness of Your Emotions

Like many of the psychological skill labels, the phrase "awareness of your emotions" refers to several things. The first is the ability to simply name the emotion you're feeling. The second is figuring out why you're feeling that way – what situation you're responding to. The third is to recognize the thoughts and interpretations of the situation that mediate between the events and the emotions. To give an example, one person simply feels lousy on Sunday night and tends to drink alcohol a lot. He's irritable with family members. But for him, that's as far as the emotional exploration goes.

A second person also feels bad on Sunday night. He starts to put names on these feelings. He says, "This is a feeling of dread, discouragement, depression, anger." Then he thinks, "What makes me feel this way?" He lets his mind wander. He notices that when he imagines going to work the following morning, the emotions intensify. This gives him an unmistakable clue that going to work in the morning is the trigger for the emotions. He recalls the verbal brutality and sadistic attitude of his boss. He realizes he dreads the hostile criticisms his boss makes. He realizes the depressed feeling is connected with the thought, "I'm trapped and hopeless; I have no escape from this situation." He connects the feeling of anger to thoughts such as "I'm being taken advantage of! I'm being mistreated! He has no right to do this to me!"

These realizations spur the man to look for other options, find another job with a favorable emotional climate, and live more happily ever after. His research has fortunately given validity to the thought of "I shouldn't have to put up with this," and not to his thought of "There's no way out."

But the point is this: there's no way he could have either validated or invalidated those thoughts had he not become aware of them; there's no reason to be aware of them without identifying the feelings. Thus, one of the major purposes of getting in touch with your feelings is that the awareness of them triggers chains of thought and action that make life better. Feelings are signals that sometimes say, "You should do more of this," or "Quit doing this." They can say, "Look for an escape route," or "Keep on; things are going great." These are very important signals for us. We ignore them at our peril.

In the 1970s, two psychiatrists, Peter Sifneos and John Nemiah, invented the word *alexithymia* to refer to a problem certain people have. The word *alexithymia* is derived from roots that mean "a lack of words for feelings." This word really refers to a skill deficiency in recognizing feelings and expressing them. Sifneos and Nemiah hypothesized that this skill deficiency was found particularly frequently in people with psychosomatic illnesses. And one hypothesis to explain this is that the reduced effectiveness in coping with situations that comes from lack of awareness of emotions actually disposes people to psychosomatic conditions. A great deal of research has been done on alexithymia, and although there's still uncertainty, many studies have confirmed that alexithymia is frequent among those with psychosomatic illnesses, and more frequent than among other comparison groups.

Let's engage in what could turn out to be pure fantasy, but what could perhaps sometimes be a reasonable explanation of the causal link. Let's imagine two people. Both are dissatisfied with something their spouse is doing – spending too much money perhaps. The first one suppresses and denies the fact that he feels angry about this. But he is still aware on some level of the situation he doesn't like, and his reaction is to tighten the head muscles and get headaches.

The second one recognizes he is feeling angry at his spouse about the financial problem, and has a conversation with his spouse about the problem. The conversation helps the person understand some of his spouse's expenditures and also results in the spouse's agreeing to try to save more. This person now relaxes, because the situation has been improved, and he no longer gets tension headaches.

Or here's another fantasy. Two school children are being bullied at school. One doesn't recognize how bad she feels about this, but finds herself getting stomachaches in the morning. Because she sometimes gets to stay home from school because of the stomachaches, they're reinforced and tend to happen more often.

The second child recognizes and expresses the fact that she's fearful about going to school. Her expression of emotion mobilizes her parents to have conferences with the principal and the teacher and to get them to protect this child from bullying. Because the problem gets reduced, this child doesn't find somatic symptoms reinforced, and they don't persist.

In these two fantasies, what would have happened if the people had expressed the emotion, but NOT solved the problem that caused the negative emotion? Would they have been just as likely as the alexithymic person to have somatic symptoms? This is still a mystery according to my reading of research literature, as is a great deal having to do with the mechanism by which psychosomatic illnesses get started and maintained.

The research literature does suggest to me, however, that if someone does have symptoms best explained as psychosomatic, and if the person is deficient in the skill of recognizing and expressing feelings, that person should probably work on this skill and see whether it makes things better.

Typically specific negative emotions carry specific signals to us. If we feel guilty, the signal is saying, "You've done something bad; don't do that again." Anger tells us, "This person is taking advantage of you; figure out how to stop him." Fear tells us, "You're in danger! Protect yourself!" Fun and exhilaration tell us "Yay, this is great! I don't want to stop!"

But sometimes the signals emotions give us are incorrect. Sometimes, for example, we feel guilty about things over which we had absolutely no control. Sometimes we fear non-dangerous situations, and sometimes we have fun in situations where we should fear the consequences!

In the case where our emotions are sending false signals, though, it is still useful to become aware of them. The awareness helps us to figure out that the signal is false. For example, when I become aware that I'm feeling guilty about the death of my relative, I can remind myself that there was nothing I could have done to prevent it. When I get scared of the dark, I can remind myself there's not really a danger lurking in it. When I get in touch with my feeling of exhilaration and pleasure from watching the good guy kill the bad guy in a movie, I can question whether I want to succumb to the movie's exploitation of the base instinct for sadistic revenge.

One of the goals for the fully functioning person is to gradually cultivate the accuracy of her emotional reactions. Accuracy of emotions means you feel bad about things you really would do well to avoid, and good about things you really would do well to approach. There are maximum true signals and minimum false signals coming from your emotions.

A second goal is that the degree of the negative emotion be great enough to send good signals, but not so great as to cause incapacitating pain. For example, when you lose a book that belongs to a friend, you want to feel bad enough to do something about it and take care not to do it again, but not so bad that you want to kill yourself and can't function for three months.

Emotional self-training is often a very long-term task. It's very difficult to do this task without being skilled at becoming aware of your emotions. It's difficult to gradually change a variable favorably, without having some way of measuring that variable.

The guess-the-feelings game

What exercises give practice in the skill of awareness of your emotions? One of them is called the guess-the-feelings game. You look at a list of feeling words, such as angry, sad, happy, surprised, and proud. You tell the story of something that happened to you. You include your thoughts, that is, what you said to yourself about the situation. Then you let the other person guess how you felt about it. (To make it easier for a correct guess to be made, you give several feelings for the guesser to choose among.) Both people win if there's a correct guess.

In another variation, you don't tell about your own experience, but just make up a story or tell about someone else. This is useful in those times when you don't want to do lots of self-disclosure to people for whom it wouldn't be appropriate.

It's easier doing this game as the guesser than as the teller. As the guesser, you get model after model of hearing someone else narrate situations, recognize feelings, and tell the thoughts that give rise to those feelings. Those models should help you to do the same thing as the teller.

Doing this game gives you practice in connecting up your experience with words for emotions. It's hard to imagine someone doing this for several hundred or thousand repetitions without getting better at this skill and becoming less "alexithymic."

If there isn't someone else you feel like playing this game with, another option is simply to keep a log of situations you've expressed, thoughts you've had about the situation, and emotions you've felt. (With a little more work, you can complete the STEB and also record the behavior you did.)

Here's a short list of feeling words for use in such exercises. I find this list is often enough to cover the bases fairly well. With a short list like this, it's easier to guess the particular word someone was thinking of.

A short list of feeling words

Angry (Mad)
Scared (Frightened, Afraid, Fearful)
Sad
Guilty
Ashamed
Disappointed
Bored
Lonely
Worried

Happy (Joyful, Glad)
Proud
Grateful
Relieved
Confident
Interested
Liking or Loving
Compassionate
Fun

In case you'd like more of the "full whammy" of feeling words to think about and draw upon, here's a longer list.

Some feeling words: a longer list

Positive: accepted, amazed, appreciative, amused, awed, attracted, calm, cheerful, close, compassionate, curious, confident, contented, elated, excited, free, friendly, fun, glowing, grateful, happy, hopeful, interested, jolly, light-hearted, liking, loving, moved, playful, pleasant, pleased, proud, relaxed, relieved, satisfied, self-assured, serene, silly, slaphappy, sympathetic, tenderness, thankful, thrilled, tickled, warmth, wonder

Negative: afraid, angry, annoyed, anxious, ashamed, bitter, bored, bothered,
brokenhearted, burdened, confused, depressed, disappointed, discouraged, disgusted, displeased, disturbed, drained,
embarrassed, envious, fearful, frazzled,
frightened, frustrated, guilty, harried,
hate, hopeless, horrified, hurt, impatient, irritated, jealous, lonely, low,
pain, rage, regret, resentment, scared,
self-critical, shocked, startled, tense,
terrified, threatened, tormented, troubled, turmoil, uncomfortable, uneasy,
unfriendly, unpleasant, upset, worried
Other: amazed, astonished, bewildered,
concerned, flabbergasted, indifferent,
excited, pity, worn out, suspicious,
stirred, wonder

The attitude to cultivate when
using these lists is that it's celebration-
worthy whenever you can accurately
connect a situation (and the accompany-
ing thoughts) with a feeling – that doing
so has made a step toward understanding the situation and dealing with it successfully.

Skill 33: Awareness of Control

Awareness of control means coming to accurate judgments about the causes of things that go on in your life. Three questions are useful to ask yourself about the causes of things, as follows.

1. How much did you cause this event to happen, versus how much was it caused by something outside you?

2. How much is the cause of this event something temporary or something permanent?

3. Is the cause of this event general or specific? That means, does it apply to lots and lots of other events, or just this one (and maybe a few others).

Let's look at these three areas one by one.

Internal versus external control

How much responsibility lies in your hands, how much in other causes? If an event is under your internal control, you cause it; if it's externally controlled, something or someone else causes it. The well known Serenity Prayer, which is a paraphrase of a prayer written by Reinhold Niehbur, goes: "Grant me the courage to change the things that I can change, the serenity to accept the things that I can't change, and the wisdom to know the difference." Awareness of internal versus external control is the wisdom to know the difference.

Awareness of internal or external control means figuring out what is luck and what isn't. In bridge or poker or other card games, your ability to win the game depends partly on what cards you're dealt; it also depends partly on how you choose to play the cards you're dealt. The first part is luck, and the second part is skill.

People make two types of errors on internal and external control. One occurs when you to see things as externally controlled, as due to luck or other people's choices, when in fact you could do something about the event. This is the error of falsely denying control. The second is the tendency to take too much responsibility for things that were really due more to other people's decisions or to fate. This is the error of falsely believing in control.

The word "power" is very relevant to the question of internal versus external control. When you feel that events are under your own control, you feel power over them; you feel "empowered" to affect them.

People's notions about how much they can control a situation sometimes become self-fulfilling prophecies. For example, two people find it very difficult to learn to read. The first one thinks, "It's hard because of the way my brain is made. I don't have responsibility for it. I'll just have to live with it." The person remains a poor reader. The second thinks, "It may take me much more work than other people, but I have the power to do that work." The second person logs in hundreds of hours in reading drills, and eventually becomes a good reader.

Because the first person believed he had no control over the situation, he never gained the experiences to show that he could have controlled it. Because the second person believed in his own power, he gained experiences that confirmed it. We often don't know for sure how much power we have, before we exert a great deal of work; our guess about our power determines whether we will expend that work or not.

Sometimes people think about control in an all-or-nothing fashion, with assumptions like these: either my reading problems are my fault, or else they aren't; either my dispute with this other person is all my fault or all his fault. An antidote to this way of thinking is to imagine a pie graph that divides up the responsibility for a certain event. What percent of the responsibility is mine, and what percent is due to other causes? This is what a jury is asked to do in a lawsuit having to do with an accident. In one case, where a motorist struck two pedestrians, the jury assigned 80 percent of the responsibility to the motorist, 5 percent to the pedestrians, and 15 percent to the township that required the pedestrians to board a bus from an unsafe place.

Here's another example. A teacher gives an assignment very quickly, and I fail to get it written down. I don't turn in my homework the next day. How should I divide up the responsibility for this? Perhaps 25 percent goes to the teacher for giving the assignment too quickly. Another 25 percent goes to the fact that I'm not good at writing quickly. And 50 percent goes to my not bothering to ask the teacher to repeat the assignment, and not bothering to ask someone else what the assignment was. Of course there's no way of assigning precise numbers to the segments on the graph. But you can usually come up with more reasonable answers when you think of it in this way than when you try to give all the responsibility to one cause.

Here's a second example: Suppose I put on a piano concert, and I get very nervous and mess up a song I had played perfectly dozens of times in practice. How do I assign the percentages for responsibility? Maybe 10 percent to the fact that I don't have the innate talent of a Chopin or Mozart. Maybe 10 percent to the fact that I could have practiced even more. But 80 percent to the fact that I got too nervous, and this interfered with my playing.

Here's a third example. Suppose I weigh thirty pounds more than I want to. I attribute 20 percent of the cause to the family member who buys a lot of junk food that tempts me. I attribute another 30 percent of the cause to my genes. The remaining 50 percent I divide between my insufficient self-discipline on eating and my insufficient self-discipline on exercise.

Why is awareness of internal or external control so important? Because life is about making good things happen. But, if you don't know what causes things to be better, you can't make them better. If you think there's nothing you can do to cause things to be better, you have no motivation to do anything. On the other hand, if you think there's something to do or to have done when there really isn't or wasn't, you just frustrate yourself or make yourself feel guilty unnecessarily.

Awareness of control directs your effort into the right channels. Let's think again about the examples above. Suppose someone thinks: "I didn't turn in my assignment purely because the teacher gave it too fast; I messed up the piano concert purely because I didn't inherit talent; I'm overweight purely because of my genes." What can that person do about making things better in any of these areas? Nothing. He is helpless.

But if he sees a significant portion of the cause as something he can affect through effort, he can motivate himself to ask about assignments when he misses them, systematically desensitize himself to the fear of performing in public, and cultivate self-discipline in eating and exercise.

When many people go to a psychotherapist, they find it more pleasant to complain about the causes they can't control than to find and work on the causes they can control. Here's how my family member makes me unhappy; here's how the school I have to go to is terrible; here's how my work situation is so bad. Awareness of internal or external control means figuring out what part of any situation one can change, and what part one can not change, and putting the effort toward changing the changeable rather than complaining about the unchangeable. In the words of the proverb, "It's better to light a candle than to curse the darkness."

Why is awareness of internal or external control sometimes such a difficult skill? There are two reasons. First, it's often difficult to come to an intellectual understanding of what causes what. The rules for inferring that one thing causes another are complex and challenging. Much of the scientific method and the study of research design have to do with trying to figure out causal relationships in accurate ways.

One of the problems with drawing inferences about a cause is that you have to know how long to keep trying. For example, suppose a parent is trying to help a child learn to quit hitting. Someone advises the use of "time out" as punishment. The parent does one time out after the child hits. The child comes right out of the time out and hits again. The parent concludes, "This obviously didn't work." But those with more experience with the effects of time outs on hitting behavior could have told the parent that she should continue with the time out strategy consistently for a week or two, and expect a change in the frequency of hitting then, rather than giving up too soon. With more time in the experiment, she can conclude that time outs do cause reduced hitting; with too little time, she concludes no causal relationship.

If it were easy to make causal inferences, there would be much less disagreement in the world. If you read any newspaper, you see many examples of people disagreeing over what causes what. Some people think public funding of a stadium will cause great economic development for the region; opponents predict it will cause much less development than other uses of public money. The proponents of gun control think more restrictive laws will reduce violent crime; opponents predict these laws will raise violent crime. One group feels welfare causes dependency and lowers character; another group feels this effect is negligible. Environmentalists feel a coke plant causes health problems; the coke company thinks the plant is perfectly safe. Getting to the correct answer on causal relations requires very careful experimentation, data gathering, and data analysis.

Sometimes even more difficult than the intellectual task of drawing causal inferences is an emotional factor. Seeing your own power to control events often involves doing something very difficult: admitting a mistake or failure. It's never pleasant to admit your own imperfection. It's much easier to say, "There's nothing I could have done about that," than to say, "I could have done something to prevent that bad outcome, and next time I will." Thus, the skill of handling mistakes and failures is strongly related to awareness of internal or external control.

If you're assigning responsibility for events in a reasonable way, the percentages of responsibility don't vary based on the identity of the people involved. For example, suppose I argue it's your fault when your car scratches my parked car, even though I was parked very close to you, saying that whoever drives a car should always be able to avoid scraping a parked car. Suppose, however, that when my car scratches your car, it's your responsibility, because no one should park too close to someone else. Obviously my judgments on responsibility conveniently change to keep me from being held responsible! We look more at this criterion of reversibility when we discuss the skill of choosing just options.

Sometimes people have grown up with a reinforcement history that works against the awareness of internal or external control. Someone in your family breaks a vase, for example. Your parent says, "Who's responsible for this?" If you deny responsibility for it, you escape punishment, since there isn't any proof. If you accept responsibility you get punished. If this type of vignette is repeated often enough, you learn never to admit that anything is your responsibility, even to yourself. This is a bad habit, because you arrive at the idea that there's nothing you can do to make things better.

Some people have just the opposite problem. In making a responsibility graph, they tend to give themselves all of it. For example, a child has trouble with math at school. His mother attributes 100 percent of the responsibility for this to the fact that she didn't lobby hard enough for his getting a different math teacher; she gives 0 percent of the responsibility to his not working hard enough.

For another: A person has an argument with his father, and later that day his father has a heart attack and dies. The man is ridden with guilt, and gives 100 percent of the responsibility for the heart attack to himself for arguing with his father, and 0 percent to the fact that his father has chain smoked for decades, has gotten no exercise, and has refused to get checked by doctors.

A mother forgets to buy a certain type of cereal for her daughter, and her daughter has a tantrum the next morning; the mother attributes 100 percent of the responsibility for this unpleasantness to her own forgetting and none to her daughter's low frustration tolerance skills. Or even more extreme, a wife is beaten up by her husband, but she says to herself, "If I were a better wife, he wouldn't do it; it's my fault."

People who do this tend to endure too much immature or abusive behavior from others and cause themselves too much guilt. It's not a good feeling for a parent to realize, after years of self-sacrifice, that she has produced not eternally grateful admirers, but spoiled brats.

In the psychological literature there are questionnaires that measure "internal locus of control" (the tendency to give yourself responsibility) versus "external locus of control" (the tendency to give other people or fate responsibility). People with more of an internal locus of control tend to do better in lots of ways. There's usually an element of every situation that we can control, even if it's only a small part. It makes sense for us to find that part we can control and focus on it. By doing this, we avoid the feeling of powerlessness and helplessness.

It's often difficult to practice awareness of internal or external control, because sometimes no one is really sure how much of something is caused by what. There's often a lack of a reliable "gold standard" for the truth. You can practice taking guesses, but you may be practicing incorrect guesses. One way around this problem is to practice with hypothetical situations where the answer is fairly clear. There are practice problems of this nature in *Programmed Readings For Psychological Skills*.

Permanence and generality

When an event happens, do you think the cause is permanent or temporary? Specific or general? Let's look at some examples of what this question means. Suppose I win a swimming meet. If I say to myself, "I had an unusually good day today," I'm thinking about a temporary cause; if I think, "I'm a fast swimmer," I'm thinking about a more permanent cause. If I say to myself, "This shows I trained well for this swimming meet," I'm thinking about something specific; if I think, "This shows that when I really work hard at things, I can be successful," I'm drawing a much more general conclusion.

Suppose a friend of mine moves to a different state. If I think to myself, "I'll never have a friend like this again," I'm thinking permanent causation; if I think, "It will take me a while to find someone I enjoy as much," I'm thinking more temporary causation. If I think, "I'll miss my friend," I'm thinking something more specific than if I think, "Life is totally different now."

Suppose I find myself in a gloomy mood. If I think, "It's happening again that I'm feeling gloomy for a few hours," I'm imagining a temporary cause. If I think, "I don't see much hope for things to ever get better," I'm thinking of permanent causes. If I think, "This lousy mood is a pain in the neck; I wish it would go away right now," I'm sticking to a specific; if I think, "Life is really not worth living," I'm getting much more general.

Suppose I read a good book that enlightens me about some very important ideas. If I think, "I enjoyed reading

that. Now what am I going to do next?" I'm thinking of temporary causes. If I think, "This book has given me some ideas that will help me the rest of my life!" I'm thinking of permanent causes. If I think, "I liked what the book said about writing a to-do list," I'm thinking of specific causes; if I think, "I can read and hear things that help me live my life better, and that is wonderful," I'm thinking of a more general conclusion.

What sorts of causal attributions tend to make you feel the most optimistic and happy, feel lots of gumption and will to persist? Martin Seligman and his colleagues have collected much evidence that people do better in many ways when they give the "benefit of the doubt" to temporary and specific explanations for bad events, and to permanent and general explanations for good events. In many cases, people's habits of thinking have more influence on the causal attributions they come up with than the data from the situation itself.

The moral of this story is: when something good happens, you should not overlook the possibility it was caused by something permanent and general. When something bad happens, you should not overlook the possibility it was caused by something temporary and specific. "The truth shall set you free," but in the world of incomplete information under which we operate, why not give at least equal chance to the hypotheses that make us feel optimistic?

Skill 34: Decision-making

Decision-making is a crucial psychological skill. People make themselves happy or miserable, rich or poor, alive or dead, productive or nonproductive, depending on what decisions they make. Everything you do or say is the product of a decision you have made. Some decisions are made with a lot of thought, and some with little or no thought. If you can recognize what decisions are most important and can think very carefully and well about these decisions, you can greatly improve your life.

This chapter goes into some detail about the skill of decision-making. Before doing so, however, I want to give a brief overview that will show you how to do this skill well.

Brief overview

If you concentrate on the following five points, you'll probably improve your decision-making skills.

1. Recognize you're at a choice point worth devoting some thought to, and describe the choice point to yourself in words. For example, say to yourself, "This person is behaving to me in a very angry and aggressive way. I want to think carefully about how to respond." Or, "I might have a serious illness. I want to decide what steps to take."

2. Think about what your goal or goals are in this situation. For example:

"What am I trying to accomplish, in handling this aggressive person? Is it my goal to teach this person a lesson? I think my main goal is just to leave this situation unharmed." Or: "My goal is to protect my health, and this is more important than saving money, time, or effort."

3. List several options about what you could do at this choice point; don't just do the first thing that comes to mind. For example: "I could just listen to him empathically. I could walk or run away immediately. I could speak calmly to him explaining what I see as going on. I could call the police on my cell phone."

4. Get more information if it's available and can help you. For example, regarding my health problem, I'll check out some books from a medical library and read them, read journal articles, and seek consultation with experts.

5. State to yourself in words what the advantages and disadvantages are of the options that seem best. For example, with the aggressive person: "Speaking calmly may calm him down, but anything I say might just trigger him to get more angry. If I start to call the police, he might physically try to stop me. Listening empathically might have the best chance of not making him angrier. I could at the same time be edging away from him.

After doing these things you're ready to decide.

If you recognize the choice points of your life and practice going through these steps with them, preferably writing out your decision-making process, you may drastically improve your ability to make good decisions.

Now let's describe the skill of decision-making in a much more detailed way.

Two ways to make better decisions

Let's talk about two ways to make better decisions. One way is to get more information that bears upon the decision. And the second way is to learn to make more systematic and logical use of the information you do have. Players of the game of bridge have an expression that summarizes these two ways: "One peek is worth two finesses." A "finesse" is a way of playing the cards that maximizes your score, given that you're uncertain what cards one of your opponents holds. But if you get a "peek" and actually see what cards your opponent holds, you know even more about how to play the cards.

One very useful way to organize the information you do have, when making a difficult decision, is to sit down and use pencil and paper or a keyboard to write, and keep track in that way of the thoughts you have about the decision. If someone asked you to multiply 628 by 321 (without a calculator or computer), you would not think of do-

ing it without using pencil and paper as an aid to your memory. But most people try to make decisions that are much more complex than this arithmetic problem without ever writing anything down. The problem is that we can only hold a limited amount in memory. If you don't use writing as a memory aid, you tend to remember one aspect of the situation, and this gives you the urge to act in one way; then you remember another aspect of it, and this gives you the urge to act in another way. By writing, you can better integrate all that you know about the situation.

Writing or stating a situation summary

When you start to analyze a decision, one of the first things to do is briefly summarize the situation: you state who is involved, what your goal is, what the immediately obvious choices are, and what is at stake. This is just a concise summary of the situation you're facing.

Here's an example of this sort of concise summary:

"A kid who lives near me likes to play mischievous pranks. He gets into a lot of trouble over this, and, if I hang out with him, I think I'll get into some trouble too. I've already gotten into a little trouble. I like him and want to be nice to him, and I enjoy being with him. I don't want to get a bad reputation. I wish he didn't do this stuff, although sometimes it's funny."

Doing this is called problem-identification. Just identifying a situation and telling about the nature of the decision is in some ways the simplest of the steps in decision-making. But for many people, it's the most difficult. Many decisions are not made correctly for one major reason: they're never really identified and addressed.

Suppose someone asked you, "What decisions have you faced lately?" Would you be able to give that person many answers? Just about every waking moment involves a choice, a decision of some sort. If you can become aware of what the situations you're in, you can help yourself make decisions.

How high are the stakes?

A reasonable next step is to make a decision about the decision: How much is at stake in this decision, how important is it, how much time and effort does it deserve? Some decisions deserve a great deal of time and energy, and some deserve almost none. As you read the following, think about how much time and effort you think each would deserve:

Which type of apples to get at the grocery store

Whether to have another child

Whether to buy a house or rent an apartment

Whether to get married to a certain person

What to wear on a certain day

Whether to take a certain course in school

What sort of television to buy

Whether to take the bus or walk to a certain place

Which restaurant to go out to on a certain night

Whether to buy self-sticking envelopes or the type you have to lick

How to strengthen my "social support network," how to have more mutually rewarding relationships with other people

People seldom put enough effort into decisions such as "What shall I do with my time?" "What are my goals?" Where do I want to put my effort? Should I watch the evening news each evening, as I am doing, or is there something I could do that's more rewarding to me? How should I spend my day today? What sorts of things do I want to do with my friends? How can I be of greater service to humanity? How can I accomplish more worthwhile things?"

Few of us put time and effort into the decision process in proportion to how important the decision is. Some of us err by making important decisions impulsively, some by obsessing over small decisions deserving little more than a random choice; most of us make both sorts of errors. We can make our lives better by devoting more energy to the more important decisions.

Posing more questions

If a decision is important enough to warrant some time and energy, a next step is to pose to yourself questions helpful to ask in making the decision. For example, with the decision about the mischievous friend that we talked about a while ago, here are some other questions to think about:

How important is it to me to be friends with him?

How important is it for me to try to help him stay out of trouble?

How likely is it that his pranks will get me in trouble?

How likely is it that I could persuade him to stop doing these pranks?

How likely is it that I could persuade him to stop doing them when I'm with him?

Are there other friends I care about as much, whom I'd like to spend more time with?

After the questions have been raised, the next step is to go through them again and think about the answers. And this may trigger more questions to add to the list. If the decision is very important, it will be useful to write down what you know about the answers. If the decision is not as important, it may suffice just to think about the answers to the questions without writing.

Getting more information

Another decision about the decision should be made at about this time. When the relevant questions have been raised, the next question is, "Can I, and should I, get more information, in any way, that will help me know the answer to this question, and thus make the decision better?" Here is where the "One peek is worth two finesses" strategy comes in.

Here are some examples of getting more information:

Someone who is deciding whether or not to accept a recommendation regarding a surgical operation gets a second opinion from a highly regarded surgeon and goes to a medical library and reads articles and textbooks about the condition he has.

A person who is thinking of hiring a certain person to remodel his house obtains the names of other people who have employed this person and calls them on the phone to see what their experiences with him were like.

A person thinking of using a certain baby-sitter decides to watch the baby-sitter interacting with the children for a couple of hours before ever leaving the children alone with the baby-sitter.

A person who is worried about whether the baby-sitter is supervising the children adequately decides to come home for brief periods of time unexpectedly to see what's going on at those times.

A couple who disagree with each other about what to do about their child's behavior problems consult an expert on that topic, and ask for readings about how to solve behavior problems.

A doctor who's not sure whether a child needs stimulant medication for hyperactivity gives the drug on some days and gives placebo on other days, and gets behavior ratings done each day by parents and teachers. At the end of the trial, he compares the ratings for drug days and placebo days.

A person who's hiring a secretary gives prospective candidates a test in the skills they'll need on the particular job they're applying for.

A teacher who's not sure which of two ways of instructing children works best sets up an experiment in which children are randomly assigned to the two methods. After instructing them, the teacher gives a test to see how well each member of each group learned the things that were taught.

These examples illustrate several ways of getting more information: reading books and articles on the topic, consulting an expert or several experts, getting information from friends or acquaintances, asking systematic questions of the person who wishes to transact something with you, doing an experiment yourself, giving a test, making systematic observations yourself, enlarging the "behavior sample" you have observed.

Brainstorming and listing options

Another important part of the decision-making process is brainstorming as you "list options." This means

that you address the question, "What could I do in this situation?" It's very helpful at this point to aid your memory with writing. It's also helpful not to censor your options, but to let as many different ideas come into your mind as you can. A wild or unreasonable option might suggest another one that turns out to be just the one you want.

For example: A parent is deciding what to do about his or her child's problems of not doing well in school. After "peeking" at some information by talking with the teacher and talking with the child, the parent lists the following options, some of which are options for "peeks" at more information, and some of which are options for making things better:

Get the child a tutor.

Learn how to tutor the child myself.

Bribe the child with money for doing better.

Persuade the teacher to give a daily report card so I can celebrate days when the child tried hard.

Have the child tested to get more information on his or her ability level.

Transfer the child to a different school.

Transfer the child to a different type of class.

Have the child go to school only a half day, to avoid turning him off to academic work even more than he has been, and teach the child at home the rest of the time.

Get the child a better table and lamp and a quiet work place for him to do his homework.

Do some of my work from the office while sitting near him at night, so he won't be so lonesome while doing his homework.

Get a book on study skills and read it and teach it to him.

Consult an expert on whether medication would help the child; read about this question too.

Consult a child psychiatrist about how to make things better.

Ask other parents, especially the parents of children who are doing well, about their ideas on how to help the child achieve more.

Explore more with the child whether emotional problems are getting in the way of his schoolwork

In this example, the person really wasn't very seriously considering the option of "bribing the child with money for doing better," but listing this option anyway led the person to think about another option, that of having a daily report card and a celebration about the days when the child did well. This is an example of how options can trigger other options in your mind.

A very useful exercise is to take a decision you're facing, and to list as many options as you can about what to do about it. You may wish to stop reading now, and do this exercise.

Predicting consequences

Then, with options listed, a logical next step is to try to predict the consequences of the options that are being seriously considered.

Here, as in almost all stages of the decision process, there's uncertainty. You can never know with total certainty what will happen if you try a certain option. So for that reason, it's useful to think of several different consequences that may occur for any option you're considering, and to think about how likely each consequence is. It's often important to remind yourself to think of long-run consequences as well as short-run consequences.

For example, a teacher at a preschool sees two children bickering with each other and saying hostile things to each other. The teacher is trying to predict the consequences of going to the two children and directing them to do something that will distract them from their conflict. As the teacher thinks of possible consequences, the following come to mind:

Short term:

They will go to the new activity, and their hostility will cease (fairly likely).

They will refuse to go to the new activity, and their hostility will continue (a little less likely).

They will go to the new activity, and another similar conflict will arise very soon (a little less likely).

Longer term:

Their hostility will be reinforced by my attention to them, and their tendency to be hostile will increase (very likely.

They will have less of a chance to practice hostility because I interrupt the activity, and their tendency to be hostile will decrease (somewhat likely).

They will get the message from me that hostility is not acceptable, and this will decrease their tendency to be hostile (somewhat likely).

Other children will notice that I pay attention to them for this behavior, and the other children who want my attention will have their tendencies to be hostile increased (fairly likely).

Sometimes when listing possible consequences of an option, it's useful to divide them into positive and negative consequences, or advantages and disadvantages. Sometimes a very useful guide in making a decision is to write down the advantages and disadvantages of each major option you're considering. In the example above, it's not very hard to tell which possible consequences are advantages and which are disadvantages.

In the example above, the teacher judged the likelihood, or the probability, that each consequence would occur, in terms like "very likely" and "fairly likely."

There is, of course, a more precise way to do it: using numbers. If I guess that there's a .5 or 50 percent chance that something will happen, that means that, if the situation were re-peated over and over, I would expect the thing to happen about half the time. I'm guessing that there's about the same chance of the thing happening as getting "heads" when flipping a coin. If I guess that there's a one in six, or one sixth, or 17 percent chance that something will happen, I'm guessing that there's about the same chance of the thing's happening as rolling a "one" when rolling a die.

Why think in terms of numbers, when all you're doing is taking a wild guess anyway? Even a wild guess, when you understand what the guess is, is better than one where you're not sure what's meant. And when you use numbers, you can also think about how "wild" your guess is, how wide your range of confidence is.

Suppose you're thinking of taking a trip in a space shuttle. An engineer tells you, "I think there's a pretty good chance the shuttle will blow up." Suppose instead that the engineer were to tell you, "My best guess is that the chances are 75 percent that the shuttle will blow up." Which statement gives more information about whether to take the shuttle flight or not?

Summing outcomes' utility times probability, for each option

Once you have predicted consequences and have taken your best guess at how likely each possible consequence is, the next important step in decision-making is to decide how much you like each possible consequence, that is, how much you want or don't want it to happen. The word that has been given to this "goodness" or "badness" of a consequence is "utility." If something is more desirable, more preferable, it has higher utility. It is usually of higher utility to live than to die, to be healthy than to be sick, to get money rather than to lose it, and to experience pleasant things rather than unpleasant things.

Here's a concept very central to living a good life: try to select the option with the highest "expected utility."

Expected utility means how good you would expect things to come out, on the average, if you were to do this option many times in just the same circumstances, that is, if you were to let the random elements in the outcome average themselves out over time.

If you know exactly what will happen if you do a certain option, you don't have to do as much calculation. For example, if it's one hundred percent certain that option A will produce a very good outcome, and it's also totally certain that option B will produce a so-so outcome, option A obviously has a higher expected outcome than B. The challenge comes when you aren't certain about the outcomes, but all you can do is estimate probabilities.

For example, you're introduced to a stranger who extends his hand for you to shake. You have a choice of whether to shake the hand or not. If you refuse to shake it, you have a chance of offending the stranger and the person introducing him. If you shake it, you

have a chance of catching a dreaded illness from him and dying, or of being dragged off and kidnapped or mugged.

Even if you've never heard the formula I'm going to give, you intuitively know how to make such decisions. You have to take into account how likely the different outcomes are, as well as how bad they are. You weight the goodness or badness of each option's possible outcome by multiplying it by the probability of its actually happening. You do this for the various outcomes possible for each given option, and add them up. This gives the "expected utility" for the option, and the option with the highest expected utility is the one to choose.

To put this mathematically: Expected utility = sum of (utility of the outcome, times the probability of the outcome) over all possible outcomes.

I intuitively think, yes, I could catch a dreaded illness and die, and that would be very bad. But the probability is so low that this takes away very little from the expected utility of the option of shaking hands. I also judge the probability of getting mugged or kidnapped to be low, because I'm much bigger than the stranger and I'm in a crowded public place. If I refuse to shake hands, the chance of offending is high, and this takes away a good deal from the option of refusing to shake hands. So I shake the stranger's hand.

Here's another example: Someone offers you a chance to make a bet on a coin flip. If you pick "heads" or "tails" correctly, you win $1. If you pick incorrectly, you lose $10. The chance of your guessing correctly is 50 percent. Should you make the bet, or shouldn't you? (We'll temporarily forget about your feelings about gambling in general or the long-term consequences of setting a precedent in favor of gambling.)

Without even multiplying probabilities by utilities, this sounds like a bad deal, doesn't it? (When you do multiply probabilities by utilities, you find that, if you were to accept this deal many times, you would on the average lose $4.50 each time. You get that by adding a half times 1 and a half times minus 5.) On the other hand, by raising a utility or probability, we can turn it into a good deal. What if your chance of winning, rather than being 50 percent, were 99.9 percent? Or what if the amount you would win if you guess right, rather than being one dollar, were a million dollars?

Maybe these examples will convince you that, if you're like most people, you've been intuitively multiplying probabilities by utilities and adding them up all your life, even if you haven't been aware of it.

Here's another example: Suppose that a friend tells you the following: "I've been having some pain. There's an operation that has a good chance of taking away the pain. But there's also a chance that I'll die during the operation. What do you think I should do?" Now what would you want to know before you would begin to advise your friend?

Most people would want to know how bad the pain has been. If it has been very mild, the benefit of relieving it would be smaller; if it has been very severe, the benefit of relieving it would be larger. The "benefit" we are talking about here is a utility. Most people also want to know, how big is the chance that the operation will relieve the pain? And how big is the chance that you'll die? The bigger the chance of relief, and the smaller the chance of death, the better an idea it is to have the operation. These chances are probabilities.

These examples illustrate that, in making decisions, most people have some sort of rough way of estimating and calculating with utilities and probabilities, even if they don't use those words.

So what I've said is that, in making a decision, you take any given option. You list the possible consequences of that option. You figure out how well you like each consequence; that is, you assign a "utility" to it. You guess how likely it is that that consequence will occur; that is, you assign a probability to it. You give a score to each consequence (the higher the score, the better the consequence is and the more likely it is to happen) – and you do this by multiplying the probability by the utility. Then you add up the score of all the possible consequences of the option to get a score for that option.

Then you do this for any other options, and you pick the option with the highest score.

Does anybody ever really do this in real life? How useful is this way of thinking?

Like most of the actions suggested in this decision-making chapter, you don't have to carry it out completely to benefit from it. Just having the notions of utility and probability in your mind may help you in systematically making a decision. If you have a very important decision to make, you may wish to actually do the multiplying and adding.

In general, I think this notion of "maximizing the expected utility" is one of the most important and profound principles that anyone has ever figured out. It's worth quite a bit of effort to understand it.

How to rate utility

How do you assign numbers to utilities? A useful approach is to anchor yourself by defining the best and worst outcomes in this particular decision, and calling them 100 and 0. Then you rate the utility of all other outcomes as somewhere between.

Let's imagine that you're deciding whether to get an operation to relieve some pain. Let's assign the number 0 to dying on the operating table. Let's assign the number 100 percent to it being fully relieved of all pain. Suppose I hurt so bad that it would be about an even bet for me to get the operation

even if I had only a 5% chance of pain relief. Then staying as I am would rate 5 on a scale of 100. On the other hand, if it would be about an even bet for me only if I had a 95% chance of pain relief, staying the way I am rates 95.

Using rating scales

Now let's go to a different sort of problem in assigning utilities. Here the problem is that there are different aspects of a given consequence, and you want to decide how to weight them.

For example, you're trying to decide which baby-sitter to hire, out of several different possibilities. Each person you're considering offers attractive qualities. You think about one person, and how that person is very enthusiastic, and you lean toward choosing that person. Then you think of another person, and how that person is probably more mature and less impulsive, and you lean toward choosing that person. You think of another person, and the fact that this person charges less attracts you. When you think of certain aspects, you lean in one direction, and when you think of others, you lean in another direction. The problem is that your memory can't hold all aspects of each consequence in mind at the same time.

A solution to this problem is to make yourself a rating scale, very much like the rating scales used for research purposes. You have one item on the scale for each important aspect of the situation you're evaluating.

Here's a sample rating scale that may be made up by our hypothetical searcher for a child-care worker.

My Child-Care Worker Search Rating Scale

0 = Very bad
2 = Bad
4 = So-so
6 = OK
8 = Good
10 = Very Good

_____Doesn't want to compete with the parent for the favor of the child
_____Enthusiastic and fun way of dealing with child
_____Big repertoire of mutually gratifying activities with child
_____Child seems to have positive feelings about person
_____Quality of conversation, language use modeled for the child
_____ Kindness
_____ Knowledge of safety precautions
_____ Knowledge of first aid techniques
_____Nonimpulsiveness, good judgment
_____Honesty
_____Refrains from unnecessary directives
_____Good at responsive interactions
_____Uses appropriate assertion
_____Ease of transportation to and from here
_____Price the person charges
_____Wide range of times available

_____Uses differential attention and excitement well

The simplest way to use a scale like this is to assign a rating to each item, add up the scores, and pick the option with the highest score. This method makes every item just as important as every other. Research has found that this simple method usually works just about as well as adjusting the weights of the items so that the ones that are more important get weighted more heavily.

Suppose that when you simply add up the ratings, you have the gut feeling that you like a different option better, one that didn't get the highest score? Then maybe you need to make the rating scale more precise by assigning different weights to the items, according to their importance. Each item score will be multiplied by the weight when the total score is calculated. The more important items will have higher weights, so that they will contribute more to the total score.

Let's say our searcher for a childcare worker decides the "price the person charges" is least important. This item gets an arbitrary weight of 1. All the other items will be weighted according to how much more important they are than the person's wage. Knowledge of safety precautions gets weighted four times as high, as does honesty; appropriate assertion skills gets weighted two times as high. Now our searcher notices that safety precautions are weighted twice as important as assertion skills; if this still rings true, then the weights are left as they are; if not, they're adjusted.

Then he scores the scale again, this time multiplying each item score by its weight and adding up all the products. He picks the option with the highest score. Again, if the option with the highest score somehow doesn't seem most desirable to him, he fiddles with the weights and the ratings until the total scores are in accord with his feelings.

One may ask, if he's going to go with his gut feelings, why go through this process in the first place? The process of figuring out the important aspects of the situation, assigning the proper weight for each aspect, and rating each choice according to those aspects and summing the score may change his gut feelings, because it causes him to focus systematically on first, one, then another of the important aspects of the choices.

You can use a rating scale for most other sorts of decisions: buying a car, hiring an employee, choosing a job, deciding whether or not to have another child, or even choosing a spouse. (If you use a rating scale to choose a spouse, you may give special meaning to the opening lines of Elizabeth Browning's poem: "How do I love thee? Let me count the ways.")

What if there aren't several other options for comparison? For example, suppose someone gets only one job offer, and is choosing whether or not to take it? It still helps, in evaluating an option, to have some standards for comparison (even if at this moment they are only hypothetical) if similar options will present themselves later. The person evaluating a job offer may compare it to all other jobs he has had.

Including precedent-setting as part of outcomes

When evaluating the utilities of consequences, there's one aspect that is often overlooked. People often overlook the effect the option will have on the precedents they set for their own behavior and for other people's behavior. If the option involves violating some important principle, undermining the precedent of that principle can be harmful, even though the other consequences of the action are positive.

For example: A person knows he can drink alcohol in moderation and not suffer ill consequences. However, in making a decision, he takes into account the precedent he will be setting for other people who admire him, including his children; he's not so sure that alcohol will never be a problem for them. When he takes into account the chance that he could set a precedent for them that drug use is permissible, he decides not to use alcohol.

A person calculates that, if he were to cheat on his income tax return, he could claim ignorance of the situation if he were audited, and would lose nothing more than having to pay the back taxes. If, on the other hand, he is not audited, he saves the money he does not pay. So far, the utility equation seems to be in favor of cheating. However, when he takes into account that by cheating he is undermining his own habit of honesty and is weakening his personal precedent for honesty, this consideration shifts the balance in favor of paying the extra tax.

A legislator is deciding about laws regarding euthanasia. It appears there are some cases of terminal and painful illness where actively giving drugs to end someone's life is the most merciful thing to do. On the other hand, allowing this may undermine society's precedent against murder. When this aspect of the outcome is taken into account, the decision is not so easy.

Satisficing versus optimizing

How should one make low-stakes decisions? What about deciding which envelopes to buy, which parking place to take, whether to get red apples or golden apples, and so forth?

Some useful concepts in thinking about decisions are "optimizing" and "satisficing." Optimizing means you go through the process of generating all the options you can, gathering information, predicting consequences, estimating utilities, and choosing an option by maximizing the expected utility. Optimizing means trying to pick the very best option. The only trouble with optimizing is that it takes time and energy. But if the decision is important,

time invested in optimizing may be the best time you can spend.

Satisficing, on the other hand, is a strategy for less important decisions. When you satisfice, you search through options until you come to the first one that's "good enough." You then stop searching, enact the option, and get on with the next thing in life.

Here are some examples of satisficing. A person is in a town on a business trip. He wants to get a quick lunch at a restaurant while he's planning important things that will occur in the afternoon. He walks down the street until he finds the first restaurant that looks acceptable. Without gathering any more information on any other options, without rating any of those options on the ten aspects of restaurants he finds desirable, he sits down in the restaurant. He looks quickly at the menu; he stops reading as soon as he sees something that looks acceptable, and he orders it for lunch.

A mother is picking out a story to read to her child. She looks through the books until she finds one she feels like reading, and, without bothering to compare with all the other books, she says, "Here's a good one!"

Two people are spending an afternoon together, and they're deciding what to do. One scans through options in his mind; the first option that strikes him as fun is to go for a walk in the park. He suggests that. It's also a "good enough" option for the other person, and they do it without contrasting it with all other possible options.

Satisficing is one way not to spend a lot of time and energy on a decision. Another way is doing abbreviated optimizing. You can list some options, not necessarily all possible ones. You can think about the most likely consequences, not all possible ones. You can make an intuitive appraisal of utilities rather than using preference probabilities or a rating scale. You can spend no time peeking at new information. The principle to keep in mind is that you want to spend time and energy in proportion to how much the decision deserves it.

The small sample size error

Errors in decision-making can be committed by spending too much, or not enough, time and energy on a decision relative to what the decision deserves. The person who obsesses over what color scarf to buy, or the person who quits his job in a moment of anger at his boss, is likely to be making this type of error.

Even when the decision is carefully considered, a frequent error is making a conclusion based on too small a sample of data, i.e. not enough peeks.

A person concludes on the basis of one thirty-minute interview, and a great deal of thought, that someone is a wonderful candidate for a job. A person concludes on the basis of knowing someone for a month that a person is a wonderful marriage partner. A doctor decides after trying a medication with a child for one day that the medication is not helping and discontinues it. Someone knows one person who had an operation and suffered no ill effects of it; the person concludes that the operation is very safe. Someone is cheated by a person of a certain race and concludes that all people of that race are dishonest. Someone's Aunt Hattie smoked a pack of cigarettes a day and lived to be ninety years old; the person concludes that smoking is safe. These are all examples of the "too small a sample size" error. No amount of thinking can substitute for adequate numbers of data points in making a conclusion.

The sunk costs error

Another interesting error is the failure to ignore "sunk costs." Sunk costs are the time, money, and effort that have been put into something so far, that will never be recoverable no matter what option you choose. Because they can't be changed and they're the same for all options, they're of no help in making the decision and should be ignored.

For example, suppose a person buys a movie ticket, not knowing much about the movie. He intensely dislikes very violent movies. After the first fifteen minutes of the movie, he can tell it's very violent, and he hates watching it. He overhears someone who has already seen it, who says things that confirm his impression that it will continue to be this violent. We assume he cannot get a refund.

Should he walk out? He calculates that he will enjoy the next two hours very much more if he does leave than if he doesn't. He decides that leaving will maximize utility relative to staying. Therefore he should leave.

But wait. We don't know how much he paid to get into the movie. If he paid nothing, he would feel no hesitation in leaving. Suppose, instead, that he paid $10 for this performance. He thinks, "If I leave I will just be throwing away $10."

If he lets this thought influence him, he's making the "sunk costs" error. The essential point is that, at the time of his decision point, his $10 is already lost no matter what he does. Whether he had paid $500 or $1, that money is gone. The only question now is whether he wants to spend the remaining time of the movie doing something more valuable, or something less valuable to him. A good way of putting his decision is, "Would you rather pay $10 to do something you don't like, or pay $10 to do something you like better?" The rational thing to do is to forget about what he paid to get in, and walk out.

Here's another example of the "sunk costs" notion. A person owns shares of stock that have gone down in price. She is trying to decide whether to hold them or sell them. She concludes that the money she could recover by selling now she will probably grow more in some other investment, and she decides to sell. But someone says to her, "How much did you pay for the stock? . . . You've lost money? If you sell now you'll lock in your loss. Are you sure you don't want to hang on longer? It's likely to go up eventually."

If she lets this sort of thinking influence her, she's making the sunk costs error. The money she paid for the stock is a sunk cost, no matter what she does. The only question is whether the money recoverable now should be employed in this stock or somewhere else.

Here's another example. A nation is fighting a war. As people study the situation more, they realize that fighting the war was not a good decision in the first place. More to the point, they realize that the losses they would entail from now on by continuing to fight would exceed the gains that they and other people would get by continuing to fight. This is true, people decide, even if you take into account the undesirability of the precedent of failing to finish something that was started with a great show of commitment.

But when it's proposed that they simply pull out their troops and stop fighting, some people argue, "But we've already lost thousands of lives in this war. If we pull out now, those lives will have been wasted."

If the country decides to keep fighting on this basis, it's making the "sunk costs" error. The lives that have been lost have been lost whether or not the fighting continues.

Here's another example. A couple moves into a neighborhood where the property taxes are very high, but the reputation of the public school district is very good. They send their children to public school. One of their children hates school, does very poorly, and seems to have special needs that this school cannot meet. Someone suggests the couple consider private school or homeschooling. They say, "We couldn't possibly do that, not with all the money we're paying in property taxes for this public school system." The money they're paying in taxes is a sunk cost. The only relevant question is, "Is the benefit to the child that we could get by private schooling or homeschooling worth the cost or effort of either of those options?" If the answer is yes, then they should choose that option regardless of how much money has been sunk into the public school system.

Postdecisional regret and bolstering

Postdecisional regret occurs when someone makes a decision and does something to signal a commitment to it. As soon as the commitment has been made, all the disadvantages of the options decided upon come into great prominence in the person's mind, and he regrets his decision.

Some people get into such a strong habit of postdecisional regret that they predict they'll regret whatever decision they make. Since the expectation is of regret, some people with this pattern fear making decisions, and tend to postpone them whenever possible. The decision process is very painful if this pattern is strong enough.

Bolstering is the opposite. When a person makes a decision, sometimes he then successfully convinces himself that the option he picked was obviously the best one or only good one. He's much more confident after making the commitment than before. After making the decision, he is sold on all the advantages, and ignores the disadvantages. He has an advantage of not being plagued by doubts as he does the work necessary to enact the course of action he has decided upon.

Is postdecisional regret always bad, and is bolstering always good? Not necessarily. If someone made a bad decision, and further information reveals all the more clearly it's a bad decision, bolstering can distort the truth and keep someone on an unwise course. Postdecisional regret can work on the side of rationality when further information, or more careful reexamination of the information, reveals the decision was wrong.

Too much bolstering leads a person to be set in his ways and stubborn; too much postdecisional regret leads a person to be wishy-washy and tormented.

Here's a technique that may help people avoid too much postdecisional regret and too much bolstering after the decision is made. This technique is to use your imagination to vividly project yourself into the future. Imagine that a certain alternative has been chosen, and that a firm commitment to it has been made. Imagine the setting you'll be in, and the other people who will be in the setting; imagine yourself doing the things you'll be doing. Create as detailed a "movie" as you possibly can about the ways things will go if you decide upon the option. It may be useful to use writing as an aid to memory, and to write your own description, your own movie script. If in your movie your natural tendency toward postdecisional regret or bolstering starts to come forth, you know you're doing a vivid job of imagining.

Having done this, then do the same thing with the other option. Create just as vivid an image of what will happen with this option. Let the movie unfold in as great detail as you can. Note your feelings in this situation. If you feel postdecisional regret or bolstering at work, take note of it.

Then come back to reality and remember your movies. Did postdecisional regret operate in both, so that for each option you ended up wishing you'd taken the other? Did bolstering operate in both, so that for each option you felt this was by far the best choice and that there could never be a good argument for deviating from it?

If you decide you're overusing postdecisional regret or bolstering, you can set as a goal for yourself not distorting the truth so much. You can consciously try to focus your attention more on the advantages of the decision you made (if you're trying to do less postdecisional regret), or to focus your attention more on the criteria that would make you reverse your course (if you're trying to do less bolstering). You can monitor how well you're able to change your postdecision patterns. You can celebrate when you make those patterns more useful to yourself.

What if, when you do your mental movies, you decide both options will work out just fine, and that both will lead to happy, but different, outcomes? This prediction may often be true. Fortunately, there are very often many right answers to a decision. Sometimes if someone is equipped with an optimistic and cheerful spirit and a willingness to work to make things better, he or she can make the best of many different decisions. However, some options make it very difficult for the heartiest spirit to remain hearty.

When the problem is enacting the decision, not making it

Suppose someone has made all sorts of good decisions. He has decided to quit smoking, to avoid yelling at his child when he misbehaves in order not to reinforce him with excitement, and to get to bed early enough that he's not irritable the next day. His problem is doing the things he's decided to do. He just doesn't do them, even though he's unwavering in his decision that they're best.

If the problem is enacting the decision rather than making it, the "methods of influence axis" is useful to think about. The methods of influencing a child are the same ones you can use to influence yourself. For example, affirming to yourself repeatedly that the new pattern is your goal, setting up a hierarchy of small steps toward the goal, reinforcing yourself for moving closer to the goal, enlisting the aid of other people in reinforcing you for steps toward the goal, monitoring your own progress, making the stimulus situations more conducive to progress, reading instructional materials that remind you how to make progress, repetitively practicing the desired pattern in fantasy and role-playing as well as in real life, and observing models of the desired pattern are likely to help you carry out the pattern you've decided upon.

Here's a summary of the decision-making techniques recommended here.

1. Make a decision about how much effort and energy this decision requires.

2. On very important decisions, write your thoughts, to keep up with them in all stages of the decision process.

3. Start with a concise description of the situation and of the goal, the choices, and what is at stake.

4. Be careful not to avoid the decisions about your goals and the use of your time.

5. List questions, the answers to which would give you more information with which to make an important decision.

6. Seek the answers to those questions, by reading, asking questions, and making observations, so as to get information that will help you with the decision.

7. Brainstorm options for what to do about the situation, without censoring them.

8. Try to predict the consequences of the most prominent options.

9. When predicting consequences, give thought to long-run consequences as well as short-run consequences, and to precedents and habits as well as to effects on this situation only.

10. Get into the habit of guessing the probability that a certain consequence will occur, expressed in numbers.

11. Rate the utility of the various consequences. "Preference probability" is a way of rating the utility of outcomes other than the best and worst. A preference probability is the odds of getting the best outcome, rather than the worst, that you think would make an even swap between taking a gamble on the best or worst and taking the intermediate one.

12. Pick the option with the highest expected utility. Expected utility is a sum you get by taking the utility of each consequence, multiplying it by its probability, and adding up those products for all possible consequences.

13. To help yourself weight all the important aspects when judging the utility of an outcome, make up a rating scale for yourself and get a summary score for each outcome. Most of the time you can simply add up the scores for each item; sometimes you'll want to weight the items so that some are more important than others.

14. On unimportant decisions or decisions where there's a great deal of time pressure, you may wish to "satisfice," or take the first acceptable option you come across. Or, you may wish to do a much-abbreviated version of the "optimizing" process described above.

15. Make sure that, on important decisions, you get enough data before deciding.

16. Don't let "sunk costs" influence you when deciding what's the best course of action.

17. If you find you have a prevailing pattern of too much postdecisional regret, or too much bolstering, try to change these patterns over time, the same way you try to change any other habit.

18. Make mental movies of your guess of what outcomes certain options will lead to. Notice your tendency toward postdecisional regret or bolstering, and practice in fantasy using less of those patterns if you decide that's what's best.

19. If the problem is getting yourself to enact the decision you know to be best, use the techniques of self-influence listed in the methods of influence axis.

20. Keep in mind that, for some decisions, there are many right answers, meaning many options that will lead to a happy outcome given a cheerful, optimistic, and hard-working attitude.

Exercises in mental maneuvers for decision-making

The following are some decision-making maneuvers. Try to:

1. fully understand each of them,

2. log in a good number of hours practicing each of them with hypothetical situations,

3. look through your real-life experience for real situations to add to the list,

4. practice using these maneuvers with real-life situations from the past, to rehearse for the next time a similar situation comes up,

5. practice using these with real-life situations when they come up, and

6. celebrate it in your mind when you're able to do any of these things.

If you spend enough time doing these things, I can almost guarantee that your decisions will be better.

Goal-setting

What is your purpose in dealing with a given situation? What are you trying to do? Developing aims, goals, or objectives allows you to have a sense of purpose rather than just respond by habit or imitation. Goal-setting lets you be "proactive" rather than "reactive."

Example: Think of yourself at this stage of your life. What are your goals?

Example: You go to a party. What are your goals for the party?

Example: You read a book. What might your goals be?

Example: You and your spouse disagree about how the yard should look. What are your goals?

Identifying choice points

In every activity, there are lots of choice points. In identifying choice points, you bring to awareness what decisions have to be made in successfully carrying out that activity. This is a list of questions to be answered. Probably one of the most frequent causes of bad decisions is someone's failure to identify a certain decision as a choice point of high priority. (See prioritizing as the second half of this process.)

Example: Someone is starting up a business. For three minutes, list as many possible choice points as you can for this person.

Example: Think about your current life situation, and list choice points facing you now.

Listing the factors

When you make a decision, you're usually trying to get as much or little of certain factors as you can. For example, suppose you're a parent choosing a baby-sitter. You're trying to maximize the amount of fun your child

has, your child's safety, the positive influence on your child's psychological skills, the degree to which you'll feel unworried when you child is with the baby-sitter, and so forth. You're trying to minimize the chance the child will be mistreated, the chance the child will be spoiled, the length of time you have to spend driving the baby-sitter home, and so forth.

When you list the factors, you are in effect making a rating scale. You can use this rating scale to evaluate any candidate for what you're choosing.

Example: A person has the chance to choose what college to go to. List the factors for this choice.

Listing options

This is the process of listing alternatives, possible choices, options. You try to brainstorm to think of as many ideas as you can about what to do in a given situation, or how to explain or understand a situation.

Example: You're having trouble keeping up in a certain course in school. List options on what you could do.

Example: One person likes to play loud music, and another person in the household finds this very disturbing. List options as to what they could come up with as solutions for their problem.

Information-seeking

This is a special case of listing options; it's listing the options for ways of finding out more information about a certain issue. Making decisions is only as good as the information you have, and often finding more information on the topic is the key to making a good decision.

Example: A person is looking for a job. How can the person find information about what jobs are available?

Example: A person thinks he has a medical problem. How can the person get information on it?

Listing pros and cons

When listing pros and cons, you take an idea, or a proposal, or an option that you might try, and list for yourself the advantages, or points in favor of it (the pros), and the disadvantages, or points against it, (the cons). The pros are the things you like about the idea, and the cons are the things you don't like.

Most people have an "all or none" response to options, giving them their total approval or total disapproval. Listing pros and cons helps to get you into the habit of giving more careful consideration to ideas, seeing both sides of a question, weighing the pros against the cons, rather than just having a gut reflex that accepts or rejects an option.

It's not good to keep vacillating back and forth about an option without ever making a definite commitment to it. But the idea of listing pros and cons is that you can do this better after you have thought carefully about the option.

Example: List pros and cons for three minutes on the following idea:

Children should be taught to tutor other children in school, and lots of time should be spent at schools with older children tutoring younger children.

Predicting consequences

You try to predict the consequences for a certain option. You try to predict

Immediate consequences: Less than one year

Short to medium-term consequences: one to twenty-five years

Long-term consequences: more than twenty-five years

Some people are in the habit of thinking of consequences that will occur only in the next few seconds, or not thinking of consequences at all. Predicting consequences helps to lengthen your time perspective and to get you trying to predict what will happen later.

Example: Someone considers becoming a vegetarian. Predict consequences for this option.

Prioritizing

When you have made a list, as in some of the other maneuvers described here, you have been trying to come up with as many ideas as you can. When you prioritize, you try to pick out from that list the most important ideas, the ones you want to give the most weight to. You arrange the ideas in order of priority.

Example: Someone is choosing whom to employ for a job. First list the factors and then prioritize by picking the three most important priorities in order.

Example: List the choice points in your life at present, and then select the three most important ones.

Perspective-taking

Here you try to imagine what another person's point of view on something is; you try to see things from the other person's perspective. You can do any of the other maneuvers, imagining what the other person might be thinking. For example, you can set goals from someone else's perspective. Perspective-taking is meant to be an antidote to selfishness.

Example: A parent and a teenager have differing points of view on how late the teenager should be allowed to stay out at night. Please list thoughts that might occur to each, first the teenager's perspective and then the parent's perspective.

Estimating probabilities

In making decisions, you try to predict consequences and try to guess how likely those consequences are. In this exercise, you guess what the probability is of something happening in a certain situation. If two or more people guess, they can compare their guesses with one another.

Example: Someone doesn't drink or use drugs, is in good physical condition, has reasonably good reflexes, drives within the speed limit, and drives about ten hours a week. What do you guess the probability is that this person will have a serious auto accident in a given year?

Someone else drinks several beers while driving, at least once a week, and drives thirty or so miles at a rate well above the speed limit several times a week. What do you guess the probability is that this person will have a serious auto accident in a given year?

Estimating utilities

How good or bad is a certain outcome? In making decisions it's good to have a sense of perspective on how desirable or undesirable a certain situation is. The "utility" of a situation is how good or bad, how desirable or undesirable it is.

Exercise: Please arrange the following outcomes in order of how desirable they are, that is, how much their utility is. Then add other situations from your life, and say where they would fall on the rank ordering.

Winning a couple of million dollars in a lottery

Doing work that wins the Nobel Prize

Figuring out a way to cure AIDS

Having someone call you a name

Finding a dollar bill on the sidewalk

Getting to eat what you like the best in the world

Having to have an appendix taken out and being in the hospital for a few days

Losing a pen

Skill 35: Toleration, Non-bossiness

Toleration is the skill of liking, or at least putting up with, people as they are. It's avoiding an overly strong urge to either change people or reject them because they're separate and different from you.

A simple example is the person who tells other people what to do all the time, bossing others to do whatever he feels they should do. This person doesn't stop to see things from the other person's perspective, and doesn't realize that the other person likes freedom. As a more specific example: A child invites another child over to his house and then bosses her around so much that the guest wants to leave.

Another example is the parent or teacher who gives too many unnecessary commands to a child. "Don't sit there; sit over there. Take your coat off. Hold still. Don't fidget so much. Eat more of your beans. Don't eat so much bread." When an adult is too bossy with a child, the child usually rebels after a while. Each experience of being controlled induces resentment that seems to accumulate over time.

Some adults who give children too many unnecessary commands do so not because of a rational decision that each command is necessary. Rather, they do it because similar commands they were given as children are recorded in their memories. They duplicate this as though playing a tape recording. Eliminating unnecessary commands can greatly improve adult-child relationships.

Another example of low skill in toleration is the irrational empire builder. There are countless people in business and government who are more obsessed with the desire to bring more and more people under their power and control than they are with figuring out what is the best direction to lead those people.

The most pathological example of an empire builder was Adolph Hitler, who wanted to control the world, decide which races should live and die, and constantly increase power by whatever means necessary. History has been kinder to other empire builders, such as Napoleon, Julius Caesar, and Alexander "the Great" – all of whom distinguished themselves by amassing power to bring other people under their control against their will.

The business world contains untold stories of leaders who were doing a good job of running a small organization, but as they felt the need to acquire more and more units in order to build their own power, lost touch with the people they were leading and sped to failure. These stories probably don't get as much publicity as those of the empire builders who became fabulously wealthy, and, partly for this reason, the drive for empire-building continues.

Another example of skill deficiency in toleration, seen frequently among children, perhaps less frequently among adults, is bullying. One person causes pain or distress to another, not to get something out of the person, but for the pure pleasure of having power over that person. For example, a child calls another child names at the bus stop, not wanting the child to give him anything, not trying to get revenge on the child, but simply glorying in the fact that he's powerful enough to do this to the other person and get away with it. This skill deficiency is not remedied by practicing the steps of rational problem-solving; it is remedied by the person with the tyrannical motives learning to live and let live, learning not to need power over other people so much.

This brand of skill deficiency in toleration has a certain contagious quality: the person who has been bullied often tends to want to bully others. For A child who victimizes other children brings forth nothing but righteous indignation from adults who see his bullying. But when the adults learn that this child is mercilessly bullied by an older sibling, they become a little more sympathetic. Then perhaps they learn how the older sibling is mercilessly bullied by a parent, and how the parent is bullied by almost everyone in his life.

Another motive for lack of toleration is, strangely enough, people's natural desire for a strong social network, their need for belonging in a group. Out of a need for belonging, people define certain characteristics as defining "our group," and the absence of those characteristics as defining "the other people." For example, in order to be in our group you have to be an athlete, or to be wealthy, or to have a body part pierced, or to be a drinker, or a nondrinker, or to be a member of a certain religion, or not be overweight, or to have certain social skills, or to be a certain sex, or to be a certain race. Or in order to be in our group you have to drive one of several types of cars. Or wear a certain type of hat.

Why define the group in these terms? Because if you have the defining characteristic, you can be sure you're in the group; you don't have to worry about exclusion. If you define the group with more abstract terms – such as people of good character, interesting people, nice people – then you can never be totally sure whether you fit the definition or not. But you can be very sure, for example, that you're white, you have an expensive house, and you drive a Mercedes.

Once people get the idea that one or more of these characteristics define their social network, they can reject or seek to change people who don't have those characteristics. They can't define their social network as potentially including all decent people they meet and have time to relate to. Thus, an element of the skill of toleration is to appreciate human diversity, and to appreciate differences from oneself as interesting and enriching.

The skill of toleration, interestingly, is a very important one for people who seek to help other people with their problems.

Here's what might happen when the helper has too great a desire to control the other person, too great a desire for power over the other person. The helpee presents a problem: "My boyfriend treats me badly," or, "I can't get my work done on time." The helper then figures out a certain solution, and advises the helpee to do that. For example: "If he treats you like that, you should dump him!" Or, "Sit down right here and now and do it right away!"

Then suppose the helpee doesn't want to enact that particular option. Now sometimes the helper is very frustrated by the helpee's failure to enact that option successfully, and becomes angry with the helpee. Now the helpee has another problem: "The helper is angry at me." The helper now has a problem too: "I can't get the helpee to do what she should do." The two may become locked in a power struggle.

One way of talking about what the helper should do in this situation is to say that the helper needs to let the helpee "own the problem." That is, the helper doesn't have a personal need for the problem to be solved in a particular way, or even for the problem to be solved at all. The only need the helper has is to offer high-quality help; if the other person still is not able to solve the problem, at least the helper has done his job. The helper gives the helpee the freedom not to solve the problem if she, or fate, so chooses. And giving other people freedom is the core of the skill of toleration.

How does one overcome the habit of bossiness, the wish to control others too much, an overly great need for power? The answer lies in being able to take the perspective of the other person and to exercise the Golden Rule. One of the most eloquent statements of this was made by Abraham Lincoln, who said, "As I would not be a slave, I would not be a master." If you don't want other people bossing you too much, don't boss them too much.

Another change that happens as people grow and develop in this skill is the redefinition of someone else's wish to be different from them as not their problem, not my problem, but no problem. For example, suppose a family member enjoys watching lots of athletic contests. Suppose I feel that, for me, watching athletic contests would be a colossal waste of time. Part of the skill of toleration is defining whatever gives the other person happiness as no problem, if it is not harmful to me or others.

But sometimes this isn't a simple decision. This is part of what often makes this skill difficult. Sometimes other people's seemingly private choices indirectly harm me or others by changing the general character of the culture. Suppose my family member entertains himself by watching boxing matches. I might reasonably argue that his behavior encourages brain damage among the boxers and the admiration of violence by the rest of the culture. Thus, his entertainment is harmful, and I should use the skill of assertion, not the skill of toleration. For an even more obvious example, if my family member has a habit of driving drunk at high speeds, then that habit is very likely to do lots of harm. Thus, it would be easy to argue that I have a moral obligation to use any influence, control or power I possess to change my family member's behavior.

The choice of whether to control people or let them make their own choices is constantly an issue in political decisions. Political leaders often say, "I personally do not believe in (abortion, use of guns, use of drug x), but I would not interfere with someone else's choice to get those things." Other leaders say, "Because I personally do not believe in these things, I have a moral obligation to keep other people from choosing it." In many cases the question of whether to try to control the other person or give him his own choice is determined by just how bad you think the effects of his behavior will be. At some point you draw the line and feel that "live and let live" must give way to "I can't let you do that." But people will inevitably disagree on where to draw that line.

The skill of toleration is listed in the conflict resolution group because toleration tends to reduce conflict. Not all toleration is good, however, and not all conflict is bad. When people are do-

ing truly harmful and wrong things, it's good that other people are intolerant of those things and are in conflict with them.

However, many of the conflicts that people get into, and directives people give to other people, have to do with extremely trivial points which by no stretch of the imagination are great wrongs that must be righted. The person with the skill of toleration can at least let these obviously trivial things go by without bothering about them.

Skill 36: Rational Approach to Conflict or Joint Decisions

Let's think about the words, conflict and joint decision. Conflict is a situation where two people's wishes are opposed. One person wants one thing to happen, and another person would prefer something else to happen. For example, two people are playing tennis, and one thinks a certain shot fell in bounds and the other thinks it was out. Or a mother prefers that her son would do homework immediately; the son would put it off. A husband would like to spend time golfing, whereas the wife would prefer that he spend time playing with the kids at home. A two-year-old child wants to play with a toy all by himself, and another two-year-old child wants to play with the same toy at the same time.

Joint decisions occur even more frequently than conflicts. In a joint decision, people have to figure out what they will do about a decision that affects both of them. Their interests may or may not be opposed. For example, there's a family vacation coming up, and people need to decide what to do. This is a joint decision; if people want different things, it's also a conflict. Two children get together to play, and there are various choices as to what they will do. This is a joint decision; if they want to do different things, this is also a conflict. Two people get married and need to decide whether and when to try to

have children. This is a joint decision; if they disagree, there's a conflict.

What do we mean by an irrational or rational approach to joint decision and conflict? A rational approach means to think hard, using your reasoning and calculation abilities, to try to figure out what option would work out best in the long run. When certain options work better for one person and others work better for another, things get complicated. But in rational joint decision-making, the two people at least take into account the welfare of both people.

It's easy to illustrate what irrational approaches to conflict are. When I lived in Chicago, there was a heavy snowstorm, and one man had shoveled out a parking place on the road. When he drove up to the space to park his car, he discovered that another man had parked there. The resulting conflict ended with one of the two men killing the other. This is what rational conflict resolution is not: when a low-stakes issue such as a parking place winds up being settled with high-stakes consequences such as killing. Another time I heard of a killing that occurred over a seemingly trivial conflict: who would get to use a pay phone first. Sadly, deaths over such minor issues occur with considerable frequency.

When people find themselves in conflicts, there's a tendency for their bodies to respond with the fight-or-flight response. When someone perceives himself as threatened, his body starts secreting adrenaline and other hormones, which are designed to protect the person from getting hurt by mobilizing his body for strenuous exercise. Blood goes to the muscles, the heart beats faster, sweating starts, breathing is faster, and heightened muscle tone can cause trembling. The person is physiologically ready to run away from the enemy or to fight physically. The fight-or-flight response is not conducive to cool, calm, calculating deliberation. It's meant for quick motion.

Centuries of evolution have selected for the fight-or-flight response. Animals able to run away the quickest or fight the hardest have tended to survive and pass their genes on.

But at some point the human race gained the capacity to generate options, predict consequences, and think about the advantages and disadvantages of options. They became able to communicate with one another in words about these ideas. The newer responses – rational thinking and talking – are in competition with the older responses, fighting or fleeing.

Sometimes people talk in a way that's close to flight-or-fight, without physically hitting or running away. It's like fight when people yell and scream at each other and get very angry, even without hitting. And it's like flight when someone feels scared of talking about a joint decision and therefore avoids ever talking about it. For example, a wife doesn't like the tone of voice with which her husband talks to her, but she's scared of talking about this topic, and so she never gets around to mentioning it.

Let's think about choosing how you want to act in a certain joint decision situation. Some people don't consciously choose how to act for a certain situation – instead, they go into a certain way of acting by reflex. They get locked into a certain response to joint decisions, rather than tailoring their response. For example, some people tend to get angry; others try to do what the other person wants; others start bargaining and negotiating. The person with the best habits with regard to conflict has various ways of acting in his repertoire, and makes a choice based on the particular situation.

Let's talk about the stance that's variously called self-sacrifice, giving behavior, conciliation, or "being nice." The person who takes this stance basically says, "Hey, it isn't that big a deal to me; let's do what you want." For example, one person in a family wants to go out to eat supper one night, and the second would slightly prefer not to, but he says, "OK, if it will make you happy, let's do it!" Or suppose a family is playing games together. One person would prefer to play charades first, and the other would prefer to play twenty questions first. One of the people says, "Okay, we'll do what you want first." It's very difficult for people to get along, unless at least one of them can use giving behavior on many of the very low-stakes joint decisions that come up.

Sometimes problems come up when each person is locked into using giving behavior and neither will be assertive about their own wishes. In such cases, you hear dialogues like, "What would you like to do?" "Whatever you'd like to do." "Well, I'll do whatever *you'd* like to do." "No, you pick." Someone has to be at least a little assertive in order for joint decisions to be made. Also, there can be problems when the same person in a relationship is the one who always gives in and the other always gets his way. If this happens, the giver tends to become resentful and the taker tends to become spoiled and bratty.

The opposite of the giving behavior stance is the assertive stance. In this stance you're inclined to hold your ground, stick up for what you want, refuse to give in, and avoid self-sacrificing. But you only oppose the other person to the extent necessary to get what you want.

By contrast, in the aggressive stance, you don't just try to get what you want; you want to attack, defeat, and punish the other person. The assertive stance is very much compatible with cooperative negotiation, whereas the aggressive stance is very much a competitive situation.

The stance of the expert negotiator is complex. The best negotiator is flexible and is able to go into any of the other stances as necessary. The best negotiator has certain interests and realizes that the other person has some interests. The negotiator attempts to figure out what these interests are and to come up with some sort of bargain. The negotiator hopes the other person will agree to the deal, and wants to meet the other person's wishes at least enough to accomplish this. The negotiator often does a lot of tactful persuasion – talk meant to persuade the other to go along, but not to make the other person lose face.

Sometimes the conflict of interests is over something that has already happened and can't be undone. For examples, you have already broken my object that I liked; or your dog has already bitten my child; or you have already lost control of your emotions and yelled at me in a very inappropriate way. Any of the stances already mentioned can be assumed when figuring out what to do about these, either how to make restitution for these things or how to assure that the injury won't happen again.

Let's mention two more stances people take with injuries that have happened in the past. One is punishment: making someone feel bad for doing something that was a wrong act. The other is forgiveness: letting go of the urge to punish the person for their wrong act, or letting go of a sense of pain that will persist until the other person has been punished.

As a general rule, giving punishment and taking an aggressive stance toward conflict tend to be greatly overused in the world, and the negotiator stance tends to be greatly underused. Giving behavior or self-sacrifice is overused by some people and underused by others, as is assertion. None of these general stances is always right or always wrong. The important thing is to pick the stance that's appropriate to the situation at hand.

Another stance may be called "refusal to engage in the conflict." This occurs when one person refuses to define a situation so that it creates a conflict. For example: One child says to another, "I think you're an ugly dork." The child expects this will create a conflict, as follows: "I want to think badly of you, and you want me not to do that." But suppose the other child shrugs and says, "Well, you have a right to your opinion." Then the second child is refusing to engage in the conflict. The nonverbal message is, "The fact that you think I'm a bad person doesn't cause me a problem I consider worth solving."

Let's talk about a general paradigm for joint decisions and conflicts, a set of criteria for making joint decisions rationally and well. These criteria are compatible with any of the stances we've mentioned so far, with the exception of the aggressive stance. People having joint-decision conversations in real life rarely meet all these criteria. But many conversations that don't go well could have been made better by changing just one of these criteria from the "not done" to the "done" column. If people could practice these criteria in many role-played conversations as part of their education, the world would be a much better place.

Checklist for joint decision-making

1. Defining. Each person defines the problem from his or her point of view, without blaming, and without telling what the solution should be.

2. Reflecting. Each person reflects to let the other person know he understands the other person's point of view.

3. Listing. They list at least four options.

4. Waiting. They don't criticize the other's options until they've finished listing.

5. Advantages. They think and talk about the advantages and disadvantages of the best options.

6. Agreeing. They pick one to try.

7. Politeness. They don't raise their voices or put each other down or interrupt.

Now, let's think about each of these seven. Let's consider why they're worth doing and how to do them.

The first criterion is that each person defines the problem from his or her point of view, without accusing the other person or dictating the solution to the problem. What do you do if you don't tell how to solve the problem or describe what the other person is doing badly? You name the situation and tell what your own interests are. Let's look at some examples of the contrast between describing the solution and talking about the other person's bad points as opposed to defining the situation and your interests.

Suppose the problem is that music the first person is playing is disturbing a family member, the second person. Suppose the second person's opening problem statement is, "Turn off that stupid music!" This dictates what the solution to the problem is: the music is to be turned off, not turned down, listened to with headphones, listened to outside, or any other option. The opening statement also accuses the other person of having bad taste in music, liking stupid music. This opening is likely to provoke a defensive response from the first person.

Suppose instead the second person says, "When the music is as loud as it is, and when it's that particular music, I have trouble concentrating on my homework." Now the problem situation has been named, and the second person is also stating his own interests, namely doing the homework successfully. Of course, it's still possible the first person would feel defensive or touchy. But there's much less reason for the first person to feel threatened than with the first opening.

Suppose the problem is that the first neighbor's dog is barking very loudly and keeps the second neighbor awake at night. Suppose the second person opens by saying, "You've got to get rid of that out-of-control mutt of yours!" This again dictates a particular solution to the problem; it accuses the first person by saying he has an out-of-control mutt. Suppose instead the second neighbor had opened with "I have a problem. When your dog barks in the middle of the night, it keeps me awake, and I can't get as much sleep as I would like." That is naming the problem situation and stating one's own interests.

One guideline for defining problems in this way has been referred to as "I Messages" or "I Feel Statements." They take the following form: "When this certain thing happens, I experience this because of that. When X, I experience Y because of Z." For example, "When you pulled into that parking place, I felt upset, because I just spent fifteen minutes digging out that parking space from the snow. I just went to get my car and come back and put it in." Contrast this opening statement with "Get the heck out of that parking space now!"

Another example: "When I see that balls are left on the stairway, it bothers me a great deal. I worry that someone is going to step on them and slip and hurt herself." Contrast this with "Who around here is so thoughtless as to leave balls on the steps?"

Why is it important to define the problem in terms of interests rather than simply telling the other person what to do? Often when the first person tries to dictate to the second what should be done, the second doesn't like being ordered around and will resist. Then it becomes a power struggle between the two of them. If you can define the problem without saying what the solution should be, then both people are freer to think of various options rather than to fight over just one of them. You want to make the problem statement in such a way as to not lock yourself prematurely into any one particular option.

For example, in our problem with the two men wanting the parking place, suppose that instead of saying, "Get the heck out of that parking space right now," the person who shoveled the snow had said, "I'm sure you didn't know this, but I spent the last fifteen minutes shoveling the snow out of that space so I could put my car into it." That leaves the second person open to options like, "I'm in a big hurry for a very important meeting. Suppose I pay you $50 for the privilege of parking here, and you dig out another space?" This option might be a great one for our snow-shoveler, but, if his opening line had dictated only one option, he never would have heard it.

The second step in the rational problem-solving paradigm is for each person to do a reflection of the other's point of view. This lets each make sure he understands other person's problem statement, and, perhaps more important, lets the other person know he understands.

As an example of step two, using the barking dog problem: When the one person says, "Your dog's barking is keeping me awake at night," the second person says, "So, as I understand it, this is happening frequently enough that you're losing a lot of sleep and it's something we need to do something about," and the other person says, "Yes."

So far one person has made a problem-definition statement and the other person has reflected it. The reflection gives a chance to clear up misunderstandings. For example: The first person says, "Your dog's barking is keeping me awake at night." The second says, "So you're insisting I get rid of the dog, and you're going to sue me if I don't?" This incorrect reflection gives the first person the opportunity to say, "No, that's not what I'm saying at all. I'm simply saying that this is a problem and I wanted to talk with you about how to solve it." Now the second person should reflect again until he has heard it right.

The next task is for the second person to describe the problem from his point of view and to define his own interest, and for the first person to reflect accurately. So the second person says, "Well, my dog is very dear to me and is perhaps the best friend I have. Furthermore, I work on the night shift. I depend on the dog to guard the house and make sure I don't get robbed at night."

Now the first person has a turn at doing a reflection, "So, what I hear you saying is that your dog is not only a dear friend to you, but also the protector of the house when you're working on the night shift." The second person says, "Yes, you understand it." Each of them may wish to talk longer and to further clarify their points of view on the problem and do further reflections. But, by making one statement of their own interests, they have at least progressed a great deal further than many people do in having a rational conflict-resolution conversation.

Step three is listing options. This has been called "brainstorming." It's good to actually take out a piece of paper and write down the options as they are listed. Both people think of several options. In the exercise, together they should list at least four options.

While they are doing this, as criterion four states, they don't criticize the options, at least not until the listing is over. They concentrate on listing them.

When a conflict is not being settled well, one person usually suggests an option and the other person usually criticizes it. The first person defends it, and the second criticizes it in a different way. The more they argue, the more the defender of the option comes to believe in it, and the more the attacker comes to believe that it's a dumb idea. The more

the two people talk, they more they disagree.

Meanwhile, they may be overlooking a better option that could solve the problem very well, an option that has not occurred to either of them. If they list more than one option, and if they don't criticize before listing for a while, they avoid this premature commitment for or against an option. When each person generates at least two options, each gets into a more flexible frame of mind: each at least acknowledges the possibility that there's more than one way to solve the problem.

Why is it a good idea to separate the option-listing from the option-evaluating? When you start criticizing options, you tend to shut down the creative process of generating more options. The idea of brainstorming is to generate as many ideas as possible; they don't have to be perfect options, or even good ones. Even ridiculous options may suggest to you or the other person another idea that will really work well.

Only after both people have agreed to stop listing options, should they start thinking about advantages and disadvantages of the options. For example, the first person says, "That's all the options I can think of. Can you think of any more?" The second says, "No. Let's go ahead and evaluate the options." The people are thereby agreeing on what stage of the process they are in.

When trying to pick an option, the two people should keep an image in mind of options competing with one another rather than people competing with each other. Which option will maximize the joint welfare of both people? If they can focus on that question, rather than on the question of which person will win, they'll be much more likely to solve their problem. In the ideal image, the two people work in cooperation to try to predict which option will work best, rather than competing with each other.

When you evaluate options, you think about what consequences you predict for them. A good consequence is an advantage of the option, and a bad consequence is a disadvantage of the option.

Suppose that, in our dog problem, one person has said, "One option is that you could get an electronic alarm system to protect your house at night rather than relying on your dog."

Suppose the other person says, "Oh yeah, right. I should go out and spend $2,000 on an alarm system and have to pay some company $30 a month to keep it up. You rich people think working people like me are made out of money. You never think someone else might not have as many dollars to throw away on things as you do." This statement doesn't stick to the disadvantage of the option. It spills over into talking about the good and bad points of the other person. It implies that the other person is selfish and inconsiderate of other people's points of view, and that the other person has lived a life of ease at the expense of people who have had

to work harder. The other person might be tempted to begin defending himself against this charge, and lose sight of the original problem.

How could the person talk about the disadvantage of the option without making a statement about the other person? It would be better to say, "Getting an electric alarm system is certainly an option for protecting the house. A major disadvantage is that it would probably cost at least a couple of thousand dollars to install and maybe $30 a month to keep it going." Now the other person would find it much easier to say, "Well, the cost is a disadvantage, but I happen to have a brother-in-law who can do it for considerably less than that. Plus, the problem is important enough for me that I would be willing to contribute something toward the cost of it." You can bet the second person would not have volunteered any of his own resources if he had just been insulted.

When evaluating options, it's good to think about how the advantages compare with the disadvantages. A complex but very good way of thinking about how good an option is involves the concept of "expected utility." Utility means the happiness of the people involved. The word "expected" means what's the most likely amount of happiness to result from the option. To get the expected utility of an option, you first think of the possible consequences that might occur if that option were tried. You rate how good or bad each of those consequences is. Then you weight the rating of each consequence according to the chance that it will actually happen. When you add up the weighted scores, you get the expected utility.

Here's an example of using expected utility in thinking. Suppose the conflict is between two neighbors. One neighbor has hewn out dirt from the hillside and has made a wall that's really a high cliff. If a child were to fall off that cliff to land on the concrete driveway below, it's almost certain the child would be hurt badly or even killed. The option being considered is building a fence to keep the neighbor's children from the cliff. But the neighbor who owns the cliff doesn't want an unsightly fence in that place.

Suppose the best guess is that the chances would be 1 in 300 that the child would fall off the cliff if there's no fence. How do you think about this? With the no-fence option, you have a 1 in 300 chance the child will get hurt very badly or killed. With the fence option you have 100 percent chance of having something one neighbor considers unsightly. How do you weigh these? You multiply the disutility of a child's being hurt or killed by a 1/300 probability. You compare that to the disutility of the sight of the fence multiplied by a probability of 1. (For simplicity, we're assuming that the fence lowers the probability of the fall to zero, and we're ignoring the cost of the fence, etc.)

So the calculation comes down to this: Is the disutility of the death or serious injury of a child more than 300

times worse than the disutility of the unsightliness of the fence? If so, it's rational to put up the fence. If you feel that a child's being hurt or killed is less than 300 times worse than the unsightliness of the fence, then you don't build the fence. In my system of values, the death or serious injury of the child would be weighted at least thousands of times more important than any considerations about appearances, and the option of building the fence would win hands down.

This weighing of probabilities and utilities is central to the rational process. It is NOT true that only mathematicians think in this way. We constantly weigh probabilities and utilities in real-life decisions, most of the time without even realizing we are doing so.

A game I made up called the decisions game gives practice in weighing probabilities and utilities. I found that even young children can make decisions in fairly accurate ways when given information on probabilities and utilities, despite the fact that they don't know what the words *probability* and *utility* mean and despite their not having studied enough mathematics to actually calculate expected utilities.

The next criterion for our exercise in rational problem-solving is that they finally agree on something. They don't have to agree on the final solution to the problem. They can agree on an intermediate step. For example, they agree that they don't have enough information now, and that they need to make some calls to find out how much an electronic burglar alarm system costs. Or they agree on the need to find out how dogs are affected by being kept in small spaces. Or they agree that they need more time to think about this and will talk more about it later. If they decide that, on a certain political issue, one will vote one way and the other one will vote the other way, then they are "agreeing to disagree," but it's still an agreement. Sometimes these agreements to disagree are really agreements to stay friends despite never seeing eye-to-eye on a certain issue.

The last criterion for this exercise is that, during all the conversation, they don't insult each other or raise their voices at each other or interrupt each other. And, of course, they don't use physical violence against each other.

Why shouldn't they raise their voices? Some people think that, if people yell more, they'll get their anger out of their system. This notion is almost always wrong. Extensive research has found that trying to get anger out by yelling usually only tends to increase the anger. When people yell, they stimulate each other to become angrier. Screaming in anger makes physical violence more likely, not less likely. It raises the arousal level to the point where people don't think rationally or clearly.

Why shouldn't people interrupt each other? When they do interrupt

each other often, they're usually competing on at least two levels: what should be done about the problem, and who gets to talk at any moment. The frustration of not being able to talk when one wants to can make people angrier.

I've taught conflict resolution to people who had a strong habit of interrupting each other. The following technique helped. I took a piece of paper and wrote on it the words "the floor." Then I established the rule that people could speak only when they were physically holding "the floor" in their hands. When they were through speaking, they literally gave "the floor" to another person. This rule focuses attention on yielding one's turn to speak to someone else.

This concludes the explanation of the seven criteria for rational joint problem-solving. There's one more criterion that perhaps should be added to the list: that people actually carry out the agreement that they made. This presents a challenge to do in role-playing, but it's always possible given enough imagination.

Suppose two people go through the rational problem-solving process and come to agreements, but one or the other of them repeatedly fails to abide by those agreements. The other person will rightly mistrust the whole process. They now have a different problem to deal with: the agreement isn't being kept. It may be because the first person never had any intention of keeping it. It may be because the person wanted very much to keep it but just lacked the strength, willpower, or organizational skills to keep it. If the first person never intended to keep the agreement and was lying when the agreement was made, then there are big problems that will be solved only when the person stops lying.

If, on the other hand, the person just isn't organized enough, can't remember, or doesn't have enough willpower, then there are possible solutions. Better ways can be found to remind the other person to carry out the agreement. Incentives can be set up to help the other person gain the will to do it. Penalties can be imposed if the person doesn't do it. The person can engage in fantasy practice repeatedly to help himself do it. The other person can model how to do it better. The person can engage in psychotherapy meant to help the person overcome barriers that block his doing it. How to get the agreement carried out can be treated as a separate problem for which options can be listed and discussed.

In my vision of utopia, people would practice solving hundreds of joint decisions in role-playing, trying to meet each of the criteria and trying to come up with the best solution possible. After extensive role-playing practice, the process starts to become second nature. But a very small amount of practice, e.g. three or four role-played situations, usually doesn't do much of anything.

Much repetition is necessary before habits change.

Sometimes parents are very reluctant to do such practice with their children, because they feel that parents should be the authorities who make the decisions and children should carry out those decisions. I too am a believer in parental authority. But even when the parent reserves the right to make the final decision, often much can be accomplished by listening to the child's point of view on the problem, listing options together, and considering advantages and disadvantages together, before the parent has the final say on the choice. Often the parent is much better equipped to choose after getting the information from the child.

Secondly, at other times the parent doesn't need to use authority; on a subclass of joint decisions, the parent can give the child more power. Thus, with a five year old, when it's a joint decision on "What fun thing shall we do together now?" the child should be given more power, whereas in the decision on "Is it bedtime now?" the child should be given almost no power.

Joint problem-solving is quite different when the two people will have a continuing relationship with each other than when they'll never see each other again. For example, it's very different when a husband and wife negotiate with each other than when someone negotiates with a used-car salesman. When the relationship is an ongoing one, there's much more interest in preserving the quality of the relationship. Thus, there's more incentive to be gracious and rational and to give in. On the other hand, there's also more incentive *not* to give in: you don't want to start the precedent of giving in, you don't want the other person to expect you'll give in the next time and the time after that.

The rational joint-decision paradigm I've described requires both people to contribute. What happens when one person tries it and the other doesn't? Sometimes one person can lead a conversation that approximates the rational conflict-resolution steps, even though the other person isn't used to thinking in this way. You can, for instance, unilaterally make a problem statement of your own point of view. You can keep searching for accurate reflections until you've accurately stated the other person's point of view. You can paraphrase the suggestions the other person makes as options. You can unilaterally list options. You can unilaterally comment about the advantages and disadvantages of the options. You can unilaterally state which options would be acceptable and unacceptable to you, although you can't make the other person agree on one. You can also unilaterally refuse to engage in yelling, insulting, or interrupting.

Often, the more one person does these things, the more the other person reciprocates. Over time it's possible to influence someone toward this rational process just by doing it yourself.

This is not to say that it's possible to have a rational conflict-resolution conversation with everyone in the world. Rational conversations with Adolph Hitler would have done no good. Sometimes the pure exercise of power is called for. Some people are so convinced their point of view is right that they'll not be persuaded by any appeal to rationality or reason. This is why armies, courts, police forces, and prisons exist. These are methods of forcing people to do what is just and right, when they can't be persuaded to reach that decision on their own.

Nonetheless, it's good to envision a future world where rational conflict resolution is learned so universally and so thoroughly that there would be much less need for armies, courts or prisons.

In the meantime, it's very desirable for people to cultivate niches of relationships that rely on rational joint problem-solving rather than the use of force. Family members should make the rational solving of problems a very high priority. Supervisors of workplaces should see to it that joint decisions are made rationally. Even when working with someone we think will not respond to rational conflict- resolution methods, attempting these methods usually doesn't cost us anything.

The best way to learn the rational problem-solving process is by practicing role-playing. Although there are many varieties of two-person problems, when you begin to role-play them you soon find similar features among them. Practicing in role-playing should be part of the general education of children. If family members can practice repeatedly, the functioning of the family can be improved. The *Options and Consequences Book* I composed will be useful for people who want to practice role-playing.

Here are four more topics related to the rational approach to joint decision-making and conflict resolution. One is understanding nine methods of influence and drawing on all of them. The second topic is using tact and other ways of talking that help negotiations come out better. The third topic is sources of power in negotiations. And the fourth is the skill of awareness of alliances and group structures, a subskill of negotiation and joint decision.

Methods of influence

The process of listing options, predicting consequences, and choosing wisely among the options is a skill that should precede the skills of influencing other people. It does little good to be able to influence others if you're unsure of the options you want them to choose.

But let's assume you've done a good job of listing and choosing, and you want to help the other person do his part in the plan. How do you influence the other person? Or more generally, how does anyone influence another person to do anything?

I want to think about methods of influence that aren't usually thought of as part of the negotiation process. But if we broadly define negotiation as the whole set of strategies meant to help people come to good joint decisions, and to resolve their problems with one another, then these nine methods are of paramount importance.

We can remember these methods by the mnemonic "Oh am prism." Each letter in this nonsensical phrase stands for a method of influence, as follows:

O - Objective formation or goal-setting
H - Hierarchy
A - Attribution
M - Modeling
P - Practice
R - Reinforcement and punishment contingencies
I - Instruction
S - Stimulus situation control
M - Monitoring

Let's spend some time thinking about what each of these means.

Objective formation

Objective formation or goal-setting means setting your sights, or helping someone else set her sights, on achieving something, such as getting better at a skill. If someone decides that peace and nonviolence are worthy goals, that person will probably be less likely to hit someone else. If a person frequently hears people speak with admiration for people who've made accomplishments in peaceful and nonviolent ways, that person will be much more likely to adopt this goal than if the admired characters are boxers and fighters.

Sometimes objective formation in a young child can be fostered simply by a parent's repetitively stating his or her earnest hope for the child: "It's my earnest hope for you that throughout your life, you'll be able to make other people happy, and to be happy yourself while doing so." At other times asking a person whether he would like to be able to do something better tends to heighten the consciousness of the goal: "I'm curious. Are you interested in learning to be braver when you try things like school work, and not be so afraid of failing?" or "How interested are you in having everybody in the family pitch in to keep the house more organized?" Objective formation is served in families and organizations by slogans, mottoes, oaths, mission statements, and theme songs. For example, the references to helping and kindness in the promises of the Girl Scouts and Boy Scouts are intended to serve the cause of conflict resolution, since kindness and helping are incompatible with violent and selfish conflict-resolution tactics.

Hierarchy

Hierarchy means setting up a series of baby steps that will lead to the goal, rather than trying to reach it in one great big jump. For example, suppose a teacher is in conflict with a child; the child can't concentrate on his work and sit still long enough. The teacher finds that the best solution to the conflict is to arrange a series of tasks that require fairly short concentration and sitting and allow the student to have successful experiences at them, and that gradually work their way up the hierarchy until the child is concentrating and sitting longer. Or, as a second example: A boss has a conflict with an employee who can't seem to do a certain complex procedure right. Rather than using punishment, reward or bargaining, the best method for resolving the problem is to let the employee go through a computer training that simulates the process. This training takes him step by step along the hierarchy of difficulty, with lots of practice at each step.

Attribution

The word *attribution* has to do with the causes we attribute to events. One major class of attributions seeks to explain behavior by means of permanent or long-lasting traits the person has. If a parent says to a child, "You're lazy," the parent is usually explaining some lack of work the child has done by the trait of laziness. The message may become a self-fulfilling prophecy. The child may act even lazier because he comes to think of himself as lazy. He doesn't take on tasks that require a lot of work, because that's not something lazy people do.

On the other hand, suppose the parent says, "You haven't learned how to use self-discipline to do tasks like these yet, but if you do learn that, it's going to be great." Now the parent is attributing to the child at least the possibility of learning the skill that's deficient. Now the child might be more likely to take on the hard task and succeed at it, because it would be a sign that he's learning self-discipline skills and things are going to be better because of that.

Modeling

Modeling means you show the person examples of how to do the skillful pattern. Modeling can take place in real life, as for example in the models family members give each other; it can also take place through fiction and fantasy, as in the examples that television characters give people for imitation, or the examples given in stories we read or tell about people we admire or dislike, and so forth.

When we see or hear models of thought, feeling, and behavior, we lay down in our memory banks patterns that we can then access when a decision point faces us. In some way we search through the patterns laid down in our memory bank, seeking one that will be most appropriate in the current situation. The more positive, adaptive, reasonable, psychologically skillful patterns we have laid down in our memory banks, the more likely we are to land on something that works well.

What does this have to do with conflict resolution? Suppose a husband has a problem with his wife: he feels

she is not upbeat and cheerful enough. It's possible that he might be able to resolve this conflict better by modeling upbeat and cheerful behavior himself, rather than by verbally negotiating an agreement with her that she will smile more and be more enthusiastic.

Practice

Providing practice opportunities means giving someone a chance to try out and rehearse the skillful patterns. A kid who's learning to share should play with someone else so that he can practice this skill. But practice opportunities are helpful only if the person practices positive patterns. A person learning conflict resolution benefits from dealing with the conflicts of daily life if she is practicing positive patterns, but she is harmed if she is practicing only negative patterns. A person learning to socialize with friends benefits if he is practicing socializing well, but he does not benefit if he is practicing socializing poorly.

The more we practice the patterns of thought, feeling, and behavior laid down in our memory bank by modeling, the more they become accessible and the more likely they are to be chosen.

Fantasy rehearsal means practicing things in imagination: imagining yourself doing the thing you want to do more often. Fantasy practice makes patterns more accessible, just as real-life practice does. Some early research on this topic involved ski racers. After skiing a course a few times, half the racers were asked to practice going down the hill in their imaginations, planning how they could best make each turn, creating a movie in their minds in which they ski the hill as well as possible. The other half of the racers did some unrelated activity during the same time. When the race was performed, the racers who had rehearsed in fantasy did better, on the average, than those who had not. Numerous other studies have concluded that rehearsal in fantasy "deepens the groove" for the pattern that's rehearsed.

Every time someone makes a mental representation of a concrete pattern of thought, feeling, and behavior, that person is performing a fantasy rehearsal of it. This means a fantasy rehearsal is taking place whenever you tell about a past event, vividly imagine the event while someone else tells about it, act out a behavior sequence with toy people, cause video game characters to enact a behavior, sing a song about a behavior sequence, or simply sit and imagine the pattern.

A special case of fantasy rehearsal is called *desensitization*. Suppose I'm afraid of starting to socialize with new people. If I repeatedly imagine myself doing so skillfully, and imagine a pleasant, non-punishing consequence, I'm practicing socializing in an unfearful way, and the fear gradually goes away. We can undo associations with negative feelings by repeatedly practicing a certain image in a safe and pleasant context. By this means, people

have overcome fears of heights, thunderstorms, being in public places, and many anxieties.

Sometimes undoing the connections between situations and negative emotions is good, but at other times it can be very bad. For example, most children seem to have a built-in empathic response of distress when seeing another person hurt and in distress. But by repeatedly being exposed to cartoons in which people are hurt as funny music plays in the background and no negative consequences occur, children can gradually lose the ability to feel distress over another's pain, and can even learn to laugh at another's misfortunes. In such cases, the child has become desensitized to images of people being hurt.

Society often acts toward children as if the principles of modeling and fantasy practice were nonexistent. People nag at children not to hit one another and often punish them when they do so, while at the same time giving them thousands of violent models on television and giving them thousands of opportunities for violent fantasy practice in video games.

Reinforcement

Reinforcement means something similar to reward: reinforcement is something that happens after a behavior that makes it more likely to happen again. Why did psychologists add the word *reinforcement* to the language, rather than just talking about rewards? Partly because something intended *by the person who does it* as a punishment, and experienced *by the person who receives it* as unpleasant, can still be a reinforcer, i.e. something that increases the behavior rather than decreasing it. For example, yelling at children when they misbehave sometimes actually tends to reinforce the misbehavior, rather than reduce its frequency. Children who are stimulus-seekers may be more reinforced by the excitement than they are punished by the disapproval.

You're reinforcing a behavior any time you do anything someone wants you to do, or any time you furnish someone a situation he prefers to what was going on before. Usually you're reinforcing whatever the person did just before you gave your reinforcer. Furthermore, any time you stop doing something that someone doesn't like, you're reinforcing the behavior the person did just beforehand. This means that, as long as you're with someone and your behavior is changing, you almost constantly reinforce the other person.

For example, a big brother is reading a book in a two-year-old child's presence, and the small child is playing with some toy people. The child has a toy person hug another person, and say "Nice baby." The big brother looks up from his book and observes the play.

If the child wanted the big brother's attention, (and it's a safe bet that he did, for most children), the big brother has just reinforced the episode of prosocial fantasy practice in the child's dramatic play, even though he hasn't said a word or lifted a finger.

Or for another example, a mom comes home and hugs her husband in the child's presence. The child screams jealously, and the mom immediately stops hugging her husband and looks at the child. She has just reinforced the screaming: the screaming was followed by the stopping of something the child didn't want (the hugging) and the starting of something the child did want (the look in his direction).

Attention, interest, enthusiasm, and signs that you like another person are important reinforcers for most people.

Another very important type of reinforcement is called internal reinforcement. When I do something smart or good and say to myself, "Hooray, I did a good job," I'm delivering a reinforcement to myself. The goal of education is to learn to do smart and good things, not because someone is ready to hand you a sticker or because someone is ready to pay attention to you, but because you have an internal value system that recognizes good acts and feels pleasure in them.

Here's one more important point about reinforcement: "vicarious" reinforcement also exerts an effect. This means people are influenced by the reinforcement they see other people getting as well as the reinforcement they get directly themselves. Suppose an adult asks three preschool children to sit down to eat and one of them sits down.

The adult says to the one who sat down, "Thanks for doing what I asked! That makes it so much more convenient for me!" The other two are probably receiving the information that compliance with the request is reinforceable by appreciation; in other words, they get vicarious reinforcement that tends to lead them to comply also.

Punishment is the other side of the coin from reinforcement. It's something that comes after a behavior that makes that behavior less likely to happen again. If yelling at a child for whining really reduces the whining, then the yelling is functioning as punishment; if the yelling increases the whining, then the yelling is functioning as reinforcement and not punishment. If, on the other hand, looking and speaking to the child with a grave and serious demeanor decreases the behavior, then that response is functioning as punishment.

To emphasize: we do things that *we predict* will be reinforcing or punishing; we *find out* whether those acts are reinforcing or punishing only after observing for some time whether the frequency of the behavior increases or decreases.

Here's a reason for relying as little as possible on punishment: it's difficult to punish without at the same time modeling doing something unpleasant. Punishment usually makes the other person want to do something unpleasant back. If a kid hits another kid because he called him a name, the hitter may be punishing the misbehavior, but he's also modeling for the other kid how to hit, and probably making the other kid want to hit back.

Instruction

Instruction means teaching or telling someone what to do or how to do it. For example, a boss has a conflict with contractors who are reporting the number of hours they worked as too high. The boss considers firing them, yelling at them, and punishing them in other ways. He considers having a problem-solving conversation. But he finally realizes he has never taught his employees how to accurately calculate the number of hours they have worked. He writes an instruction manual that clearly explains how to calculate the hours, and he finds the problem is greatly reduced.

Here's a central principle of instruction: instruction is much more effective when the instructed person is *not* feeling criticized, threatened, or defensive, but instead when he's interested and receptive to the instruction. Instruction given immediately after someone has done something undesirable is usually less effective than instruction given either at a routine, neutral time, or immediately after a person's positive behavior.

Stimulus control

Stimulus control means arranging the things in the environment, the stimuli, so they elicit desirable behavior. Suppose a man is overeating junk food, and his wife has a problem with this because she thinks it's endangering his health. She decides it's *not* a good use of stimulus situation control to have bowls of potato chips placed on numerous tables in the house. Before resorting to yelling at him or arguing with him, she decides to alter the stimuli of the house so it requires a greater effort to have access to junk food.

A girl likes to put together jigsaw puzzles. Her little sister tends to mess them up. The older girl decides that, in this two-person problem, rather than arguing with the younger sister, she'll use stimulus control: she puts the puzzle on a high table the younger sister can't reach.

Monitoring

Monitoring means that you keep up with how well the person is doing over time, measuring the results. Suppose a child and his parents have a problem: the parents think the child is not practicing the piano enough and is wasting the money the parents are spending on piano lessons. They decide to keep track of how much time the child actually does practice. This has the effect of letting the parents be aware of when the child is practicing, and it also gives the child an incentive to practice more.

Or two people in a family have a conflict with each other about who does chores. They decide to keep records of who does what chores at what time. This not only lets people get credit for

the work they do, but also gives them an incentive to do more. "That which gets measured tends to get improved," applies to families as well as schools, factories, and offices.

This brings us to the end of the discussion of the nine methods of influence. In thinking about negotiating for solutions of two-person problems, one will usually do well to consider each of the nine methods of influence as ways of helping either the other person or oneself to do more of the behavior that will solve the problem.

Using tact in negotiations

Tact is the art of not embarrassing people: making other people lose face as little as possible. It's the art of saying things without making it look as if you've defeated the other person. It's giving the other person no reason to defend his image.

We spoke in the previous section about the attribution of positive traits to other people, or the possibility of their developing positive traits. This is also a good example of the use of tact.

Suppose someone is playing with a little child who won't share anything. This child tends to grab everything from the hand of anyone else who's playing with it. Suppose the person says, "You're just selfish and grabby! You can't share!" This person, by attributing a negative trait to the child, is probably making the child defensive. On the other hand, suppose the person says, "If you'd share more, I'd have more fun playing with you, and I bet you'd enjoy it more too." Now the person implies the person has the potential for a positive trait and doesn't embarrass the other person.

Here's another example: Suppose one family member says to another, "You're so terribly disorganized. You're a mess. You're a slob!" These statements are NOT tactful. They attribute negative traits to the other person. Suppose instead the first person says, "If you ever get around to organizing this room, I sure will appreciate it; I bet you'll be happier with it too."

This wording prophesies that the desired behavior may take place. It talks about the positive outcomes the desired behavior will produce. Tactful talk is a kind way to communicate with the other person: it stars the other person in a play with a positive outcome rather than making the other person a villain.

Another example of tact is carefully exploring the other person's objections to options. If the person hasn't fully stated all his interests at the beginning of the conversation (and this is usually the case), then listening to the person's reasons for supporting or opposing various options will help to understand the other person's interests. The more you know about the other person's interests, the more likely you are to be able to find a way to meet those interests without forfeiting your own.

Here's another example of tact: resisting the temptation to say, "You're totally wrong," but instead sharing with the other person the data you used to come to a different conclusion. For example, someone says, "There's no evidence at all that any child was harmed by being spanked." A disagreeing person who isn't interested in tact might say, "You're totally wrong; you don't know what you're talking about; there's all sorts of evidence. How can you even say that? You're just trying to make excuses for your own behavior."

The person who's interested in tact might reply, "Some of the evidence may be hard to find. I have here a study of 1,200 families, where they looked at the punishment methods and also looked at how aggressive the children became . . . " The tactful person shares with the other person the same data that influenced his conclusion; there's as much reference to the facts as possible and no reference to the bad traits or bad motives of the other person.

The good negotiator keeps in mind that people almost never win arguments once people become angry at each other. Almost never does it then happen that someone says, "I was wrong; you were right. I had an opinion, but your superior logic and knowledge has changed my mind." Most people simply can't do that. They can't tolerate losing face by backing down once they've become angry.

Therefore the good persuader tries to avoid getting into an angry argument with the other person if at all possible. The good negotiator values keeping an open mind and keeping focused on the data. The good negotiator tries to make the options compete with one another, rather than people competing with one another; he tries to have the conclusions be data driven and not personality driven.

To negotiate in a data-driven way, the negotiator must do two things that a lazy person can't do. First, she must work hard to find out data and study it carefully. She should keep an open mind to the questions until enough information has accumulated for her to make her decisions. Second, she should be prepared to listen and be influenced by the other person's data. In this way the good negotiator models and reinforces data-driven decision-making. This is particularly important in families, where people have a strong interest in modeling and reinforcing good negotiation tactics in family members.

Sources of power in negotiations

When we talk about sources of power in negotiations, we're talking not about the power to make the other person do what you want and resent it, but to help the other person come to a rational agreement with you. We've already talked about the fact that doing the homework, looking up the data about effects of options, can be a way of helping the other person come to a good conclusion. Another source of power is

doing the work and practice necessary to present that data eloquently.

One power source is the power to give tangible rewards. For example, a parent has the power to give or withhold toys, clothes, food or other tangible rewards from a child. A rich person has the power to influence people by paying them to do what he wants.

Another source of power is called organization-defined power. Negotiators should also be aware of the power hierarchies that exist in the organization they may be in. Most organizations in the corporate world have different levels of power defined by people's position in that hierarchy, similar to the ranks that exist in the military. People who are higher than you in the power structure have the ability to set your salary, influence your job ratings and recommendations for further jobs, determine the size and niceness of your working quarters, and so forth. In schools, teachers, principals, and students are organized into levels of power on a hierarchy. Anyone who's negotiating with someone on a different level of power in a hierarchy should be aware of this and take it into account.

People who are in power in an organization should be careful not to let their organization-defined power influence people away from data-driven decisions. For example: People in an engineering department are trying to decide which of several types of parts that could go into a car will work the longest and cause the fewest repairs. This should be a purely data-driven question. But if the boss, who has the power to decide how much people are paid, has a very strong guess about what the answer should be, this power might make the engineers agree with him even though the data don't. If the boss rewards people for agreeing with his guess rather than making a data-driven decision, the car, the employees, and the customer will all eventually suffer.

Another type of power is "walk-away power." This is the power to walk away from a deal and say, "No. I don't want any of the options you want. Let's just not make a deal with each other."

A type of walk-away power used constantly in business can be called creating an auction. This means you don't just deal with one person; you deal with that person's competitors, and you let them compete with one another to make the best deal for you.

For example, suppose I get my heart set on buying one particular car. I can use any sort of posturing I want, but if it's obvious that I've made up my mind to buy this car and I'm just bickering about the price, my power in the negotiation is very low. On the other hand, suppose I find four different places where essentially the same sort of car is sold. Suppose I let the competitors know I'll take the best deal I can get. Now I have lots of walk-away power. I'm letting the car sellers compete with one another rather than compete just with me. Each car seller knows

I'm prepared not to make a deal with him at all.

Walk-away power also applies to love relationships, and to bonds of friendships between people. Some people in relationships will put up with physical and verbal abuse from the other person, whereas other people will invoke their walk-away power very soon.

What gives some people more walk-away power in relationships than others? One is the ability to form relationships with other people; another is the ability to live happily without a relationship of the type that one is in. Another one is having low separation fear that would prevent one from ending the relationship. Thus the person who's more willing to end the relationship has more walk-away power when conflicts come up.

But that person invokes his walk-away power at the peril of both people and quality of the relationship. Threatening to use walk-away power in a friendship threatens the other person's security in the relationship. It often reduces the capacity of both people to fully love each other. The person who's threatened gets an incentive to gradually increase his own walk-away power. When both people invoke that sort of power, the relationship often ends. If the people had invoked more gentle types of power with each other, the relationship might have continued happily.

For example: One five-year-old says to another, "If you won't let me have that cookie, I won't be your friend anymore." This may succeed in getting the cookie, but this tactic, if repeated, should make the second child start looking for other friends. Or, a husband is in an argument with his wife over spending $50 or not. He says, "Maybe if you can't see it my way, you should find someone else to be married to." Threats of this nature might end up causing just this outcome.

A gentler source of power is one that simply expresses dissatisfaction, without tying it to any consequence. This is the simple communication, "I'm not happy with this option. If this is the option we choose, it will not leave me satisfied." Communicating this dissatisfaction usually gives at least some incentive to the other person to remedy the dissatisfaction. The willingness to communicate that dissatisfaction, and to feel it in the first place, thus represents a source of power.

On the other hand, the willingness on one person's part to tolerate and ignore the other person's dissatisfaction also represents a type of power. Suppose you say, "I really dislike this option," and I say, "Tough; that's what we are doing. I don't care whether you like it or not." Then I'm invoking the power of tolerating and disregarding your dissatisfaction. Again, when you use this power, you should think about the effect it might have on your relationship.

One of the marks of a good relationship is that each person uses the power to express dissatisfaction or to ignore dissatisfaction judiciously. They save this power for times when the data support a certain decision and the decision is very important. If someone overuses the power of expressing dissatisfaction, the other person is stimulated to overuse it himself, or to begin overusing the power of ignoring dissatisfaction.

For example, when a family member constantly whines and complains over minor trifles, other family members usually complain back to him, or start to ignore his complaining, even when he has a valid point, as in the story of "The Boy Who Cried Wolf." However, some people can't stand other people's dissatisfaction and handle it by giving the complainer whatever he wants. This creates a different side effect. The complainer can actually learn to be more dissatisfied and unhappy than he would be if his unhappiness didn't give him so much power.

For example, suppose there's a two-year-old child who cries, wails, and has a tantrum whenever he doesn't get a cookie, doesn't get to sit just where he wants, doesn't get to wear certain clothing, or whatever. The parent has a very low tolerance for the child's dissatisfaction and gives the child whatever he wants when he wails and cries. The consequence for this child is that he learns that wailing and crying is a powerful thing, and he learns to do it more and more often. He's also learning to be a very unhappy person in the course of doing so. What this parent should do is learn to increase her own power of tolerating and ignoring the other person's dissatisfaction.

If people in relationships overuse their power of tolerating and ignoring the other person's dissatisfaction, there are dangers. Sometimes the other person will step up to other power tactics. For example, a wife has over a long time expressed dissatisfaction, and the husband has used his power to ignore her dissatisfaction. She may find herself with no better option than to invoke her walk-away power and end the relationship. Or, a child whose dissatisfaction is ignored, even when that dissatisfaction is very reasonable and just, might decide to go to power tactics such as hitting someone, threatening suicide, and so forth, to get people to take notice.

Violence is the power tactic that all the others should be used to avoid. From the three-year-old who says, "If you don't give me the toy, I'll hit you," to the government leader who says, "If you don't do what we want, our troops will invade," the threat and use of physical violence is a power tactic vastly overused by the human race. The measure of how much humanity has progressed should be not how fast we can encircle the globe, not how much our computers can do, not the size of our economies, but how much we can avoid using violence to influence one another.

The final power tactic that I'll mention is one that's underused as much as violence is overused. This occurs when people develop a positive relationship, and they each cultivate the wish to please each other. They each develop a sincere desire to make the other feel good. Then the expressions of feeling good from the other person become important rewards. Thus each person's approval becomes a method of influence for the other. It's important not to give approval to others capriciously or unconditionally; if this happens, approval ceases to be a source of reward. It becomes disconnected from data-driven decisions about whether the other person did something good.

It's possible to arrange these power tactics in order of how much you would like them to be the prevailing tactics in your family. What would you like? Here's my list, in approximate order from least wanted to most wanted:

Physical violence

Walk-away power

Power of ignoring dissatisfaction

Power of expressing dissatisfaction

Organization-defined power (e.g. the parents are in charge)

Power to give or withhold tangible rewards

Power of eloquence in presenting data

Power from approval, in relationship with mutual sincere wishes to please one another

Power of careful research on data-driven decisions

I have data-driven decisions as best on this list because, if people make joint decisions based on careful examination of data and careful prediction of outcomes, sometimes they can come to the same conclusion as to what would be best without either of them having to "use power on" the other. But if people are to use power on one another, as all but the most idealistic dreamers realize happens all the time, it's best that it be done in the most pleasant ways people can come up with.

Awareness of alliances and group structures

What do we mean by this subskill? Up until now, we've been talking about conflict resolution and joint decision-making as though there were just two people involved. But people organize themselves into larger and more complex bargaining units. They organize into groups that have different structures.

The simplest is an alliance between two people: a partnership, a strong friendship, a marriage. Involving more people is a clique; here what's important is whether someone is in or out. Another example of such a group is a hierarchically arranged power structure. The classic example of this is the military, with its commander in chief, its generals, and its various other ranks down to privates. Another example of such a structure is that of most corporations, with a main boss who bosses other bosses, who boss other bosses;

finally you get down to the workers who don't tell anybody what to do, but just work.

Sometimes not being aware of alliances and group structures can cause major conflicts and bad feelings.

To give a simple example, a college-aged man meets a woman and says, "I think you're really attractive, and I think we'd get along together well. How would you like to go out with me sometime?" Unfortunately, the boyfriend this woman is steadily committed to is standing with the two of them and listening to the conversation. Because the asker didn't take the time to find out the nature of the alliance between the two people, he caused himself embarrassment and engendered some hostility. Even if the young lady were dissatisfied with how she was being treated by her boyfriend and interested in exploring other relationships, she would be extremely unlikely to do so with her boyfriend there. The moral of this vignette is that the "homework" required before taking many interpersonal actions is to explore and consider the nature of the alliances among people. Is your action working against some loyalties that have already developed?

Another large set of examples involves the keeping of secrets. Any time you ask someone to share a secret with you and to keep it from someone else, you're in a sense asking that person to be more loyal to you than to the other person. Unless there's a clear reason why you deserve loyalty more than the other person, the request for secrecy can cause troubles in the relationship.

For example: A husband and wife work for the same company. A coworker of the wife starts saying things to her like, "Don't tell your husband I said this, but I think he should never have hired that supervisor." After a few instances of this, the coworker notices the wife is starting to avoid her and is being much more distant from her. If she has developed no skill in awareness of alliances, she might not realize that her request for secrecy is putting the wife into conflict with her loyalty to her husband, which is greater than her loyalty to her coworker.

Or for another example, suppose a baby-sitter gets a visit from her boyfriend while she's baby-sitting for a child at the child's house. She then starts to worry the child's parents might not approve of the visit. So she says to the child, "Please don't tell your parents that my boyfriend visited." When the parents find out about this request for secrecy, they immediately dismiss the baby-sitter. The baby-sitter thinks, "That's not fair. It isn't such a big deal. He's very responsible; he only visited for a few minutes, and I was keeping a watchful eye on the child the whole time."

In thinking this way, she misses the point that the request for secrecy is the major transgression. In asking the child to keep a secret from the parents, she's putting the child's loyalty to her in conflict with the child's loyalty to the parents. Since a major portion of a baby-sitter's job is not to induce loyalty conflicts, the baby-sitter should not be asking a child to keep secrets from his parents.

Here's another example with a baby-sitter. A baby-sitter becomes very attached to a child. The child wants a very expensive present. The parents have said they couldn't afford it now; maybe they can later. When the child's birthday comes, the baby-sitter makes a financial sacrifice to get this present for the child. The child is overjoyed, but the parents are angry. Why? The baby-sitter thinks, "I was generous and giving. How could they possibly be angry with me?"

The answer is that the baby-sitter's present showed up the parents' present. The baby-sitter is fostering the loyalty of the child to her at the expense of the child's loyalty to the parents. Since the parents have already said the present was too expensive, the baby-sitter is giving the child the message that she can provide something for the child that the parents cannot. The baby-sitter has failed to see her proper place in the hierarchy of loyalties the parents wish to develop in the child. If she wanted to give the child that present, she should at least have asked the parents first.

Another element of awareness of alliances has to do with being aware of the "chain of command" in an organization. By the chain of command, we refer to how organizations are set up where a boss has a boss, and that boss has another boss, and so forth. The general rule is that, if you skip someone and go "over his head," dealing with his boss rather than him, you often embarrass and anger the person you skipped over.

Here's an example: Suppose a worker discovers that the way the company is disposing of waste products creates a hazard. If something isn't done soon, the company could do lots of damage and get sued. But quick action can save the reputation of the company, along with lots of money. The worker is very excited with what he has found out. Instead of telling his own boss this information, he goes directly to his boss's boss. The boss's boss realizes this is important information. The company uses the information, and the worker is praised. The worker feels good.

However, later on, the worker notices lots of unexpected hostility from his own boss. What has happened? The worker's boss was quite embarrassed that he had been left out of the decision. He didn't like having heard the information from his own boss rather than from the worker. The worker didn't follow the unspoken rule that you don't skip a position in the chain of command when you're reporting important information.

Here's another example about chain of command. A parent feels that a teacher is yelling at her child and the other students too much. She writes a letter to the superintendent of the school system, detailing his problems. When the superintendent gets the letter, she does what comes naturally in a hierarchical organization: she calls the principal and says, "Are you aware that this is a problem?" The principal is not aware of the problem, and feels embarrassed at the idea that the parent would be aware of a problem that she knows nothing about.

So the principal denies that a problem exists. The principal forms an alliance with the teacher and one or two other parents who are satisfied with the teacher, to oppose the parent who had complained. The superintendent refers the parent to the principal. By the time the parent gets to the principal, the parent encounters a unified wall of opposition.

Suppose instead, the parent had found several other parents who were also dissatisfied, and had gone first to the teacher, with the notion of going next to the principal and next to the superintendent if change did not occur. Now there's motivation for the teacher or the principal to bring about the desired changes in order to keep the complaint from going further up the chain of command, rather than defensiveness about the fact that they were skipped.

The general rule we're speaking about in this section is to be aware of all the people who are parties to a certain joint decision, and at least be aware of what their interests and positions are.

You may end up opposing them because of principle, but you want to avoid offending people out of ignorance.

Here's another example of this rule. A student is giving a speech at a school assembly. The student finds out that it's the principal's birthday. So the student decides that, before his speech, he will wish the principal a happy birthday and lead everybody in singing "Happy Birthday." By doing this innocent action, he incurs a great deal of hostility from other students.

Why? Because another group of students had prepared a birthday celebration for the principal that was meant to be a big surprise. The speaker stole the spotlight from the other students. If the speaker had bothered to ask the other students who were on the program for the assembly what they were going to do, he could have planned accordingly.

Another general rule is that, when you're dealing with groups, it's often good to float your ideas by an individual member of the group with whom you have an alliance before proposing it to the whole group.

Here's an example of that. A young adult joins a soccer club. The club has a large meeting attended by club members as well as their friends and relatives. The person proposes to the group that the club have a beer party. There's a very strained and uncomfortable look on the faces of almost everybody in the room. The person

who's leading the group explains to the new group member that shortly before he joined, the club did have a beer party. The leader of the club, while driving home under the influence of alcohol, had an accident in which he and another person were was killed. After that, everybody in the club unanimously felt that no such parties should be repeated for a long time. If the new member had floated his idea by even one group member he knew, he would have learned information that would have saved him embarrassment.

Here's another example. In a corporation, a department has a meeting. There someone fairly low in the hierarchy announces there's a strong expectation that everyone in the department will fork over a fairly large amount of money for a certain cause. One person who has never heard of this plan is quite outraged by it. He makes an impassioned speech against it in the group meeting. The person doesn't know that the head of the department, his boss's boss, is the one came up with the idea. The head of the department is quite sensitive about any opposition to this idea and very much resents any public opposition to it. The worker finds himself targeted by his boss.

If the worker wanted to oppose the plan, there would have been a politically wiser way to do it. He should have listened to the announcement, said nothing at that time, and then started gathering information. He should have found out how the decision came about and who along the chain of command supported it. Armed with that information, he could then have found out the extent to which other people were willing to join him in opposing the plan. He could then decide whether his forces were strong enough to change the policy, and also decide whether a win in this battle would be advantageous with respect to his position in the corporation.

The point here is NOT that one should never oppose powerful people. The point is that, when one takes on groups of people in a conflict, it's more intelligent to do it knowing whom you're opposing rather than being ignorant of that. If you really want to make changes, often the best way to do it is to arrange for no one to lose face.

Suppose the worker in the last story went around individually to other workers and found that many people had strong feelings against paying the money. Then they all conveyed this information to their boss, who reports to the department head. Their boss then tells the department head this, in a closed meeting. Now, if the department head changes his decision, he comes across as someone who listens to the wishes of his workers, rather than as someone who caves in to a single disgruntled worker. In other words, it's much easier for the department head to make a change without losing face.

All of these examples illustrate that the currency in dealing with groups and alliances is information: knowing the power structure of the group, who is allied with whom, who favors what. Thus, the person who wishes to deal successfully with alliances and groups will carefully cultivate sources of information.

There will be times when people choose to take on an opponent seemingly so powerful that there's no possibility that the option they favor will prevail. They choose to speak forthrightly about their data-driven and value-driven decision, even though there are strong alliances and coalitions thoroughly organized in the opposite direction. At times people choose not to bother with understanding alliances, but simply speak their minds honestly and openly whenever they get the chance. This is sometimes a very courageous and admirable attitude.

However, you shouldn't do this with the expectation of "having your cake and eating it too." If you ignore alliances and speak openly, you can't expect people to listen to reason. You have to expect that on many occasions you will be a "voice crying in the wilderness," rather than successfully implementing the options you think are right.

Let's summarize the main ideas in this section on negotiation skills. First, speak with tact, so that there's minimal necessity for the other person to have to lose face. Second, be aware of the various sources of power in negotiations, and make conscious decisions about which to use. Third, since joint

decisions often involve more than two
people, be aware of alliances and group
structures, and take them into account
when proposing options.

Skill 37: Option-Generating

Option-generating is the skill of thinking of creative options for solutions to problems. The skill of option-generating is useful in joint decisions and in individual decisions. This skill has been called "divergent thinking." Divergent means going in different directions, and when you generate lots of options, you let your mind go in many different directions to come up with as many different ideas as you can.

Why is it good to be able to generate many options? The more options you can think of, and the more creative your options are, the more likely you are to land on a really good one. Perhaps for this reason, research has demonstrated that children who are good at option-generating seem to be better liked by their peers and by their teachers. This isn't surprising. Which would you rather have as a friend: someone good at figuring out solutions to problems, or someone bad at it?

Listing options is also an important antidote to impulsiveness, the habit of acting without thinking. The impulsive person needs to consider various options rather than doing the first one that comes to mind.

How do think of lots of options? One way is to have categories of options in memory, and use these to prompt yourself. Suppose the conflict is that one person cooks a dish made of fish and sauerkraut; the other hates the smell. One category of option is for one person simply to give the other what he wants, with no strings attached. For example, the first person stops making fish and sauerkraut. Or the second person simply puts up with the smell without complaining. A similar option is for one person to give in to the other, in return for the other's appreciation. Another type is for one person to give the other what he wants in return for the other person's reciprocating in some other way. For example: "I'll stop cooking the fish and sauerkraut, if you'll stop leaving your socks on the living room floor." Or "I'll put up with the fish and sauerkraut, if you'll put up with my playing my flute late at night."

Another category of option is a compromise: each person moves closer to what the other person wants, and they meet somewhere in the middle. For example, rather than cooking the fish and sauerkraut twice a week, I'll reduce it to twice a month in consideration of your wishes, and you'll tolerate that reduced frequency.

Another category involves someone's learning to do something he couldn't do before. For example, the second person learns to hypnotize himself to enjoy the smell of fish and sauerkraut.

Another category involves a person's continuing to get what he wants, but shifts the time or place so it doesn't interfere with what the other person wants. For example, one person cooks the fish and sauerkraut only at the times when the other person is going to be out of the house. Or, one person shifts the place of the cooking so that he does it on an outdoor grill.

Another category is technological solutions. For example, they get a fan that will pull the air out of the house and prevent the smell from invading the house. Or they get an airtight container that will allow the dish to be cooked without giving off a smell. Or, they cook the food while the other person is away and put it in airtight containers that can be heated up later on.

Another category is taking turns. One of our two people could do what he wanted on cooking one month, and the other could do what he wanted the next month. They could take turns getting their way. Or, for a better example of this type of option: Suppose two people in a family disagree on vacation plans. They decide to let one person choose for one vacation and let the second person decide on the next vacation.

Another category of solutions is figuring out a way of choosing randomly. For example, we flip a coin to decide who gets what.

Another category is to pick an option totally different from the original positions. For example: The mother wants to name the son "Sedgwick" and the father wants to name him "Biff." They finally settle on naming him "Alfonso." Or, to return to the fish and sau-

erkraut problem, they experiment with new dishes until they find that the fish and sauerkraut lover savors tofu and stir-fry vegetables even more than he loves fish and sauerkraut; the other person happens to love the smell of tofu and stir-fry vegetables.

Perhaps you can think of even more categories of options. But if you prompt yourself with these categories, you can usually stretch your mind to think of more options than you could have otherwise.

Several of these categories of options are "win-win" solutions: solutions where both people end up getting what they want. For example, if the first person likes cooking the food on an outdoor grill, then both of them get what they want with that option. This sort of solution is much more desirable than one person's winning and the other's losing.

It is much easier to come up with "win-win" solutions if the two people clearly know the interests of both people. A classic story of a "win-win" solution involves two people, each of whom wanted to use the last orange in the house. A problem definition such as "Give me that orange!" or "That's MY orange," or "What do you think you're doing with that orange?" would start them jockeying for a win-lose solution. One would get it, or the other would. Or perhaps they would have come up with compromise where each gets half the orange.

But this story has the happier ending of a win-win solution, since each stated her interest clearly. One said, "I had my heart set on eating that orange because I'm hot and thirsty. I've been thinking about how juicy it is and how it would feel in my mouth." The other one says, "I wanted to use the peeling of the orange for a cake recipe." When they stated their interests, the "win-win" option was obvious. The moral of the story is that the skill of generating creative options is greatly helped by the skill of defining the problem well.

Generating options takes time and patience. Often people don't succeed at this skill because they don't allocate enough time to think of creative options. The more patient they are, the more options they can come up with.

In the section on concentration skills, I will describe more thoroughly the "return to the center" exercise. In this exercise, you pose a question to yourself, and you start listing possible answers. You keep thinking, even after you feel you have run out of answers. The mind-stretching process of continuing to concentrate even when no answer comes immediately is one that yogis have used to develop mental power.

Considering a two-person problem or joint decision, and asking oneself, "What are all the options I can think of," is a wonderful way to do the "return to the center" exercise. For those who would like a list of problems and a list of options for comparison with the list you generate, this may be found in the *Options and Consequences Book.* In my vision of the ideal education, daily exercises in generating options for hypothetical or real problems would be included.

The benefits of increasing your skill at option-generating are enormous. Every day you're faced with one decision after another. At almost every moment you have a choice. A lifetime presents millions of decisions. The more you can make good ones, the better your life will be. And the more good options you can think of, the better your decisions will be.

Skill 38: Option-Evaluating

In dealing with conflict situations, the skill of option-evaluating can also be called having a good sense of justice. When people are in a conflict, an option that is fair, right, and reasonable is called a just option; when people choose to do that option, we say that justice has been done.

A sense of justice and reasonableness is at the heart of the joint decision-making process. If people can't tell a reasonable option from an unreasonable option, then they find it impossible to solve problems well.

What's the most common example of a skill deficiency in justice or option-evaluating? Probably it's having too much of a feeling of entitlement. When you feel entitled to something, you feel that it's only right and just that you should get it. Some people with extreme feelings of entitlement seem to always decide that the option most reasonable, fair, and just is the other person's doing exactly what they want.

An entitled three-year-old might feel that it's absolutely right that, if another child picks up a toy, he should hand it over to me immediately. And then when he goes and gets another toy and I become more interested in it because he has it, he should give me that too! An entitled child might feel that his parent should get him anything he wants to eat, any time he wants it. Another entitled child might feel that it's

only right that other children should want to play with him and not reject him, even though he hit them for no reason. An entitled married person might feel that it's only right that his mate make large amounts of money for the family by working long hours, but that she also spend most of her time with the children. An entitled person might feel that a terrible injustice has been done if she leaves a phone message and it isn't returned right away. If I'm an entitled person, I might think it only fair and reasonable that, if I climb over a fence onto someone else's property, clearly marked with "No Trespassing" signs, and then I hurt myself, the other person should pay me lots of money.

One of the hallmarks of overly entitled thinking is that it only applies when I'm the one on the receiving end; it doesn't apply if I'm the giver and the other is the receiver. For example, it's only right that the other children should let me take their toys away, but if one tries to take one away from me, I show my indignation with a major tantrum. It's only right that people return my phone calls right away, but I have very good reasons why I can't always do that. It's only right that my spouse do lots of work, but I would be unwise to work so much that I'd get burned out. It's only right and just that I put a fence right on the boundary line between my property and my neighbor's property, but the neighbor should put up a fence at least a foot back onto the neighbor's property so that my property isn't encroached upon. In all these cases it's illogical to argue that something is right if I'm the receiver, but wrong if I'm the giver in the same situation.

Sometimes we find ourselves on opposite sides of a certain conflict at various times. For example: My friend shows up late when she is meeting me, and I have a feeling of injustice. A few weeks later I show up late when she's waiting for me. Now I may have a chance to revise my sense of how inexcusable and unjust the act of lateness is. Now I have some direct experience that teaches me what it's like to try to get from one side of my city to the other in traffic jams. One of the marks of a psychologically mature person is the ability to profit from these experiences: not to exact harsher justice on the other person than you would exact on yourself in the same situation.

But in some situations we never have the opportunity to switch places. I happen not to be able to rely on my actual experience to know what it's like to be gay or a member of a minority ethnic group or drug addicted or suffering with a psychotic illness or in poverty. I won't be able to directly experience prejudice and rejection for one of these causes. And the same is true for thousands of other conditions other human beings experience that I will never directly experience. Thus, in deciding what is just,

I need to use the skill of empathy. Empathy is the ability to imagine oneself in some other person's place, and to use such imagination to get a feeling from the other person's point of view. The power of imagination and empathy in helping people to come to more just decisions is not used often enough in the world.

A person with too much feeling of entitlement is often known as a spoiled brat. Some adult spoiled brats, instead of throwing tantrums, screaming, and throwing things, tend to make righteously indignant statements about how they're deserving something or other, how they've been treated unfairly, how other people's behavior is appalling, and so forth. And others actually scream and throw things just as some three-year-old children do! Usually in both cases there's a skill deficiency in deciding whether an option is just or not, in deciding just how large an injustice one has suffered.

There's a very different way that people can have low skill in option-evaluating. Some people have the opposite of an overblown sense of entitlement: too little entitlement. This means a feeling that, whenever there's a joint decision, it's the other person who is entitled. This sort of person tends to think, "It's my own duty and obligation to make sure the other person is satisfied." The person with an overblown sense of entitlement gets called selfish, grabby, and narcissistic. The person with a sense of undeservingness tends to called a wimp, to be told, "You're a doormat; you're letting the other person walk all over you." If those with overblown senses of entitlement are extreme *takers*, those with too little entitlement are extreme *givers*. Some extreme givers stay in relationships with abusive people because they feel they don't deserve any better and they have a duty to help the other person, no matter how much it costs them. Some extremely giving parents work almost constantly to give to their children, only to find as their reward that their children have become spoiled brats.

How do you nurture the ability to decide on the justice and reasonableness of options? Again, my recommendation is to use imaginary situations. Pondering and discussing what are the most just and reasonable options to solve a conflict when you have no personal interest in it will prepare you to take an objective stance when you do have a personal interest in the conflict.

Another useful exercise is to practice role reversal by role-playing. For a hypothetical two-person problem, you act it first from one person's point of view, and then from the other's. Or, for a real-life problem, you can actually pretend that you're the other party to the conflict and let someone else pretend to be you. You can negotiate the conflict from each other's point of view.

If you want to choose options that are just and reasonable, the best advice is "Don't be a selfish spoiled brat, but don't be a wimpy doormat either." Looking after your own interests, but giving some weight to the other person's interests is key. If that's enough for you right now, you can skip the next paragraphs of headier thoughts and go to the next skill.

But some of you may want to think in more depth about justice. How do we decide which options are just and reasonable in solving problems between people? What principles do we use? First, let's think about what sometimes gets passed off as justice but is not justice.

Justice is *not* summarized by the statement, "Might makes right." When two children want to play with the same toy, justice is not done when the bigger, tougher, and more powerful child gets what he wants. When a brother is making noise with his drums and disturbing his sister who wants to study, justice is not done if the person who's stronger and more aggressive gets his or her way. Or suppose a farmer has been watering his crops from a stream. When a powerful company pollutes that stream and poisons the farmer's crops, justice in no way depends on the fact that the corporation has lots of money to give to politicians and the farmer has none. This is one of the first lessons we have to learn about justice: it's something totally different from power.

Justice also doesn't mean, "Everybody gets exactly equal amounts of whatever there is that's good." For example, two children each get a cookie, but one's cookie was just a little bigger than the other. So the one with the smaller cookie feels entitled to get something else to make up for it. Or a brother was invited to a birthday party, and the sister was not; the sister feels entitled to get something else on that day that will be just as much fun as the birthday party. It's useful for children to get over this literal idea of fairness early in their lives; it seems to give rise to endless bickering.

Justice also isn't summarized by the statement, "The majority rules." While the opinions of people about what is just and reasonable are impor-tant, there can be times when most peo-ple want things that are very wrong and unjust. For example, most people in some communities in America's past felt it was perfectly just and reasonable for one person to own another as a slave.

Public opinion swings back and forth and is not the source of reliable decisions about what is reasonable and just. If the majority of people feel it's fine to be entertained by gladiators fighting to the death, or boxers fighting to the point of brain damage, that doesn't make their point of view supe-rior to a minority who feel such enter-tainments should be outlawed.

So if justice isn't the principle of power, equal division, or a public opin-ion poll, what is it?

One principle of reasonableness and justice is that people should be able to make exchanges with each other if those exchanges are OK with each per-son. These exchanges are especially reasonable if they make both people better off. If I have a guitar and you have a wagon, and I want the wagon more than the guitar, and you want the guitar more than the wagon, then we can trade and both of us will be better off. A huge amount of human activity is based on this principle. Every day there are countless transactions by which people enter voluntary exchanges. Was it reasonable for you to make that trade with me? Yes, because I wouldn't have done it voluntarily with you if I hadn't expected it would make me happier.

A basic principle that helps peo-ple make exchanges is that people should be able to make promises and expect that those promises will be kept. Suppose you lend me a book, on the condition that I'll give it back in a cou-ple of weeks. I agree to this. Then I find out that I like the book probably much more than you ever will, and I'll use it more than you will. Suppose I argue that, because I'll get more use out of it, I should be able to keep it for a couple of years, not a couple of weeks. If we have a dispute over this, your expecta-tion that I give it back is totally just and my expectation of being able to keep it is totally unjust. I entered into an agreement and I should be expected to follow through on my promise.

But things get complicated soon. Suppose people make an agreement, but one person was forced to make the agreement. If I twist your arm so hard that you agree to pay me $50 for my hoe, when I bought it for $5, you shouldn't have to keep that promise. Likewise, if I make an agreement based on a lie that someone told me, I usually shouldn't have to keep the agreement. Suppose I promise to buy a house based on information the owner gave me that the basement never leaks. If I discover after the next heavy rain that the basement has filled up with five inches of water, I should not be held to my promise to buy the house.

When we speak of justice, a guiding principle is *the rule of law*. Suppose one group of people decide they will simply claim a piece of land that belongs to another group of people. The rule of law means that you shouldn't have to sit down and figure out what is justice in this situation as though it were happening for the first time in human history. Under the rule of law, people have already made agreements that say what it means to have something belong to you, and how you start and stop owning something. You look at those laws to help decide what is just in the dispute between the two groups. If there are agreements that people can refer to, the rule of law can effectively substitute for the rule that might makes right. In other words, people can check laws rather than fight each other to settle the dispute.

One person wants to drive forty miles per hour on a road, and the person behind him is very angry that he isn't going at least sixty. If the rule of law operates, the fact that the speed limit is forty on that road should make a difference; if it does not, then the two people may be driven to fight about their dispute.

Laws were a wonderful invention of the human race. They made it possible for people to settle disputes on some basis other than the power held by the two people. They made it possible for there to be a principle of *equal rights under the law*: that is, if I take something that is rightfully yours, justice dictates that I give it back, no matter whether I'm famous, attractive, rich, powerful, and in the majority group, or whether I'm ugly, obscure, poor, and a member of a minority group. This principle is sometimes stated by saying that the law is not a "respecter of persons": the law applies without regard to who I am.

The rule of law and equal rights under the law are more mature useable versions of the notion of fairness than the one we discarded earlier. The one we discarded was, "The goodies get divided up exactly equally." The notion of equal rights under the law is, "A law should not apply differently to one person than to another."

Most of us will not spend time writing laws or dealing with laws created by legislatures. How does the principle of the rule of law apply to our everyday lives? The principle applies to everyday situations, even when there are no written laws. For example, suppose a teacher lets some children talk without raising their hands and being called upon; others of a certain race or a certain physical appearance get severely reprimanded if they do the same thing. Justice is not being served, because the rule of law is not being used.

In everyday situations, when thinking about the reasonableness of an option, we can think, "Is the principle I'm using here one that I can wish everyone would use?" Thus, even if the principle isn't a law, can we wish it were one that everyone would go by? For example, suppose someone has accidentally spilled some food, and someone considers harshly punishing that person, for example, by not giving the person food for a whole day. Would we want the principle of harsh punishment for unintentional mistakes that don't do much harm to be one that's used for everyone, including ourselves? If not, this gives a clue that this isn't a good option to use with someone else. This way of thinking is one I discussed earlier; it's Kant's "categorical imperative": act so that you can wish the principle guiding your action would be used by all people. This is very similar to the Golden Rule: "Do unto others as you would have them do unto you."

The utilitarian ethical rule we discussed earlier is also central in deciding what options should be chosen. According to this rule, the best option is the one that makes all the people involved happiest in the long run. When two children want the same toy, the option of letting the most powerful child grab whatever he wants from the less

powerful one makes for immediate unhappiness for the less powerful child. In a less obvious way, it promotes longer-term unhappiness for the more powerful child, because he gets reinforced for grabbing things away, and gets further into the habit of grabbing rather than following some rule.

And the same thing goes for almost all conflicts between a more powerful and less powerful person. If an adult guides the children into the option of "The person who was playing with it first will tell the second when he's done with it," then the long-term happiness of both children is promoted.

Sometimes an option makes people happier except for the precedent it sets. When you take into account the precedent, that is, the fostering or the undermining of a custom or rule, sometimes you get a different answer about whether the option is good. For example, some people with terminal illnesses and great suffering may be better off dead than alive. It may be, in some of these cases, that the sick person would be better off if someone would just kill him. But the rule against killing people is such an important one, so close to universally useful, that undermining this rule would be quite harmful.

So an act of "mercy killing" might do good for the family, even good for the person being killed, but it's still harmful enough for society in general that society has an interest in forbidding it. The type of utilitarian thinking that takes into account the effects of actions on customs and rules is called "rule utilitarianism." Rule utilitarianism incorporates some of Kant's thinking into utilitarian theory.

Let's return to the main question we're wrestling with: what makes an option just and reasonable? Here's another very useful principle: unless you have a really good reason to do otherwise, let other people do what they want. One of the main utilitarian thinkers, John Stewart Mill, wrote an essay on this called "On Liberty." Mill asked the question, "What gives someone the right to use physical force or coercion on another?" His answer was that forcing someone to do something, as contrasted with persuading them or influencing them to do it of their own will, was justified only to keep that person from harming you or someone else.

One exception that Mill made to this idea is the situation where someone has to make decisions for a child or someone with impaired judgment. Any sensible person would agree I, as a father, have a right to physically coerce my one-year-old daughter to get a diaper change, even though she may not feel like it. I'm making a decision on her behalf using my mature judgment.

Of course, many cases are not so clear cut as this. What about when I want to set a curfew for my seventeen-year-old daughter? What if I want to provide involuntary sterilization to a severely retarded person? What if I want to do this to a mildly retarded per-

son? When should someone be sent to a mental hospital against his will?

And what about when the person on whose behalf I'm acting is impaired, not by mental maturity, but by ignorance of the particular issue? Is it just to compel people to pay tax money to pay for regulation of toxic wastes, even if most of them don't want to, because they're ignorant of the problems that would occur without such regulation? Deciding when one person may act in another person's behalf is often tricky business.

There are various philosophical issues involved in option-evaluation, including those of how you weight the other person's interests relative to your own interests, and how you weight long-term interests relative to short-term interests.

But there are also scientific issues. How good or bad an option is depends on what its outcome is. But deciding on an option ahead of time requires that we be able to predict outcomes. Here's where science comes in. A father thinks his child should get a certain medicine; the mom thinks the child should not. One of three outcomes will occur: the child will do better, do worse, or do the same on the medicine as without it. The difficulty is in knowing the answer. In cases like this, the cause of option-evaluation is often best found by someone's digging into the scientific literature and reading it thoroughly, looking for the best answer to the question, or consulting an expert who has already done so.

There are countless conflicts between people that revolve around imperfect knowledge of outcomes. One group of people feels that using tax money to build a sports stadium will do much more good for the people of a region than investing the money in tutoring for poor children; another group predicts just the opposite. One parent thinks the amount of fruit juice the child is drinking will have bad effects on the child's growth and development; the other parent feels no harmful outcome will occur. One person feels lowered speed limits will save lots of lives; another doubts this. In conflicts like these, my motto is "One peek is worth two finesses": a long peek at what's known about predicting the outcome in question will do much better than arguing over what seems best in the absence of good data.

Skill 39: Assertion

The skill of being assertive has a lot to do with what we spoke of in the section on option-evaluating. Assertiveness is being neither an aggressive brat nor a wimp. Assertiveness is being willing to insist upon one's own wishes. It's being able to state very firmly, confidently, and strongly what one thinks should be done. It's making requests and commands of other people, even if the other people aren't inclined to do those things. It's to state one's intentions and carry out those intentions, even when other people don't like it. The skill of assertion is refusing to let people make you into a doormat. But it is NOT making other people into doormats.

One of the hallmarks of skill deficiency in assertion is not being able to say "no" to requests. Some people find themselves doing many things they would rather not do, simply because people ask them. Then, oftentimes, people who have said "yes" to these things find themselves resenting the other person for making them do these things, when all the other person did was ask.

Many teenagers find themselves getting into unwanted sexual activity or unwanted use of drugs simply because a peer asks them to do so. Skills of assertion make it easier to refuse requests.

We mentioned in the section on negotiation, the power that comes from expressing dissatisfaction and from being able to tolerate or ignore someone else's dissatisfaction. The person with low assertion skills has given up those sources of power. He's unable to say to people, "I don't like that. Please stop doing that. I don't want it. I'm not going to do it. I'm not satisfied with that. I'm not going to put up with it." Or to say, "I am going to do this, and if you don't like it, that's tough. I'm still going to do it because it's right."

People with low assertion skills sometimes have a huge buildup of anger. They feel they're being taken advantage of – which is often exactly right. Their anger communicates to themselves that they're being used.

At other times, people with low assertion skills get depressed. Depression is often the feeling we get when we think that a) something very bad is happening, and b) we can't do anything about it. Depression is feeling powerless to change bad things. The person with low assertion skills often needs to reclaim the power to influence interpersonal events, a power that he has given away.

Sometimes low assertion skills show themselves in competitive situations. Some people fear winning. They're afraid that, if they win, they'll disappoint the other person. So, if they get a little bit ahead in a game or sport, they start letting up on their efforts and end up losing when they had the ability to win.

The fear of winning a competition is not limited to games and sports. It occurs also in competitions for business, for academic success, or for success in scientific discovery, or success in competing for a desirable mate.

A central element in low skills of assertion is the fear of being disliked, rejected, disapproved of, or criticized. Fear comes from thinking you're in danger. The conclusion that you're in danger involves two separable ideas. The first is that something is really bad. The second is that there's a decent chance this bad thing might happen. If the thing that happens isn't bad, or if there's a low enough chance that it will happen, then the fear is unrealistic, and the person isn't in real danger. Sometimes the key to gaining assertion skills is convincing oneself that the fear of being disliked or rejected is unrealistic: that the feared bad results are either not bad enough or not likely enough to worry about.

Suppose a mother is turning her daughter into a spoiled brat by giving the child what she wants whenever she wants it. If the mother doesn't give the child what she wants, the daughter tends to have a tantrum, cry, look angry, or speak in an angry tone of voice. The mother gives into this and gives the child what she wants. The mother becomes aware that she tells herself, "If I don't give my daughter what she wants, she's going to hate me. She'll shun me in favor of the other parent. That will be horrible."

The mother is held hostage by this belief system. A key to her gaining assertion skills is revising her guess of how likely it is that her daughter will continue to hate her if she doesn't do what she wants. When she looks at the evidence, she notices that other people, who are much more assertive with their children, are not hated by their children. The mother also revises her rating of how awful it is when her child is temporarily angry or rejecting of her. The mother concludes that her fear is unrealistic and begins to act more assertively toward the child.

For another example: Someone is asked for money by a professional panhandler who's constantly on the streets asking people for money. The person correctly predicts that, if he doesn't give money to the panhandler, the panhandler will feel and express hostility and rejection. But the person becomes more assertive when he reminds himself that whether the panhandler likes him is not important. The fear of disappointing this person is an unrealistic fear.

For another example: Suppose someone has a fear of winning competitions. First he thinks about how likely it is that the bad thing, i.e. rejection, disapproval, will happen. He considers the evidence that people often respect and admire someone more, not less, when the person has beaten them in a competition. He also considers the evidence that, even though some people do resent someone for winning, the winner can handle that. That's not awful, terrible, or the end of the world.

Or, for a fourth example: Suppose someone realizes he has a fear of succeeding, based on his fear that succeeding will make people envious or jealous. In thinking about how likely it is that they will feel envious toward him if he succeeds, he acknowledges that misery loves company and that some unsuccessful people do get very jealous of anybody who succeeds.

But he then considers that most people will probably like him more because he's successful. He considers how bad it is that some people will be jealous of him, and he decides that this is not awful. He cultivates the courage to succeed in spite of those who want him to stay a loser because they'll feel better about being losers themselves.

Being skilled in assertion does NOT mean you always insist on something without ever giving in. It does NOT mean you keep insisting on what you want without listening to what the other person says. People who do this invariably run into other people who do the same thing, and thus encounter major conflicts over very minor things.

Some things are not worth insisting on. In the conflict between the two men over the parking space on the snowy day, where one ended up killing the other, both would have been much better off if one of them had had the sense to say, "OK, I give in; this isn't worth it. You park here and have a nice day." The psychologically healthy person is skilled at both assertion and at conciliation and submission. He makes intelligent decisions about when to use each of these interpersonal styles.

How does one decide how assertive to be? I want to insist more on a certain option when: 1) the data strongly support it; 2) my values strongly support it; and 3) the stakes are very high for me.

For example, suppose my neighbor is using chemicals to kill weeds in his lawn, and the rain washes them into my yard. If I look up the data on these chemicals and find that there's clear evidence the chemicals cause cancer in children, and if I value the health of children much more than the weedlessness of the neighborhood, and if I consider the issue of whether my children get cancer a very high stakes issue for me, then I should be very assertive.

Suppose, instead, that my next-door neighbor, whom I don't know well, is drinking a whole bottle of whiskey every night. The data show that this is a very bad decision for his health, and I strongly value health, but his drinking alcohol is not a high stakes issue for me – although it is for him. But because it's not really my business, I probably would not be assertive on this issue unless someone asked me for help. On the other hand, if he were my relative or close friend, I'd have a stake in his health and would have more reason to be assertive about insisting that he do something about his problem.

Suppose I'm invited to a boxing match for a birthday party. I'm very familiar with the data on the fact that boxing often causes brain damage to the people who do it, and violent entertainment tends to make the people who watch it more violent. Nonviolence is one of my strongest values, and I feel I have a very high stake in helping to promote a nonviolent world. I would then want to be assertive in declining this invitation or protesting the plan. In this case, my three criteria of data, values, and high stakes have been met.

Suppose I order a sandwich at a busy restaurant, and when I get it I discover that, rather than having mustard on it, as I requested, it has ketchup. Do I ask the waitress to take it back? Here the "data" involve my previous experiences with mustard and ketchup, and, though there's a slight preference in favor of mustard, it's not a strong preference. Regarding my values, I value the time that would be saved by not bothering with this much more than I value the preference of mustard over ketchup, and I also value not hassling the poor waitress much more than I value getting my way on this particular preference. And the stakes of the issue are very low for me. So I choose to forget it and enjoy the sandwich with ketchup on it.

There are countless situations like this that will come up, where the data and/or one's values support a certain option, but the stakes are so low

that it's not worth insisting on. If someone has the thought, "I MUST stick up for what I want," and is firmly insistent upon every single preference, that person is likely to be seen as a pain in the neck by other people.

If you restrict your assertion to the situations that really deserve it, there's a side benefit. The people you know will gradually learn you don't insist on things without good reason. They'll then at least have the chance to be more influenced by your assertiveness.

The skills of tactfulness and listening are not separate from assertiveness. The skill of assertion means not being afraid to insist on, and get, your own way. But you usually come out ahead by doing this in the nicest way you can.

Sometimes the skill of assertion means speaking very forcefully, with anger, with great authority. Sometimes it means speaking very gently, making a request in the most polite and even tentative terms. And sometimes it means taking a middle ground. When should one use each? This varies with the situation. Part of being expert in assertion is matching your degree of forcefulness to the situation.

Useful exercises on assertion are to practice discriminating different degrees of forcefulness in assertion when you hear different things that people say. Can you tell the difference between mild, moderate, and very forceful assertions? *Exercises for Psychological*

Skills and *Programmed Readings on Psychological Skills* contain exercises in telling the difference. After this, the next exercise is to practice making up communications with different degrees of forcefulness. If, in any situation, you can easily compose one response that's very gentle, one that's very forceful, and one that's in the middle, then you're more likely to come up with the right response to any given situation.

Skill 40: Submission or Conciliation

The skill of assertion is central to a happy life. But just as central is the skill of giving in, admitting being wrong, not fearing losing, submitting to another's will, giving the other what he wants.

We can think of three stages of development some people experience with respect to assertion and giving in. At the first stage, the person always gives in, out of sheer cowardice or ignorance of anything better. Whatever the other person wants, he does, because he doesn't want to disappoint or anger the other person and doesn't have much of an idea of what's better to do. This is the stage of being intimidated, of fearing assertion. It's not a fun stage to be in.

At the second stage, the person discovers a certain meaning of courage: the courage to stand up to someone else and oppose that person, to be assertive. But each instance of assertion is an effort to prove oneself, to show, "I can do it. I'm not a wimp." The courage to be assertive is so fragile that it must be proven over and over, and thus a fear of submission develops. Giving in means I'm a wimp, and I couldn't have that happen. Above all, other people should never see me back down, because they would laugh at me and think I'm a wimp, and that would be so horrible I couldn't take it. The stakes of any joint decision are much higher than just the interests involved; they involve proving whether I'm a coward or a brave person. But in this stage there's still great fear: not the fear of disappointing or angering the other person, but the fear of disappointing the imaginary or real audience who value assertion.

Adolescent boys sometimes find themselves in fatal fights with each other, simply because neither of them has graduated from this stage. Some minor reason for a conflict turns into a showdown in which each one's reputation for courage is at stake. An audience watches to see who will back down. Both boys are so afraid of losing face before this audience that neither can back down, and one or both is killed. We can call this the "fear of submission" stage.

In the third stage, the person doesn't have an unrealistic fear either of disappointing the other person or of seeming cowardly to the audience. In this stage, the person is finally able to judge the issue on its merits. He can take a stand based on the data he has and the values with which he interprets that data. Then, if more data come in that change the decision, he can change his stand without fearing that people will ridicule him for backing down. In this stage, there's neither an unrealistic fear of assertion nor an unrealistic fear of submission. We can call this the stage of freedom from fear, or the stage of flexibility.

The person in this third stage realizes that other people are often fickle and that their values are often not strong. He has his own internal evaluation of himself that can stand firmly, even if other people are rejecting and criticizing him for giving in.

When two people who are in the stage of fear of assertion enter a relationship, such as marriage, it's hard for decisions to get made. Conversations tend to go like this: "We'll do whatever you want." "No, you decide. Whatever you want."

When someone in the stage of fear of assertion marries someone with fear of submission, the second dominates the first. Unless the second makes very wise decisions, it usually happens that the first comes to resent being dominated by the second. If the first person becomes more assertive graduates to the second stage, heated conflict can take place and divorce often results.

This is because the relations between two people with fear of submission are marked by life-and-death-like struggles over little things. When any little conflict comes up, each person must prove himself by not giving in to the other. Obviously harmonious joint decisions are very difficult.

The best relations occur between two people who are in the freedom from unrealistic fear stage. They have the freedom to evaluate options on the basis of the data and their values, and not to be very concerned about whether they are winning or losing the competition. They can now afford to let options compete with one another rather than feeling that something about their own worth is at stake in a competition with another person. Both people feel free to insist upon something if their objective evaluation warrants it, or to give in if their evaluation warrants that.

Probably at some point in the past, women were particularly vulnerable to getting stuck in stage one, assertion-fear, and men in stage two, submission-fear. Today that may have changed somewhat, but it's still probably true that submission-fear is more common among men.

Men often equate the courage to be assertive with masculinity. If I back down, my manhood is at stake, goes this reasoning. If someone insults me, I have only two options, according to this reasoning: to prevail over this person, or to lose my manhood. If I were to think rationally, I might realize that in a fight I'll likely get hurt, even if I "win" the fight. I furthermore might conclude that my fighting is contributing to a culture of violence that's not good for other people.

But if I believe strongly enough that I'm a wimp and sissy and not a real man unless I prevail, these rational considerations bypass me. If I have these beliefs, I give everyone in the world the power to engage me in a contest whenever they'd like. I'm shackled by the need to defend my masculinity.

Many men are killed because they're ignorant of or can't understand the courage required at times for conciliation or submission. The person with a fear of submission is a coward about being called a coward. He's a scaredy cat when it comes to losing face. Overcoming such fear is a courageous act. But it's more abstract than the fear of physical danger, and it goes over the heads of most people. It's too complicated to understand.

Since losing in competition is a type of submission, sometimes people with unrealistic submission-fear avoid entering competitions in the first place. The reasoning goes: "Losing face is so dangerous that I will avoid any situation where I might not win." This results often in the underachiever syndrome. I'm so afraid of losing that I don't play the game.

When I speak of "games," I refer to almost anything that measures performance. Academic achievement can be an arena where the fear of losing prevents someone from competing at all. For example: In a family there's an older brother who makes great grades and wins academic honors. The younger brother thinks, "I could never beat my older brother at the game of academic achievement. Therefore I won't even enter it. I'll tell myself that it's all stupid and pointless and it makes no sense and I'll be above it. I'll protect myself from the great humiliation I would suffer if I really tried my hardest and he still beat me." Often people don't even realize they're thinking in this way until they consciously pay attention to their thoughts.

People who have this problem can sometimes solve it by a new pattern of thinking. In this new pattern, I compare my performance to two standards other than what everyone else is doing. One is my own past performance. For example, I feel good about being able to do things in mathematics I couldn't do before, and I feel good at doing better on tests than I could do before, and I don't worry about how I do relative to my older brother, the math whiz.

The second, and even more important standard is: how good a performance is necessary to make myself and other people happier. There's a "good enough" level I deserve to feel OK about, even if someone else's performance is better. For example, if my farm produces 100,000 bushels of corn, and someone else's farm produces 100,001 bushels, I've been "beaten" in the competition of who can produce the most.

But that doesn't matter to the people who eat my corn, nor to my family members who are supported by the sale of my corn. If my performance is good enough to feed hundreds of people and support my family, I don't need to worry. The point of growing corn is to do good for myself and others by doing so, not to prove I'm an OK person. For another example, if I'm a doctor and I learn to give excellent care to every patient who comes to me, those patients don't care that someone else beat me in the competition for the top slot in medical school. The point of learning medical skills is to use them to help people, not to prove how smart I am.

Let's contrast how these two different styles of thinking might affect someone considering competition, for example in the game of tennis. The person who measures his performance only in comparison to other people might not want to play against a better player, because he'll prove himself not OK by losing. But he doesn't want to play against a less skilled player, because then he would be even more humiliated by losing and would not feel OK unless he gained an overpowering victory. So, if his fear of losing is great enough, he might not play at all. Accordingly, he loses many chances to get better.

The person who measures himself against the standard of his own past performance, by contrast, will seek to play opponents who are a little better than he, because they'll tend to bring out his personal best performance. Even if he loses the match, he triumphs if his play is better than it was in the past. Furthermore, he thinks about the point of the game, and what he's trying to accomplish. If he improves his own play, gives the opponent enough of a match that the game is fun for him and for the opponent, and gets exercise to boot, he has performed well enough.

The person who measures his performance against his own past performance and against the standard of

what's good enough to accomplish his goals will not have the "sore loser" syndrome. This person realizes the purpose of games is to have fun and to learn about improving performance and not to prove that he's an OK person.

The fear of submission can also cause problems in the workplace. In most corporations, there's a hierarchy by which almost everyone reports to some boss. Someone who has the attitude that "No one tells me what to do," and "My self-worth is less if I let someone boss me," is headed for big troubles in most workplaces. Sometimes people with submission fears end up getting fired from several jobs before they become motivated enough to increase their skills in giving in to a boss.

The skills of giving in also find great usefulness when people make mistakes and realize they were wrong and need to change course. The person with an inordinate fear of backing down often continues in the same wrong course, because he can't admit he made a mistake. He thus compounds the original mistake rather than correcting it. For example, suppose a leader of a country gets his country into war. This seemed like the best thing to do at the time, given the information available. Then, gradually more information comes in, making it clear that getting into the war was a bad mistake. Nothing is getting accomplished and lives are being lost needlessly, not to mention money, equipment, and other resources.

The leader considers options. One option is to forge ahead and to keep fighting, telling himself that he has to stick by the original decision without wavering. Many patriotic people in the country would support this option.

The other option is for the leader to admit that the war effort has been a mistake, and to abandon it before more lives are wasted. What skill gives the leader the courage to do this? It's the skill of conciliation, of backing down, of conceding that one was wrong. This is the courage to face the fear of losing face and to triumph over that fear. The most courageous act is to let one's decisions be data-driven and values-driven.

The initial data seemed to indicate that more lives would be saved by going to war, but subsequent data indicated the opposite. If the leader places a higher value on saving lives than on his own political career, he'll change the course of action even though many people will call him a coward and a wimp. In this case, exercising the skill of backing down is much more courageous than being assertive and standing one's ground. Few people in the world seem to realize this, but if more did, the world would be a much better place.

Skill 41: Differential Reinforcement

The skills in the joint decision and conflict resolution group all have to do with how people influence one another. People who are more skilled can influence one another in kinder and gentler ways; those who are less skilled rely on more hostile and forceful ways.

A *reinforcer* is something that happens after a behavior that makes that behavior more likely to happen in the future. The word *reinforcer* or *reinforcement* means almost the same as *reward*. When you use differential reinforcement, you give more reinforcement for some things than for others: there's some systematic pattern in how you give out your rewards.

One of the reinforcers that people give other people is their attention. People need to be noticed. If you simply pay attention to certain things people do, and ignore other things they do, you usually increase the first set of things relative to the second set.

Differential reinforcement is one of the most powerful tools an adult has in helping to influence the behavior of a young child. Unfortunately, adults often unwittingly use differential reinforcement in ways that encourage the behavior they *don't* want from the child.

For example, a two-year-old quietly asks for her mother's attention while her mother is talking with her father. The mother ignores this. Gradually the two-year-old starts screaming and grabbing at the mother's face. Now the mother turns her attention to the two-year-old and says, "What do you want?" Or, the mother turns her attention to the youngster and says, "Please don't do that." Either way, the attention has probably reinforced the screaming and grabbing, even though in the second case the words were meant to discourage them. If the parent wanted to use differential reinforcement in the other direction, the parent would pay attention to the gentler requests for attention but turn attention away from the child when the child screamed and grabbed.

For another example, a child wanders around lonely in a day-care center while the adults attend to other children. Then the child hits another child. Suddenly an adult comes to him, kneels down, looks him in the face, and says, "No, Johnny, we mustn't hit. We use words when there's something we want." The child was ignored for his nonviolence, and his violence was reinforced by attention. If the adult wants to use differential attention in the other direction, the adult would try to attend more often to the child when he was behaving nonviolently, and withdraw attention (for example by a time out) when the child behaved violently.

A child wakes up in the middle of the night and wants to come into the parent's room. The parent isn't interested. Later the child wakes up complaining of being scared. Now the parent holds the child, comforts the child, rubs the child's back, and sings to the child. The child has now been reinforced for being fearful because of the attention he received when he was fearful, attention he didn't get otherwise. So the next time the child gets lonesome in the middle of the night, the child becomes scared.

If the parent wanted to use differential reinforcement in the other direction, the parent would bring the child into her bedroom and give the child lots of attention first thing in the morning when the child wakes up, after he has slept in his room throughout the night. Similarly, if the child had fears in the middle of the night, the parent might comfort the child for a short time but would send the child back to his own bed.

For another: Two parents talk with each other while two children pleasantly play with each other. But when the children start arguing and calling each other names, the parents go and pay attention to the children and try to get them to act properly. Again, the attention reinforces the hostile behavior among the children. If the parents wanted to use differential reinforcement in the other direction, they might observe and comment when the children are being nice to each other, and turn their attention away at the first hostile tone of voice the children use toward each other.

Differential reinforcement of course does not apply only to the relations of adults to young children. Suppose there's a college teacher who gives a lecture to his students and walks out, ignoring each of the individuals in the class. But one day he says that, if anyone has any complaints about the class, he wants to pay attention to those. A couple of students do make a complaint, and he listens very carefully and thanks the students for what they have said. Soon the rate of complaints goes way up, and the students actually are getting more and more dissatisfied with the course. The teacher is using differential reinforcement of dissatisfaction and complaining. If instead the teacher used the same differential reinforcement to encourage interested questions about the subject matter of the course, he might foster fascinating discussions among the students.

A husband decides he should compliment his wife. So he tells her frequently, I like your dress. That's a pretty scarf. Your hair looks nice today. Gradually the portion of her budget and time spent on clothing and appearance rises more and more. He gripes to someone about her having superficial values. The other person points out to him that these are the values he has brought out by using differential reinforcement. If he had reinforced her for working hard, being kind to the children, coming up with interesting ideas, or being cheerful, he might have seen more of those behaviors and less attention to clothes and hair.

The head of a college department gives the teachers in her department recognition, pay raises, and promotions based almost exclusively on how many articles they have published in scientific journals. She finds that her faculty members are writing lots of articles, but they seem to be doing a poor job of teaching. Then she decides she'll give these rewards based on how highly the students rate the teachers in their courses. She finds that the number of picnics and parties teachers have for their students rises enormously, that the grades teachers give students experience a big jump, and that the number of funny stories teachers tell in class also goes way up. She concludes that differential reinforcement definitely has an effect, but perhaps using students' popularity ratings wasn't the best measure of proficiency in teaching.

What do all these examples have to do with conflict resolution? In every case, there's something someone wants someone else to do. One approach to getting the person to do it would be to sit down and have a problem-solving discussion. Another approach would be to yell at the other person and have a heated disagreement. But if the influence provided by differential reinforcement can bring about the desired change in behavior, this can sometimes be the most pleasant and workable way to solve the problem. With differential reinforcement, the person has not just knowledge of what the other person wants him to do, but a continuing incentive to do it.

Here are three types of differential reinforcement that are important enough to deserve names of their own. Differential attention means you reinforce by looking at the person, listening, talking to, touching, and otherwise attending to the person, and in response to other behaviors you ignore the person and pay attention to other things.

Differential excitement means you become more excited over some things than others: you get a louder, higher-pitched, and faster tone of voice. Differential excitement is particularly important for people who are "stimulus-seekers," or people for whom excitement is particularly reinforcing.

Differential request-granting means you grant requests at some times and not at others. With children, for example, differential request-granting might mean you give the child what he asks for much more often when the request is both reasonable and politely stated than when it's not.

If you want to try to use differential reinforcement to resolve a problem with another person, think in the following way. First think about what the other person is doing that you don't like. Then think about what you would like the other person to be doing instead. Then try to give much more attention, excitement, or whatever else the person wants when they do the preferred behavior than when they do the unpreferred behavior.

Here's an example: A boy wants to practice the piano. But he has a two-year-old sister who comes up and bangs on the piano when he practices. He decides he would like the younger sister to sit on the floor and play with toys and listen while he plays the piano. So he gets some toys and puts them on the floor and starts practicing.

When his younger sister goes for thirty seconds playing on the floor without banging on the piano, he speaks to her nicely and pats her on the back. After she goes a minute at a time without banging on the piano, he gives her another toy from his briefcase. After she goes five minutes and claps at the end of the song, he gets down on the floor and pays attention to her for a while. After a good while of working at this, he finds that he not only has someone who doesn't interfere with his practice; he has a pleasant and appreciative audience.

Here's another example: A family is troubled by the tendency of a two-year-old to scream loudly. The family members all decide that they would rather have the two-year-old speak to them in a normal tone of voice. They realize they have unwittingly used differential reinforcement to get the child to scream: they have on many occasions spoken with one another, while ignoring the two-year-old, but finally paying attention to her when she screamed. So they decide to reverse the direction of differential attention. They try to be particularly attentive to her when she speaks in a normal voice; the minute she starts screaming, they all start talking to one another and ignoring the two-year-old. They find the screaming goes down drastically.

Group 7: Nonviolence

One might argue that a separate skill group on nonviolence is superfluous. If you're kind, and if you do joint decisions well, don't those skills in themselves imply nonviolence? I include a separate group for nonviolence because of the importance of the idea of nonviolence for the world. The survival of the human race might well depend on respect for the concept of nonviolence. At the individual level, your life may depend upon someone's belief in the principle of nonviolence.

I include in this group forgiveness and anger control, and commitment to the principle of nonviolence. Many other skills are related, including all those in the kindness and joint decision group, frustration tolerance, self-discipline, carefulness, and others.

Skill 42: Forgiveness and Anger Control

Why is forgiveness an important skill? Because not all conflicts get resolved the way we want, no matter how good we are at all the other skills. People choose to exercise power over us in ways we don't like. People will take advantage of us. People will be cruel or selfish. Well-meaning people will make errors and mistakes. As Alexander Pope said, "To err is human, to forgive divine."

Some people make it hard for themselves to forgive because they don't realize how human it is to make mistakes. Doing scientific research, or quality control in business, or anything else where errors are systematically checked, will impress you about this fact of human nature. If you select individuals for their intelligence and their carefulness, and if you have them do anything often enough, whether it's entering numbers into a computer, watching people and counting how many times they do something, deciding whether someone did one thing or another, you'll almost never find that two different people agree 100 percent. At least one of them has made an error.

A certain fraction of the choices people make in hiring will be wrong. A certain fraction of the times a doctor does an operation, he'll make a mistake. A certain fraction of the time people are presented with a social situation, they'll handle it in a way that needlessly offends someone. A fraction of all cars that are fixed will be fixed incorrectly. A certain fraction of computers that are shipped will be defective. A certain fraction of the conflicts you have with a partner or spouse, that partner will not handle well. If it's possible to do something, it's possible to do it wrong. There's a certain error rate in everything people do.

This is true even when they're trying as hard as they can not to make errors. When they're not motivated, there are even more errors. To err is human. This attitude is not a cynical one, but rather a realistic view that perfection in any human endeavor is impossible. The person who comes to this realization will find it easier to forgive people than the person who feels everyone should be perfect 100 percent of the time.

Now let's talk about the meaning of forgiveness. Many people think of forgiveness as something they do for another person, the person who wronged them. But, there's another meaning of forgiveness that's not quite so unselfish. This is the act of forgiving in one's own best interest. Carrying around unbridled fury is usually not pleasant. It can keep you awake at night. It can make you irritable toward innocent bystanders. In some people it seems to raise blood pressure. It's not a pleasant thing to do. A person with the skill of forgiveness can decide to quit doing this for her own sake. The skilled person thinks, "I want to quit roasting this person in my mind. I want to quit working myself up about how bad a thing he did to me. I still acknowledge that he did a very bad thing and I dislike that he did that thing. But I wish to quit blaming him and going over in my mind how evil and horrible he is. I want to do this for my own good, to help myself."

This version of the skill of forgiveness is more of a communication to yourself than to the other person. Rather than saying, "That's OK; don't worry about it," to the other person, you send a message to yourself that says, "Cool it. It's not doing me any good to remain worked up about this any longer." Or the message is, "I'd rather feel something other than anger."

This line of reasoning brings up the question, "What's the purpose of feeling angry?" Certainly our ability to feel anger did not evolve without a reason. Anger is usually the signal that we need to take action to oppose someone else, that he is doing something we need to stop him from doing. Anger serves a signal function, just as other emotions do. Guilt signals us we should not do something harmful. Fear signals us we should look out for danger. It's important to listen to the signals the emotions give us, and anger is no exception.

It's also useful at times to think in such a way that stirs up anger. Suppose a boss has an employee who has been very pleasant to her and whom she

likes. But then the boss finds out the employee has been embezzling money from her for quite some time. The boss may find it easier to fire that employee and get back the embezzled money if she works up a certain degree of anger toward the employee.

For another example: Suppose a woman is being abused by her boyfriend. If she feels only compassion and pity for the poor man who hasn't yet learned how to act right, she might end up getting herself killed or into a long-term state of unhappiness. If she can work up a healthy dose of anger, it might help her to break off the relationship and find a better one.

So far we've talked about two functions of anger. First, it can be a signal that it's rational to oppose someone else's wishes. Second, it can also help you mobilize the energy, strength, and courage necessary to oppose the other person's wishes.

A third function of anger is to reduce guilt when guilt isn't appropriate. Suppose the abused woman we mentioned breaks off the relationship with the abusing man but now feels guilty about it. The types of thoughts that tend to mobilize and stir up her anger probably reduce her guilt. Suppose she finds herself thinking, "Oh. I caused him to feel so bad; maybe I did something wrong. Maybe I should go back and take care of him." Those thoughts are probably reduced by anger-inducing thoughts such as "What did he care about my welfare? If he cared about me, he wouldn't have beaten me up. He bullies people weaker than he is, like the coward he is!" These thoughts may serve a function of helping her stick by her decision to stay away from him.

Thus, sometimes it's useful to "do anger." But sometimes it isn't. The person with the skill of forgiveness can decide when it isn't useful to anger oneself, and stop doing it; she can also decide it is useful, and keep doing it.

You'll notice that I use a rather unusual syntax when I speak of anger as a useful or not useful thing to do, or when I speak of angering oneself. People are accustomed to thinking of anger as something we have or don't have, rather than as something we do or don't do.

Which is it? I think the distinction is important. If it's something we have, like too much urine in the bladder or too much trash in the house, the only way to get rid of it is to get it out, to expel it. Many people have tried to "get their anger out" by yelling, throwing things, or beating on things or people. On the other hand, if anger is something we do, like jumping up and down or tightening a fist, then it's possible simply to stop doing it, without worrying about what will happen to it or where it's going to go.

Much observation and research has strengthened the view of angering ourselves as something we do, not something we have. One can express anger for a lifetime and still not get rid of it. Anger is mobilized by certain sorts of thoughts. We think them, rather than have them. When we remind ourselves that a certain person is putting us at a disadvantage in a very unjust way and that we strongly need to oppose that person, we think thoughts that will usually mobilize anger. Thus we can choose not to anger ourselves by altering our thought patterns.

It's also possible to cultivate the ability to directly influence one's emotions. One can turn on anger or turn it off. Actors on the stage do this all the time. They don't simply make the physical motions of feeling angry or feeling sad. They make themselves feel angry or sad so they'll be able to play the part convincingly. Acting well means being able to turn on and turn off emotions according to whether it's useful at that point in the play. The skill of forgiveness is similar: it involves the ability to turn on or off anger according to whether it's useful at that point in life.

Suppose someone was teased and picked on when he was a junior-high school student. He is now forty-five-years old. Still, bringing back those memories brings up tremendous fury and fantasies of violent revenge. These thoughts make it difficult to calm himself and fall asleep. The person thinks to himself, "What am I accomplishing by getting angry? Am I giving myself a signal that I need to pay attention to, to keep myself from being taken advantage of? No. Does getting angry helping me mobilize my energy in a useful way? No. It's too late for that. Is it keeping me from feeling guilty? No. There's no chance of my feeling guilty about this. It's really not doing me any good. Therefore, I would prefer not to get angry so much."

This decision, that the intensity of the anger is not helpful, is central to the skill of forgiveness. I realize that ceasing to anger myself so much at someone may or may not do that person a favor, but it does do me a favor.

In fact, here's one way to think about a situation like this: to continue to feel bad about the oppression is to continue to be defeated by the other people. In other words, to continue to feel bad lets the harm they did compound itself over the years. Freeing oneself of the anger and rage one has toward the other person means finally getting the power not to let those actions hurt you any more. Thus, in a paradoxical way, ceasing to rage about the person's misdeeds defeats the other person's wish to harm. It defeats the wishes he had to be powerful over you and make you feel bad. Forgiving the other person is a victory over his ill intentions toward you.

Let's make an important distinction between two types of forgiveness. In one type, you say to yourself, "I can't be friends with this person; I don't want this person around me. But I choose to stop being so angry at this person, for my own good."

The second type goes further. In this type, you say to yourself, "Even though this person did something harm-

ful, I want to stay in the relationship. I can still be a friend. I want to stop being so angry at the person, not only for my own good, but also for the sake of the other person and the relationship." In the second type, there's often a communication to the other person, a saying of something that means, "We can still be friends; we're OK with each other again."

The second type of forgiveness is vital for anyone who wants to stay in a family, or almost any other relationship. People do harmful things to each other. In the best relationships, those harmful things aren't very harmful, are done infrequently, are unintentional, and are sincerely regretted by the other person. But no one should expect to be in a relationship, especially a family relationship, without experiencing some harmful or at least irritating actions from the other person.

There are many times, unfortunately, when people have to decide they don't want to stay in relationships: that the harm is too great, too often, too intentional, not regretted enough. There are times when people need to use punishment or a stern or angry tone of voice in an effort to keep the other person from repeating harmful actions. There are times when they have to use lawsuits to try to recover some of the damage the other person has inflicted. There are times when they have to use force to keep the other person from being harmful. Anger, of a modulated sort, can sometimes assist in carrying out these actions. Unbridled rage, on the other hand, usually interferes with the careful decision-making these actions entail.

The vision of highest skill in this area is someone's making a rational choice about what's the best response to other people's harmful or unpleasant behavior and feeling no more anger than is necessary for enacting that response in the best way.

Let's look at some examples of the use of this principle. A small child comes into the office of a counselor who works with troubled children. The first thing the child does is kick the counselor. The counselor calculates that punishing this child by making him stay in the corner for several minutes is much more useful to him than, say, ignoring the kick. The counselor holds the child with crossed arms in the corner in such a way that the child cannot move. The child yells obscenities at the counselor until the time is up. But he is less likely to kick again.

Meanwhile, the counselor is not feeling rage toward the child. He realizes there are reasons why the child acted aggressively. He doesn't get so angry that he wishes to hurt the child or cause the child unnecessary distress. He does feel indignant enough, though, that he doesn't feel guilty or apologetic about using punishment the child doesn't like.

Here's another example: A child is being teased by another child at school. The child chooses what his re-sponse will be: he makes humorous comments that make other children laugh and cause them to admire his quick wit. His emotion is one of light-hearted fun. If he had reacted with great rage, he would not have been able to respond the way he did.

Here's another example of the principle of "just enough anger to enact the rational choice." A prosecuting attorney is seeking to get life imprisonment of a person who carried out a violent crime. The attorney uses rational decision-making to choose what penalty to seek and how to seek it. She'll probably find it easier to prosecute that person if she works up a little indignation at him. She thinks about the victims of his crime and how unjustly he treated them. But she thinks mainly about what strategies will work best. She will not find herself best served if she becomes so angry with the defendant that she screams curses at him during the court testimony.

On the other hand, the defense attorney in the same case finds her interest best served by not being at all angry at the deeds of her client. She works up some indignation over the adverse social circumstances that have made this person resort to violence, and sees her client as a victim of an unjust society. She feels sorry for him more than indignant toward him. But she modulates this; if she feels so sorry for him that she offers to take him home with her, she's not serving her own interest.

The example of the two attorneys illustrates ways you can increase or decrease anger so as to help yourself do what you need to do. To understand the strategies, we first have to digress into a brief discussion of dramatic roles.

Of all the stories people entertain themselves with, a large portion seem to revolve around the joint struggles of a persecutor (bad guy, villain), a victim (the one the bad guy is bad to), and a rescuer (our hero!) The roles of persecutor, rescuer, and victim are such prominent roles in dramas that they're firmly fixed in most people's minds. In a movie you can tell almost instantly whether a character is a persecutor, a rescuer, or a victim. We get very used to casting people into these familiar roles.

What does this have to do with anger? If you want to make yourself MORE angry with someone, you cast him in the role of persecutor in your mind, and focus your thoughts upon the effects he's having on the innocent victim (such as yourself) with whom your sympathies lie. You can also cast yourself as the hero who will rescue the victim from the persecutor.

On the other hand, if you want to make yourself LESS angry with someone, you cast that person in the role of victim. You see the stresses, the unfortunate life experiences, the biological predispositions, the other people who have treated that person badly, and perhaps an unjust society in general, as the persecutors that make that person a victim and make the person act wrongly. In your role as hero, you side with that victim against the forces that victimize him.

In achieving a balanced, modulated, rational response, it's often best to see things from both points of view. For example, the counselor kicked by the small child thinks about the unjust treatment the child has received, the models of violence he has been exposed to, his victimization by older children, the genes for impulsivity he probably inherited, and so forth; these tend to increase sympathy for the child.

If we want to be forgiving, we can always think about the hereditary and environmental reasons why people do what they do; those reasons are always there. On the other hand, the counselor thinks about the victims of the child's aggression, the other children the child has scared or hurt, and the pain in his own shin, and these thoughts produce some indignation toward the child.

It would be wrong to end a discussion of the skill of forgiveness without returning to our previous categorization of thoughts:

Awfulizing
Getting down on yourself
Blaming someone else
Not awfulizing
Not getting down on yourself
Not blaming someone else
Goal-setting
Listing options and choosing

Learning from the experience
Celebrating luck
Celebrating someone else's choice
Celebrating your own choice

When people are low in the skill of forgiveness, they tend to do lots of awfulizing and blaming someone else. "It's awful that the other child is playing with something that belongs to me! He's a horrible person for doing that!" Or, "It's terrible that this person laughed at me when I slipped! He deserves eternal punishment for that, that worthless excuse for a human being!"

When people gain in the skill of forgiveness, they do less awfulizing and less blaming of someone else. "How bad is it that the other child is playing with my toy? Not so bad. I didn't want to be playing with it right now anyway. The other child isn't a villain. He just saw it and picked it up, the same way I might have done."

You can do "not blaming someone else" even when the other person is totally to blame. For example, when a bully has hurt me badly, intentionally, purely for sadistic pleasure, I can think, "He IS a bad person. Punishment might do him lots of good. But I don't want to keep running the idea of how bad he is through my mind, because I've got better things to do with my mind."

Not awfulizing and not blaming someone else often set the stage for a good round of goal-setting and rationally listing options and choosing. Figuring out the different responses to the situation that are possible, predicting consequences, using one's value system to evaluate those consequences, and enacting the chosen option are good uses of mental and physical energy.

So one way of thinking about the skill of forgiving is that the expert in it can do a good job of not awfulizing, not blaming someone else, goal-setting, and listing options and choosing when other people act badly. Given the imperfections of humanity, opportunities for the exercise of this skill arise very often.

Skill 43: Nonviolence

Skill 43 is commitment to the principle of nonviolence, the fundamental value of not hurting or killing.

I include commitment to this principle for two reasons. The first is its importance. To eliminate, or greatly reduce, violence and cruelty is one of the most significant steps the world could take toward both ensuring the survival of humanity and improving mental health. The second reason is that in my opinion, the most fully functioning person not only is nonviolent, but also works for nonviolence in the world – devotes effort to keep people from hurting one another. Working toward nonviolence in the world is, in my opinion, the highest calling that human beings can carry out. Nonviolence activism provides a constant reminder of how desirable it is to exercise fortitude, kindness, and conscience on a personal level.

Violence classified by its arena

Violence is very prevalent in several different arenas. Domestic violence is physical hurting that occurs within families. Violence in schools is part of the widespread phenomenon of bullying. Criminal violence is reportable in crime statistics: armed robberies, murders, assaults. Violence between gangs also falls into the category of criminal violence. The most dangerous category is warfare. Though it's not against the law, and its perpetrators win medals and become heroes, it's the form of violence that's most likely to end the life of all humanity on earth. Becoming more and more prevalent in the twenty-first century is the blend of criminal violence and warfare known as terrorism.

Violence classified by motive

There are several possible motives for violence. Two broad categories are 1) motives that depend on the existence of strong emotion, and 2) motives that result from calculation about the achievement of goals. Violent crimes in these categories have been referred to as crimes of passion and cold-blooded crimes, respectively.

If a man finds his wife involved with another man, flies into a rage, and strikes out violently at the other man, this is an example of violence accompanied by strong emotion. By contrast, if a drug dealer finds that someone is encroaching upon his territory, he hires someone to kill that person. He's using violence to achieve his goals. The striking aspect of this cold-blooded crime is how little emotion the criminal feels rather than how much.

Cold-blooded violence is often tied to the motive for power. Obviously a credible threat of violence affords someone a certain power over someone else, at least in the short term. Extortion of lunch money among school children and full-fledged armed robbery both use the threat of violence to get the power to make others hand over their money. Of course, the armed robber often finds himself in a very powerless position, i.e. in prison; the long-term consequences of the violence are different from the short-term consequences.

A motive for violence that can involve elements of both strong emotion and calculation of goals is the motive for retaliation, for revenge. A first person or group has been harmed by a second person or group. The first feels anger that makes it feel gratifying to imagine taking revenge. But the first also calculates (or perhaps rationalizes) that retaliation will prevent further victimization.

A related motive is the fear of harm: violence is seen as self-defense. If Jack thinks that Bill wants to kill him, Jack may become motivated to kill Bill first.

Jack's judgment, even if wrong, can become self-fulfilling: Bill finds out that Jack wants to kill him, and now Bill really does want to kill Jack. People who act as if people are out to get them usually eventually find that they have real enemies.

Another motive for violence is the fear of loss of face. One person or group perceives an insult or injury from a second. Unless the person or group retaliates violently, that person will lose face among the other members of the group who have somehow gotten the notion you must retaliate to protect your honor. This source of motivation invokes the notion of a dominance hierarchy, a pecking order. Sometimes people carry out violence against others purely to establish that they're higher on the dominance hierarchy than someone else, for example the bully who victimizes those less powerful than he. At other times people use violence to resist being put in a low position on the dominance hierarchy, for example the bully's victim who uses a weapon against the bully.

Effects of retaliation

What are the usual effects of retaliation and revenge-seeking? Much of people's readiness to use violence probably has to do with their expectations about its results. The results the user of violent retaliation desires are usually a pure and uncomplicated punishment paradigm. You punish the person who did bad things, and the person doesn't do those bad things anymore. Or, you eradicate the bad person, and it's impossible for him to do bad things any more.

Unfortunately, the person or group you're punishing, or the allies of that person or group, are highly likely to see the violent retaliation you use as a bad act that in turn justifies and necessitates retaliation against you. Thus, rather than suppressing the violence against you, the violent retaliation you use can sometimes foster an even greater degree of violence coming in your direction. This is the vicious cycle of punishment. This vicious cycle is responsible for huge amounts of human unhappiness and destruction.

When does violent retaliation work as its users intend, and when does it result only in more violence? This is an important question for both psychological researchers and historians. My observation of both human relationships and of the history of warfare is that violent retaliation appears to produce the desirable intended results rather infrequently. Sometimes a group of people is crushed by the power of an opponent, and in the short run it appears the violence did its intended job. But the hatred and humiliation of the defeated person or people linger and smolder, and retaliatory violence sometimes erupts after a long delay. "He who lives by the sword, dies by the sword," expresses accurately the effects of violent retaliation in many, if not most cases.

When the perpetrators of violent deeds are brought to justice in some manner, who should do it? In the best of circumstances, justice is enforced under the "rule of law," by governments whose interests are in preserving precedents that will be fair and most effective, rather than under "vigilante justice," in which people take the law into their own hands.

Actions to end violence

What can people do to end violence? The following are some specific actions that may be taken. Not everyone will agree with these. But at present, all of these appear to be viable ways of working toward a nonviolent world.

Methods applicable to all forms of violence

1. Boycott entertainment violence and promote anti-violent art.

When we live in a culture where our main forms of fun are watching people shoot and kill one another in movies, and enacting simulations of violence in video games, the principle of fantasy rehearsal is working against us. Any individual who takes a stand against violent entertainment is doing something so unusual that it will probably have noticeable effects.

By anti-violent art, I mean songs, stories, movies, and other art forms that promote the idea of nonviolence. Art is a major way of influencing the ideas of a culture.

2. Work toward making weapons less available.

The availability of very lethal weapons, especially guns, is a major factor that contributes to the likelihood of killing and severe hurting. The availability of nuclear weapons contributes to the likelihood of a nuclear war. If nonviolent dispute-resolution methods are strengthened, people's perceived need for weapons will be greatly reduced.

Opponents of weapons control have correctly pointed out that unilaterally disarming when there's an enemy who hates you and who wishes to kill you is naive. Thus weapons control should be accompanied with progress toward the rule of law, toward thoroughly enculturating nonviolent means of dispute resolution.

3. Avoid drinking alcohol.

A substantial portion of domestic and criminal violence is carried out by someone who's drunk. Alcohol intoxication lowers the barriers to violence between family members. But the use of alcohol is a cultural phenomenon; each person's use of it, even if that person is never violent, contributes to the precedent that enables other people to use it. Any individual who wishes to reduce domestic violence makes a contribution to the cause by abstaining from alcohol and thus weakening the perception that "everyone does it."

Domestic violence

1. Become familiar with rational decision-making skills and teach them to others.

One of the antidotes to domestic violence is calm, rational joint decision-making conversation. This is a major group of skills emphasized in this book. Anyone who learns these skills well, and who teaches them to others, makes violence of all sorts less likely, including domestic violence.

2. Study and teach the subject of parenting.

There are very workable methods of influencing children other than threatening to physically hurt them. Even if you're a child or teenager, you can start to study the subject of how to be a good and nonviolent parent, and can work toward the inclusion of this subject in your school's curriculum.

3. Support shelters and refuges for victims of domestic violence.

If people find themselves in a violent home, there should be an escape route. Women's shelters are one example of these.

Violence in schools

Work toward applying the rule of law among children and youth in schools.

If you're a student or a teacher, or if you have a child in a school, does the school have clear-cut procedures for determining whether someone was violent, and clear-cut consequences that effectively deter violence? Does the rule of law also apply to verbal abuse of one student by another, which is often a predecessor to physical violence? If not, you can work toward a set of written laws and procedures that are carried out in the case of violence or verbal abuse among individuals in the school.

Criminal violence

Avoid the purchase of illegal drugs and persuade others to do the same.

When someone purchases an illegal drug, he's supporting an industry that's built on violence. How does one drug dealer establish the exclusive right to sell in a certain territory? You can bet the threat of violence is the key to that drug dealer's economic existence.

Work toward the training of high-risk individuals in the skills that are alternatives to crime.

Many people turn to crime in part because they lack the skills to succeed, i.e. to get legitimate sources of power, in noncriminal ways. Earning money using some expertise at a trade is a source of power that can be an alternative to violence. If people are taught the basic skills of literacy, persistence, self-discipline, knowledge of a specific trade, and the other skills necessary to work successfully, the threat of criminal violence is reduced.

Warfare

Promote the idea of a world government and the rule of international law.

If two states within a country have a dispute with each other, they do not assemble armies; they assemble lawyers. They argue their case in courts. The legal process is highly imperfect and subject to deserved criticism, but it's far more humane as a method of resolving conflicts than warfare is. If someday disputes between nations can be solved by international courts rather than by armies, the world will have taken an enormous step forward. The World Federalist Association is an organization that promotes this idea.

Group 8: Respectful Talk, Not Being Rude

This skill group could have been subsumed under kindness. And respect-ful talk is a crucial part of kindness. But sometimes people forget the importance of the words and tones of voice they choose in speaking. To emphasize this, and because the categorization of ways of speaking respectfully and disrespect-fully is a large topic, respectful talk gets its own group.

Skill 44: Respectful Talk

What are the benefits of respectful, polite, words, spoken in a polite tone of voice? I believe these benefits are much more far-reaching in their mental health consequences than most people realize. Let's consider a few psychiatric disorders and their possible links to respectful versus disrespectful talk.

Depression: Depressed people are very often in the habit of harsh self-criticism. Where does this habit come from? Often (not always) it comes from hearing someone else be harshly critical of them or others.

Anxiety: A major anti-anxiety agent is a warm, supportive social network. Why is this? Because when scary things happen, if people can work together and support one another, they are much more likely to prevail over the danger. Conversely, when people speak to one another with disrespect and hostility, they themselves are more likely to present threats to one another; they are more justified in fearing one another, and in fearing dangerous situations from the outside, which they must face alone.

Conduct disorder and oppositional defiant disorder. Children with these problems typically act in a defiant, hostile manner; often they have learned these patterns by imitation.

Borderline personality disorder. People with this sort of problem tend to have big problems with relationships, and frequently have relationships ended or disrupted by very hostile talk or actions. The childhood histories of people with this problem are often characterized by lots of verbal abuse.

Even schizophrenia and bipolar disorder, two of the psychiatric illnesses with the most evidence for biological causation, are influenced by hostile or respectful talk. The courses of these disorders are altered for the better or worse, depending on the degree of respectful talk that goes on in the families of the people who have these problems.

Types of messages

What exactly do we mean by respectful talk? I've worked on categorizing the types of utterances people make to each other. I've tried to divide them into two classes: one is the class of utterances that tend to make people angry and get them irrational, and the other is the class of utterances that tend to lead people to think carefully. I call these two classes "obstructive messages" and "facilitative messages." The obstructive messages are sometimes useful, and it's impossible to say that people should never use them. But many people can improve things by using obstructive messages less often, and facilitative messages more often.

Obstructive messages:

1. Criticizing. "You're bad." "You did something bad. "You're a pig." "You're lazy." "You hurt other people, without thinking about anybody but yourself."

2. Put-down question. "What makes you think you can do that?" "Who do you think you are?" "Why can't you see what's plain as day?"

3. Silent resentment. Greatly resenting something someone has done and keeps doing, but feeling powerless to do anything about it.

4. Acting out anger. Hitting someone else, slamming a fist on a table, slamming a door.

5. Threatening. "If you keep doing that, you're going to get hurt badly."

6. Commanding. "Get over here, right this minute."

7. Sarcasm. "Yeah, right. Tell me about it. Oh, sure, that's really a funny one."

8. Defending oneself. "No, I don't waste money. How could you possibly accuse me of something like that?"

9. Overgeneralizing. "You never think about anyone but yourself." "You never do any work around this house."

10. Communication cutoff. Hanging up the telephone in the middle of a sentence. Walking out of the room in the middle of a conversation.

11. Nonverbal hostility. Tones of voice and facial expressions of hostility.

12. Attacking with a new issue. "You accuse me of wasting money, while you waste all your time playing video games, just getting fatter, and never cleaning up after yourself."

13. Overlong statements. Speaking for more than a minute or two without giving the other person at least a chance to respond.

14. Indefinite words or phrases. "You are so, I don't know, so icky." "You need to get your act together."

15. Unrequested advice. "You shouldn't be indulging your child so much. You should say no to him when he asks for so much attention."

Facilitative messages:

1. Mutual topic-finding. "Is now a good time to talk about the problem with your friend?"

2. I want statement. "I wish we could all turn out the lights when we aren't using them."

3. I feel statement. "When you tease me like you just did, it doesn't feel good, because it feels like you aren't being loyal to me." "When you compliment me like that, it makes me feel great."

4. Defining the problem. "Could we talk about a problem? When you stay up till midnight playing your music, it keeps me awake; I naturally get ready to sleep about ten."

5. Reflection. "So you're saying the noise I'm making is messing up your sleep rhythm, huh?"

6. Listing options. "I could go somewhere else to play the music. I could play with headphones so you couldn't hear them. I could not play at all after ten o'clock."

7. Citing advantages or disadvantages. "The advantage of headphones is that I could play music all I want. The main disadvantage is that they cost money to get."

8. Bargaining. "If you do this for me, I'll try to be really quiet when I get up in the morning, so you can sleep later."

9. "You are good" statements and "You did something good" statements. "You did a great job on that." "You're a true friend."

10. Asking for more specific criticism. "Tell me more about what I did that you didn't like."

11. Agreeing with part of criticism or argument. "You're right. I'm not the neatest person in the world." "I'll admit, there's room for improvement in how I talk." "You're right; this shirt is not the most beautiful one."

12. Communication postponement. "How about if we both cool off and think about this some more, and talk about it more tomorrow night?"

13. Nonverbal kindness. Approving tones of voice, smiles, pats, hugs.

14. Quantification of wants and feelings. "This is important to me, close to 10 on a scale of 10."

15. Citing specific observations. "I didn't like it when you said to me, 'Only a jerk would do that.'" (Versus: "I don't like it when you're mean.") "The last five times I've given you homework assignments, you've not done any of them." (Versus: You're lazy.) "I really like how when your sister told you how much work she did, you said 'All right!' and smiled at her. Some kids would have tried to one-up her by saying, 'I did lots more than you.'"

16. Open-ended question. "Tell me about yourself." "Tell me about what you've been doing lately." "What are your thoughts about that?"

17. Follow-up question. "Oh, what kind was it?" "What was it like for you when that happened?"

18. Asking for feedback. "What's your reaction to what I've just said?"

19. Facilitation. "Humh!" "Oh." "I see." "Yes." "Uh huh." "Is that right!" "Wow."

Two simple theories

Here's a theory. The higher people can make the ratio of facilitative to obstructive messages in their speech, the better they'll get along and the happier they'll be with one another (all other things being equal). This theory predicts that, if you listened to family members talk to one another, those families using more facilitative messages would do better on other measures of how well they got along with one another.

Here's a second theory. The higher the ratio of facilitative to obstructive messages in what a person says say to himself (his own self-talk), the happier that person tends to be.

Does this mean the very simple act of trying to express things in facilitative ways rather than in obstructive ones can do a huge amount of good? That's what the theory predicts.

Motives that lead to hurtful talk

Why is it so hard for people to switch from obstructive to facilitative messages? Here are some motives that lead people to hang on to obstructive messages:

1. Excitement and stimulation. One person insults or picks on another as an escape from monotony and a form of entertainment.

2. Punishment. Someone wants to change another person's behavior by using talk designed to punish unwanted actions.

3. Dominance Hierarchy, Power. One person uses hurtful talk toward another to show he has the power to do so without the other's retaliating, and is thus higher on the dominance hierarchy than the other.

4. Anger. One person feels anger and has a habit of using hurtful talk when angry.

5. Imitation learning. Someone imitates someone else who has modeled hurtful talk.

6. To command attention. To be listened to or attended to by someone who would otherwise not pay attention.

Vicious cycles and virtuous cycles

When one person speaks disrespectfully to the second, the second is made angry, wishes to punish the speaker, and perhaps wants to protest the implication that the other is higher on the dominance hierarchy. In addition, the second can learn habits of disrespectful talk from the first by imitation learning. So the second person often tends to speak disrespectfully back to the first. The first responds to the disrespectful talk by speaking back even more disrespectfully. A vicious cycle has started.

On the other hand, kind and respectful talk that makes the other person feel good, tends to elicit respectful talk for most of the same reasons. The second feels good, wishes to reward the first, and learns habits of respectful talk by imitation learning. So the second tends to talk back respectfully, which elicits more respectful talk from the first. This is called a virtuous cycle.

If you're starting a family, forming a social group, or getting into a relationship with one person, it's good, from the very beginning, to try to get the habits of respectful talk started toward a virtuous cycle. Once these cycles get started, they can be hard to stop.

Group 9: Friendship-Building, Relationship-Building

The quality of life is to a large extent determined by the quality of our relationships with other people. The skills in this group are some of the most important ones in making and keeping good relationships. They include the ability to decide whom to count on for what, how to start social interaction and how to continue it, how to be a good listener, and how to disclose and reveal yourself when that's appropriate. They include the communication of positive emotions to others.

The skill of loyalty and sustaining attachment would be included in this group if it did not have its own group. Many friendships are destroyed because of problems with other skills, such as fortitude or with joint decision-making. Nonetheless, the friendship-building group is a good place to look if you want to make and improve relationships.

Skill 45: Discernment and Trusting

Discernment is awareness of others' skills and personalities. It means being able to see other people as they really are, without distorting your view of them. Trusting means being able to enter into relationships with people where you count on them to act a certain way. These are basic skills that make it possible to get into relationships.

How people act doesn't just depend on the other person, but on you too

Some people fall into what I will call the "consumer" approach to relationship-building. They see themselves as picking people to have relationships with, in the same way that they view picking out a pair of pants or a bicycle. Or, they're like young children who are picky eaters. The picky eater's prevailing comments on foods of various sorts are "I don't like that kind," "No, that doesn't please me," "That doesn't meet with my approval," "I don't like that either." Sometimes the young child is so afraid he will not like something new that he won't try it. And many people act the same way toward new relationships.

A variant of the consumer approach is snobbery. The essence of snobbery is the idea that only a select few people are good enough for you to spend time with or get into relationships with. The thought pattern seems to be, "I can prove what a good person I am by identifying most people as unworthy of my friendship." Of course, most people who engage in snobbery don't consciously say this to themselves.

In the consumer approach you view the other person's qualities as fixed and unchanging, and as being the same no matter whom the other person is with.

The flip side of the "consumer" attitude toward relationships is the "consumee" attitude. The person with this attitude sees himself, not as the person picking items off a shelf, but as the one on the shelf being picked. Will I be deemed OK? Are my qualities good enough that anyone will choose me? This attitude is common in people with a great fear of rejection, or a history of rejection by others.

A different mind-set toward relationships is what we can call the efficacy approach. The word *efficacy* means the power to bring about a desired result. With the efficacy approach, in forming relationships or being with people you ask the question: "How can I bring out some part of what this person is capable of, and some part of what I'm capable of, in a way that will be mutually satisfying?" "How can I find the part of this person that will be in harmony with some part of me?" Here you regard the other person, not as a fixed commodity, but as a person who has many different possible ways of acting, depending upon how you act to that person. In using the efficacy approach, you acknowledge your own power to make your enjoyment of another person greater, depending on how you act. Your power is not unlimited, but it is substantial.

Let's give some examples of the difference between the consumer and consumee approaches and the efficacy approach.

Imagine that a woman has a roommate who acts very shy. If the woman used the picky approach to relationships, she might say, "Nope, that person is boring. Doesn't say enough to keep me entertained. Cross that person off the list of candidates for friends." If she took the snobbish variation of the consumer approach, she might think something very similar: "I want a more dynamic class of people in my circle. This person doesn't make it." With the consumee approach, she might think, "She can't relate to me. I guess this proves I'm not acceptable to her."

But instead, with the efficacy orientation, she thinks, "Some shy people need longer to warm up than others. And this person may be afraid of disapproval; if I can give her approval and a feeling of success, perhaps I can bring out a part of her I can enjoy." She gradually makes her roommate feel very comfortable, and they have many enjoyable times together.

Or suppose someone finds himself living next door to someone whose religious beliefs he finds not just different from his own, but downright offensive. If he were to take the consumer approach, he would think, "This is a good enough reason to leave this person alone altogether." However, he instead takes the efficacy oriented approach, and thinks, "I'll avoid talking about religion when the subject comes up, and I'll steer us in other directions." He finds a common ground with his neighbor in the fact that they both like to play folk music, and they often spend some enjoyable time together doing this.

For another example: The first person remarks to the second about someone they both know, "That person is so stingy!"

The second, surprised, says "Really? I've found him to be very generous."

The first says, "I've asked him to lend me some things, and he just refuses me."

The second says, "That's strange; he's been willing to lend me almost everything I've ever asked for."

It turns out the difference lies in the fact that the first person has in the past borrowed things and has never returned them! The second has always returned everything faithfully. For this reason, the man acts stingy toward the first, but generous toward the second. But people tend to explain other people's actions in terms of fixed traits they see the other person as having, rather than in terms of their own behavior that has influenced the other. It would be useful for the first person to get beyond the consumer mentality and recognize his own efficacy in affecting the other person's behavior.

It's good not to overdo your perception of your own efficacy in bringing out the best in others. You don't want to make commitments to long-term relationships with very difficult people just to see if you can meet the challenge of bringing out the best in them! But most people tend to make the opposite error more often.

What do we mean by the skill of trusting?

Sometimes people use the word trust to mean, "believing that the other person is telling the truth." I'm using it here to mean more than that. Here I'm talking about trusting as "believing that the other person will treat you as you want to be treated," or "believing that you can happily interact with this person, in a certain way." If I'm standing at the top of some stairs with a friend, it's trust if I believe my friend won't give me a push down the stairs just to see what would happen. I'm trusting my friend, even though he never made a promise that he wouldn't push me down stairs!

Obviously, the skill of trusting doesn't mean you believe that everyone you meet will treat you just as you want to be treated at every moment. That

would be foolish. There are some people in the world who are not trustworthy for much of anything. No person will always act the way you want him to.

But, there are some people you can trust for lots of things, and there are lots of people you can trust for some things. The skill of trusting means having reasonable ideas and beliefs about what you can and cannot count on people for. You want to enjoy people in the ways you can enjoy them, and not count on them for things they won't come through on.

Two types of mistakes in trusting

Having the skill of trusting means staying away from two types of mistakes as much as possible. The first mistake comes when you trust someone when you shouldn't. This might be called gullibility. Or you could call it getting your hopes too high. Here's an example: Someone comes up to you on the sidewalk and asks you for a loan of $50, saying he'll mail you a check to pay you back. He plans to keep the money. If you trust him and lose $50, you make the first type of mistake. You're being too gullible.

The second mistake comes when you fail to trust someone when you should. This might be called being too cynical or too paranoid. Here's an example: A person is diagnosed with cancer. The doctor tells him about an expensive treatment that would really help. The person thinks the doctor is just out for money and doesn't get the treatment. It turns out the treatment would have helped tremendously, and the person pays for his non-trusting with his life. When someone is extremely untrusting for no reason, the word *paranoid* is used. Here's an example of being paranoid: Someone sees some people talking and laughing, and the person thinks the people must be saying bad things about him behind his back and laughing at him. The person feels angry or fearful of these people, even though there's no evidence to justify his feelings.

Here are some other examples of the mistake of failing to trust someone when it would be wiser to trust.

Someone has been teased and rejected by a kid in his neighborhood. There's another kid who's nice to him, but he's afraid to get to know the nice kid because he's afraid he'll get teased and rejected again.

Someone gets her car inspected. The mechanic says her car needs to be fixed or it will break down very soon. She has heard stories about car mechanics' doing work that isn't necessary to get people's money. She drives away because she doesn't trust the mechanic. Her car does break down, and it's very inconvenient for her to get it fixed.

Being with other people depends upon trust

When you think about it, it would be hard for people to be together at all without trust. Imagine if nobody could trust anybody for anything. It would be very difficult to ever buy food or anything else. The one with the money would say, "Give me the food I'm buying first, so I'll know you won't run off with my money." The one who was selling the food would say, "Give me the money first, so I'll know that you won't run off with the food without paying me."

But that's not all. If no one in the world could trust that other people weren't out to hurt them and rob from them, they would all try to stay away from one another, or even kill one another before they got killed first. It would be a very sad life if people couldn't trust anybody else.

Trust is one of the qualities that make the world fit to live in. Fortunately, we can trust some people and some things. But there are very few people we can trust for everything in the world. An important skill is to figure out whom you can trust for what.

Here's an example of trusting people for some things but not for others. Suppose Ms. Smith has a friend, Mr. Jones. Ms. Smith knows that she can count on Mr. Jones to be nice to her. He always has a smile for her and says kind things to her. He will always listen to her if she wants to talk about something that's bothering her. If someone else says something mean to her, her friend will always stick up for her and say something nice. Mr. Jones is a good friend.

But can Ms. Smith count on him for everything? Mr. Jones is a very reckless driver. So if Ms. Smith wants to ride somewhere in a car, she won't ride with Mr. Jones. She trusts him for the things he's good at, and not the things he's bad at.

Suppose Ms. Smith has another friend named Ms. Lee. Ms. Smith doesn't like to talk with Ms. Lee when she has a problem; Ms. Lee is usually very critical. She says things like, "Well, if you'd thought about that enough, you wouldn't have gotten into that problem. It's your own fault." But Ms. Lee happens to be one of the most careful drivers in the whole world. She watches like a hawk for any car that might cause a problem; she's always sure to make sure her car is in good condition. So if Mary wants to count on someone to ride in a car with, she'd count on Ms. Lee before she'd count on Mr. Jones.

So the skill of trusting is not so simple as deciding whom to trust and whom not to trust. You can count on some people for some things and other people for other things. If you do the skill of trusting well, you'll trust people for what they're trustworthy in. You won't count on them for things they aren't trustworthy in.

In deciding whom to trust, the past predicts the future

People have tried many ways to figure out whom to trust for what. Whenever a person decides whom to hire for a job, she's wondering, "Can I trust this person? Can I trust this person not to steal from my company? Can I trust this person to do the job right? Can I trust this person not to say mean things to customers? Can I trust this person to work hard and not want to get paid for goofing off?"

Here's a rule to go by when trying to decide whom you can trust for what: The past predicts the future. The way people have acted in the past predicts how they're going to act in the future. The older someone gets, the more their past behavior predicts their future behavior.

The second rule is: if you want to know how someone will act in a certain situation, see how the person has acted in similar situations. So the best way to predict whether or not someone is going to be a good worker, friend, husband, or wife is to see how he or she acts in just the sort of situations that are important that the person handle well.

Do you want to see if a worker is trustworthy? Then let her work for you for a while and see how she does. In all human relations people spend time getting to know each other and deciding how much they can trust each other for what. It's best if they spend this time before making big commitments to each other. A commitment is an agreement where people have something to lose if they can't count on each other, but they have something to gain if they can. When two people get married and have a child, that's a huge commitment. When someone hires someone for a job, that's a commitment, although not such a huge one. If people make a commitment without having enough knowledge of each other, they may not be able to keep it.

It's good to be aware of how big a commitment you're getting into. A commitment that I'll pay someone $15 if he'll mow my lawn is not a very big commitment. It doesn't require a whole lot of trust. On the other hand, suppose I sign a contract with someone that he will cut my grass for the next three years. By this contract I'm not going to let anybody else cut my grass. Also, I'll have to pay $100 if I decide to break this contract. This is a bigger commitment. But it's still not nearly as big as the commitment involved in getting married to someone.

The bigger the commitment you're going to make, the more information you're going to need about the person. You want to see how the person acts in the sorts of situations that the person will have to handle well.

You decide whom to trust for what by observing how people handle situations

You decide who is trustworthy for what things by getting to know people.

What does it mean to get to know someone? It means you watch and notice what the person does. You listen to what the person says. You see what sorts of things she does in certain situations. The more you've watched and observed someone, the more you

know what sort of things you can trust him for. You only know how he'll act in certain situations if you've seen him in lots of similar situations.

Do you remember fairy stories where two people who hardly know each other get married and live happily ever after? A certain prince, for example decided to marry Cinderella after dancing with her for one evening. If the prince lived happily ever after with Cinderella, it was because he was very lucky. Deciding to count on someone to be your spouse takes a great deal of trusting. Except in fairy stories, it takes a great deal of data-gathering before you're ready to decide whether to trust someone enough to take the major step of marrying that person.

So when you're trying to decide whether you can count on someone for something, you first ask yourself, "What do I want to count on him to do, in what situations?" You think about the important things, not the little ones. Then you watch what he does in those same situations. If he always handles the situations in a way you like, you're in luck. If he usually handles the situations just the way you don't want him to, you'd better not stake too much on his changing his ways.

Some people have trouble trusting because of overgeneralizing

You decide whether to trust based on your experience with people. Sometimes people make a mistake in trusting called overgeneralizing. They have bad experiences with someone, and generalize that to other people who would be much nicer if they were given the chance. Some people who have been treated unkindly have lots of trouble trusting that anyone else will treat them kindly.

This can cause big problems. If you expect that others are going to be mean to you, you sometimes act mean first. This may cause the other person to act mean even when they weren't going to act mean in the first place. Expecting other people to be mean can be a "self-fulfilling prophecy." A self-fulfilling prophecy is something that happens because you act as if you think it will happen.

Here's an example of someone who barely stopped himself from doing a self-fulfilling prophecy. A boy named Billy went to a school where he got picked on by everyone. Lots of times at school when someone said, "Hey Billy!" he would turn around to find the person saying, "You're a fatso!" or "You're ugly!" Then Billy would say something like, "Oh, shut up!" He got so used to saying this, that it got to be a habit.

Then he transferred to a new school. Someone sitting behind him said, "Hey, Billy!" He started to turn around to the person and say, "Oh, shut up!" But he thought better of it. He thought something like, "Let's see now. I couldn't trust those people in the other school to be nice to me. But I don't know about this person now. Maybe I'll

give him the benefit of the doubt and get to know him a little better."

So Billy turned around and looked at him and said, "Yes?" and the other boy said, "My name's Tommy. I just wanted to welcome you to our school. I hope you enjoy it." When he heard this, Billy was so glad he hadn't said, "Oh, shut up." to Tommy. And he said to Tommy, "Thank you so much for saying that. That really makes me feel good." That was the start of a friendship between Billy and Tommy. But if Billy had said, "Oh, shut up," it's possible that acting as if he expected Billy to be mean would have made Billy act mean back to him.

Once some people did a study. They found some boys who were mean to other people and compared those boys with another group of boys who were nice to people. They showed both groups many pictures of people doing things with one another. You couldn't tell exactly what was going on. For example, one person had his hand up, and he was facing another person. The experimenters would ask the boys what was going on in the pictures.

The mean boys would usually say something like, "he's got his hand up so he can hit the other person." The nicer boys more often guessed something like, "Maybe he's got his hand up so he can shake hands with the other person." or, "Maybe he's got his hand up so he can pat the other person on the back." The point of the study was that mean people more often are the ones who think other people's actions are mean or threatening.

So one of the most important things in the skill of trusting is to realize that even though there are a lot of people in the world who act mean, there are also a lot of people in the world who act nice. The key to figuring out whether you can trust a person and for what things is to get to know that person better over a long period of time.

Reasons for distorted views of others

What are some reasons why people distort their views of other people? Suppose a person has low skills of tolerating aloneness and rejection, and a very desperate need to be in a relationship with someone. But the person also has a core belief that "The person must be perfect in these several ways, or else the person is no good, and it's very dangerous to have a relationship with him." The person may have a very high fear of trusting, and a core belief of "If you get into the relationship with the wrong person, it's extremely dangerous. If you trust the wrong person, it's curtains!" The person has very much an all-or-nothing viewpoint about other people – either someone is the right type or the wrong type. There are not shades of gray. Now suppose the person gets into a relationship. The relief of the desperate loneliness is so great that there's great pleasure. The person wants so badly to be in a relationship that she

will distort reality to see the other person as perfect, as a savior.

But as the relationship continues, the evidence keeps coming that the other person is not perfect – as no person is. Plus, the closer the relationship becomes, the more the fear of closeness is activated. Suddenly the balance tips and the person acknowledges that the other person is not all good. Given the all-or-nothing viewpoint, this means the other person is all bad. The person can become very angry and rejecting of this impostor, this false savior.

The fear of closeness gets taken care of as the relationship ends in a stormy way. Then the fear of aloneness sets in, and the cycle starts over again. A good many people oscillate back and forth in this way, driven by the fear of closeness and the fear of aloneness, alternating between seeing someone else as an angel and seeing that person as a devil.

What's the answer to this sort of problem? The answer is fixing the skill deficiencies in handling aloneness and handling closeness, intimacy, trusting, and depending, as well as replacing the tendency to see other people as either all good or all bad with an attitude that allows others to fall on all sorts of points on all sorts of spectra.

Thinking about the psychological skills axis, the list of skills that organizes this book, in many ways provides an antidote to all-or-none thinking. If we imagine that each person gets a rating from 0 to 10 on all sixty-two of these skills, we come up with huge numbers of possible variations of how people can be. Almost no one gets a rating of "all good" or "all bad."

The syndrome I just described represents a major pattern of distorting one's views of other people. But people can distort without being locked into that oscillating pattern. Almost everyone falls prey at some point or another to wish-fulfilling distortions. Someone wishes to be in a romantic relationship. Someone comes along who is willing to play the role of Prince or Princess Charming, person of dreams. Perhaps Prince or Princess Charming also casts the first person in the role of a similar Prince or Princess Charming. The notion of simultaneously having a dream lover and being a dream lover is intoxicatingly pleasant. It's what many people refer to when they speak of being in love.

And if Prince and Princess Charming both have high psychological skills, particularly loyalty, kindness, frustration-tolerance, self-discipline, and good decision-making; and if the two have enough commonality in interests, goals, and preferences about how to live, they might be able to sustain that feeling of being in love, at least to some extent, throughout a lifetime with each other. Stranger things have happened in the history of the world!

But the chances of selecting the right person for a long-term relationship, based upon that person's answering the casting call for a role in the "dream lover" play, are not huge. Therefore it's necessary to take time for the intoxication of being in love to wear off and to do some rational evaluation of the other person as a candidate for mate, separating one's wishes from what reality truly is.

Here's another way in which people distort their views of others. We all tend to cast new people into the roles played by other people in our relationship histories. This person gets cast as my father, this person as my competitive sister, this person as the class bully who terrorized me, this person as the beautiful classmate I worshipped from afar, etc.

For example, a man's father had very high standards, expected very high performance, and was impeccably fair and honest. The man wanted his father's approval very strongly, but never could quite get enough of it. Then the man gets a job; the boss has very high performance standards and is very hardworking himself. The boss gets cast by the man into the "father" role. The boss leads the man into one shady deal after another, getting the man to do his dirty work. Because the real father was very fair and honest, the man assumes the boss is also that way. It takes an unusually large amount of experience before it finally begins to dawn on the worker that the boss is not at all fair and honest like his father.

The nearly universal tendency to see people in the present as reincarnations of people in the past has gone by various names. Sigmund Freud called this *transference*. We transfer the perceptions appropriate for one person to someone else they in some way resemble. Harry Stack Sullivan called the distortions of people based on past experience *parataxic distortions*.

In the viewpoint of many analysts, the inability to see people as they really are and respond to them in ways appropriate to the current situation is at the heart of neurosis. Therefore resolution of the transference is at the heart of psychotherapy. Obviously, my own point of view is that there are many other psychological skills that need to be developed independently from this one. Nonetheless, this one is important.

One of the major thought patterns useful in overcoming distortions of our views of others is, "that was then, this is now." The assumptions about the character traits and personalities of people in the past do not necessarily generalize to people in the present.

How do you come to an undistorted picture of someone's skill in one of these sixty-two dimensions, anyway? You collect a data sample, noticing how the person responds in situations calling for that skill. If you observe the person experiencing twenty-five frustrations, and he has a tantrum or other immature response after twenty-three of them, you're pretty safe in inferring his frustration tolerance is low. If you see him in thirty opportunities to be kind, and he is kind in twenty-eight of them, he gets a high rating on kindness skills. If out of

ten conflicts, the person acts totally selfish and irrational in nine of them, he gets a low conflict-resolution rating. The higher your sample size, the more confidence you can put in your inference. If you collect enough good data, you can come to good information.

But the sample of situations has to be relevant to the situations you want to generalize to. All over this country, men and women are making inferences about whom they want to marry by observing the partner's behavior on dates. They're trying to predict who is good to negotiate finances with, clean vomit off kids with, read kids bedtime stories with, and declutter a garage with. They predict this by collecting a data sample on who is good to go out to dinner with, listen to concerts with, and see movies with. They're trying to predict success in the work of family life by observing how someone participates in being entertained. My guess is that those contemplating marriage would make better decisions if they could teach a religious education class together, do a tutoring project together, or jointly conduct some other work project, preferably one involving the nurturing of children.

Skills of discernment can also provide an antidote to prejudice. Despite advances in this arena, prejudice still abounds: racial prejudice, prejudice against women or men, or people of certain nationalities, or homosexuals, or those of certain religions, or those of a certain age groups. Prejudice is the tendency to think all members of a certain group are alike – all of them fit a certain stereotypical image – "if you've seen one you've seen them all." Stereotyping means overgeneralizing far beyond the data. There's so much variation within any large group of people that seeing all of them as the same is making a very large distortion of reality.

The task of discernment is made difficult because of limitations in the amount of time available to get to know people. This is especially true in a culture where people deal so much with anonymous strangers. In a small town with a stable population where everyone gets a large amount of data on everyone else over a long period of time, it becomes possible to know people better than in the fluid, mobile, big-city culture that is the norm for the United States.

But another barrier to discernment is a failure to turn one's attention fully to the task of getting to know another person. An exercise for the skill of discernment, therefore, is to take some time to get to know someone else. Collect that person's biography; listen to the story of that person's life. Observe and record that person's behavior and see whether the generalizations you would make about that person can be supported with specific, concrete examples. If no one else is available, you can let this person be yourself. The skills of knowing others and knowing oneself are closely tied to each other.

Skill 46: Self-Disclosure

Another word related to self-disclosure is "intimacy." It refers to the ability to talk about what's really meaningful to you, personal things, things that make life meaningful, things that people have feelings about.

Here are some questions that people would probably consider fairly intimate questions. How happy am I with my relationships? How satisfying, how meaningful, is my life? What would make my life more meaningful? What are the obstacles to my living life most fully? What are the things I'm most proud of doing? What are the things I'm most ashamed of? What goals do I want to dedicate myself to? What, and whom, do I really care about? What makes my relationships good or not good? What do I worry about and fear? How do I want to change myself? What emotions am I feeling, about what events? These are a sample of what we mean by "intimate questions."

There are plenty of topics to think and talk about other than intimate questions. What's the weather likely to do today? How do I get my computer to do a certain thing? What do I think is going to happen in a certain sports contest that's coming up? Who won the latest political race? Where can you get a certain thing least expensively? What's the best kind of car to buy? How do you win a certain video game?

What's the difference between the first group of questions and the second group? The second group deals with things outside myself, whereas the first group deals with what's inside me. With the questions about things outside myself, probably lots of people other than I could talk about them, and say just the same things. The first group has answers that are unique to me.

Why would anyone want to be able to talk and think about the first set of questions rather than just the second? What's the value of the skill of intimate self-disclosure? Or put another way, what's the problem with NOT being able to think and talk about the first type of questions, and only the second?

In answering that question, the first thing we should realize is the link between talking and thinking. When we talk about certain things, we get words in our vocabularies for certain ideas. When we practice using those words and putting them together; we become able to think about them better. On the other hand, if we never talk about certain things, we tend not to be so expert at thinking about them. Thinking is often a process of talking to oneself about something; by talking to someone else we practice talking to ourselves, and vice versa.

Sometimes people don't talk about their intimate feelings and thoughts because they keep them hidden even from themselves. Being able to tell someone else about something means that you can think about it yourself.

The second thing to realize is that intimate questions are important. Indeed, they may feel more threatening simply because they are more important, and the stakes are higher. Why does it feel more intimate if I talk about whether my wife and I are getting along well, and less intimate if I talk about whether I think the Braves are going to beat the Pirates? It's because the first question is infinitely more important – to me at least – than the second. If I'm feeling really sad, discouraged, or hopeless, it's much more important for me to figure out why I feel that way than to think about whether I like Buicks better than Toyotas.

Therefore, if I'm unable to think and talk about intimate questions, I'm in danger of ignoring the important things about my life in favor of the less important things. For example, while I'm spending my energy trying to figure out which sports team is going to hire a certain player, I'm ignoring the quality of the relationships in my life.

A special case of self-disclosure is being able to talk about problems to someone who might help you with them. The following story has happened millions of times: The first person has a problem that the second person could help with. But the first person doesn't want to talk about it, because talking about it is too embarrassing or otherwise painful. The first person avoids the subject, and thus avoids solving the problem.

A special sort of problem is a situation that you handled badly. Suppose a child is in a classroom, and a special person comes into the classroom to help her. She's embarrassed by having to get help that her classmates don't need. She knows her classmates might tease her about this. So she's rude to the helping person, saying, "Get out of here. I don't need you." She gets into trouble that proves much more embarrassing than the original problem.

Now it's a couple of days later. The child gets the chance to talk about the situation. If she has good self-disclosure skills, she can talk about the situation at length. She can look back and decide why she acted as she did. She can decide what she wishes she had done in this situation. She can rehearse in fantasy what she would like to do in a similar situation. In short, she can learn from the experience, and make herself a more competent person.

But if she says, "I don't want to talk about it," and shifts the subject to talk about a television show, she loses that opportunity. Then, the next time a similar situation comes around, she's no more prepared for it than she was the first time.

Most of what has been called psychotherapy depends upon the person's being willing to self-disclose and talk about problems. People who are willing to talk about problems can do much more learning from experience than those who are not willing to do so.

It takes courage to self disclose, whether to a therapist or any other helping person. You run several risks. You run the risk the other person will respond in a punishing, critical, or humiliating way. You run the risk the other person will use the information against you. You run the risk the other person will get too bossy about telling you what you should do or what you should have done. And finally, even if the other person responds in a way that avoids all these unpleasant effects, you still risk feeling bad about bringing up the memories of the problem situation rather than shoving them out of your mind and thinking of something more pleasant.

For this reason, you have to pick and choose whom you want to self disclose to. Even among those people lucky enough to have someone good to self-disclose to, many fail to take advantage of the opportunity. This is one of the reasons many people fail to solve their problems, but just hang on to them indefinitely.

Here's another reason to work at the skill of intimate self-disclosure. It lets people get the feeling they gradually know each other better and better. It lets people feel closer to each other, and to become close friends. Sometimes people stick to the more non-intimate areas in order to keep their distance from the other person, to avoid a feeling of closeness. But most people seem to

be happier when they can feel close to at least one person.

If intimate self-disclosure has so many good points, why not do it almost all the time? There are risks. One risk is humiliation. For example, a middle school kid confides that she has a "crush" on someone. The person who hears this news tells several other people who taunt and tease the person who made the self-disclosure. It would not take many experiences like this to make someone stick to talking about what movies are good, what clothes people like, and other non-intimate details.

For this reason, people who have had much experience with being embarrassed and humiliated by other people often find it very difficult to be intimate. It can sometimes take lots of conscious thought to realize that not everyone is out to humiliate and embarrass you, and that some people are trustworthy with intimate disclosures.

There's another risk. If you talk about personal things to someone you don't know well, it might make the other person uncomfortable. There are unwritten rules about when it's OK to make intimate self-disclosures. If you break these rules, you can expect some surprise, perhaps discomfort, on the part of the other person. So part of the skill of intimacy is knowing when to speak of intimate details and when not to.

As people get to know each other better, they usually progress from talking about less intimate details to more intimate disclosures. In this way you gradually test the waters. You see whether you and the person can trust each other with minor intimate details before revealing more major ones.

When people don't know each other well and aren't going to get to know each other well, sometimes it's more fun to talk about external things than to talk about intimate disclosures. You have to care about someone before you want to hear about whether he's happy with his work or his family; but you can be entertained by his telling funny jokes whether you care about him or not.

There will be many people whom you'll choose not to reveal intimate information to. Sometimes it will be because you don't trust the person not to embarrass you. Sometimes it will be because you don't know the person well enough and you don't want to make the other person uncomfortable. And sometimes it's because you realize the other person doesn't know you well enough to care much about the intimate details of your life.

If someone is not good at talking about important aspects of his life, how does he get better at it? Sometimes developing the skill of handling teasing and criticism is what helps the most. For example, if I'm totally confident that what I did, thought, or felt was OK, no matter who teases or criticizes, then I'm less vulnerable. If I'm able to maintain that confidence when people try to criticize or tease, then those who would want to humiliate and embarrass me

find they don't get much of a reaction from me. Then they tend to back off that issue, because their attempt to become powerful in this way doesn't work.

The more this happens, the more I feel free to own all parts of myself without fearing that someone will reject me. But getting totally confident that I'm OK regardless of others' taunting or rejection is easier said than done. This is especially true if I myself believe that I've done something weak, wrong, or shameful, as all people do from time to time.

Many people live their lives with an underlying feeling that everyone would reject them if they only knew their terrible secrets. It's a tremendous liberation to get over that feeling. One of the ways people get over that is to hear other people tell about their lives, and to find that they're not alone in doing whatever they're ashamed of. Other people get over that feeling by participating in the type of psychotherapy where they gradually reveal more and more of the things they were afraid of revealing. In doing so, they find that the therapist doesn't reject or humiliate them, and that what they have experienced is common human experience.

Here are some exercises with the skill of intimacy. First, think of various questions you might think of asking other people, and rate them on a scale of 10 as to how personal versus how safe they are. For example, "Looks like it's going to rain, doesn't it?" would rate approximately 0 on this scale, and "Tell me about your romantic or erotic fantasies" would rate close to 10. "What sorts of things do you enjoy doing?" would rate perhaps 2, whereas "If you could have three wishes, what would they be," would rate perhaps 6 or 7. This exercise will help sensitize you in making choices about what feels right to ask someone and what to tell someone, given the degree of trust that currently exists.

The second exercise is to think of things you could reveal about yourself, and rate your own degree of comfort with these disclosures. For example, my comfort in revealing that I like cloudy weather might extend to everyone. I might feel comfortable telling everyone (except my history teacher) that I like math more than history. I continue, until I get to the parts I perhaps wouldn't tell anyone, and list those. Then if I'm feeling brave and strong, I might explore the parts that take great courage to acknowledge, even to myself. By doing this exercise, I come to understand more thoroughly my own fears of disclosure of certain things. I should be able to decide more rationally what I do – and don't – want to disclose to whom.

Skill 47: Expressing Gratitude and Approval

So much of human happiness or misery depends on the approval or disapproval we communicate through our words. To be in relationships where approval is frequently exchanged is a recipe for happiness; to be in relationships where disapproval is constantly exchanged is a recipe for misery.

Skill of expressing approval doesn't equal flattery

Let's think about the difference between the skill of expressing approval, on the one hand, and deceitful flattery, on the other hand. The difference lies in whether the person sincerely believes the approving words he's speaking.

For example: Let's suppose Madame Fifi has a lot of money and may be making a contribution to an organization. The head of that organization knows Madame Fifi is very concerned with how she dresses and what her clothes look like. So the person showers Madame Fifi with lots of words of this sort: "Madame Fifi, what a beautiful dress you have on! Oh, the colors just go so well together. I just love the textures of that material, and your shoes just go so well with that dress!" If, however, the person really either dislikes or is utterly indifferent to Madame Fifi's clothes, but is expressing fake approval simply to get something out of her, that's not honest and is not a good

example of the skill described in this chapter.

Consciously looking for things to approve of is good

On the other hand, suppose a first person wants to build a relationship with a second person. He says to himself, "I'll be very watchful of what the other person does. I'll be on the lookout for something she does that really goes along with my own value system." The second person makes a comment in a discussion about a book she's reading, and the person recognizes this as an idea he really values. He says to the second person, "You know, I think that's really a good comment you made. I think that was very smart. I'd like to hear more of your ideas about that." He has now spoken honestly about his own positive feelings. But he first made it more likely they would come by looking for them and watching for them.

This is like so many other things that our minds do. We're much more likely to come up with answers to questions if we consciously ask the questions. If we never pose the question to ourselves, "What has the other person done that I admire, that I like, that I can get excited about in a positive way," then the answer is much less likely to come. On the other hand, if we're constantly asking the question, we will often find the answer coming to us.

The importance of tone of voice

Our tone of voice and facial expressions are at least as important as the words we say.

Let's imagine a teenage girl has given a teenage boy a poem she has written for him to read. After he reads it, he says to her in a monotone voice, "That's a very good poem. I like it very much." He doesn't smile, and his face doesn't move much when he says this to her. Will she feel very complimented? Probably not. Has he done well in expressing positive feelings to another person? He has expressed positive thoughts, but the feelings are not present, or at least they haven't been communicated through his tone of voice or facial expression.

Now, let's imagine a similar situation with two other people. The boy really likes the poem, but this time he gets through reading it, and he sits for a few minutes with an amazed look on his face and says, "Wow! Wow! That was powerful!" and his eyebrows are raised high. He has probably communicated much more effectively his positive feelings. His tone of voice and facial expression probably communicated more than his words did.

Imagine a tutor working with a child. The child gets the right answer to a question, and the tutor says in a monotone, "That was very good." By contrast, imagine that tutor saying, with great excitement and pleasure, "Hey! Hey!" The second utterance is meaningless semantically, but it probably will be much more reinforcing to the child than the monotone words.

Praise should take into account the person's past performance

When expressing approval and positive feelings toward another person, especially that brand of positive feelings known as praise, we evaluate what the other person has done. It's important to know well enough what the standard is for the other person, where that person is on his own progression up the ladder of skill.

For example, someone is learning the skill of anger control. On a certain occasion, he becomes angry, and responds by pounding his fists on the table and growling, and then sitting and moping for another five minutes before going on. Is this something to give approval for, or disapproval? It depends on whether it's a movement up or down the hierarchy of skill. If the person's previous habit had been to resort to physical violence almost consistently, then avoiding that in this instance would be cause for great celebration. On the other hand, if the person had previously reached the point where he could respond with some rational talk about the problem, trying to solve it, the performance in this instance would be more cause for curiosity than for celebration.

For another example: A student almost always gets 100 percent right on his math test. There's a substitute teacher, who hands back a test he did;

he missed three of the questions. The substitute teacher says, "You did really well! You got all of them right but three. You keep studying, and maybe someday, you'll get them all right." The student doesn't appreciate this compliment because the substitute teacher doesn't know this student's past history. The teacher doesn't know if the performance is a move up or down on the hierarchy of skill.

Approval doesn't necessarily equal praise

Expressing approval doesn't have to take the form of praise. You can just describe or mention what the other person did, and let the context of the situation and the tone of voice and facial expression communicate the approval without any obvious evaluation of what the other person did. Another way of expression positive feeling without evaluating the performance is to simply name the feelings the performance (or whatever) gave to you without rating or judging the other person's behavior.

For example: Someone says to a broad-jumper, "It really gives me a thrill to see you float though the air each time you jump." This isn't evaluating, judging, or measuring the jump; it's simply communicating the feelings the jump gives to the person who's watching it.

Or, suppose someone has just given a speech. If someone wants to praise and evaluate it, they would say,

"That was really a good speech; it was really well done." Someone who wants to express her own feelings about it, on the other hand, would say, "I really feel good after hearing you talk. I think I can use the things you've said. I'm excited about trying." This expresses approval, without explicitly evaluating the performance.

Here's another example. The first person is singing, and the second person listens. If the second is evaluating the other person's performance, she might say, "You were on pitch, and your regulation of your volume was really good. You sang all the notes perfectly! Congratulations!" On the other hand, someone who's telling their own reaction to it might say, "I heard you sing that song and felt really stirred. When you got to the end, I felt shivers going up and down my back." This is an example of stating the feelings the other person's actions bring out in you.

Here are some examples of simply describing and naming the other person's action, letting the tone of voice communicate the positive feelings.

A college student has been working really hard on a project for school. His parent knocks on his door and walks into his room and says, "Boy, you've been working on this for three hours without stopping!" That statement is just naming what the person has seen rather than saying, "You're doing a good job! You're really sustaining attention to your task for a very long time."

I'm proud of you for that. That's a good job! Congratulations!"

Sometimes people like it better if you just name what they've done rather than actually evaluate their performance.

Here's another example: Two young children are doing dramatic play. They are pretending one of them is about to go over a waterfall in the river and the other is saving him. If an adult wants to give praise for this, he might say, "Boy, you're being so imaginative, and you're also acting out such positive things with each other." But if the adult wants to communicate positive feelings without using an evaluation, the adult might just watch with really rapt attention and have an interested and curious expression on his face, and that might be enough in itself. Or he might say, "Wow! That person is getting saved from going over the waterfall!" That would be an example of just describing what's going on, but using a positive tone to communicate the positive emotion.

These techniques of describing the feelings the other person's actions gave you, describing the other person's actions, and communicating the feelings in your tone of voice are an answer to the following question: "How can we have a world where people are very frequently communicating positive feeling toward one another without having a world where people are constantly judging one another?"

Barriers to approval

What are some of the barriers to people's communicating positive feelings to one another? One barrier, probably, is the fear you'll admire someone who won't admire you back. This is the fear that I'll say, "Wow! That really made me feel good when you did that," and the other person will say, "Who asked you, anyway?"

For this reason and others, the skill of expressing approval takes some courage. It's helped by an attitude of "Hey, here is what I feel, and I feel it whether or not the other person appreciates it. I can handle it if the other person doesn't appreciate it back."

Here are some other barriers to expression of approval. Sometimes people are angry at each other. For this reason, they can't feel good about one good behavior because they're angry about the previous behaviors. Sometimes people are afraid of expressing positive feeling for fear it will take on sexual implication to the other person and will be understood the wrong way. Sometimes people in authority are hesitant to praise the people under them too much for fear they'll get complacent and slack off. In fact, the opposite is probably more likely to be the case in such a situation.

Sometimes people don't express positive feelings about what the other person has done because they're so depressed that they aren't feeling very positive about anything; or else they're so wrapped up in their own problems that they really don't have the mental energy to observe the positive things other people are doing. A similar mentality is expressed by "If it ain't broke, don't fix it": if things are going well and done well, that means you don't have to do anything. The approval of things being done well is, however, often the preventive maintenance that's absolutely necessary if things are to continue to go well.

The following is a table of things people can say to create and maintain a positive emotional climate in relationships. I believe it's not too simplistic to say that, if people will simply watch for the opportunities to say these sorts of things and say them more often, a great deal of good can be done.

Things to say to create a good emotional climate

Expressing gladness that the other person is here: Good morning! Good afternoon! Good evening! I'm glad to see you! It's good to see you! Welcome home! Hi!

Expressing gratitude and appreciation: Thanks for doing that for me! I really appreciate what you did. I'm glad you told me that! Yes, please! That's nice of you to do that for me! This is a big help to me. Thanks for saying that!

Reinforcing a good performance of the other person: You did a good job! That's interesting! Good going! Good point! Good job! Congratulations to you! You did well on that! That's pretty smart!

Positive feelings about the world and the things and events in it: Wonderful! That's really great! Wow! Hooray! I'm so glad it happened like that! Sounds good! Look how beautiful that is!

Wishing well for the other person's future: I hope you have a good day. Have a nice day! Good luck to you! I wish you the best on (the thing you're doing).

Offering help or accepting a request for help: May I help you with that? I'd like to help you with that. I'll do that for you! I'm going to do this job so you won't have to do it! Would you like me to show you how I do that? I'd be happy to do that for you!

Expressing positive feelings about oneself: I feel good about something I did. Want to hear about it? Hooray, I feel so good about that!

Being forgiving and tolerating frustration: That's OK; don't worry about it. It's no problem. I can handle it. I can take it. It's not the end of the world.

Expressing interest in the other person: How was your day today? How are you? How have you been doing? How have things been going? So let me see if I understand you right. You feel that _____. So in other words, you're saying _____. I'd like to hear more about that! I'm curious about that. Tell me more.

Consoling the other person: I'm sorry you had to go through that. I'm sorry that happened to you.

Apologizing or Giving In: I'm sorry I said that. I apologize for doing that. I think you're right about that. Upon thinking about it more, I've decided I was wrong. I'll go along with what you want on that.

Being Assertive in a Nice Way: Here's another option. Here's the option I would favor. An advantage of this plan is . . . A disadvantage of that option is . . . Unfortunately, I can't do it. I'd prefer not to. No, I'm sorry; I don't want to do that. It's very important that you do this.

You can increase your ability to say these positive utterances by using fantasy rehearsal. A very useful exercise is to go through this list, and to vividly imagine yourself saying each utterance to someone in your family or your social network.

Skill 48: Social Initiations

Social initiations are how people get started talking together or playing together or interacting.

Most people seem to need to do things with other people a fair portion of their waking moments, rather than staying alone. People are social animals. Sometimes when people don't know good ways of making social initiations, they'll fall into bad ways simply because they need interaction of some sort.

For example, a boy at school doesn't know exactly how to start talking with another boy and get interaction going well, so he walks over and pushes the other kid. Or he comes up and grabs something away from the other child and runs off with it. This child's motive is simply to start some social interaction. If he can figure out better ways of doing it, he won't need to do it in ways that make other people angry.

There are differences in the ways popular and unpopular children do social initiations, according to one study. Unpopular children tend to do social initiations in a way that interrupts what other children were doing. For example, they ask a question about something the other child is not paying attention to, or make a statement about a new topic, or request that people stop doing something else to look at them and play with them.

The popular children, on the other hand, tend to go up and check out the scene and see what the other children are doing. Then they join in with what they're doing. That way they don't interrupt them or pull their attention away from what they're working on. So being too pushy and too demanding of other people's attention is not the best way to start interacting.

On the other side of the coin, some people are too shy. They find it hard to get themselves to make social initiations. Often this is because they fear they'll make a mistake. So there's an issue of balance. If you're too pushy and intrusive, you might turn people off, but if you're too scared of being pushy and intrusive, you won't get social initiation started.

As people get older, their social initiations are more likely to be verbal, whereas those of younger children are more likely to be simply joining in playing.

When people get older, it becomes simpler to make social initiations. It's very easy simply to go up to someone and say, "Hi, how are you? My name is Peter," and most of the time the person will say their name back. The next step in the social initiation process is usually some sort of question about the other person. At the beginning, this should be not a personal question, but something very nonthreatening. Examples of non-personal questions are: "You just moved into this neighborhood a while ago, didn't you?" or, "Have you been coming here long?"

When one is doing this simple act, there are several things to keep in mind. One is the importance of making eye contact first. If you don't make eye contact first, the other person will probably not know exactly whom you're talking to. When people have said things to me without making eye contact first, I've usually looked in the direction they were looking to see if someone was there. At times I've asked, "Are you speaking to me?" You can avoid putting someone in this position by looking at her when you speak to her.

Walking up to someone and introducing yourself is best done in a context or social situation where people expect others to introduce themselves. For example, when people are neighbors, or when people are standing around at a party, or when people are working in the same building or going to school in the same class, there's an unwritten rule that it's polite and nice to make social initiations.

On the other hand, suppose someone were to walk up and introduce himself in a grocery store, or while walking down a sidewalk on a busy city street, or while standing in an elevator. The other person might experience it as strange, simply because these aren't situations where people customarily introduce themselves. The unwritten rule

seems to be that if you're in a situation where you'll be seeing each other again, it's expected you will introduce yourself. If you're in a situation where strangers commonly pass one another without speaking or acknowledging one another, you're not expected to introduce yourself.

To make things more complicated, in some situations where it would feel strange to start social interaction by introducing yourself, it would not feel strange for one person to start a conversation without introducing himself. For example: Let's imagine that two people are standing together waiting for a bus to come. It would feel natural for one person to say to the other person, "Do you ride this bus often enough to know whether it usually comes on time?" Whereas it might feel a little strange if the person were to say, "Hi, my name is John Smith. What's your name?"

Here are some other examples of this idea of starting a conversation but not introducing yourself first. Suppose two people are now sitting on the bus together. Or, let's say two people are sitting next to each other in the type of crowded restaurant where people sit at the same table with one another, for example, at food courts. Or people are sitting close to one another on the side of a swimming pool or are in the pool close together. In many of these situations it seems more socially acceptable to make social initiation in a way that says, "I want to talk to you for some reason other than just wanting to make friends." When people really do want to make friends in situations like these, they sometimes play a game of cooking up some other reason to start talking to one another.

What we've said so far has to do with social initiations toward strangers. Now, let's talk about social initiations with people you do know.

Suppose that Gina and Suzanne are in a class together and they see each other often. Then one day, they're both at the grocery store, and Gina notices Suzanne, but Gina is too shy to do a social greeting ritual. Gina turns her eyes away to avoid eye contact with Suzanne. She doesn't say anything, and she walks past looking at the cans on the grocery store shelf. If Suzanne sees this, Suzanne might feel offended. She might imagine Gina isn't saying "Hi" because she doesn't like her, rather than just because she's shy.

So a very important rule of social relationships is that, when you see someone you know, you look them in the eye and say "Hi" to them. It's much better if you remember their name and remember to say their name. If Gina had simply looked over at Suzanne and said, "Hi Suzanne," that would have changed the whole situation around. If she had smiled while saying it, that would have been even better.

Of course, once Gina does this, Suzanne should definitely say, "Hi, Gina," and smile back. If someone says hello to you and you don't say hello back, that's almost always taken as a sign of unfriendliness. Failing to greet someone you know and failing to return a greeting from someone you know are two social errors people should avoid making. Why turn people off by making these errors when it's so easy just to say "Hi"?

Often if people want to continue social contact after saying, "Hi," they'll go to "How are you?" or "How are you doing?" If they know each other really well, or if they want to signal they have time for a longer conversation, they'll answer the "How are you?" by really telling about things that have happened to them.

For example: When Suzanne says, "How are you doing?" and Gina says, "Doing okay now, but there was a real scare. My brother was lost for two hours!" On the other hand, if people don't know each other well or can't spend time chatting, the answer to "How are you?" is something like, "Doing fine. How are you?"

Of course, when people know each other well, they can initiate social contact in all sorts of creative and interesting ways. They don't have to be quite so careful. They can skip the greeting ritual altogether, if they want.

Gina might go up to Suzanne, and initiate social contact by saying, "Suzanne, are you still surviving after that test today!" Or she might immediately start off by saying, "Looks like you pick the grocery store that all the smart people pick, huh?" or whatever.

The important thing is that people like the existence of the relationship to be acknowledged by the other person. This applies to members of your own family as well.

Let's imagine you're sitting in the front room of your house looking at a magazine and a family member who has been out comes into the house. Suppose you continue to read the magazine and ignore the other person as he comes into the house. What message is the other person getting from this? It probably goes something like "I'm not glad to see you; I don't care whether you're here or not."

On the other hand, suppose the family member comes home and the first sentence out of your mouth is, "I need to borrow some money tonight, please." What is your family member likely to think about this sort of social initiation? Probably the family member will just think. "This person is not really interested in me. They just want to get something out of me."

On the other hand, let's imagine that the family member who's home runs to the front door and says, "Hello! I'm glad to see you! How did things go for you today?" Now the person coming home is probably feeling very valued by the interest the person shows. So much good feeling can be generated by such small amounts of effort, that it's a shame when people pass up the opportunities to create good feelings in these ways.

What's the group of people with whom it's most important to have good relationships? Usually that group is family members. Making enthusiastic social initiations is one way to get interactions between family members started out on the right foot. These social initiations acknowledge the other person and give a message that you value the other person.

When we talked about expressing positive feelings, we talked about the importance of tone of voice and facial expression. The same thing goes with social initiations. The two words – "hello" and a person's name – can be said with an almost infinite number of tones of voice and facial expressions that will communicate everything from, "I hate you!" or "I'm in love with you," to "I feel guilty about what I just did, and I want your forgiveness," to "I've been waiting to see you for a long time and I'm overjoyed to see you."

One exercise is to just say "hello" and someone's name in as many tones of voice as you can simply to get the feeling of the wide variety of facial expressions and tones of voice that can be used. If you can greet someone in an enthusiastic way, this is a simple way to give a little happiness and pleasure to someone.

Greeting rituals vary from sub-culture to sub-culture in our society, and some of them change quickly with the times. One sub-culture might say, "How do you do?" while another says, "How are you doing?" Another might say,

"What's up, man?" and another might say, "What's happening?" Although greeting rituals go in and out of fashion, they all mean the same thing: "I acknowledge you; you're at least a little important to me; we can talk further if you wish."

Skill 49: Socializing

The art of social conversation is the art of continuing friendly talk after the social initiation has been made. What do you say after you say "hi"?

We can think of social conversation in terms of content and process. The content is what people talk about: the weather, their work, their family members, their ideas on how to make the world better, and the conditions under which happiness occurs. The process has to do with how long each person talks before letting the other talk, whether they interrupt each other, how they signal it's time for the other to take a turn, how they jointly decide on a topic, and so forth. This process has been called the "pragmatics" of conversation.

First let's think about the content of conversation. What sort of things do people find out about each other as they talk and get to know each other better? We can use the word "Paper" as a mnemonic for topics of "getting to know you" conversation. Each of the five letters in the word "Paper" stands for a topic area, as follows:

P = Places
A = Activities
P = People
E = Events
R = Reactions and Ideas

Here are some examples of things people find out in each of these areas:

PLACES:
Where do you live?
Where did you live before you came here?
How long have you been living here?
Whose class are you in?
What school are you in?
Where do you go after school?
Where do you like to go the most?
What are your favorite places?

ACTIVITIES:
What do you like to do for fun?
What are your favorite things to do?
What are your least favorite things to do?
Do you have any hobbies?
What are your favorite foods to eat?
What are your favorite games to play?
What are your favorite books?
What sports do you like to play?
What games do you like to play?
Do you play a musical instrument?
Do you like acting?
Do you like art?

PEOPLE:
Do you have any brothers or sisters?
How old are they?
Who else is in your family?
What do they like?
Who are some of your friends?
Tell me about your friends?

Do you have cousins and aunts and uncles?
Do you have grandparents?
Tell me about your other family members?
Do you have any animals?
What are your animals like?

EVENTS:
What have you been up to lately?
What has been happening to you?
Are you going on vacation anytime soon?
What are you going to do over the summer?
Do you have any fun things planned?
What's the scariest thing that ever happened to you?
What's the funniest thing that ever happened to you?
What event are you looking forward to the most?
What are you dreading the most?

REACTIONS/IDEAS: (Includes the person's responses to any of the above named things.)
How did you feel when that happened?
Do you like that place?
What was your reaction to moving from one place to another?
Do you still like doing that activity, or have you begun to tire of it?
What's your reaction to this particular person?
What are your ideas/reactions about events happening in the news?

IDEAS ABOUT LIFE AND CURRENT EVENTS:
Ideas about how to reduce violence
Ideas about the problem of poverty
Ideas about the problem of pollution of the environment
Religious ideas
Philosophical ideas
Most important ideas to live by

These are some of the areas of content that people talk about as they're getting to know each other or long after they've gotten to know each other.

Let's remind ourselves of something we talked about earlier, when discussing the skill of intimacy and self-disclosure. When you're just starting to get to know someone, you want to ask about, and tell about, areas that are not too threatening, not too "heavy," things that will have a safe bet of not making the other person uncomfortable. As you gradually get to know the other person better, you can venture into more risky territory, because now you know what will make the other person comfortable or uncomfortable.

For example, let's imagine you're talking with someone for the first time, and the person asks, "Do you ever have problems with constipation?" or, "Do your parents fight with each other much?" If you're like most people, you'd be inclined to think, "That's none of your business!" or "Don't be so nosy!" On the other hand, if the person asked, "Did you hear the weather report for today?" or "What sorts of things do you like to do the most?" then, if you're like most people, you wouldn't consider these questions too nosy at all.

The same principle applies to what people tell each other about themselves. Suppose someone you didn't even know came up to you and started talking with you, and said, "I've got this problem about my feet stinking. When I take off my shoes, the people in my house want to throw me out." Or suppose the person said, "I can't stand my little brother. Sometimes I have these horrible fantasies about what I want to do to him. They even scare me, that I think this way."

You'd probably feel that something strange was going on. Why would a person who doesn't know me at all be telling me such intimate details? On the other hand, if the person said, "Boy, I love this cloudy weather. This is my favorite type of day," or if you were eating and the person said, "I think this lasagna is great! I wonder how they made it so good!" then these are very nonthreatening details that would make almost no one uncomfortable.

So in social conversation, be aware of how personal any given question or statement is. Also be aware of how well you know the other person and how much that person feels comfortable with the topic you're thinking of asking or telling about. You want to make the topic fit the person's tolerance for it.

People can make errors in either direction on this. On the one hand, if

you tell or ask about personal issues when you don't know the other person well, you make the other person think you're strange. On the other hand, if you continue to confine your conversation only to the least threatening topics, like the weather and sports, as you get to know a person better and better, the person might feel bored with you or think you're superficial.

Now let's think about the process, the pragmatics of conversation.

One way not to do social conversation is just to go through the list of PAPER topics above and ask every one of these questions one by one. This would probably feel very unnatural. If you were to do that, the other person would probably feel as if you were filling in a form, rather than having a regular social conversation. Another way not to do social conversation is to tell the other person the answers to those questions about yourself, without stopping. In this case, the other person might be thinking, "Who asked you?" or "I wish he would shut up."

When the "pragmatics" of conversation are going well, the two people explore together what topic to talk about, and by sending messages to each other, sometimes in subtle ways, they come up with a topic that's interesting to both of them. They give signals to each other about what they're interested in and what they're not interested in, and they each pick up on the other person's signals. They finally land on something that gives both of them fun to think and talk about.

There's something else very important that also happens when the pragmatics of conversation go well. The two people give each other signals that allow them to take turns, to decide who gets to talk at any given moment. They work it out so they take turns talking and listening in a way that feels good for both of them.

A third thing happens when the pragmatics are going well: the two people give each other evidence that they're listening to each other. They show that what the other person says has registered with them, that it has made an impact on them in some way. They respond to the other person's words and signals; they don't each have a preset speech they take turns giving.

The term we use to describe a conversation where two people take turns responding to each other is *reciprocal interaction*. This doesn't happen when one person talks and the other just listens. It doesn't happen when one person asks a preset list of questions and the other answers them. It happens when each person listens to the other person and says something back that shows that he listened.

For most people, it's fun to talk when each person influences the thoughts and words of the other. The two people are going along together on a thinking trip, and both of them have a say in the direction of this trip. On the other hand, when the first person goes off in his own direction without picking up on the signals about where the second person would like to go, the second person usually feels discomfort or irritation. Sometimes the second person doesn't even know why she's feeling irritated, but just knows the other person "rubs her the wrong way."

Conversation with another person is not something you do with your mouth only; you do it with your ears and your brain. You listen very carefully to what the other person is saying, and you let it sink in and think about it. It's sometimes hard work to pay attention to what the other person is saying. Often you'd rather be thinking about something else. But if you don't want to listen when someone else is speaking, try to excuse yourself altogether from the conversation. One sure way to turn off someone else is to "tune out" while she's talking to you, and for her to realize nothing she's saying is registering in your mind.

How do you avoid irritating people by not giving them enough say in how the conversation goes? We can list some guidelines on how to do this.

One guideline is to stop talking frequently so you can let the other person react to what you've said. When you see the other person's reaction, you can tell whether the conversation is on the right track, or whether the direction should be changed. Stopping talking usually means that you don't talk for more than a minute without stopping.

The second guideline is that, when you stop talking, and even while you're talking, pay close attention to the other person's reaction. Use the information you get to decide whether the conversation is on track or not. Suppose that while you're talking, the person is looking around the room, looking at other people, starting to fiddle with something in his hands, looking up at the ceiling, taking a big breath, sighing, looking at his watch, looking bored. You're getting clear signals that should tell you, "Stop talking now, whether you're finished or not. Get the other person's reaction so as to get the conversation back on the right track."

Suppose that while you're talking, the person is looking right at your face, is nodding, is saying "Uh huh," every now and then, and is looking very interested. Then you're getting signals the conversation is on the right track.

Suppose that when you stop talking, the other person changes the subject. Or suppose the other person doesn't say anything at all about what you were just talking about. Then you're getting a signal the other person doesn't want to continue along this line. You're getting a signal that you should invite the other person to pick a topic, such as by saying, "So, what have you been up to lately?" On the other hand, if when you stop talking, the other person looks very thoughtful, as if they're processing what you just said and thinking of a reply, then you should wait for them to reply to what you've said.

Here's another guideline. In the conversations that occur in most relationships, you should have a balance between telling about your own experience and paying attention to the other person's experience. If you're telling about things that happened to you, and thoughts and feelings you've had or that you're having, and things about your own life, then you're telling about your own experience. If you're listening to what the other person is saying about her own experience, or asking about the other person's experience, or asking the other person to tell you more, or checking out whether you heard it right, then you're paying attention to the other person's experience.

Some people tend to tell about their own experience too much. Other people don't reveal anything about their own experience, and can only have conversations with people who are content to tell about their own experience all the time. Someone who's good at the pragmatics of conversation will have a balance between talking and listening, one that's suitable both to herself and to the other person. Of course, any one conversation may focus on one or the other person more than the other. Not every conversation has to be balanced. But over time, it's good that balance take place.

In thinking about the process of conversation, it's useful to define some words to refer to the types of things people say. If you know words for these ways of talking, you can think more clearly about how you want to achieve a balance of them in your conversation. We've already talked about telling about your own experience and paying attention to the other person's experience. Let's list some other types of utterances under each of those.

1. Telling about your own experience:
    1.1: New topic statements
    1.2: Follow-up statements
2. Paying attention to the other person's experience:
    2.1 New topic questions
    2.2 Follow-up questions
    2.3 Facilitations
    2.4 Reflections
    2.5 Tracking and describing

Let's define these. Telling about your experience, as we have already said, is telling any of your thoughts or feelings, recounting anything that has happened to you, telling what you're going to do in the future, telling your ideas. In other words, it's giving any information at all that resides in your brain to the other person. In computer jargon, it's uploading information from you to the other person. If the statement you make changes the topic, we call that a new topic statement. If it's on the same topic the other person was already talking about, we call it a follow-up statement.

For example: Let's say one person says, "I have a dog; I love to spend lots of time taking care of him and playing with him," and the other one says, "I belong to the Catholic Church." That's a new topic statement. On the other hand, if the second person says, "I have a dog too; mine is a Labrador." That's a follow-up statement because it's on the same topic the first person was discussing.

Suppose the other person says, "Oh, so playing with your dog is one of your favorite things to do, huh? One of my favorite things to do is to play basketball." In a sense, this would still count as a follow-up statement because it's still on the topic of things we like to do, even though it isn't on the topic of dogs.

As you can tell from the examples given so far, the more your "telling about your own experience" comes in response to, and is on the same topic as, what the other person was just talking about, the more natural and pleasant the conversation feels. In other words, the more your comments come in the form of follow-up statements, the better, because this doesn't jerk the other person's attention away from something and onto something else.

On the other hand, often you finish talking about some topic, and you can feel that you and the other person are finished with that. At times like this, new topic statements are good. When telling about your own experience, you should work for a balance. The best balance is usually loaded heavily in the direction of follow-up statements.

When you request information to be "downloaded" from the other person's brain to yours, or signal that you're receiving it and want to keep receiving it, you're paying attention to the other person's experience.

Questions can be either follow-up questions or new topic questions, depending on whether they're on the same topic the person is already talking about or whether they introduce a new topic.

Suppose someone says, "I have a dog, and I spend a lot of time taking care of him." and the other person says, "Oh, what kind is he?" Or suppose she says, "Oh, how do you play with him? What sort of things do you do with your dog?" These are follow-up questions. On the other hand, if the second person were to say, "Do you like your teacher at school?" That's a new topic question; it changes the subject.

You want to achieve a balance between follow-up questions and new topic questions. The best balance usually has many more follow-up questions than new topic questions. That way, the other person will not have the sensation you're jerking her attention around from topic to topic in a way that may be unpleasant to her.

What is a facilitation? By this word, we refer to the little grunts and utterances that don't mean much, other than "I'm receiving your message; keep going." Here are some examples of facilitations.

"Oh?"
"Is that right?"

"Hmmm.",
"What do you know!"
"That's interesting."
"Umm Hmmm."
"Yes."
"Wow."

These little utterances are all translated to mean, "I'm listening to you; I'm hearing what you're saying; please feel permission to keep going." Looking at the other person and nodding is also a facilitation, even though it isn't done in words. The word "facilitation" means something that makes something else easier. When you send these little messages, you make it easier for the other person to talk, because they know you're listening.

A reflection is the most complex type of utterance. This is a statement that says, "What I hear you saying is _____." or, "The message I'm getting from you is _____."

Here's an example of someone's using reflections, based on the conversation about the dog we talked about earlier.

First person: I have a dog, and I spend lots of time taking care of him and playing with him.

Second person: Sounds like that dog is a real good friend of yours.

First person: Yeah. I'd really be upset if anything ever happened to him. He's really been so close to me for so long.

Second person: He's really valuable to you.

First person: Yes, and I worry about that, because he's getting old. He is eleven in people years, but I know that in dog years, he's getting up there.

Second person: It must not feel good to know he'll be leaving you some day.

First person: It bothers me, and I don't guess that there's anything I can do about that, but at least I can take good care of him and help him enjoy whatever life he has left.

Second person: So, you know you can't keep him from aging, but at least you can help him have a happy life for the rest of it, huh?

The art of doing accurate, empathic reflections is difficult. It involves really listening very closely to what the other person says. It involves saying back to the other person what you hear, but not just parroting back the other person's own words. You translate the meaning of what the person says into your own words. The art of listening in this way is so important that I've listed it as a separate skill, the skill of listening.

Tracking and describing is like a reflection, only it's naming the other person's physical actions rather than their verbal message. For example, suppose an adult is watching a child make up a bed. The adult says, "There goes one corner of the sheet, nice and tight . . . and there goes the other. Now the blanket . . . and now the bedspread! There go the pillows, and you've done it!" This is tracking and describing. For a second example, suppose an adult is watching a child play with a puzzle: "There's an interesting piece. You're looking for where it fits. You found it! There it goes. On to the next one." This is tracking and describing.

The most natural and pleasant conversations are usually those where there are mixtures of several of the types of utterances we've mentioned so far. If you have conversations where you don't ever do reflections or facilitations or follow-up questions or statements, you're probably not listening much to the other person. If you have conversations where you're constantly making new topic questions and statements rather than follow-up questions and statements, you're probably not focusing on any topic. If you don't ever tell about your own experience, you may be acting shy or guarded. If you don't pay enough attention to the other person's experience, you may be focused on yourself. If any of these things are not OK with the other person, there's a problem.

Of course, it's possible to carry the idea of balance too far. You don't want to feel that every conversation has to have a certain distribution of these utterances. When someone else is really into talking about something, for instance, and you're very interested in hearing it, the other person may simply go on and on telling about their own experience, and you may go on and on doing little but facilitations. And that can be fine with both people. The goal is that both people seem satisfied with the conversation, not that you have a certain mathematical ratio of utterances. Still, keeping in mind the types of utterances and trying to keep a balance can be a guideline that may make it easier to achieve the goal of creating a satisfying experience for both people.

Let's introduce more words that help us think about the pragmatics of conversation. Two important concepts are overlong statements and interruptions. When someone goes on talking for much over a minute without letting the other person have a chance to talk or at least do a reflection or a facilitation, the chances are that person is making an overlong statement. The other person may be getting restless and may want to say something, but not getting the chance to and may be feeling frustrated.

Overlong statements tend to lead other people to do interruptions. In fact, sometimes the only way to get some people to stop talking is to interrupt them. But this is usually not pleasant for the people having to interrupt.

Sometimes people talk to each other at the same time. This is called overtalk. When both people are talking, who is listening? This defeats the whole point of communicating. The fewer overlong statements people make, the less need there is for interruptions and overtalk.

People often tend to interrupt each other when they get into an arguing mood. When someone interrupts you in an argument, you have two reasons to be angry. The first is hearing that you're wrong. The second is that you couldn't finish saying what you wanted to say, that you couldn't feel that you were heard. Thus interrupting simply adds fuel to the flame of anger when people argue with each other.

Thus   when two people have a problem they're trying to solve together, it's very important for them to discipline themselves to stop talking, to listen to what the other person is saying, to make sure they understand the other person correctly, and only then to come out with their own idea. This takes lots of self-control, and many people don't know how to do this well.

Let's add two more terms to our list of ways of talking about the process of conversation. Let's think about the difference between open-ended questions and specific questions.

An open-ended question gives the other person lots of latitude as to what he wants to talk about. For example: "Tell me about yourself" is a very open-ended question. Or if someone says, "I went on vacation recently," and the other person says, "Oh, tell me about it," that's an open-ended question. If the other person were to say, "Oh, what was it like?" or "How was it?" those would be open-ended questions. On the other hand, if someone were to say, "Where did you go?" or "How long were you gone?" those would be specific questions. If the person says, "Did you have a good time?" that's a specific question. Questions that you answer yes or no or with a short answer are specific.

The good conversationalist knows that open-ended questions will give the other person the most freedom to land on a topic the person would most like to land on. On the other hand, specific questions give the other person the best idea of what the questioner wants to hear about. Sometimes the other person mainly wants freedom; sometimes he's most comfortable with direction. To be the best conversationalist, you ask in a way that makes the other person most comfortable. But you keep in mind that things can change at any point. After breaking the ice with a few specific questions, the person you're talking to might want to have the freedom of some open-ended questions.

Or sometimes you let people land on a topic with an open-ended question, and show your interest in that by asking more specific questions. For example, someone asks an open-ended question, "What have you been up to?" This would let someone answer by telling almost any of his or her recent experiences, thoughts, or ideas. Suppose the other person answers by saying, "Oh, I'm pretty tired today; I just got through chopping down a very big tree." Now the person has defined a topic he's interested in, and now the first person can ask more specific ques-

tions about this topic, such as, "Oh, how did you happen to have to cut a tree down?" "Where was it?" or "How did you cut it down? With an ax or a saw?" "How did you keep it from falling over on you?" etc. The more specific questions usually feel good to people once they've been allowed to land on a topic they're interested in.

Open-ended questions are good because they give the other person freedom. Specific questions are good because they probe into areas the other person might not have thought about mentioning, and they might stimulate the other person to think of things they haven't thought of before. They also give the other person the clear indication you're interested in the topic you're asking about.

There's something else about your conversation that's perhaps most important of all. When the other person says something, your response usually communicates a message that says "I approve," or "I don't approve," or "I don't care." One of the things that makes another person want to talk with you is getting signals of approval and excitement from you in response to what they say.

Suppose someone says, "I just won a prize for a math contest." Suppose you respond with a facilitation, and say, "Is that right!" in a very excited, happy, and approving tone of voice. The person has been reinforced for talking to you.

On the other hand, suppose when the person says, "I just won a prize for a math contest," you say, "Oh, you did, huh," in a very sarcastic tone of voice, as though you think the person is bragging too much. Now the person is being punished for telling you this.

Now suppose when the person tells you about the math contest, your response is, "I'm going to be taking a vacation soon." The person is getting the message, "I don't care about what you told me," and will probably feel hurt or angry.

You can use facilitation such as, "Oh, is that right?" or "What do you know?" or "Humh," in all sorts of different tones of voice. These tones can communicate anything from, "I'm bored with this," to "This is about the most exciting thing I've ever heard of." If you can consistently give the other person the message, "What you have to say is interesting, good, and worthwhile," you'll always have friends. Almost everyone in the world wants to be around someone who finds what they have to say noteworthy, pleasing, and smart.

Let's put together a rating scale by which people can measure whether they've followed the guidelines we just gave for any bit of conversation. This also draws some from the ideas discussed for the skill of listening.

Rating Scale for Conversations

0 = Not successful at all

2 = Only a little success
4 = Some success
6 = Pretty much success
8 = High degree of success
10 = Very high degree of success

1. Did you tune in to, and respond to, the signals from the other person about whether the content of the conversation, the topic, was something the other person was interested in?

2. Was the content of the conversation not too "personal" so as to be threatening to the other person, but personal enough to be interesting?

3. Did you do your part toward making a good balance between telling about your own experience and paying attention to the other person's experience?

4. Did you talk enough so that the other person didn't have to feel that having a conversation was too much effort on his part?

5. Did you stop talking soon enough that the other person had plenty of chances to influence the direction of the conversation?

6. Did you take turns talking and listening in a way that seemed to feel good for the other person? (Usually this means there's no need for interruptions or overtalk.)

7. When the other person talked, did you respond in a way that showed you had listened?

8. Did you show you had paid attention to the other person with some

facilitations, follow-up questions, and follow-up statements?

9. Did you use reflections to show you had paid attention to the other person?

10. If you used reflections, did you put them into your own words rather than just "parroting" by repeating the exact words of the other person?

11. If you used reflections, were they accurate in expressing what the other person said and how strong the person's feelings were?

12. Did your responses to what the other person said reinforce that person for talking with you? In other words, did you give messages of approval and enthusiasm about what the other person said, with your tone of voice and with your words?

13. If you asked questions, did you choose well between open-ended questions (to allow the other person to land on a topic of her own choosing) and specific questions (to show interest in a particular topic)?

14. Did you give eye contact to the other person a reasonable portion of the time, especially when the other person was talking, but not steadily stare at the other person?

15. Was a good portion of what you said of a positive, upbeat nature?

16. How much do you think the other person enjoyed this conversation?

Skill 50: Listening

This has already been mentioned as part of the skills of social conversation, but it's so important that it deserves a listing of its own.

What do we mean by being a good listener? Partly we mean being able to use facilitations and to make follow-up questions and follow-up statements that show the other person we're responding to what they said, not just giving a prearranged speech.

One of the things most central to the skill of listening is the art of doing good empathic reflections.

What is a reflection? It's a statement or question where you say back to the other person what you heard from them, to make sure you got it right.

Sometimes the easiest way to learn to do reflections is to prompt yourself with some "fill in the blank" sentences.

Prompts for doing reflections

So you're saying _____?"
"What I hear you saying is _____?"
"In other words, _____?"
"So if I understand you right, _____?"
"It sounds like _____,"
"Are you saying that _____?"
"You're saying that _____."

In the practice exercise, you listen to the other person tell or read a story or just talk about what's on his mind. Each time the other person stops, you respond in one of these ways, and fill in the blank with whatever you understood the other to say. After you've done this for a while, you can leave out the first part of each of these sentences and just fill in the blank. That's another way to do a reflection.

Here's an example of two people doing this exercise.

First person: "Sometimes I think I should just not watch the news and read the newspaper any more. It's so depressing, all the violence that's going on these days."

Second person: "So you're saying you find the violence so discouraging that you get the urge to just shield yourself from any news of it, huh?"

First person: "Yes. It really makes me sad when I hear of someone hurting or killing another person. It's all so needless and unnecessary."

Second person: "What I hear you saying is, it gets you down when you hear of violent things going on because it all seems such a waste."

First person: "Yes, it's a waste because it could all be prevented if we would just put the effort into stopping it. I don't think I realized this before.

Before, I just thought it was just part of the nature of human beings to be violent. But, now that I think it could be prevented, it bothers me even more than ever to see it going on."

Second person: "In other words, if you felt there was nothing that anybody could do about it, then you would accept it more. But because you think it can be stopped, it bothers you more. Is that right?"

First person: "Yes. There are so many things we could do to stop it, like getting rid of guns; we could teach people conflict resolution; we could teach people to be nicer to one another from a very early age; we could stop entertaining ourselves by watching people hurt each other so much. There are all sorts of things we could do."

Second person: "So if I understand you right, you know all sorts of ways to try to stop violence, and it bothers you that people don't do them more, right?"

First person: "That's right. But you know something? It's a good kind of being bothered. It's a being bothered that I want to have. It gives me a sense of direction and purpose. I wouldn't like to go back to the place where I feel numb to it."

Second person: "It sounds like you would rather feel bad about the violence, because that dissatisfaction will propel you to do good things to try to end it?"

First person: "Yes, that's right."

People don't often get into the pattern of one person speaking and the other person reflecting every time he opens his mouth. But doing this is a very good exercise. It helps you practice listening and concentrating on what someone else is saying.

Why are empathic reflections so important? Why would the world be a lot better if people did more reflections?

Let's list some reasons here. First, people very often misunderstand one another, and reflections can prevent a lot of misunderstanding. It's not surprising that people misunderstand one another so much. In order for an idea to be communicated from one person's mind to another's, the first person has to translate the idea into words, and the second has to translate those words back into the idea. Whenever translation takes place, there can be errors. The first person can make a mistake when choosing the words he uses to communicate the idea. The second can make a mistake in interpreting those words. A great deal of anger comes from people's misunderstanding one another.

But when the listener reflects, he translates the idea back into other words and sends it back to the speaker. If the speaker recognizes it as the correct message, both people now know that understanding has taken place. If the speaker sees that the original idea is not correctly reflected, he has a chance to say, "No, that's not what I meant to communicate to you. Let me try it again." They can keep trying until understanding is confirmed.

Another purpose served by reflections is to help people be *nondirective* with one another. When you ask a new topic question or even a follow-up question, you're directing the person's line of thought. You're telling them, "Think about this and give me the answer to it." When you give advice to them, you're seeking to direct their thought and their actions. "Think about doing this and then do it."

Reflections, by contrast, don't direct the person to do anything, other than just to confirm that the message was heard right. The speaker can then decide what he wants to say next. He's given the freedom to let his mind go wherever it wants to. Certain therapists who use a lot of reflections are sometimes called non-directive therapists. Just having someone listen to you without directing you can often be very helpful.

Reflections also send what I have called a "value message" to the other person: a message of, "I care about you; I'm interested in you; I value you." Why do reflections communicate these things? On the one hand, they let the other person see that "I'm working really hard to understand and hear and remember the messages you're giving me," and, on the other hand, they say, "I'm giving you the freedom to decide what you want to say next and what you want to do next." For this reason, most people find it's pretty pleasant to speak with someone who can do accurate empathic reflections.

Reflections are also very useful when the first person is talking about a problem, because they let the first person continue to own the problem and to be in charge of solving it. They don't transfer ownership of the problem to the listener. Reflections prevent something from happening that happens quite often: the first person starts talking about the problem. The second starts to assume ownership of the problem and tries to solve it. The second gives advice. But the first doesn't want that advice, and rejects the second person's plan. The second person becomes angry at the first for not accepting his solution to the problem.

In other words:

The first person says, "I've got this problem."

The second person says, "Why don't you try this?"

The first person says, "I have tried it, it doesn't work."

The second person says, "How about this instead?"

The first person says, "That wouldn't work either."

They continue like this until after a while the second person becomes angry at the first person and says, "Well, if you don't want any of the solutions I have to offer, why did you even bring the subject up?"

And, maybe the first person is thinking, "I didn't want you to try to solve my problem, I just wanted you to listen while I tried to work on it and solve it myself."

As a general rule, the person who has the problem knows a lot more about the situation than the person who has just heard about it. So it's often very important to let the first continue to own the problem rather than try to take it on yourself.

These are some of the "whys" of empathic reflection. Let's now talk about the "hows." It's a very difficult art. One of the mistakes some people make when they're just beginning to practice this skill is called "parroting the code." If you parrot the code, instead of really receiving the message the other person is giving you and then translating it into your own language, you just repeat the language the other person used. A parroting reflection confirms only that you heard what they said and not that you understood what they meant.

For example:

The first person has been working on writing an article for a long time. The first person says: "Oh, I'm about to crash!"

The second person reflects: "So, you're just about to crash, huh?"

The first person's reaction to this might be, "Yes, that's what I said. Why are you repeating it back to me?"

The first person has a right to be puzzled because this reflection is just a simple repetition of the words the first person used.

On the other hand, suppose the second person said, "So you're really sick of working on that article?"

Then perhaps the first person says, "No, actually I'm enjoying it thoroughly. It's just that I'm about to crash because I'm so exhausted. I've been up so long, and I'm really sleepy."

The second person says, "Oh, now I see. You're still enthusiastic about it, but you need some rest, huh?"

The first person says, "Yes."

So you do a reflection that really accomplishes something when you translate the other person's message into your own words. If the person still confirms that this is what she meant to say, a meeting of the minds has taken place.

To translate the other person's message into your own words is one thing; to change it around by adding your own ideas and opinions is another. For example, suppose a high school kid says to his father, "I've been thinking of taking off a year and working before I go to college. I could get a job as a waiter in a restaurant, or working construction, or anything for a while."

Suppose the father says, "So, what I hear you saying is you'd rather spend a year of your life in mindless, low-class work rather than cultivating your mind to really do something useful and get ahead."

This is not an empathic reflection. This is a little editorial by the father. If you're going to give advice or an editorial, don't disguise it in the format of an empathic reflection.

Making some guesses as to what the other person is thinking and feeling, or as to why they are thinking and feeling that way, is often a legitimate and good part of doing an empathic reflection.

For example: A girl says, "That brother of mine, I could just lock him up!"

The listener reflects: "Sounds like your brother must have done something recently that really got you angry, huh?"

Here the listener is guessing a little bit, rather than just purely reflecting what she heard, but it's a reasonable guess and if it's wrong, the speaker can always correct the listener.

On the other hand, suppose the first person says, "That brother of mine! I could just lock him up!"

Suppose the second person says, "Sounds like you're really angry at your brother because you want your mother's attention and he's always getting her attention when you want it, huh?" The first person would have every right to say, "Where did you get that idea?" It may or may not be correct, but it's not a reflection of the message the person was trying to send.

Another way people can improve the quality of their reflections is to make sure they accurately reflect the degree of emotion the other person feels.

Suppose the first person says, "This is a really important art project for school. I've spent hours upon hours on it! Now, finally I've finished it up in a way that I like, and then I go in three hours later and find my little brother has just torn it up! Not just one tear, but he totally destroyed it. Aargh!"

Suppose the second person's reflection to this is, "So, it sounds like you would have preferred he didn't tear it up."

This particular restatement would probably irritate the speaker. Why? The reflection is accurate, but it doesn't go far enough. A more accurate reflection would be, "So you're saying all those hours and all that creative energy went down the drain? It must be taking an enormous effort for you to stay in control at this moment!"

On the other hand, part of being a good empathic listener is not joining the other person in wallowing in thought patterns that aren't useful, for example non-useful awfulizing, getting down on yourself, and blaming someone else.

For example: The speaker says, "I'm so stupid. I don't have half a brain in my head. Even a dog or cat would have been smart enough to have put that painting where a two-year-old kid couldn't have gotten at it. But not idiot me!"

Suppose the listener reflects as follows: "So, in other words, you think you're such a dumb, bird-brained imbecile? Just a stupid jackass fool, huh?"

425

This may be an accurate reflection of what the other person is feeling, but the most useful reflection finds the healthiest and most useful portion of what the other person has been thinking. So, for example, a better reflection would have been to say:

"Huh! In other words, you're not blaming your brother, but you're kicking yourself for not putting it in a safer place."

Now let's think about some of the attitudes and thought patterns that seem to make it easier to be a good empathic listener.

Often someone starts out listening to someone else. But something the other person says triggers an idea. So the listener starts rehearsing what he's going to say when the speaker stops speaking. But as the listener does this, he tunes out the speaker, and stops listening. Other times the listener gets so impatient to make a point that he interrupts the other person.

This pressure to have the other person hear is often one of the biggest obstacles to listening. One of the biggest aids to listening is an attitude of patience and knowing that your own ideas and your own points can wait a while. You can spend some energy understanding the other person's points of view before giving your own.

Sometimes the pressure to interrupt and give one's own point comes from the fear of forgetting what you were going to say. In this case, the listening process requires doing two things

with your brain: logging away in memory the point you eventually want to make, but still devoting enough brain power to listening.

Another barrier to the listening process is the attitude that the other person doesn't have anything worth saying or worth listening to: the other person is blabbering on and wasting time. To concentrate fully on what the other person is saying and really try to understand thoroughly the other person's point of view often requires some sacrifice. It's a sacrifice of time, effort, and brainpower that might be more pleasurably spent watching television, reading a book, or having a fantasy. Devoting your brain to the other person's words is a gift to the other person.

You're not always obligated to give that gift every time the other person opens his mouth. Sometimes people do talk on and on about things that aren't very important even to themselves. Sometimes this stems from a fear of talking about what really does matter. Sometimes it stems from a bad conversational habit of just saying everything that comes to mind.

The expert listener needs to decide when to be patient and when to be assertive. Sometimes it's a good idea to interrupt and say, "I'm sorry. I'm having trouble following exactly what point you're making. Could you please try to make it in a few words?"

On the other hand, there are times when this might be just exactly the wrong thing to do for the developing relationship – what the speaker needs is someone who will hang in there and simply keep working, listening, and trying to understand with full effort in the faith that eventually the person will get to what's really important. Sometimes the speaker may need to test the waters with the less important ideas. It's often hard, but important, to decide when to be patient and when to hurry the other person.

Sometimes the best thing I can do as a listener is to guide the person to a topic I'm interested in. Suppose someone is very interested in talking about professional sports and about politics. Suppose I'm not interested in professional sports, but very interested in politics. It's silly for me to try to appear interested while the person talks for a long time about professional sports, when we could be having a conversation about politics that's fun for both of us.

Here's another barrier to listening: a shortage of one-on-one time for people to spend paying attention to each other. In a family with several members, a parent may hardly ever be alone with one of the children. The time that would be spent listening to that child is always spent with some other child's competing for the parent's attention. And even when people are alone together, if the television or some other sort of electronic medium is competing for the attention of each, people can't listen as well. People can't really concentrate on each other.

Occasionally, I hear statistics on how little time parents in our society actually spend in one-on-one interaction with their children. These numbers always strike me as shockingly low. It would not surprise me if there were a similarly low amount of time allocated by husbands and wives to actually paying attention to what the other one was saying. The same can probably be said about bosses and employees and other important relationships that make up the fabric of our society.

My guess is, that if we could take just a portion of the amount of time people in our culture spend listening to television and other electronic media, and have them spend that time listening to the real people in their lives, the world would be a much better place.

Group 10: Self-Discipline

Self-discipline, also known as self-control, self-regulation, and delay of gratification, is the ability to choose and enact options that are less pleasurable, but have a better long-term effect. Having self-discipline means being "tough" in the best sense of the word. It means having the power to say "No" to your brain's demands of "Give me pleasure! I want it right now!"

Skill 51: Self-Discipline

This book presents many good ways to make you more productive, happier, more capable of serving humanity, and psychologically healthier. However, most of the techniques I speak about have a "catch." Let's talk about what that catch is.

I have on many occasions mentioned how useful it is to do fantasy rehearsals of the types of situations you need to improve in the most. You imagine yourself thinking, feeling, and behaving the way you've decided you would like to in that situation. The catch is this: it's work to do fantasy rehearsals of your difficult situations, and it's much more fun to watch television.

In the section on courage skills and fear reduction, I mention exposing yourself to the situations that you fear unrealistically, and keeping yourself from escaping the situation until the fear habituates, or reduces itself. There's one big catch: this is no fun. It's much more pleasant to sit down and have some cookies than to expose yourself to a feared situation.

In the section on concentration skills, I recommend repeatedly concentrating on something difficult to concentrate on, rating how well you concentrate, and then trying again, watching what you do with your mind when you concentrate best and trying to duplicate this in future sessions of concentration. There's one catch to this: it's a lot of work. It's usually much more fun to call up a friend on the phone and chat, or to listen to music.

For anybody who's addicted to cigarettes, I have a foolproof program. Here it is: you don't smoke another one for the rest of your life. You gut out the discomfort you feel while withdrawing, and celebrate when you feel better. Huge numbers of people have used this method successfully. But there's one major catch to it: it's so pleasant to have another cigarette when you're right in the midst of the worst withdrawal pains, and it's very unpleasant at that moment to avoid smoking.

For anyone who has trouble learning to read, I have an answer. You sit down and drill on several tasks arranged in a hierarchy of increasing difficulty, for perhaps half an hour a day for a year. I can almost guarantee that, at the end of that year, you'll be reading much better. There's just one catch. It's much more fun to goof off and play with toys, or play with a pet, or play video games than it is to do those drills.

Is there someone who needs higher education but doesn't have the money for it? Here's how that person can learn what an educated person knows. There are lots of great textbooks in college bookstores; you find reading lists for the courses you're interested in and study those books diligently and steadily. Even without the benefits of hands-on experience and social interaction about the ideas you're studying, if you can study steadily and methodically, you'll probably learn more than most college students do. There's just one catch. This takes tremendous self-discipline. When people pay college tuition, they're paying for behavior modification programs for themselves (not to mention credentialing programs), perhaps more than for the information per se.

Are you overweight? Here's a simple program. You use some formulas described in many books to figure out how many calories it takes to maintain your present weight, and eat 300 calories less than that per day in the form of well-balanced meals. Also you get some strenuous exercise at least thirty to sixty minutes a day. There's only one catch. At any given moment, it usually feels better to break these rules than to follow them.

Would you like to have a lot of money? Here's how. You work very hard to prepare yourself for a well-paying job, and when you get one, you work hard to do it extremely well. In the meantime, you realize that whatever your income is, there are people who live on half that much. So you save half (or a quarter, or 15 percent) of what you make, and study carefully how to invest it. Unfortunately, this too is not a get-rich-quick program. The catch is that it's much more pleasant in the short run to spend money than to save it, and working very hard is often less pleasant than playing.

Is there a world out there filled with mishandled conflict and violence? Here's a solution to that. When people have conflicts, they should meet at least one of the seven criteria discussed earlier in the section on conflict resolution and joint decision-making: they should refrain from interrupting, putting each other down, and raising their voices at each other. Here's the catch: when you're angry, it's often more gratifying, for the moment, to interrupt, insult, and yell than to use the self-discipline it takes to withhold these responses.

I could go on in this vein for a long time. But let me give just one more program with a catch. Do you want to know a lot about psychological skills? Read this book, as well as the others that accompany it, several times, think very carefully about what you're reading, and regularly do all the exercises that are suggested. Here's the catch: it takes many hours to do this well, and there are many more enjoyable things for you to do with your time. This book is not written to be entertaining, and it will never be able to compete in entertainment value with others that are.

Now the interesting thing about all these programs is that none of them takes superhuman skill or talent. They don't require the ability to withstand agony. Everything I've mentioned can be done, and has been done, by people with ordinary intelligence and ability. But the thing that distinguishes people who can do these things from people who can't is the skill of self-discipline, or delay of gratification. This skill means you do what you've decided will achieve your goals best rather than what feels best at the moment. It's doing what you decide will be best, rather than doing whatever you feel like. It's passing up the temptation of what feels good now in order to accomplish a goal you've set.

The skill of self-discipline makes working to get better at any other psychological skill more likely to succeed. To put this another way, all the very useful techniques that people have discovered for making yourself happier and more productive will be useless to you unless you have the self-discipline to use them.

It should come as no surprise that self-discipline skill is correlated with success in almost every area of human endeavor, because self-discipline means the ability to get yourself to do the things necessary to succeed. Some research studies have come to the more surprising conclusion that you can measure self-discipline among young children, and the amount of self-discipline you measure has predictive power many years later.

How did the researchers measure self-discipline? They gave children the opportunity to have a small amount of very desired reward right away, or to wait and have a larger amount after the waiting period. For example, the children were allowed to have two pieces of candy immediately, but if they could wait in front of the candy without eating it for ten minutes, they could have five pieces. This choice between something pleasurable right now versus doing without it now for a greater reward later is the essence of delay of gratification skill.

According to a variety of indicators, the children who were able to wait for the greater but more delayed reward were more successful years later. This brings up the question, what if the children who were not successful had been trained? Is it possible to train people in self-discipline skills?

It turns out that it is possible to train, not only people, but also animals such as pigeons and rats. How do you train an animal in this skill? You start out with a very small delay, and work your way up. For example, the animal gets to press one of two bars. One bar gives a food pellet immediately (but you can only get the reward one time from it), and the other gives two pellets after a two-second wait. The animal learns by trial and error to pick the delayed reward. Then the trainer uses the strategy of shaping to gradually increase the delay, perhaps sweetening the reward by having a higher ratio of payoff after the delay.

What if all children learned to delay gratification in a paradigm like this? It's one worth trying, in my opinion.

Why is self-discipline so hard?

It's often true that things are pleasurable because they're good for us in some way. Evolution did not produce in us the capacity for pleasure for no good reason. For example, people throughout the centuries who have taken pleasure from eating have been less likely to starve than people who have not taken pleasure from eating. Thus, selection favors people who like to eat, and thus almost all of us enjoy eating. People who have sexual urges tend to pass their genes along more than those people who don't. Thus, almost all people have the capacity for sexual pleasure. Pleasure from eating and from sexuality is meant to serve two very important goals: preservation of the individual and preservation of the species.

And yet acting on every urge to eat and every sexual urge would result in bad consequences for most people. Similarly, sleep is good for us, and it's not without reason that we're programmed to want to continue sleeping until our wish to sleep is fulfilled and we naturally wake up. But people who can't take control of their sleep rhythms and reset them tend to get fired for lateness.

So, rather than maximizing present pleasure, the fully functioning human being has to calculate what is going to produce the greatest payoff in the long term, taking into account the needs of others as well as oneself. Sigmund Freud spoke of this sort of long-term calculation as using the "reality principle," whereas doing whatever feels best in the short run he called the "pleasure principle."

Other examples of the need for self-discipline

When ingenious people figured out how to produce drugs that produce pleasure, they created a vast market for the exercise of self-discipline skills. At any moment, there's probably some drug you could swallow, inject, sniff, or smoke that would give you a temporary "high" or feeling of pleasure. But that pleasure, which should be saved up to reinforce behaviors leading to happiness or productivity, is now instead reinforcing only more drug-seeking behavior. Even disregarding the pernicious side effects of "recreational" drugs, the way of life such drugs reinforce is ultimately selfish, empty, and meaningless. But once drug-seeking behavior has been powerfully reinforced many times, it takes a great exercise of self-discipline to stop the habit.

Similar to drug use in many ways is an addiction to high stimulation from television, video games, or other electronic devices. Cultivating the ability to turn off the external stimulation and be at peace within oneself, or to tolerate low-stimulation experiences such as reading this book, takes a great amount of self-discipline for some people. It has been argued cogently by Neil Postman, Jane Healy, and others that we as a culture are losing our capacity for rational discourse because we're getting too lazy to decipher written words, and we're letting television create mental images for us.

Self-discipline is also required in the countless choice points when you decide to either do something productive or to amuse yourself. What if everyone in the world started to use the immediate pleasure principle all the time? Factories would cease to produce things – it's much more fun to do almost anything else than work on an assembly line. Health care workers would decide whether or not it was more amusing to take care of your illness than to play golf or watch television, and would often choose the latter. If you stopped at a restaurant, the waiters would say, "Get your own food!" And the cook would say, "Cook it yourself if you want it! I'm out of here!"

The garbage that people produce would lie around and pile up and fester, for who would choose to clean up garbage rather than do something more pleasant? Farmers might eat the food they produced, but no one would choose to do the laborious tasks of picking it and trucking it off to other people and stocking grocery stores. Why do that boring work when you could be playing a video game? Civilization would quickly dissolve.

Self-discipline is also a very important part of our relationships with other people. What's the most immediately gratifying thing to do when someone angers you? For many people, the answer to this is to scream at him or hit him. Delay of gratification consists in curbing those impulses and working for the delayed gratification achieved by speaking rationally to the other person.

Lack of skill in delaying gratification causes other problems in relationships. Without these skills, people view other people as good for what they can get out of them at the present moment. The minute someone stops meeting their immediate wishes, they run to someone else. Or, they're so selfish that other people flee from relationships with them. Having relations with others requires being able to balance giving and taking, rather than constantly taking.

Deficiency in self-discipline skills greatly interferes with happiness. Long-term happiness requires calculation for long-term gains. The trouble with working for immediate pleasure is that you're usually left with little when the immediate pleasure goes away. The seekers of immediate pleasure tend to find themselves without loyal friends, with drug withdrawal symptoms, without money, and without the meaning in existence that comes from having something to look forward to in the intermediate and long-term future. Accordingly, there's a real emptiness to existence which then must be escaped by another round of drug use, drinking, overeating, sexual indulgence, another spending spree, another gambling venture, etc. Thus, all human beings should place a high premium on attaining delay of gratification skills.

Probably few people – especially those who have had the self-discipline to read this far in this book, or even this chapter – can identify with the picture of the person with absolutely no self-discipline skills. But probably all of us have some area where we would like to use more self-discipline. Interestingly, people can show very high delay of gratification skills in some areas and low skills in other areas.

For example: Someone is very hard working, thrifty, and honest. But he has an addiction to cigarettes that he can't break. Another person does a high volume of work, but has a procrastination habit that leads him to get work done just before deadlines under extreme stress during frantic all-nighters. Another person can work for very long periods, to total exhaustion, in practicing sports skills, but the same person wimps out quickly when practicing academic skills.

How to develop self-discipline

Setting goals and wanting them very much. Self-discipline is choosing to do what will accomplish your goals rather than what will just give you short-run pleasure. Obviously it's hard to do this if you don't have goals! It's easier to delay gratification on doing homework if you really have your heart set on making straight A's. It's easier to delay gratification if you have your heart set on running a mile in four minutes and forty seconds, on having a million dollars with which to start a charitable foundation, on winning a prize for research, on publishing an article in the *New England Journal of Medicine*, on getting into Harvard graduate school, on contributing 10 on a scale of 10 to a positive interpersonal climate in your family, on playing a Chopin piano piece expertly, or on being able to rate yourself at least 8 on a scale of 10 for each of these psychological skills.

In setting goals, it doesn't do to simply say, "I'd like to have ten million dollars." Setting goals also means getting in mind how much work and sacrifice it will take to accomplish the goal, and deciding that the goal is worth the effort. This is where the "wanting them very much" comes in. I'd like to have someone give me a billion dollars, but being a billionaire is definitely not a goal of mine, because I don't want to do what it takes to become a billionaire. I'd love it if I could play complex piano pieces beautifully, but this is not a goal of mine, because I don't want to spend the time it would take to learn to do this.

Here are some other guidelines for setting goals. It's good to be specific, so you can definitely tell whether you achieved the goal or not. Thus if I say, "I want to be good in tennis," how good is good? On the other hand, if I say, "I want to be ranked in the top five in my district," that's more specific. It's good to be specific with respect to time, as well. If I want to weigh 178 pounds, that's a nice goal, except that I can put it off indefinitely. If I want to weigh

178 pounds by January 1, 2005, that's more specific.

Another guideline on goals is to vividly imagine what it will be like to achieve the goal. Thus, if I have a goal that I will contribute 10 on a scale of 10 to a positive interpersonal climate in my family, I want to imagine very vividly what my behaviors will look and sound like in all sorts of situations.

Believing that work can accomplish goals. Some people with poor self-discipline skills have a core belief that the good things that come your way do so regardless of the work you put into achieving them – that work on goals is uncorrelated with achieving goals. We'll talk more about this when we discuss the skill of awareness of control, the skill of figuring out what you can control and what you can't. The experience of working very hard for something, and accomplishing it because you worked hard on it, is worth more than gold. Experiences like this teach you that work does have a connection with accomplishment.

Highly valuing self-discipline, and using the internal sales pitch. What do you get out of delaying gratification? Why bother? Unless you're really convinced of the answer to this, temptation will be too hard to resist.

Here's an example of an internal sales pitch: Why should I use self-discipline in setting up and keeping an organized filing system for my papers? So that I won't have to go through the agony of needing information and hav-ing to search through piles of paper to find it. So I won't feel a twinge of pain each time I see those piles of paper waiting to be organized. So that I don't have to live in fear of a tax audit. So that I can pay bills on time and not pay huge amounts of interest on credit cards. So that dust mites won't breed in my papers and cause allergies that make my family members sneeze. So that I'll get better at self-discipline in general. If this happens, I may find it easier to lose that twenty pounds and look much better.

Remembering the paradigm of habituation to painful emotion. Do you remember that, in the chapter on courage skills, we talked about how exposing yourself to a situation that evokes unrealistic fear or other unrealistic painful emotion gradually lessens the painful emotion? You can do this with the fatigue and restlessness that comes from practicing or working on something. You can do this with the physical fatigue of endurance training. You can do it for the deprivation feeling that comes from not indulging yourself in sweets and fats. If you tough out those bad feelings long enough, you can habituate yourself to them.

Remembering that you're working on delay and not absence of gratification. If people try to be too ascetic, they have a way of swinging back and forth between self-denial and self-indulgence. They think, "I will go on this very austere diet to lose weight," and for a while they are successful.

They really do lose weight when they eat nothing but grapefruit without sugar and black beans.

But then the part of the personality that desires gratification rebels and wins out over that part that's an overly severe master. The person then swings into the extreme of overeating and bingeing. That's why striving for moderation is much more likely to be successful than striving for extremes of self-denial. A useful image is that of gradually turning up self-denial to the point necessary to achieve the goal, but not much further.

This idea has its limits, however. It needs to be considered separately for each area of indulgence. It does appear that, for people who have trouble with alcohol, for example, it's wiser to strive for a zero alcohol intake than for alcohol intake in moderation. The same is probably true for those with addictions to cocaine or heroin.

Nonetheless, even for those people who are trying to totally give up certain sorts of pleasures, it's good to keep in mind the goal of increasing their access to other sorts of healthier pleasures. You don't want to try to convince your mind and body to give up pleasure altogether.

Cultivating the ability to celebrate progress toward the goal. Everything we said in the chapter on self-reinforcement and pleasure from accomplishments is crucial to delay of gratification. It's crucial to be able to say to yourself sentences like this:

"Hooray for me! I'm getting started in this task. I'm glad I'm able to do something for myself that isn't immediately gratifying for the sake of my future goal. I'm making progress. Good for me! I've finished a sub-task. This is an important milestone. This is great. The project is completed, even though the payoff is still far off down the line."

Being able to say these sorts of things to oneself means you don't have to forgo gratification quite so much in order to practice delay of gratification skills. In fact, if you get good enough at delivering these reinforcing thoughts to yourself, and taking pleasure in them, the activity in question can become positively pleasurable. This is what I call "advanced self-discipline."

In advanced self-discipline, you not only get yourself to do the thing that will advance yourself to your goal, you get yourself to enjoy it. For example, a writer who at one time had to force himself to write can start to take enough pleasure in writing that he greatly looks forward to and cherishes his daily writing time.

Cultivating the ability to imagine the future. Self-discipline is greatly helped by visualizing future outcomes. Suppose two runners are training. One of them is only focusing on the moment: "My body feels tired. It'd be nice to stop and catch my breath. Putting out this effort is not very pleasant."

The other one has an image in mind of his muscles, heart, and blood vessels gradually reshaping themselves into a more smoothly running system. He also has an image in mind of future races being won, future races being run fast, even if they are not won, images of the acclaim from friends, acclaim from strangers, images of the admiration of teammates, and all sorts of other images of how nice it would be to attain the desired goal. Which of the two runners will find it easier to exercise delay of gratification skills? The one who envisions the future will have an enormous advantage.

A not-too-bad one-sentence summary of the works of Jean Piaget on cognitive development is as follows: As people mature, they develop more ability to think about things that are not physically present. In other words, they transcend the limitations of the here and now.

One of the most harmful messages of certain forms of psychotherapy, for example Gestalt therapy, as articulated by its founder Fritz Perls, is that one should stay only in the here and now and should not worry about what will happen in the future. The fully functioning person is constantly working to create the kind of future that will be best. It's impossible to devote oneself to this task without the capacity to imagine, predict and visualize the sort of future consequences that come from decisions.

If you're new to the skill of visualization of the future, you can start with practicing visualizing anything not physically present. Very soon, you start to practice visualizing the positive results of your delay of gratification activities. You imagine these positive results; you imagine yourself doing the work to achieve them; you imagine yourself imagining the positive results at the same time you're doing the work.

Some people simply don't visualize a future for themselves. They imagine that life will end at a fairly early age, or they simply have no image of what it will be like after a certain point in time or no image of what it will be like in the future at all. One of the interesting aspects of transactional analysis, as developed by Eric Berne, is called script analysis. This is looking at and making conscious your images of your own life script.

For example: When do you imagine yourself dying? If you're sixteen and you imagine yourself going out in a blaze of glory at age twenty-five, it's much more difficult to practice delay of gratification skills than it is if you imagine yourself going through various stages of life and ending up as a very wise old person of ninety or one hundred. Do you envision yourself having a pleasant retirement period of life? If so, it makes more sense to save money for that time than if you refuse to imagine this. Do you imagine yourself gradually accumulating a greater and greater reputation for successful work? If so, it's probably easier to do some work right now than if you did not incorporate this image into your life script.

Cultivating beliefs consistent with the practice of self-discipline. If your core belief about existence is "Eat, drink, and be merry, for tomorrow you may die," it's not very easy to cultivate self-discipline skills. The problem with this belief is that the overwhelming probability is you won't die tomorrow.

What are some beliefs that foster self-discipline? Here are some:

1. The best things in life do not come easy. Things such as happy family life, success in work, staying educated and enjoying the complexity of the universe take some effort.

2. Life throws at us many challenges requiring us to bear discomfort; it's good to take pride in your ability to bear discomfort if you need to. It's foolish to bring on discomfort for its own sake. But when the greatest good for humanity and for yourself can be achieved by forgoing pleasure and bearing discomfort, it's the mark of a superior human being to be able to do so.

3. Some of the discomfort and painful feelings we encounter are signals that we need to avoid something harmful or dangerous to us. Other pain and discomfort is to be toughed out and withstood without running away from the situation. The healthiest people can discriminate well which is which.

4. Payoffs sometimes come only after huge amounts of work. Practically speaking, this philosophical approach translates into the question, "How long do you have to keep working on something without getting the payoff you want before you conclude that the effort is in no way productive of the payoff?"

For some people the answer is in seconds. If I try for a few seconds and don't get something, it must be that trying has no causal connection to getting it and therefore it's time to give up. For other people at the other extreme, the answer to this question is measured in lifetimes. For example, in working for the cause of peace and nonviolence on earth, many people are able to sustain their efforts toward peace and nonviolence despite an almost certain conviction that the goal they seek will not be attained in their lifetime.

A subset of delay of gratification skills is the skill of bearing actual physical pain. Many people are afflicted with conditions that cause pain every day, perhaps every second of their lives. With many chronically painful conditions, the most gratifying pathway in the long run is gradually to learn to cease focusing on the pain and to focus instead on what other gratifications one can achieve despite continuing to have the pain. This attitude can turn the attention away from the painful stimuli and thus actually reduce the pain somewhat.

Using memories of successes in self-discipline as resources. I have discussed this technique for a few other psychological skills. It really applies to all of them. If you can memorize your success experiences in self-discipline, and then call to memory the way you thought, felt, and behaved in that successful experience just before taking action on another challenge, you're more likely to be able to transfer the formerly successful patterns to the present challenge.

For example, when I'm trying to lose weight and I'm offered ice cream, I recall the time I successfully turned down the cookies. I recall how good I felt about myself for using self-discipline. Then I step into this image and reenact it as I turn down the ice cream. Or when I'm trying to get myself to do my income tax, I remember how I successfully got myself to do the annual report for a project recently. I recall how I reinforced myself for getting started even when I didn't feel like it. Then I try to reenact a similar pattern.

Doing lots of fantasy rehearsals. If you want to get better at anything, you practice it. If you want to get better at self-discipline, you practice self-discipline. One way to practice is by fantasy rehearsals. You imagine yourself at a choice point where self-discipline skills are necessary: the time when you choose to get out of bed or sleep late, the moment you choose to stop eating or to overeat, the moment you choose to do your work or goof off, the moment you choose whether to drink alcohol or not, the moment you choose to spend money or save it.

You describe the situation out loud as if it were happening in the present. You think aloud the thoughts that you would like to think in this situation, and you describe yourself acting and feeling as you would like to act and feel. After you have done this, you've done one repetition of a fantasy rehearsal out loud. If you do several hundred of them, it's very likely you will increase your self-discipline skills.

Below is an outline for fantasy rehearsals of self-discipline:

Steps in Practicing Delay of Gratification

1. Situation:
    Describe the situation. What are the sights, sounds?
2. Thoughts:
    Here's an opportunity.
    What are the reasons for doing the less enjoyable vs. the more enjoyable option? (Visualize benefits of delaying gratification, visualize consequences of not delaying gratification)
    How bad is what I have to endure by delaying gratification now?
    Let me remember a time when I handled a situation like this well. I want to see and hear it in my mind.
    It will be an accomplishment if I can tough this out and handle it well. It will toughen me for the future.
    How can I celebrate finishing this by rewarding myself with some gratification?
    It won't kill me to do the less enjoyable option.

If I really play my cards right maybe I can figure out a way to enjoy this.

I want to reinforce myself for every step along the way.

3. Emotions:

I feel determined.

I imagine myself feeling the way I want to feel: confident, excited, resigned, calculating, proud of the way I'm handling this, or . . .

4. Behavior: I'm doing the option I chose. I'm doing something that makes sense.

5. Celebration: Hooray, I did a good job!

Group 11: Loyalty

The sixteen skill group names are chosen to include the most important principles for living. The art of sustaining relationships over time is another skill that's so important it gets its own group.

Skill 52: Loyalty

Loyalty is also called the skill of sustaining attachments to other people. Sustaining means keeping, not throwing away. Attachments are bonds with other people, sticking together with someone. Loyalty means continuing to be friends over time, rather than drifting apart and not being in touch.

The opposite of the skill of loyalty is being fickle. A fickle friend is here today and gone tomorrow. As soon as someone else better comes along, the fickle friend is gone.

Why is the skill of loyalty so important? Human beings don't just need food, air, water, and so forth; they also need relationships. Human beings bond to other people. They need attachments, and they need people they can go to when they need help and people who come to them for help.

People who have several really close, true friends, tend to do much better when bad things happen to them than people who don't have close and true friends. Having a few people whom you can help, who will help you, whom you get along with, and whom you can have fun with is called having a social support system.

Family members can be part of a social support system. If you're lucky enough to have brothers, sisters, parents, children, uncles, aunts, cousins, or grandparents whom you get along with, whom you like, then you have what's called a family support system.

People who have weak family support systems have to do more work to cultivate a support system of friends. They also have to be particularly interested in keeping those friends over a long time because, although cousins don't stop being cousins, and brothers and sisters don't stop being brothers and sisters, friends sometimes stop being friends and just drift away from each other.

The person with low loyalty skill tends to think, when things go wrong in a relationship, "I'll just never talk to that person again. I'll just stay away from that person from now on."

People who do have the skill of loyalty tend to end relationships as a last resort. When there's a problem that comes up in a long-term relationship, they think first in terms of, "How can I work this out? How can I make things go better? How can I get the relationship back in good shape?" Rather than just thinking, "I'll leave the relationship and forget about it."

One of the other skills we've talked about in very great detail is joint decision, or conflict resolution. The skill of problem-solving goes hand in hand with the skill of loyalty, because problem-solving is a good alternative to leaving relationships when things go bad.

With the skill of loyalty, realistic goals lead to greater success. You can't be loyal to everyone. You only have room in your life for so many really close, important relationships. If you try to have too many really close relationships, you'll find you just don't have time. It takes time to develop a relationship with someone. You have to spend time together, first of all, getting to know each other, to decide whether you want to make the commitment to a friendship that lasts. After that, it takes time to build that friendship and time to enjoy it. Sometimes, if two people are close friends and then one person moves away from the other person, they can still be close friends, but they still have to spend time somehow or another: time spent on the phone, or time spent writing and reading letters, or time visiting.

So, If you want to be good at the skill of loyalty, think: who are the ten, twenty or thirty people in your life who are the most important to you, whom you most want to cultivate and nurture friendships with? Then put your time and energy into these relationships. Even when time is short, if you want to keep these relationships going, you have to make the time to put into them.

I mentioned that one of the tests of loyalty comes when people have conflicts. Another test of loyalty comes when other people have conflicts with your friend.

For example, suppose Jerry and Tim are friends. Then they each start in a new school. Jerry becomes popular, but even though Tim is nice, Tim gets teased for being fat. If Jerry were not good at the skill of loyalty, Jerry would pretend not to know Tim, or even join in with the other boys and girls in teasing him. But if Jerry is really good at the skill of loyalty, Jerry will say, "Hey, I don't like that when you tease him. He's a good friend. You should get to know him better and learn what a good friend he can be."

A friend who will stick up for you even when other people are picking on you is a truer friend than one who will desert you when the going gets rough.

How do you decide whom you want to be loyal to? Remember, you can't be loyal to everyone. A lot of what we said about the skill of trusting has to do with selecting who will receive your loyalty. You get to know people over time, and you decide over time how much you can trust them for what things. That helps you to decide whom you want to be loyal to and whom you don't.

There's a difference between being loyal to someone and just being polite and courteous to someone. You can be polite and courteous to almost everyone. But if you're loyal to someone, you're willing to sacrifice something for that person. First of all, you want to spend your time in continuing to be with them. And you're willing to sacrifice time, effort, and money to help them out if they need it.

Loyalty to a woman is a very important issue for men. Often you see men bouncing from one woman to another. In movies sometimes characters who do this are depicted as sexy and admirable because they can attract all sorts of new women, one after the other. But the skill of attracting new people and getting into new relationships over and over and then leaving them is a very superficial skill.

The skill of loyalty is a much more important one. The man who's able to be loyal to one woman over a long period of time has a skill that's really valuable for the world. Why is this so valuable? One obvious reason is that it results in families where children will have two parents who are interested in taking care of them and helping them develop. But even when children are not involved, stable couples are good for the world because at least there are two people who will look after each other's welfare and help each other out.

Of course, what I've just said goes for women as well as men. Some women also tend to want to prove their desirability by going from one romantic relationship to another rather than remaining loyal to one person. But the problem seems to be somewhat more common for men than women.

Some people have trouble with the skill of loyalty because they really don't consider themselves too likable. They figure if someone really gets to know them well, they will be rejected by that other person. This leads them to reject the other person before there's any chance of getting rejected. They bounce from one person to another, trying not to let the other person know them well enough to really see who they are.

The skill of loyalty doesn't mean you have to stay in relationships where you get treated badly over and over. Suppose a woman finds herself married to a man who beats her up and is otherwise violent with her. Or suppose he isn't physically violent, but constantly says mean things to her. Does the skill of loyalty mean that she has to stick with him anyway? Of course not. It usually means she should have gathered more information before she made a commitment to him.

But people make mistakes. The goals of preserving life and limb, living in peace, and living with someone whom you can be happy with are more important than the goal of being loyal to someone whom one can't be happy with.

Throughout people's lives, one of the most important things for their happiness is the quality of their long-term relationships. Do they have people whom they've had good relationships with for years and years? The answer to this question often makes the difference between happiness and misery.

Group 12: Conservation

The principle of conservation is the value that's the opposite of decadent consumption and waste.

Skill 53: Conservation and Thrift

One way to practice delay of gratification is to save money rather than spending it. This is such an important skill for the well-being of people that I've listed it as a separate psychological skill.

Like many other skills, this one calls for some balance. It's possible to have too much thrift. If you go through life scrimping on every penny, to die with lots of money that you can't take with you, you haven't just delayed gratification; you've forgone it altogether. There's a certain skill of pleasure in using money. The skill of pleasure from spending money will get less emphasis here because in present culture of the United States, the skill of pleasure from spending is so widely practiced compared to the skill of thrift.

Through advertising, our present culture presents almost ubiquitous indoctrination toward the pleasures of consumption. Anyone who takes part in any of the mass media receives countless messages urging her to consume, and hardly ever a message telling her not to consume so much.

Financial decisions and money management don't seem to be at the forefront of most psychotherapists' work. However, money management affects psychological health in a variety of different ways. Conflicts between husbands and wives over money play a large part in many divorces, which in turn have great effects on psychological health. The necessity for both fathers and mothers to work long hours to make ends meet plays a large role in the psychological health of children. The stress in families caused by not being able to pay the bills creates all sorts of stress symptoms, as well as more conflict among family members. The more money families have available to meet their consumption demands, the less stress is generated over money.

Consumption: when is enough too much?

Consuming less is also an ethical issue. Whenever someone spends money on a certain good or service, he's directing some of the labor and resources of the world to be channeled into producing that good or service, as opposed to some other. Dollars tell people what to do. If I spend money on violent entertainment, it's as if I'm hiring someone (or a portion of a someone) to produce it, to deliver it, to market it, and so forth. If, instead, I spend that money on contributing to a fund for educating poor children, I hire someone (or a part of someone) to do education. The way I channel my dollars affects what people do with their time and the world's resources. In a world where people are starving, going uneducated, and living amid violence, to spend money on luxuries instead of solving these problems is hard to justify.

Let's examine some information put out by the United Nations Human Development Report, 1998.

Here's how much it would take to provide, for all the world's citizens, for a year, in U.S. dollars:

Basic education for all: $6 billion

Water and sanitation for all: $9 billion

Reproductive health services for all women: $12 billion

Basic health and nutrition: $13 billion

Here are some of the ways money is currently spent:

Cosmetics in US: $8 billion

Perfumes in Europe and US: $12 billion

Pet foods in Europe, US: $17 billion

Business entertainment in Japan: $35 billion

Cigarettes in Europe: $50 billion

Alcoholic drinks in Europe: $105 billion

Narcotic drugs in the world: $400 billion

Military spending in the world: $780 billion

One source listed entertainment expenditures in the U.S. at 27 percent of the gross national product. The movie *Terminator II* grossed over $200,000,000 in its first year of release. That single movie grossed enough to pay for individual tutoring for a 200-day school year, at $15 per hour, one hour a day, for nearly 67,000 children. Society could have chosen to direct that money into individual tutoring rather than into *Terminator II*.

Let's think more about the consumption of our society, and how much of it could be forgone if there were really an ethical choice between our luxuries and feeding and clothing and giving health care to people who are going without it.

Huge amounts are spent on advertising meant simply to persuade us to consume products. Much of our spending on clothing, homes, cars, etc., isn't meant to simply provide warmth, transportation, and shelter, but it is meant to establish one's position in the dominance hierarchy – to show how much money you have.

We see huge consumption of fast foods, convenience food, and snack foods, increasing our gross national product; then we have a huge weight-loss industry trying to counteract the results of the convenience food industry. We see huge spending on alcohol and tobacco, and huge health-care costs trying to counteract the effects of the success of the alcohol and tobacco industry. There's huge spending on lobbyists to influence the tax code in ways favorable to certain groups, and huge spending on accountants trying to figure out the complex tax laws the lobbyists have been successful in enacting.

We spend vast amounts of dollars on attractive packaging of products; this necessitates huge dollars spent on waste management, to get rid of the packages once we throw them away. We spend huge amounts on guns, and then need to spend huge amounts on police to try to solve the crimes committed by those guns. There's a huge gambling industry, which necessitates an industry of providing treatment to people who can't stay away from the gambling industry.

Each of these expenditures adds to the gross domestic product, the sum total of goods and services our society produces. This is the number that's supposed to indicate the economic health of a country. But what portion of it actually does anybody any good, versus what portion of it, in addition to diverting resources from causes that would do good, creates problems that absorb still further resources?

In order to buy and produce all the unnecessary things our society buys, we have to go to work for long hours and spend time away from our children. We send our children to spend most of their time in herds of other children rather than learning from those who are older and wiser.

How can society help to channel human efforts and activities into the areas that really do produce the greatest good for humanity? This is the real question for economics. This is a very different question from that of how can the economy produce the highest degree of activity. Much of that activity may be totally wasteful or even counterproductive.

The answer to this important question lies in the individual choices people make on how to spend their money. The economy will produce what people want to pay for.

Thus, the societal problem comes down to individual choices. Any individual can use the skill of financial delay of gratification to refuse to waste money on things that don't contribute to the greatest good of humanity. It also involves rearranging one's pleasure mechanisms so we derive more enjoyment from spending money on things that contribute to the greatest good rather on things than vainly waste resources.

A program for thrift skills

Thrift is a delay of gratification skill, and it can be practiced with fantasy rehearsals just as any other type of delay of gratification skill. Here are the steps.

1. You make a list of the types of situations that are triggers or temptations. These are situations that have successfully tempted you to waste money and the world's resources. Or these can be situations that you make up, that might tempt you in the future. Here are some examples:

a. I get a catalogue in the mail with lots of interesting gadgets advertised, and I look through it just to make sure I haven't missed anything; I see a particularly fun-looking gadget.

b. I don't have anything planned, so I consider going to the shopping mall and wandering around looking at things.

c. I notice that a neighbor has bought something particularly nice, and I consider getting the same thing. Keep going until you have listed many, many situations.

2. You decide what you want to think, feel, and do in each of these situations. It's good to write down these thoughts, emotions, and behaviors. What would the ideal you do? As you decide on your thoughts, consider "not awfulizing" about the amount of deprivation you would experience by not spending the money. For example: "If I don't have this new computer, I'll still be better set up with computing power than 98 percent of people in the world, and I'll still be able to do all I really need to do just fine."

Consider visualizing more ethical alternatives: "If I don't spend money on this, I'll be able to contribute that money to basic education, nutrition, and health care for the world if I choose. I'll be able to shift production a little away from more junk luxuries, and toward more basic goods and services."

3. You do many fantasy rehearsals of the desired patterns of thought, emotion, and behavior in the situations you've listed. You do these often and regularly.

4. When real-life successes come up, you celebrate them greatly. You also include these in your list of desirable patterns and fantasy rehearse them just as the other situations.

5. When real-life failures happen, you learn from the experience. You add the trigger situation to the list of practice situations, and do the other steps with that situation.

6. Meanwhile you expose yourself to models of people who've been exemplars in this skill, and you read further instructions on how to do the skill well. (I recommend reading about the material consumption habits of Mohandas Gandhi and reading the detailed instructions on this skill as contained in the book *Your Money or Your Life* by Dominguez and Robbin.)

Group 13: Self-Care

The first skill in this group is carefulness and appropriate caution. Part of carefulness has to do with not harming other people, as well as taking care of oneself.

The skill titled "habits of self-care" could prevent countless unnecessary deaths, diseases, and injuries.

The self-care group is where I've placed the skill of relaxation. It could have gone in the joyousness group. But some people have to work at this skill rather than just enjoy it!

The skill of self-nurturing talk is one of the best ways of being on your own side and helping yourself.

This group of skills is just as important as the more altruistic ones, such as kindness. In order to help others, you first must take care of yourself.

Skill 54: Carefulness

Carefulness skills should balance courage skills. Courage skills let you act without unrealistically high levels of fear, avoidance, adrenalizing, and mobilization of energy to protect yourself. Courage skills keep fear from interfering too much with a happy life. But carefulness skills help you to have reasonable levels of fear, avoidance, adrenalizing, and mobilizing of energy to protect yourself when you need them. Carefulness skills do something even more important than courage skills: they keep you alive. They also keep you from getting hurt and from damaging your reputation and losing your friends.

If no fears were realistic and if danger did not exist, there would be no need for carefulness skills. But danger does exist.

It's interesting that deficiencies in courage skills don't necessarily provide surpluses in carefulness skills. A person can be greatly afraid of public speaking and very shy about meeting new people, and yet very reckless about driving fast, drinking alcohol, and smoking cigarettes.

Each year millions of teenagers start smoking cigarettes. This behavior is, in my opinion, face-valid evidence of deficiency in carefulness skills. The evidence for the dangers of starting smoking is overwhelming. Cigarettes are highly addictive and cause numerous health problems, including emphysema, lung cancer, heart disease, strokes, and bladder cancer. Smoking causes other bad effects, ranging from premature aging of the skin to increased risk of house fires. It costs money that could be spent on other things. All of these bad outcomes represent danger that's associated with the option of starting to smoke. Disregarding those dangers is not courageous, but foolish. But decisions like these are made very frequently.

To give another example, approximately one in six male drinkers of alcohol becomes a "problem drinker" or alcoholic, and approximately one in sixteen female drinkers has this outcome. A boy might react to these statistics by saying, "Hey, the chances are very good that I won't be an alcoholic. They're way over 50 percent. In fact, the odds are 5 to 1 that I won't become a problem drinker. No problem."

Let's think a little bit about this sort of reasoning. The odds are also five to one that, if you take a revolver pistol with six chambers for bullets, put one bullet in, spin the chambers, put the gun to your head, and pull the trigger, you won't die. So if someone offered you $100 to play Russian roulette in this way, would you take him up on the offer? If you would, then you know how highly you value your life – at somewhere less than $500.

How did I arrive at the figure of $500? You can take my word for it, and skip the next few paragraphs of mathematical explanation, if you want.

One simple way of arriving at this number is to think, you should sell one in five odds of dying for a cost no less than one fifth of the value of your life. If the cost of your life is anything over $500, you shouldn't sell one in five odds of dying for $100.

But for those who've had a little algebra, and are more interested in using math to help decision-making, there's a more rigorous way. In the chapter on decision-making there's a discussion of getting the expected value of an option by adding up the products of the utilities of different outcomes and their probabilities. If you play Russian roulette, the chance of dying is 1/6 and the chance of living is 5/6. The expected value of the option of playing roulette is 1/6 times whatever the negative utility of dying is, plus 5/6 times the utility of winning the game, which is $100.

The expected value of not playing the game at all is 0, no change in your fortunes. So under what circumstances does 1/6 of the negative value of dying plus 5/6 times $100 exceed zero? If you solve the inequality $1/6(X) +5/6(100)>0$, you find it's true only when X has a disutility less than $500. If you value the disutility of dying as less than $500, your life is worth less than $500 to you.

Most people would feel tremendously insulted if someone told them their life was worth less than $500. Yet, with insufficient carefulness skill, they often proclaim the low worth of their lives to themselves.

Suppose a few friends dare an adolescent to dive off a big rock into a river. The adolescent feels the odds are 5 to 1 he'll live; the chances are only 1 in 6 he'll hit a rock and die. But he'll get lots of approval from the gathered gang of friends if he does it. If he does it, by the same calculations listed above, he places a value on his life of only five times the worth of the momentary approval he'll get from his friends. This is a pretty low value! Insufficient carefulness skills lead people to risk things of high value for things of much lower value. It's a foolish decision, because the calculation is never made in the first place.

Let's go back to the example of starting up drinking alcohol. Let's suppose the benefits are feeling close to some peers who also drink, and having more fun with them, and the risks are a one-sixth chance of becoming an alcoholic. If you consider the quality of life that's destroyed by alcoholism, how much is that worth to you? If it's worth any more than five times the value of having fun with the peers, it's not smart to take up drinking.

When I discuss courage skills, I mention that, when there's real danger, often what's necessary is not a strong unpleasant feeling of fear, or the fight-

or-flight response. Often what's most useful is simply mobilizing energy to protect yourself, and avoiding the dangerous situation. For example, riding motorcycles is such a dangerous activity that the people who work in transplant surgery call them "donorcycles." Motorcycles result in many deaths of healthy people who are potential organ donors. If you look at the statistics on riding motorcycles, you find that you don't need to feel fear; you don't need to pump adrenaline; you just need to stay off them, if you value your life highly.

The examples we've examined highlight the fact that carefulness skills are most challenged in situations where there's no certainty of a bad outcome; that is, the chances of an OK outcome are pretty good, but there's a significant chance of a very bad outcome. Other examples are as follows:

In putting herbicides and pesticides on your lawn, there's a good chance of having a lawn that's "better" in some ways and a small chance of giving cancer to yourself or your children.

In driving at high speeds on the highways, (only 10 or 15 miles per hour over the speed limit, as is the current custom), there's a good chance of arriving safely at your destination, but a small chance of being killed.

In being significantly overweight, there's a good chance of escaping serious health problems, but a significant chance of incurring them.

In moving into an old house, without checking for lead in the paint or the pipes, there's a good chance of nothing bad happening, but a significant chance of children getting permanent brain damage from lead toxicity.

When someone confronts you with angry and profane language, if you thoroughly put him down and mention your willingness to fight him, there's a good chance you'll be able to say to yourself, "I told that unpleasant person off; I saved face; I didn't act like a wimp," and a significant chance that you'll get into a fight resulting in death or permanent brain damage, or being imprisoned.

It's not difficult for most people to take protective action when the dangerous situation has already caused them physical pain. If you've been stung by bees several times, for instance, you're probably more careful about going near bees' nests. But when it's possible to escape negative consequences for a long time, you can become desensitized to the danger.

Adolescence is a time of life when carefulness skills are in particularly short supply. That's why auto insurance rates are much higher for adolescents than they are for adults. Driving fast, using drugs, using alcohol, getting into fights, taking risks in sporting and recreational activities, making suicide gestures – these are some of the areas of risk-taking that claim the lives of thousands of adolescents each year. These are by far the most prevalent causes of death in adolescents. Accidents, homicides, and suicides, in that order, are the top three causes of death among adolescents in the U.S.

Why do so many adolescents have such problems with carefulness skills? Perhaps one explanation is that adolescents have very few people whose lives and welfare depend on their careful behavior. A young adult who's a parent and who does not want to leave a child fatherless or motherless has a much bigger incentive to be careful than does an unattached adolescent.

A second possible explanation is that many adolescents are trying to prove themselves independent of their parents; doing dangerous acts that any rational parent would prohibit is a way of saying, "I'm now grown up. I'm now able to make my own decisions."

A third possible explanation is that there's something built in to the evolutionary heritage of the adolescent male, in particular, that makes him want to demonstrate courage to other males and to females, even if that courage is sometimes demonstrated in foolish ways. That is, over the centuries, the more courageous males perhaps enjoyed some sort of advantage in getting their genes passed on.

And, finally, part of the blame could be on our cultural customs that segregate adolescents into settings (e.g. high schools, athletic teams, teenage hangouts) where they have relatively little contact with either adults who could reinforce carefulness, or younger children who require it, but where they're primarily engaged in winning the acceptance of others their same age.

How do we decide which forms of courage are rational, good, and praiseworthy, and which types of fearless or risk-taking behavior are simply foolish? For the person with no beacon that directs decision-making, one form of courage is as good as any other. But for the person who's guided by the beacons of a sound set of ethical principles, such as those listed in the chapter on kindness, decisions are easier.

For example, a doctor decides to take a risk in going to a foreign country devastated by war and poverty to help the people there. He knows there's risk involved, but he calculates that he can do good for humanity and fulfill his purpose of improving the world, and that his chances of succeeding in this venture justify the risks. On the other hand, if he were to take an equally large risk to his life by driving fast, just in order to see how fast his car will go and experience the thrill of speed, the expected payoff does not justify the risk. In fact, this action violates the ethical principle that you should take care of your own health and welfare, so that you can help others.

Now let's talk about some ways of increasing carefulness skills.

Identify important choice points. By the phrase "choice point," I mean a time when you have to make a decision that makes a difference. In a sense, almost every waking moment of life is a choice point. At any given second, you have choices about what to do. When you're watching a videotape, at any moment you can choose to turn it off, switch to another, or keep watching. If you keep watching, you can choose to concentrate fully, or let your mind drift to other things.

But some choice points are more important than others, and those that involve danger and risk are important ones. I believe that for many people with insufficient carefulness skills, the one thing that would help the most is simply to increase their tendency to say to themselves, "Hey, wait a minute. This is an important choice point. Let me think about this a while." Many dangerous behaviors are undertaken impulsively, without thinking before acting.

There's an exercise you can do to practice this subskill of identifying important choice points. You can do it anywhere and any time. You can do it while you're stuck in a traffic jam or while you're listening to a boring speech. You simply think of choice points and rate how important they are. You particularly think about choice points that have happened to you or might happen to you. In rating their importance, you can use an all-purpose rating scale of "how much," as follows:

0 = None
2 = Very little
4 = Some, but not much
6 = Pretty much

8 = High
10 = Very high

Here's an example of someone who's doing this exercise. "Deciding whether to wear my old running shoes or my even older running shoes today: 0 on a scale of 10 importance. Deciding whether to start smoking cigarettes or not: 10 on a scale of 10 importance. Deciding whether to be cheerful or grumpy to my aunt today: 7 on a scale of 10 importance. Deciding whether to drive very fast or drive near the speed limit: 10 on a scale of 10 importance. Deciding whether to get married to a certain person or not: 10. Deciding whether to have 1 percent fat milk or skim milk this morning, 3. Deciding whether to take up playing a very violent video game, 8."

Practice predicting consequences. When people make bad decisions demonstrating low carefulness skills, they often did not stop to think at all about what could happen as a consequence of the option they chose. Another of the major antidotes to low carefulness skills is to spend lots of time predicting consequences of actions. I wrote *The Options and Consequences Book* to help people get practice in thinking of possible consequences. You can look at the options considered there, and think of possible consequences, and see how your list of possible consequences compares with mine. If you work hard, you can probably think of many more than I listed. Or, if the consequences book is not handy, you can simply think of different actions people might consider taking, (especially yourself), and practice listing as many possible consequences as you can for those actions.

When you predict consequences, it's very important to think about the consequences of your behavior on precedents that are set, on habits you're strengthening, and on expectations to act the same way in the future. For example, the immediate consequences of someone's drinking a glass of wine may be of no harm at all. But if, by drinking that glass of wine, the person sets the precedent for himself that drinking alcohol is OK, and if he makes it much more likely he'll drink a lot more in the future, then the action may have very important negative consequences. If a person tells a lie one time, it may have no consequences at all, but if doing it and getting away with it strengthens his habit of being dishonest, that may have very serious consequences for his life.

Think about probabilities and utilities. When you predict consequences, you need to have a gut feeling, if not a numerical estimate, of how good or bad that consequence would be and how likely it is. You can disregard the consequences of very low probability. Someone considers the option of not doing his homework and playing basketball instead. One consequence that occurs to him is that he could get discovered by a talent agent for a professional basketball team and hired on the spot. It is indeed a possibility, but the chances of this happening are so very low that this consequence doesn't even register on the likelihood scale. On the other hand, if taking a certain drug increases the risk of cancer to say, 1 in 50 rather than a much lower risk, then when you multiply the disutility of cancer by the probability of getting it, you still get a very significant number. If there are high disutilities with any significant probabilities, you need to realize that there's danger.

Vividly imagine the negative consequences. When you're trying to increase courage skills, you want to imagine vividly the positive outcome, knowing that the emotions often respond more to mental images than they do to calculations. You use the same principle with carefulness skills, only this time vividly imagining the possible negative consequence that could occur if you take an overly dangerous option.

If you're contemplating driving at too high a speed in a residential neighborhood, you imagine what it might be like if someone rides a bicycle out in front of you. If you're contemplating trying a drug of abuse, you imagine what might happen if you like it so much that you can't stop using it. If you're contemplating using profane and angry language to someone else, you imagine what consequences might occur if there's physical violence between you.

Reinforce carefulness by canceling the image of the bad consequence.

Sometimes people with fearfulness problems sustain their problems by doing the following things: they imagine a bad consequence of the scary situation, avoid the scary situation, and reinforce themselves for avoidance by "canceling" the image of the bad consequence. For example, someone with a fear of social situations gets an image in mind that if he goes to a party, people will laugh at him and look down on him. He decides to stay home from the party, and is reinforced for this decision by the "canceling," or getting out of his mind, the unpleasant image. In this case, the presentation and canceling of a scary image serve to reinforce avoidance in a way that's probably not helpful.

But when you're trying to increase your carefulness skills, you can use the same technique in the service of reinforcing avoidance that's good. For example, someone contemplates riding a bike at high speed with no helmet. She imagines crashing, hurting her head, and becoming brain-damaged for life. When she decides to put her helmet on and ride in a safe place at reasonable speed, her canceling the image of getting brain damaged reinforces her carefulness.

Do fantasy rehearsals. Write down as many examples as you can recall of situations where low carefulness skills have produced bad effects for you. Imagine any other choice points between a reckless and a careful choice. Do fantasy rehearsals out loud of encountering those situations or similar ones and choosing a careful rather than a reckless option. Here's an outline for doing such fantasy rehearsals.

Steps in practicing carefulness

1. Situation:
   Describe the situation. What are the sights, sounds?
2. Thoughts:
   Here's an important choice point. I need to stop and think now.
   What do I have the urge to do? What are the possible consequences of that?
   How bad are the bad consequences? How likely are they?
   I want to think about consequences on habits, expectations, and precedents, not just immediate consequences.
   I want to imagine vividly any bad consequences that are important in this decision.
   I value my life, my safety, and my social reputation very highly. It's not ethical to endanger any of those without a good reason.
3. Emotions:
   Feeling fear of real danger, or the urge to avoid real danger, is a good thing, not a cowardly thing.
   I want to feel proud of being reasonable about this.
4. Behavior:
   I'm doing the option that I chose. I'm doing something that makes sense. I'm avoiding taking foolish risks.
5. Celebration:
   Hooray, I did a good job!

Habits of self-care are a special set of self-discipline skills, the ones that preserve our health and safety. Many health problems spring from preventable causes. In other words, if all people followed the health and safety practices that are the subject of this chapter, a vast amount of unnecessary suffering and premature death could be prevented.

Ethyl alcohol

Throughout history, ethyl alcohol has probably caused more damage than any other drug of abuse because of its ubiquitous presence and because it's a far more dangerous drug than most people seem to realize.

Of all the psychiatric diagnoses given to males in the United States, alcohol abuse is the most frequent – the number one diagnosis. In females, alcohol abuse accounts for a high portion of psychiatric diagnoses.

Of drinkers, and excluding abstainers, about 14 to 16 percent of male drinkers and 6 percent of female drinkers report a moderate level of tangible negative consequences associated with alcohol abuse. Thus, if a male takes up drinking, the chances are about one in six or seven that he will suffer negative consequences from abuse.

A study of criminal offenders convicted of violent crimes revealed that 54 percent of them had used alcohol just before the offense. Alcohol involvement was particularly prevalent in cases of manslaughter (68 percent) and assault (62 percent).

A substantial portion of people who commit homicide had used alcohol shortly before the time of the crime. Among homicide victims, one study found that 33 percent of them were legally intoxicated at the time of their murder (with a blood alcohol concentration of 0.10 percent or higher). Another study was very similar, finding that 30 percent of murder victims were legally intoxicated. The increased risk of being a murder victim, if one is drunk, is partly based on the fact that homicide offenders are more likely to have been drinking if the victim has been drinking and vice versa.

Alcohol is also related to suicide. Suicide is one of the three leading causes of death among males 15-34 years old. (The other two are homicides and accidents.) An analysis of 3,400 violence-related deaths in which the victim's blood alcohol concentrations were tested found that suicide was the cause of 21 percent of those deaths. In 35 percent of those suicides, the victims had been drinking; intoxication was present at the time of death in 23 percent.

Alcoholics have a very high suicide rate. Suicide rates of 8 to 21 percent were found in a review of several follow-up studies of alcoholics. One study of patients who survived unsuccessful suicide attempts found that 50 percent of male suicide attempters had a drinking problem, with 25 percent of them classed as alcohol-dependent. The proportion of female suicide attempters with drinking problems was about 23 percent in this study. According to the same study, 74 percent of the male suicide attempters and 51 percent of the female suicide attempters had been drinking shortly before the suicide attempt.

Alcohol is also strongly related to motor vehicle crashes. According to one study, about 43 percent of fatally injured drivers were legally drunk at the time of their deaths.

Liver disease has long occupied a place on the top ten causes of death in the U.S. It's generally agreed that at least 50 percent of all cirrhosis deaths are alcohol related, although some estimates are as high as 95 percent.

Adding together deaths due to suicide, homicide, accidents, cirrhosis of the liver, and all other alcohol-related causes, the yearly death toll for alcohol has been estimated at approximately 100,000 people.

The Wernicke-Korsakoff syndrome is a disorder of the brain resulting from the combination of protracted alcoholism and deficiency of the vitamin thiamine, or vitamin B-1. One of the major symptoms of this disorder is the inability to form new memories. Thus, the person with this syndrome cannot remember recent events and cannot learn new material. But, even if someone receives adequate amounts of thiamine, that doesn't necessarily make him immune to the brain damage and memory problems produced by alcohol. There's now impressive evidence in studies of rodents that chronic alcohol consumption, unaccompanied by malnutrition, results in permanent learning deficits and significant brain damage.

One study in humans analyzed the frequency of CT-Scan abnormalities and deficiencies in psychological testing results in a group of thirty-nine drinkers who consumed less than five ounces of pure alcohol a day. This study also looked at the diet and nutritional status of these people. Thirty-one of these subjects showed some degree of atrophy of the brain on CT-Scan, and twenty-five of these people also performed poorly on psychological tests of brain functioning. Sixteen of these subjects were nutritionally deficient, and fifteen of those had abnormal CT-Scans or psychological tests results. However, there was a lack of correlation between nutritional indexes and the severity of abnormalities in the CT-Scans and psychological tests. These findings suggest the abnormalities are probably due to alcohol effects themselves, rather than only to the nutritional deficiencies associated with alcoholism.

There are also short-term effects on memory caused by a dose of alcohol. Studies indicate that the tendency of heavy drinkers to forget things they've done while drunk can be replicated in experiments. Acute doses of alcohol are reported to have disruptive effects on human memory. A blood-alcohol concentration of .04 grams per 100 milliliters of blood (40 percent of the way toward being legally drunk) can disrupt memory functions, and memory impairment progresses as the blood-alcohol concentration rises.

There's some evidence that alcohol can cause permanent reductions in "cognitive efficiency," or intellectual functioning, in social drinkers. The investigations of intellectual functioning in nonalcoholic social drinkers have yielded inconsistent results. Some studies do not demonstrate an effect. However, at least five studies have found an effect on the cognitive efficiency of even moderate social drinkers. The final answer to this question is not in, but there's some evidence suggesting that moderate doses of alcohol may be somewhat harmful to the brain, just as high doses of alcohol are definitely harmful to the brain. One review concluded, "It is clear that the cognitive efficiency of moderate social drinkers can be compromised."

Alcohol affects sex hormones in men. Chronic alcoholic men sometimes become "feminized," with female hair patterns and enlargement of their breasts. In carefully controlled research ward studies, it has been found that alcohol causes a decrease in the levels of testosterone, the major male sexual hormone, in the bloodstream. It has

been suggested that alcohol is a direct toxin to the cells of testes that manufacture testosterone. At some point, after a certain amount of ingestion of alcohol, the changes in the testosterone-producing cells become irreversible.

The ingestion of alcohol by pregnant women is so harmful to the brain of the fetus that it constitutes the number-one cause of mental retardation in the United States.

The most obvious cases of the ill effects of alcohol are referred to as "Fetal Alcohol Syndrome." The research on this question started in the early 1970s. In 1973, investigators described a number of gross physical deformities in eleven very young children of severely alcoholic mothers who drank during pregnancy. These children had small openings of the eyes, drooping eyelids, small eyes, underdeveloped midfaces, skin folds in the corners of the eyes, an underdeveloped philtrum (the depression just above the upper lip), an exaggerated space between the nose and the upper lip, and small head circumference. Ten years later, eight of these eleven children were re-examined. Four of them had an I.Q. in the range between 70 and 86, which is borderline retarded to low-normal range of intelligence. The other four had an I.Q. ranging from 20-57 and were in the severely retarded range. The degree of intellectual impairment they had correlated with the severity of their physical malformation. Another prominent problem in these children was growth deficiency.

The finding that such serious problems resulted when severely alcoholic mothers drank a lot of alcohol during pregnancy raised questions about how frequent such problems are in the population as a whole, and how much of a problem is caused in fetuses when the alcohol intake of their mothers is relatively milder.

Fetal Alcohol Syndrome, as defined by deformities, growth problems and/or intellectual problems has been estimated to occur in somewhere between one and three babies per 1,000 live births. If you take the lower figure of 1 in 1,000, this would imply that, of some 250 million Americans, some 250,000 of them are affected by Fetal Alcohol Syndrome.

If a mother drinks heavily during pregnancy, it's not automatic that the child will have Fetal Alcohol Syndrome. For some reason, some fetuses are more susceptible than others. In one study, among the 5 percent of pregnancies where the mothers drank the most heavily, only 5-10 percent of the infants scored abnormally low on mental and psychomotor tests when tested at eight months of age. In another study, only five babies among the 204 offspring of a group of heavily drinking women had Fetal Alcohol Syndrome.

However, the lowering of intelligence does not necessarily require the full presence of Fetal Alcohol Syndrome. In one study, the children of alcoholic mothers scored 15-19 I.Q. points lower than the comparison group of children. The results of this study suggested that, although the children with clear-cut Fetal Alcohol Syndrome, and its attendant deformities and growth problems, showed the lowest I.Q. scores, children of alcoholic mothers can have their I.Q. scores depressed by their mother's drinking during pregnancy, even without the physical deformities of Fetal Alcohol Syndrome.

According to one review, "The prevailing view . . . is that the obvious developmental and behavioral [problems] of Fetal Alcohol Syndrome represent only the most severe end of a continuum of fetal damage that can be produced by prenatal alcohol exposure, and that lower levels of maternal drinking may also have some measurable effect upon the fetus."

In other words, if a lot of alcohol can do a lot of damage, a little alcohol can do a little damage. One large-scale study looked at effects on children compared with the average intake of alcohol by the mother during the pregnancy. The data from this study showed that even a very small amount of alcohol consumption by mothers can have an effect on the unborn child. This same longitudinal study has found that alcohol-related neurological and behavioral effects have persisted in children of heavier-drinking mothers to at least four years of age. Furthermore, the more sensitive laboratory tests continue to show reduced attention and slower information processing even in four-year-old children who were exposed before birth to lower levels of alcohol.

The authors advise caution in interpreting these findings. A variety of possible drinking patterns during pregnancy were grouped together in the same average daily consumption categories, and some drinking patterns within each average consumption level could be riskier than others. For example, going on a drinking binge, especially at a critical period of vulnerability of the fetus, may be especially harmful, even though the average level of alcohol per day is not that great.

Also, we should note that, although neurological and behavioral deficits in children were found to be associated with low to moderately heavy alcohol consumption during pregnancy, the deficits were relatively small, and measurements in a large number of such children were required to achieve statistical significance.

Another study looked at eighty-four children of mothers who drank at moderate levels primarily during their pregnancies. Only one woman during this sample consumed more than an average of one-and-a-half ounces of alcohol a day throughout pregnancy. Binge drinking was very infrequent in these women. Nonetheless, tests performed when the children were thirteen months of age suggested that social drinking during pregnancy was associated with lower scores on tests of spoken language and verbal comprehension in the children.

The evidence clearly recommends that pregnant women should not drink alcohol at all. The same recommendation would hold for a woman who's attempting to get pregnant, or who is fertile, sexually active, and without a foolproof method of birth control.

If someone has alcohol problems, aiming toward "moderate drinking," as contrasted with total abstinence, seems to be a bad idea. One very interesting study on this topic looked at sixty-two chronic alcoholics. Thirty of them received training in "nonproblem drinking skills." In other words, this subgroup was taught to drink at moderate levels, rather than to abstain from alcohol. Six months later, this subgroup had experienced more abusive drinking days than the thirty-two people who had not received this training. In other words, in this study the attempt to teach moderate drinking to problem drinkers was a failure.

Other studies have compared heavy drinkers who have set the goal of total abstinence with those who have set the goal of moderate drinking. The relapse into alcoholism was higher in those who had attempted to drink moderately.

Another study looked at 1,300 alcoholics and measured how many of them went on to become moderate drinkers. Only 1.6 percent of them had been able to do this.

In general, the evidence supports the idea that, once significant dependence on alcohol has occurred, the alcoholic no longer has the option of returning to social drinking, and that abstinence is the most appropriate goal.

National surveys of drinking practices indicate that approximately one third of the U.S. population ages 18 and over are abstainers from alcohol. Drinking alcohol is a social phenomenon, so abstaining from alcohol decreases the probability that those in your social network, i.e. family members and friends, will become alcoholic.

My own conclusion is that a drug that constitutes the number-one cause of mental retardation is, by that fact alone, too dangerous for our society to play around with, and that, in a rational society, the custom of social drinking would be abandoned, just as the custom of indoor smoking in public places has been.

Effects of tobacco

Tobacco addiction rivals alcohol addiction with respect to total damage done. The word "tobacco addict" is probably a more accurate rendering of reality than the word "smoker."

Tobacco is a highly addictive substance; difficulty in withdrawing from cigarettes has been compared with the difficulty in escaping addiction to heroin. Among smokers who receive formal help with their problem, only about twenty to forty percent are still not smoking a year after treatment.

Cigarette smoke comprises several different substances. Nicotine is probably what makes tobacco addictive; some of the other components, such as benzopyrene, nitrosamines, and other chemicals are documented to cause cancer; formaldehyde and acetaldehyde inhibit the cilia (the little hair-like cells that help clean the respiratory system).

Smoking makes it more likely for someone to get coronary artery disease, strokes, and peripheral vascular disease. Smoke accelerates atherosclerosis. A wide variety of cancers, including lung cancer, are far more common in cigarette smokers. Smoking dramatically increases the likelihood of getting chronic bronchitis and emphysema. Emphysema is irreversible damage to the sacs that make up lung tissue, reducing the total surface area available for oxygen to get into the blood. In pregnant women, smoking leads to an increase in miscarriages, reduced birth weight of the children, increased perinatal mortality, and increased likelihood of sudden death of infants. Smokers have more sleep difficulties, and tend to have more depression, anxiety, and irritability.

Cigarette smoke inhaled by non-smokers can cause cancer, asthma, lung dysfunction, and angina. When addicted smokers stop, there's often a withdrawal syndrome consisting of drowsiness, headaches, increased appetite, insomnia, restlessness, irritability, hostility, anxiety, upset stomach, and difficulty concentrating. Smoking wrinkles the skin of smokers, so they tend to look older than other people their age; thus, if the desire for health and life isn't enough to make some smokers quit, vanity might provide a motivation.

Effects of marijuana

Marijuana (its most active component is tetrahydrocannabinol) has a reputation as relatively safe drug, among drugs of abuse. However, that reputation is deserved mainly because marijuana's companions in the set of illegal drugs are even worse. In the short term, marijuana interferes with short-term memory, attention span, recall, the ability to store knowledge, verbal expression, and the capacity to carry out tasks requiring multiple mental steps. People under the influence of marijuana have a tendency to confuse past, present, and future. I believe a way of summarizing these facts is that marijuana users pay money for a substance that makes them temporarily more stupid.

Balance and stability of stance are hampered even at low doses. Driving impairment lasts four to eight hours, long after the user perceives the effects of the drug. Higher doses can produce hallucinations, delusions, paranoid feelings, and confused and disorganized thinking. Exposure of pregnant women to marijuana results in lower birth weight and possible persistent effects on the learning of the offspring. Chronic use of marijuana is associated with bronchitis and asthma.

The "tar" produced by burning marijuana is more carcinogenic to animals than tar from cigarettes, because marijuana cigarettes contain more tar and respiratory irritants than tobacco smoke. Chronic use of marijuana may lead to an "amotivational syndrome" consisting of apathy, dullness, and impairment of judgment, concentration, and memory, and loss of interest in pursuit of goals. Marijuana may have an effect on sexual functioning: anovulatory cycles and lowered concentrations of testosterone have been reported. Temporarily lower sperm counts and inhibition of the hypothalamic-pituitary axis have also been reported.

Effects of cocaine and amphetamine

Cocaine and amphetamine are similar in their pharmacologic effects. The person who takes them for the purpose of getting high usually finds that a higher and higher dose is required over time for the high to occur. As higher doses are used, toxic effects appear. Grinding of the teeth, picking of the face and hands, suspiciousness, and a feeling of being watched can occur. The user can start having hallucinations: a feeling of bugs on the skin or visions of lights. Disorganization of thinking occurs. After a period of using these drugs and then stopping, the user will usually sleep for a long time, and wake up feeling hungry, depressed, and lethargic. The lethargy can last for many days, until the use of the drug again interrupts the lethargy and the cycle starts over. Those who get delusions and hallucinations with cocaine or amphetamine may experience a "kindling" process in which a smaller dose, or perhaps only environmental stimuli, may be sufficient in the future to elicit the same response. The paranoia, delusions, and hallucinations that occur with these drugs can be indistinguishable from a schizophrenic syndrome.

Cocaine use has been linked by some research to manic-depressive illness. Some researchers feel that a recent increase in manic-depressive illness may be attributable to the rise in cocaine abuse.

Use of cocaine in high doses has been reported to do damage to blood vessels and to adrenergic neurons in the brain. Long-term use has led to exaggerated startle reactions and abnormalities of muscle movement.

Overdoses of these drugs can be fatal.

Effects of narcotics

Heroin is the prototypical narcotic of abuse, and it's usually injected intravenously to get the maximum high. Morphine is very similar to heroin, and oxycodone, codeine, and several other prescribed drugs are in this class.

In terms of damage to body organs, the narcotics are not nearly as bad as alcohol or tobacco. But the longer narcotics are used, the more the brain becomes dependent on them for the ability to feel good. There's an extremely unpleasant withdrawal syndrome that lasts a week or two, and a much more prolonged state of feeling bad after that. This bad feeling can be relieved temporarily by another dose of narcotic. Thus the motivation to get more narcotics becomes extremely high, and the narcotics user becomes trapped in a cycle of delivering more and more money to the supplier of the drug. If the user doesn't have enough money, he will have to steal it. The difference between the bad feeling of withdrawal and the good feeling of an injection of narcotic is so high that many narcotics users cannot avoid this reinforcement; they will use dirty needles and risk infecting themselves with AIDS.

The two worst drugs in my estimation

Which drugs of abuse do you think are most dangerous? It would be very interesting to find a rank ordering of the danger of the entire set of drugs of abuse by experts in this field. According to the evidence I've read, first place for the worst drug class goes to the inhalants: the chemicals one gets by sniffing glue and other organic solvents. These can cause death or irreversible damage to the brain (as well as to the liver and kidneys). People who use these solvents to get high have been found to have shrinkage of the brain and lowered IQ scores. In other words, they make you permanently more stupid, that is, if they don't kill you.

My second-place designation for the worst illegal drug in prominent use at this time goes to MDMA or "ecstasy." Accumulated good evidence shows that "ecstasy" in the doses people ordinarily use to get high can do permanent damage to memory functions and other brain functions. This drug particularly damages serotonergic neurons, the ones whose functioning the class of Prozac-like drugs seeks to increase in treating depression, anxiety, and a variety of other disorders.

Some other factors in risk-benefit calculations

When one is contemplating taking a drug of abuse, one should take into account the effects on other people as well as the effects upon oneself. Suppose I give a party in which one of the activities is Russian roulette. Six people play, and one is killed. Do the other five players or the host bear no responsibility for the one who died? If the other five had all said, "No way am I going to play that dumb game," the other one probably would not have done so either. Thus the five players created the social environment that killed the sixth.

The same is true with "social" drinking. The five men in six who don't become alcoholics create the social climate that ruins the sixth one's life. (I speak of men because the rates of alcoholism are higher among men than women. But with slightly different numbers, the same arguments can be made for women too.)

Other drugs of abuse, including cocaine, heroin, and marijuana, all present a choice between the instant gratification of the pleasure the drug gives and the long-term gratification of avoiding the negative health consequences they produce.

With all these drugs, and with the health skills group in general, another exercise in delay of gratification involves the relatively unexciting and unstimulating activity of reading and learning about the side effects of these drugs. Which is more pleasant?: to watch an exciting movie, or to read about how carcinogenic marijuana smoke is? But such a delay of gratification exercise can be literally life saving.

Before leaving this brief discussion of drug abuse, it's good to think about the ethics of supporting the illegal drug economy. Probably not many people enjoy the idea of contributing financially to murder. It may be helpful for someone trying to get off illegal drugs to consider that the competition among various suppliers of illegal drugs is not done primarily by catchier advertising, a friendlier sales force, more efficient manufacturing, and so forth: the dominant suppliers at most points along the chain are those who have successfully threatened the competition with death, or killed them. The buyers of illegal drugs vote with their dollars to support the most ruthless and brutal members of society.

Weight control

In some ways avoiding obesity is even more difficult than avoiding a drug of abuse: you can totally abstain from drugs and gradually build up that habit of total avoidance, but you can't do the same with food. Avoiding obesity results in large health advantages, among them lower rates of adult onset diabetes, high blood pressure, and cardiovascular illness.

In the United States, the problem of obesity is more the rule than the exception, despite increased awareness of health risks and despite often cruel and vicious discrimination against obese people.

What advice can be given to the person interested in weight control? The following summarizes what I've gleaned from studies and experience.

It's important to see the goal of weight control in perspective. Attainment of ideal body weight does contribute to health and well-being. But this goal isn't worth the risk of developing a life-threatening eating disorder (such as anorexia or bulimia), or hating yourself. Life is too short to go through it obsessed with one's weight. There are more important goals.

It's important to recognize the long-term nature of the weight control goal. Too many people think in terms of going on a diet and losing x number of pounds. To escape this perspective, think about the fact that your total weight at this point reflects the total energy intake through food and the total expenditure of calories over all your life so far. To think about this in another way: suppose two people start a decade at their ideal weight. Ten years later, one of them is forty pounds overweight, and the other is still at the ideal bodyweight. Suppose we define "positive caloric balance" as more calories ingested than expended. What average daily positive caloric balance would result in the forty-pound weight gain over ten years? The answer (assuming about 3,500 calories per pound) works about to about forty calories per day.

How long does it take to expend forty calories per day? Moderate exercise burns about ten calories per minute. So the person who's forty pounds overweight could have eaten exactly the same things he ate for those ten years, yet remained at ideal bodyweight by simply adding four minutes a day of moderate exercise! Or: that person could have remained at ideal bodyweight by the subtraction of a mere forty calories a day of food intake. That's less than three teaspoons of sugar!

You often read that diets don't work. It is true that "going on a diet" aimed at short-term weight loss, involving great deprivation, is usually followed by regain of weight. However, many people have successfully lost weight and have kept it off. And most of these have set some sort of rules for themselves, and have followed them.

What sorts of rules are these? One extremely sensible rule has to do with the distribution of food in the diet, and shifting food intake away from "junk food," the type of food that has high caloric density and not much nutritional substance. I believe a reasonable rule is to take in a maximum of a couple of hundred calories (or more, or less, depending upon your energy expenditure) of junk food per day. Some people can achieve good weight control simply by limiting the junk and eating as much as they want of the nonjunk. It can be helpful to try to eat more nonstarchy vegetables, because they induce a feeling of fullness with little caloric load. Distributing the whole dietary intake so that the staples are whole grains, vegetables, and fruits will make weight control much easier. Nobody gets fat by bingeing on broccoli, spinach, lentils, and eggplant.

A second very sensible rule is to increase the daily exercise to a much higher level than most people achieve. The health benefits of exercise go far beyond those of weight control. The human body, through centuries of evolution, has been in almost constant motion during the waking hours, in a never-ending search for food through "hunting and gathering." In many ways the hours of sitting that make up most people's lifestyles are not what the body was designed for. The cardiovascular benefits of exercise keep increasing up to at least the level of about 500 calories a day, which is achievable from fifty minutes a day of moderate exercise. Increasing caloric expenditure by this much per day can make it drastically easier to achieve weight control.

Another reasonable rule is to restrict the circumstances for eating. For those people who nibble many times during the day, it may be possible to lower caloric intake the little bit that makes the difference between success and failure by restricting eating to three or four discrete meals. In each of these meals, a reasonable amount of food is chosen, placed on a table, and eaten, without additions (with the exception of nonstarchy vegetables). In choosing the food for those meals, you simply take a guess at what amounts will give you a slightly negative caloric balance for the day.

If curtailing junk food, increasing exercise, and curtailing eating between meals do not work by themselves, and if the goal of weight control is of very high priority, then the next rule is to make *sure* to achieve a small to moderate negative caloric balance daily. If this is the rule, then you have to weigh or measure, write down, and calculate the caloric load from all the food you eat during the day. When you reach the level that's about 500 to 800 calories under your estimated caloric intake, you stop eating for the day. This is tedious effort and requires great self-discipline, but it will succeed if it's continued long enough.

Exercise

Exercise has very positive health consequences, partly by contributing to less obesity and partly through other pathways. One of the most interesting health benefits of exercise is as an anti-depressant. A controlled study recently contrasted daily aerobic exercise with one of the antidepressant drugs as a treatment for middle-aged depressed people. In the short run, the two treatments were approximately equally effective, but upon longer-term follow-up, the exercise group did even better than the antidepressant drug group. In other studies, exercise has also reduced anxiety. One of the mechanisms for the mental health effects of exercise may be the effect upon sleep and daily rhythms.

Both strength-training (e.g. lifting weights) and aerobic training (e.g. running, swimming, biking) are useful in weight control. Strength training builds muscle, and muscle tissue burns calories.

A major challenge is to find a form of exercise that can be enjoyable enough to do regularly and frequently. At the beginning stages of an exercise program, if exercise is unpleasant, the best advice is to lower the intensity of exercise until there's no pain, but to continue daily exercise. Over time, people tend to habituate to the unpleasant aspects of exercise and to cultivate the pleasures of it; this is a very positive form of "addiction."

Sleep habits and circadian rhythms

One of the most important habits of self-care is that of maintaining a regular sleep rhythm, or as some researchers have come to call it, good "sleep hygiene."

A significant portion of the bad feelings human beings have may come from their bodies' not fully "knowing" whether they're supposed to be asleep or awake. Huge numbers of people can't sleep well at night, yet feel tired or doze off during the day. It's as though the body is constantly straddling the fence on whether to be awake or be asleep. This appears to be particularly true in the state of depression.

How does the body know whether to be awake or asleep? The regulation of the sleep-wake cycle is a very important circadian rhythm. The word "circadian" literally means "about a day" – the times when you want to go to sleep and wake up recur about a day after the times you most recently went to sleep and woke up. A variety of hormones rise and fall in a daily rhythm. Melatonin is one of the hormones that have an influence on sleep, but others do as well. Body temperature also follows a daily rhythm, which is tied to the sleep cycle.

How does the body fall into a rhythm where it "knows" when to be asleep and when to be awake? First of all, the very idea of a rhythm suggests you should strive for regularity in your times of going to bed and getting up. If there's wide variation, you're losing the power of circadian rhythms to help the body know when to wake up or go to sleep. So the first rule in setting circadian rhythms is to try to go to bed and get up as close to the same time each day as you can.

Right away we run into problems with a culture where "night life" on weekends might last until 2 a.m., and morning classes or work time on weekdays might start at 8 a.m. It's impossible to maintain a good circadian rhythm around those parameters unless you happen to be that very rare sort of person who only needs four or five hours of sleep.

Especially for adolescents and young adults, a very common problem is "delayed sleep phase disorder." This means your circadian rhythm is telling you to go to sleep, for example, at 3 a.m. and sleep until 11 a.m., (and you do this on weekends and holidays), but the morning school bus ride or morning commute to work starts at 7:30 a.m. The body is saying, "It's in the middle of the night," while the person is trying to wake up and start the day.

What problems does this cause? Falling asleep at class or work, missing class or work, feeling irritable or tired, and being much less productive at class or work are big problems with this pattern. Another problem is insomnia. If someone's body is set to have night begin at 3 a.m., and he goes to bed at 10 p.m., he will usually lie there fully alert, because his body is telling him it's still

time to be awake. Circadian rhythm disorders are a big and very prevalent problem. Almost all high school and college students either have this problem or know someone who has it.

How do you reset circadian rhythms? How do you get yourself falling asleep and waking up earlier? The sleep researchers use the word *zeitgebers* to refer to those stimuli that reset circadian rhythms. There are four main ones to know about.

The first we have already mentioned: what time you go to bed and what time you get out of bed.

The second is bright light. Bright light falling on the retina in the morning tends to move the circadian rhythm earlier. Bright light late in the evening tends to move it later. So if you want to wake up earlier and get sleepy earlier, expose yourself to bright light upon awakening, for at least half an hour, perhaps as long as two hours. If sunlight is not available or convenient, a variety of companies make bright lights especially for this purpose.

The third zeitgeber is exercise. Exercise first thing in the morning also tends to move the sleep cycle earlier. It's as though exercise tells the body, "Yes, it really is time for the awake cycle to begin."

The fourth zeitgeber is food. People with delayed sleep phase disorder tend not to be hungry in the morning, and to get hungry late at night. If you avoid eating after, say, 7 p.m. and try to eat first thing in the morning, you can use this to set your sleep rhythm earlier.

If you keep all four of these zeitgebers recurring in your life on a very regular daily rhythm, your chances for good sleep and alert wakefulness are vastly greater than if you don't.

Here's how this might work. Suppose you're in a habit of falling asleep at 3 a.m. and getting up at 11 a.m. You want to get into a rhythm of going to sleep at 11 p.m. and waking up at 7 a.m. To do this, you try as hard as you can to stay awake between the hours of 7 a.m. and 11 p.m., and you give yourself every possible opportunity to sleep between 11 p.m. and 7 a.m.

How do you wake yourself up at 7a.m.? First, by getting up out of bed, and then by getting exercise, bright light, and a substantial breakfast. Throughout the day you use exercise to help yourself stay awake. After about 8 p.m. you avoid exercising and eating. Then when 11 p.m. comes around, you lie down in bed, in the dark, with no music and no TV on. If you can get to sleep within twenty to thirty minutes, you sleep. If you can't get to sleep, then you get up and do something useful: clean the house, write about the worries on your mind, write about the things you're glad to have done, read this book, study schoolwork, pay bills, etc. You avoid bright light, eating, or exercise.

After about an hour or so, you lie down, relax, and let pleasant images of kindness, beauty, and calmness go through your mind. If you fall asleep during this time, that's good; if you can't fall asleep after half an hour or so, get up and spend another hour doing something useful. If you wake up before 7 a.m. and can't get back to sleep, go back into the same cycle of getting up, doing something useful for an hour, and then lying down for twenty to thirty minutes. When 7 a.m. comes around, you get up, exercise, get bright light for at least half an hour, eat a big breakfast, and try to keep yourself awake till 11 p.m.

If you have the self-discipline to follow this plan immediately, this is the quickest way to reset the circadian rhythm. If you can not get yourself out of bed at 7 a.m., an alternative is to work backwards from 11 a.m. to 7 a.m. more gradually, getting up as early as possible each morning and getting the light, exercise, and breakfast as soon as possible upon awakening.

Suggestions for sleep hygiene

The following list summarizes some suggestions on sleep hygiene and the reasons for them.

1. Try to go to bed and get up within a half-hour of the same time each day and night. Even better is exactly the same time each day and night. Here's the reason: this sets your circadian rhythm in a consistent pattern. Cultivating circadian rhythms that will tell you very clearly whether to be awake or asleep, with no ambiguity, is key to the reconditioning process.

2. If you're not sleeping well, let your regular bedtime be late enough and your regular time of arising be early enough so that you're a little sleep deprived. After your sleep habits improve, then you can lengthen the sleep time if you wish. Here's the reason: you want sleep deprivation working on your side so you'll associate your bed with sleeping. After this association builds up strongly, you can gradually lengthen your sleep time if you need more sleep per day.

3. Use the bed only for sleeping, and no other activity, such as doing homework, reading, discussing important decisions. (There's one exception: The sleep researchers, who are very familiar with the "art of the possible," don't try to prohibit couples who sleep together from having sex in bed.) The reason for using your bed for sleeping only is that you want to establish a conditioned association between lying down in bed and going to sleep. The longer you use the bed for some activity that requires you to be awake, the more you break up the association between the bed and sleep.

4. If you lie down in bed and can't go to sleep for twenty to thirty minutes, get out of bed and do something useful but nonexciting, something that doesn't involve eating, bright lights, or exercise, for about an hour. (Reading this book is an excellent activity for those times.) Then lie down again. Here's the reason: You don't want to spend a lot of time in bed awake, because this breaks up the association between the bed and sleeping. The exception to this is when you're doing such pleasant drifting and relaxing that you could enjoy it even if it went on all night long.

5. If you can't go to sleep, try to do something you can celebrate having completed. This reduces how bad it seems to you to be sleepless. If you desperately fear sleeplessness, that fear can keep you awake. Remind yourself that sleep deprivation is not horrible. The more you can want to be able to stay awake, to get more done, the less the fear of sleeplessness keeps you awake. You stay out of the vicious circle where such fear creates sleeplessness and sleeplessness leads to more fear.

6. If you find that, while you're in bed, lots of worries or things you need to do are running through your mind, get up and write down all those things, and, if possible, schedule a time to do the things you need to do. Here's why: sometimes the business of the day keeps you from remembering important things to do, and they rush into your mind when you go to bed. If they're written down and scheduled, then you don't need to be trying to remember them.

7. Study your master to-do list, make a daily to-do list, put the to-dos in priority order, and schedule the highest priority to-dos each day. Here's why this helps: If you will make a routine of doing this, the things you need to do

will get taken care of and scheduled, so you won't need to do the previous suggestion so often.

8. Get at least twenty minutes of strenuous exercise each day, preferably much more. Preferably get some of it the first thing in the morning. Here's the reason: the exercise gets you tired and helps you sleep. Exercise first thing in the morning helps to set your circadian rhythms into motion so your body will start the clock running in the morning and will know it's time to go to sleep at your bedtime. During the centuries in which the human body evolved, people had to get much more exercise than they do today, if they wanted to live. The body was not built for sitting around as much as most people do.

9. Avoid anything containing caffeine after the noon meal. Caffeine can keep you awake.

10. Practice the relaxation response during the day when you get a chance. This includes noticing any tension in your muscles, and trying to reduce that tension. Use biofeedback if available. Relaxing is a skill that needs practice. You should cultivate it by working at it regularly. Biofeedback can measure your degree of expertise at it.

11. Practice relaxing for a few minutes each night before going to sleep. (Please see the chapter on relaxation skills in this book.) Reason: getting your body relaxed helps you get ready to go to sleep.

12. While you're lying in bed, practice the art of imagining or remembering pleasant but not too exciting fantasies. Imagine stories as in picture books for young children where all the characters are nice, everything will turn out OK, and there's never any real danger. Do the "pleasant dreams exercise" in which you let a stream of images of kindness, calmness, and beauty go through your mind. Such stimuli are conducive to peaceful transition to sleep for adults as well as children.

13. Make sure the stimuli present when you go to sleep are the same ones that will be present if you wake up briefly in the middle of the night, preferably no stimuli at all (dark room, quiet.) Everyone tends to wake up briefly in the middle of the night; you want to be able to fall back asleep at those times. That's why you want to condition yourself to fall asleep with those stimuli present. Some people go to sleep with stimuli such as TV or music; when they wake up, they "don't know how" to fall back to sleep in a dark, quiet room.

14. If your sleep is disrupted by nightmares, use the strategy of revising the nightmare in your mind, practicing being in control of your own fantasies. While you're awake, replay the nightmare up to the point where you begin to feel anxious. Then call up whatever imaginary allies you need (people, machines, magic wands, etc.) to make yourself safe. If there's a scary character, find out what he wants. If what he wants is bad, ask him what he accomplishes by getting that, and keep going

backward until you come to some basic motive that can be fulfilled in positive ways as well as harmful ways. Work out a way that you and the scary character can make an exchange with each other. Turn the scary character into an ally who will use its powers to help you in the future, rather than work against you. Or if there's some other sort of scary event in the nightmare, figure out a way to imagine yourself triumphing over it and coming out safe and sound. In summary: you make the nightmare a story with a happy ending.

Other health and safety habits

Let's list some other health and safety habits that can require self-discipline skills.

Avoiding riding in autos at "excessive speed" or with an intoxicated driver

Using seat belts

Getting adequate sleep (so as, for example, not to fall asleep at the wheel while driving)

Complying with prescribed medical treatments (for example, medication for people with high blood pressure, proper insulin dose for diabetics, proper self-catheterization for those with certain neurological problems with bladder functioning)

Proper dental self-care and compliance with dental treatment

Using sunscreen and clothing to minimize sun exposure to the skin and avoid skin cancer

Avoiding loud noise exposure (to prevent hearing loss)

Avoiding herbicides and pesticides (to prevent cancer, Parkinson's disease, and other health problems)

Avoiding anything that propels one at high speed without adequate crash protection, e.g. motorcycles

Avoiding being in high places without adequate protection against falls (e.g. rock climbing on cliffs without being adequately belayed, working on rooftops without securing oneself)

Avoiding exposure to high crime regions, if possible, especially at night and when alone

Avoiding any activity that causes blows to the head, e.g. boxing

Avoiding being outside in lightning storms

Avoiding situations where violent conflict with others is likely

Being careful with or avoiding the use of fire in and around houses, and making sure electrical systems in houses are not conducive to fire

Keeping weapons such as firearms locked up securely

Watching constantly over the activities of toddlers, closely supervising preschoolers, giving appropriate supervision to older children

Preventing circumstances where heavy objects can fall over onto people

Wearing helmets in activities where head injury is possible, e.g. biking, skating

Becoming a skilled swimmer before spending much time around bodies of water or on boats

Treating with great caution any machinery that grinds, cuts, crushes, drills, or pierces

Avoiding being around highly flammable materials such as gasoline vapors

Avoiding taking risks with fireworks

Avoiding inhaling dust, gases, smoke, or anything else other than air

Avoiding entrusting your health or safety to people whose dependability is not demonstrated: e.g. by accepting rides with strangers, accepting drugs from strangers

Many health and safety hazards stem from sources of energy that can possibly be applied to the body. Guns, motorcycles, fast-moving cars, heavy objects that can fall over, electrical outlets, lightning storms, bright sunlight, being in high places, fires, highly flammable materials, electric machinery, and the fast motion of skating or skiing all represent energy sources that potentially can be harmful. Whenever there's an energy source, safety precautions need to be taken.

Cognitive strategies in avoiding unnecessary risks

The skill of cultivating positive health habits involves using some mathematics. Weighing the risks and benefits of certain behaviors is a quantitative exercise. You have to get information on probabilities and utilities and put your effort where the greatest payoff lies. For example, suppose someone scrupulously avoids sugar that has been obtained from sugar beets or sugar cane and substitutes for it sugar that has been obtained from rice or fruit juice. Yet this person fairly frequently smokes marijuana cigarettes. The choice of sugars has an impact on the person's health of approximately zero, and the health risk from carcinogens in marijuana smoke is hundreds of times greater.

To give another example: Someone doesn't give up smoking for fear of gaining ten pounds of weight. But to incur the same health risk incurred by smoking, this person would have to gain perhaps 150 pounds of weight. Stopping smoking is much more important than losing ten pounds of fat. But coming to such realizations requires another delay of gratification exercise: reading and studying the health literature to figure out the relative weights that should be assigned to certain healthy or unhealthy behaviors.

Sometimes the main barrier to choosing healthy behaviors is not ignorance as to the risks and benefits, but psychological defense mechanisms that distort the truth, such as denial. Denial is a classic defense mechanism of alcoholics. Countless people are known by all their friends and relatives to be alcoholics. Yet they themselves continue to say they can quit any time, that drinking is not a problem, and that even though a few negative consequences may have occurred, they will not occur in the future.

Denial allows people to see reality quite differently from what it is. Denial is a "defense" against bad feelings, because the distorted view of reality is more pleasant than seeing things the way they are. It's no coincidence that among the first steps in the twelve-step approach to alcoholism and other addictions are admitting the effect alcohol has had upon one's personality and taking a "fearless inventory" of the ways in which the drug has caused one to harm others. This is what is known as breaking through the defense of denial.

Throughout this book, I've referred to a list of types of thoughts:

awfulizing
getting down on yourself
blaming someone else
not awfulizing
not getting down on yourself
not blaming someone else
goal-setting
listing options and choosing
learning from the experience
celebrating luck
celebrating someone else's choice
celebrating your own choice

When we spoke about courage skills and frustration tolerance skills, the pitfalls of awfulizing, getting down on oneself, and blaming other people were explained. But in the skill of positive health habits, often people don't awfulize enough, in the sense that they deny the badness of a bad reality. They get away with this temporarily because the bad consequences may occur years later or may be only probable and not certain.

Here's an example of what I mean. Suppose people dump carcinogenic chemicals onto their lawns, thus raising by several times the chances their children will get cancer. Rational thinking would lead to thoughts such as, "What a bad idea to raise the risk of cancer in my family members! This is stupid and unconscionable that we're doing this!" The bad feelings engendered by such awfulizing and getting down on oneself supply a motive for change of behavior. If the next step is listing options and choosing, people can make rational choices as to what the behavior change should be. If the person were to not awfulize by saying, "Hey, lots of other people do it, and get away with it. It's no big deal," that would be a distortion of reality.

Here's another example. Someone plans to go to a party, drink five or six drinks or more, and drive home. If the person uses not awfulizing only, he might say something to himself like, "It's not a big deal. I've done it before and have lived through it. Lots of other people do it too." Doing a little awfulizing and getting down on oneself, however, would result in a more accurate view of reality: "This is a terrible idea.

If I don't change my plans, I'm going to do something really stupid and bad."

As I've mentioned several times before, negative emotions such as fear and guilt did not evolve for no reason. Human beings developed the capacity for such feelings so those feelings could spur us to avoid bad actions and move toward good actions. It's very possible and easy to have too much fear and guilt. But to have none, when some would be helpful, is often a major obstacle to developing the skill of cultivating health habits.

Thus, when doing fantasy rehearsals of the desirable ways of thinking, feeling, and acting in these areas, it's sometimes useful for people who have been using denial to practice a *reasonable, moderate, nonexcessive* amount of awfulizing and getting down on oneself. Rather than saying to oneself, "This violent video game is entertaining," it's less of a distortion to say, "This provides fantasy rehearsals of hundreds of violent acts; that's a terrible thing for society. My supporting it is a selfish act." Rather than saying to oneself, "This cigarette tastes good; I'm sure glad for that good feeling," it's less of a distortion to say, "I'm raising the chances my family members will suffer from asthma, respiratory infections, and even cancer. I'm doing something selfish and stupid."

If I awfulize and get down on myself so much that I commit suicide or get so depressed I can't do anything, or become paralyzed by fear, obviously I've gone overboard. But, if my thinking of negative thoughts and creating some negative feelings provides some motivation for me to avoid the unhealthy behavior, and if I indeed avoid it, the pain I created was well worth bearing.

If I do avoid the unhealthy behavior, the end of the story should involve a great deal of celebration. "Hooray for me! This is another day that I've gone without smoking!" "I have done something very wise by choosing not to drink and drive; congratulations, self." "I feel good about the moral choice to boycott violent entertainment such as this." Thus a happy ending to the chain of thinking, feeling, acting, and thinking some more is the desired goal, not wallowing forever in negative thinking and self-blame.

Here's another angle on ways of thinking about these health habits. People can get distorted ideas about what's strong and brave. Lots of men can get distorted ideas about what's manly. Who is the stronger and braver and tougher man? The one who goes to the bar and drinks lots of shots, smokes cigars, takes on all comers in a fight, rides a motorcycle without a helmet at high speed, etc.? Or the man who disciplines himself not to smoke and drink, to watch his weight, to exercise and to drive very carefully?

The first type of man is often celebrated and revered as macho and tough. But those who've had the opportunity to work in hospitals and to see the results of such reckless behavior have a much more realistic perspective on it: it should be realistically called stupid behavior.

Failure in the skill of cultivating health habits is often the failure of imagination. One factor that led me to abstain from smoking was the vivid images people had given me of various physiological processes: the paralysis of the cilia that clean the bronchi; the lungs gradually getting blacker and dirtier; the sacs in the lungs breaking down; the image of having emphysema and gasping for every single breath. One of the major mental maneuvers making delay of gratification skills feasible is to bring the future into the present by imagination. An example is to see in one's mind the contrast between emphysema and health, even though the outcome would occur many years into the future.

Using the nine methods of influence on yourself

If you want to stop smoking, to lose weight, to exercise more, to quit drinking, or to cultivate any other health habit, how do you do it? Countless books have been written on these questions. Many of them try to sell the reader on a method that can be carried out without any discomfort or without large amounts of effort. Fewer of them seem to advertise that the method involves getting used to exerting very large amounts of effort and cultivating the skill of enduring discomfort. The

short answer to the question of how to do these things is to start doing them, endure the discomfort that comes, and gradually habituate yourself to that discomfort as you continue to do the positive health habit. The same mechanism of habituation to discomfort occurs with self discipline as occurs with habituation to fear in the case of desensitizing unrealistic fears.

A slightly longer answer involves reexamining the nine methods of influence we've spoken about before, and trying to mobilize them in the service of the positive health habit one is trying to cultivate. Let's think of these nine methods and how they would be used for some of these health habits.

1. Objective formation or goal-setting. For example, if I want to quit smoking, I might write down that this is my goal. I also write down the advantages of quitting smoking, the internal sales pitch. I decide how much time I'm willing to allocate to activities (such as fantasy rehearsals) that will help me in my goal. I make time for such activities and put them in my schedule.

2. Hierarchy. If I want to quit drinking alcohol, it's not a good idea to go from a very large amount drunk per day to nothing. I should get some help with gradual detoxification. (This usually involves using one of the benzodiazepine drugs rather than alcohol itself.) If I want to cultivate the exercise habit, I might start with walking half a block, and gradually work my way up the hierarchy until I am running several miles.

3. Attribution. I attribute to myself the capacity to do the positive health habit. I say to myself, "I'm capable of existing very happily without cigarettes," rather than saying to myself "I'm a smoker and always will be one."

4. Modeling. I expose myself to positive models of patterns useful in cultivating the health habit. These can be real-life models or imaginary ones. For example, in quitting drinking I expose myself as often as possible to the success stories of people who have stopped drinking; I do this by attending Alcoholics Anonymous meetings. Or in cultivating exercise habits or positive eating habits, I read about people who have achieved their goals and exactly what they have done, thought, and felt.

5. Practice. I do fantasy rehearsals as well as real-life rehearsals of the positive patterns, in great numbers. For example, I fantasy rehearse many times how I will turn down offers of alcoholic drinks at parties. I practice reminding myself of the importance of self-discipline. I practice reminding myself that enduring some discomfort in the service of long-term happiness is a great thing to be able to do.

6. Reinforcement and punishment. I try to arrange consequences for the desired and undesired behavior that will push me in the right direction. For example, I allow myself to buy a computer only when I have achieved my goal of reducing my blood lipids through diet and exercise. I make a large deposit of money to someone and gradually receive the money back only if I'm successful in staying off cigarettes. I use internal reinforcement, by celebrating my own choice when I carry out positive patterns. I recall those and celebrate them again when remembering them.

7. Instruction. I study how people have successfully accomplished this goal. I listen to speeches, watch videotapes; I become an expert in the health habit in question. I recycle information through my brain, not only to learn it, but also to remind myself of it.

8. Stimulus situation control. I avoid tempting myself when I am not 100 percent confident I can withstand the temptation. For example, when quitting drinking, I don't allow myself to go onto the property of a bar. I also arrange stimuli to prompt myself toward positive habits. I move the treadmill up to the room where I spend the most time, and out of the dingy and dusty basement.

9. Monitoring. I keep logs of the total time of exercise per day, or the total number of calories consumed per day, or the number of days I've gone without alcohol. I celebrate my successes.

Most successful programs combine these methods of influence in some ways. If you can mobilize them, your chances of succeeding at any given health habit are greater.

Skill 56: Relaxation

There are at least four separable meanings of the skill of relaxation, as follows.

1. Getting into a relaxed, pleasant state
2. Controlling what your body does
3. Being able to "goof off"
4. Tolerating low stimulation

The first meaning is being able to get into a relaxed, pleasant state when you want to. And what's a relaxed state? It's a subjective feeling of peace and calm. It's a quiet, restful feeling. It's a bodily state where the muscles aren't any more tense than they have to be for whatever is going on. Breathing tends to be on the slow side. All the bodily reactions that go along with the flight-or-fight response tend not to be happening. It's a state that tends to re-charge you and give you more energy for expenditure of effort later on.

The second meaning of relaxation is gaining control over various aspects of what your body does. The part of your body that most people think of as being under conscious control is the skeletal muscular system, the muscles that attach to our bones. We can choose how we want to move our hands, feet, tongues, and jaws. We choose whether we want to pick something up, put it down, whether we want to write something or not, whether we want to say

something with our mouths or not. A large part of our brain is devoted to sending information to the muscles so the conscious choices that we make can be carried out.

However, the brain is also in charge of the autonomic nervous system. We can think of the autonomic nervous system as affecting the body's readiness for various types of activities. The flight-or-fight response is only one set of reactions governed by the autonomic nervous system; there are several others.

Many of these responses are mediated by "smooth muscles," muscles that look different from skeletal muscles under a microscope. There's smooth muscle in the stomach and intestines. People don't usually think of these muscles as under voluntary control. But misactivity of these smooth muscles probably contributes to diarrhea, abdominal pain, and irritable bowel syndrome.

There are also smooth muscles in the blood vessels. The contraction and relaxation of these smooth muscles determine how large the blood vessels are. When the blood vessels get smaller, blood pressure goes up. When blood vessels get smaller in an arm or leg, that limb is colder. A problem called Raynaud's Disease results from the constriction of blood vessels in limbs. The dilation and constriction of the blood vessels in the head and brain are probably related to migraine headaches.

One of the most interesting discoveries of recent decades was that people can learn to control some of the bodily reactions we previously thought involuntary. One method of teaching people to do this is biofeedback. Biofeedback means using some sort of device (for example, a thermometer) to measure something the body is doing, and figuring out how to control it (for example, learning to raise or lower the temperature of the hands). There's usually some sort of mental or bodily sensation that goes along with whatever you do to change the parameter in question. People can learn to create the frame of mind that produces an increase or decrease in heart rate, blood pressure, skin temperature, the movement of the intestines, and so forth.

Biofeedback gave us measurements to prove that people could learn to affect these parameters. But for a long time prior to that, people have been controlling frames of mind and bodily functions. Some used the term *hypnosis* or *self-hypnosis* to refer to what they were doing. Eastern practitioners of yoga have been doing similar things for many centuries.

One corollary of the notion that we can control more than we thought we could about ourselves is that people can control their emotions. Some people have the idea that emotions are not under voluntary control, that you can't help it if you feel angry, depressed, or scared, and the only thing you can do is to handle those feelings well. This notion is false. Although it's often more difficult and less straightforward to learn to control emotion than to learn to control visible behavior, it's very much possible.

The third meaning of relaxation is being able to "goof off." It seems that, for most people, this is the least of their worries. In a world where there's poverty, violence, and environmental destruction, how can we justify wasting time on "idle chatter," playing games, watching entertainment, or just wandering around and watching the clouds go by? Some people are such compulsive workers that they interfere with their family lives, their relationships, and even their own health. They earn the title of workaholics. For them, learning to give themselves permission to "waste time" is a real virtue.

The final meaning of relaxation is being able to handle low stimulation. This is a very important skill. Many people have problems caused by a pattern of sensation-seeking or stimulus-seeking. Some of them call themselves "excitement junkies". Some of them need to stir something up so much, and dislike boredom so much, that they will do maladaptive things just to escape the monotony of existence they feel. Some will make people angry or hurt people's feelings; others will take unnecessary risks.

Learning to tolerate low stimulation is discussed under the skill of relaxation, but for many sensation-seekers it feels anything but pleasant, and feels much more like frustration tolerance. But many of the same exercises that develop the skill of relaxation also develop the skill of tolerating low external stimulation. These exercises involve turning inward and learning to be at peace with yourself. Most of these exercises will help with relaxation in all four meanings discussed here.

Benefits of relaxation

Why should people spend time on this skill? Relaxation skills help to reduce both migraine and tension headaches. The prevalence of painful headaches is reason enough for everyone to learn relaxation as a preventive measure. Insomnia is also a pervasive problem, and relaxation skills also help with getting to sleep at night. Irritable bowel syndrome (abdominal pain, diarrhea) exists in a large portion of the population, and relaxation has also helped with this.

Bruxism is a fairly common condition in which people grind their teeth while asleep; this can result in great damage to the teeth. Learning to relax the muscles of the jaw and face can help or sometimes cure bruxism. Relaxation can also prevent teeth-clenching, which can cause pain in the temporo-mandibular joint where the jawbone joins the skull. Hypertension, or high blood pressure, is an extremely common and damaging problem. Although not everyone can learn to lower their blood pressure through relaxation, some people can. Raynaud's disease, mentioned earlier, is greatly helped by learning relaxation skills. Relaxation can treat other illnesses involving a strong brain-peripheral organ connection.

But preventing and curing physical problems is not the only role of relaxation skills. These skills also help us to reduce or eliminate unwanted negative emotions. In the chapters on anger control and fear reduction, I discussed the role of relaxation skills. A relaxed, peaceful, calm state is incompatible with great fear or anger. Fantasy rehearsals of situations that provoke unrealistic fear or anger, in which you rehearse responding in a relaxed and calm way, can play a major role in fear reduction and anger control. There's hardly a person who does not need to reduce unrealistic fear or anger at one time or another.

In addition, some people feel relaxation skills aid in creative thinking, in getting the mind into a state where it can generate new and interesting ideas.

By helping people to feel at peace within themselves, relaxation skills reduce the need for chemical methods of relaxation such as the use of alcohol or narcotics.

And finally, the skills of tolerating low stimulation that come from relaxation practice can reduce many of the negative side effects of dependence upon sensation-seeking. We'll talk about this later.

The benefits of relaxation skills are so great that these skills should be taught to everyone.

Match or mismatch between state of mind and situation

Is the goal of relaxation skills a state of relaxed, dreamy, blissful calmness at all times? Of course not. Our bodies evolved the capacity for excitement, arousal, and tension for a reason: these states of mind are useful at times.

If I'm going to give a speech to a group, I want to be full of energy. I don't want to feel as if I'm ready to fall asleep. If I'm going to run a sprint, or perform a dance, or take a math test in a competition, or finish writing a proposal in time for a deadline, I want to be "up."

In all these circumstances I want to be in control, and thinking well; I don't want to be panicked. I want just the right combination of concentration, relaxation, and arousal in just the ways that will allow me to perform best. In friendly, active socialization, I want to be in a frame of mind different from my frame of mind when I'm enjoying introverted drifting of the mind. Sexual arousal involves a certain type of relaxation and a certain type of excitement.

The point is there are lots of different ways our bodies can be tuned. There are many ways the settings can be set to make us ready for a certain type of activity.

What we want, for best functioning, is the best possible match between our body's state of arousal and relaxation and the task we're taking on. Many people get into trouble because of mismatches. They are falling asleep in the middle of the chemistry exam or highly charged with energy just after turning off their lights to go to bed. In a conflict-resolution situation, where they need to be calm, they're too excited. And, while trying to give an exciting speech, they're too calm.

How do we arrive at the best match? For a person who has learned to vary his own state of arousal and relaxation, consciously or unconsciously, the following strategy is available: you start doing the task, and try various states of arousal, until you home in on the one that works best for that task. It's similar to turning the station-selecting dial on a radio until you reach the place where the signal comes in clearest.

Researchers did a very interesting experiment with headache control. One group of people learned to raise the temperature of their hands. This procedure had previously been found to help headaches; raised temperatures in the hands are associated with greater relaxation. Another group learned to *lower* the temperature in their hands, and a third group did nothing. Both of the groups who learned to control hand temperature reduced their headaches, whereas the control group did not. I interpret this study to mean that the useful thing is to learn to vary your own physiologic states, so that you can range around and tune in to the one that's most comfortable (e.g. least painful) and most useful at any given time.

Awareness and measurement as a first step in controlling the state of mind

One of the first steps in learning to control your state of mind is learning awareness of it and measurement of it. How relaxed are you at this moment on a scale of 0 to 10? How focused versus scattered; how inward directed versus outward directed; restless and under pressure to move versus content to sit still; tight versus loose in muscle tone? How energized versus fatigued? Are you confident-excited versus scared-excited? Learning self-observation is a first step in gaining conscious control of these states of mind. For purposes of the activities that follow, it will usually do simply to rate your own relaxation, using our "how much" rating scale:

0 = None
2 = A little
4 = Some
6 = Pretty much
8 = High amount
10 = Very high amount

Once you've learned to observe and recognize whatever state of mind you're in, the next step is experimenting with various things to do in your head until you find some combination of them that will get you into the desired

state. Of course, some self-congratulation for moving successfully into the desired state is very useful; self-criticism and awfulizing over not immediately moving into the desired state of mind is usually counterproductive.

Five relaxation techniques

I'll describe five different techniques, as follows: simple rest, progressive muscular relaxation, meditation using a mantra, relaxation assisted by imagery, and cognitive restructuring. First, however, I'll go over some of the aspects shared by all these relaxation methods.

It's important to remember that none of these techniques should be used like a pain pill and employed only when anxiety and tension are at their worst. Instead, they should be practiced on some sort of regular basis, for example, for fifteen minutes a day, and should not be neglected on days when you're already feeling relaxed.

The suggestion is based on conditioned association learning. If one does a certain maneuver only when tension is at its worst, that maneuver may become associated with the feeling of tension. This, of course, is just the opposite of what's desired in a relaxation technique. So whatever technique is used, it should be practiced especially when it's not immediately needed.

Relaxing for fifteen minutes a day, every day, is something that's very hard for many people to continue to do indefinitely. Once your relaxation skills have been refined by daily practice, an alternative for maintenance is to relax for about three seconds, thirty times a day. Just a few seconds of relaxation, a couple of times each waking hour, may be enough to do the trick for many people.

A second suggestion relevant to all these techniques is that you should try to relax, but not try so hard that the goal of relaxation becomes just another test where one may succeed or fail. It's important to think of the relaxation practice periods as times where it's impossible to fail, where every possible outcome is OK and nothing to worry about, even if some occasions turn out not to be relaxing at all.

A third suggestion common to all these techniques is that the physical setup of the environment should be arranged so that interruptions may not intrude, and one's physical position is conducive to relaxation. Taking a telephone off the hook or putting a "do not disturb" sign on an office door and lying down on a mat are examples of what can facilitate this.

The fourth suggestion for all these techniques is to imagine that using the technique will gradually bring about the desired results. This suggestion comes from studies of the placebo effect: often when people expect a positive result to occur from a treatment, a positive result actually tends to occur. What techniques used by people when inducing a placebo effect in themselves can you consciously and purposely mo-

bilize? One might be the belief that the remedy will indeed produce positive effects. In the case of relaxation for certain tension-related problems, many outcome studies show adopting such a belief doesn't require any self-deception. A second factor, perhaps separate from the belief, is the mental image of the desired results. In other words, one who doesn't believe can always imagine.

Now for the first technique, which is simple rest. For some people this might work just as well as the more elaborate techniques I'll mention later, as it has in at least one controlled study. This technique is simply a combination of the four suggestions I've already mentioned as common to all the techniques. You simply take out fifteen minutes a couple of times a day, get into a place where it's possible to relax, sit or lie down, and don't try to do anything in particular – you just rest. Whatever your mind wants to do, let it. Try to relax, but don't try so hard that you induce performance anxiety. You peek at your watch whenever you want do, and when the allotted time is up you get up and go about your business. So much for technique number one.

The second technique is progressive muscular relaxation. First used by Jacobsen in the 1930s, it's the method Joseph Wolpe used with success in desensitizing phobias. It rests on the following theory: first, that one can learn, through practice, a high degree of control of the tension in the skeletal muscles; and, second, that relaxing those muscles is conducive to emotional relaxation as well.

There are two stages to learning this technique, one involving purposeful tension and relaxation, and the second involving purposeful relaxation alone. The purpose of the first stage is to sensitize your mind to the perceptions of muscle tension, and to give yourself practice in undoing tension. For example, you tense your forearm muscle by gripping with your hand; then you let off the tension and pay careful attention to how it feels to uncontract your muscle fibers. Once the muscle has gone back to the normal state of relaxation, you try to go even further in the direction of relaxation than you have already gone.

You do the same thing with all the major muscle groups of the body, contracting them, paying attention to the tension, and then relaxing them as far as you can. It's helpful when doing this procedure not to induce a high degree of tension, as though you were doing isometric exercises, but to induce a very mild and slight degree of tension, so that you'll become expert at discriminating fine differences in muscle contraction.

When doing these exercises pay particular attention to the muscles around the head, because they seem to be particularly associated with emotion. The clenching or unclenching of the jaw, the tension of the muscles of the forehead, the tension of the neck mus-

cles and the muscles around the mouth should get a good deal of attention.

In the second stage of progressive muscular relaxation practice, you don't contract the muscles to begin with, but you just let your attention go to the various muscle groups and try to reduce the degree of muscle contraction in each of them. Many people like to time this relaxation with their breathing: that is, every time you breathe out, you let your muscles get a little more limp and loose. You do this for fifteen minutes a couple times of day, and hopefully enjoy the pleasant sensations the relaxation induces.

When Wolpe used this technique to desensitize fears, he would first ask the person to relax, and then alternate the relaxation activity with imagining the situations that trigger unrealistic anxiety, starting with the least scary scenes and gradually working up to the more scary ones. If particular imagined scenarios tend to make one more tense, one option is to gradually desensitize oneself to those scenarios. But simply doing the relaxation practice a couple of times a day probably tends to accomplish the same thing over time, because the unpleasant outcomes one worries about do sometimes tend to pop into the mind during relaxation. If one notices this happening, one can then turn the attention back to relaxing the muscles, and count it as a little desensitization trial.

The third technique is meditation using a mantra. This is the technique that was given a great deal of publicity during the 1960s and 1970s under the name of "transcendental meditation." Back then, people were given a Sanskrit word to say to themselves while meditating; researchers found that using the word "one" as a mantra worked just as well. Some people may not like the word "one," and may want to choose a different mantra. A mantra is simply an auditory or visual image to which you return your attention during the relaxation practice. Some people have used an imagined spot of light as a mantra. Others have used as a mantra paying conscious attention to their own breathing. Perhaps the mantra functions as a means of turning the attention away from other thoughts, such as worrisome ones.

To use this technique, then, you prepare to relax, and then turn your attention to the mantra. It's important not to worry about how relaxed you become. Also, don't measure your success by how conscientiously you keep repeating the mantra. If you realize your attention has been on something else other than the mantra for a few minutes, don't worry about it, and let your attention gently return to the mantra.

The fourth technique is relaxation assisted by imagery. Here you don't have just one image you keep returning to; you have your imagination carry out something similar to a pleasant dream. You might go in your imagination to a very pleasant place. You might hear pleasant things happen. You generate stories in your mind, stories with positive emotional tone throughout. I think generating stories of people being kind, helpful, and supportive of one another are the best type to use, since a positive emotional climate among people is perhaps the central element of a feeling of safety and security.

The goal in practicing this technique is to be able to drift into a pleasant and relaxing fantasy at will. Keep in mind the maxim: "You're the director of your own fantasy world." If you find this is not true at first, and unwanted images intrude, keep practicing – not at trying to get unwanted images out (it's best to just let them run their course), but at bringing to mind the desirable images. With practice you'll gain confidence that you can present to yourself the sorts of stories most helpful to you.

The fifth technique is cognitive restructuring. Tension and anxiety usually result from anxiety-provoking thoughts. Sometimes we don't even notice these thoughts enough to remember them, unless we consciously keep a log of them. Such thoughts include self-statements such as "This situation that I'm in is terrible"; "Something awful is about to happen if I don't watch out"; "I'm going to fail terribly if I don't watch myself, and that will be terrible"; "I'm putting in a performance I should be ashamed of"; "I'm not doing well enough"; "I should do better than this"; "This other person should be acting better and the fact that he isn't is terrible," and so forth.

Sometimes the beliefs underlying such thoughts are things like "Nothing short of perfection is good enough," or "Everything has to be just right in order for me to feel good." Such cognitive patterns in general tend to estimate highly the awfulness of situations and the blameworthiness of oneself and others.

The opposites of such cognitive patterns are self-statements like, "This situation is unpleasant, but it's not terrible," or "My performance was not perfect, but the only way I learn is to try things repeatedly," or "Sometimes it's a waste of time and energy to want everything perfect," or "I'll decide what the highest priorities are and put energy there, and not worry if the lower priorities fall to the wayside," or "The purpose of this situation is for me to try to do some good for someone or learn to do good rather than for someone to evaluate my worth as a person," or "I can put up with a very wide range of other people's actions," or any of hundreds of other thoughts that tend to reduce the awfulness of situations and reduce blameworthiness of oneself and others. By becoming aware of when you're exaggerating awfulness or blameworthiness and substituting thoughts that don't do so, you can greatly reduce negative emotion, including tension.

In using cognitive restructuring you may become aware of certain sorts of situations that tend to trigger the thoughts of awfulness or blameworthiness – situations of interpersonal conflict, rejection, disapproval, criticism, failure, frustration, being alone, or not knowing how to do something, etc. Once you understand these connections, you can then practice in imagination facing these trigger situations but doing so with the more desirable cognitive patterns in mind.

All these techniques have much potential, provided that you persistently use them. They do require some systematic effort and allocation of time before gains begin to appear, and many people who believe the techniques will work never actually carry them out. However, the increase in quality time and energy brought about by improving the skill of relaxation far outweighs the time required to devote a substantial effort to one or more of these techniques.

The following script incorporates several of the techniques mentioned above. You might find it useful to record it onto audiotape and listen to it.

Relaxation tape script

The ability to relax your body and your mind, whenever you want to, is a skill that is very useful in many different ways. It allows you to calm yourself so you can think better. It makes it easier to go to sleep. It lets you undo any tension in muscles that would be uncomfortable or painful. It has been found helpful in preventing several physical problems, including headaches and certain types of stomachaches.

It gives you practice in controlling your own mood. It allows you to get rid of restlessness. It allows you to better handle and enjoy being by yourself. It is very useful in reducing fearfulness, when you want to do that. It can prepare you for getting good and thoughtful ideas. It helps you in resolving conflicts with other people. It is a skill that's worth working on for a very long time, if that's what it takes to master it.

One of the most important ways of relaxing is to notice any tension in your muscles, and to reduce that tension, and let your muscles stop pulling. As you sit or lie down comfortably, it often feels pleasant to let your muscles relax themselves. The more relaxed your muscles are, the more your mind will tend to drift in ways that are also calm and peaceful.

Here is one way you can practice relaxation of your muscles. You can think about the different muscles of your body, and go through the different muscle groups one by one. You can notice the tension that is already in the muscles, or you can tense those muscles just a little bit. Then you make that tension go away, as totally as possible. If you can notice the difference between full relaxation and even a very small amount of tension in a muscle, you have a very important skill. Because as long as you can notice tension, and even

make tension greater, you have the power to make that tension go away.

All you have to do to produce relaxation is the opposite of what you do to create tension. When you let off the tension, you let the muscles become very loose and relaxed. You do this for all the muscle groups in the body. You notice what happens when you relax muscles. You feel the difference that happens when you relax. When you have done this enough times, you will know very well how to tense and relax all the muscles of your body.

You will not have to tense the muscles very hard, but only very lightly, or maybe not at all, to feel the difference that happens when you relax the muscles.

You might start with gripping your hands into fists, not hard, but very lightly. Even if you do it very lightly, you can feel a tension in the muscles of your forearms and hands. Once you feel that tension, you can let it off, and let your forearms relax and get very loose. Pay attention to the feeling of relaxation, and how it's different from the feeling of tension.

You might next make your upper arms a little tense by trying to make a muscle as though you were going to feel the muscle in your upper arms. You do this by pulling so as to bend your arm at the elbow, but at the same time trying to straighten out your arm. Feel the tension in your upper arm muscles. Then you can release the tension and let those muscles become loose and re-laxed.

You might next make your shoulders a little tense by starting to shrug your shoulders a little, the way people do when they say, "I don't know." Then you relax those shoulder muscles.

If someone wants to make their neck muscles tense, they try to pull their head forward, and at the same time pull it back, so that the muscles are pulling against each other. Then when they feel that tension, they can relax those mus-cles, and let those muscles be very calm.

If someone wants to tense the muscles that are at the side of the face, the jaw muscles, they do it by biting so as to clench the teeth together, while at the same time trying to open the mouth. This produces tension in the jaw mus-cles, the muscles on the side of the head, and the muscles on the upper part of the neck. Then you can relax those muscles by letting your jaw relax. When you do this, your jaw will usually be hanging open just a tiny bit.

If you want to tense the muscles of the upper part of your face, you lift your eyebrows and at the same time try to push your eyebrows down. Then when you feel that tension, ever so slightly, you can let it off.

If you want to tense the muscles of the lower part of your face, you push your lips together a little bit, and pull the corners of your mouth back as though you were smiling, and at the same time you try to purse your lips back as though you were trying to whis-tle. Then you let all that tension off, and you feel the relaxation of the muscles of the lower part of your face.

Many people find that relaxing the muscles of their face and jaws and neck is just what makes them feel the most calm and peaceful. You might try it if you want to, thinking about the muscles of your jaws, your upper face, your lower face, and your neck.

Some people like to think about their breathing as they're relaxing, and let their muscles get a little more re-laxed each time they breathe out. So the rhythm is: breathe in, relax out, breathe in, relax out.

Now you might experiment with how to make the muscles tight in your back. If you try to arch your back as if you're bending backward, you can tense the long muscles that run down your back. Then when you feel that tension, you can let it off. If you pull your shoulders back, you can feel tension in the muscles in the upper part of your back, and then let that tension off.

You can also experiment with tensing and relaxing the muscles of your chest and your abdomen, or belly. To tense those of your chest, pull your arms as if you're going to clap your hands together, then relax that tension. To tense the muscles of your abdomen, if you're lying on your back, pretend that you want to sit up, and feel just a little tension in those muscles. Then you can let them off. Or if you're sitting in a chair, you can tense your belly and back muscles by trying to lean forward, while at the same time trying to lean backward. When you feel that tension, let it off, and as always, pay attention to the different degrees of tension and relaxation you're feeling.

You can make the muscles in your upper legs tense by trying to bend the leg at the knee and trying to straighten it out at the same time. Then you can let off that tension, so your upper legs are very relaxed. You can tense your lower legs by trying to push your toes down and trying to pull your toes up at the same time. Then you can let off that tension too, so your lower legs are relaxed.

There are many muscles in the body, including some I didn't mention. It can be fun to experiment with finding out how it is that you make a certain muscle tense. Over time, you'll be able to tense or relax any muscle in the body any time you want to.

After you go through and actually practice tensing and relaxing your muscles, you can just let your attention go first to one muscle group and then another, seeing whether you can make that muscle group any more relaxed, loose, and limp than it already is.

You might want to think about your breathing again, and feel the air going in and out, and each time you breathe out, feel some part of your body getting just a little more relaxed than it was before.

The skill of getting your muscles relaxed will be very useful to you, for the rest of your life. It's one people can gradually improve at over time, simply by noticing what sort of effort tends to tense what muscles, and what sort of relaxation of that effort relaxes those muscles. You'll start to find which particular muscles are the most important ones for you.

Relaxing your muscles is only a part of the interesting and pleasant things you can do while you're relaxing.

Another very useful way of relaxing is to practice imagining beautiful and relaxing scenes, nice and pleasant places to be. You may want to think of the following scenes, briefly, when I mention them, and then come back to them later when the tape stops and imagine them more thoroughly.

Different scenes are relaxing for different people. How does it feel when you imagine a beautiful sunset? How does it feel to imagine the sound of wind gently blowing among the tree leaves? How about the image of beautiful flowers? How about the sight and the sound of a waterfall? How about listening to rain fall on a roof? How about imagining waves rolling in where you're relaxing on a beach? Or the image of how you feel just as you're awakening on a morning when there are no responsibilities you have to carry out? Or the image of sitting in a cool room, with a warm blanket around you, looking at a fire burn in a fireplace?

Or what is it like to imagine yourself drinking cool water when you're very thirsty? Or watching snow drifting slowly to the ground? Or can you imagine a rag doll, and then imagine your body as being that loose and relaxed? What is it like to imagine watching white clouds drifting by on a day in the spring? Or can you just become conscious of the chair or the bed that is holding you up, and feel yourself being held?

Sometimes the most relaxing images are not just of places, but also of people, and people acting kind and gentle and loving and giving with one another. These images let people feel peaceful and relaxed.

You can imagine stories of people's kindness. For example, you may want to imagine that someone is searching for something, and someone else in a very calm and kind way helps that person find it. When they find it, the people feel good about each other. If you want to, you can fill in your own details about where they are, what is being searched for, where they look, and what it looks like when they find it. You can do this in a different way every time if you want, or the same way every time you do it, or sometimes one way and sometimes another. You're in control of your own imagination, and you can lead yourself wherever you choose.

Or you may imagine that someone leads someone else on a very interesting and pleasant journey, showing that person something that is very fun or interesting to see. If you want to, you can imagine your own details, about where the first person takes the second, what sorts of things they see and experience. You can imagine the faces of the first person as that person enjoys what they're doing, and the face of the other person feeling good about giving the other a pleasant experience.

Or you may imagine that someone teaches someone else something that person really wants to know. The teacher is very kind and patient. The teacher wants to let the learner learn at his own pace, and does not rush him. The learner is very grateful to the teacher. The teacher is also grateful to the learner. The teacher realizes that someone who allows you to teach them something is giving a nice gift, a pleasant memory that the teacher will have for a lifetime. You can fill in your own details of where they are, what is being learned, and how they are learning it.

Or you may imagine that someone helps someone with a job of some kind. As you do, imagine the two people feel very good about each other. You can see and hear what they're doing together and what sorts of words they're saying to each other, if they are saying anything.

Or you may imagine that people are being kind and loving to each other by playing together. They know in the backs of their minds that the most important thing when they're playing with each other is to be kind and caring with each other. They each take pleasure whenever they can see that they have helped the other feel good. If you want to let a story about this come to your mind, you can imagine where they are and what or how they're playing and what they're saying to each other.

Or you may imagine people showing their love and caring about each other by noticing and commenting on the other person's good acts or accomplishments. You can imagine that people rejoice and feel good when their friends and loved ones have successes. If you want to, you can imagine exactly what someone is doing and how someone else feels good about it, and how that person lets the other person know his pleasure.

Or you may imagine people sharing things with each other, making it so there is enough to go around. You can imagine whether they are taking turns with some toy or tool they want to use, or whether the are sharing something to eat or drink, or someone else's attention and time, or something else.

Or, you may imagine one person showing love and caring for another by being a good listener when the other speaks. As one person tells thoughts and feelings, the other very patiently tries to be understanding.

Some people enjoy recalling the things they have done in real life that they're glad they have done. Some people like to think back about the kind things they have done for other people, or the work they have done to educate themselves and make themselves better or the work they have done to make the world a better place, or the times they have lived joyously, or the times they have made good decisions and carried them out. They may want to celebrate the times they have been honest, or the times they have been strong and brave.

Some people enjoy thinking about the ways in which they are blessed, and feeling gratitude for those. If they are able to have any material things that make life easier, if they are able to eat and drink so they do not have to be hungry and thirsty, if they have someone who can take care of them when they need it and be of support to them, if they have friends or loved ones they can care for and support, they may want to feel gratitude for these blessings.

You can let your mind drift, and think about any stories or images of these things you want to. You're perfectly free to let your mind drift in any way you choose. Sometimes people enjoy not choosing, but simply letting the mind drift wherever it wants to go, and observing what happens.

In fact, sometimes it's a very pleasant experience just to imagine that your mind is a blank screen, and to simply wait and see what comes on it, and to observe it with interest and curiosity, not trying to control it in any way. You can practice relaxing your muscles, imagining relaxing scenes, thinking of stories of people being kind to each other, or you can simply let your mind drift and see where it takes you. Or you can let your mind drift and not observe it, but simply rest. You can guide your own experience to make it pleasant, relaxing, peaceful, and enjoyable to you. As you do so, you have reason to celebrate practicing such an important skill.

Overcoming workaholism

Many great people have seemed to be consumed by their calling and have devoted a high portion of their waking moments to it. It appears not to have hurt Mohandas Gandhi that he didn't take time off to play cards and golf and have a few beers and watch television sitcoms. If someone realizes that his work is of crucial benefit to humanity, that it's deeply fulfilling to himself, and that it's the best use of time he can possibly devise, is it workaholism if he spends almost all his time doing it? It's not, in my opinion, unless there's something else such as a commitment to a child that he's neglecting by attending to it.

Similarly, if someone works two low-paying jobs to support his family, because those jobs are all that are available, and otherwise his family would be in dire poverty, is that person a workaholic? Not unless there's a better way out of poverty that he's ignoring.

What is a pathological compulsion to work? How do we separate that from the intense dedication that's often necessary to be great or to lift a family out of poverty? There's no way of telling the difference unless there's some

ethical beacon that gives us direction. Here are some ethical principles that were listed earlier, in the chapter on kindness:

The "greatest good" rule: make as much happiness as you can. Or: "make the greatest good for the greatest number." Or: "improve the world as much as you can."

You owe more loyalty to family members and friends than to strangers; but it's good to help any human being.

Take care of your own health and welfare, so you can help others.

The first principle suggests that you ask the question, "Does working an additional hour, versus doing something else, increase or decrease the total happiness of the world?"

The second principle suggests you should weight the happiness of your family members and friends you're already committed to more highly than the happiness of those who aren't depending on you. Thus, if you're a head of a company and you manufacture a product that makes many people happy, you still may not be making the right choice if you're neglecting the welfare of your own spouse and children.

The third principle suggests you need to take care of yourself for the long term. If your solution to the demands of work and family is to give up most of your sleep and stress yourself tremendously, you haven't made the right choice if you give yourself a premature heart attack. Another ethical principle is, "Since cheerfulness is contagious, be of good cheer if it is at all appropriate." If you stress yourself from work so much that you don't feel like being cheerful, but instead you're irritable and snappy at people, you probably aren't making the right choice.

Many people who overwork themselves are consumed with games designed to establish themselves in a good position on a dominance hierarchy. Can I build an empire? Can I become more powerful than the next person? Can I make more money than the other person? (And not, can I make enough money so that I can accomplish certain things with it?)

Some people overwork themselves because they feel they need the money, but they never make a crucial calculation. They're spending money on things that give them much less pleasure, fulfillment, and meaning than would be obtained by working the correspondingly lower amount of time.

For example, someone gets paid $15 an hour, after taxes. He fairly frequently spends $30 on restaurants. But if given the choice between the restaurant meal and working even one hour less, he would much rather work an hour less. The same thing goes for many other things he consumes. He's exchanging a valued resource, his time, for things that are less valuable to him! If he can work out a way of working less and consuming less, he will be much better off.

The skill of avoiding workaholism is one that is largely accom-plished by systematic decision-making on this question: where is my time best used? What method of conducting my life will lead to the best results? The chapter on decision-making is very relevant to this skill.

Tolerating low stimulation, overcoming stimulus addiction

The skill of handling low stimulation is probably important enough to be a separate psychological skill. But I list it as a subskill of relaxation, because the relaxation techniques listed earlier are good ways of working on this skill.

People who are poor at handling low stimulation get into trouble by their "sensation-seeking," "stimulus-seeking," or "risk-preferring" habits. Here are some questions meant to help identify the sensation-seeking pattern.

Sensation-seeking questionnaire

1. Do you often get into conflicts with people or provoke other people just to get some excitement going?

2. Would you often rather have someone yell at you in anger than have a boring conversation?

3. Are you more easily bored than other people?

4. Do you have little tolerance for waiting? Are you impatient?

5. Do you usually prefer taking risks to playing it safe?

6. Is the feeling of an adrenaline "rush" a positive high for you?

7. Would you enjoy parachute jumping, hang gliding, rappelling off

cliffs, bungee jumping, mountain climbing, and other exposures to high places?

8. Would you enjoy driving fast, riding roller coasters, speed boat racing, being a test pilot, riding motorcycles, and other exposures to great speed?

9. Do your tastes in entertainment run more toward action, adventure, and thriller movies than toward explorations of interpersonal relations?

10. Do your tastes in music run more toward loud, jarring music with shocking lyrics rather than toward lyrical and beautiful music?

11. Are you attracted to danger, such as emergency rescues?

12. Do you tend to get into high-pressure, deadline situations because you take pleasure from the excitement produced by brinkmanship?

13. Do you tend to take speculative financial risks rather than play it safe with money?

14. Are you a "yeller," and do you often provoke other people to yell?

15. Does making a powerful authority figure very angry strike you as gleefully funny?

16. When you were a child, did you tend to climb up anything you could climb, or zoom down anything you could zoom down?

17. Have you received injuries from risk-taking activities?

18. Do you find the pressure of close, intense, and high-stakes competition very pleasant? For instance, if you were a basketball player, would you like to be the one who takes the last shot in a tied-up game?

19. Does getting disapproval from people tend to make you laugh more than it tends to make you feel devastated?

20. Would boycotting violent entertainment represent a very great loss for you?

21. Do you find displays of large emotion entertaining, even if the emotion is an unpleasant one, such as anger or fear?

22. Do you greatly prefer to be the center of attention than to let someone else be the center of attention and take a position in the background?

23. Are you more tempted by the thrill of new romantic relationships than by the stability of old ones?

24. Is it unpleasant for you to sit by yourself and think?

25. Is it unpleasant for you to sit by yourself and read or write?

26. Are the moments of lying in bed before going to sleep unpleasant for you?

It's important to realize how much of a stimulus-seeker you are and how much the significant people in your life are, if you wish to understand what is going on. When stimulus-seeking is the motive behind human conflict, different solutions are called for than when the motives are different.

For example, a parent sees two siblings fighting and yelling at each other over a toy. The parent seeks to help the children find rational, win-win solutions to their conflict – take turns, decide who gets to use it first by a coin flip, etc. But these solve the problem only if you assume the children are motivated by a desire to use the toy. What if the payoff one or both of them are seeking has very little to do with the toy? What if one or both siblings simply want the stimulation of making the other one angry? Then coming to a rational and calm agreement on an option doesn't solve the real problem at all. The real problem is, "How can I (or we) inject some excitement and stimulation into life right now?"

Countless parents and other family members have made the mistake of trying to scream at a stimulus-seeker to get him to stop doing something. For many stimulus-seekers, screaming is reinforcement. It's as though the screamer said, "Here, have several dollars just for doing what you just did." So that when the parent screams at the stimulus-seeking child, "Didn't I tell you not to DO THAT!" the child is being made MORE likely to do that again, not less likely.

When dealing with stimulus-seeking children, it's prudent to yell when they do good things and to speak very quietly and slowly and in a low tone of voice when speaking about the bad things they do. That way, you don't use differential reinforcement in the wrong direction.

Like most characteristics human beings are capable of, stimulus-seeking evolved for a reason. Those who be-come rich and famous and those who are recognized as heroes or leaders are often stimulus-seekers. You don't achieve any of those things by playing it safe and avoiding excitement and risks. Could anyone who is not a fairly extreme stimulus-seeker aspire to become president of the United States? Could someone who isn't a stimulus-seeker borrow huge amounts of money and start a new company? Even in the sometimes staid world of science, the truly innovative and great scientists are sometimes obvious sensation-seekers. Some people who are stimulus-seekers in smart ways seem to have a great time doing it. Being a stimulus-seeker is lauded by such expressions as "nothing ventured, nothing gained," and "faint heart never won fair lady."

Although stimulus-seeking sometimes motivates what people admire the most, it also sometimes motivates that which we admire least. The phenomenon of thrill-seeking murders is sensation-seeking at its most degraded. Bullying and sadistic cruelty often appear to be motivated by stimulus-seeking. Drug addiction often appears motivated by stimulus-seeking. Stimulus-seekers often wind up dead – from being killed in fights, high-speed traffic accidents, and drug overdoses. Those who are addicted to sensation enough that they prefer anger from other people to quieter positive regard often end up friendless, isolated, and very lonely.

From the observation of many individuals given diagnostic labels of attention-deficit hyperactivity disorder, it appears that the stimulus-seeking trait is what causes many of them the most problem. Disruptive behavior in school or in families, enough to elicit anguished emotion from teachers and parents, is often the only antidote children can come up with to a highly unpleasant prevailing boredom. Trouble-making behavior in groups is the antidote to the boredom the child would experience if he were being quiet and listening to one person at a time.

Researchers appear to be moving toward isolating at least one gene for stimulus-seeking. Several studies have found a certain gene present much more frequently in stimulus-seekers than non-stimulus-seekers. The gene seems to have to do with dopamine in the brain pathways, and this is a logical pathway for stimulus-seeking to create itself.

But as is always the case, whenever a certain human characteristic has a genetic contribution, it's almost always possible to override the genetic disposition, at least to some extent, by new learning.

What forms does this learning take? The goal should not be for the stimulus-seeker to stop enjoying the excitement of high-stimulation situations. The goal is for him to be able to tolerate and even enjoy low stimulation when desirable. The goal is to enlarge the person's repertoire, to give him a bigger range of things he can do comfortably.

Because the centers of emotion in the brain are initially programmed to enjoy the excitement of unwise risks, the centers of the brain that control calculation and logical thinking have to do more of the job of avoiding unwise risks.

For instance, the emotional centers may be saying, "Hey, this person is all red in the face and is screaming at me. Isn't this funny?!" It's the job of the logical centers to say, "It's not to my advantage to be making this person hate me. This is not something I want to feel good about." The emotional centers may be saying, "Wow, this car can go fast! What fun!" It's up to the logical centers to say, "Hey, the probability of my getting killed is higher if I go too fast. It's not worth it. I should avoid this danger, even if I don't feel scared." We discussed this sort of thinking in the chapter on carefulness skills.

Here's a way of measuring or testing your skills of handling low stimulation. Sit in a room with nothing particularly interesting in your visual field, and no sounds – no radio, CD player, or television in the background. Just sit still for several minutes. Do anything you want in your own mind. You can recall interesting memories. You can work on decisions. You can have pleasant, even exciting fantasies. You can make up and solve problems. You can let your mind drift. You can do whatever you want except generate external stimulation.

After the five minutes are up, rate how pleasant and how useful it was to spend the time in that way. If it was not useful and very unpleasant, you're getting a clue that handling low stimulation is a skill you could improve.

Here's a similar exercise. This time, you sit with nothing but a pencil and paper (or word processor and blank screen, *without* pop-up messages from the Internet or action games to turn to). You just write anything you want, or you sit and think about writing. You can write a plan for accomplishing something, a poem, a story, a list of goals, a set of questions about your life and corresponding answers, or whatever else you wish. Again, all the stimuli come from within your own mind. You're using paper or word processor as an aid to remembering what went on in your mind.

After spending a certain amount of time on this exercise, rate how pleasant and how useful you were able to make this time. Remember, though, that you're not really rating the exercise; your rating gives you one measure of your own skill at handling low stimulation.

And finally, try any of the relaxation techniques listed above or any of the exercises listed in the chapter on the skill of concentration. If sitting in a comfortable chair and visualizing pleasant scenes and kind acts is torture for you, and you feel the overpowering urge to switch to visualizing earthquakes and warfare, you need to work on the skill of handling low stimulation.

How do you learn to handle low stimulation? Very little has been written about teaching sensation-seekers to handle low stimulation, as contrasted with techniques of teaching phobic people to handle the situations they're scared of. But my guess is that the principles are very similar. Almost all the techniques mentioned in the chapter on courage skills are probably useful. In particular, the central principle is exposing yourself to the situation you have an aversion to, and continuing the exposure long enough for some habituation to occur.

For example, you sit silently in a comfortable chair with your eyes closed. If this causes uncomfortable feelings that rate 8 on a scale of 10, you "gut it out" and keep sitting silently. Gradually the distress level subsides to 2 or 3. If this happens, you've had a major success in using exposure to reduce your aversion to low stimulation. If the next time you try it, your distress level starts out at only 6, you know you're making rapid progress.

Perhaps another principle just as central as prolonged exposure is getting clear in your mind that you want to get better at handling low stimulation, that you value this skill, and that any times you do handle such situations well are cause for celebration. This is a totally different mindset from that held by many stimulus-seekers, who think something like, "This is a boring situation. The goal is to get out of this situation and into a more exciting one, not to become more able to tolerate such boring situations."

Questing for internal growth rather than external excitement is a major paradigm shift. It could be that the people who make this shift are the ones who can learn to tolerate or enjoy low-stimulus situations by practicing. Being in a low-stimulus situation affords the opportunity to practice the skill; it does not guarantee that the person will take that opportunity.

Before leaving this topic I want to give one more guideline for stimulus-seekers. If you're attracted to risks, go for risks where the expected outcome (that is, the utility of the outcome, multiplied by the probability of the outcome, and summed over all possible outcomes) is positive. For example, putting $5,000 dollars into a horse race and putting it into a highly volatile stock are both risky ventures. But the average outcome from volatile stocks is to make money; the average outcome from horse races is to lose money. Risking by starting a business is a smarter way of getting thrills than risking by trying drugs. There are winning and losing ways of being a stimulus-seeker.

Skill 57: Self-Nurture

Being kind to yourself or being your own best friend is another name for this skill.

Some people find that they treat themselves worse than they would ever think of treating other people. Or they say rude things to themselves that they would never think of saying to someone else.

Let's think just a little bit about the whole notion of how you act toward yourself and what you say toward yourself.

Sometimes people aren't aware of how important this is and how frequently they're saying something to themselves. But what you say to yourself is very important in determining how you feel about things, including how you feel about yourself, and it's also very important in determining how you're going to act.

Let's suppose I knock over a glass of water when I'm at the table. The glass doesn't break, but the water spills everywhere, and I say to myself, "Oh! You stupid idiot!" My saying this to myself has much the same effect upon me, and perhaps an even greater effect, as if someone else had said it to me. If someone else calls me a stupid idiot, I could possibly say kinder words to myself. I could say, "No, I'm not a stupid idiot. I just made a mistake. It's not such an awful thing." Then I probably wouldn't feel so bad because I don't

agree with what the other person has said. But when I put myself down and get down on myself, then who's there to defend me?

On the other hand, if, when I knock over the glass of water and I say to myself, "It's not such a big deal. You can clean it up. It is a correctable error. It's no problem. Maybe you can learn from this and watch your motions next time and be less likely to knock it over." Then I've spoken to myself as though I were a friend to myself.

What we say to ourselves really makes a difference. By being harshly critical, one part of me can make the rest of me feel bad.

Sometimes people don't put their automatic thoughts into words. Sometimes they think in wordless images that nonetheless mean something like "You stupid idiot! Why did you do such a dumb thing?" It's hard enough to be aware of these automatic thoughts when they're put into words; it's even harder to be aware of them when they're just fleeting images. So if you're working on the skill of self-nurture, one of the first steps is simply becoming aware of what you're saying to yourself and putting those thoughts into words so you can hang onto them and examine them.

A person was trying to write a thesis for school. He found he just couldn't get himself to write it. He experienced "writer's block": whenever he tried to write, he would find himself putting it off.

Once someone asked him, "What are you saying to yourself as you're trying to write?" His first answer was, "I don't think I'm saying anything." The other person said, "Observe yourself a little more closely, please. Try to put your thoughts into words as you write, so you can realize what they are."

The next time he sat down to write, he made up his mind he was going to think his automatic thoughts in words this time. As soon as he sat down, he said to himself, "Oh, you're probably going to screw up. You're going to fail at doing this again this time. That will mean you're just not good at writing. You're just not smart enough." Then he wrote one sentence and he sat back and said to himself, "That sentence sounds so stupid. When people read this, they're just going to laugh at you and wonder what you're doing even trying to write this thesis." Then he tried to write another sentence or two, but before he even got started, he'd say, "No. That's no good. Why are you coming out with something so stupid?"

When he sat back and observed the thoughts that he was thinking to himself, he now noticed that the self-instructions, the self-talk he was using, caused a big problem with writing. He discovered that his own self-talk was chewing himself out the whole time he was trying to write. This getting-down-on-himself type of self-talk was interfering with his writing by making him feel bad all the time and by really punishing him for trying to work.

When he gradually started working on the skill of self-nurture, he tried to stop saying those negative things to himself and started talking to himself as he would talk to someone he liked and wanted to help and wanted to do well. Gradually, he taught himself to speak to himself in this way. Now, when he sat down to write, he would say, "Congratulations. You sat down and got to work. That's the most important part. You can't get anything done unless you start. Hooray, you started!"

Then, when he wrote the first sentence, he said to himself, "Hooray! I got something down. I may need to revise it later. It doesn't come out perfectly the first time, but that's okay. At least I'm moving along."

When he had written the first section, he said to himself, "Hooray for you! You persevered; you kept on going at it. Now you can go back and revise, but I'm proud of you for getting so much done already."

When he learned to speak to himself in this way, he found that writing was even fun. He'd learned a very important secret about life and not just about writing: how much we enjoy many, many things has more to do with what we say to ourselves about them than it does with the activities themselves. If we can speak to ourselves in friendly ways, we will enjoy almost everything that we do more than if we spoke to ourselves in ways that are unfriendly.

Here's a caution, though. When we talked about kindness to others, we talked about looking after people's long-run good rather than just their short-term pleasure. The same thing goes with the skill of self-nurture. In the long run, it isn't kind to a child you're taking care of to give her a lunch consisting only of brownies and soda pop. It's also not kind to do such a thing to yourself.

Sometimes the best self-talk is tough self-talk. Sometimes the kindest thing you can say to yourself is, "Quit acting selfish and lazy, and do what you know is best." A good coach or teacher sometimes gives constructive criticism; likewise, it's useful for you to give it to yourself. But you want to use just enough criticism to motivate yourself to do better, and not so much that you make yourself miserable and interfere with your own productivity.

Finding the proper balance between being good to yourself and having high standards for yourself involves a lot of judgment. If people are thinking only about their short-term pleasure, they might decide that the most self-nurturing thing to do is to give themselves some sort of drug that will make them feel good temporarily. But the skill of self-nurture involves figuring out what is best in the long run and being kind enough to yourself to do that for yourself.

On the other hand, some people become so involved in self-denial and being ascetic that this interferes with their skill of self-nurture. For example, suppose someone won't let himself eat anything that tastes very good, but restricts himself to rice, broccoli, peas, and water all day long. He won't let himself have fun listening to music and wants to make himself work all day long. He won't let himself have fun laughing and joking around, but rather wants to keep himself serious all day long.

This person probably isn't doing a good job at the skill of self-nurture. He's being too hard a taskmaster on himself. The skill of self-nurture involves figuring out some way of finding a balance between getting self-gratification right now and trying to do the less pleasant things that will be better off for you in the long run.

Fortunately, there's room in life for both having fun now and working for more long-term interests. Being good at the skill of self-nurture entails becoming good at figuring out how to do what's really best for you in the long run, but at the same time giving yourself some pleasure in the short run. Sometimes the best plan is to reward yourself for the hard work in the future by letting yourself do something that's fun right now.

Does the skill of self-nurture mean you never say anything critical to yourself? No, it doesn't, just as the skill of kindness doesn't mean you never say anything critical to anybody else. But, it does mean that, when you do say critical things, you say them for the sake of making things better off in the long run.

I can be self-nurturing and still say to myself, "I made a really big mistake here. I did something very harmful. I should not have done that. It's very important for me to undo my mistake as much as I can and to spend lots and lots of work trying to practice and rehearse not ever doing this again. I shouldn't let up on myself until I've practiced this a lot and am sure I'm not going to make the same mistake again."

This sort of talk is self-critical, of course, but there's a difference between this and the sort of talk that just insults oneself. The difference is this: the criticism supports the basic belief that I want to make things come out well for myself in the long run. My being hard on myself is actually a loving way for me to act toward myself sometimes because it's trying to make things come out better in the long run.

The following idea lies behind helpful critical talk: "If you'll work very hard at not repeating this mistake, you'll be happier in the long run. That's what I want for you because I love you and want the best for you." This is the spirit that a good parent has when reprimanding a child, and it's the spirit a healthy person has when delivering a reprimand to himself.

Self-nurture doesn't entail feeling that you're perfect in any way. The skill of self-nurture doesn't mean that I say to myself, "Oh, I'm a great dancer. I'm great at getting along with people in every situation. I'm great at math. I'm great at soccer." The skill of self-nurture, rather, means that you want yourself to be happy and you're going to work to help yourself be happy, even if you're not great at something, or even if you're not great at anything. You're looking out for yourself, despite your imperfections.

Being good at self-nurture often requires that you desire to get better at skills constantly, because this is how you become happier. A person who says to himself, "I like myself just the way I am. I don't want to get better at anything" is usually making a big mistake. If you like yourself, then the thing to do is to help yourself get better and better at lots of different skills and to not be satisfied with staying unskilled at anything that's really important to your happiness. On the other hand, saying to yourself, "I don't deserve to feel good until I'm perfect at many different skills" is a mistake too. The task is to tolerate your own imperfection and enjoy life while working toward being better.

Here's an idea that has helped lots of people to speak to themselves in self-nurturing ways. If you're too harsh on yourself, start speaking to yourself more about what you *have permission* to do, rather than what you *should* do.

Suppose I find myself feeling guilty over some low-stakes action that has most likely had no effect. Let's say, for example, that I used an unenthusiastic tone of voice during a long conversation with someone. Saying to myself, "I haven't done anything bad; I shouldn't feel guilty" could lead me, if I believe it, to feel guilty about feeling guilty – I'm doing something I shouldn't do!

On the other hand, if I say to myself, "I haven't done any harm to this person. It's OK for me to feel no guilt, and that's what I'd like. It will also be OK if I do feel guilt for a while; it will go away sooner or later." Now I'm making it clear to myself that, whatever way I feel, I won't be breaking some big rule.

A very useful exercise for self-nurturing skills is fantasy rehearsal. Imagine any situation, and practice speaking to yourself in the same sorts of words that a kind, wise, nurturing parent would use to speak to you. This exercise has generated major positive effects for some people.

Group 14: Compliance

How do we achieve the opposite of violence, terrorism, and anarchy? How do we make nonviolent dispute-resolution the rule and not the exception? If we try to do it only by trying to teach everyone to be kind and to have reasonable expectations of others and to mutually agree on fair and just solutions to problems, we have a long way to go, possibly forever, before a nonviolent world can come about.

But another strategy posits that the opposite of violent dispute-resolution is the *rule of law*. We decide what is just and what is not just, and we make the best laws we can. If there's a dispute we go to the law books rather than running for the guns.

But the rule of law is impossible without compliance, which is the skill of obeying laws and directives that are reasonable and just. Compliance skills permit the rule of law to be a possibility.

As I mention both here and in other parts of this book, not all laws and not all directives that authorities give are good. There is a place for disobedience of peers and disobedience of authority. The skill of compliance is to be balanced with the skills of independent thinking and courage.

Skill 58: Compliance

The capacity of countries and individuals to use destruction and terrorism to influence one another has grown tremendously within the last century. Now when people attempt to resolve disputes by violence, the roots of civilization and the continued existence of life on this planet are at stake. For the human race to survive there must be increased reliance upon the rule of law in human affairs: rational, clear, written decisions about what is just and fair: these are called laws. If laws are to have any positive effect, people must be willing to sacrifice a certain part of what they would otherwise like to do in order to obey those laws. Obedience to laws or to an authority who gives directives in accordance with the idea of the rule of law is the skill of compliance.

When a speaker says to a group of adults, "May I have your attention, please?" and the audience continues talking to one another, ignoring the speaker's request, that's noncompliance. A parent says, "Please stay out of the street," and a child ignores this and runs out into the street as he pleases. A seven-year-old is picking up a one-year-old toddler; the toddler's parent, fearing that the younger child will be dropped, commands, "Please do not pick her up." Minutes later, the older child picks up the toddler again.

The speed limit on a road is forty miles-per-hour; someone routinely drives at sixty-five miles-per-hour. A tutor asks a child, "Please come and sit with me, and let's work on these exercises." The child runs off and opens a file cabinet and takes out the papers. A boss says, "Work begins at 8:30 in the morning. Please be on time." A worker routinely comes in at 9 o'clock. A parent has taken a child swimming. The parent says, "We have to go now." The child ignores this, and keeps on swimming.

A Sunday school teacher says to a boy, "Please don't ever push other people like that." The boy responds by giving an impish grin, running over to a little girl, and pushing her. There's a law against stealing, but an employee steals lots of money from the business he works for and winds up in prison.

A country enters into a contract to pay dues to an international organization; the country refuses to pay those dues when the organization's member states make a decision this country doesn't like. A treaty says that a country will not develop certain weapon systems; the country develops them anyway on the sly.

All of these are examples of noncompliance, of poor compliance skills. In each instance, there is someone who's in authority, someone who by written or unwritten agreement is in the position to tell someone else what to do. And in each of the examples above, that person received a response that seemed to reflect a "You-don't-tell me-what-to-do" attitude.

If you can identify with the authority figure in the above examples, you know how maddening it can be to run up against noncompliance. But the person doing the disobeying – or his peers – is also harmed. The interpersonal climate of the classroom with even one very noncompliant child is changed for the worse. The child who disobeys the rule about running into the street could get killed. The speeder increases his risk of getting killed and his fellow drivers' risk of being killed. The person who steals from the employer sets up an atmosphere of mistrust that affects all relations in the workplace from then on.

The role of compliance in the safety of children

Why is compliance important for children? For one thing, it could make the difference between life and death, injury and health. For example: A parent runs into a store, and says to the children, "Please stay in the car. I'll be out in just a minute." After thirty seconds, one of the children unbuckles herself and runs after her mother, getting hit by a car driving through the parking lot. For another example: A parent says, "Please don't touch that cup of coffee. It's hot." The child ignores this request and grabs it quickly, spilling it on his hand and burning himself.

For another example: A parent says to her child, "Please stay with me" as they are walking on a crowded downtown street. The child ignores this command and runs away from the parent. While the parent is searching for the child, someone kidnaps the child. Or: the parent shows the child a gun and tells the child, "If you ever see one of these in someone's house, don't touch it. Stay away from it. It's a gun, and it could kill you." The child does see a gun at someone's house, and has a great interest in doing whatever is forbidden. The child shoots himself with the gun.

One could imagine hundreds of similar examples. The conclusion from them is: if a parent loves a child and wishes to preserve the child's life and health, the parent should train the child to obey. Compliance skills can literally save a life.

One corollary of this is that children without good compliance skills should have a much more restricted range of activities than those with good compliance skills. For example, there's a pretty state park with beautiful trails beside a river. A trip to this place would be a great idea for a parent with a compliant child. But there's a rocky cliff along the way, and a noncompliant child who cannot be counted on to obey commands to stay back from the cliff's edge simply shouldn't be taken on such a trip.

There's a big fair, a fun place to take a compliant child; a noncompliant child who might run away simply shouldn't be allowed in such a crowd. There's a series of big climbing tubes at a playground, sized just for children. But the noncompliant child who will ignore adults' requests to get out of the climbing tubes when the adult asks can never be allowed in them in the first place.

The role of compliance in relationships with a child

There's another reason for teaching children compliance skills that's only slightly less compelling than their relationship to health and safety. It's difficult for an adult to enjoy being with a very noncompliant child. When a parent or teacher can't depend on the child to obey the parent's directions to, "Please put that down," or "Please come with me now," or "The rule is not to hit," or "Please give me your attention," being with that child is very unpleasant.

Noncompliant children irritate parents and teachers. And when parents and teachers are irritated, they often speak in angry tones of voice and are themselves not as pleasant to be with. A vicious cycle can start going back and forth in which both people are acting more and more unpleasant to each other. Even if this doesn't happen, it's difficult for the adult to be joyous and lots of fun. In summary, the quality of adult relations with noncompliant children is usually much poorer than the quality of adult relations with compliant children.

It hardly needs to be said that the quality of the child's relationship with parents and teachers is a very important factor in the development of all other psychological skills. Psychological skills flourish in a climate where there's lots of good feeling in the relationship.

Because compliance with the parent is so important for a child's safety and for the development of positive relationships, parents should put a very high priority on teaching compliance skills to children. In most cases this involves making the consequences for compliance so much better than the consequences for noncompliance that a command or request from the parent becomes an "offer you can't refuse" for the child. It also involves helping the child understand the reasons why compliance skills are important and useful, giving good models of compliance skills, and giving frequent enough indoctrination of the child about the importance of compliance.

The relation between compliance and self-discipline

Compliance is the "interpersonal equivalent and predecessor of self-discipline." What's meant by this?

In most of the examples of self-discipline I present in the chapter on that skill, someone gives himself commands, and then complies with them. For example: You order yourself to cut out junk food so you can lose some weight, and you follow your own command. You do something that you don't necessarily "feel like" doing. Self-discipline can be divided into two parts: figuring out what to command yourself to do, and following your own commands. As is known by anyone who has made resolutions, New Year's or otherwise, the second part of this is much harder than the first.

With compliance, the command originates with someone else. But otherwise, the task is similar. You're responding to a directive to do something that you otherwise might not have done, or that you might be very strongly inclined not to do. Because there are two people involved, one who gives the commands and one who follows them, we may say that compliance is the interpersonal equivalent of self-discipline.

Why do we say that compliance is the "predecessor" of self-discipline? Self-discipline means subordinating your momentary desires to your long-term goals. But compliance can begin in a child's life before the child is even capable of forming long-term goals. The child complies with a request to go to bed, even though he doesn't feel like it. This compliance occurs before she can understand that getting enough sleep helps to attain the goal of having stable moods. Or the child complies with a request to cooperate in a diaper change before the child has the capacity to set a goal of avoiding diaper rash and before she understands the causal relation between diaper changes and avoiding rashes.

The child who practices complying with requests from adults to do things he doesn't "feel like" doing is practicing the hardest part of the skill of self-discipline. If you get good enough at following the command to do something that isn't immediately pleasurable, it should be easier to follow your own commands to yourself to do something that isn't immediately pleasurable.

Kids who do whatever they feel like doing, with no habit of compliance, are often correctly labeled spoiled brats. The adult equivalent of the spoiled brat child is the person without self-discipline. The child no one can get to do any work is analogous to the adult who can't get himself to do any work.

Two games: frustrate-the-authority and meet-the-challenge

One of the amazing characteristics of human beings is our ability to make up games. If we define the object of a game as getting the most marbles, we crave marbles; if we define the object of the game as having the least marbles when the game ends, we get rid of them as rapidly as we can. In either case, the marbles have no intrinsic value but are valuable only according to our arbitrary definition in the context of the game.

Just as we define games with formal rules, we also can find ourselves playing other games with arbitrarily defined goals. In the process of education or child-rearing, children are given many "challenges" by authority figures.

For example: "Can you read these words?" "Can you do these math problems?" "Let's see how fast you can get your room cleaned up." "Your assignment is to write a three-page article on the following topic." "Everyone please stop talking and give me your attention."

Children tend to get into the habit of responding to these challenges in one of two ways. In the meet-the-challenge game, the child thinks, "The object of the game is to meet this challenge. Can I do it? I'll try. If I succeed at meeting it, I will feel good. If I don't succeed, I won't feel as good." The student defines the game in the way the teacher wants him to define it. If the challenges are at the right level of difficulty, worth carrying out, balanced with enough rest time, and so forth, the game can be a great deal of fun for all concerned.

But some children define the game in a different way. When the authority figure wants you to do a certain thing, can you get away with doing something differently and frustrating the authority figure? For example, when the authority says, "Please stop talking and give me your attention," the game is "How long can I keep talking?" When the authority figure says, "You can touch anything on the table but this thing," the game is, "Can I touch it as soon as the authority figure isn't looking?" When the tutor wants you to do a certain drill, the game is "Can you make it unpleasant enough for the tutor that

he will not ask you to do it any more?" When the authority figure says to clean up the room, "Can I frustrate the authority figure by ignoring that request and watching the authority figure become angrier and angrier?"

Why do people get into the frustrate-the-authority game? For one thing, it's a game that's often possible to win. If the challenges given the child are consistently too hard, too easy, too stifling, or too meaningless, the child can find the-meet-the-challenge game too unpleasant or too impossible, and fall into the "'frustrate-the-authority" game instead. Perhaps children fall into the "frustrate the authority" game from watching too many cartoons. An archetypal plot of cartoons is that a cat, coyote, or other powerful predator figure opposes a less powerful figure such as a mouse or a roadrunner, whereupon the less powerful figure repeatedly frustrates the predator, with great glee and humor.

When a child is playing the meet-the-challenge game, a display of anger from the authority figure is an unpleasant, punishing event. But when a child gets thoroughly enough into the frustrate-the-authority game, anger from the authority figure becomes a reward, not a punishment. The child looks at the authority saying, "Didn't I tell you to do that? Why aren't you doing it?" with glee, and has the thought of "I'm winning the game." The usual pattern in which anger functions to give negative feedback and decrease behavior is thwarted. Sometimes the authority figure yells even louder and gets an even more pained expression on his face, turning up the volume of the display of anger; this strategy usually results only in the authority figure's becoming more frustrated.

This pattern is obviously a very unpleasant one for the authority figure; it's even more destructive, however, for the child. If the pattern generalizes enough, the child can find himself gleefully frustrating almost everyone he comes into contact with, and can find himself universally disliked. The child can realize too late that the game has incurred for him the lasting contempt of those he has frustrated.

If someone is the authority figure, the most loving way to help someone out of this game is to make sure it's never reinforcing for the child to play it. One way to do this is to maintain calm and composure, i.e. not to become frustrated, but to impose a severe enough penalty for the game that the child will think twice before playing it again.

For example, the adult says, "Now it's time to get out of the swimming pool and go home." The child gleefully refuses, and flees from the adult. The adult calmly announces that this is the last swimming trip the child will get for a month, and that if the child does not get out immediately, this will be the last trip for two months. And the adult never fails to enforce a penalty once given.

While this type of interaction may come across as harsh, it's infinitely better for the child in the long run than letting the child take pleasure from the frustrate-the-authority game and fall into a stronger and stronger habit of playing it.

Eric Berne's terminology

Eric Berne developed a set of words useful in thinking about compliance skills, as well as other psychological skills; he called his system of thinking "transactional analysis." In explaining the ways people think, feel, and behave, Berne identified several parts of the personality.

The nurturing parent is the part of ourselves that wants to take care of someone (example: I'll be happy to show you how to do that, my good girl.) The critical parent is harsh, limiting, and condemning (example: "You know better than that; you're going to get a punishment.") The adult calculates risk/benefit ratios and calculates expected utilities of outcomes (example: "I think the chances are that this option will work out better; I'll try it.") The natural child likes to play, frolic, and be happy (example: "Yay, this is fun chasing each other!") The adapted child follows rules and stays out of trouble (example: "Yes sir, I'll do it right now.") The rebellious child rebels against authority and can delight in frustrating the authority (example: "You can't tell me what to do.")

Berne posited that the parent part of the personality is created by memories of how authority figures acted toward us during childhood. The child, according to Berne, is created by memories of how we actually felt, acted, and thought in childhood. The adult is the part that makes calculations based on data, observations, and predictions. The adult uses any information relevant to the decision.

It's often a good exercise to translate between different types of language. Berne spoke of some people being stuck in the adapted child "ego state." To rephrase this in the language of psychological skills, these people need to improve in the skills of independent thinking and assertion. Berne spoke of other people who seemed to be stuck in the rebellious child. In the language of psychological skills, these people are poor at the skill of compliance. Berne would say that each of these people would do well to strengthen the adult ego state. In the language of psychological skills, we'd say that becoming skilled at independent thinking and rational decision-making would help people learn when to comply with someone and when not to.

Let's give a little more detailed description of the rebellious child. The hallmark of the rebellious child is mischievous laughter. It's fun and it's funny to put one over on the authority figure. It's pleasurable for the rebellious child either to be defiant or to be sneaky in disobeying.

Imagine a class of students who make spit wads of paper. The instant the teacher turns his back to write on the board the students throw them at one another with great glee, only to assume a posture of innocence when the teacher turns around. This is a large group reveling in the rebellious child ego state. It's not the throwing of the spit wads that's fun in itself; it's the excitement, pleasure, and risk-taking involved in putting one over on the authority figure.

Entering the rebellious child mode is even more fun if the authority figure operates mainly from the critical parent. When the authority figure can't have fun and would try to inflict upon the people under his authority a lifestyle of constant work, no play, and no fun, then the rebellious child emerges with a sense of a strong right to exist. Conversely, the more the authority figures show that they themselves can have fun and enjoy life, and that following their rules doesn't keep others from greatly enjoying life, the less need there is for rebellion.

Why do we give people authority?

Some people with poor compliance skills can't understand why anyone would ever willingly give someone else the authority to issue commands and expect obedience. In these people's philosophy, the best form of government is anarchy: a system where there are no authorities whatsoever. For these people, there's only one answer to the question "Why do you give people authority?" That answer is "Because I can't help it. The other person has the power to make me. But when I get the power to resist that authority, I will."

Why should there be speeding laws? For no reason, according to this viewpoint – they just restrict my freedom of choice. Why should there be police? For no reason – police are just "pigs." Why should teachers have authority over students? For no reason – students should have the power to do what they want.

Yet the person who doesn't believe in authority often shifts philosophy very quickly when the authority might protect his own rights from being trampled on by other people. When someone else going 100 miles-per-hour hits my car, suddenly I believe the authorities have every right to punish him. When someone steals from me or threatens me, suddenly I feel it's good that police exist. When another student is calling me names and physically hurting me, suddenly I feel it would be useful for a teacher to have authority to stop him.

Without the existence of authority and rules, every dispute between people can devolve to the question of who is more powerful. Suppose my neighbor builds a tool shed on my property. "Hey," I say. "What are you doing? That's my property!" My neighbor replies, "I think it's MY property."

What is my response? Do I get into a physical fight with my neighbor? Do we both get guns? Do we fight it out with bombs? These are all real possibilities in a world where there is no authority. What happens in a world where authority prevails is that legal action is taken, and the authorities would look at the surveys of the property, and compel my neighbor not to build on my property. Police would come and stop him, if necessary. Because there's a structure of authority, I don't need to fight over such disputes.

Suppose there's a river that flows from Arizona to California. The people in Arizona are using the water; the people in California feel they Arizonans are using too much. A dispute arises. How is the dispute resolved? Does Arizona mobilize an army to fight California? Fortunately not. An authority structure and rule of law exist so that representatives from the states can argue their case in federal court. The federal judges decide what happens, and they speak with authority. Because of this authority, the two states don't have to fight each other.

Suppose a big kid at school would like a little extra money. He tells a little kid that every day he should pay him a dollar unless he wants to get beat up. In a world without authority, the little kid has little choice but to comply. But when there is authority, the teachers and principal can expel the older student who has practiced such extortion, in order to keep the school a safe place.

Someone might say, "People should be able to resolve these disputes without the use of authority. If people were good enough at conflict resolution, at recognizing just options, and at kindness, ethics, and good decision-making, there would be no need for authority." If all people had all these skills in abundance, it's true that there would be less need for authority. But that time has not arrived. And let's not try holding our breath until it does.

What if everyone were really good at acting reasonably to one another, solving disputes rationally, choosing just options, and so forth? Would there then be no need for authority? In fact, because people have unequal skills and expertise, we would still need to let people have authority over others in order for organizations to work smoothly.

Let's imagine a book-publishing business where every decision is made by a vote of all the people who work for the company. The person who's the computer expert for the company doesn't just fix a computer problem. He explains the problem to everybody, and lets them discuss their ideas. Everyone votes on what solution he should take. The accountant for the company doesn't just figure out how much taxes they owe. She explains every financial transaction to everybody, and the final amount paid is put to a vote. The authors find that everyone in the company makes a number of suggestions about how to change their books, and each

separate change goes according to the vote. The secretaries find they have a hard time getting their work done, because they're constantly being called on to vote on how the books should read, how much employees should be paid, how to fix the computers, and so forth. The sales manager for the company has a good idea on how to sell more books, but the computer department and the shipping and delivery departments, who don't like her idea, vote it down.

Would you invest in this company? Or would you rather invest in a company that lets the computer expert be the boss of what happens with the computers, the sales expert be the boss of the sales strategy, and the authors and editors be the boss of what's in the books?

This fanciful example illustrates a good reason for the existence of bosses. It simply takes too much time to let every person in an organization work on every single decision. In the interest of efficiency, you have to let people be in charge of things and make decisions and enforce them. Certain decisions are delegated to certain people and, when they make them, other people comply with them. Other decisions are delegated to other people, and people comply.

Because the skill of compliance exists, organizations that can do things no one individual can do. You can let the experts in each area have authority, and the others defer to and comply with their decisions.

An irrational belief leading to noncompliance

One of the major obstacles that can interfere with the skill of compliance is the following belief: there should be no one who's better than I am in anything. Or: If anyone is more competent than I am in any area, that's an intolerable affront to my self-esteem. The person who really believes this finds it more difficult to delegate authority to someone else, and to comply with the decisions of others. But obviously only a few people can ever be the most competent in any one area, and no one can be the most competent person in everything. Anyone who thinks about this belief system even a little bit will recognize it as false.

Much compliance results from exchanges people make

In his essay, *On Liberty*, John Stewart Mill wrote that one person has the right to force someone else to do something only to prevent harm from taking place. But, much more frequently, one person takes some control of another person or gives orders, commands, or requests to another person not to prevent harm, but in an exchange agreement, as in a contract. In other words: I agree to give up some control to you in exchange for what I hope to get out of the arrangement. The employee gives authority to the employer in exchange for being paid. The student gives up some control to the teacher in exchange for learning more. The people on the committee surrender some control to the chair of the committee in exchange for the efficient functioning of the committee. The people in a country allow other people to make laws that will govern their behavior in exchange for a better society in which to live.

This sort of voluntary giving of authority is what Thomas Jefferson referred to when he spoke of government based on the consent of the governed. These agreements to yield authority in exchange for something you want are very different from the situation of a dictatorship. In a dictatorship, people yield control to the dictator, not in a voluntary exchange, but simply because the dictator has more power. The people fear the consequences if they don't comply.

When you're complying with any authority, it's often helpful to realize you're making an exchange. This often makes it easier to comply. In a classroom, you give some authority to the teacher in exchange for a sense of order. If you want the sense of order without being willing to comply, you want to have your cake and eat it too.

What about complying with unreasonable authority?

The skill of compliance sometimes can be useful even in those situations analogous to facing a dictatorship. If someone holds me at gunpoint and demands my wallet, it's much more rational for me to give it to him and lose a fairly small fraction of my net worth if doing so will decrease my chance of getting killed. Thus, despite the title of this skill as "compliance with reasonable authority," there are times when it's extremely rational and wise to comply with very unreasonable authority. Obviously, it's even more desirable to avoid or escape the situations where it's necessary to do this.

Compliance requires rationality and frustration-tolerance

If you've mastered the skill of compliance, you base your decisions about whether or not to comply on what will make things come out the best, what will produce the best outcome, and what will produce the greatest good for oneself and humanity in the long run. The skill of compliance means not basing your decision on trying to prove you can stand up to your father or mother, or to prove that you can make your own decisions, or to prove that authority figures in your past have been conquered. The skill of compliance involves substituting rationality for all these neurotic motivations to comply or not comply.

Once a rational decision to comply has been made, you must often invoke the skills of delay of gratification or frustration tolerance to carry it out. But if you practice complying with requests that are good to carry out but which you don't feel like doing, you practice the skill of delay of gratification and self-discipline.

Compliance must be balanced with independent thinking and assertion

The skill of compliance with reasonable authority must be balanced with the skills of assertion and independent thinking. Why? Because people who would like to see themselves in authority issue many *unreasonable* requests or commands that you don't have to obey and you should not obey. One of the difficult parts of the skill of compliance is discriminating between a reasonable rule or command and one that's unreasonable.

The psychologist Stanley Milgram carried out some very famous experiments demonstrating people's willingness to comply with unreasonable requests. The person in charge of the experiment asked his subjects to inflict shock upon another person. Most of the subjects obeyed, even though they felt a great deal of conflict about it and seemed to know it was wrong. (In actuality, the person who was supposedly getting shocked was an actor, a confederate of the experimenter.) These experiments and others like it showed that many people are way too obedient to unreasonable or immoral authority. One motivation for these experiments was the atrocities carried out by people obeying authority during the Holocaust of the 1940s.

There is definitely a place for disobeying authority. Leo Tolstoy, the Russian writer, drew inspiration from the American writer Henry David Thoreau; both wrote about the necessity for civil disobedience when the authority of the state ordered one to carry out acts of violence contrary to one's moral principles. Tolstoy exerted a large influence on Mohandas Gandhi, who led a nonviolent revolution in India. Gandhi in turn influenced Martin Luther King, Jr. All of these people distinguished themselves by nonviolently disobeying unreasonable rules. They chose to exercise the skills of independent thinking and assertion rather than compliance, and the world was better off for their choice.

Another famous noncomplier is Rosa Parks, the African-American woman who disobeyed an order to give up her seat on a bus in the days when bus seating was segregated by race. She chose to exercise assertion and independent thinking rather than compliance. Her defiance, when combined with other civil rights actions, led to the abolition of many unreasonable laws.

These examples illustrate that compliance is not simply blind obedience to anyone who tells you to do something. You must think about whether what you're obeying serves the greater good of humanity. But, in most situations, people don't want to comply, not because their consciences dictate noncompliance, but because they don't feel like doing the work necessary to comply, or they don't feel like curbing the impulse to do whatever they want.

Compliance skills are important early in a child's life, long before the child has the reasoning capacity to de-cide whether a request is reasonable or unreasonable. When dealing with young children, adults have the sacred responsibility to give requests and commands that are reasonable and moral.

The attempt of child-rearing experts to find balance

I've read several books about child-rearing (and have written a couple). It's interesting to see the wide differences and shifts in attitude that happen over the decades regarding authority, compliance, freedom, nonbossiness, independent thinking, and assertion. It's also interesting to see how many writers feel other writers have been "too permissive" or "too authoritarian."

In a sense, it's only natural and expected that there should be endless tension and argument about compliance with authority versus individual freedom and nonbossiness. This is a classic case where balance is necessary. A child who has strong compliance skills but few independent thinking and assertion skills is very handicapped, and is vulnerable to any bossy people who come around looking for a follower. A child who's expert at opposing authority but who has no compliance skills may end up dead or in very bad relations with adults. It's not good to be either a hypercompliant wimp or a spoiled brat.

Another reason why the pendulum of permissiveness versus authoritarianism continues to swing endlessly back and forth is that dealing with very compliant people is dangerous for the order-giver. For most of us, it's pleasurable to give an order and have someone else carry it out!

But this pleasure can be an addictive one. If you get too hooked on it, you can start venturing from reasonable and necessary commands to those that simply fulfill your own whims. It can take great self-discipline not to abuse one's power when one is dealing with compliant people.

So let's imagine that everyone agrees today's children are too spoiled and they are, as a group, noncompliant brats. Writers persuade parents that they need to increase their skills of enforcing authority. Suppose adults actually do this, and children become more compliant. Then it's likely to be true that many of the order-giving adults have become unreasonable, and are abusing their power. So it then becomes necessary for other writers to become the champions of nonbossiness skills in dealing with children.

The notion of balance does not mean, however, that the best of all possible worlds occurs when the child obeys 50 percent of commands. Instead, the ideal to strive for in any given family is that 100 percent of parental commands are reasonable and necessary, and that the child obeys 100 percent of those reasonable and necessary commands. In this ideal world the parent also makes suggestions that are clearly different from commands, and the child uses independent thinking skills to decide whether to follow those suggestions.

For example: "Please put your coat on now" is a command. "If you're hot, you can take your coat off" is a suggestion. "Would you like to work on your writing now?" is a suggestion. "It's time for you to work on your writing now" is a command.

If parents can fulfill the obligation to give only reasonable commands, and if children can fulfill the obligation to obey those commands, the chances for happy family life will be dramatically increased.

Group 15: Positive Fantasy Rehearsal

This is the skill group that reminds us that what we imagine is just as important as what we do. Cultivating positive habits in using the imagination can enhance almost all other psychological skills.

Skill 59: Imagination and Positive Fantasy Rehearsal

At various places throughout this book, I've referred to the skill of using the imagination in productive ways. This chapter will recap some of those ideas.

Our culture is constantly engaging in imaginary activities. It's difficult to be in public places without being exposed to a work of the imagination, sometimes several simultaneously. Songs depict imaginary situations between imaginary people. Television shows have imaginary characters interacting with one another. Video games direct imaginary characters to interact. Polls find that the figures young people admire most are often actors, actresses, and singers – purveyors of imaginary situations and events. Make believe is very important – and to adults, as well as children.

Imaginary events can be the vehicle for two of the most important methods of influence: modeling and practice. Whenever you observe an imaginary character doing something, that image is downloaded into your memory. When you choose a behavior, the stored image of that behavior becomes accessible as you search your memory bank.

Thus one very important function of imaginary vignettes is transmission of patterns of thought, feeling, and behavior from one person to another. The more the culture as a whole can

develop a vast storehouse of models that are positive, good, and appropriate for a wide variety of different situations and for all of the psychological skills, the richer that culture will be. Conversely, the more the culture has a storehouse of negative models, and constantly downloads it, the worse the culture will become. It's pleasant to envision a culture where, for each of the sixty-two skills of this book, there are vast numbers of readily accessible models in the form of stories, plays, songs, and movies, for every age group.

A corollary of this idea is that it would behoove parents to engage with their children in a continual and regular exposure to models of psychological skills. Whenever the child exhibits troublesome or troubled behavior, one of the responses a parent can make is to download many stories that model the psychological skills the child needs in order to handle the situations better. *Programmed Readings for Psychological Skills*, a book of concrete vignettes I have written, is meant to serve this end.

In addition to modeling, imagination permits practice. A great deal of research has demonstrated that fantasy rehearsals can increase skill. In one study of ski racers, half were assigned to fantasy-rehearse skiing the hill, and the other half were assigned to perform an unrelated mental activity. The fantasy rehearsal group delivered faster times in the ski race. Other studies of fantasy rehearsal have involved interpersonal behavior, such as the skill of assertion.

Fantasy rehearsal is vastly underutilized. You can use it for any of the psychological skills discussed in this book. You store in your mind many concrete images of what it would look, feel, and sound like to do positive examples of a psychological skill. You run the images of these positive patterns through your mind many times. Real-life successes can be replayed as fantasy rehearsals; real-life failures and mistakes can have their scripts rewritten to replace the undesirable pattern with the desirable one. Then these desirable patterns can be used for fantasy rehearsals.

With enough work on fantasy rehearsals, and with correct choices as to what the positive pattern would look, feel, and sound like, it's almost a sure thing that the worker will improve in the skill. But a very important proviso is that enough repetitions must be carried out. The mistake most people make in doing fantasy rehearsal is to think that one or two practices are sufficient. This is as misguided as thinking that practicing a piece of music once or twice on the piano is enough to prepare for a performance.

Fantasy rehearsal can produce dramatic changes in people, but few people are willing to repeat the rehearsals enough times to achieve mastery.

How does one do the technique of fantasy rehearsal? Some people attempt to do it by simply closing one's eyes and imagining oneself in the situation – thinking, feeling and behaving. You can certainly do it this way, but it's awfully easy to get off task. Also, if you have an instructor, your instructor can't give feedback on your technique. I think it's usually more useful to do fantasy rehearsals out loud or in writing, describing in words the situation and the thoughts, emotions, and behaviors you experience in response to it.

Here's an example. A person is trying to get into the habit of starting his homework right away at a certain time each day, rather than putting it off.

(Situation) "I'm at home, and there are lots of interesting and fun things to do. But I look at the clock, and I see it's the time I want to start my homework each day."

(Thoughts) "This is a challenge to my delay of gratification skills. I don't feel like working now, but if I can make myself do it, and even find a way of enjoying it, that will be quite an accomplishment. I'll deserve to congratulate myself and feel good if I do that. It won't kill me to sit down and work. People have put up with far worse things in human history. I want to relax and keep my eyes out for ways to make this interesting for me. I'm getting started, I'm sitting down, I'm looking at my to-do book, I'm opening my books. Hooray for me for getting started! I want to reinforce myself for the small steps as I do this."

(Emotions) "As I do this, I'm feeling determined and confident. I'm feeling proud that I'm able to control myself."

(Behavior) "I'm continuing to do this work. I'm challenging myself, and I'm meeting my challenges. I'm getting it finished."

(Celebration) "Hooray for me! I've finished it now. And hooray that I did this fantasy rehearsal!"

One way of performing repetitions is to write out the words to the fantasy rehearsal and read those words several times. Another way is to make a tape recording of the fantasy rehearsal and listen to it over and over. These techniques make it easier to check off on a tally sheet how many fantasy rehearsals have been done.

Imagination in the decision-making process

Without the use of imagination, it's impossible to be a good decision-maker. Why? Because you use imagination to call to mind the problem itself, to envision options for solving it, and to envision consequences of each option. For example: Suppose I'm sitting at my desk, thinking about how to educate my children. All I see at my desk is a computer, a clock, and a phone. But in my mind I see a child reaching schooling age and various paths diverging. I hear words in my mind, my own self-talk, formulating the problem in words – what would be the best way to educate

this child? This sentence and the picture of my child are just imaginary.

Now I start to envision options. I call to mind the public school and some private schools, and I call to mind an image of homeschooling. None of these are exactly accurate. They are images, the product of my imagination. But there's enough information, enough memories, to draw upon that I can make very detailed and elaborate images of what the child's experience would probably be like.

Then I call to mind consequences. I try to predict what things will be like in a year, in five years, in ten years, in twenty years with these options, and I give mental pictures and inner sentences to my predictions. What imagined consequences do I like best and which option will product them? I choose on that basis.

I recall working with a child who had great difficulty visualizing anything. Not surprisingly, this child tended to bypass the thoughtful process of decision-making described above and react impulsively to situations. By cultivating the ability to imagine problem situations, options, and consequences, the decision-making process is vastly improved.

Imagination in communication

Abstract language provides a general idea of the ideas we're trying to communicate. But specific examples, the words that create clear mental images, really nail down what we're trying to say. When someone says, "Today has been a wistful day for me," you're given an abstract picture of what the day has been like. But when the person goes on to give concrete images, we learn much more. "Today I've been listening to tape recordings of my father. On one he's singing 'It's a Lovely Day Tomorrow.' I've been imagining what it would be like if he could have lived long enough to know my children. I'll bet they would have loved to hear him tell his stories. I'll bet they would have loved to see his warm smile."

Here's another example. A parent says to a child, "Settle down!" This abstraction communicates something. But if the parent says, "Please use a voice no louder than the one I'm using now. You can walk around; you don't have to sit, but don't run. You can play with the toys, but please don't touch these china figurines." If the child can remember all that, he has very clear images of what the parent wants.

Here's a different kind of example. Someone could say, in abstract terms, "I feel low these days, sort of like the best part is over." Contrast that with a few lines from one of Shakespeare's sonnets: "That time of year thou mayest in me behold, When yellow leaves, or none, or few do hang/ Upon those boughs that shake against the cold/ Bare ruined choirs, where late the sweet birds sang." Such concrete sensory images are found, not only in good poetry, but also in all sorts of effective writing and speech.

Imagination in reading

When you read, all you really see on the page are little black squiggles. When the written word names a witch, an angel, a Thanksgiving harvest or courage, where do the pictures and sound effects come from? They come from your own imagination, your own ability to conjure up the images the author wants you to see. So reading is really an act of imagination. Conversely, without the skill of imagining well, reading comprehension suffers. Much of education consists in teaching people to make accurate pictures and sounds out of words.

Imagination in mathematics and science

Has anyone ever seen an electron? No one has, yet people who have studied electricity all have some sort of image in their heads of little balls that flow along through wires when you plug them in. No one has ever seen an atom or a chemical bond, or smelled or tasted a photon. No astronomer has ever seen a "black hole." Many of our most basic scientific ideas are concepts we imagine rather than directly see, hear, smell, touch, or taste.

It's also impossible to do mathematics without imagining. "A boat can go 30 miles an hour in still water. The current of the river goes 10 miles an hour. How long will it take the boat to go 40 miles upstream?" When you do a problem like this, do you see a boat and a river, and do you see the river moving? If you can't see these things, this sort of problem will be more difficult than if you can.

But word problems aren't the only element of math that calls for imagination. Someone adds 38 and 26 and gets 298. Does this answer make sense? You know off the bat that it doesn't if you have a mental image of roughly how big the three numbers are. You know the sum is bigger than it should be, without having to add the numbers. Many school children who can do the mechanical processes of addition and subtraction can't tell whether their answers are reasonable because they don't have some sort of mental image of what numbers really mean.

Imagination is necessary in all of mathematics. Can you understand what a negative number is, without being able to visualize a number line, or a thermometer, or a time line, or some such representation? Can you understand what a fraction is without ever visualizing a pie or a cup or a pattern of squares or something that's divided up into parts? Who can understand derivatives and integrals without visualizing lines tangent to curves or areas under curves? Much of mathematics is a training of the imagination.

Imagination used in calling up psychological resources

Let's return to imagination in the service of solving psychological challenges. Here's a technique for helping yourself respond to a situation with the emotions you choose. It strongly resembles fantasy practice. But I list it as a separate technique because the idea isn't so much to increase the habit strength of positive patterns, as to select and activate a positive pattern for use in a given situation.

Suppose there's a town meeting coming up about whether or not to allow schools to compel children to watch advertising. A person has very strong feelings on this matter, and he hopes to communicate those feelings in the town meeting. But ordinarily he's rather timid and tentative in expressing his thoughts and feelings. He doesn't want to act this way. He asks himself, "How do I want to feel and think? What style of behaving do I want to enact?" He decides he would like to be determined, confident, impassioned, serious, and forceful. This is step 1: deciding how he would like to handle the situation.

In step 2, he searches his memory bank for images of such a pattern. He tries to recall himself acting in that way, but can't do so. But he can recall very clearly an image of someone else acting that way, in a debate that he recently watched. The debater, whom he admired, used exactly the style he would like to use.

Now for step 3: he runs that recalled image through his mind in as much detail as he can, pulling up the sights and sounds to activate them. In step 4, he rehearses what he's going to do in the town meeting, trying to keep the same pattern from the recalled image activated. In other words, he transfers the style from the recalled situation to the upcoming situation. In step 5, he goes into the real-life situation and does what he has rehearsed in his mind.

These steps of activating a desired pattern have been used in curing phobias. For example: Someone is deathly afraid of bugs. In step 1, he decides he'd like to be more slaphappy and silly than scared – the silliness will be a good antidote to the fear. In step 2, he lands on memories of being with friends, acting out crazy scenes, laughing. In step 3, he runs these memories through his mind in great detail. In step 4, he sees himself acting really silly rather than scared when he first sees a ladybug, then a cockroach. He imagines politely asking each bug to dance, dancing with each bug, singing romantic songs to each bug, and otherwise entertaining his friends with his silliness. In step 5, he does this in real life when he encounters the bug.

Imagination in dealing with trauma

When something horrible happens to someone – they get raped, they fight in a war, a child dies – the memory of the event is stored. Part of the problem many people have is intrusive images, imaginings they can't control, that cause great distress. Nightmares are one manifestation of this; waking images of the traumatic scene are another. To keep these traumatic memories from coming to consciousness, people sometimes go to elaborate lengths to avoid either physical reminders of the experience or other associated memories that remind them of it.

When people deal with remembered trauma, it's often useful to bring the distressing images back to mind on purpose. But here the goal is to respond to them in a different way than being overcome with distress. In a method some therapists have used, the person purposely calls to mind the traumatic memory, while simultaneously doing a task such as moving the eyes back and forth from left to right. The eye movements are apparently not essential to the method; people have obtained good results from making clicks near one ear and then near the other.

The essential elements of such a program are as follows. First, it's a familiar principle that purposeful exposure to a feared situation, including a feared memory, tends to cause habituation. Second, calling up the feared image while simultaneously doing another attention-demanding task gives practice in not letting the scary image incapacitate you and keep you from functioning. At any rate, purposely doing the thing that's most scary to do, in this case calling to mind a set of mental images, has a familiar ring, from our chapter on courage skills.

Here are some more imagination-centered techniques therapists have used in helping people deal with traumatic memories or scary scenes. One such technique is to take a traumatic memory and to run it rapidly backwards, as if one were watching a videotape in fast reverse. Another such technique is to call to mind the scary scene and move it farther away, make it smaller, change it from color to black and white. These methods too involve purposely calling to mind scary images, but doing things with the images to show that you can control them, and to practice controlling them, i.e. by changing them around.

Imagination for self-exploration

Two personality tests that have been used extensively for many decades, despite the fact that evidence for their reliability and validity is rather poor, are the Rorschach test and the Thematic Apperception Test. In the Rorschach, you imagine things in inkblots, and in the Thematic Apperception Test you make up stories about pictures. Although I don't feel these devices are useful as "tests," they contain a kernel of truth: the fantasies you produce tell you something about yourself. If nothing else, these tools reveal some of the images available in your fantasy repertoire.

You don't need pictures to associate to; if you simply blab out a story as quickly as you can, you get a picture of the contents of your imagination at one particular moment. The psychoanalytic treatment of dreams and people's associations to dreams are similar. People tell what thoughts and fantasies come to mind with respect to each element of the dream and the dream as a whole. This is the process of letting the imagination go and then sitting back and observing what the imagination has created. The exercise I mentioned in the concentration chapter, of letting the mind drift and observing what it does, can also produce interesting results.

Finally, people have used guided fantasy, where part of a story is told and the participant must fill in its other parts, as a means toward self-awareness. For example: A magician brings you to a table where a dinner is served, and allows you to choose three people from your past to be your companions. Whom do you choose? You get to ask each one a question. What do you ask? You get to tell each one a statement. What do you say?

Imagination as entertainment

The techniques I just discussed may be more entertainment than edification. But they can be fun, as can all sorts of other uses of imagination. Observing the products of other people's imaginations, as in watching plays and movies and reading novels, is for many people a source of great joy in life. The creation of one's own imaginings, for example in story writing, poetry composition, and improvisational drama, or in dramatic play as children do, or in simply daydreaming wish-fulfilling fantasies, not only entertains and gives pleasure, which is reason enough for its existence, but exercises the imagination muscle, and readies it for the more utilitarian purposes I listed earlier.

Group 16: Courage

Included in this group are the skills of overcoming anxieties and fears of all sorts. I include as separate skills in this group handling two very different interpersonal stances: that of depending and accepting help, and that of being independent and resisting the influence of another. The fear of being dependent and the fear of being disliked or independent are the basis of many other fears.

Skill 60: Courage

Courage skills are useful in dealing with real danger. They are also useful in dealing with situations that feel more dangerous than they really are.

Fear serves a purpose

Some people think it would be good to be "fearless." This is not true. Fear is the brain's signal that there may be danger. There's a good reason why we're able to feel fear! Fear tells us, "You'd better protect yourself!" It's our brains' way of making danger stand out and be noticed. Because of fear, we don't find ourselves thinking like this: "Humh, what's the best thing for me to do now? Plan a vacation? Make up a poem? Or get out of the street so I won't get run over by that big truck coming straight at me?" When dangerous situations come up, fear helps them take over our attention and get us moving quickly toward safety.

Some people seem relatively fearless. Being fearless poses problems. When fearless people are children, they often wind up in emergency rooms. Some wind up dead. They're not afraid of climbing into high places or leaping from them. They're not afraid of running into streets. If they make it through childhood, fearless people often get killed during risky ventures like motorcycling, reckless driving, or fighting. Fear is meant to keep us out of trouble. Much of the time, it does that.

Fear was not invented just to keep us alive. It's also meant to help us avoid losing precious things, such as our money and our reputations. People who have no fear of losing money often throw it away on risky deals. People who have no fear of losing their reputation often blow it by making fools of themselves. Suppose a person is so fearless that he challenges someone else to a public debate. He knows little about the subject and does no work to prepare himself. He comes away from the debate looking foolish. He would have been better off if some fear had given him a signal that said, "Watch out!"

So having good courage skills is not so simple as just trying to get rid of all your fear. We need fear to alert us to danger, whether physical, financial, or social.

Too much fear interferes with life

On the other hand, you can have too much of a useful thing! And many, many people do have too much fear. Fear is very unpleasant. Fear is the emotion that goes along with blood-curdling screams and thoughts like "Aaah! Let me out of here!" If you feel that emotion too often, you enjoy life much less. It's a problem to solve.

Almost everyone feels a certain amount of "unrealistic fear." Unrealistic fear is fear that's too big for the amount of danger. Suppose someone crossing a very well built bridge feels huge fear, 10 on a scale of 10, that the bridge will collapse. He feels this even though he can say it's almost impossible that the bridge will actually fall. This is unrealistic fear. It's a problem to solve.

Sometimes people don't use the word "fear" in describing the bad feeling that's attached to a situation. Someone is "afraid" of doing homework, for fear that she will mess it up and do badly at it. But she might have other thoughts that make her feel angry about it, bored with it, upset about it, or disgusted with it. She may feel these other bad feelings more than fear. We'll talk about fear in this chapter. But most of what we'll say goes for any bad feeling that is attached to a certain situation.

Luckily, there are some good ways of reducing fear. This chapter will talk about these ways. If you have too much fear, you'll benefit from learning these ways very well, and using them very often. But first we need to talk about ways of assessing danger and ways of dealing with real danger.

Assessing danger

To have good courage skills, you need to be able to assess danger, to figure out how much danger there is.

Here's a formula for assessing danger:

Danger = Chance that bad things will happen x How bad they are

That is, you multiply the chances of bad outcomes by a rating of how bad the outcomes are.

Suppose I'm walking outside on a sunny day. It occurs to me that I could get struck by lightning. How bad would it be if that happened? Very bad, close to 10 on a scale of 10. Yet I'm in no danger. Why? Because the chance this will happen is very close to zero. If I felt a lot of fear, it would be unrealistic. I'd be feeling tremendous fear with low danger. On the other hand, if there's a storm and lightning is striking very close to me, the chance of the bad outcome is much higher.

Suppose a student goes to take a test with a hundred questions on it. The student is well prepared. The student thinks, "Oh, no. I might miss a question!" Even for well-prepared students, the chance of missing at least one question is usually pretty high. But how bad is this outcome? It's not terrible to miss a question. So there's still not much danger.

If a fear is unrealistic, usually someone is overestimating something. Sometimes it's the chance that a really bad thing will happen. Sometimes it's how bad something is.

See if you can figure which one the person is overestimating. Suppose there's a man who has lots of money saved up. He can support his family for the rest of his life, just on his savings. He hears from a very reliable person that at his job, his pay will soon be reduced. He feels great fear over this. Which is he overestimating?

A child is lying in bed. She feels very scared. She feels that a kidnapper might come into the house and steal her away. She guesses that the chances of this happening tonight are about 50 percent.

Both of these people have fairly unrealistic fears, don't they? Neither of them is in much danger. The man is overestimating the badness of the outcome. The child is overestimating the chance of a bad outcome.

What to do about realistic fear and danger

Not all fears are unrealistic. And even fears that are fairly unrealistic often have a realistic part.

Take the example of the man who feared his pay would be reduced. It's not horrible if his pay is reduced, but it is undesirable. So if he can do something to prevent that, so much the better. If he can find another job he likes just as well that pays more, he has dealt with the danger. Or take the example of the child fearing kidnappers. The chance of a kidnapping may be very low, but if the doors are unlocked, it makes sense to lower the chances by locking the doors.

Very often, there's something we can do to reduce danger, whether the danger is great or small. Here are three types of things we may choose to do: pump adrenalin, avoid or escape the situation, and work toward skill in handling the situation well.

1. Pumping adrenalin. Adrenalin is one of our hormones. Our body often pumps it out into the bloodstream when we're scared. It helps us if we need to run fast, fight hard, or otherwise use lots of energy quickly. It prepares our bodies ready for lots of hard exercise.

Once I was walking by myself in a rough section of Chicago, late at night. (And, yes, this is a very bad example of decision-making skill.) Three big, mean-looking guys started following me. Then they started running after me. I'm very thankful that my body pumped adrenalin. It helped me to run the fastest 200 yards of my life. We pump adrenalin when we're scared, so that we can save ourselves in situations like this.

Sometimes, though, pumping adrenalin gets in the way. Suppose I'm going to perform at a violin concert. Pumping adrenalin makes my muscles ready to work hard. The muscles are so ready to move that they tremble. I don't want trembling muscles when I play the violin. I need to teach my body not to pump too much adrenalin. Pumping adrenalin does not help me perform at a violin concert, the way it helps get away from mean guys. Let's look at other things we can do about danger and realistic fear.

2. Avoiding or escaping. This means to stay away from the situation that causes the danger. Or, if I'm already in the situation, it means to get out of it. For instance, I went to the park on the night of my narrow escape from the thugs because I wanted some exercise. Realistic fear might have led me to lift weights inside rather than walk

around outside. Avoidance would also be a good way for me to reduce danger in presenting a violin concert. To reduce the realistic danger of looking foolish, I avoid scheduling violin concerts for myself. I stick to an instrument that I have learned how to play!

Suppose that I'm out with some friends and someone dares me to dive off a cliff into a river below. If don't have total certainty that I won't land on some rocks and kill myself, I surely have reason for realistic fear! Avoidance is the best strategy in this situation.

Avoidance and escape are often extremely wise choices. I wish that I could magically give more people realistic fear of alcohol, cigarettes, and other recreational drugs, and promote more vigorously a strategy of avoiding these substances.

But sometimes avoidance has big costs. Suppose I'm very afraid of doing a bad job on a paper I'm assigned to write. Every time I think of writing, I feel scared. So I avoid this fear by not thinking about it. I end up not turning in a paper, and getting a grade of zero. I would have been better off writing a bad paper!

Suppose I'm lonely and would like to invite someone to do something with me. I think about calling up someone and inviting this person. I have some fear I'll look foolish and will just be rejected. If I use avoidance and escape, I might simply decide not to invite the other person. The loneliness is the price I pay for avoidance.

3. Skill-building and preparing. This means to build the skills necessary to handle the situation well. If you're a violin player, it means practicing the song so thoroughly that you can almost do it in your sleep. It also means practicing getting worked up to just the right degree of excitement – not too much, not too little, but just the right amount. It means practicing playing the song in front of people. It means practicing in your mind playing it in front of the people at the concert.

Suppose someone has "test anxiety." When tests come up at school, the person becomes very scared. Skill-building and preparing means working very hard to prepare for the test. It could mean making up tests on the material and practicing taking them. If someone has made up very difficult tests and taken them, scored them, and passed them with flying colors, the person has less cause for realistic fear of failing the test.

Suppose I'm scared of looking foolish by calling someone up and inviting the person to do something with me. Skill-building and preparing means that I prepare myself thoroughly in the art of social conversation skills. I rehearse in my mind various comfortable and genuine conversations. I prepare so much that I'm sure I'll act appropriately and will not feel foolish, even if my invitation is declined.

Suppose I sign up for a sports team. I'm afraid of being embarrassed. I'm afraid that other people will be much better than I. Skill-building and preparing means that I do my homework ahead of time. I observe to see how good the people I'll be playing with are. I check to see where my skills are now. I work and practice to see whether I can raise my skills to a level where I'll realistically feel confident. If lots of work and practice can get me to that level, I've used skill-building and preparation successfully. If I find I can't get to that level, then my preparation has at least led me to make a wise choice of avoidance.

Suppose I have a fear of driving a car. If I use avoidance, I simply stay away from the steering wheel. Skill-building and preparation, however, might involve lots of careful watching while someone else drives. It might involve extensive study of a manual. It might involve practicing with a computer simulation. It might involve going out to practice on a parking lot in the wee hours of the morning when no one else is there. I can do many fantasy rehearsals of handling difficult traffic.

Suppose I find out I'm at risk for heart disease. This causes some realistic fear. The strategy of avoidance might lead me to turn my eyes away whenever I catch a glimpse of an article on heart disease. Skill-building and preparation might involve eating a very healthy diet, building a sensible exercise program, and so forth.

Suppose someone is very much afraid of living his life in poverty. In order to defend against this fear, he spends a great deal of time studying to decide how he can make enough money. He spends time building the skills he needs for a high-paying profession. He spends time deciding how to save and invest the money he makes.

Suppose someone is very scared of writing badly and having her writing look foolish. She studies manuals on how to write well; she studies good writing so she can imitate it; she practices writing very often; she does lots and lots of revision; she starts very early to give herself lots of time before any deadline.

There's one short word that summarizes what we need for skill-building and preparation strategies. When I say it, you'll immediately know why many people don't use these strategies enough. The word is *work*. It takes lots of work to get really prepared and to build skills. But work can make great things happen. People who are in a habit of working hard and long to improve their prospects of success are very lucky. They have a great way to defend themselves against fear.

To summarize: Pumping adrenalin, avoidance and escape, and skill-building and preparation all have their place in dealing with real danger and realistic fear. Having good courage skills involves choosing appropriately among these strategies.

Reducing unrealistic fear

Now let's talk about reducing unrealistic fear.

First I'll outline techniques of fear reduction; then I'll explain these steps more fully.

Techniques of fear reduction

1. Recall and list situations.
2. Rate your handling of them.
3. Use behavior, not feeling, as the measure of your success at the beginning.
4. Move up the hierarchy of difficulty.
5. Use prolonged enough exposure.
6. Choose your self-talk.
   6.1 Accurately assess danger; use not awfulizing if possible.
   6.2 Think about advantages of cultivating toughness.
   6.3 Use self-reinforcement.
7. Choose your Imagery.
   7.1 Use positive imagery.
   7.2 Transfer the image of success to the scary situation.
   7.3 Habituate to scary images.
8. Use relaxation.
9. Use fantasy rehearsal.
10. Reinforce courage, not fear.

Recalling and listing situations

Remember that you don't want to get rid of all fear. You want to work on those situations where the fear is out of proportion to the danger. Without a specific situation, you can't decide whether the fear is realistic or unrealistic.

You need specific, concrete situations to practice with. To get those situations, you search through your memory for times when you had unrealistic fear. Write down these situations. As you continue to work on this, add to the list. Any time a situation comes up that causes you unrealistic fear, write it down.

If one of your fears is of social embarrassment, then showing someone this list may be a scary situation in itself! Or perhaps even the prospect of telling someone about these situations is scary. If recounting the real situations is too scary for now, you can still do work by making up stories. Make up situations that are like the ones you're afraid of, situations you would be afraid of, but which have not happened. You can envision these situations as happening to someone else, not you, if you like. Or someone else can make up specific situations for you, based on some knowledge of the type of situations that are hard for you to handle.

Sometimes the hardest task is figuring out exactly what situations you're afraid of. Sometimes what really triggers the fear are thoughts or images that you forget about soon after having them.

Here's an example: A man notices himself becoming anxious during the same month each year. He doesn't know why. He just feels "imminent doom." He finally spends some time posing the question, "What am I afraid of," and letting his mind drift to an answer. The image of his dying of a heart attack comes to mind. He then remembers it was at this time of year that his own father died of a heart attack. He conjures the image of his own children struggling and being victimized after he dies. His thoughts are, "Their lives are going to be terrible." Now he has "gotten in touch with" what he's really afraid of.

Here's another example. A teenage girl finds herself with a pounding heart, trembling, and vomiting on certain mornings during the week. At first she thinks something is physically wrong with her. She finally asks herself why the symptoms come on certain days and not others. She realizes that on those days she's scheduled to come in contact with a couple of boys at her school who harass her. They sometimes poke or grab her in very unwanted ways. She becomes aware of how much she mistrusts the school authorities. She's afraid that if she tells, she will only be doubted, laughed at, and embarrassed. She now has some very real problems to solve. But the fear is now attached to concrete situations rather than being mysterious and unknowable.

A boy finds it very hard to get to sleep at night. He gets very "wired up" and tense. The next morning he can't remember what he was tense about. He resolves to keep track of the thoughts that go through his mind. He lies down in his bed at night and immediately the image comes to his mind that a criminal will sneak in his window and kidnap him. He once saw this image in a movie, and he recalls it vividly. He now realizes this is what's scaring him.

I have talked about this process earlier in this book. I have referred to it as filling in the STEB matrix. You become aware of what situations you're having trouble with, what thoughts you're having in those situations, what emotions you're feeling, and what behaviors you're doing.

How do you come to realize what's really scaring you? Sometimes you just ask yourself questions and give your mind time to answer. What bad things am I worried will happen? What's the worst that could happen in this situation? What would happen as a result of that? What scary scene am I trying to keep out of my mind? Answering these questions can be very uncomfortable. You answer them when you're ready to handle that discomfort, in exchange for having a better chance to solve the problems.

When you make lists of the types of situations you want to handle better, you're really on the road to improvement. This is often a very hard step. It's much easier for most people to tell themselves that something or someone else is the problem, not that their own reactions are the problem. For example:

Instead of "I have math anxiety," the person thinks, "Math is stupid and boring."

Instead of "I'm scared of meeting new people," the person thinks, "These parties are a stupid waste of times."

Instead of "My fear of failure makes me anxious all the time at school," the person thinks, "All the teachers are bad, and nothing that I'm taught is worthwhile."

Instead of "I'm scared I might say the wrong thing and embarrass myself," the person thinks, "I don't want to meet those people; I have nothing in common with them."

Blaming other people or other things is a tempting pattern to get into, because it saves face. It allows us not to have to admit any imperfection in ourselves. But we pay a severe price for doing this. First, it doesn't lead us toward making the changes in ourselves that we need to make. Many people have spent their whole lives complaining about other people and other things and avoiding making changes that would make them much happier.

There's another severe price. When there are lots of negative thoughts and beliefs about the world, other people, and activities, these thoughts are very depressing. Perhaps this is a reason why anxiety and depression tend to go together.

In summary, a very important first step in overcoming fears and gaining courage is simply to admit to yourself, "Here's a situation that scares me more than I'd like it to." If you can have the courage to say that to yourself, you're on the way.

Rating your handling of the situations

How good was your handling of each of the situations? Or how good is your imaginary handling of it, now? You can use the following scale:

0 = Very bad
2 = Bad
4 = So-so
6 = OK
8 = Good
10 = Very good

Or you can rate the sheer degree of discomfort or distress you would feel in this situation. This is referred to as a SUD rating: subjective units of discomfort.
0 = None
2 = Very little
4 = Some, but not much
6 = Moderate amount
8 = Great amount
10 = Very great amount

These two ratings measure very different things: how successfully you behave in the situation, and how you feel in the situation.

If you want to change something, it's important to measure it. If you want to improve your responses to situations that are scary to you, measure those responses.

Use behavior, not feeling, as the measure of success at the beginning

I recommend rating situations in both of the above ways. But then, when you start practicing with the situations, I recommend making your first measure of success whether you behaved the way you want.

The reason for this is to avoid vicious cycles. Suppose I'm really intent on giving a speech without fear. I stand up on the stage. I think, "Am I scared?" I notice my trembling hands, and my rapid breath, and my sweaty palms. I notice the urge to run out the side door. The answer is, "Yes, I'm scared!" Now I can think, "Oh, no, my fear-reduction techniques aren't working! I'm failing at the goal I had wished for so strongly!" These thoughts make me even more scared. When I notice this happening, I say to myself, "Oh, no. I'm even more scared than before! When is this going to stop!" A vicious cycle has set in. I am monitoring my fear, and when I find it, that makes me more scared.

On the other hand, suppose my main criterion is behavior. I'm thinking, "My goal is to get my ideas across. It doesn't matter if I'm terrified the whole time. I just want to get these words out." I start giving the speech. This time, if I notice my sweaty palms and pounding heart, I think, "Who cares? The words are coming out! I'm succeeding!"

Eventually, I want not only to handle the situation well, but also to enjoy myself while doing it. Eventually, I want the SUD level to go down. But the first priority is establishing some memories of "success experiences," of behaving the way I wanted to in the situation.

Move up the hierarchy of difficulty

Once you have listed the scary situations, you want to arrange them in order – in a "hierarchy." You arrange them in order of their SUD rating. Which are the 2s and 3s and 4s that are uncomfortable but not terribly so? Which are the 8s and 9s and 10s that are the big fear-provokers? And which are the 5s, 6s, and 7s that are in the middle range?

After you arrange the situations in order, you'll usually want to start out with the low-level ones, and work your way up. This way you get some success experiences under your belt before tackling the really tough situations. This way, before you take on the biggest fears, you learn to trust that the fear reduction techniques will really work,

In research studies, sometimes people have jumped right to the scariest situation and have stuck with it for a long time. If you can hang in there and stick with it, this seems to work for fear reduction just as well as moving gradually up the hierarchy does. But I still recommend working up the hierarchy if possible. This is because you want to avoid attempting the scariest situation, getting too scared of it, and escaping from it. As we'll see in the next section, escaping when your fear is greatest can do more harm than good.

There are many instances in which you'll have no choice but to start high on the hierarchy. For example, you take on a very important job, and you're anxious about your ability to perform in it, but there are very great costs if you try to escape or avoid it. Or you find yourself in a school situation that causes great anxiety, but the costs of dropping out are far greater than those of staying in. In situations where you can't have the luxury of gradually working your way up the hierarchy of difficulty, you're going to need to get tough and tolerate some pain. The consolation is that you can probably get over the problem more quickly than you would have if you had approached it gradually.

Use prolonged enough exposure

There have been lots of different programs for fear reduction, and many of them have been successful. But the one thing that successful programs seem to have in common is prolonged exposure. This means that you have to be in the situation that you're unrealistically afraid of – you have to expose yourself to it. And you have to stay in it long enough – the exposure has to be prolonged enough – that the fear goes way down.

This is one of the main secrets of fear reduction that most people don't know. It's important to understand this principle.

Suppose someone says, "I get exposed to the scary situation all the time. If I didn't, I wouldn't have a problem. If exposure cures fears, why doesn't the fear go away?"

Let's understand the difference between prolonged exposure and short exposure. Let's imagine I'm working with a fear of being on an elevator.

Suppose I get on an elevator and I notice myself feeling scared. I feel a great urge to escape. Now the door finally opens, and I get off in a hurry. "Thank goodness I'm off," I say to myself, and my fear goes down.

The students of behavior speak of "negative reinforcement." This means that a behavior is rewarded by the turning off of something unpleasant. For example, there's an unpleasant noise coming from an alarm clock; the stopping of the noise rewards the behavior of turning off the clock. Is negative reinforcement occurring in the situation of brief exposure to the elevator? And what is being reinforced?

The reduction of fear is the turning off of something unpleasant. And the behavior that it rewarded was hurrying off the elevator. In other words, fear-reduction rewarded escape behavior.

But what is fear? It's largely the urge to escape. Rewarding escape has much the same function as rewarding fear itself. The fear is likely to be just as great, or greater, the next time I get on the elevator.

On the other hand, suppose I make myself get on the elevator and just stay on it. I ride up and down and watch the door open and close. At first my fear is very great. Then it starts to go down. The emotional part of my brain is gradually finding out that nothing horrible is happening. I'm gradually starting to really appreciate that I'm not in big danger. It takes time for this to get through. But over time, it does, and the fear goes down. My SUD rating gradually goes from 10 down to 1 or 2.

Now the fear-reduction has not rewarded escape behavior. If anything, it has rewarded courage behavior, that is, staying with the feared situation. The next time I get on the elevator, the fear is very likely to be less. If I repeat the prolonged exposure enough, I can reduce the fear to a very low level, or to zero.

This story has a very important moral for all who would reduce unrealistic fear. Once you've decided a fear is unrealistic, you want to avoid becoming scared of the situation and then escaping from it before the fear has gone down. You want to set yourself up for prolonged exposures.

Suppose a girl has stage fright. Suppose someone says to her, "Well, just come to the recital. If you feel too scared, you don't have to play. If you're not scared, you can play." Is this a good plan? The reasoning we just went through helps us know that it isn't. You don't want to reward fear by making escape or avoidance depend on it.

Suppose the same girl is given a choice. "You can have a recital in front of just a few people you know well, and play all the songs you know well. Or you can perform in a big recital and just play a very short piece. That way you won't have to be on the stage very long."

For fear-reduction, which would be better for her to choose? The longer she can be on the stage, the better. And if having a small group makes it easier for her to put on a long recital, then she should go for it. The best thing for her would be to have an audience who was willing to keep listening until her SUD rating was low.

In talking about the effects of exposure, there's a word worth knowing. The word *habituation* refers to the fact that we gradually get used to things. If we stay in scary but non-dangerous situations long enough, we habituate to them.

Consciously choosing your self-talk

One of the most helpful discoveries in the field of fear-reduction is that you can change how you feel by what you think. If you're saying to yourself, "This is going to be awful! I can't stand this! I'll never live this down. I'm going to be so humiliated!" then it's easy to see why there would be some fear. But people often say things like this to themselves without even being aware of it, or at least without remembering it well enough to recount later. So one of the first steps in choosing your self-talk is becoming aware of what you automatically say to yourself.

If you notice that you're saying things to yourself like, "Something horrible is about to happen," this is not something to regret or to punish yourself for. This is something to celebrate! Why? Because you have become aware of your self-talk, and this is an important step in changing it. Try to congratulate yourself for taking this important step.

In thinking about your own thoughts, it's useful to refer to the categorization we've used several times before in this book:
1. Awfulizing
2. Getting down on yourself
3. Blaming someone else
4. Not awfulizing
5. Not getting down on yourself
6. Not blaming someone else
7. Goal-setting
8. Listing options and choosing
9. Learning from the experience
10. Celebrating what happened to happen
11. Celebrating someone else's choice
12. Celebrating your own choice

If you want to reduce fear, you want to choose things to say to yourself that are "celebrating" statements and "not awfulizing" statements, rather than "awfulizing" statements. You want to choose statements such as the following:

"I am safe, because . . ."

"I know that I can handle this situation successfully, because . . ."

"There's no need for me to escape. This will come out OK."

"I'm so glad I prepared for this situation well."

"I'm glad that I can trust another person to make it come out OK because . . ."

"I'm glad it so happens that the danger level is very low."

What if you don't believe that these statements are true? What if you're really in great danger? Then you're dealing with realistic fear. Maybe you really do need to escape or avoid. But if you have carefully figured out beforehand that you're not in danger and that any fear you will feel is going to be unrealistic, you need to remind yourself of the reasons for this.

In addition to reminding yourself that you're not in grave danger, there's another useful line of self-talk. This is to remind yourself of the advantages of being tough and strong. These fall into the category of goal-setting. These are self-statements such as:

"I want to make myself tougher."

"If I can tough out this situation, I'll be better able to handle others."

"I won't have to be bothered so much by fear if I can get tougher."

"I'll like myself better if I can learn to be strong on this."

"If I can just get over this hump, I'll save myself a lot of pain from then on."

As you continue to stay in the scary situation, there's still another line of self-talk that's very useful: self-reinforcement, or celebrating your own choices. This includes self-statements like this:

"Hooray for me! I'm gutting it out!"

"I'm doing it. I'm being brave."

"Some people may not have thought I could do it. But I'm doing it! I'm making a triumph for myself."

Consciously choosing your imagery

What you say to yourself in words is an important portion of your thoughts. But another important portion is the mental images you give yourself. Suppose you're trying to write an article, and you're struggling against the fear that causes writer's block. It doesn't do much good to say the words "I am safe," if you're visualizing a committee of readers frowning at you, and hearing in your mind their highly critical tones of voice.

It's good to cultivate, consciously, an image of getting positive feedback, perhaps accompanied by some useful criticism. You "keep your eyes on the prize," and imagine the good consequences that writing the article will bring.

Choosing positive imagery

If you're afraid of flying, it doesn't help to say, "I know the chances of a safe flight are very high," if the image you're seeing and hearing in your mind is of the airplane plummeting toward the earth as people scream. But, if you can visualize the airplane flying safely and uneventfully on a boringly routine flight, your statement about a safe flight is more effective in reducing your fear.

If you're giving a speech, you might imagine that at least one person will enjoy it, find it useful, or be excited by it. You may know that others will disagree, but you focus at least some attention on the sympathetic listener.

Some people are helped by calling to mind the image of a very nurturing, loyal, strong, and dependable friend to take with them into scary situations. Some people have referred to this as the "inner guide" image.

Transferring a success image to this situation

Here's an imagery technique that many people have found useful. You first ask yourself, "How would I like to feel and act in this situation?" Perhaps the answer is relaxed, perhaps brave, confident, silly, slaphappy, assertive, or pleasantly excited. Then you search through your memory bank for at least one memory of feeling and acting that way. If you haven't ever felt and acted that way yourself, then you search for an image of someone else's doing so. (I have written some "modeling stories" for the purpose of providing suitable images.) We can call a memory of the desirable pattern the "resource," because we draw upon this resource in handling the scary situation.

The next step is to imagine very vividly the resource image. You run it through your consciousness perhaps several times, as though playing a videotape.

The next step is to take the scary situation, and imagine yourself handling the scary situation in the same way that you (or someone else) handled the resource situation. In other words, you take the desirable pattern and just transfer it over to the situation you want to handle well. You run this sequence through your imagination repeatedly. Then you step into the situation in real life, and enact the sequence you've been imagining. If you're successful, then the success experience you've just created can be a new resource!

Here's an example: One afternoon I spoke with a woman who was experiencing great anxiety. She was retiring, and there was to be a dinner in her honor later that evening. She would be asked to say a few words, and she faced this prospect with terror. I asked her how she would like to feel, instead, during these moments. She said she would rather feel relaxed, humorous, grateful, and in charge of things. I asked her whether she had ever had these feelings before, especially in public speaking situations. She was a schoolteacher,

and could retrieve many memories of times she had felt that way, in front of her classes. I asked her to retrieve memories of very specific times and places, and to run these images through her mind in great detail.

After she had done so, I asked her to take the same pattern of her thoughts, feelings, and behaviors and lift it over to the scene she would be experiencing later in the evening. I asked her to imagine feeling and acting the same way at the dinner. She was able to do so. I asked her to keep practicing this fantasy. She later told me the evening had gone well.

Habituating to negative images

There's sometimes a problem with consciously choosing your imagery. If you try NOT to think of a certain image, it will often pop right into your head. A story by Tolstoy had to do with someone's trying not to think of a white bear. If you try, right now, not to think of a white bear, does the image pop into your head despite your efforts?

This brings up another imagery technique worth using. If the worst outcome pops into your head, you can go ahead and expose yourself to it in your imagination and become less scared of it. You purposely keep imagining one of the worst outcomes. You imagine yourself handling it, maintaining your courage and dignity, prevailing, even in this unwanted event. For example, I imagine myself coming to the end of the speech I'm giving. The people don't applaud.

One by one they start hissing and boo-ing. I remain calm, pack up my materi-als, and stand proudly as they yell in-sults at me.

Here's another example. I imag-ine calling someone, to invite the person to do something with me. The person says, "With you? You think I would get together with you? Ha! Ha! No way! You're such a klutz. I would never want to be seen near you! If you ever come close to me, I'll get out a sign that says, 'I did not invite this ridiculous person to come near me.'"

But in the image, you're not devastated. Instead, you're thinking, "I can handle this. It's not the end of the world if this particular person doesn't like me. I'm not giving this person the power to determine how I feel. I can be strong."

Or I imagine that the airplane I'm riding on is going straight down and people all around me are screaming. I relax and give thanks that I have had the opportunity to be alive. I review some of the best moments of my life. I check to see if there's anyone I can comfort by my calmness in the remaining seconds of my life.

Or I imagine that I hand in a written article. Rather than getting an A, it not only gets an F, but it also gets loudly criticized before a whole group of people. The critic very sarcastically comments on every paragraph, after which he rips the paper into small pieces. Meanwhile, I take some pleasure in being able to watch this spectacle calmly and with dignity. Perhaps if the critic makes some good points, I tell him so, and if I disagree, I voice my op-posing opinions.

The same principles of exposure that apply to real situations also apply to imaginary situations. If there's an image that scares you more than you'd like, you can habituate to it by prolonged ex-posure. You can remind yourself that the image itself is not dangerous, even though the real-life situation may be dangerous.

If I find that one of these images is too scary at the beginning, I can change it around until it's at the right point on the hierarchy of difficulty. Per-haps I imagine the critic of my article with a banana peel draped across his head. This image is so silly that the whole scene is sapped of some of its ability to scare me.

There are other ways to make a scary image more tolerable at the be-ginning. You can choose to see it in black and white rather than in color. You can see it on a television screen rather than in real life. You can make the image small and far away. You can see yourself as though watching your-self from the outside, rather than look-ing out from your own eyes.

Some people have found, with scary memories, it helps to visualize the whole scene running very rapidly backward, as in a videotape played backward very quickly. When this method does help, perhaps its most helpful feature is learning you can control the frightening image. You learn that imagining it is not something that just happens to you, but that it's something you can change around in any way you wish.

If you become an expert in manipulating the images in your own imagination, you're well on your way to conquering any problems with unrealistic fear.

Relaxation

When most people become scared, they tense up. They may clench their teeth, tighten their face muscles, or grip with their hands. For this reason, you've probably come to associate tense muscles with scary situations, and relaxed muscles with safe and secure situations. If you can learn to relax your muscles on purpose, you can help yourself to feel safe and secure.

It takes some people a great deal of work and practice to learn to relax their muscles thoroughly and completely. Many people are not willing to do this work. But the work of refining this skill can be of great benefit.

How do you work at developing muscular relaxation skill? You practice noticing how tense your muscles are. You make them a little more tense on purpose, and pay attention to the feeling. Then you let the tension off, and pay attention to how the feeling changes. You do this separately for every muscle group of your body. If you have access to an EMG (electromyogram) biofeedback machine, you

can help yourself by measuring your degree of muscle tension, rather than just feeling it.

If your hands tend to become sweaty when you get scared, this is a clue that your "skin conductance" is a measure of how nervous you are. It may be useful to get a machine that measures skin conductance and use it as you train yourself to relax. Having dry hands tells you that you're relaxed. Likewise, if your hands become cold when you're scared, you can train yourself to warm your hands, using a suitable thermometer for feedback.

Sometimes thinking of comforting and relaxing images works well in relaxing your muscles. Some people practice saying a "mantra" to themselves, such as the word "one"; this gives themselves a signal to relax. There are many techniques for doing this, and I have written more about these in the chapter on relaxation skills.

You first practice relaxing at those moments where there is no pressing need to relax (and no big barrier to relaxation), for example at a regular time each day. When you have become very good at relaxing, you're then ready to use your relaxation skills to help in fear reduction. You get yourself relaxed, and then you practice handling the scary situation (using role-playing or fantasy rehearsal, or real-life exposure) while trying to stay as relaxed as you can.

Fantasy rehearsal

I've spoken in previous chapters about the technique of fantasy rehearsal. Let's review this crucially important way of practicing.

Positive fantasy rehearsal means imagining yourself handling a situation as you would most like to handle it. You imagine yourself coming out with the thoughts, emotions, and behaviors that are the very best you can pick.

Each fantasy rehearsal builds up the habit strength of the new and better response just a little bit. You have to do lots of fantasy rehearsals to build up the habit strength to the point where you will automatically act this way in real life.

One type of fantasy rehearsal is the "fantasy rehearsal out loud." You speak aloud, describing the situation, your thoughts, your emotions, and your behaviors. Let's imagine I have a fear of spiders. Here is what a fantasy rehearsal out loud might sound like:

Situation: I'm walking through the front hall of my house, and in front of me I see a spider dangling on a thread from the ceiling. It's a brown spider, and not a poisonous one. I stop and look at it.

Thoughts: I can handle this. I'm many times bigger than this creature; it's not dangerous to me. I could easily kill it if I wanted to. What do I want to do? I want to try to put it outside without harming it. Dealing in a brave yet gentle way with this spider will be a big accomplishment for me. I'm relaxing my muscles.

Emotions: I'm feeling compassion for the spider. I'm feeling calm and safe.

Behavior: I'm getting a tissue; I'm lowering the spider to the floor and trapping him gently in the tissue. I'm opening the front door and putting him outside. I'm wishing him a good life.

Celebration: Hooray, I handled this situation well!

Here is a generic outline for fantasy rehearsals of courage skills.

1. Situation:

Describe the situation, as if it's happening now. What are the sights and sounds?

2. Thoughts:

Here's an opportunity.

It will be an accomplishment if I can tough this out.

What bad could happen? How bad is it? How likely is it? How much danger am I in?

Let me remember a time when I handled a situation like this well. I want to see and hear it in my mind.

I want to relax my muscles.

This is not the end of the world; this is not awful.

Here are my options: . . . Here's the one I want to pick.

4. Emotions:

Excited? Brave? Confident? Happy? Relaxed? Having fun?

Behavior:

I'm doing something that makes sense. I'm doing something that is reasonable.

5. Celebration:

Hooray for me! I handled this situation well!

If there are situations you really want to handle differently, I strongly recommend that you tape your fantasy rehearsals of these situations. Then listen to the tape or read the words every day. Experience these patterns over and over until they become second nature.

Millions of people are plagued with overly great fears. Very few of them have ever written or taped a fantasy rehearsal to present to themselves over and over. I believe this powerful technique is vastly underused.

Real-life exposure and practice are great, if available. But sometimes real-life exposure can't last long enough, as with fears of certain fleeting social situations. Sometimes, as with the fear of nuclear war, going crazy, or death, real-life exposure is not practical. With fantasy rehearsals you can meet your own needs by engineering the length of exposure and the response you make.

Reinforce courage, not fear

It's often easier to work toward goals if you can rig up some reward for achieving them. Can you find a way of being rewarded for each step toward success? For example, suppose someone is afraid of public speaking. He sets a goal of successfully giving five speeches. He gives $100 to a friend, and the friend gives back $20 for each speech he gives. This arrangement is called "contingency contracting."

By the same token, it's important to make sure you aren't being rewarded for the fear itself. Suppose someone receives a paid "sick day" off from work whenever his anxiety becomes too high. The holiday is a reinforcer, a reward for most people. It's hard to get rid of anxiety when you're receiving a powerful reinforcer for it. If you discover any rewards you're receiving for having anxiety, you should try to eliminate them.

Skill 61: Depending

I put the skill of depending under the category of courage skills because many people appear to be terrified of doing it. The skill of depending means you can get help when you need it and feel OK about that. It means you aren't scared to ask someone to help you. It means you don't have to feel ashamed about getting someone to help you with something.

Reasons for fear of depending

Why do people sometimes feel scared or ashamed to ask for help?

Sometimes the answer is found in the skill of trusting. Some people can't really believe that someone else is trustworthy enough to help them in the way that they want to be helped.

There are other reasons too. Some people feel they should already be perfect. If you need help, you aren't perfect. To admit you need help is to admit you're imperfect.

Most people wouldn't be so bold as to claim they are perfect in every way. However, for many people, the pain of admitting they're imperfect in any one way seems too much to bear.

But refusing to admit that you're imperfect doesn't make you any better. In fact, if it keeps you from obtaining help and working on getting better, it keeps you from getting better.

For example, suppose someone is not doing well in math. Suppose this person believes that getting extra help in math is only for people who are stupid. The person refuses extra help so he won't feel stupid. But the decision not to get extra help keeps him working at a low level. His very fear of being exposed as inadequate is one of the main factors that keep him performing inadequately.

For another example: One person is unhappy with his life and considers going into psychotherapy. But he doesn't do this because he's scared this would be admitting he's crazy or screwed up.

Someone else, who is braver in this way, goes into psychotherapy and receives lots of help. This person uses what he learns in order to make life much happier over time. Because this person wasn't afraid to admit he was imperfect, he got much closer to perfect than the other person did.

Here's a third example: Two people drink too much alcohol, and both greatly impair their judgment and threaten their health by doing so. The first one admits he has a problem and gets help. He learns how to work at the psychological skills that will help him overcome his addiction. The second refuses to admit that a problem exists. Because he doesn't get help, he doesn't work on anything, and the problem gets worse.

Fear of depending sometimes leads to denial of problems

Suppose someone is extremely afraid of getting help for a certain problem. One way to escape the fear is for the person to trick himself into thinking there's no problem. Tricking yourself in this way is called denial.

For example, suppose two children in a family are continually yelling at each other, calling each other names, and hurting each other. The kids are very unhappy and make each other unhappy. Suppose the father and mother say to themselves, "Oh well. Kids are like this. It's no big deal." If the parents trick themselves into believing everything is OK because it's too painful to try to solve the problem, they're using denial.

Of course, denying a problem exists doesn't make it go away; nevertheless, denial is something most human beings tend to do, at least a little bit. It's often difficult to admit to yourself the problems you have.

Attitudes that reduce denial

People are less likely to use denial if they think in certain useful ways. For example: With most skills, it's not where you start out that's important; it's where you end up that's important. It's not so important how competent you are at something right now; it's how competent you become at it over time. So there's no shame in admitting you're imperfect at something now. The important thing is to be getting better at it over time.

Some skills are very important to a given person, and other skills aren't. When the skill is very important, it's even more necessary to accept help than when it isn't. For example: For the brain surgeon, it's very important to be good at brain surgery; it's not as important to be good at folk dancing. But if the brain surgeon is not competent at some part of brain surgery, it's even more important that he get help than if he's not competent at folk dancing.

So if a skill is very important, you'd better be able to accept help at it. If the skill is unimportant, then it's not a big problem that you're not good at it yet. In the first case, denying the problem exists is dangerous; in the second case, it's unnecessary.

Some people associate asking for help with being a baby

Here's another reason why some people are scared to get help: We start out in life almost totally helpless, needing to depend on other people for everything. We cannot even move much without help. We can't feed ourselves; we need help cleaning ourselves up, and so forth. As we get older, we learn to do more things on our own. Doing things without help feels like being a "big boy or girl."

This is fine much of the time. When you're a young child, it's great to take pride in being able to put your clothes on by yourself.

But some people go too far in thinking that not needing help is good and needing help is bad. They feel they have to do everything by themselves, and they can't ask for help for anything. And sometimes they make themselves miserable or waste a lot of time this way.

For example: A man is new in town. He's in his car, trying to find a certain store. He knows he's near it. He keeps driving around, trying to find it, for a whole hour. Meanwhile, there are lots of people walking around who know where the store is. They would be happy to tell him where it is.

But he's too ashamed of asking for help to ask. So he wastes his time and makes himself unhappy. He's not asking for help, and he's making a bad decision.

There has to be some reasonable balance about when to ask for help and when to take pleasure in doing something on your own.

How do you decide when to ask for help?

How do you decide when to ask for help? Making this decision well is key to the skill of depending.

Let's imagine that three people want to become really great piano players. The first tries to figure out how to play without any help from anybody in any way. The second one tries to figure out how to play by reading a book. The third one reads the book, but also hires the very best teacher she can possibly find to help her.

Let's pretend that the three people have equal talent, and that they work equally hard. Which one is most likely to become a great piano player? Probably the one who receives the most help.

Getting help is especially unshameful if you're giving the other person something in return for helping you. The piano teacher receives two things: money and the satisfaction of helping a good pupil.

When should you not ask for help? Sometimes you can do a job yourself, and it's right that you do it yourself, and you can't offer anyone else something in return for helping you. For example: A boy asks another for help on math homework. The second boy says, "Have you tried these problems yet?" The first says, "Well, no, I haven't." The second says, "Did you read in the book about how to do them?" The first says, "No." The second says, "Do you remember in class how the teacher explained how to do them?" The first says, "No. I was playing a hand-held video game during that time."

How would you feel if you were the second person? You might feel irritated. You're being asked to do work in order to make up for the other person's laziness. If you were the person asking for help, you might feel rightly ashamed, especially if you weren't offering the other person anything in return for his help. The first person is asking for help but not making a good decision.

Here's another situation: John, who is Mary's brother, says to Mary, "We have to clean up some rooms of the house. Why don't we do all these rooms together? I'll help you do your rooms, and you can help me do my rooms. That way we'll get to keep each other company while we're working, and it'll probably be more fun." John could do his job by himself, but it wouldn't be as much fun. He's offering Mary something in return for the help. He's offering her his company and the chance to have a better time. He's asking for help, and it's probably a good decision.

On the other hand, suppose John were to say, "Mary, would you please do me a favor? Go clean up those rooms I have to clean up. I just don't feel like doing it. I'd rather watch television." Mary probably wouldn't like that. Asking for this sort of help would be a bad decision.

The person helping you will feel much better if she sees you're trying to help yourself and put some effort into it too.

For example: Someone decides he wants to become a great scientist. He asks a person who's already a great scientist, "Can I learn from you? Can I come and work in your lab with you? I can notice how you do things, so that I can become a great scientist like you!"

The great scientist replies, "Sure, come on!" Suppose the person

shows up every day, works really hard, takes very detailed notes on what goes on, and tries to help out whenever there's something to do. The great scientist is likely to feel just fine about helping him. The person has received help and has made a good decision.

On the other hand, suppose he doesn't show up much of the time, comes in late, leaves early, and doesn't pay much attention to what's going on. The great scientist would be likely to think, "Hey, I'm trying to help him, but he's not doing his part." The person has asked for help, but he has made a bad decision. He shouldn't have asked for help unless he was willing to do his part in return.

Here's a third thing that makes people enjoy giving help: getting appreciation for it. We talked about giving people something in return when you get help from them. Sometimes all they want or need is a sincere "thank you."

Have you ever given someone directions on how to get somewhere? Perhaps the person said something like, "Thank you. That really is a big help. I appreciate that!" For most people, just being able to help someone else and having the person appreciate it is enough payment for your offering that few seconds of help.

And yet the fellow in one of the stories we looked at a while ago was afraid to ask other people for directions. Maybe he didn't like to admit he couldn't find everything all on his own. Maybe he didn't feel he had enough to offer the other person in return, when saying "thanks" would have been enough.

Here's another story. Let's say a parent has a child who's starting to become sick. The parent thinks, "Let's see. Should I call the doctor and ask what to do? If I do, the doctor is likely to think I'm stupid because I don't already know what to do. So maybe I'll put it off and just hope things get better."

Then the child becomes sicker. Finally, the parent calls the doctor. The doctor says, "Why didn't you call sooner? If we had started treatment sooner, your child would have been a lot better off." In deciding not to ask for help, this person made a bad decision. Here the problem was that the person was afraid of what someone else would think. He was afraid of looking stupid or incompetent. But he looked more incompetent because of being afraid to ask for help.

Here's another reason some people don't ask for help. They feel nobody knows anything about their problem because they're the only person in the world who has ever had it. This is almost never true.

For example: Once someone had a problem. He felt he had to count the number of footsteps he took in going someplace. If he made a mistake, he felt he had to go back and count again. Later he felt he had to wash his hands a certain number of times. He became scared of germs, even though he knew

his hands were already clean. He'd never heard of anybody with these kinds of problems. He thought he was the only one in the world who had ever had them. He thought that asking for help must be silly, because nobody would know anything about it, and people would just think he was strange.

Then this person finally mustered the courage to ask for help. He read in the library, talked to friends, and went to experts. He found out there are large numbers of people – millions of them – with problems like his. He found out that his troubling behaviors were called "compulsions." He learned there was even a sort of club of people who had this problem and wanted to learn more about how to help it. He learned about several good ways of helping himself, and he became much happier. The person wished he had asked for help sooner. When he finally did ask for help, he made a good decision.

One of the reasons people need to think about helping one another is the idea that nobody is good at everything. Some people are skilled in some ways and some in others. For this reason, it makes sense that people should form teams, where people can do the things they're best at.

Suppose one person forms a company that makes and sells cars. He decides he will design the cars, build them, advertise them, and sell them. He will also take care of all the paperwork and taxes. He will ask no one for help.

He has to become skilled at every single one of these tasks.

On the other hand, a second person also decides he wants to form a company that makes and sells cars. This person decides to find the best designers to design his cars, and the best car builders to build them. He hires people to advertise the cars even though they might not know a thing about how to build cars. He hires people who are good at selling to sell the cars, and people who are good at numbers and paperwork to keep track of the expenses and taxes. In other words, he asks for help from people who are much better at these different skills than he is. He doesn't try to do it all himself.

Which of the two is making the best decision? Almost certainly the second person is. This is why you don't see one-person car companies. This is what cooperation is all about. Each of us has our strengths and weaknesses. If many imperfect people, with all sorts of weaknesses, can work together in a way that can combine their strengths, they can do some really great things. If we require that any single person be wonderful at everything, very few things would get done.

The results are more important than the means

Suppose you had an illness. You have your choice between two doctors. The first says, "I pride myself in never getting help from any other doctor. I always handle every case myself." The second says, "I can't know about every illness in the world. If you have a problem that some other doctor can handle better than I can, I'll ask that doctor to help and send you to that doctor."

Which doctor would you rather go to? If you're like me, you'd choose the second. The first is interested in proving himself, whereas the second is interested in getting good results. That is, getting your illness taken care of and getting you well. If the second doctor sent you to someone who could cure your illness, you probably wouldn't think, "He was a wimp. He had to ask for help." You'd think, "He knew just the right person to ask for help. I'm grateful to him." His decision to get help would be a good decision.

Suppose two people who have problems with depression. They both feel no energy to do anything, and feel very unhappy. Not everybody who is unhappy can be helped by medicine, but, in this story, we're going to suppose that each of these two people could be helped to feel a lot better by taking antidepressant medicine.

The first person says, "I've got to prove that I can handle this myself, without taking medicine." He rejects help, and toughs it out. But, while doing this for a couple of years, he can't do his work, help anybody else, or be a good father for his kids.

The second one hears that medicine may help him. He says, "Hey, I'll take whatever help I can get. There are people out there depending on me." So, with the help of the medicine, in six weeks he's able to help people by doing his job, be a good father for his kids again, and feel better.

Suppose the first person says to the second, "You were a wimp. You had to get help, while I was tough." If I were the second, I'd think: "It's results I'm interested in. The results are that I'm helping people at work, helping my kids, and enjoying myself more. The people I'm helping are glad I chose not to be tough in this way." I think the second person, the one who got help, made the better decision.

The words 'independent' and 'interdependent'

In thinking about the skill of depending, it's useful to think about the words "independent" and "interdependent." The more you're able to do something without help, the more you're independent. The more you're connected with other people who can help you, and whom you can help in turn, the more you're part of an interdependent group.

Figuring out when to be independent and when to be interdependent is one of the main skills a psychologically healthy person learns to do well.

Skill 62: Independent Thinking

Ralph Waldo Emerson, in his famous essay titled "Self Reliance," wrote this sentence: "To be a man is to be a non-conformist." (If he were writing today, I'm sure he would have used nonsexist language: "To be a mature person is to be a non-conformist.") The skill of independent thinking is the skill of not simply going along with a crowd or with one other individual who says, "Think this way," or "Do this thing." Independent thinking means coming to an independent conclusion about what's the best thing to do.

A lot that passes for non-conformity is rebellion against a prevailing set of ideas without having any better ideas to replace them. For example: If I refuse to take baths, I'm certainly being a non-conformist, but I don't think this is the type of non-conformity Emerson was referring to. If I refuse to bathe, I'm certainly making a statement that I don't wish to follow the conventions and expectations that most other people have. But unless I can come up with some good reason for not bathing, my thinking is in no way superior to that of the people I'm rebelling against.

Do robots and don't robots

In thinking about the skill of independent thinking, it's useful to imagine two types of robots: "do robots" and "don't robots." A do robot is pro-grammed to do whatever you tell it to do. You can tell it to bang itself in the head or jump off a bridge, and it will comply; it has no choice. A don't robot has been programmed to do exactly the opposite of what you tell it to do. If you tell it not to bang itself in the head, it will bang itself in the head. If you tell it to not jump off the bridge, then it will jump off the bridge. Again, it has no choice; it is programmed to do the opposite of whatever you tell it.

Some people are like "do robots": they have so few assertion skills and independent thinking skills that they comply blindly with anybody who gives them an order, whether that person is a reasonable authority or an unreasonable authority. If an acquaintance from school tells a "do robot" kid to take a certain drug, he does it.

On the other hand, there are some people who are so intent on rebelling that they're like the don't robots. Whatever a parent wants, the don't robot must do the opposite. If the parent wants him to succeed in school, he fails. If the parent wants him to have nice friends, he finds losers to be friends with. He's so driven to prove he's not a do robot that he becomes a don't robot. Although he's seeking to be independent from authority, he still has not achieved freedom.

What is lacking in both these hypothetical robots is a beacon to guide decision-making, other than what someone else wants you to do. The person who makes decisions based on what will produce the greatest good for himself and others will find that sometimes his calculations lead him to agree with other people and sometimes to disagree. But he has attained freedom to choose by adopting an ethical beacon, rather than simply choosing to agree or disagree.

In other words, the person who is truly skilled at independent thinking has a standard of judgment, a method that will tell her what's the best thing to do. She has some way of calculating what to do other than by polling other people. If the calculations come out that it's better to do something different from what others are doing, then the independent thinker can do it anyway. But she does it, not because she wants to be different from other people, but because she has made her own calculations.

For example: Let's say someone lives in a culture where almost everybody drinks alcohol. She studies the risks and benefits of alcohol consumption and concludes that the risks far outweigh the benefits and that the best thing would be not to drink alcohol at all. She makes this calculation on the basis of the probability of becoming a problem drinker; the probability of having an auto accident; the probability of suffering a memory decline from great alcohol consumption; the probability of fostering a custom that will result in

women of child-bearing age drinking in large numbers and the probability that a certain portion of these women will harm their fetuses by drinking alcohol.

Against this, she weighs the increased pleasure she might feel at social functions and the decreased incidence of heart attack she might have as a result of the protective effect of alcoholic beverages. She may base her calculation on what will make her happiest and what will make other people happiest. She's a utilitarian thinker if she tries to produce the greatest good for the greatest number. She's not necessarily trying to do the opposite of what anybody else does or non-conform to anybody. She is simply trying to make the world as good a place as she can make it.

The independent thinker knows that many, many people can all be wrong. In some societies, for instance, almost everyone has condoned slavery. In others, almost everyone has condoned cannibalism or human sacrifice. The mere fact that everyone believes a certain thing is good doesn't mean it's good. So one of the attributes of an independent thinker is a lack of blind trust in everyone else: a belief in the fallibility of other people's judgments.

Here's another example of a situation where independent thinking is called for: Let's assume someone lives in a culture where the habit of almost everyone around him is to use violent entertainment: to watch violent movies, to watch violent television shows, to participate in violent video games, to buy their children toys that enable those children to very easily act out violent fantasies. If this person avoids violent entertainment and boycotts it simply because everybody else is doing it, he's indulging in non-conformity for non-conformity's sake alone.

On the other hand, suppose he thoroughly reads the research data about the relationship between violent entertainment and real-life violence. As a result, he decides that, by boycotting violent entertainment, he can reduce by at least a little bit the rate of violence in real life and thus make the world a better place. Now he is non-conforming for a different reason. He non-conforms based on his calculations of what will make the world a better place.

Suppose someone else sees everyone on the highway around him going seventy-five or eighty miles-per-hour in a zone that has a posted speed limit of fifty-five miles-per-hour. The person reads the data on traffic accidents and deaths at various speeds. Suppose he decides that fifty-five miles-per-hour is the speed that would minimize his chances of having an accident. He decides that going much lower than that would probably increase danger by making people slow down too much as they pass, but that going at higher speed would make him less safe by increasing the distance it takes for him to stop. Once he decides this, he drives at the speed he calculates is best.

If he were driving at the speed limit simply to be different from everybody else, that would be rebellion against the existing order without any well-reasoned replacement for it. Making the decision on the basis of carefully considered calculations and then being willing to oppose the prevailing custom to carry it out is the skill of independent thinking.

The person who's best at independent thinking does not simply ignore the reactions of other people to his non-conformity but takes them into account when making his calculations. For example: Suppose someone calculates it would be a better society if men would give up wearing ties around their necks. This person figures out how many wasted hours and minutes are spent tying and untying ties, buying them, picking them out, getting them cleaned, etc. The person reasons that this time would be much better spent to people's listening to each other or tutoring children.

But suppose the person works in a place where the clear standard is that every man wears a tie. He calculates that, if he non-conforms, the amount of hassle he would have to endure would not be worth the trouble. He decides not to draw the battle lines over this issue. He decides the world will be a little better place if he saves his energy for more important issues and conforms on this one.

There are two parts to the skill of independent thinking. The first is calculating what's the best thing to do. We'll talk more about this in the skill of decision-making. The second part is tolerating people's negative reactions when you do something different.

It's a sad truth that many people dislike other people's doing anything differently from what they do. If they use a certain recreational drug, they want their friends to. If they wear their hair in a certain way, they want their friends to. If they like certain music and hate others, then their friends should feel the same way. The thought pattern is, "There's only one right way to be." This is not an admirable characteristic of human beings, but it's one that's very common.

The independent thinker, therefore, must be ready to tolerate the disapproval or perhaps even the rejection of people who see him as different. How does the independent thinker do this? One way is by liking himself in a way that makes him less dependent on what other people think of him. In other words, the thought pattern is: I like myself; I don't need everyone else in the world to like me.

A second coping mechanism independent thinkers use is to seek out a subculture or a social network that does tolerate their brand of independent thinking. For example, the person who boycotts alcohol finds kindred spirits in Students Against Drunk Driving. Or the boycotter of violent entertainment finds kindred spirits in the local peace organization. The one who believes most people drive too fast finds a small group of people working to resist increases in the speed limits. For almost any belief that goes against the crowd, there's a certain subculture that adheres to that belief. So the independent thinker reasons: I will find kindred spirits who accept my belief, and therefore I don't need all others to accept it.

Seeking a kindred subculture is a different strategy from that of liking oneself so much that one doesn't need the approval of anyone. Though it may sound less noble than going it alone, seeking a kindred subculture is usually more realistic. This strategy recognizes that people do need other people. They need social networks; they need friends. There is only a certain amount of rejection that anybody should put up with, especially when there's an alternative.

Another reason for forming a subculture of kindred spirits is that, by organizing, people can have a greater chance of persuading the larger society and of having a positive effect on how the world operates.

The strategy of first making carefully reasoned calculations and then looking for others who concur in that judgment is very different from the strategy most people use. Most people find themselves in a social network first, and that social network then determines their beliefs.

Part of the skill of being an independent thinker is refusal skills, ways of saying no to the pressure to conform. We spoke in some detail about this under the skill of assertion. But let's make just a couple of points here. An overly apologetic refusal to go along with someone may appear to be done out of weakness, rather than out of strength of conviction. On the other hand, an overly hostile rejection of the other person's personality and character is usually not productive either.

Usually the best strategy of refusal is to take your different path in a spirit of friendliness and acceptance of the other person, despite the difference in your choices. Only when the other person becomes hostile or rejecting does the independent thinker feel the need to use skills of ending relationships or tolerating distancing.

Index